KU-693-181

GULAG

ANNE APPLEBAUM

GULAG

A HISTORY OF THE
SOVIET CAMPS

ALLEN LANE
an imprint of
PENGUIN BOOKS

ALLEN LANE
THE PENGUIN PRESS

Published by the Penguin Group
Penguin Books Ltd, 80 Strand, London WC2R ORL, England
Penguin Putnam Inc., 375 Hudson Street, New York, New York 10014, USA
Penguin Books Australia Ltd, 250 Camberwell Road, Camberwell, Victoria 3124, Australia
Penguin Books Canada Ltd, 10 Alcorn Avenue, Toronto, Ontario, Canada M4V 3B2
Penguin Books India (P) Ltd, 11, Community Centre, Panchsheel Park, New Delhi – 110 017, India
Penguin Books (NZ) Ltd, Cnr Rosedale and Airborne Roads, Albany, Auckland, New Zealand
Penguin Books (South Africa) (Pty) Ltd, 24 Sturdee Avenue, Rosebank 2196, South Africa

Penguin Books Ltd, Registered Offices: 80 Strand, London WC2R ORL, England

www.penguin.com

First published in the USA by Random House, Inc. 2003
First published in Great Britain by Allen Lane The Penguin Press 2003

2

Set in 9.75/12.75 pt Sabon and Eurostile
Typeset by Rowland Phototypesetting Ltd, Bury St Edmunds, Suffolk
Printed and bound in Great Britain by Clays Ltd, St Ives plc

ISBN 0-713-99322-7

Contents

Part III
The Rise and Fall of the Camp-Industrial
Complex, 1940–1986

List of Illustrations

Within the Text

List of Maps

Acknowledgements

No book is ever really the work of one person, but this book truly could not have been written without the practical, intellectual and philosophical contribution of many people, some of whom count among my closest friends, and some of whom I never met. Although it is unusual, in acknowledgements, for authors to thank writers who are long dead, I would like to give special recognition to a small but unique group of camp survivors whose memoirs I read over and over again while writing this book. Although many survivors wrote profoundly and eloquently of their experiences, it is simply no accident that this book contains a preponderance of quotations from the works of Varlam Shalamov, Isaak Filshtinsky, Gustav Herling, Evgeniya Ginzburg, Lev Razgon, Janusz Bardach, Olga Adamova-Sliozberg, Anatoly Zhigulin, Alexander Dolgun and, of course, Alexander Solzhenitsyn. Some of these number among the most famous of Gulag survivors. Others do not – but they all have one thing in common. Out of the many hundreds of memoirs I read, theirs stood out, not only for the strength of their prose but also for their ability to probe beneath the surface of everyday horror and to discover deeper truths about the human condition.

I am also more than grateful for the help of a number of Muscovites who guided me through archives, introduced me to survivors, and provided their own interpretations of their past at the same time. First among them is the archivist and historian Aleksandr Kokurin – who I hope will one day be remembered as a pioneer of the new Russian history – as well as Galya Vinogradova and Alla Boryna, both of whom dedicated themselves to this project with unusual fervour. At different times, I was aided by conversations with Anna Grishina, Boris Belikin, Nikita Petrov, Susanna Pechora, Aleksandr Guryanov, Arseny Roginsky and Natasha Malykhina of Moscow Memorial; Simeon Vilensky of Vozvrashchenie; as well as Oleg Khlevnyuk, Zoya Eroshok, Professor Natalya Lebedeva, Lyuba Vinogradova and Stanislaw Gregorowicz, formerly of the Polish Embassy in Moscow. I am also extremely grateful to the many people who granted me long, formal interviews, whose names are listed separately in the Bibliography.

Outside of Moscow, I owe a great deal to many people who were willing to drop everything and suddenly devote large chunks of time to a foreigner who had arrived, sometimes out of the blue, to ask naïve questions about subjects they had been researching for years. Among them were Nikolai Morozov and Mikhail Rogachev in Syktyvkar; Zhenya Khaidarova and Lyuba Petrovna in Vorkuta; Irina Shabulina and Tatyana Fokina in Solovki; Galina Dudina in Arkhangelsk; Vasily Makurov, Anatoly Tsigankov and Yuri Dmitriev in Petrozavodsk; Viktor Shmirov in Perm; Leonid Trus in Novosibirsk; Svetlana Dointsena, director of the local history museum in Iskitim; Veniamin Ioffe and Irina Reznikova of St Petersburg Memorial. I am particularly grateful to the librarians of the Arkhangelsk Kraevedcheskaya Biblioteka, several of whom devoted an entire day to me and my efforts to understand the history of their region, simply because they felt it was important to do so.

In Warsaw I was greatly aided by the library and archives run by the Karta Institute, as well as by conversations with Anna Dzienkiewicz and Dorota Pazio. In Washington, DC, David Nordlander and Harry Leich helped me at the Library of Congress. I am particularly grateful to Elena Danielson, Thomas Henrikson, Lora Soroka and especially Robert Conquest of the Hoover Institution. The Italian historian Marta Craveri contributed a great deal to my understanding of the camp rebellions. Conversations with Vladimir Bukovsky and Aleksandr Yakovlev also helped my comprehension of the post-Stalinist era.

I owe a special debt to the Lynde and Harry Bradley Foundation, the John M. Olin Foundation, the Hoover Institution, the Märit and Hans Rausing Foundation and John Blundell at the Institute of Economic Affairs for their financial and moral support.

I would also like to thank the friends and colleagues who offered their advice, practical and historical, during the writing of this book. Among them are Antony Beevor, Colin Thubron, Stefan and Danuta Waydenfeld, Yuri Morakov, Paul Hofheinz, Amity Shlaes, David Nordlander, Simon Heffer, Chris Joyce, Alessandro Missir, Terry Martin, Alexander Gribanov, Piotr Paszkowski and Orlando Figes, as well as Radek Sikorski, whose ministerial briefcase proved very useful indeed. Special thanks are owed to Georges Borchardt, Kristine Puopolo, Gerry Howard and Stuart Proffitt, who oversaw this book to completion.

Finally, for their friendship, their wise suggestions, their hospitality and their food I would like to thank Christian and Natasha Caryl, Edward Lucas, Yuri Senokossov and Lena Nemirovskaya, my wonderful Moscow hosts.

In the terrible years of the Yezhov terror I spent seventeen months waiting in line outside the prison in Leningrad. One day somebody in the crowd identified me. Standing behind me was a woman, with lips blue from the cold, who had, of course, never heard me called by name before. Now she started out of the torpor common to us all and asked me in a whisper (everyone whispered there):

'Can you describe this?'

And I said: 'I can.'

Then something like a smile passed fleetingly over what had once been her face . . .

– Anna Akhmatova,
'Instead of a Preface', *Requiem 1935–1940*

This Book is Dedicated to
Those Who Described What Happened

Introduction

And fate made everybody equal
Outside the limits of the law
Son of a kulak or Red commander
Son of a priest or commissar . . .

Here classes were all equalized,
All men were brothers, camp mates all,
Branded as traitors every one . . .

> – Alexander Tvardovsky,
> 'By Right of Memory'[1]

This is a history of the Gulag: a history of the vast network of labour camps that were once scattered across the length and breadth of the Soviet Union, from the islands of the White Sea to the shores of the Black Sea, from the Arctic Circle to the plains of central Asia, from Murmansk to Vorkuta to Kazakhstan, from central Moscow to the Leningrad suburbs. Literally, the word GULAG is an acronym, meaning *Glavnoe upravlenie lagerei*, or Main Camp Administration. Over time, the word 'Gulag' has also come to signify not only the administration of the concentration camps but also the system of Soviet slave labour itself, in all its forms and varieties: labour camps, punishment camps, criminal and political camps, women's camps, children's camps, transit camps. Even more broadly, 'Gulag' has come to mean the Soviet repressive system itself, the set of procedures that prisoners once called the 'meat-grinder': the arrests, the interrogations, the transport in unheated cattle cars, the forced labour, the destruction of families, the years spent in exile, the early and unnecessary deaths.

The Gulag had antecedents in tsarist Russia, in the forced-labour brigades that operated in Siberia from the seventeenth century to the beginning of the twentieth. It then took on its modern and more familiar form almost immediately after the Russian Revolution, becoming an integral part of the Soviet system. Mass terror against real and alleged opponents was a part of the Revolution from the very beginning – and by the summer of 1918, Lenin, the Revolution's leader, had already demanded that 'unreliable elements' be locked up in concentration camps outside major towns.[2] A string of aristocrats, merchants and other people defined as potential 'enemies' were duly imprisoned. By 1921, there were already eighty-four camps in forty-three provinces, mostly designed to 'rehabilitate' these first enemies of the people.

From 1929, the camps took on a new significance. In that year, Stalin decided to use forced labour both to speed up the Soviet Union's industrialization and to excavate the natural resources in the Soviet Union's barely habitable far north. In that year, the Soviet secret police also began to take control of the Soviet penal system, slowly wresting all of the country's camps and prisons away from the judicial establishment. Helped along by the mass arrests of 1937 and 1938, the camps entered a period of rapid expansion. By the end of the 1930s, they could be found in every one of the Soviet Union's twelve time zones.

Contrary to popular assumption, the Gulag did not cease growing in the 1930s, but rather continued to expand throughout the Second World War and the 1940s, reaching its apex in the early 1950s. By that time the camps had come to play a central role in the Soviet economy. They produced a third of the country's gold, much of its coal and timber, and a great deal of almost everything else. In the course of the Soviet Union's existence, at least 476 distinct camp complexes came into being, comprising thousands of individual camps, each of which contained anywhere from a few hundred to many thousands of people.[3] The prisoners worked in almost every industry imaginable – logging, mining, construction, factory work, farming, the designing of aeroplanes and artillery – and lived, in effect, in a country within a country, almost a separate civilization. The Gulag had its own laws, its own customs, its own morality, even its own slang. It spawned its own literature, its own villains, its own heroes, and it left its mark upon all who passed through it, whether as prisoners or guards. Years after being released, the Gulag's inhabitants were often able to recognize former inmates on the street simply from 'the look in their eyes'.

Such encounters were frequent, for the camps had a large turnover. Although arrests were constant, so too were releases. Prisoners were freed because they finished their sentences, because they were let into the Red Army, because they were invalids or women with small children, because they had been promoted from captive to guard. As a result, the total number of prisoners in the camps generally hovered around two million, but the total number of Soviet citizens who had some experience of the camps, as political or criminal prisoners, is far higher. From 1929, when the Gulag began its major expansion, until 1953, when Stalin died, the best estimates indicate that some eighteen million people passed through this massive system. About another six million were sent into exile, deported to the Kazakh deserts or the Siberian forests. Legally obliged to remain in their exile villages, they too were forced labourers, even though they did not live behind barbed wire.[4]

As a system of mass forced labour involving millions of people, the camps disappeared when Stalin died. Although he had believed all of his life that the Gulag was critical to Soviet economic growth, his political heirs knew well that the camps were, in fact, a source of backwardness and distorted investment. Within days of his death, Stalin's successors began to dismantle them. Three major rebellions, along with a host of smaller but no less dangerous incidents, helped to accelerate the process.

Nevertheless, the camps did not disappear altogether. Instead, they evolved. Throughout the 1970s and early 1980s, a few of them were redesigned and put to use as prisons for a new generation of democratic activists, anti-Soviet nationalists – and criminals. Thanks to the Soviet dissident network and the international human rights movement, news of these post-Stalinist camps appeared regularly in the West. Gradually, they came to play a role in Cold War diplomacy. Even in the 1980s, the American President, Ronald Reagan, and his Soviet counterpart, Mikhail Gorbachev, were still discussing the Soviet camps. Only in 1987 did Gorbachev – himself the grandson of Gulag prisoners – begin to dissolve the Soviet Union's political camps altogether.

Yet although they lasted as long as the Soviet Union itself, and although many millions of people passed through them, the true history of the Soviet Union's concentration camps was, until recently, not at all well known. By some measures, it is still not known. Even the bare facts recited above, although by now familiar to most Western scholars of Soviet history, have not filtered into Western popular consciousness. 'Human knowledge,' once wrote Pierre Rigoulot, the French historian of communism, 'doesn't accumulate like the bricks of a wall which grows regularly, according to the work of the mason. Its development, but also its stagnation or retreat, depends on the social, cultural and political framework.'[5]

One might say that, until now, the social, cultural and political framework for knowledge of the Gulag has not been in place.

I first became aware of this problem several years ago, when walking across the Charles Bridge, a major tourist attraction in what was then newly democratic Prague. There were buskers and hustlers along the bridge, and, every 15 feet or so, someone was selling precisely what one would expect to find for sale in such a postcard-perfect spot. Paintings of appropriately pretty streets were on display, along with bargain jewellery and 'Prague' key chains. Among the bric-à-brac, one could buy Soviet military paraphernalia: caps, badges, belt buckles and little pins, the tin Lenin and Brezhnev images that Soviet school-children once pinned to their uniforms.

The sight struck me as odd. Most of the people buying the Soviet paraphernalia were Americans and West Europeans. All would be sickened by the thought of wearing a swastika. None objected, however, to wearing the hammer and sickle on a T-shirt or a hat. It was a minor observation, but sometimes it is through just such minor observations that a cultural mood is best observed. For here, the lesson could not have been clearer: while the symbol of one mass murder fills us with horror, the symbol of another mass murder makes us laugh.

If there is a dearth of feeling about Stalinism among Prague tourists, it is partly explained by the dearth of images in Western popular culture. The Cold War produced James Bond and thrillers, and cartoon Russians of the sort who appear in Rambo films, but nothing as ambitious as *Schindler's List* or *Sophie's Choice*. Steven Spielberg, probably Hollywood's leading director (like it or not), has chosen to make films about Japanese concentration camps (*Empire of the Sun*) and Nazi concentration camps, but not about Stalinist concentration camps. The latter haven't caught Hollywood's imagination in the same way.

Highbrow culture hasn't been much more open to the subject. The reputation of the German philosopher Martin Heidegger has been deeply damaged by his brief, overt support of Nazism, an enthusiasm which developed before Hitler had committed his major atrocities. On the other hand, the reputation of the French philosopher Jean-Paul Sartre has not suffered in the least from his aggressive support of Stalinism throughout the post-war years, when plentiful evidence of Stalin's atrocities was available to anyone interested. 'As we were not members of the Party,' he once wrote, 'it was not our duty to write about Soviet labour camps; we were free to remain aloof from the quarrels over the nature of the system, provided no events of sociological significance occurred.'[6] On another occasion, he told Albert Camus that 'Like you, I find these camps intolerable, but I find equally intolerable the use made of them every day in the bourgeois press.'[7]

Some things have changed since the Soviet collapse. In 2002, for example, the British novelist Martin Amis felt moved enough by the subject of Stalin and Stalinism to dedicate an entire book to the subject. His efforts prompted other writers to wonder why so few members of the political and literary Left had broached the subject.[8] On the other hand, some things have not changed. It is possible – still – for an American academic to publish a book suggesting that the purges of the 1930s were useful because they promoted upward mobility and therefore laid the groundwork for perestroika.[9] It is possible – still – for a British literary editor to reject an article because it is 'too anti-Soviet'.[10] Far more common, however, is a reaction of boredom or indifference to Stalinist terror. An otherwise straightforward review of a book I wrote about the western republics of the former Soviet Union in the 1990s contained the following lines: 'Here occurred the terror famine of the 1930s, in which Stalin killed more Ukrainians than Hitler murdered Jews. Yet how many in the West remember it? After all, the killing was so – so boring, and ostensibly undramatic.'[11]

These are all small things: the purchase of a trinket, a philosopher's reputation, the presence or absence of Hollywood films. But put them all together and they make a story. Intellectually, Americans and West Europeans know what happened in the Soviet Union. Alexander Solzhenitsyn's acclaimed novel about life in the camps, *One Day in the Life of Ivan Denisovich*, was published in the West in several languages in 1962–3. His oral history of the camps, *The Gulag Archipelago*, caused much comment when it appeared, again in several languages, in 1973. Indeed, *The Gulag Archipelago* led to a minor intellectual revolution in some countries, most notably France, converting whole swathes of the French Left to an anti-Soviet position. Many more revelations about the Gulag were made during the 1980s, the glasnost years, and they too received due publicity abroad.

Nevertheless, to many people, the crimes of Stalin do not inspire the same visceral reaction as do the crimes of Hitler. Ken Livingstone, a former British Member of Parliament, now Mayor of London, once struggled to explain the difference to me. Yes, the Nazis were 'evil', he said. But the Soviet Union was 'deformed'. That view echoes the feeling that many people have, even those who are not old-fashioned left-wingers: the Soviet Union simply went wrong somehow, but it was not fundamentally wrong in the way that Hitler's Germany was wrong.

Until recently, it was possible to explain this absence of popular feeling about the tragedy of European communism as the logical result of a particular set of circumstances. The passage of time is part of it: communist regimes really did grow less reprehensible as the years went by. Nobody was very frightened of General Jaruzelski, or even of Brezhnev, although both were responsible for a great deal of destruction. The absence of hard information, backed up by archival research, was clearly part of it too. The paucity of academic work on this subject was long due to a paucity of sources. Archives were closed. Access to camp sites was forbidden. No television cameras ever filmed the Soviet camps or their victims, as they had done in Germany at the end of the Second World War. No images, in turn, meant less understanding.

But ideology twisted the ways in which we understood Soviet and East European history as well.[12] A small part of the Western Left struggled to explain and sometimes to excuse the camps, and the terror which created them, from the 1930s onwards. In 1936, when millions of Soviet peasants were already working in camps or living in exile, the British socialists Sidney and Beatrice Webb published a vast survey of the Soviet Union, which explained, among other things, how the 'downtrodden Russian peasant is gradually acquiring a sense of political freedom'.[13] At the time of the Moscow show trials, while Stalin arbitrarily condemned thousands of innocent Party members to camps, the playwright Bertolt Brecht told the philosopher Sidney Hook that 'the more innocent they are, the more they deserve to die'.[14]

Even as late as the 1980s, there were still academics who continued to describe the advantages of East German health care or Polish peace initiatives, still activists who felt embarrassed by the fuss and bother raised over the dissidents in Eastern Europe's prison camps. Perhaps this was because the founding philosophers of the Western Left – Marx and Engels – were the same as those of the Soviet Union. Some of the language was shared as well: the masses, the struggle, the proletariat, the exploiters and exploited, the ownership of the means of production. To condemn the Soviet Union too thoroughly would be to condemn a part of what some of the Western Left once held dear as well.

It is not only the far Left, and not only Western communists, who were tempted to make excuses for Stalin's crimes that they would never have made for Hitler's. Communist ideals – social justice, equality for all – are simply far more attractive to most in the West than the Nazi advocacy of racism and the triumph of the strong over the weak. Even if communist ideology meant something very different in practice, it was harder for the intellectual descendants of the American and French Revolutions to condemn a system which *sounded*, at least, similar to their own. Perhaps this helps explain why eyewitness reports of the Gulag were, from the very beginning, often dismissed and belittled by the very same people who would never have thought to question the validity of Holocaust testimony written by Primo Levi or Elie Wiesel. From the Russian Revolution onwards, official information about the Soviet camps was readily available too, to anyone who wanted it: the most famous Soviet account of one of the early camps, the White Sea Canal, was even published in English. Ignorance alone cannot explain why Western intellectuals chose to avoid the subject.

The Western Right, on the other hand, did struggle to condemn Soviet crimes, but sometimes using methods that harmed their own cause. Surely the man who did the greatest damage to the cause of anti-communism was the American Senator Joe McCarthy. Recent documents showing that some of his accusations were correct do not change the impact of his over-zealous pursuit of communists in American public life: ultimately, his public 'trials' of communist sympathizers would tarnish the cause of anti-communism with the brush of chauvinism and intolerance.[15] In the end, his actions served the cause of neutral historical inquiry no better than those of his opponents.

Yet not all of our attitudes to the Soviet past are linked to political ideology. Many, in fact, are rather a fading by-product of our memories of the Second World War. We have, at present, a firm conviction that the Second World War was a wholly just war, and few want that conviction shaken. We remember D-Day, the liberation of the Nazi concentration camps, the children welcoming American GIs with cheers on the streets. No one wants to be told that there was another, darker side to Allied victory, or that the camps of Stalin, our ally, expanded just as the camps of Hitler, our enemy, were liberated. To admit that by sending thousands of Russians to their deaths by forcibly repatriating them after the war, or by consigning millions of people to Soviet rule at Yalta, the Western Allies might have helped others commit crimes against humanity would undermine the moral clarity of our memories of that era. No one wants to think that we defeated one mass murderer with the help of another. No one wants to remember how well that mass murderer got on with Western statesmen. 'I have a real liking for Stalin,' the British Foreign Secretary, Anthony Eden, told a friend, 'he has never broken his word.'[16] There are many, many photographs of Stalin, Churchill and Roosevelt all together, all smiling.

Finally, Soviet propaganda was not without its effect. Soviet attempts to cast doubt upon Solzhenitsyn's writing, for example, to paint him as a madman or an anti-Semite or a drunk, had some impact.[17] Soviet pressure on Western academics and journalists helped skew their work too. When I studied Russian history as an undergraduate in the United States in the 1980s, acquaintances told me not to bother continuing with the subject in graduate school, since there were too many difficulties involved: in those days, those who wrote 'favourably' about the Soviet Union won more access to archives, more access to official information, longer visas in the country. Those who did not risked expulsion and professional difficulties as a consequence. It goes without saying, of course, that no outsiders were allowed access to any material about Stalin's camps or about the post-Stalinist prison system. The subject simply did not exist, and those who pried too deep lost their right to stay in the country.

Put together, all of these explanations once made a kind of sense. When I first began to think seriously about this subject, as communism was collapsing in 1989, I even saw the logic of them myself: it seemed natural, obvious, that I should know very little about Stalin's Soviet Union, whose secret history made it all the more intriguing. More than a decade later, I feel very differently. The Second World War now belongs to a previous generation. The Cold War is over too, and the alliances and international fault lines it produced have shifted for good. The Western Left and the Western Right now compete over different issues. At the same time, the emergence of new terrorist threats to Western civilization make the study of the ways in which the old communist threats to Western civilization were combatted all the more necessary.

In other words, the 'social, cultural and political framework' has now changed – and so too has our access to information about the camps. At the end of the 1980s, a flood of documents about the Gulag began to appear in Mikhail Gorbachev's Soviet Union. Stories of life in Soviet concentration camps were published in newspapers for the first time. New revelations sold out magazines. Old arguments about numbers – how many dead, how many incarcerated – revived. Russian historians and historical societies, led by the pioneering Memorial Society in Moscow, began publishing monographs, histories of individual camps and people, casualty estimates, lists of the names of the dead. Their efforts were echoed and amplified by historians in the former Soviet republics and the countries of what was once the Warsaw Pact, and, later, by Western historians too.

Despite many setbacks, this Russian exploration of the Soviet past continues today. True, the first decade of the twenty-first century is very different from the final decades of the twentieth century, and the search for history is no longer either a major part of Russian public discourse, or quite so sensational as it once seemed. Most of the work being carried out by Russian and other scholars is real historical drudgery, involving the sifting of thousands of individual documents, hours spent in cold and draughty archives, days spent looking for facts and numbers. But it is beginning to bear fruit. Slowly, patiently, Memorial has not only put together the first guide to the names and locations of all of the camps on record, but has also published a ground-breaking series of history books, and compiled an enormous archive of oral and written survivors' tales as well. Together with others – the Sakharov Institute and the publishing house Vozvrashchenie (the name means 'return') – they have put some of these memoirs into general circulation. Russian academic journals and institutional presses have also begun to print monographs based on new documents, as well as collections of documents themselves. Similar work is being carried out elsewhere, most notably by the Karta Society in Poland; by historical museums in Lithuania, Latvia, Estonia, Romania and Hungary; and by a handful of American and West European scholars who have the time and energy to work in the Soviet archives.

While researching this book, I had access to their work, as well as to two other kinds of sources that would not have been available ten years ago. The first is the flood of new memoirs which began to be published in the 1980s in Russia, America, Israel, Eastern Europe and elsewhere. In writing this book, I have made extensive use of them. In the past, some scholars of the Soviet Union have been reluctant to rely upon Gulag memoir material, arguing that Soviet memoir writers had political reasons for twisting their stories, that most did their writing many years after their release, and that many borrowed stories from one another when their own memories failed them. Nevertheless, after reading several hundred camp memoirs, and interviewing some two dozen survivors, I felt that it was possible to filter out those which seemed implausible or plagiarized or politicized. I also felt that while memoirs could not be relied upon for names, dates and numbers, they were none the less an invaluable source of other kinds of information, especially certain crucial aspects of life in the camps: prisoners' relationships with one another, conflict between national, religious and ideological groups, the behaviour of camp guards and administrators, the role of corruption, even the existence of love and passion. I have consciously made heavy use of only one writer – Varlam Shalamov – who wrote fictionalized versions of his life in the camps, and this because his stories are based upon real events.

As far as was possible, I have backed up the memoirs with an extensive use of archives – a source which, paradoxically, not everyone likes to use either. As will become clear in the course of this book, the power of propaganda in the Soviet Union was such that it frequently altered perceptions of reality. For that reason, historians in the past were right not to rely upon officially published Soviet documents, which were often deliberately designed to obscure the truth. But secret documents – the documents now preserved in archives – had a different function. In order to run its camps, the administration of the Gulag needed to keep certain kinds of records. Moscow needed to know what was happening in the provinces, the provinces had to receive instructions from the central administration, statistics had to be kept. This does not mean that these archives are entirely reliable – bureaucrats had their own reasons to distort even the most mundane facts – but if used judiciously, they can explain some things about camp life which memoirs cannot. Above all, they help to explain why the camps were built – or at least what it was that the Stalinist regime believed they were going to achieve.

It is also true that the archives are far more varied than many anticipated, and that they tell the story of the camps from many different perspectives. I had access, for example, to the archive of the Gulag administration, with inspectors' reports, financial accounts, letters from the camp directors to their supervisors in Moscow, accounts of escape attempts and lists of musical productions put on by camp theatres, all kept at the Russian State Archive in Moscow. I also consulted records of Party meetings, and documents that were collected in a part of Stalin's *osobaya papka* collection, his 'special archive'. With the help of other Russian historians, I was able to use some documents from Soviet military archives, and the archives of the convoy guards, which contain things such as lists of what arrested prisoners were and were not allowed to take with them. Outside of Moscow, I also had access to some local archives – in Petrozavodsk, Arkhangelsk, Syktyvkar, Vorkuta and the Solovetsky islands – where day-to-day events of camp life were recorded, as well as to the archives of Dmitlag, the camp that built the Moscow–Volga Canal, which are kept in Moscow. All contain records of daily life in the camps, order forms, prisoners' records. At one point, I was handed a chunk of the archive of Kedrovy Shor, a small division of Inta, a mining camp north of the Arctic Circle, and politely asked if I wanted to buy it.

Put together, these sources make it possible to write about the camps in a new way. In this book, I no longer needed to compare the 'claims' of a handful of dissidents to the 'claims' of the Soviet government. I did not have to search for a median line somewhere in between the accounts of Soviet refugees and the accounts of Soviet officials. Instead, to describe what happened, I was able to use the language of many different kinds of people, of guards, of policemen, of different kinds of prisoners serving different kinds of sentences at different times. The emotions and the politics which have long surrounded the historiography of the Soviet concentration camps do not lie at the heart of this book. That space is reserved, instead, for the experience of the victims.

This is a history of the Gulag. By that, I mean that this is a history of the Soviet concentration camps: their origins in the Bolshevik Revolution, their development into a major part of the Soviet economy, their dismantling after Stalin's death. This is also a book about the legacy of the Gulag: without question, the regimes and rituals found in the Soviet political and criminal prison camps of the 1970s and 1980s evolved directly out of those created in an earlier era, and for that reason I felt that they belonged in the same volume.

At the same time, this is a book about life in the Gulag, and for that reason it tells the story of the camps in two ways. The first and third sections of this book are chronological. They describe the evolution of the camps and their administration in a narrative fashion. The central section discusses life in the camps, and it does so thematically. While most of the examples and citations in this central section refer to the 1940s, the decade when the camps reached their apex, I have also referred backwards and forwards – ahistorically – to other eras. Certain aspects of life in the camps evolved over time, and I felt it was important to explain how this happened.

Having said what this book is, I would also like to say what it is not: it is not a history of the USSR, a history of the purges, or a history of repression in general. It is not a history of Stalin's reign, or of his Politburo, or of his secret police, whose complex administrative history I have deliberately tried to simplify as much as possible. Although I do make use of the writings of Soviet dissidents, often produced under great stress and with great courage, this book does not contain a complete history of the Soviet human rights movement. Nor, for that matter, does it do full justice to the stories of particular nations and categories of prisoner – among them Poles, Balts, Ukrainians, Chechens, German and Japanese POWs – who suffered under the Soviet regime, both inside and outside the Soviet camps. It does not explore in full the mass murders of 1937–8, which mostly took place outside the camps, or the massacre of thousands of Polish officers at Katyń and elsewhere. Because this is a book intended for the general reader, and because it does not presume any specialized knowledge of Soviet history, all of these events and phenomena will be mentioned. Nevertheless, it would have been impossible to do all of them justice in a single volume.

Perhaps most importantly, this book does not do justice to the story of the 'special exiles', the millions of people who were often rounded up at the same time and for the same reasons as Gulag prisoners, but who were then sent not to camps but to live in remote exile villages where many thousands died of starvation, cold and overwork. Some were exiled for political reasons, including the kulaks, or rich peasants, in the 1930s. Some were exiled for their ethnicity, including Poles, Balts, Ukrainians, Volga Germans and Chechens, among others, in the 1940s. They met a variety of fates in Kazakhstan, central Asia and Siberia – too wide a variety to be encompassed in an account of the camp system. I have chosen to mention them, perhaps idiosyncratically, where their experiences seemed to me especially close or relevant to the experiences of Gulag prisoners. But although their story is closely connected to the story of the Gulag, to tell it fully would require another book of this length. I hope someone will write one soon.

Although this is a book about the Soviet concentration camps, it is nevertheless impossible to treat them as an isolated phenomenon. The Gulag grew and developed at a particular time and place, in tandem with other events – and within three contexts in particular. Properly speaking, the Gulag belongs to the history of the Soviet Union; to the international as well as the Russian history of prisons and exile; and to the particular intellectual climate of continental Europe in the mid-twentieth century, which also produced the Nazi concentration camps in Germany.

By 'belongs to the history of the Soviet Union', I mean something very specific: the Gulag did not emerge, fully formed, from the sea, but rather reflected the general standards of the society around it. If the camps were filthy, if the guards were brutal, if the work teams were slovenly, that was partly because filthiness and brutality and slovenliness were plentiful enough in other spheres of Soviet life. If life in the camps was horrible, unbearable, inhuman, if death rates were high – that too was hardly surprising. In certain periods, life in the Soviet Union was also horrible, unbearable and inhuman, and death rates were as high outside the camps as they were within them.

Certainly it is no coincidence that the first Soviet camps were set up in the immediate aftermath of the bloody, violent and chaotic Russian Revolution either. During the Revolution, the terror imposed afterwards, and the subsequent civil war, it seemed to many in Russia as if civilization itself had been permanently fractured. 'Death sentences were meted out arbitrarily,' the historian Richard Pipes has written, 'people were shot for no reason and equally capriciously released.'[18] From 1917 onwards, a whole society's set of values was turned on its head: a lifetime's accumulated wealth and experience was a liability, robbery was glamorized as 'nationalization', murder became an accepted part of the struggle for the dictatorship of the proletariat. In this atmosphere, Lenin's initial imprisonment of thousands of people, simply on the grounds of their former wealth or their aristocratic titles, hardly seemed strange or out of line.

By the same token, high mortality rates in the camps in certain years are also, in part, a reflection of events taking place throughout the country. Death rates went up inside the camps in the early 1930s, when famine gripped the entire country. They went up again during the Second World War: the German invasion of the Soviet Union led not only to millions of combat deaths, but also to epidemics of dysentery and of typhus, as well as, again, to famine, which affected people outside the camps as well as within them. In the winter of 1941–2, when a quarter of the Gulag's population died of starvation, as many as a million citizens of the city of Leningrad may have starved to death too, trapped behind a German blockade.[19] The blockade's chronicler Lidiya Ginzburg wrote of the hunger of the time as a 'permanent state . . . it was constantly present and always made its presence felt . . . the most desperate and tormenting thing of all during the process of eating was when the food drew to an end with awful rapidity without bringing satiety'.[20] Her words are eerily reminiscent of those used by former prisoners, as the reader will discover.

It is true, of course, that the Leningraders died at home, while the Gulag ripped open lives, destroyed families, tore children away from their parents and condemned millions to live in remote wastelands, thousands of miles from their families. Still, prisoners' horrific experiences can be legitimately compared to the terrible memories of 'free' Soviet citizens such as Elena Kozhina, who was evacuated from Leningrad in February 1942. During the journey, she watched her brother, sister and grandmother die of starvation. As the Germans approached, she and her mother walked across the steppe, encountering 'scenes of unbridled rout and chaos . . . The world was flying into thousands of pieces. Everything was permeated with smoke and a horrible burning smell; the steppe was tight and suffocating, as if squeezed inside a hot, sooty fist.' Although she never experienced the camps, Kozhina knew terrible cold, hunger and fear before her tenth birthday, and was haunted by the memories for the rest of her life. Nothing, she wrote, 'could erase my memories of Vadik's body being carried out under a blanket; of Tanya choking in her agony; of me and Mama, the last ones, trudging through smoke and thunder in the burning steppe'.[21]

The population of the Gulag and the population of the rest of the USSR shared many things besides suffering. Both in the camps and outside them, it was possible to find the same slovenly working practices, the same criminally stupid bureaucracy, the same corruption, and the same sullen disregard for human life. While writing this book, I described to a Polish friend the system of *tufta* – cheating on required work norms – that Soviet prisoners had developed, described later in this book. He howled with laughter: 'You think prisoners invented that? The whole Soviet bloc practised *tufta*.' In Stalin's Soviet Union, the difference between life inside and life outside the barbed wire was not fundamental, but rather a question of degree. Perhaps for that reason, the Gulag has often been described as the quintessential expression of the Soviet system. Even in prison-camp slang, the world outside the barbed wire was not referred to as 'freedom', but as the *bolshaya zona*, the 'big prison zone', larger and less deadly than the 'small zone' of the camp, but no more human – and certainly no more humane.

Yet if the Gulag cannot be held totally apart from the experience of life in the rest of the Soviet Union, neither can the story of the Soviet camps be fully separated from the long, multinational, cross-cultural history of prisons, exile, incarceration and concentration camps. The exile of prisoners to a distant place, where they can 'pay their debt to society', make themselves useful, and not contaminate others with their ideas or their criminal acts, is a practice as old as civilization itself. The rulers of ancient Rome and Greece sent their dissidents off to distant colonies. Socrates chose death over the torment of exile from Athens. The poet Ovid was exiled to a fetid port on the Black Sea. Georgian Britain sent its pickpockets and thieves to Australia. Nineteenth-century France sent convicted criminals to Guyana. Portugal sent its undesirables to Mozambique.[22]

The new leadership of the Soviet Union did not, in 1917, have to look quite as far away as Greenland for a precedent. Since the seventeenth century, Russia had its own exile system: the first mention of exile in Russian law was in 1649. At the time, exile was considered to be a new, more humane form of criminal punishment – far preferable to the death penalty, or to branding and mutilation – and it was applied to a huge range of minor and major offences, from snuff-taking and fortune-telling to murder.[23] A wide range of Russian intellectuals and writers, Pushkin among them, suffered some form of exile, while the very possibility of exile tormented others: at the height of his literary fame in 1890, Anton Chekhov surprised everyone he knew and set off to visit and describe the penal colonies on the island of Sakhalin, off Russia's Pacific coast. Before he left, he wrote to his puzzled publisher, explaining his motives:

We have allowed millions of people to rot in prisons, to rot for no purpose, without any consideration, and in a barbarous manner; we have driven people tens of thousands of versts through the cold in shackles, infected them with syphilis, perverted them, multiplied the number of criminals ... but none of this has anything to do with us, it's just not interesting ...[24]

In retrospect, it is easy to find, in the history of the tsarist prison system, many pre-echoes of practices later applied in the Soviet Gulag. Like the Gulag, for example, Siberian exile was never intended exclusively for criminals. A law of 1736 declared that if a village decided someone in its midst was a bad influence on others, the village elders could divide up the unfortunate's property and order him to move elsewhere. If he failed to find another abode, the state could then send him into exile.[25] Indeed, this law was cited by Khrushchev in 1948, as part of his (successful) argument for exiling collective farmers who were deemed insufficiently enthusiastic and hard-working.[26]

The practice of exiling people who simply didn't fit in continued throughout the nineteenth century. In his book *Siberia and the Exile System*, George Kennan – uncle of the American statesman – described the system of 'administrative process' that he observed in Russia in 1891:

The obnoxious person may not be guilty of any crime . . . but if, in the opinion of the local authorities, his presence in a particular place is 'prejudicial to public order' or 'incompatible with public tranquility', he may be arrested without warrant, may be held from two weeks to two years in prison, and may then be removed by force to any other place within the limits of the empire and there be put under police surveillance for a period of from one to ten years.[27]

Administrative exile – which required no trial and no sentencing procedure – was an ideal punishment not only for trouble-makers as such, but also for political opponents of the regime. In the early days, many of these were Polish noblemen who objected to the Russian occupation of their territory and property. Later, exiles included religious objectors, as well as members of 'revolutionary' groups and secret societies, including the Bolsheviks. Although they were not administrative exiles – they were tried and sentenced – the most notorious of Siberia's nineteenth-century 'forced settlers' were also political prisoners: these were the Decembrists, a group of high-ranking aristocrats who staged a feeble rebellion against Tsar Nicholas I in 1825. With a vengeance that shocked all of Europe at the time, the Tsar sentenced five of the Decembrists to death. He deprived the others of their rank, and sent them, in chains, to Siberia, where a few were joined by their exceptionally brave wives. Only a few lived long enough to be pardoned by Nicholas's successor, Alexander II, thirty years later, and to return home to St Petersburg, by then tired old men.[28] Fyodor Dostoevsky, sentenced in 1849 to a four-year term of penal servitude, was another well-known political prisoner. After returning from his Siberian exile, he wrote *The House of the Dead*, still the most widely read account of life in the tsarist prison system.

Like the Gulag, the tsarist exile system was not created solely as a form of punishment. Russia's rulers also wanted their exiles, both criminal and political, to solve an economic problem that had rankled for many centuries: the underpopulation of the far east and the far north of the Russian land mass, and the Russian Empire's consequent failure to exploit Russia's natural resources. With that in mind, the Russian state began, as early as the eighteenth century, to sentence some of its prisoners to forced labour – a form of punishment which became known as *katorga*, from the Greek word *kateirgo*, 'to force'. *Katorga* had a long Russian prehistory. In the early eighteenth century, Peter the Great had used convicts and serfs to build roads, fortresses, factories, ships and the city of St Petersburg itself. In 1722, he passed a more specific directive ordering criminals, with their wives and children, into exile near the silver mines of Dauriya, in eastern Siberia.[29]

In its time, Peter's use of forced labour was considered a great economic and political success. Indeed, the story of the hundreds of thousands of serfs who spent their lives building St Petersburg had an enormous impact on future generations. Many had died during the construction – and yet the city became a symbol of progress and Europeanization. The methods were cruel – and yet the nation had profited. Peter's example probably helps explain the ready adoption of *katorga* by his tsarist successors. Without a doubt, Stalin was a great admirer of Peter's building methods too.

Still, in the nineteenth century, *katorga* remained a relatively rare form of punishment. In 1906, only about 6,000 *katorga* convicts were serving sentences; in 1916, on the eve of the Revolution, there were only 28,600.[30] Of far greater economic importance was another category of prisoner: the forced settlers, who were sentenced to live in exile, but not in prison, in underpopulated regions of the country, chosen for their economic potential. Between 1824 and 1889 alone, some 720,000 forced settlers were sent to Siberia. Many were accompanied by their families. They, not the convicts labouring in chains, gradually populated Russia's empty, mineral-rich wastelands.[31]

Their sentences were not necessarily easy ones, and some of the settlers thought their fate worse than that of the *katorga* prisoners. Assigned to remote districts, with poor land and few neighbours, many starved to death over the long winters, or drank themselves to death from boredom. There were very few women – their numbers never exceeded 15 per cent – fewer books, no entertainment.[32]

On his journey across Siberia to Sakhalin, Anton Chekhov met, and described, some of these exiled settlers: 'The majority of them are financially poor, have little strength, little practical training, and possess nothing except their ability to write, which is frequently of absolutely no use to anybody. Some of them commence by selling, piece by piece, their shirts of Holland linen, their sheets, their scarves and handkerchiefs, and finish up after two or three years dying in fearful penury . . .'[33]

But not all of the exiles were miserable and degenerate. Siberia was far away from European Russia, and in the East officialdom was more forgiving, aristocracy much thinner on the ground. The wealthier exiles and ex-prisoners sometimes built up large estates. The more educated became doctors and lawyers, or ran schools.[34] Princess Maria Volkonskaya, wife of the Decembrist Sergei Volkonsky, sponsored the building of a theatre and concert hall in Irkutsk: although she had, like her husband, technically been deprived of her rank, invitations to her soirées and private dinners were eagerly sought after, and discussed as far away as Moscow and St Petersburg.[35]

By the early twentieth century, the system had shed some of its previous harshness. The fashion for prison reform which spread through Europe in the nineteenth century finally caught up with Russia too. Regimes grew lighter, and policing grew laxer.[36] Indeed, in contrast to what came later, the route to Siberia now seems, if not exactly pleasurable, then hardly an onerous punishment for the small group of men who would lead the Russian Revolution. When in prison, the Bolsheviks received a certain amount of favourable treatment as 'political' rather than criminal prisoners, and were allowed to have books, paper and writing implements. Ordzhonikidze, one of the Bolshevik leaders, later recalled reading Adam Smith, Ricardo, Plekhanov, William James, Frederick W. Taylor, Dostoevsky and Ibsen, among others, while resident in St Petersburg's Schlüsselberg Fortress.[37] By later standards, the Bolsheviks were also well fed, well dressed, even beautifully coiffed. A photograph taken of Trotsky imprisoned in the Peter and Paul Fortress in 1906 shows him wearing spectacles, a suit, a tie and a shirt with an impressively white collar. The peephole in the door behind him offers the only clue to his whereabouts.[38] Another taken of him in exile in eastern Siberia, in 1900, shows him in a fur hat and heavy coat, surrounded by other men and women, also in boots and furs.[39] All of these items would be rare luxuries in the Gulag half a century later.

If life in tsarist exile did become intolerably unpleasant, there was always escape. Stalin himself was arrested and exiled four times. Three times he escaped, once from Irkutsk province and twice from Vologda province, a region which later became pockmarked with camps.[40] As a result, his scorn for the tsarist regime's 'toothlessness' knew no bounds. His Russian biographer Dmitri Volkogonov characterized his opinion like this: 'You didn't have to work, you could read to your heart's content and you could even escape, which required only the will to do so.'[41]

Thus did their Siberian experience provide the Bolsheviks with an earlier model to build upon – and a lesson in the need for exceptionally strong punitive regimes.

If the Gulag is an integral part of both Soviet and Russian history, it is inseparable from European history too: the Soviet Union was not the only twentieth-century European country to develop a totalitarian social order, or to build a system of concentration camps. While it is not the intention of this book to compare and contrast the Soviet and the Nazi camps, the subject cannot be comfortably ignored either. The two systems were built at roughly the same time, on the same continent. Hitler knew of the Soviet camps, and Stalin knew of the Holocaust. There were prisoners who experienced and described the camps of both systems. At a very deep level, the two systems are related.

They are related, first of all, because both Nazism and Soviet communism emerged out of the barbaric experiences of the First World War and the Russian civil war, which followed on its heels. The industrialized methods of warfare put into wide use during both of these conflicts generated an enormous intellectual and artistic response at the time. Less noticed – except, of course, by the millions of victims – was the widespread use of industrialized methods of incarceration. Both sides constructed internment camps and prisoner-of-war camps across Europe from 1914 onwards. In 1918 there were 2.2 million prisoners of war on Russian territory. New technology – the mass production of guns, of tanks, even of barbed wire – made these and later camps possible. Indeed, some of the first Soviet camps were actually built on top of First World War prisoner-of-war camps.[42]

The Soviet and Nazi camps are also related because they belong, together, to the wider history of concentration camps, which began at the end of the nineteenth century. By concentration camps, I mean camps constructed to incarcerate people not for what they had done, but for who they were. Unlike criminal prison camps, or prisoner-of-war camps, concentration camps were built for a particular type of non-criminal civilian prisoner, the member of an 'enemy' group, or at any rate of a category of people who, for reasons of their race or their presumed politics, were judged to be dangerous or extraneous to society.[43]

According to this definition, the first modern concentration camps were set up not in Germany or Russia, but in colonial Cuba, in 1895. In that year, in an effort to put an end to a series of local insurgencies, imperial Spain began to prepare a policy of *reconcentración*, intended to remove the Cuban peasants from their land and 'reconcentrate' them in camps, thereby depriving the insurgents of food, shelter and support. By 1900, the Spanish term *reconcentración* had already been translated into English, and was used to describe a similar British project, initiated for similar reasons, during the Boer War in South Africa: Boer civilians were 'concentrated' into camps, in order to deprive Boer combatants of shelter and support.

From there, the idea spread further. It certainly seems, for example, as if the term *kontslager* first appeared in Russian as a translation from the English 'concentration camp', probably thanks to Trotsky's familiarity with the history of the Boer War.[44] In 1904, German colonists in German South-West Africa also adopted the British model – with one variation. Instead of merely locking up the region's native inhabitants, a tribe called the Herero, they made them carry out forced labour on behalf of the German colony.

There are a number of strange and eerie links between these first German-African labour camps and those built in Nazi Germany three decades later. It was thanks to these southern African labour colonies, for example, that the word *Konzentrationslager* first appeared in the German language, in 1905. The first imperial commissioner of German South-West Africa was one Dr Heinrich Goering, the father of Hermann, who set up the first Nazi camps in 1933. It was also in these African camps that the first German medical experiments were conducted on humans: two of Joseph Mengele's teachers, Theodor Mollison and Eugen Fischer, carried out research on the Herero, the latter in an attempt to prove his theories about the superiority of the white race. But they were not unusual in their beliefs. In 1912, a best-selling German book, *German Thought in the World*, claimed that

nothing can convince reasonable people that the preservation of a tribe of South African kaffirs is more important for the future of humanity than the expansion of the great European nations and the white race in general . . . it is only when the indigenous peoples have learned to produce something of value in the service of the superior race . . . that they can be said to have a moral right to exist.[45]

While this theory was rarely put so clearly, similar sentiments often lay just beneath the surface of colonial practice. Certainly some forms of colonialism both reinforced the myth of white racial superiority and legitimized the use of violence by one race against another. It can be argued, therefore, that the corrupting experiences of some European colonists helped pave the way for the European totalitarianism of the twentieth century.[46] And not only European: Indonesia is an example of a post-colonial state whose rulers initially imprisoned their critics in concentration camps, just as their colonial masters had.

The Russian Empire, which had quite successfully vanquished its own native peoples in its march eastwards, was no exception.[47] During one of the dinner parties that takes place in Leo Tolstoy's novel *Anna Karenina*, Anna's husband – who has some official responsibilities for 'Native Tribes' – holds forth on the need for superior cultures to absorb inferior ones.[48] At some level, the Bolsheviks, like all educated Russians, would have been aware of the Russian Empire's destruction of the Kirgiz, Buryats, Tungus, Chukchi and others. The fact that it didn't particularly concern them – they, who were otherwise so interested in the fate of the downtrodden – itself indicates something about their unspoken assumptions.

But then, full consciousness of the history of southern Africa or of eastern Siberia was hardly required for the development of European concentration camps: the notion that some types of people are superior to other types of people was common enough in Europe at the beginning of the twentieth century. And this, finally, is what links the camps of the Soviet Union and those of Nazi Germany in the most profound sense of all: both regimes legitimated themselves, in part, by establishing categories of 'enemies' or 'sub-humans' whom they persecuted and destroyed on a mass scale.

In Nazi Germany, the first targets were the crippled and the retarded. Later, the Nazis concentrated on Gypsies, homosexuals and, above all, on the Jews. In the USSR the victims were, at first, the 'former people' – alleged supporters of the old regime – and later the 'enemies of the people', an ill-defined term which would come to include not only alleged political opponents of the regime, but also particular national groups and ethnicities, if they seemed (for equally ill-defined reasons) to threaten the Soviet state or Stalin's power.

At different times Stalin conducted mass arrests of Poles, Balts, Chechens, Tartars and – on the eve of his death – Jews.[49]

Although these categories were never entirely arbitrary, they were never entirely stable either. Half a century ago, Hannah Arendt wrote that both the Nazi and the Bolshevik regimes created 'objective opponents' or 'objective enemies', whose 'identity changes according to the prevailing circumstances – so that, as soon as one category is liquidated, war may be declared on another'. By the same token, she added, 'the task of the totalitarian police is not to discover crimes, but to be on hand when the government decides to arrest a certain category of the population'.[50] Again: people were arrested not for what they had done, but for who they were.

In both societies, the creation of concentration camps was actually the final stage in a long process of dehumanization of these objective enemies – a process which began, at first, with rhetoric. In his autobiography, *Mein Kampf*, Hitler wrote of how he had suddenly realized that the Jews were responsible for Germany's problems, that 'any shady undertaking, any form of foulness' in public life was connected to the Jews: 'on putting the probing knife to that kind of abscess one immediately discovered, like a maggot in a putrescent body, a little Jew who was often blinded by the suddenness of the light . . .'[51]

Lenin and Stalin also began by blaming 'enemies' for the Soviet Union's myriad economic failures: they were 'wreckers' and 'saboteurs' and agents of foreign powers. From the late 1930s, as the wave of arrests began to expand, Stalin took this rhetoric to greater extremes, denouncing the 'enemies of the people' as vermin, as pollution, as 'poisonous weeds'. He also spoke of his opponents as 'filth' which had to be 'subjected to ongoing purification' – just as Nazi propaganda would associate Jews with images of vermin, of parasites, of infectious disease.[52]

Once demonized, the legal isolation of the enemy began in earnest. Before the Jews were actually rounded up and deported to camps, they were deprived of their status as German citizens. They were forbidden to work as civil servants, as lawyers, as judges; forbidden to marry Aryans; forbidden to attend Aryan schools; forbidden to display the German flag; forced to wear gold stars of David; and subjected to beatings and humiliation on the street.[53] Before their actual arrest in Stalin's Soviet Union, 'enemies' were also routinely humiliated in public meetings, fired from their jobs, expelled from the Communist Party, divorced by their disgusted spouses, and denounced by their angry children.

Within the camps, the process of dehumanization deepened and grew more extreme, helping both to intimidate the victims and to reinforce the victimizers' belief in the legitimacy of what they were doing. In her book-length interview with Franz Stangl, the commander of Treblinka, the writer Gitta Sereny asked Stangl why camp inmates, before being killed, were also beaten, humiliated and deprived of their clothing. Stangl answered, 'To condition those who actually had to carry out the policies. To make it possible for them to do what they did.'[54] In *The Order of Terror: The Concentration Camp*, the German sociologist Wolfgang Sofsky has also shown how the dehumanization of prisoners in the Nazi camps was methodically built into every aspect of camp life, from the torn, identical clothing, to the deprivation of privacy, to the heavy regulation, to the constant expectation of death.

In the Soviet system, the dehumanization process also began at the moment of arrest, as we shall see, when prisoners were stripped of their clothes and identity, denied contact with outsiders, tortured, interrogated and put through farcical trials, if they were tried at all. In a peculiarly Soviet twist on the process, prisoners were deliberately 'excommunicated' from Soviet life, forbidden to refer to one another as 'comrade', and, from 1937 onwards, prohibited from earning the coveted title of 'shock-worker', no matter how well they behaved or how hard they worked. Portraits of Stalin, which hung in homes and offices throughout the USSR, almost never appeared inside camps and prisons, according to many prisoner accounts.

None of which is to say that the Soviet and Nazi camps were identical. As any reader with any general knowledge of the Holocaust will discover in the course of this book, life within the Soviet camp system differed in many ways, both subtle and obvious, from life within the Nazi camp system. There were differences in the organization of daily life and of work, different sorts of guards and punishments, different kinds of propaganda. The Gulag lasted far longer, and went through cycles of relative cruelty and relative humanity. The history of the Nazi camps is shorter, and contains less variation: they simply became crueller and crueller, until the retreating Germans liquidated them or the invading Allies liberated them. The Gulag also contained a wide variety of camps, from the lethal gold mines of the Kolyma region to the 'luxurious' secret institutes outside Moscow, where prisoner scientists designed weapons for the Red Army. Although there were different kinds of camps in the Nazi system, the range was far narrower.

Two differences between the systems strike me as fundamental. First, the definition of 'enemy' in the Soviet Union was always far more slippery than the definition of 'Jew' in Nazi Germany. With an extremely small number of unusual exceptions, no Jew in Nazi Germany could change his status, no Jew inside a camp could reasonably expect to escape death, and all Jews carried this knowledge with them at all times. While millions of Soviet prisoners feared they might die – and millions did – there was no single category of prisoner whose death was absolutely guaranteed. At times, certain prisoners could improve their lot by working in relatively comfortable jobs, as engineers or geologists. Within each camp there was a prisoner hierarchy, which some were able to climb at the expense of others, or with the help of others. At other times – when the Gulag found itself overburdened with women, children and old people, or when soldiers were needed to fight at the front – prisoners were released in mass amnesties. It sometimes happened that whole categories of 'enemies' suddenly benefited from a change in status. Stalin arrested hundreds of thousands of Poles, for example, at the start of the Second World War in 1939 – and then abruptly released them from the Gulag in 1941 when Poland and the USSR became temporary allies. The opposite was also true: in the Soviet Union, perpetrators could become victims themselves. Gulag guards, administrators, even senior officers of the secret police, could also be arrested and find themselves sentenced to camps. Not every 'poisonous weed' remained poisonous, in other words – and there was no single group of Soviet prisoners who lived with the constant expectation of death.[55]

Second – as, again, will become evident in the course of this book – the primary purpose of the Gulag, according to both the private language and the public propaganda of those who founded it, was economic. This did not mean that it was humane. Within the system, prisoners were treated as cattle, or rather as lumps of iron ore. Guards shuttled them around at will, loading and unloading them into cattle cars, weighing and measuring them, feeding them if it seemed they might be useful, starving them if they were not. They were, to use Marxist language, exploited, reified and commodified. Unless they were productive, their lives were worthless to their masters.

Nevertheless, their experience was quite different from that of the Jewish and other prisoners whom the Nazis sent to a special group of camps called not *Konzentrationslager* but *Vernichtungslager* – camps that were not really 'labour camps' at all, but rather death factories. There were four of them: Belzec, Chelmno, Sobibor and Treblinka. Majdanek and Auschwitz contained both labour camps and death camps. Upon entering these camps, prisoners were 'selected'. A tiny number were sent to do a few weeks of forced labour. The rest were sent directly into gas chambers where they were murdered and then immediately cremated.

As far as I have been able to ascertain, this particular form of murder, practised at the height of the Holocaust, had no Soviet equivalent. True, the Soviet Union found other ways to mass-murder hundreds of thousands of its citizens. Usually, they were driven to a forest at night, lined up, shot in the skull, and buried in mass graves before they ever got near a concentration camp – a form of murder no less 'industrialized' and anonymous than that used by the Nazis. For that matter, there are stories of Soviet secret police using exhaust fumes – a primitive form of gas – to kill prisoners, just as the Nazis did in their early years.[56] Within the Gulag, Soviet prisoners also died, usually thanks not to the captors' efficiency but due to gross inefficiency and neglect.[57] In certain Soviet camps, at certain times, death was virtually guaranteed for those selected to cut trees in the winter forest or to work in the worst of the Kolyma gold mines. Prisoners were also locked in punishment cells until they died of cold and starvation, left untreated in unheated hospitals, or simply shot at will for 'attempted escape'. Nevertheless, the Soviet camp system as a whole was not deliberately organized to mass-produce corpses – even if, at times, it did.

These are fine distinctions, but they matter. Although the Gulag and Auschwitz do belong to the same intellectual and historical tradition, they are nevertheless separate and distinct, both from one another and from camp systems set up by other regimes. The idea of the concentration camp may be general enough to be used in many different cultures and situations, but even a superficial study of the concentration camp's cross-cultural history reveals that the specific details – how life in the camps was organized, how the camps developed over time, how rigid or disorganized they became, how cruel or liberal they remained – depended on the particular country, on the culture and on the regime.[58] To those who were trapped behind barbed wire, these details were critical to their life, health and survival.

In fact, reading the accounts of those who survived both, one is struck more by the differences between the victims' experiences than by the differences between the two camp systems. Each tale has its own unique qualities, each camp held different sorts of horrors for people of different characters. In Germany you could die of cruelty, in Russia you could die of despair. In Auschwitz you could die in a gas chamber, in Kolyma you could freeze to death in the snow. You could die in a German forest or a Siberian wasteland, you could die in a mining accident or you could die in a cattle train. But in the end, the story of your life was your own.

I

The Origins of the Gulag, 1917–1939

1

Bolshevik Beginnings

But your spine has been smashed,
My beautiful, pitiful era,
And with an inane smile
You look back, cruel and weak,
Like an animal past its prime,
At the prints of your own paws.

– Osip Mandelstam, 'Vek'[1]

One of my goals is to destroy the myth that the cruellest era of repression began in 1936–37. I think that in future, statistics will show that the wave of arrests, sentences and exile had already begun at the beginning of 1918, even before the official declaration, that autumn, of the 'Red Terror'. From that moment, the wave simply grew larger and larger, until the death of Stalin . . .

– Dmitri Likhachev, *Vospominaniya*[2]

In the year 1917, two waves of revolution rolled across Russia, sweeping imperial Russian society aside as if it were destroying so many houses of cards. After Tsar Nicholas II abdicated in February, events proved extremely difficult for anyone to halt or control. Alexander Kerensky, the leader of the first post-revolutionary Provisional Government, later wrote that, in the void following the collapse of the old regime, 'all existing political and tactical programmes, however bold and well conceived, appeared hanging aimlessly and uselessly in space'.[3]

But although the Provisional Government was weak, although popular dissatisfaction was widespread, although anger at the carnage caused by the First World War ran high, few expected power to fall into the hands of the Bolsheviks, one of several radical socialist parties agitating for even more rapid change. Abroad, the Bolsheviks were scarcely known. One apocryphal tale illustrates foreign attitudes very well: in 1917, so the story goes, a bureaucrat rushed into the office of the Austrian Foreign Minister, shouting, 'Your Excellency, there has been a revolution in Russia!' The minister snorted. 'Who could make a revolution in Russia? Surely not harmless Herr Trotsky, down at the Café Central?'

If the nature of the Bolsheviks was mysterious, their leader, Vladimir Ilyich Ulyanov – the man the world would come to know by his revolutionary pseudonym, 'Lenin' – was even more so. During his many years as an émigré revolutionary, Lenin had been recognized for his brilliance, but also disliked for his intemperance and his factionalism. He picked frequent fights with other socialist leaders, and had a penchant for turning minor disagreements over seemingly irrelevant matters of dogma into major arguments.[4]

In the first months following the February Revolution, Lenin was very far from holding a position of unchallenged authority, even within his own Party. As late as mid-October 1917, a handful of leading Bolsheviks continued to oppose his plan to carry out a *coup d'état* against the Provisional Government, arguing that the Party was unprepared to take power, and that it did not yet have popular support. He won the argument, however, and on 25 October the coup took place. Under the influence of Lenin's agitation, a mob sacked the Winter Palace. The Bolsheviks arrested the ministers of the Provisional Government. Within hours, Lenin had become the leader of the country he renamed Soviet Russia.

Yet although Lenin had succeeded in taking power, his Bolshevik critics had not been entirely wrong. The Bolsheviks were indeed wildly unprepared. As a result, most of their early decisions, including the creation of the one-party state, were taken to suit the needs of the moment. Their popular support was indeed weak, and almost immediately they began to wage a bloody civil war, simply in order to stay in power. From 1918, when the White Army of the old regime regrouped to fight the new Red Army – led by Lenin's comrade, 'Herr Trotsky' from the 'Café Central' – some of the most brutal fighting ever seen in Europe raged across the Russian countryside. Nor did all of the violence take place in battlefields. The Bolsheviks went out of their way to quash intellectual and political opposition in any form it took, attacking not only the representatives of the old regime but also other socialists: Mensheviks, Anarchists, Social Revolutionaries. The new Soviet state would not know relative peace until 1921.[5]

Against this background of improvisation and violence, the first Soviet labour camps were born. Like so many other Bolshevik institutions, they were created *ad hoc*, in a hurry, as an emergency measure in the heat of the civil war. This is not to say the idea had no prior appeal. Three weeks before the October Revolution, Lenin himself was already sketching out an admittedly vague plan to organize 'obligatory work duty' for wealthy capitalists. By January 1918, angered by the depth of the anti-Bolshevik resistance, he was even more vehement, writing that he welcomed 'the arrest of millionaire-saboteurs travelling in first- and second-class train compartments. I suggest sentencing them to half a year's forced labour in a mine.'[6]

Lenin's vision of labour camps as a special form of punishment for a particular sort of bourgeois 'enemy' sat well with his other beliefs about crime and criminals. On the one hand, the first Soviet leader felt ambivalent about the gaoling and punishment of traditional criminals – thieves, pickpockets, murderers – whom he perceived as potential allies. In his view, the basic cause of 'social excess' (meaning crime) was 'the exploitation of the masses'. The removal of the cause, he believed, 'will lead to the withering away of the excess'. No special punishments were therefore necessary to deter criminals: in time, the Revolution itself would do away with them. Some of the language in the Bolsheviks' first criminal code would have thus warmed the hearts of the most radical, progressive criminal reformers in the West. Among other things, the code decreed that there was 'no such thing as individual guilt', and that punishment 'should not be seen as retribution'.[7]

On the other hand, Lenin – like the Bolshevik legal theorists who followed in his wake – also reckoned that the creation of the Soviet state would create a new kind of criminal: the 'class enemy'. A class enemy opposed the Revolution, and worked openly, or more often secretly, to destroy it. The class enemy was harder to identify than an ordinary criminal, and much harder to reform. Unlike an ordinary criminal, a class enemy could never be trusted to co-operate with the Soviet regime, and required harsher punishment than would an ordinary murderer or thief. Thus in May 1918, the first Bolshevik 'decree on bribery' declared that: 'If the person guilty of taking or offering bribes belongs to the propertied classes and is using the bribe to preserve or acquire privileges, linked to property rights, then he should be sentenced to the harshest and most unpleasant forced labour and all of his property should be confiscated.'[8]

From the very earliest days of the new Soviet state, in other words, people were to be sentenced not for what they had done, but for who they were.

Unfortunately, nobody ever provided a clear description of what, exactly, a 'class enemy' was supposed to look like. As a result, arrests of all sorts increased dramatically in the wake of the Bolshevik coup. From November 1917, revolutionary tribunals, composed of random 'supporters' of the Revolution, began convicting random 'enemies' of the Revolution. Prison sentences, forced-labour terms, and even capital punishment were arbitrarily meted out to bankers, to merchants' wives, to 'speculators' – meaning anyone engaged in independent economic activity – to former tsarist-era prison warders and to anyone else who seemed suspicious.[9]

The definition of who was and who was not an 'enemy' also varied from place to place, sometimes overlapping with the definition of 'prisoner of war'. Upon occupying a new city, Trotsky's Red Army frequently took bourgeois hostages, who could be shot in case the White Army returned, as it often did along the fluctuating lines of the front. In the interim they could be made to do forced labour, often digging trenches and building barricades.[10] The distinction between political prisoners and common criminals was equally arbitrary. The uneducated members of the temporary commissions and revolutionary tribunals might, for example, suddenly decide that a man caught riding a tram without a ticket had offended society, and sentence him for political crimes.[11] In the end, many such decisions were left up to the policeman or soldiers doing the arresting. Feliks Dzerzhinsky, founder of the Cheka – Lenin's secret police, the forerunner of the KGB – personally kept a little black notebook in which he scribbled down the names and addresses of random 'enemies' he came across while doing his job.[12]

These distinctions would remain vague right up until the collapse of the Soviet Union itself, eighty years later. Nevertheless, the existence of two categories of prisoner – 'political' and 'criminal' – had a profound effect on the formation of the Soviet penal system. During the first decade of Bolshevik rule, Soviet penitentiaries even split into two categories, one for each type of prisoner. The split arose spontaneously, as a reaction to the chaos of the existing prison system. In the very early days of the Revolution, all prisoners were incarcerated under the jurisdiction of the 'traditional' judicial ministries, first the Commissariat of Justice, later the Commissariat of the Interior, and placed in the 'ordinary' prison system. That is, they were thrown into the remnants of the tsarist system, usually into the dirty, gloomy stone prisons which occupied a central position in every major town. During the revolutionary years of 1917 to 1920, these institutions were in total disarray. Mobs had stormed the gaols, self-appointed commissars had sacked the guards, prisoners had received wide-ranging amnesties or had simply walked away.[13]

By the time the Bolsheviks took charge, the few prisons that remained in operation were overcrowded and inadequate. Only weeks after the Revolution, Lenin himself demanded 'extreme measures for the immediate improvement' of food supplies to the Petrograd prisons'.[14] A few months later, a member of the Moscow Cheka visited the city's Taganskaya prison and reported 'terrible cold and filth', as well as typhus and hunger. Most of the prisoners could not carry out their forced-labour sentences because they had no clothes. A newspaper report claimed that Butyrka prison in Moscow, designed to hold 1,000 prisoners, already contained 2,500. Another newspaper complained that the Red Guards 'unsystematically arrest hundreds of people every day, and then don't know what to do with them'.[15]

Overcrowding led to 'creative' solutions. Lacking anything better, the new authorities incarcerated prisoners in basements, attics, empty palaces and old churches. One survivor later remembered being placed in the cellar of a deserted house, in a single room with fifty people, no furniture and little food: those who did not get packages from their families simply starved.[16] In

December 1917, a Cheka commission discussed the fate of fifty-six assorted prisoners – 'thieves, drunks and various "politicals"' – who were being kept in the basement of the Smolny Institute, Lenin's headquarters in Petrograd.[17]

Not everyone suffered from the chaotic conditions. Robert Bruce Lockhart, a British diplomat accused of spying (accurately, as it happened), was imprisoned in 1918 in a room in the Kremlin. He occupied himself playing Patience, and reading Thucydides and Carlyle. From time to time, a former imperial servant brought him hot tea and newspapers.[18]

But even in the remaining traditional gaols, prison regimes were erratic, and prison wardens were inexperienced. A prisoner in the northern Russian city of Vyborg discovered that, in the topsy-turvy post-revolutionary world, his former chauffeur had become a prison guard. The man was delighted to help his former master move to a better, drier cell, and eventually to escape.[19] One White Army colonel also recalled that in the Petrograd prison in December 1917 prisoners came and left at will, while homeless people slept in the cells at night. Looking back on this era, one Soviet official remembered that 'the only people who didn't escape were those who were too lazy'.[20]

The disarray forced the Cheka to come up with new solutions: the Bolsheviks could hardly allow their 'real' enemies to enter the ordinary prison system. Chaotic gaols and lazy guards might be suitable for pickpockets and juvenile delinquents, but for the saboteurs, parasites, speculators, White Army officers, priests, bourgeois capitalists and others who loomed so large in the Bolshevik imagination, more creative solutions were needed.

A solution was found. As early as 4 June 1918, Trotsky called for a group of unruly Czech war prisoners to be pacified, disarmed, and placed in a *kontslager*: a concentration camp. Twelve days later, in a memorandum addressed to the Soviet government, Trotsky again spoke of concentration camps, outdoor prisons in which 'the city and village bourgeoisie . . . shall be mobilized and organized into rear-service battalions to do menial work (cleaning barracks, camps, streets, digging trenches, etc). Those refusing will be fined, and held under arrest until the fine is paid.'[21]

In August, Lenin made use of the term as well. In a telegram to the commissars of Penza, site of an anti-Bolshevik uprising, he called for 'mass terror against the *kulaks* [rich peasants], priests and White Guards' and for the 'unreliable' to be 'locked up in a concentration camp outside town'.[22] The facilities were already in place. During the summer of 1918 – in the wake of the Brest-Litovsk Treaty which ended Russia's participation in the First World War – the regime freed two million war prisoners. The empty camps were immediately turned over to the Cheka.[23]

At the time, the Cheka must have seemed the ideal body to take over the task of incarcerating 'enemies' in 'special' camps. A completely new organization, the Cheka was designed to be the 'sword and shield' of the

Communist Party, and had no allegiance to the official Soviet government or any of its departments. It had no traditions of legality, no obligation to obey the rule of law, no need to consult with the police or the courts or the Commissar of Justice. Its very name spoke of its special status: the All-Russian Extraordinary Commission for Combating Counter-Revolution and Sabotage – or, using the Russian abbreviation for 'Extraordinary Commission' – the Ch-K, or Cheka. It was 'extraordinary' precisely because it existed outside of 'ordinary' legality.

Almost as soon as it was created, the Cheka was given an extraordinary task to carry out. On 5 September 1918, Dzerzhinsky was directed to implement Lenin's policy of Red Terror. Launched in the wake of an assassination attempt on Lenin's life, this wave of terror – arrests, imprisonments, murders – more organized than the random terror of the previous months, was in fact an important component of the civil war, directed against those suspected of working to destroy the Revolution on the 'home front'. It was bloody, it was merciless, and it was cruel – as its perpetrators wanted it to be. *Krasnaya Gazeta*, the organ of the Red Army, described it: 'Without mercy, without sparing, we will kill our enemies in scores of hundreds. Let them be thousands, let them drown themselves in their own blood. For the blood of Lenin . . . let there be floods of blood of the bourgeoisie – more blood, as much as possible . . .'[24]

The Red Terror was crucial to Lenin's struggle for power. Concentration camps, the so-called 'special camps', were crucial to the Red Terror. They were mentioned in the very first decree on Red Terror, which called not only for the arrest and incarceration of 'important representatives of the bourgeoisie, landowners, industrialists, merchants, counter-revolutionary priests, anti-Soviet officers' but also for their 'isolation in concentration camps'.[25] Although there are no reliable figures for numbers of prisoners, by the end of 1919 there were twenty-one registered camps in Russia. At the end of 1920 there were 107, five times as many.[26]

Nevertheless, at this stage, the purpose of the camps remained ambiguous. The prisoners were to carry out labour – but to what end? Was labour meant to re-educate the prisoners? Was it meant to humiliate them? Or was it supposed to help build the new Soviet state? Different Soviet leaders and different institutions had different answers. In February 1919, Dzerzhinsky himself made an eloquent speech advocating a role for the camps in the ideological re-education of the bourgeoisie. The new camps would, he said,

make use of the labour of those persons under arrest; for those gentlemen who live without any occupation; and for those who are unable to work without being forced to do so. Such punishment ought to be applied to those working in Soviet institutions who demonstrate unconscientious attitudes to work, tardiness, etc . . . In this way we will create schools of labour.[27]

When the first official decrees on the special camps were published in the spring of 1919, however, slightly different priorities appeared to take precedence.[28] The decrees, a surprisingly lengthy list of rules and recommendations, suggested that each regional capital set up a camp for no fewer than 300 people, 'on the border of the city, or in nearby buildings like monasteries, estates, farms, etc.'. They mandated an eight-hour workday, with extra hours and night work allowed only 'in agreement with the labour code'. Food packages were forbidden. Meetings with members of the immediate family were allowed, but only on Sundays and holidays. Prisoners attempting escape could have their sentence multiplied by ten. A second attempt could be punished by death – an extremely harsh sentence in comparison with the lax tsarist laws on escape, which the Bolsheviks knew only too well. More importantly, the decrees also made clear that the work of the prisoners was intended not for their own educational benefit, but to pay for the cost of the camp's upkeep. Prisoners with disabilities were to be sent elsewhere. The camps were to be self-financing. Optimistically, the camps' original founders believed that they would pay their own way.[29]

Thanks to the irregular flow of state financing, those running the camps quickly became interested in the idea of self-finance, or at least in making some practical use of their prisoners. In September 1919, a secret report shown to Dzerzhinsky complained that sanitary conditions in one transit camp were 'below criticism', largely because they rendered so many people too ill to work: 'During wet autumn conditions they will not be places to collect people and make use of their labour, but will rather become seedbeds for epidemics and other illnesses.' Among other things, the writer proposed that those incapable of work should be sent elsewhere, thereby making the camp more efficient – a tactic that would later be deployed many times by the leadership of the Gulag. Already, those responsible for the camps were concerned about sickness and hunger mostly in so far as sick and hungry prisoners are not useful prisoners. Their dignity and humanity, not to mention their survival, hardly interested those in charge at all.[30]

In practice, not all camp commanders were concerned with either re-education or self-financing. Instead they preferred to punish the formerly well-off by humiliating them, giving them a taste of the workers' lot. A report from the Ukrainian city of Poltava, filed by a White Army investigating commission after the temporary recapture of the city, noted that bourgeois captives arrested during the Bolshevik occupation had been given jobs which were 'intended as a way of scoffing at people, trying to lower them. For example, one arrestee . . . was forced to clean a thick layer of dirt from a filthy floor with his hands. Another was told to clean a toilet, and . . . was given a tablecloth in order to do the job.'[31]

True, these subtle differences in intention probably made little difference to the many tens of thousands of prisoners, for whom the very fact of being arrested for no reason at all was humiliation enough. They probably did not affect prisoners' living conditions either, which were universally appalling. One priest sent to a camp in Siberia later recalled soup made from entrails, barracks without electricity, and virtually no heat in winter.[32] Aleksandr Izgoev, a leading tsarist-era politician, was sent to a camp north of Petrograd. On the way, his party of prisoners stopped in the town of Vologda. Instead of the hot meal and warm apartments they had been promised, the prisoners were marched from place to place in search of shelter. No transit camp had been prepared for them. Finally, they were lodged in a former school, furnished with 'bare walls and benches'. Those with money eventually purchased their own food in the town.[33]

But this sort of chaotic mistreatment was not reserved only for prisoners. At crucial moments of the civil war, the emergency needs of the Red Army and the Soviet state overrode everything else, from re-education to revenge to considerations of justice. In October 1918, the commander of the northern front sent a request to the Petrograd military commission for 800 workers, urgently needed for road construction and trench digging. As a result, 'a number of citizens from the former merchant classes were invited to appear at Soviet headquarters, allegedly for the purpose of registration for possible labour duty at some future date. When these citizens appeared for registration, they were placed under arrest and sent to the Semenovsky barracks to await their dispatch to the front.' When even this did not produce enough workers, the local Soviet – the local ruling council – simply surrounded a part of Nevsky Prospekt, Petrograd's main shopping street, arrested everyone without a Party card or a certificate proving they worked for a government institution, and marched them off to a nearby barracks. Later, the women were released, but the men were packed off to the north: 'not one of the thus strangely mobilized men was allowed to settle his family affairs, to say goodbye to his relatives, or to obtain suitable clothing and footwear'.[34]

While certainly shocking to the pedestrians thus arrested, that incident would have seemed less odd to Petrograd's workers. For even at this early stage in Soviet history, the line between 'forced labour' and ordinary labour was blurred. Trotsky openly spoke of turning the whole country into a 'workers' army' along the lines of the Red Army. Workers were early on forced to register at central labour offices, from where they might be sent anywhere in the country. Special decrees were passed prohibiting certain kinds of workers – miners, for example – from leaving their jobs. Nor did free workers, in this era of revolutionary chaos, enjoy much better living conditions than prisoners. Looking from the outside, it would not always have been easy to say which was the work site and which the concentration camp.[35]

But this too was a harbinger of what was to come: confusion would beset the definitions of 'camp', 'prison' and 'forced labour' for most of the next decade. Control over penal institutions would remain in constant flux. Responsible institutions would be endlessly renamed and reorganized as different bureaucrats and commissars attempted to gain control over the system.[36]

Nevertheless, it is clear that by the end of the civil war, a pattern had been set. Already, the Soviet Union had clearly developed two separate prison systems, with separate rules, separate traditions, separate ideologies. The Commissariat of Justice, and later the Commissariat of the Interior, ran the 'regular' prison system, which dealt mainly with what the Soviet regime called 'criminals'. Although in practice this system was also chaotic, its prisoners were kept in traditional prisons, and its administrators' stated goals, as presented in an internal memorandum, would be perfectly comprehensible in 'bourgeois' countries: to reform the criminal through corrective labour – 'prisoners should work in order to learn skills they can use to conduct an honest life' – and to prevent prisoners from committing further crimes.[37]

At the same time, the Cheka – later renamed the GPU, the OGPU, the NKVD and finally the KGB – controlled another prison system, one that was at first known as the system of 'special camps' or 'extraordinary camps'. Although the Cheka would use some of the same 're-education' or 'reforging' rhetoric within them, these camps were not really meant to resemble ordinary penal institutions. They were outside the jurisdiction of other Soviet institutions, and invisible to the public eye. They had special rules, harsher escape penalties, stricter regimes. The prisoners inside them had not necessarily been convicted by ordinary courts, if they had been convicted by any courts at all. Set up as an emergency measure, they were ultimately to grow larger and ever more powerful, as the definition of 'enemy' expanded and the power of the Cheka increased. And when the two penal systems, the ordinary and the extraordinary, eventually united, they would unite under the rules of the latter. The Cheka would devour its rivals.

From the start, the 'special' prison system was meant to deal with special prisoners: priests, former tsarist officials, bourgeois speculators, enemies of the new order. But one particular category of 'politicals' interested the authorities more than others. These were members of the non-Bolshevik, revolutionary socialist political parties, mainly the Anarchists, the Left and Right Social Revolutionaries, the Mensheviks, and anyone else who had fought for the Revolution, but had not had the foresight to join Lenin's Bolshevik faction, and had not taken full part in the coup of October 1917. As former allies in the revolutionary struggle against the tsarist regime, they merited special treatment. The Communist Party's Central Committee would repeatedly discuss their fate up until the end of the 1930s, when most of those who remained alive were arrested or shot.[38]

In part, this particular category of prisoner bothered Lenin because, like all leaders of exclusive sects, he reserved his greatest hatred for apostates. During one typical exchange, he called one of his socialist critics a 'swindler', a 'blind puppy', a 'sycophant of the bourgeoisie' and a 'yes-man of blood-suckers and scoundrels', fit only for the 'cesspit of renegades'.[39] Indeed, long before the Revolution, Lenin knew what he would do with those of his socialist comrades who opposed him. One of his revolutionary companions recalled a conversation on this subject:

I said to him: 'Vladimir Ilyich, if you come to power, you'll start hanging the Mensheviks the very next day.' And he glanced at me and said: 'It will be after we've hanged the last Socialist-Revolutionary that the first Menshevik will get hanged.' Then he frowned and gave a laugh.[40]

But the prisoners who belonged to this special category of 'politicals' were also much more difficult to control. Many had spent years in tsarist prisons, and knew how to organize hunger strikes, how to put pressure on their gaolers, how to communicate between prison cells in order to exchange information, and how to organize joint protests. More importantly, they also knew how to contact the outside world, and who to contact. Most of Russia's non-Bolshevik socialist parties still had émigré branches, usually in Berlin or Paris, whose members could do great damage to the Bolsheviks' international image. At the third meeting of the Communist International in 1921, representatives of the émigré branch of the Social Revolutionaries – the party ideologically closest to the Bolsheviks (some of its members actually worked briefly in coalition with them) – read aloud a letter from their imprisoned comrades in Russia. The letter caused a sensation at the Congress, largely because it claimed prison conditions in revolutionary Russia were worse than in tsarist times. 'Our comrades are being half-starved,' it proclaimed, 'many of them are jailed for months without being allowed a meeting with relatives, without letters, without exercise.'[41]

The émigré socialists could and did agitate on the prisoners' behalf, just as they had before the Revolution. Immediately after the Bolshevik coup, several celebrated revolutionaries, including Vera Figner, the author of a memoir of life in tsarist prisons, and Ekaterina Peshkova, the wife of the writer Maxim Gorky, helped relaunch the Political Red Cross, a prisoners' aid organization which had worked underground before the Revolution. Peshkova knew Dzerzhinsky well, and corresponded with him regularly and cordially. Thanks to her contacts and prestige, the Political Red Cross received the right to visit places of imprisonment, to talk to political prisoners, to send them parcels, even to petition for the release of those who were ill, privileges which it retained through much of the 1920s.[42] So improbable did these activities later seem to the writer Lev Razgon, imprisoned in 1937, that he listened to his second wife's stories of the Political Red Cross – her father had been one of the socialist prisoners – as if to 'an unbelievable fairy tale'.[43]

The bad publicity generated by the Western socialists and the Political Red Cross bothered the Bolsheviks a great deal. Many had lived for years in exile, and were therefore sensitive to the opinions of their old international comrades. Many also still believed that the Revolution might spread to the West at any moment, and did not want the progress of communism to be slowed by bad press. By 1922, they were worried enough by Western press reports to launch the first of what would be many attempts to disguise communist terror by attacking 'capitalist terror'. Towards this end, they created an 'alternative' prisoners' aid society: the International Society to Aid the Victims of Revolution – MOPR, according to its Russian acronym – which would purportedly work to help the '100,000 prisoners of capitalism'.[44]

Although the Berlin chapter of the Political Red Cross immediately denounced MOPR for trying to 'silence the groans of those dying in Russian prisons, concentration camps and places of exile', others were taken in. In 1924, MOPR claimed to have four million members, and even held its first international conference, with representatives from around the world.[45] The propaganda made its mark. When the French writer Romain Rolland was asked to comment upon a published collection of letters from socialists in Russian prisons, he responded by claiming that 'There are almost identical things going on in the prisons of Poland; you have them in the prisons of California, where they are martyrizing the workingmen of the IWW; you have them in the English dungeons of the Andaman Islands . . .'[46]

The Cheka also sought to ameliorate the bad press by sending the troublesome socialists further away from their contacts. Some were sent, by administrative order, into distant exile, just as the tsarist regime had once done. Others were sent to remote camps near the northern city of Arkhangelsk, and in particular to one set up in the former monastery of Kholmogory, hundreds of miles to the north of Petrograd, near the White Sea. Nevertheless, even the remotest exiles found means of communication. From Narym, a distant part of Siberia, a small group of 'politicals' in a tiny concentration camp managed to get a letter to an émigré socialist newspaper complaining that they were 'so firmly isolated from the rest of the world that only letters dealing with the health of relatives or our own health can hope to reach their destination. Any other messages . . . do not arrive.' Among their number, they noted, was Olga Romanova, an eighteen-year-old Anarchist, who was sent to a particularly remote part of the region 'where she was fed for three months on bread and hot water'.[47]

Nor did distant exile guarantee peace for the gaolers. Almost everywhere they went, socialist prisoners, accustomed to the privileged treatment once given to political prisoners in tsarist gaols, demanded newspapers, books, walks, unlimited right of correspondence, and, above all, the right to choose their own spokesman when dealing with the authorities. When uncomprehending local Cheka agents refused – they were doubtless unable to tell the difference between an Anarchist and an arsonist – the socialists protested, sometimes violently. According to one description of the Kholmogory camp, a group of prisoners found that

it was necessary to wage a struggle for the most elementary things, such as conceding to socialists and anarchists the ordinary rights of political prisoners. In this struggle they were subjected to all the known punishments, such as solitary confinement, beating, starving, throwing on to the wire, organized firing by the military detachment at the building etc. It will suffice to say that at the end of the year the majority of the Kholmogory inmates could boast, in addition to their past records, hunger strikes totalling thirty to thirty-five days . . .[48]

Ultimately, this same group of prisoners was moved from Kholmogory to another camp at Petrominsk, another monastery. According to a petition they later sent to the authorities, they were greeted there with 'rude shouts and threats', locked six at a time into a tiny former-monks' cell, given bunks 'alive with parasites', forbidden any exercise, books, or writing paper.[49] The commander of Petrominsk, Comrade Bachulis, tried to break the prisoners by depriving them of light and heat – and from time to time by shooting at their windows.[50] In response, they launched another endless round of hunger strikes and protest letters. Ultimately, they demanded to be moved from the camp itself, which they claimed was malarial.[51]

Other camp bosses complained about such prisoners too. In a letter to Dzerzhinsky, one wrote that in his camp 'White Guards who feel themselves to be political prisoners' had organized themselves into a 'spirited team', making it impossible for the guards to work: 'they defame the administration, blacken its name . . . they despise the honest and good name of the Soviet worker'.[52] Some guards took matters into their own hands. In April 1921, one group of prisoners in Petrominsk refused to work and demanded more food rations. Fed up with this insubordination, the Arkhangelsk regional authorities ordered all 540 of them sentenced to death. They were duly shot.[53]

Elsewhere, the authorities tried to keep the peace by taking the opposite tack, granting the socialists all of their demands. Bertha Babina, a member of the Social Revolutionaries, remembered her arrival at the 'socialist wing' of Butyrka prison in Moscow as a joyous reunion with friends, people 'from the St Petersburg underground, from my student years, and from the many different towns and cities where we had lived during our wanderings'. The prisoners were allowed free run of the prison. They organized morning gymnastics sessions, founded an orchestra and a chorus, created a 'club' supplied with foreign journals and a good library. According to tradition – dating back to pre-revolutionary days – every prisoner left behind his books after he was freed. A prisoners' council assigned everyone cells, some of which were beautifully supplied with carpets, on the floors and the walls. Another prisoner remembered that 'we strolled along the corridors as if they were boulevards'.[54] To Babina, prison life seemed unreal: 'Can't they even lock us up seriously?'[55]

The Cheka leadership wondered the same. In a report to Dzerzhinsky dated January 1921, a prison inspector complained angrily that in Butyrka prison 'men and women walk about together, anarchist and counter-revolutionary slogans hang from the walls of cells'.[56] Dzerzhinsky recommended a stricter regime – but when a stricter regime was brought in, the prisoners protested again.

The Butyrka idyll ended soon afterwards. In April 1921, according to a letter which a group of Social Revolutionaries wrote to the authorities, 'between 3 and 4 a.m., an armed group of men entered the cells and began to attack . . . women were dragged out of their cells by their arms and legs and hair, others were beaten up'. In their own later reports, the Cheka described this 'incident' as a rebellion which had got out of hand – and resolved never again to allow so many political prisoners to accumulate in Moscow.[57] By February 1922, the 'socialist wing' of the Butyrka prison had been dissolved.

Repression had not worked. Concessions had not worked. Even in its special camps, the Cheka could not control its special prisoners. Nor could it prevent news about them from reaching the outside world. Clearly, another solution was needed, both for them and for all the other unruly counter-revolutionaries gathered in the special prison system. By the spring of 1923, a solution had been found: Solovetsky.

2

'The First Camp of the Gulag'

There are monks and priests,
Prostitutes and thieves.
There are princes here, and barons –
But their crowns have been taken away . . .

On this island, the rich have no home
No castles, no palaces . . .

– Anonymous prisoner's poem, written
on the Solovetsky islands, 1926[1]

Looking down from the top of the bell tower in the far corner of the old Solovetsky monastery, the outlines of the Solovetsky concentration camp are still visible today. A thick stone wall still surrounds the Solovetsky kremlin, the central collection of monastery buildings and churches, originally built in the fifteenth century, which later housed the main administration of the camp and its central barracks. Just to the west lie the docks, now home to a few fishing boats, once crowded with the prisoners who arrived weekly and sometimes daily here during the short navigation season of the far north. Beyond them stretch the flat expanses of the White Sea. From here, the boat to Kem, the mainland transit camp from which prisoners once embarked for their journey, takes several hours. The ride to Arkhangelsk, the largest White Sea port and the regional capital, requires an overnight journey.

Looking north, it is just possible to see the faintest outlines of Sekirka, the hilltop church whose cellars once contained Solovetsky's notorious punishment cells. To the east stands the power station built by the prisoners, still very much in use today. Just behind it lies the stretch of land where the botanical garden used to be. There, in the early days of the camp, some of the prisoners grew experimental plants, trying to determine what, if anything, might usefully be harvested in the far north.

Finally, beyond the botanical garden, lie the other islands in the Solovetsky chain. Scattered across the White Sea are Bolshaya Muksalma, where

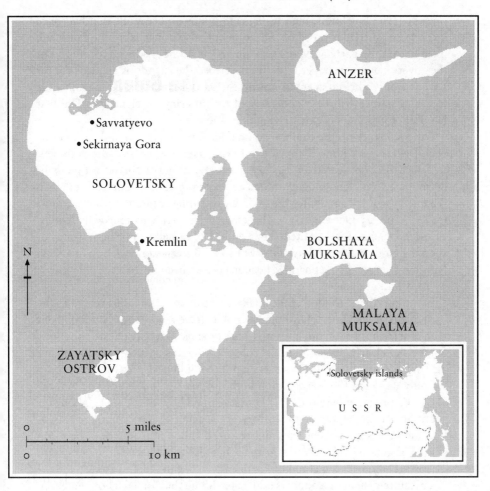

1 The Solovetsky archipelago, in the White Sea

prisoners once bred silver-black foxes for their fur; Anzer, site of special camps for invalids, for women with babies, and for former monks; Zayatsky Ostrov, the location of the women's punishment camp.[2] Not by accident did Solzhenitsyn choose the metaphor of an 'archipelago' to describe the Soviet camp system. Solovetsky, the first Soviet camp to be planned and built with any expectation of permanence, developed on a genuine archipelago, spreading outwards island by island, taking over the old churches and buildings of an ancient monastic community as it grew.

The monastery complex had served as a prison before. Solovetsky monks, faithful servants of the tsar, had helped incarcerate his political opponents – wayward priests and the odd rebel aristocrat among them – from the sixteenth century.[3] The loneliness, high walls, cold winds and seagulls that had once attracted a particular breed of solitary monk also appealed to the Bolshevik imagination. As early as May 1920, an article in the Arkhangelsk edition of the government newspaper *Izvestiya* described the islands as an ideal site for a work camp: 'the harsh environment, the work regime, the fight against the forces of nature will be a good school for all criminal elements'. The first handful of prisoners began arriving that summer.[4]

Others, higher up the chain of command, were interested in the islands as well. Dzerzhinsky himself appears to have persuaded the Soviet government to hand the confiscated monastery property, along with the property of Petrominsk and Kholmogory monasteries, over to the Cheka – by then renamed the GPU, and later the OGPU, or Unified State Political Administration – on 13 October 1923. Together they were christened the 'camps of special significance'.[5] Later, they would be known as 'northern camps of special significance': *Severnye lagerya osobogo naznacheniya*, or SLON. In Russian, *slon* means 'elephant'. The name was to become a source of humour, of irony and of menace.

In the survivors' folklore, Solovetsky was forever after remembered as the 'first camp of the Gulag'.[6] Although scholars have more recently pointed out that a wide range of other camps and prisons also existed at this time, Solovetsky clearly played a special role not only in survivors' memories, but also in the memory of the Soviet secret police.[7] Solovetsky may not have been the only prison in the Soviet Union in the 1920s, but it was *their* prison, the OGPU's prison, where the OGPU first learned how to use slave labour for profit. In a 1945 lecture on the history of the camp system, Comrade Nasedkin, then the system's chief administrator, claimed not only that the camp system originated in Solovetsky in 1920, but also that the entire Soviet system of 'forced labour as a method of re-education' began there in 1926.[8]

This statement at first appears odd, considering that forced labour had been a recognized form of punishment in the Soviet Union since 1918. It appears less odd, however, if we look at how the concept of forced labour evolved on Solovetsky itself. For although everyone worked on the island, prisoners were not, in the early days, organized into anything remotely resembling a 'system'. Nor is there evidence that their labour was in any way profitable.

To begin with, one of the two main categories of prisoner on Solovetsky did not, at first, work at all. These were the approximately 300 socialist 'politicals', who had actually begun to arrive on the island in June 1923. Sent from the Petrominsk camp, as well as from Butyrka and the other Moscow and Petrograd prisons, they were taken upon arrival immediately to the smaller Savvatyevo monastery, several kilometres north of the main monastery complex. There, the Solovetsky guards could ensure that they were isolated from other prisoners, and could not infect them with their enthusiasm for hunger strikes and protests.

Initially, the socialists were granted the 'privileges' of political prisoners that they had so long demanded: newspapers, books and, within a barbed-wire enclosure, freedom of movement and freedom from work. Each of the major political parties – the Left Social Revolutionaries, the Right Social Revolutionaries, the Anarchists, the Social Democrats and later the Socialist Zionists – chose its own leader, and occupied rooms in its own wing of the former monastery.[9]

To Elinor Olitskaya, a young Left Social Revolutionary arrested in 1924, Savvatyevo seemed, at first, 'nothing like a prison', and came as a shock after her months in the dark Lubyanka prison in Moscow. Her room, a former monks' cell in what had become the women's section of the Social Revolutionary wing, was

light, clean, freshly washed, with two large, wide, open windows. The cell was full of light and air. There were, of course, no bars on the windows. In the middle of the cell stood a small table, covered in a white cloth. Along the wall were four beds, neatly covered with sheets. Beside each one stood a small night table. On the tables lay books, notebooks, and pens.

As she marvelled at the surroundings, the tea served in teapots and the sugar served in a sugar bowl, her cell mates explained that the prisoners had created the pleasant atmosphere on purpose: 'we want to live as human beings'.[10] Olitskaya soon learned that although they suffered from tuberculosis and other diseases, and rarely had enough to eat, the Solovetsky politicals were notably well-organized, with the 'elder' of each party cell responsible for storing, cooking and distributing food. Because they still had special 'political' status, they were also allowed to receive packages, both from relatives and from the Political Red Cross. Although the Political Red Cross had begun to have difficulties – in 1922 its offices were raided and its property confiscated – Ekaterina Peshkova, its well-connected leader, was personally still allowed to send aid to political prisoners. In 1923, she shipped a whole train wagon full of food to the Savvatyevo political prisoners. A shipment of clothes went north in October of the same year.[11]

This, then, was the solution to the public relations problem posed by the politicals: give them what they want, more or less, but put them as far away from anyone else as humanly possible. It was a solution that was not to last: the Soviet system would not long tolerate exceptions. In the meantime, the illusion was easy to see through – for there was another, far larger group of prisoners on Solovetsky as well. 'Upon landing on the Solovets soil, we all felt we were entering a new and strange phase of life,' wrote one political. 'From conversations with the criminals, we learned of the shocking regime which the administration is applying to them . . .'[12]

*

With far less pomp and ceremony, the main barracks of the Solovetsky kremlin were also filling up quickly with prisoners whose status was not so assured. From a few hundred in 1923, the numbers grew to 6,000 by 1925.[13] Among them were White Army officers and sympathizers, 'speculators', former aristocrats, sailors who had fought in the Kronstadt rebellion, and genuine common criminals. For these inmates, tea in teapots and sugar in sugar bowls were much harder to come by. Or, rather, they were hard to come by for some, easier for others; for, above all, what characterized life in the 'criminal' barracks of the Solovetsky special camp in these very early years was irrationality, and an unpredictability which began at the moment of arrival. On their first night in the camp, writes the memoirist and former prisoner Boris Shiryaev, he and other new arrivals were greeted by Comrade A. P. Nogtev, Solovetsky's first camp commander. 'I welcome you,' he told them, with what Shiryaev describes as 'irony': 'As you know, here, there is no Soviet authority, only Solovetsky authority. Any rights that you had before you can forget. Here we have our own laws.' The phrase 'there is no Soviet authority, only Solovetsky authority' would be repeated again and again, as many memoirists attest.[14]

Over the next few days and weeks, most of the prisoners would experience 'Solovetsky authority' as a combination of criminal neglect and random cruelty. Living conditions in the converted churches and monks' cells were primitive, and little care was taken to improve them. On his first night in his Solovetsky barracks, the writer Oleg Volkov was given a place on *sploshnye nary*, bunks that were in fact broad planks (of which we shall hear more later) on which a number of men slept in a row. As he lay down, bedbugs began falling on to him 'one after another, like ants. I couldn't sleep.' He went outside, where he was immediately enveloped by 'clouds of mosquitoes . . . I gazed with envy at those who slept soundly, covered in parasites.'[15]

Outside the main kremlin compound, things were hardly better. Officially, SLON maintained nine separate camps on the archipelago, each one further divided into battalions. But some prisoners were also kept in even more primitive conditions in the woods, near the forestry work sites.[16] Dmitri Likhachev, later to become one of Russia's most celebrated literary critics, felt himself privileged because he had not been assigned to one of the many unnamed camp sites in the forest. He visited one, he wrote, 'and became ill with the horror of seeing it: people slept in the trenches which they had dug, sometimes with bare hands, during the day'.[17]

On the outlying islands, the central camp administration exerted even less control over the behaviour of individual guards and camp bosses. In his memoirs, one prisoner, Kiselev, described a camp on Anzer, one of the smaller islands. Commanded by another Chekist, Vanka Potapov, the camp consisted of three barracks and a guards' headquarters, housed in an old church. The prisoners worked cutting trees, with no breaks, no respite and little food.

Desperate for a few days' rest, they cut off their hands and feet. According to Kiselev, Potapov kept these 'pearls' preserved in a large pile and showed them to visitors, to whom he also bragged that he had personally murdered more than 400 people with his own hands. 'No one returned from there,' Kiselev wrote of Anzer. Even if his report exaggerates, it indicates the real terror which the outer camps held for the prisoners.[18]

All over the islands, disastrous hygienic conditions, overwork and poor food naturally led to illness, and above all to typhus. Of the 6,000 prisoners held by SLON in 1925, about a quarter died in the winter of 1925–6, in the wake of a particularly vicious epidemic. By some calculations, the numbers stayed this high: from a quarter to one half of the prisoners may have died of typhus, starvation and other epidemics every year. One document records 25,552 cases of typhus in the (by then much larger) SLON camps in the winter of 1929–30.[19]

But for some prisoners, Solovetsky meant worse than discomfort and illness. On the islands, prisoners were subjected to the kind of sadism and pointless torture of a sort found more rarely in the Gulag in later years when – as Solzhenitsyn puts it – 'slave-driving had become a thought-out *system*'.[20] Although many memoirs describe these acts, the most thorough catalogue is found in the account of an investigating commission sent from Moscow later in the decade. During the course of their investigation, the horrified Moscow officials discovered that Solovetsky guards had regularly left undressed prisoners in the old, unheated cathedral bell towers in the winter, their hands and feet tied behind their backs with a single piece of rope. They had also put prisoners 'to the bench', meaning they were forced to sit on poles for up to eighteen hours without moving, sometimes with weights tied to their legs and their feet not touching the floor, a position guaranteed to leave them crippled. Sometimes, prisoners would be made to go naked to the baths, up to 2 kilometres away, in freezing weather. Or they were deliberately given rotten meat. Or they were refused medical help. At other times, prisoners would be given pointless, unnecessary tasks: to move huge quantities of snow from one place to another, for example, or to jump off bridges into rivers whenever a guard shouted 'Dolphin!'[21]

Another form of torture specific to the islands, mentioned in both archives and memoirs, was to be sent 'to the mosquitoes'. Klinger, a White Army officer who later made one of the few successful escapes from Solovetsky, wrote that he once saw this torture inflicted on a prisoner who complained because a parcel sent to him from home had been requisitioned. Angry prison guards responded by removing all of his clothes, including his underwear, and tying him to a post in the forest, which was, in the northern summer, swarming with mosquitoes. 'Within half an hour, his whole unlucky body was covered with swelling from the bites,' wrote Klinger. Eventually, the man fainted from the pain and loss of blood.[22]

Mass executions seemed to take place almost at random, and many prisoners recall feeling terrified by the prospect of arbitrary death. Likhachev claims to have narrowly escaped execution in one mass murder in late October 1929. Archival documents do indeed indicate that about fifty people (not 300, as he wrote) were executed at that time, having been accused of trying to organize a rebellion.[23]

Nearly as bad as direct execution was a sentence to Sekirka, the church whose cellars had become the Solovetsky punishment cells. Indeed, although many stories were told about what went on in the church's cellars, so few men returned from Sekirka that it is difficult to be certain of what conditions there were really like. One witness did see one of the brigades being marched to work: 'a line of terrified people, with an inhuman look, some dressed in sacks, all barefoot, surrounded by heavy guard . . .'[24]

As Solovetsky legend would have it, the long flight of 365 wooden steps which lead down the steep hill from the Sekirka church also played a role in group killings. When, at one point, camp authorities forbade guards from shooting the Sekirka prisoners, they began to arrange 'accidents' – and threw them down the steps.[25] In recent years, the descendants of Solovetsky prisoners have erected a wooden cross at the bottom of the steps, to mark the spot where these prisoners allegedly died. It is now a peaceful and rather beautiful place – so beautiful that in the late 1990s, the Solovetsky local history museum printed a Christmas card showing Sekirka, the steps and the cross.

While the reigning spirit of irrationality and unpredictability meant that thousands died in the SLON camps in the early 1920s, the same irrationality and unpredictability also helped others not just only to live but – quite literally – to sing and dance. By 1923, a handful of prisoners had already begun organizing the camp's first theatre. At first the 'actors', many of whom spent ten hours a day cutting wood in the forests before coming to rehearsal, did not have scripts, so played classics from memory. The theatre improved greatly in 1924, when a whole group of former professional actors arrived (all sentenced as members of the same 'counter-revolutionary' movement). That year, they put on productions of Chekhov's *Uncle Vanya* and Gorky's *Children of the Sun*.[26]

Later, operas and operettas were performed in Solovetsky's theatre, which also hosted acrobatic performances and films. One musical evening included an orchestral piece, a quintet performance, a chorus and arias from a Russian opera.[27] The repertoire for March 1924 included a play by the writer Leonid Andreev (whose son Danil, another writer, would later be a Gulag prisoner), a play by Gogol, and an evening dedicated to the memory of Sarah Bernhardt.[28]

Nor was theatre the only form of culture available. Solovetsky also had a library, which eventually numbered 30,000 books, as well as the botanical garden, in which prisoners experimented with Arctic plants. Solovetsky captives, many former St Petersburg scientists among them, also organized a museum of local flora, fauna, art and history.[29] Some of the more elite prisoners had use of a 'club' which – at least in photographs – appears positively bourgeois. The pictures show a piano, parquet floors, and portraits of Marx, Lenin and Lunacharsky, the first Soviet Culture Minister, all very cosy-looking.[30]

Using the monks' old lithography equipment, the Solovetsky prisoners also produced monthly magazines and newspapers featuring satirical cartoons, extremely homesick poetry, and surprisingly frank fiction. In the December 1925 edition of *Solovetskie ostrova* (the name means 'Solovetsky islands') one short story described a former actress who had arrived on Solovetsky, was forced to work as a washerwoman, and was unable to accustom herself to her new life. The story ends with the sentence 'Solovetsky is cursed.'

In another short story, a former aristocrat who had once known 'intimate evenings at the Winter Palace' finds comfort in his new situation only by visiting another aristocrat and talking of old times.[31] Clearly, the clichés of social realism were not yet mandatory. Not all of the stories have the happy ending which later became obligatory, and not all of the fictional prisoners joyfully adapted to Soviet reality.

Solovetsky journals also contained more learned articles, ranging from Likhachev's analysis of criminal gambling etiquette to works on the art and architecture of Solovetsky's ruined churches. Between 1926 and 1929, the SLON printing house even managed to put out twenty-nine editions of the work of the Solovetsky Society for Local Lore. The society conducted studies of island flora and fauna, focusing on particular species – the northern deer, the local plants – and published articles on brick production, wind currents, useful minerals and fur farming. So interested did some prisoners become in the latter subject that in 1927, when the economic activity of the island was at its height, a group of them imported some silver-black 'breeder' foxes from Finland to improve the quality of the local herds. Among other things, the Society for Local Lore carried out a geological survey, which the director of the island's local history museum still uses today.[32]

These more privileged prisoners also participated in the new Soviet rites and celebrations, occasions from which a later generation of camp inmates would be deliberately excluded. An article in the September 1925 edition of *Solovetskie ostrova* describes the First of May celebration on the island. Alas, the weather was poor:

On the First of May, flowers are blooming all over the Soviet Union, but in Solovetsky, the sea is still filled with ice, and there is plenty of snow. Nevertheless, we prepare to celebrate the proletarian holiday. From early morning, there is agitation in the barracks. Some are washing. Some are shaving. Someone is repairing his clothes, someone is shining his boots . . .[33]

Even more surprising – from the perspective of later years – was the long persistence of religious ceremonies on the islands. One former prisoner, V. A. Kazachkov, remembered the 'grandiose' Easter of 1926:

Not long before the holiday, the new boss of the division demanded that all who wanted to go to church should present him with a declaration. Almost no one did so at first – people were afraid of the consequences. But just before Easter, a huge number made their declarations ... Along the road to Onufrievskaya church, the cemetery chapel, marched a great procession, people walked in several rows. Of course we didn't all fit into the chapel. People stood outside, and those who came late couldn't even hear the service.[34]

Even the May 1924 edition of *Solovetskii Lager*, another prison journal, editorialized cautiously but positively on the subject of Easter, 'an ancient holiday celebrating the coming of spring', which 'under a Red banner, can still be observed'.[35]

Along with religious holidays, a small handful of the original monks also continued to survive, to the amazement of many prisoners, well into the latter half of the decade. They functioned as 'monk-instructors', supposedly transmitting to the prisoners the skills needed to run their formerly successful farming and fishing enterprises – Solovetsky herring had once been a feature of the Tsar's table – as well as the secrets of the complex canal system which they had used to link the island churches for centuries. The monks were joined, over the years, by dozens more Soviet priests and members of the Church hierarchy, both Orthodox and Catholic, who had opposed the confiscation of Church wealth, or who had violated the 'decree on separation of Church and state'. The clergy, somewhat like the socialist politicals, were allowed to live separately, in one particular barrack of the kremlin, and were also allowed to hold services in the small chapel of the former cemetery right up until 1930–31 – a luxury forbidden to other prisoners except on special occasions.

These 'privileges' appear to have caused some resentment, and there were occasional tensions between the clergy and the ordinary prisoners. One female prisoner, removed to a special maternal colony on the island of Anzer after giving birth, remembered that the nuns on the island 'held themselves away from us unbelievers ... they were angry, they didn't like the children, and they hated us'. Other clergy, as many memoirs repeat, took quite the opposite attitude, devoting themselves to active evangelism and social work, among criminals as well as other politicals.[36]

For those who had it, money could also buy relief from work in the forests, and insurance against torture and death. Solovetsky had a restaurant which could (illegally) serve prisoners. Those who could afford the necessary bribes could import their own food as well.[37] The camp administration at one point even set up 'shops' on the island, where prisoners could purchase items of clothing, at prices twice as high as in normal Soviet shops.[38] One person who allegedly bought his way out of suffering was 'Count Violaro', a swashbuckling figure whose name appears (with a wide variety of spellings) in several memoirs. The Count, usually described as the 'Mexican ambassador to Egypt', had made the mistake of going to visit his wife's family in Soviet Georgia just after the Revolution. Both he and his wife were arrested, and deported to the far north. Although they were at first imprisoned – where the Countess was put to work doing laundry – camp legend recalls that for the sum of 5,000 roubles, the Count bought the right for both of them to live in a separate house, with a horse and a servant.[39] Others recall the presence of a rich Indian merchant from Bombay, who later left with the help of the British consulate in Moscow. His memoirs were later published in the émigré press.[40]

So striking were these and other examples of wealthy prisoners living well – and leaving early – that in 1926 a group of less privileged prisoners wrote a letter to the Presidium of the Communist Party Central Committee, denouncing the 'chaos and violence which rule the Solovetsky concentration camp'. Using phrases designed to appeal to the communist leadership, they complained that 'those with money can fix themselves up with the money, thereby placing all of the hardship upon the shoulders of the workers and peasants who have no money'. While the rich bought themselves easier jobs, they wrote, 'the poor work 14–16 hours a day'.[41] As it turned out, they were not the only ones feeling dissatisfied with the haphazard practices of the Solovetsky camp commanders.

If random violence and unfair treatment bothered the prisoners, those higher up the Soviet hierarchy were disturbed by somewhat different issues. By the middle of the decade, it had become clear that the camps of SLON, like the rest of the 'ordinary' prison system, had failed to meet the most important of their stated goals: to become self-supporting.[42] In fact, not only were Soviet concentration camps, both 'special' and 'ordinary', failing to make a profit, but their commanders were also constantly demanding more money.

In this, Solovetsky resembled the other Soviet prisons of the time. On the island, the extremes of cruelty and comfort were probably starker than elsewhere, due to the special nature of the prisoners and the guards, but the same irregularities would have characterized other camps and prisons across the Soviet Union at this time as well. In theory, the ordinary prison system also consisted of work 'colonies' linked to farms, workshops and factories, and their economic activity too was badly organized and unprofitable.[43] A 1928 inspector's report on one such camp, in rural Karelia – 59 prisoners, plus 7 horses, 2 pigs and 21 cows – complained that only half the prisoners had blankets; that horses were in poor condition (and one had been sold to a Gypsy, without authorization); that other horses were regularly used to run errands for the camp guards; that when the camp's prisoner blacksmith was freed, he walked away with all of his tools; that none of the camp's buildings had heating or even insulation, with the exception of the chief administrator's residence. Worse, that same chief administrator spent three or four days a week outside the camp; frequently released prisoners early without permission; 'stubbornly refused' to teach agronomy to the prisoners; and openly stated his belief in the 'uselessness' of prisoner re-education. Some of the prisoners' wives lived at the camp; other wives came for long visits and disappeared into the woods with their husbands. The guards indulged in 'petty quarrels and drunkenness'.[44] No wonder that higher authorities took the local Karelian government to task in 1929 for 'failing to understand the importance of forced labour as a measure of social defence and its advantageousness to the state and society'.[45]

Such camps were clearly unprofitable, and had been from the start, as the records show. As early as July 1919, the leaders of the Cheka in Gomel, Belorussia, sent a letter to Dzerzhinsky demanding an urgent 500,000-rouble subsidy: construction of their local camp had ground to a halt for lack of funding.[46] Over the subsequent decade, the different ministries and institutions that vied for the right to control prison camps continued to squabble over funding as well as power. Periodic amnesties were declared to relieve the prison system, culminating in a major amnesty in the autumn of 1927, on the tenth anniversary of the October Revolution. More than 50,000 people were released from the ordinary prison system, largely because of the need to relieve overcrowding and save money.[47]

By 10 November 1925, the need to 'make better use of prisoners' was recognized at the highest level. At that time, G. L. Pyatakov, a Bolshevik who would hold a series of influential economic positions, wrote to Dzerzhinsky. 'I have come to the conclusion,' his letter explained, 'that in order to create the most elementary conditions for work culture, compulsory labour settlements will have to be established in certain regions. Such settlements could relieve overcrowding in places of incarceration. The GPU should be instructed to explore these issues.' He then listed four regions which needed urgent development, all of which – the island of Sakhalin in the far east, the land around the mouth of the Yenisei River in the far north, the Kazakh steppe, and the area around the Siberian city of Nerchinsk – later became camps. Dzerzhinsky approved the memo, and sent it on to two other colleagues to develop further.[48]

At first, nothing happened, perhaps because Dzerzhinsky himself died soon afterwards. Nevertheless, the memo proved a harbinger of change. Up until the middle of the 1920s, the Soviet leadership had not been clear whether its prisons and camps were primarily intended to re-educate prisoners, to punish prisoners, or to make profits for the regime. Now, the many institutions with a stake in the fate of the concentration camps were slowly reaching a consensus: the prisons were to be self-sufficient. By the end of the decade, the messy world of the post-revolutionary Soviet prisons would be transformed, and a new system would emerge from the chaos. Solovetsky would not become just an organized economic concern, it would become a model camp, an example to be cloned many thousands of times, all across the USSR.

Even if no one was aware of it at the time, the importance of Solovetsky would become clear enough in retrospect. Later, reporting back to a Solovetsky Party meeting in 1930, a local commander named Comrade Uspensky would declare that 'the experience of the work of the Solovetsky camp persuaded the Party and the government that the system of prisons across the Soviet Union must be exchanged for a system of corrective-labour camps'.[49]

Some of these changes were anticipated from the beginning, at the highest level, as the memo to Dzerzhinsky shows. Yet the techniques of the new system – the new methods of running camps, of organizing the prisoners and their work regime – were created on the island itself. Chaos may have ruled on Solovetsky in the mid-1920s, but out of that chaos the future Gulag system emerged.

At least a part of the explanation of how and why SLON changed revolves around the personality of Naftaly Aronovich Frenkel, a prisoner who rose through the ranks to become one of the most influential Solovetsky commanders. On the one hand, Solzhenitsyn claims in *The Gulag Archipelago* that Frenkel personally invented the plan to feed prisoners according to the quantity of their work. This deadly labour system, which destroyed weaker prisoners within a matter of weeks, would later cause uncounted numbers of deaths, as we shall see. On the other hand, a wide range of Russian and Western historians dispute Frenkel's importance, and dismiss the many stories of Frenkel's omnipotence as mere legend.[50]

In fact, Solzhenitsyn probably did give Frenkel too much credit: prisoners in earlier, pre-Solovetsky Bolshevik camps also mention being given extra food for extra work, and in any case the idea is in some sense obvious, and need not necessarily have been invented by one man.[51] Nevertheless, recently opened archives, especially the regional archives of Karelia – the Soviet republic to which Solovetsky then belonged – do make his importance clear. Even if Frenkel did not invent every aspect of the system, he did find a way to turn a prison camp into an apparently profitable economic institution, and he did so at a time, in a place, and in a manner which may well have brought that idea to the attention of Stalin.

But the confusion is not surprising either. Frenkel's name appears in many of the memoirs written about the early days of the camp system, and from them it is clear that even in his own lifetime the man's identity was wreathed in myth. Official photographs show a calculatingly sinister-looking man in a leather cap and a carefully trimmed moustache; one memoirist remembers him 'dressed as a dandy'.[52] One of his OGPU colleagues, who greatly admired him, marvelled at his perfect memory, and his ability to do sums in his head: 'he never wrote anything down on paper'.[53] Soviet propaganda later waxed eloquent about the 'incredible capacity of his memory' as well, and spoke of his 'excellent knowledge of timber and forest work in general', his agricultural and engineering expertise, and his extensive general knowledge:

One day, for instance, he got into a conversation with two workers of the trust that manufactures soap, perfumes and cosmetics. He very soon reduced them to silence, as he displayed an enormous knowledge of perfumery, and even turned out to be an expert on the world market and the peculiarities of the olfactory likes and dislikes of the inhabitants of the Malay islands![54]

Others hated and feared him. In a series of special meetings of the Solovetsky Party cell in 1928, Frenkel's colleagues accused him of organizing his own network of spies, 'so he knows everything about everybody earlier than everyone else'.[55] As early as 1927, stories about him had reached as far as Paris. In one of the first books about Solovetsky, a French anti-communist wrote of Frenkel that 'thanks to his horribly insensitive initiatives, millions of unhappy people are overwhelmed by terrible labour, by atrocious suffering'.[56]

His contemporaries were also unclear about his origins. Solzhenitsyn called him a 'Turkish Jew born in Constantinople'.[57] Another described him as a 'Hungarian manufacturer'.[58] Shiryaev claimed he came from Odessa, while others said he was from Austria, or from Palestine, or that he had worked in the Ford factory in America.[59] The story is somewhat clarified by his prisoner registration card, which states clearly that he was born in 1883 in Haifa, at a time when Palestine was a part of the Ottoman Empire. From there, he made his way (perhaps via Odessa, perhaps via Austro-Hungary) to the Soviet Union, where he described himself as a 'merchant'.[60] In 1923 the authorities arrested him for 'illegally crossing borders', which could mean that he was a merchant who indulged in a bit of smuggling, or simply that he was a merchant who had become too successful for the Soviet Union to tolerate. They sentenced him to ten years' hard labour on Solovetsky.[61]

How, precisely, Naftaly Frenkel managed the metamorphosis from prisoner to camp commander also remains mysterious. Legend has it that upon arriving in the camp, he was so shocked by the poor organization, by the sheer waste of money and labour, that he sat down and wrote a very precise letter, describing exactly what was wrong with every single one of the camp's industries, forestry, farming and brick-making among them. He put the letter into the prisoners' 'complaints box', where it attracted the attention of an administrator who sent it, as a curiosity, to Genrikh Yagoda, the Chekist who was then moving rapidly up the ranks of the secret police bureaucracy, and would eventually become its leader. Allegedly, Yagoda immediately demanded to meet the letter's author. According to one contemporary (and

Solzhenitsyn as well, who names no source), Frenkel himself claimed that he was at one point whisked off to Moscow, where he discussed his ideas with Stalin and Kaganovich, one of Stalin's henchmen, as well.[62] This is where the legend grows mistier: although records show that Frenkel did indeed meet Stalin in the 1930s, and although he was protected by Stalin during the Party purge years, no record has yet been found of any visit in the 1920s. This is not to say that it did not happen: the records may simply not have survived.[63]

Some circumstantial evidence backs up these stories. Naftaly Frenkel was, for example, promoted from prisoner to guard within a surprisingly short period, even by the chaotic standards of SLON. By November 1924, when Frenkel had been resident in the camp for less than a year, the SLON administration had already applied for his early release. The request was finally granted in 1927. In the meantime, the camp administration would regularly submit statements to the OGPU describing Frenkel in glowing terms: 'in camp he conducted himself as such an exceptionally talented worker that he has won the confidence of the administration of SLON, and is treated with authority . . . he is one of the rare, responsible workers'.[64]

We also know that Frenkel organized, and then ran, the *Ekonomicheskaya kommercheskaya chast*, the Economic-Commercial Department of SLON, and in that capacity attempted to make the Solovetsky camps not merely self-supporting, as the decrees on concentration camps required, but actually profitable – to the point where they began to take jobs away from other enterprises. Although these were state enterprises, not private enterprises, elements of competition still remained in the Soviet economy in the 1920s, and Frenkel took advantage of them. By September 1925, with Frenkel running its economic department, SLON had already won the right to cut 130,000 cubic metres of wood in Karelia, outbidding a civilian forestry enterprise in the process. SLON had also become a shareholder in the Karelian Communal Bank, and was bidding for the right to build a road from Kem to the far northern city of Ukhta.[65]

From the beginning the Karelian authorities were unnerved by all of this activity, particularly since they had initially opposed the construction of the camp altogether.[66] Later, their complaints grew louder. At a meeting called to discuss SLON's expansion, local authorities complained that the camp had unfair access to cheap labour, and would therefore put ordinary foresters out of work. Still later, the mood of the meetings shifted, and those in attendance raised more serious objections. At a meeting of the Karelian Council of People's Commissars – the government of the Karelian Republic – in February 1926, several local leaders attacked SLON for overcharging them, and for demanding too much money for the building of the road from Kem to Ukhta. 'It has become clear,' summed up Comrade Yuzhnev angrily, that 'SLON is a *kommersant*, a merchant with large, grabbing hands, and that its basic goal is to make profits.'[67]

The Karelian trading enterprise, a state company, was also up in arms against SLON's decision to open its own shop in Kem. The state enterprise could not afford to open such a business, but SLON, which could demand longer hours from its prisoner employees, and could pay them far less – nothing, in fact – managed to do so.[68] Worse, the authorities complained, SLON's special links with the OGPU allowed it to disregard local laws and avoid paying money into the regional budget.[69]

The argument over the profitability, efficiency and fairness of prison labour was to continue for the next quarter-century (and will be discussed more thoroughly later in this book). But in the mid-1920s, the Karelian local authorities were not winning it. In his 1925 reports on the economic condition of the Solovetsky camp, Comrade Fyodor Eichmanns – at this point Nogtev's deputy, although he would later run the camp – bragged about SLON's economic achievements, claiming that its brick factory, formerly in a 'pathetic state', was now thriving, its woodcutting enterprises were overfulfilling that year's plan, its power plant had been completed, and fish production had doubled.[70] Versions of these reports later appeared both in Solovetsky's journals and elsewhere in the Soviet Union for popular consumption.[71] They contained careful calculations: one report estimated the average daily cost of rations at 29 kopeks, the annual cost of clothing at 34 roubles and 57 kopeks. The total expenditure on each prisoner, including medical care and transport, was said to be 211 roubles and 67 kopeks per year.[72] Although as late as 1929, the camp was in fact running a deficit of 1.6 million roubles[73] – quite possibly because the OGPU stole from the till – Solovetsky's supposed economic success was still trumpeted far and wide.

That success soon became the central argument for the restructuring of the entire Soviet prison system. If it was to be achieved at the cost of worse rations and poorer living conditions for prisoners, no one much cared.[74] If it was to be achieved at the price of poor relations with local authorities, that bothered no one either.

Within the camp itself, few doubted who was responsible for this alleged success. Everyone firmly identified Frenkel with the commercialization of the camp, and many equally firmly hated him for it. At a rancorous meeting of the Solovetsky Communist Party in 1928 – so rancorous that part of the meeting's protocols were declared too secret to keep in the archive, and are unavailable – one camp commander, Comrade Yashenko, complained that SLON's Economic-Commercial Department had accrued far too much influence: 'everything lies in its competence'. He also attacked Frenkel, 'a former prisoner who was freed after three years' work because at that time there were not enough people [guards] to work at the camp'. So important had Frenkel become, complained Yashenko (whose language contains a strong whiff of anti-Semitism), that 'when a rumour came round that he might leave, people were saying, "We can't work without him."'

Yashenko hated Frenkel so much, he confessed, that he had contemplated murdering him. Others asked why Frenkel, a former prisoner, received priority service and cheap prices in the SLON shops – as if he were the owner. Still others said SLON had become so commercial that it had forgotten its other tasks: all re-educational work in the camp had been halted, and prisoners were being held to unfair work standards. When prisoners mutilated themselves to escape work norms, their cases were not investigated.[75]

But just as SLON was to win the argument against the Karelian authorities, so Frenkel was to win the argument within SLON – perhaps thanks to his contacts in Moscow – about what kind of camp Solovetsky should become, how prisoners were to work in it, and how they should be treated.

As I have already mentioned, Frenkel probably did not invent the notorious you-eat-as-you-work system, by which prisoners were given food rations according to the amount of work they completed. Nevertheless, he did preside over the development and flowering of that system, which grew from a slapdash arrangement in which work was sometimes 'paid' with food into a very precise, regulated method of food distribution and prisoner organization.

In fact, Frenkel's system was quite straightforward. He divided the prisoners of SLON into three groups according to their physical abilities: those deemed capable of heavy work, those capable of light work, and invalids. Each group received a different set of tasks, and a set of norms to fulfil. They were then fed accordingly – and the differences between their rations were quite drastic. One chart, drawn up between 1928 and 1932, allotted 800 grams of bread and 80 grams of meat to the first group; 500 grams of bread and 40 grams of meat to the second group; and 400 grams of bread and 40 grams of meat to the third group. The lowest category of worker, in other words, received half as much food as the highest.[76]

In practice, the system sorted prisoners very rapidly into those who would survive, and those who would not. Fed relatively well, the strong prisoners grew stronger. Deprived of food, the weak prisoners grew weaker, and eventually became ill or died. The process was made more rapid and more extreme because work norms were often set very high – impossibly high for some prisoners, particularly for city people who had never worked digging peat or cutting trees. In 1928, the central authorities punished a group of camp guards because they had forced 128 people to work in the forest all night during winter, in order to fulfil the norm. A month later, 75 per cent of the prisoners were still seriously ill with severe frostbite.[77]

Under Frenkel, the nature of SLON's work changed as well: he was not interested in fripperies such as fur farming, or the cultivation of exotic Arctic plants. Instead, he sent prisoners to build roads and cut trees, taking advantage of the free, unskilled labour that SLON possessed in abundance.[78] The nature of the work quickly changed the nature of the camp, or rather of the camps, for SLON now began to expand well beyond the Solovetsky archipelago. Frenkel no longer cared, particularly, whether prisoners were kept in a prison setting, in prison buildings, behind barbed wire. He sent teams of convict labourers all over the Karelian Republic and the Arkhangelsk region of the Russian mainland, thousands of kilometres away from Solovetsky, to wherever they were most needed.[79]

Like a management consultant taking over a failing company, Frenkel 'rationalized' other aspects of camp life as well, slowly discarding everything that did not contribute to the camp's economic productivity. All pretence of re-education was rapidly dropped. As Frenkel's detractors complained, he had shut down the camp's journals and newspapers, and halted the meetings of the Solovetsky Society for Local Lore. The Solovetsky museum and theatre continued to exist, but solely in order to impress visiting bigwigs.

At the same time, random cruelty was becoming less common. In 1930, the Shanin Commission, a special delegation of the OGPU, arrived on the island to investigate rumours of ill-treatment of prisoners. Their reports confirmed the stories of excessive beating and torture on the island. In a stunning reversal of previous policy, the commission sentenced and executed nineteen of the OGPU perpetrators.[80] Such behaviour was now considered out of place in an institution that valued *trudosposobnost* – 'work capability' – above all else.

Finally, under Frenkel's leadership, the concept of 'political prisoner' changed for good. In the autumn of 1925, the artificial lines that had been drawn between those with criminal sentences and those convicted of counter-revolutionary crimes were dropped as both groups were sent together to the mainland to work in the huge forestry projects and wood-processing plants of Karelia. SLON no longer recognized privileged prisoners, but rather saw all prisoners as potential labourers.[89]

The socialist residents of the Savvatyevo barracks presented a larger problem. Clearly, the socialist politicals did not fit into anyone's idea of economic efficiency since they refused, on principle, to do any form of forced labour whatsoever. They even refused to cut their own firewood. 'We have been exiled administratively,' one complained, 'and the administration must provide us with all the necessities.'[82] Not surprisingly, that position began to inspire resentment in the camp administration. Although he had personally negotiated with the politicals in Petrominsk in the spring of 1923, and had personally promised them a freer regime on Solovetsky if they would agree to go there peacefully, Commander Nogtev in particular appears to have resented their endless demands. He argued with the politicals about their freedom of movement, about their access to doctors, and about their right to correspond with the outside world. Finally, on 19 December 1923, at the height of a particularly bitter argument over prisoner curfews, the soldiers guarding the Savvatyevo barracks opened fire on a group of politicals, killing six of them.

The incident caused an uproar abroad. The Political Red Cross smuggled reports of the shooting across the border. Accounts appeared in the Western press even before they had appeared in Russia. Telegrams between the island and the Communist Party leadership went swiftly back and forth. At first, the camp authorities defended the shootings, claiming that the prisoners had broken the curfew and that the soldiers had given three warnings before firing.

Later, in April 1924, while not quite admitting that the soldiers had failed to give any warnings – and prisoners agree they did not – the camp administration provided a more elaborate analysis of what had happened. The politicals, their report explained, were of a 'different class' from the soldiers assigned to guard them. The prisoners spent their time reading books and newspapers; the soldiers had no books and newspapers. The prisoners ate white bread, butter and milk; the soldiers had none of these. It was an 'abnormal situation'. Natural resentment had built up, the workers resenting the non-workers, and when prisoners had defied the curfew, blood was inevitably spilled.[83] To back up their conclusions, camp administrators read letters from prisoners aloud at a meeting of the Communist Party Central Committee in Moscow: 'I am feeling well, I am eating well . . . it isn't necessary to send me clothes and food now.' Other letters described the beautiful views.[84] When some of these letters later appeared in the Soviet press, prisoners insisted they had written these idyllic descriptions of life on the island only in order to calm the fears of their relatives.[85]

Indignant, the Central Committee took action. A committee led by Gleb Boky, the OGPU boss in charge of concentration camps, paid a visit to the Solovetsky camps and the transit prison in Kem. A series of articles in *Izvestiya* followed in October 1924. 'Those who believe Solovetsky is a depressing, gloomy prison, where people sit and waste time in crowded cells, are deeply mistaken,' wrote N. Krasikov. 'The whole camp consists of a huge economic organization of 3,000 labourers, working at the most varied types of production.' Singing the praises of Solovetsky's industry and agriculture, Krasikov then went on to describe life in the socialists' Savvatyevo barracks:

The life they lead can be characterized as anarcho-intellectual, with all of the negative aspects of that form of existence. Continued idleness, harping on political dissensions, family quarrels, factional disputes, and above all an aggressive and hostile attitude to the government in general and the local administration and Red Army guards in particular . . . all this combined makes these three hundred-odd people hostile to every measure and every attempt of the local authorities to introduce regularity and organization into their lives.[86]

In another journal, the Soviet authorities claimed socialist prisoners enjoyed better rations than those of the Red Army. Those prisoners were also free to meet relatives – how else could they be smuggling out information? – and had plenty of doctors, more than in normal workers' villages. Sneeringly, the article also claimed that these prisoners demanded 'rare and expensive patent preparations' as well as gold caps and gold bridges on their teeth.[87]

It was the beginning of the end. After a series of discussions, during which the Central Committee considered and rejected the idea of exiling the politicals abroad – they were worried about the impact on Western socialists, particularly, for some reason, the British Labour Party – a decision was taken.[88] At dawn on 17 June 1925, soldiers surrounded the Savvatyevo monastery. They gave the prisoners two hours to pack. They then marched them to the port, forced them into boats, and packed them off to distant, closed prisons in central Russia – Tobolsk, in western Siberia, and Verkhneuralsk, in the Urals – where they found far worse conditions than in Savvatyevo.[89] One prisoner wrote of

locked cells, the air of which is poisoned by the old, stinking toilet bucket; the politicals isolated from one another . . . our rations are worse than in Solovetsky. The prison administration refuses to recognize our *starosta* [group leader]. There is neither hospital nor medical aid. The prison consists of two floors: the cells of the lower floor are damp and dark. In these are kept the sick comrades, some of whom are consumptive . . .[90]

Although they kept on fighting for their rights, kept sending letters abroad, kept tapping messages to one another through prison walls, and kept staging hunger strikes, Bolshevik propaganda was drowning out the socialists' protests. In Berlin, in Paris and in New York, the old prisoners' aid societies began to experience greater difficulty collecting money.[91] 'When the events of 19 December occurred,' wrote one prisoner to a friend outside of Russia, referring to the shootings of the six prisoners in 1923, 'it seemed subjectively to us that the "world would be convulsed" – our socialist world. But it appeared that it did not notice the Solovets events, and then a ring of laughter entered the tragedy.'[92]

By the end of the 1920s the socialist politicals no longer had a unique status. They shared their cells with Bolsheviks, Trotskyites and common criminals. Within the decade politicals – or rather 'counter-revolutionaries' – would be considered not as privileged prisoners but as inferior ones, ranked lower in the camp hierarchy than criminals. No longer citizens with rights of the sort the politicals had defended, they were of interest to the captors only in so far as they were able to work. And only in so far as they were able to work would they be fed enough to stay alive.

3

1929: The Great Turning Point

> When the Bolsheviks came to power they were soft and easy
> with their enemies ... we had begun by making a mistake.
> Leniency towards such a power was a crime against the working
> classes. That soon became apparent ...
>
> – Joseph Stalin[1]

On 20 June 1929, the ship *Gleb Boky* docked at the small port beneath the
Solovetsky kremlin. High above, prisoners watched the scene with a great
sense of anticipation. Instead of the silent, emaciated convicts who usually
stepped off the *Gleb Boky*'s decks, a group of healthy and energetic men –
and one woman – talked and gestured as they walked on to the shore. In the
photographs taken that day, most appear to have been wearing uniforms:
among them were several leading Chekists, including Gleb Boky himself. One
of them, taller than the rest and with a heavy moustache, was dressed more
simply, in a flat workman's cap and a plain overcoat. This was the novelist
Maxim Gorky.

Dmitri Likhachev was one of the prisoners watching from the window,
and he recalled some of the other passengers too: 'It was possible to see the
knoll on which Gorky stood for a long time, together with an odd-looking
person dressed in a leather jacket, leather jodhpurs, high boots and a leather
cap. It was Gorky's daughter-in-law, the wife of his son Maxim. She was
dressed, clearly, in what was, in her opinion, the costume of an authentic
"*chekistka*".' The group then boarded a monastery carriage, drawn by 'a
horse from God knows where', and went off on a tour of the island.[2]

As Likhachev well knew, Gorky was no ordinary visitor. At this point in
his life, Gorky was the Bolsheviks' much-lauded and much-celebrated prod-
igal son. A committed socialist who had been close to Lenin, Gorky had
nevertheless opposed the Bolshevik coup in 1917. In subsequent articles and
speeches, he had continued to denounce the coup and the subsequent terror
with real vehemence, speaking of Lenin's 'crazy politics' and of the 'cesspit'
which Petrograd had become. He finally emigrated in 1921, leaving Russia

for Sorrento, where he continued, at first, to fire off condemnatory missives and angry letters to his friends at home.

Over time, his tone changed, so much so that in 1928, he decided to return, for reasons that are not entirely clear. Solzhenitsyn rather meanly claims he came back because he had not become as famous as he had expected to in the West, and simply ran out of money. Orlando Figes notes that he was miserably unhappy in exile, and could not abide the company of other Russian émigrés, most of whom were far more fanatically anti-communist than himself.[3] Whatever his motivation, once he had made the decision to return he appeared determined to help the Soviet regime as much as possible. Almost immediately, he set off on a series of triumphal journeys around the Soviet Union, deliberately including Solovetsky in his itinerary. His long interest in prisons dated back to his own experiences as a juvenile delinquent.

Numerous memoirists recall the occasion of Gorky's visit to Solovetsky, and all agree that elaborate preparations had been made in advance. Some remember that camp rules were changed for the day, that husbands were allowed to see their wives, presumably to make everyone appear more cheerful.[4] Likhachev wrote that fully grown trees were planted around the work colony, to make it seem less bleak, and that prisoners were removed from the barracks so as to make them seem less crowded. But the memoirists are divided as to what Gorky actually did when he arrived. According to Likhachev, the writer saw through all of the attempts to fool him. While being shown around the hospital ward, where all of the staff were wearing new gowns, Gorky sniffed, 'I don't like parades,' and walked away. He spent a mere ten minutes in the work colony – according to Likhachev – and then closeted himself with a fourteen-year-old boy prisoner, in order to hear the 'truth'. He emerged weeping, forty minutes later.[5]

Oleg Volkov, on the other hand, who was also on Solovetsky when Gorky visited, claims the writer 'only looked where he was told to look'.[6] And, although the story of the fourteen-year-old boy crops up elsewhere – according to one version, he was immediately shot after Gorky's departure – others claim that all prisoners who tried to approach the writer were repulsed.[7] Certainly it appears as if prisoners' letters to Gorky were later intercepted, and, according to one source, at least one of their authors was subsequently executed.[8] V. E. Kanen, a disgraced OGPU agent who had become a prisoner, even claims that Gorky visited the punishment cells of Sekirka, where he signed the prison's journal. One of the Moscow OGPU chiefs who was with Gorky wrote, 'having visited Sekirka, I found everything in order, just as it should be'. Below him, according to Kanen, Gorky added a comment: 'I would say – it is excellent.'[9]

But although we cannot be certain of what he actually did or saw on the island, we can read the essay he wrote afterwards, which took the form of a travel sketch. Gorky praised the natural beauty of the islands, and described the picturesque buildings and their picturesque inhabitants. On the boat ride to the island, he even met some of the old Solovetsky monks. 'And how does the administration treat the monks?' he asks them. 'The administration wants everyone to work. We work,' they reply.[10]

Gorky also writes admiringly of the living conditions, clearly intending his readers to understand that a Soviet labour camp was not at all the same thing as a capitalist labour camp (or a tsarist-era labour camp), but a completely new kind of institution. In some of the rooms, he writes, he saw 'four or six beds, each decorated with personal items . . . on the windowsills there are flowers. There is no impression of life being over-regulated. No, there is no resemblance to a prison, instead it seems as if these rooms are inhabited by passengers rescued from a drowned ship.'

Out on the work sites, he encounters 'healthy lads' in linen shirts and sturdy boots. He meets few political prisoners and, when he does, he dismisses them as 'counter-revolutionaries, emotional types, monarchists'. When they tell him they have been unfairly arrested, he presumes them to be lying. At one point, he seems to hint at the legendary encounter with the fourteen-year-old boy. During his visit to a group of juvenile delinquents, he writes, one of them brought him a protest note. In response, there were 'loud cries' from the children, who called the young man a 'squealer'.

But it was not just the living conditions that made Solovetsky, in Gorky's description, a new type of camp. Its inmates, the 'rescued passengers', were not just happy and healthy, they were also playing a vital role in a grand experiment: the transformation of criminal and asocial personalities into useful Soviet citizens. Gorky was revitalizing Dzerzhinsky's idea that the camps were to be not mere penitentiaries but 'schools of labour', specially designed to forge the sort of worker required by the new Soviet system. In his view, the experiment's ultimate goal was to ensure the 'abolition of prisons' – and it was succeeding. 'If any so-called cultured European society dared to conduct an experiment such as this colony,' Gorky concluded, 'and if this experiment yielded fruits as ours had, that country would blow all its trumpets and boast about its accomplishments.' Only the 'modesty' of the Soviet leaders had, he reckoned, prevented them from doing so before.

Later, Gorky allegedly said that not a single sentence of his essay on Solovetsky had been left 'untouched by the censors' pen'. We do not know, in fact, whether he wrote what he did out of naïvety, out of a calculated desire to deceive, or because the censors made him do it.[11] Whatever his motivations, Gorky's 1929 essay on Solovetsky was to become an important foundation stone in the forming of both public and official attitudes to the new and far more extensive system of camps which were conceived in that same year. Earlier Bolshevik propaganda had defended revolutionary violence as a necessary, albeit temporary evil, a transitory cleansing force. Gorky, on the other hand, made the institutionalized violence of the Solovetsky camps seem a logical and natural part of the new order, and helped to reconcile the public to the growing, totalitarian power of the state.[12]

As it turned out, 1929 would be remembered for many things other than Gorky's essay. By that year, the Revolution had matured. Nearly a decade had passed since the end of the civil war. Lenin was long dead. Economic experiments of various kinds – the New Economic Policy, War Communism – had been tried and abandoned. Just as the ramshackle concentration camp on the Solovetsky islands had become the network of camps known as SLON, so too had the random terror of the Soviet Union's early years subsided, giving way to a more systematic persecution of the regime's perceived opponents.

The Revolution had also acquired, by 1929, a very different sort of leader. Throughout the 1920s, Joseph Stalin had bested or eliminated first the Bolsheviks' enemies, and then his own enemies, partly by putting himself in charge of Party personnel decisions, and partly by making liberal use of secret information gathered on his behalf by the secret police, in which he took a particular personal interest. He launched a series of Party purges, which at first meant Party expulsions, and arranged for them to be announced at emotional, recriminatory mass meetings. In 1937 and 1938, these purges would become lethal: expulsion from the Party would often be followed by a camp sentence – or death.

With notable finesse, Stalin had also finished off his most important rival for power, Leon Trotsky. First he discredited Trotsky, then deported him to an island off the Turkish coast, and then used him to set a precedent. When Yakov Blyumkin, an OGPU agent and ardent Trotsky supporter, visited his hero in his Turkish exile – and returned with a message from Trotsky to his supporters – Stalin had Blyumkin sentenced and executed upon his return. By doing so, he established the state's willingness to use the full force of its repressive organs not only against members of other socialist parties and the old regime, but also against dissidents within the Bolshevik Party itself as well.[13]

However, in 1929, Stalin was not yet the dictator he would become by the end of the following decade. It is more accurate to say that in that year Stalin put in place the policies that would ultimately enshrine his own power and transform Soviet economy and society beyond recognition at the same time. Western historians variously labelled these policies the 'Revolution from Above' or the 'Stalinist Revolution'. Stalin himself called them the 'Great Turning Point'.

At the heart of Stalin's revolution was a new programme of extremely – almost hysterically – rapid industrialization. At that time, the Soviet Revolution had still not brought real material improvement to the lives of most people. On the contrary, the years of Revolution, civil war and economic experimentation had led to greater impoverishment. Now Stalin, perhaps sensing the growing popular discontent with the Revolution, set out to change ordinary people's living conditions – radically.

To that end, the Soviet government in 1929 approved a new 'Five-Year Plan', an economic programme that called for a 20 per cent annual increase in industrial output. Food rationing returned. For a time, the seven-day week – five days of work, two days of rest – was abandoned. Instead, workers rested in shifts, so as to prevent any factory from ever shutting down. On high-priority projects, thirty-hour shifts were not unknown, and some workers stayed on the job an average of 300 hours a month.[14] The spirit of the age, imposed from above but enthusiastically adopted below, was a form of one-upmanship, in which factory owners and bureaucrats, workers and clerks, vied with one another to fulfil the plan, to overfulfil the plan, or at least to propose newer and faster ways of overfulfilling the plan. At the same time, no one was allowed to doubt the wisdom of the plan. This was true at the highest levels: Party leaders who doubted the worth of rushed industrialization did not remain long in office. It was also true at the lowest levels. One survivor of that era remembered marching around his kindergarten classroom, carrying a little banner and chanting:

> Five in Four,
> Five in Four,
> Five in Four,
> *And not in five!*

Alas, the meaning of this phrase – that the Five-Year Plan was to be completed in four years – escaped him entirely.[15]

As was to be the case with all major Soviet initiatives, the onset of mass industrialization created whole new categories of criminals. In 1926, the Soviet criminal code had been rewritten to include, among other things, an expanded definition of Article 58, which defined 'counter-revolutionary' crimes. Formerly a mere paragraph or two, Article 58 now contained eighteen subsections – and the OGPU made use of them all, most notably to arrest technical specialists.[16] Predictably, the high tempo of change could not be met. Primitive technology, applied too quickly, led to mistakes. Someone had to be blamed. Hence the arrests of the 'wreckers' and the 'saboteurs' whose evil aims were preventing the Soviet economy from living up to the propaganda. Some of the earliest show trials – the Shakhty trial of 1928, the Industrial Party trial of 1930 – were in fact trials of engineers and technical intelligentsia. So too was the Metro-Vickers trial of 1933, which attracted a great deal of international attention because it included British citizens as well as Russians, all accused of 'espionage and sabotage' on behalf of Great Britain.[17]

But there would be other sources of prisoners too. For in 1929, the Soviet regime also accelerated the process of forced collectivization in the countryside, a vast upheaval which was in some ways more profound than the Russian Revolution itself. Within an incredibly short period of time, rural commissars forced millions of peasants to give up their small landholdings and to join collective farms, often expelling them from land their families had tilled for centuries. The transformation permanently weakened Soviet agriculture, and created the conditions for the terrible, devastating famines in Ukraine and southern Russia in 1932 and 1934 – famines that killed between six and seven million people.[18] Collectivization also destroyed – for ever – rural Russia's sense of continuity with the past.

Millions resisted collectivization, hiding grain in their cellars or refusing to co-operate with the authorities. These resisters were labelled kulaks, or wealthy peasants, a term which (much like the definition of 'wrecker') was so vague that nearly anyone could qualify. The possession of an extra cow, or an extra bedroom, was enough to qualify some distinctly poor peasants, as was an accusation from a jealous neighbour. To break the kulaks' resistance, the regime revived, in effect, the old tsarist tradition of the administrative deportation order. From one day to the next, trucks and wagons simply arrived in a village and picked up entire families. Some kulaks were shot, some were arrested and given camp sentences. In the end, however, the regime deported most of them. Between 1930 and 1933, over two million peasant kulaks were exiled to Siberia, to Kazakhstan and to other underpopulated regions of the Soviet Union, where they lived out the rest of their lives as 'special exiles', forbidden to leave their exile villages. A further 100,000 were arrested, and wound up in the Gulag.[19]

As famine kicked in, helped by poor rainfall, more arrests followed. All available grain was taken out of the villages, and deliberately denied to kulaks. Those caught stealing tiny amounts, even to feed their children, also ended up in prison. A law of 7 August 1932 demanded the death penalty, or else a long camp sentence, for all such 'crimes against state property'. Soon afterwards, the 'gleaners' appeared in the camps: peasant women who had picked up leftover grain in order to survive. They were joined by others, such as the hungry people who received ten-year sentences for stealing a pound of potatoes or a handful of apples.[20] These laws explain why peasants formed the vast majority of prisoners in Soviet camps throughout the 1930s, and why peasants would remain a substantial part of the prison population until Stalin's death.

The impact of these mass arrests on the camps was enormous. Almost as soon as the new laws came into effect, camp administrators began to call for a rapid and radical overhaul of the entire system. The 'ordinary' prison system, still run by the Commissariat of the Interior (and still far larger than Solovetsky, which was run by the OGPU), had remained overcrowded, disorganized, and over-budget throughout the previous decade. Nationally, the situation was so bad that at one point the Commissariat of the Interior attempted to reduce inmate numbers by sentencing more people to 'forced labour without deprivation of freedom' – assigning them jobs but not locking them up – thereby relieving the strain on the camps.[21]

As the pace of collectivization and the strength of repression picked up, however – as millions of kulaks were evicted from their homes – such solutions began to seem politically inopportune. Once again, the authorities determined that such dangerous criminals – enemies of Stalin's great drive for collectivization – required a more secure form of incarceration, and the OGPU prepared to build one.

Knowing that the prison system was deteriorating as fast as prisoner numbers were rising, the Politburo of the Communist Party set up a commission in 1928 to deal with the problem. Ostensibly, the commission was neutral, and contained representatives of the Interior and Justice Commissariats, as well as the OGPU. Comrade Yanson, the Commissar of Justice, was placed in charge of it. The commission's task was to create 'a system of concentration camps, organized in the manner of the OGPU camps', and its deliberations took place within clear limits. Despite Maxim Gorky's lyrical passages about the value of labour in the reformation of criminals, all of the participants used fiercely economic language. All expressed the same concerns about 'profitability' and spoke frequently about 'rational use of labour'.[22]

True, the protocol written up after the commission meeting of 15 May 1929 records a few practical objections to the creation of a mass camp system: camps would be too difficult to set up, there were no roads leading to the far north, and so on. The Commissar of Labour thought it was wrong to subject minor criminals to the same punishment as recidivists. The Commissar of the Interior, Tolmachev, pointed out that the system would look bad abroad: the 'White Guard emigrants' and the bourgeois foreign press would claim that 'instead of building a penitentiary system intended to reform prisoners through corrective labour, we've put up Chekist fortresses'.[23]

Yet his point was that the system would *look* bad, not that it *was* bad. No one present objected on the grounds that camps 'of the Solovetsky type' were cruel or lethal. Nor did anyone mention the alternative theories of criminal justice of which Lenin had been so fond, the notion that crime would disappear along with capitalism. Certainly no one talked about prisoner re-education, the 'transformation of human nature', which Gorky had lauded in his essay on Solovetsky and which would be so important in the public presentation of the first set of camps. Instead, Genrikh Yagoda, the OGPU's representative on the committee, put the regime's real interests quite clearly:

It is already both possible and absolutely necessary to remove 10,000 prisoners from places of confinement in the Russian republic, whose labour could be better organized and used. Aside from that, we have received notice that the camps and gaols in the

Ukrainian republic are overflowing as well. Obviously, Soviet policy will not permit the building of new prisons. Nobody will give money for new prisons. The construction of large camps, on the other hand – camps which will make rational use of labour – is a different matter. We have many difficulties attracting workers to the North. If we send many thousands of prisoners there, we can exploit the resources of the North . . . the experience of Solovetsky shows what can be done in this area.

Yagoda went on to explain that the resettlement would be permanent. After their release, prisoners would stay put: 'with a variety of measures, both administrative and economic, we can force the freed prisoners to stay in the North, thereby populating our outer regions'.[24]

The idea that prisoners should become colonists – so similar to the tsarist model – was no afterthought. While the Yanson commission was holding its deliberations, a separate committee of the Soviet government had also begun to investigate the labour crisis in the far north, variously proposing to send the unemployed or Chinese immigrants to solve the problem.[25] Both committees were looking for solutions to the same problem at the same time, and no wonder. In order to fulfil Stalin's Five-Year Plan, the Soviet Union would require huge quantities of coal, gas, oil and wood, all available in Siberia, Kazakhstan and the far north. The country also needed gold in order to purchase new machinery abroad, and geologists had recently discovered gold in the far north-eastern region of Kolyma. Despite freezing temperatures, primitive living conditions and inaccessibility, these resources had to be exploited at breakneck speed.

In the then-fierce spirit of inter-ministry competition, Yanson initially proposed that his own commissariat take over the system and set up a series of forestry camps in order to increase the Soviet Union's export of timber, a major source of foreign currency. This project was put aside, probably because not everyone wanted Comrade Yanson and his judicial bureaucrats to control it. Indeed, when the project was suddenly revived, in the spring of 1929, the Yanson commission's conclusions were slightly different. On 13 April 1929, the commission proposed the creation of a new, unified camp system, one which eliminated the distinction between 'ordinary' and 'special' camps. More significantly, the commission handed direct control of the new unified system straight to the OGPU.[26]

The OGPU took control of the Soviet Union's prisoners with startling speed. In December 1927, the Special Department of the OGPU had controlled 30,000 inmates, about 10 per cent of the prison population, mostly in the Solovetsky camps. It employed no more than 1,000 people, and its budget hardly exceeded .05 per cent of state expenditure. By contrast, the Interior Commissariat's prison system had 150,000 inmates and consumed .25 per cent of the state budget. Between 1928 and 1930, however, the situation reversed itself. As other government institutions slowly gave up their prisoners, their prisons, their camps and the industrial enterprises attached to them, the number of prisoners under OGPU jurisdiction swelled from 30,000 to 300,000.[27] In 1931, the secret police also took control of the millions of 'special exiles' – mostly deported kulaks – who were effectively forced labourers, since they were forbidden to leave their assigned settlements and workplaces under pain of death or arrest.[28] By the middle of the decade, the OGPU would control all of the Soviet Union's vast prisoner workforce.

In order to cope with its new responsibilities, the OGPU reorganized its Special Department for camps and renamed it the Main Administration of Corrective Labour Camps and Labour Settlements. Eventually, this unwieldy title would be shortened to the Main Camp Administration or, in Russian, *Glavnoe upravlenie lagerei*. Hence the acronym by which the department, and ultimately the system itself, would be known: GULAG.[29]

Ever since the Soviet concentration camps first came into existence on a grand scale, their inmates and their chroniclers have argued about the motives that lay behind their creation. Did they come about haphazardly, as a side-effect of collectivization, industrialization and the other processes taking place in the country? Or did Stalin carefully plot the growth of the Gulag, planning in advance to arrest millions of people?

In the past, some scholars have claimed that no grand design lay behind the camps' founding. One historian, James Harris, has argued that local leaders, not bureaucrats in Moscow, led the drive to build new camps in the Ural region. Forced to comply with the impossible requirements of the Five-Year Plan on the one hand and facing a critical labour shortage on the other, the Ural authorities increased the pace and cruelty of collectivization in order to square the circle: every time they removed a kulak from his land, they created another slave labourer.[30] Another historian, Michael Jakobson, argues along similar lines that the origins of the mass Soviet prison system were 'banal': 'Bureaucrats pursued unattainable goals of prison self-sufficiency and inmate re-education. Officials sought manpower and funds, expanded their bureaucracies, and tried to meet unrealistic goals. Administrators and warders dutifully enforced rules and regulations. Theorists rationalized and justified. Eventually, everything was reversed or modified or abandoned.'[31]

Indeed, if the Gulag's origins were haphazard, that would not be surprising. Throughout the early 1930s, the Soviet leadership in general, and Stalin in particular, constantly changed course, implemented policies and then reversed them, and made public pronouncements deliberately designed to disguise reality. It is not easy, when reading the history of the era, to detect an evil master plan designed by Stalin or anyone else.[32] Stalin himself launched collectivization, for example, only to change his mind, apparently, in March 1930, when he attacked over-zealous rural officials who had become 'Dizzy with Success'. Whatever he meant by this pronouncement, it had little effect on the ground, and the destruction of the kulaks continued unabated for years.

The OGPU bureaucrats and secret police who planned the expansion of the Gulag also seem, initially, to have been no clearer about their ultimate goals. The Yanson commission itself made decisions, and then reversed them. The OGPU also conducted policies which seemed contradictory. Throughout the 1930s, for example, the OGPU declared frequent amnesties, intended to end overcrowding in prisons and camps. Invariably, the amnesties would be followed by new waves of repression, and new waves of camp construction, as if Stalin and his henchmen were never quite sure if they wanted the system to grow or not – or as if different people were giving different orders at different times.

Similarly, the camp system would go through many cycles: now more repressive, now less so, now more repressive again. Even after 1929, when the camps had been set firmly on the path of economic efficiency, a few anomalies remained in the system. As late as 1937, for example, many political prisoners were still kept in gaols where they were explicitly forbidden to work – a practice that would seem to contradict the general drive for efficiency.[33] Nor were many of the bureaucratic changes terribly meaningful. Although the formal division between secret police camps and non-secret police camps did come to an end in the 1930s, a vestigial division remained between 'camps', supposedly designed for more dangerous and political criminals, and 'colonies', for petty criminals with shorter sentences. In practice, the organization of work, food and daily life at both camps and colonies was very similar.

And yet – there is also now a growing consensus that Stalin himself had, if not a carefully designed plan, then at least a very firm belief in the enormous advantages of prison labour, which he maintained until the end of his life. Why?

Some, like Ivan Chukhin, a former secret policeman and historian of the early camp system, speculate that Stalin promoted the Gulag's overambitious early construction works in order to build up his own prestige. At this time, he was still just emerging as the leader of the country after a long and bitter power struggle. He may have imagined that new industrial feats, achieved with the help of prison slave labour, would help him secure his power.[34]

Stalin may also have been inspired by an older historical precedent. Robert Tucker, among others, has amply demonstrated Stalin's obsessive interest in Peter the Great, another Russian ruler who deployed massive serf and prison labour to achieve enormous feats of engineering and construction. In a speech to a Central Committee plenum, made just as he was getting ready to launch his industrial programme in 1928, Stalin noted admiringly that:

When Peter the Great, conducting business with the more advanced countries in the West, feverishly built mills and factories to supply the army and strengthen the defences of the country, it was a special sort of effort to *leap clear of the confines of his backwardness.*[35]

The italics are mine: they emphasize the link between Stalin's 'Great Turning Point' and the policies of his eighteenth-century predecessor. In the Russian historical tradition, Peter is remembered as both a great and a cruel leader, and this is not thought to be a contradiction. After all, nobody remembers how many serfs died during the building of St Petersburg, but everybody admires the city's beauty. Stalin may well have taken his example to heart.

Yet Stalin's interest in concentration camps need not have had a rational source at all: perhaps Stalin's obsessive interest in vast construction projects and toiling teams of forced labourers was connected, somehow, to his particular form of megalomaniacal madness. Mussolini once said of Lenin that he 'is an artist who has worked in men as others have worked in marble or metal'.[36] This description may be better applied to Stalin, who literally enjoyed the sight of large numbers of human bodies, marching or dancing in perfect synchronization.[37] He was captivated by the ballet, by orchestrated exhibitions of gymnastics, and by parades featuring giant pyramids built out of anonymous, contorted human figures.[38] Like Hitler, Stalin was also obsessed with the cinema, particularly Hollywood musicals, with their enormous casts of coordinated singers and dancers. He might have derived a different but related form of pleasure from the vast teams of prisoners who dug canals and built railway lines at his bidding.

Whatever his inspiration, whether political, historical or psychological, it is clear that from the Gulag's earliest days, Stalin took a deep personal interest in the camps, and exerted an enormous influence on their development. The crucial decision to transfer all of the Soviet Union's camps and prisons away from the ordinary justice system and into the hands of the OGPU, for example, was almost certainly made at Stalin's behest. By 1929, Stalin had taken a great personal interest in this institution. He took an interest in the careers of the top secret policemen, and oversaw the construction of comfortable houses for them and their families.[39] By contrast, the prison administration of the Interior Commissariat was very much out of his favour: its leaders had backed Stalin's opponents in the bitter internal Party factional fighting of the time.[40]

Everyone who took part in the Yanson commission would have known all of these details perfectly well, which might have been enough to persuade them to put the prisons in the hands of the OGPU. But Stalin also intervened directly in the Yanson commission's deliberations. At one point in the tangled deliberations, the Politburo actually reversed its original decision, declaring its intention to take the prison system away from the secret police once again, and put it back in the hands of the Commissariat of the Interior. This prospect outraged Stalin. In a 1930 letter to his close collaborator Vyacheslav Molotov, he denounced this idea as an 'intrigue' orchestrated by the Commissar of the Interior who is 'rotten through and through'. He ordered the Politburo to implement its original decision, and shut down the Interior Commissariat altogether.[41] Stalin's decision to give the camps to the OGPU determined their future character. It removed them from ordinary judicial scrutiny, and placed them firmly in the hands of a secret police bureaucracy whose origins lay in the mysterious, extra-legal world of the Cheka.

While there is less hard evidence to support the theory, it may also be that the constant emphasis on the need to build 'camps of the Solovetsky type' came from Stalin as well. As mentioned earlier, the Solovetsky camps never were profitable, not in 1929, not ever. In the June 1928–June 1929 working year, SLON still received a 1.6-million-rouble subsidy from the state budget.[42] Although SLON might have appeared more successful than other local businesses, anyone who understood economics knew that it hardly competed fairly. Forestry camps which employed prisoners would always appear more productive than regular forestry enterprises, for example, simply because the latter's peasant employees only worked in the winter, when they were unable to farm.[43]

Nevertheless, the Solovetsky camps were *perceived* to be profitable – or at least Stalin perceived them to be profitable. Stalin also believed that they were profitable precisely because of Frenkel's 'rational' methods – his distribution of food according to prisoners' work, and his elimination of needless 'extras'. Evidence that Frenkel's system had won approval at the highest levels is in the results: not only was the system very quickly duplicated around the country, but Frenkel himself was also named chief of construction on the White Sea Canal, the first major project of the Stalin-era Gulag, an extremely high post for a former prisoner.[44] Later, as we shall see, he was protected from arrest and possibly execution by intervention at the very highest level.

Evidence of his preference for prison labour over ordinary labour can also be found in Stalin's continuing interest in the intimate details of camp administration. Throughout his life, he demanded regular information about the level of 'inmate productivity' in the camps, often through specific statistics: how much coal and oil they had produced, how many prisoners they employed, how many medals their bosses had received.[45] He was particularly interested in the gold mines of Dalstroi, the complex of camps in the far north-eastern region of Kolyma, and demanded regular and precise information about Kolyma's geology, Dalstroi's mining technology, and the precise quality of the gold produced, as well as its quantity. To ensure that his own edicts were carried out in the more far-flung camps, he sent out inspection teams, often requiring camp bosses to make frequent appearances in Moscow as well.[46]

When a particular project interested him, he sometimes got even more closely involved. Canals, for example, seized his imagination, and it sometimes seemed as if he wanted to dig them almost indiscriminately. Yagoda was once forced to write to Stalin, politely objecting to his boss's unrealistic desire to build a canal using slave labour in central Moscow.[47] As Stalin took greater control of the organs of power, he also forced his colleagues to focus their attention on the camps. By 1940, the Politburo would discuss one or another of the Gulag's projects almost every week.[48]

Yet Stalin's interest was not purely theoretical. He also took a direct interest in the human beings involved in the work of the camps: who had been arrested, where he or she had been sentenced, what was his or her ultimate fate. He personally read, and sometimes commented upon, the petitions for release sent to him by prisoners or their wives, often replying with a word or two ('keep him at work' or 'release').[49] Later, he regularly demanded information about prisoners or groups of prisoners who interested him, such as the West Ukrainian nationalists.[50]

There is also evidence that Stalin's interest in particular prisoners was not always purely political, and did not only include his personal enemies. As early as 1931, before he had consolidated his power, Stalin pushed a resolution through the Politburo which allowed him enormous influence over the arrests of certain kinds of technical specialists.[51] And – not coincidentally – the pattern of arrests of engineers and specialists in this earlier era does suggest some higher level of planning. Perhaps it was not sheer accident that the very first group of prisoners sent to the new camps in the Kolyma gold fields included seven well-known mining experts, two labour-organization experts and one experienced hydraulic engineer.[52] Nor, perhaps, was it mere chance that the OGPU managed to arrest one of the Soviet Union's top geologists on the eve of a planned expedition to build a camp near the oil reserves of the Komi Republic, as we shall see.[53] Such coincidences could not have been planned by regional Party bosses reacting to the stresses of the moment.

Finally, there is a completely circumstantial, but nevertheless interesting body of evidence suggesting that the mass arrests of the late 1930s and 1940s may also have been carried out, to some degree, in order to appease Stalin's desire for slave labour, and not – as most have always assumed – in order to punish his perceived or potential enemies. The authors of the most authoritative Russian history of the camps to date point out the 'positive connection between the successful economic activity of the camps and the number of prisoners sent to them'. Surely it is no accident, they argue, that sentences for petty criminal activity suddenly became much harsher just as the camps were expanding, just as more prison labourers were urgently needed.[54]

A few scattered archival documents hint at the same story. In 1934, for example, Yagoda wrote a letter to his subordinates in Ukraine, demanding 15,000–20,000 prisoners, all 'fit to work': they were needed urgently in order to finish the Moscow–Volga Canal. The letter is dated 17 March, and in it

Yagoda also demanded that the local OGPU bosses 'take extra measures' to ensure that the prisoners had arrived by 1 April. Where these 15,000–20,000 prisoners were supposed to come from was not, however, clearly explained. Were they arrested in order to meet Yagoda's requirements?[55] Or – as the historian Terry Martin believes – was Yagoda simply struggling to ensure a nice, regular inflow of labour into his camp system, a goal which he never in fact achieved?

If the arrests were intended to populate the camps, then they did so with almost ludicrous inefficiency. Martin and others have also pointed out that every wave of mass arrests seems to have caught the camp commanders completely by surprise, making it difficult for them to achieve even a semblance of economic efficiency. Nor did the arresting officers ever choose their victims rationally: instead of limiting arrests to the healthy young men who would have made the best labourers in the far north, they also imprisoned women, children and old people in large numbers.[56] The sheer illogic of the mass arrests seems to argue against the idea of a carefully planned slave-labour force – leading many to conclude that arrests were carried out primarily to eliminate Stalin's perceived enemies, and only secondarily to fill Stalin's camps.

Yet, in the end, none of these explanations for the growth of the camps is entirely mutually exclusive either. Stalin might well have intended his arrests both to eliminate enemies and to create slave labourers. He might have been motivated both by his own paranoia and by the labour needs of regional leaders. Perhaps the formula is best put simply: Stalin proposed the 'Solovetsky model' of concentration camps to his secret police, Stalin selected the victims – and his subordinates leaped at the opportunity to obey him.

4

The White Sea Canal

Where mossy cliffs and waters slumbered
There, thanks to the strength of labour
Factories will be built
And towns will grow.

Smokestacks will rise up
Under the Northern skies,
Buildings will shine with the lights
Of libraries, theatres, and clubs.

– Medvedkov, a White Sea
Canal prisoner, 1934[1]

In the end, only one of the objections raised during the meetings of the Yanson commission caused any further concern. Although they were certain that the great Soviet nation would overcome the lack of roads, although they had few qualms about using prisoners as slave labourers, Stalin and his henchmen remained exceptionally touchy about the language foreigners used to describe their prison camps abroad.

In fact – contrary to popular belief – foreigners in this era described Soviet prison camps rather frequently. Quite a lot was generally known in the West about the Soviet concentration camps at the end of the 1920s, perhaps more than was generally known at the end of the 1940s. Large articles about Soviet · prisons had appeared in the German, French, British and American press, particularly the left-wing press, which had wide contacts among imprisoned Russian socialists.[2] In 1927, a French writer named Raymond Duguet published a surprisingly accurate book about Solovetsky, *Un bagne en Russie rouge* (*A Prison in Red Russia*), describing everything from the personality of Naftaly Frenkel to the horrors of the mosquito torture. S. A. Malsagov, a Georgian White Army officer who managed to escape from Solovetsky and cross the border, published *Island Hell*, another account of Solovetsky, in London in 1926. As a result of widespread rumours about Soviet abuse of

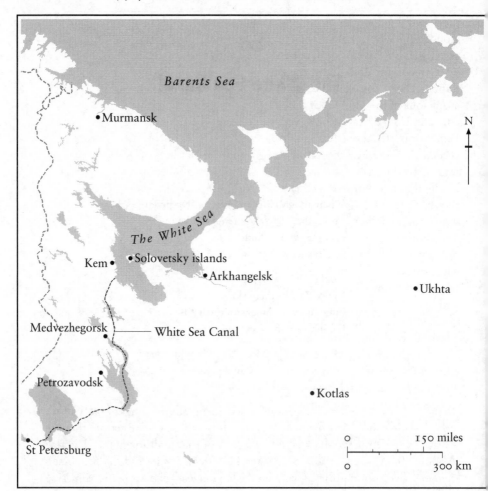

2 The White Sea Canal, northern Russia, 1932-3

prison labour, the British Anti-Slavery Society even launched an investigation into the matter, and wrote a report deploring the evidence of scurvy and maltreatment.[3] A French Senator wrote a much-quoted article based on the testimony of Russian refugees, comparing the situation in the Soviet Union to the findings of the League of Nations' slavery investigation in Liberia.[4]

After the expansion of the camps in 1929 and 1930, however, foreign interest in the camps shifted, moving away from the fate of the socialist prisoners, and focusing instead on the economic menace which the camps appeared to pose to Western business interests. Threatened companies, and threatened trade unions, began organizing. Pressure grew, particularly in Britain and the United States, for a boycott of cheaper Soviet goods allegedly produced by forced labour. Paradoxically, the movement for a boycott clouded the whole issue in the eyes of the Western Left, which still supported the Russian Revolution, particularly in Europe, even if many of the leaders were uncomfortable about the fate of their socialist brethren. The British Labour Party, for example, opposed a ban on Soviet goods because it was suspicious of the motives of the companies promoting it.[5]

In the United States, however, trade unions, most notably the American Federation of Labour, came in support of a boycott. Briefly, they succeeded. In America, the Tariff Act of 1930 prescribed that 'All goods ... mined, produced or manufactured ... by convict labour or/and forced labour ... shall not be entitled to entry at any of the ports of the United States.'[6] On that basis, the US Treasury Department banned the import of Soviet pulpwood and matches.

Although the US State Department failed to support the ban, which lasted only a week, discussion of the issue continued.[7] In January 1931, the Ways and Means Committee of the American Congress met to consider bills 'relating to the prohibition of goods produced by convict labour in Russia'.[8] On 18, 19 and 20 May 1931, *The Times* of London printed a series of surprisingly detailed articles on forced labour in the Soviet Union, concluding with an editorial condemning the British government's recent decision to grant diplomatic recognition to the Soviet Union. Lending money to Russia would, the editorialists wrote, put 'more power into the hands of those who are openly working for their overthrow and for the destruction of the British Empire'.

The Soviet regime took the threat of boycott very seriously indeed, and a number of measures were taken to prevent it from disrupting the flow of hard currency into the country. Some of these measures were cosmetic: the Yanson commission finally dropped the expression *kontslager*, or 'concentration camp', from all of its public statements, for example. From 7 April 1930, all official documents described Soviet concentration camps as *ispravitelno-trudovye lagerya* (ITL), or 'corrective-labour camps'. No other term would be used in the future.[9]

Camp authorities made other cosmetic changes on the ground, particularly in the timber industry. At one point, the OGPU altered its contract with Karellis, the Karelian woodcutting concern, so that it appeared as if prisoners were no longer being employed. At that time, 12,090 prisoners were technically 'removed' from OGPU camps. In fact, they kept working, but their presence was disguised beneath the bureaucratic shuffle.[10] Once again, the Soviet leadership's main concern was appearances, not reality.

Elsewhere, prisoners working in the logging camps were actually replaced with free workers – or, more often, with exiled 'settlers', kulaks who had no more choice in the matter than prisoners.[11] According to memoirists, this switch sometimes happened virtually overnight. George Kitchin, a Finnish businessman who spent four years in OGPU camps before he was freed with the help of the Finnish government, wrote that just prior to the visit of a foreign delegation

A secret code telegram was received from the head office in Moscow, instructing us to liquidate our camp completely in three days, and to do it in such a manner that not a trace should remain . . . telegrams were sent to all work posts to stop operations within twenty-four hours, to gather the inmates at evacuation centres, to efface marks of the penal camps, such as barbed-wire enclosures, watch turrets and signboards; for all officials to dress in civilian clothes, to disarm guards, and to wait for further instructions.

Kitchin, along with several thousand other prisoners, was marched out of the forest. He believed that more than 1,300 prisoners died in this and other overnight evacuations.[12]

By March 1931, Molotov, then Chairman of the Council of People's Commissars, felt confident that there were no prisoners left working in the Soviet forestry industry – or at least no visible prisoners – and he invited all interested foreigners to visit and see for themselves.[13] A few had already been: the Communist Party archives of Karelia record the presence, in 1929, of two American journalists, 'Comrade Durant and Comrade Wolf', American contributors to TASS, the Soviet news agency, as well as 'radical newspapers'. The two were welcomed by a rendition of the *Internationale*, the workers' anthem, and Comrade Wolf promised to 'tell the workers of America how the workers of the Soviet Union live and how they are creating a new life'. It was not to be the last such staged occasion.[14]

Yet although pressure for a boycott had collapsed by 1931, the Western campaign against Soviet slave labour had not been wholly without effect: the Soviet Union was, and would remain, very sensitive to its image abroad, even under Stalin. Some, among them the historian Michael Jakobson, now speculate that the threat of the boycott might even have been an important factor behind another, larger shift in policy. The logging business, which required a great deal of unskilled labour, had been an ideal way to make use of prisoners. But wood exports were one of the Soviet Union's main sources of hard currency, and they could not be put at risk of another boycott. Prisoners would have to be sent elsewhere – preferably somewhere where their presence could be celebrated, not hidden. There was no lack of possibilities, but one in particular appealed to Stalin: the construction of a vast canal, from the White Sea to the Baltic Sea, across a landscape largely composed of sheer granite.

In the context of its time, the White Sea Canal – *Belomorkanal*, in Russian, or *Belomor*, for short – was not unique. By the time construction began, the Soviet Union had already begun to execute several similarly grand, similarly labour-intensive projects, including the world's largest steelworks at Magnitogorsk, huge new tractor and automobile works, and vast new 'socialist cities' planted in the middle of swamps. Nevertheless, even among the other offspring of the gigantomania of the 1930s, the White Sea Canal stood out.

For one, the canal represented – as many Russians would have known – the fulfilment of a very old dream. The first plans to build such a canal had been drawn up in the eighteenth century, when tsarist merchants were looking for a way to get ships carrying timber and minerals from the cold waters of the White Sea to the commercial ports of the Baltic without making the 370-mile journey through the Arctic Ocean, down the long coast of Norway.[15]

It was also a project of extreme, even foolhardy ambition, which is perhaps why no one had tried it before. The entire route required 227 kilometres of canal, encompassed several hundred more kilometres of existing waterways, and required five dams and nineteen locks. Soviet planners intended to build it using the lowest possible technology, in a pre-industrial, far northern region which had never been properly surveyed and was, in Maxim Gorky's words, 'hydrologically terra incognita'.[16] All of this, however, may have been part of the project's appeal to Stalin. He wanted a technological triumph – one the Old Regime had never managed – and he wanted it as fast as possible. He demanded not only that the canal be built, but also that it be built within twenty months. When completed, it would bear his name.

Stalin was the chief promoter of the White Sea Canal – and Stalin specifically wanted the canal to be built with prison labour. Before its construction, he furiously condemned those who questioned whether, given the relatively light volume of traffic in the White Sea, such an expensive project was really necessary. 'I'm told,' he wrote to Molotov, 'that Rykov and Kviring want to squelch the matter of the Northern Canal, contrary to the Politburo's decisions. They should be taken down a peg and given a slap on the wrists.' During a Politburo meeting at which the canal was discussed, Stalin also wrote an angry, hastily scribbled note, which speaks of his belief in inmate labour: 'As for the northern section of the canal, I have in mind relying on the GPU [prison labour]. At the same time we must assign someone to calculate yet again the expenses in building this first section . . . Too much.'[17]

Nor were Stalin's preferences kept secret. After the canal's completion, its top administrator credited Stalin both for his 'bravery' in undertaking to build this 'hydrotechnical giant', and for the 'wonderful fact that this work was not completed by an ordinary workforce'.[18] Stalin's influence can also be seen in the speed with which the construction began. The decision to begin building was made in February 1931, and, after a mere seven months of engineering work and advance surveying, the work began in September.

Administratively, physically, even psychologically, the first prison camps associated with the White Sea Canal were an outgrowth of SLON. The canal's camps were organized on the SLON model, used SLON's equipment, and were manned by SLON's cadres. As soon as it began, the canal's bosses immediately transferred many inmates from SLON's mainland camps and from the Solovetsky islands to work on the new project. For a time, the old SLON and the new White Sea Canal bureaucracies may even have competed to control the project – but the canal won. Eventually, SLON ceased to be an independent entity. The Solovetsky kremlin was redesignated a high-security prison, and the Solovetsky archipelago simply became another division of the Belomor–Baltiiskii [White Sea–Baltic] Corrective-Labour Camp, known as 'Belbaltlag'. A number of guards and leading OGPU administrators also moved from SLON to the canal. Among them, as noted, was Naftaly Frenkel, who managed the daily work of the canal from November 1931 until its completion.[19]

In survivors' memoirs, the chaos that accompanied the building of the canal takes on an almost mythological quality. The need to save money meant that prisoners used wood, sand and rocks instead of metal and cement. Corners were cut wherever they could be. After much discussion, the canal was dug to a depth of only 12 feet, barely enough for naval vessels. Since modern technology was either too expensive or unavailable, the canal's planners deployed vast quantities of unskilled labour. The approximately 170,000 prisoners and 'special exiles' who worked on the project over the 21-month construction period used wooden spades, crude handsaws, pickaxes and wheelbarrows to dig the canal and to build its great dams and locks.[20]

From photographs taken at the time, these tools certainly seem primitive, but only a closer look reveals exactly how primitive. Some of them are still on display in the town of Medvezhegorsk, once the gateway to the canal and the 'capital' of Belbaltlag. Now a forgotten Karelian village, Medvezhegorsk is notable only for its enormous, empty, cockroach-infested hotel, and for its small local history museum. The pickaxes on display there are actually slices of barely sharpened metal, tied to wooden staves with leather or string. The saws consist of flat metal sheets, with teeth crudely cut into them. Instead of dynamite, prisoners broke up large rocks using 'hammers' – hunks of metal screwed on to wooden handles – to pound iron bars into the stone.

Everything, from the wheelbarrows to the scaffolding, was handmade. One inmate remembered that 'there was no technology whatsoever. Even ordinary automobiles were a rarity. Everything was done by hand, sometimes with the help of horses. We dug earth by hand, and carried it out in wheelbarrows, we dug through the hills by hand as well, and carried away the stones.'[21] Even Soviet propaganda bragged that stones were dragged away from the canal on 'Belomor Fords . . . a heavy truck on four small, solid wooden wheels made out of tree stumps.'[22]

Living conditions were no less makeshift, despite the efforts of Genrikh Yagoda, the OGPU chief who bore political responsibility for the project. He appeared genuinely to believe that prisoners would have to be given decent living conditions if they were to finish the canal on time, and frequently harangued camp commanders to treat prisoners better, to 'take maximum care to see that prisoners are correctly fed, clothed and shod'. Commanders followed suit, as did the chief of the Solovetsky division of the canal project in 1933. Among other things, he instructed his inferiors to liquidate queues for food in the evenings, to eliminate theft from the kitchens, and to restrict the evening head count to an hour. In general, official food norms were higher than they would be a few years later, with sausage and tea among the recommended products. Theoretically, prisoners received a new set of work clothes every year.[23]

Nevertheless, the extreme haste and lack of planning inevitably created much suffering. As work progressed, new camp sites had to be built along thecourse of the canal. At every one of these new sites, the prisoners and exiles arrived – and found nothing. Before starting work they had to build their own wooden barracks and organize their food supply. In the meantime, it sometimes happened that the freezing cold of the Karelian winter killed them before they completed their tasks. According to some calculations, more than 25,000 prisoners died, although this number does not include those who were released due to illness or accident, and who died soon afterwards.[24] One prisoner, A. F. Losev, wrote to his wife that he actually longed to be back in the depths of Butyrka prison, since here he had to lie on bunks so crowded that 'if during the night you roll from one side to another, at least another four or five people have to roll over too'. Even more desperate is the later testimony of a young boy, the son of exiled kulaks, who was deported with his entire family to one of the settlements that had just been built along the canal:

We ended up living in a barrack with two layers of bunks. Since there were small children, our family was given a lower bunk. The barracks were long and cold. The stoves were lit twenty-four hours a day, thanks to the fact that firewood was plentiful in Karelia . . . our father, and main source of food, received on behalf of all of us, one third of a bucket of greenish soup, in whose dark water swam two or three green tomatoes or a cucumber, a few pieces of frozen potato, shaken together with 100–200 grams of barley or chick-peas.

In addition, the boy remembered that his father, who worked building new houses for the settlers, received 600 grams of bread. His sister received 400 grams. That had to suffice for all nine members of the family.[25]

Then, as later, some of the problems were reflected in official reports. At a meeting of the Communist Party cell of Belbaltlag in August 1932, there were complaints about the poor organization of food distribution, dirty kitchens, and increasing incidents of scurvy. Pessimistically, the secretary of the cell wrote that 'I have no doubt that the canal will not be built on time . . .'[26]

But for most, there was not the option of doubt. Indeed, the letters and reports written by the canal's administrators over the period of its construction carry overtones of overwhelming panic. Stalin had decreed that the canal would be built in twenty months, and its builders well understood that their livelihoods, and possibly their lives, depended upon it being completed in twenty months. To speed up work, camp commanders began to adopt practices already being used in the 'free' working world, including 'socialist competitions' between work teams – races to fulfil the norm or move the stones or dig the hole first – as well as all-night 'storms', in which prisoners 'voluntarily' worked twenty-four or forty-eight hours in a row. One prisoner remembered when electric lights were strung up around the work site so that work could continue for twenty-four hours a day.[27] Another prisoner received 10 kilos of white flour and 5 kilos of sugar as a prize for good performance. He gave the flour to the camp bakers. They made him several loaves of white bread, which he ate all at once, alone.[28]

Along with the competitions, the authorities also adhered to the cult of the *udarnik* or 'shock-worker'. Later, shock-workers were renamed 'Stakhanovites', in honour of Aleksei Stakhanov, a ludicrously overproductive miner. The *udarniki* and Stakhanovites were prisoners who had overfulfilled the norm and therefore received extra food and special privileges, including the right (unthinkable in later years) to a new suit every year, in addition to a new set of work clothes every six months.[29] Top performers also received significantly better food. In the dining halls they ate at separate tables, beneath posters reading 'For the best workers, the best food'. Their inferiors sat beneath posters reading 'Here they get worse food: refusers, loafers, lazy-bones'.[30]

Eventually, top performers were also released early: for every three days of work at 100 per cent norm-fulfilment, each prisoner received a day off his sentence. When the canal was finally completed, on time, in August 1933, 12,484 prisoners were freed. Numerous others received medals and awards.[31] One prisoner celebrated his early release at a ceremony complete with the traditional Russian presentation of bread and salt, as onlookers shouted, 'Hooray for the Builders of the Canal!' In the heat of the moment, he began kissing an unknown woman. Together, they wound up spending the night on the banks of the canal.[32]

The White Sea Canal construction was remarkable in many ways: for its overwhelming chaos, for its extreme haste, and for its significance to Stalin. But the rhetoric used to describe the project was truly unique: the White Sea Canal was the first, last and only Gulag project ever exposed to the full light of Soviet propaganda, both at home and abroad. And the man chosen to explain, promote and justify the canal to the Soviet Union and the rest of the world was none other than Maxim Gorky.

He was not a surprising choice. By this time, Gorky was well and truly a part of the Stalinist hierarchy. After Stalin's triumphant steamer trip down the completed canal in August 1933, Gorky led 120 Soviet writers on a similar expedition. The writers were (or so they claimed) so excited by this journey that they could hardly hold their notebooks: their fingers were 'shaking from astonishment'.[33] Those who then decided to write a book about the building of the canal received plenty of material encouragement as well, including a 'splendid buffet lunch at the Astoria', a grand, tsarist-era Leningrad hotel, to celebrate their participation in the project.[34]

Even by the low standards of social realism, the book that emerged from their efforts – Kanal imeni Stalina (The Canal Named for Stalin) – is an extraordinary testament to the corruption of writers and intellectuals in totalitarian societies. Like Gorky's foray into Solovetsky, Kanal imeni Stalina justifies the unjustifiable, purporting not only to document the spiritual transformation of prisoners into shining examples of Homo Sovieticus, but also to create a new type of literature. Although introduced and concluded by Gorky, the responsibility for the bulk of the book was ascribed not to one individual but to a 36-writer collective. Using lavish language, hyperbole and the gentle massaging of facts, they strove together to capture the spirit of the new age.

One of the book's photographs encapsulates its theme: it depicts a woman, dressed in prison garb, wielding a drill with great determination. Beneath her is the caption 'In changing nature, man changes himself.' The contrast with the cold-blooded language used by the Yanson commission, and the economic agenda of the OGPU, could not be more stark.

For those unfamiliar with the genre, some aspects of the social realist Kanal might seem somewhat surprising. For one, the book does not attempt to disguise the truth altogether, as it describes the problems created by the lack of technology and trained specialists. At one point, the book quotes Matvei Berman, at the time the commander of the Gulag: 'You will be given one thousand healthy men,' Berman tells an OGPU subordinate:

'They have been condemned by the Soviet government for various terms. With these people you are to accomplish the work.'
    'But permit me to ask, where are the warders?' the OGPU man responds.
    'The warders you will organize on the spot. You will select them yourselves.'
    'Very well; but I know nothing about oil.'
    'Get the imprisoned Engineer Dukhanovich to be your assistant.'
    'What good is he? His specialty is the cold drawing of metals.'
    'What do you want? Are we to condemn the professors you require to concentration camps? There is no such clause in the Penal Code. And we are not the Oil syndicate.'

With those words, Berman then sent the OGPU agent off to do his job. 'A crazy affair,' note Kanal's authors. Within 'a month or two', however, the OGPU man and his colleagues are bragging to one another about the successes they have achieved with their ragtag group of prisoners. 'I've got a colonel who's the best lumberjack in the entire camp,' crows one; 'I have a field engineer on excavation work – an ex-cashier embezzler,' says another.[35]

The message is clear: material conditions were difficult, the human material was rough – but the all-knowing, never-failing Soviet political police succeeded, against all the odds, in transforming them into good Soviet citizens. Thus were actual facts – the primitive technology, the lack of competent specialists – deployed to give verisimilitude to an otherwise fanciful portrait of life in the camps.

Much of the book, in fact, is taken up with heart-warming, semi-religious stories of prisoners 'reforging' themselves through their work on the canal. Many of the prisoners thus reborn are criminals, but not all. Unlike Gorky's Solovetsky essay, which dismissed or minimized the presence of political prisoners, *Kanal* features some star political converts. Fettered by 'caste prejudice, Engineer Maslov, a former "wrecker"', tries to 'veil with iron those dark and deep processes of reconstruction of his conscience which were continually surging within him'. Engineer Zubrik, a working-class ex-saboteur, 'honestly earned the right to return again to the bosom of the class in which he was born'.[36]

But *Kanal imeni Stalina* was by no means the only literary work of the time to praise the transforming powers of the camps. Nikolai Pogodin's play, *Aristokraty* – a comedy about the White Sea Canal – is another notable example, not least because it picks up on an earlier Bolshevik theme: the 'lovability' of thieves. First performed in December 1934, Pogodin's play (eventually made into a film called *Prisoners*) ignores the kulaks and politicals who constituted the bulk of the canal's inmates, instead depicting the jolly japes of the camp bandits (the 'aristocrats' of the title) using a very mild form of criminal slang. True, there are one or two sinister notes in the play. At one point, a criminal 'wins' a girl in a card game, meaning his opponent must capture her and force her to submit to him. In the play, the girl escapes; in real life, she would probably not have been so lucky.

In the end, though, everyone confesses to their previous crimes, sees the light, and begins to work enthusiastically. A song is sung:

> I was a cruel bandit, yes,
> I stole from the people, hated to work,
> My life was black like the night.
> But then they took me to the canal,
> Everything past now seems a bad dream.
> It is as if I were reborn.
> I want to work, and live and sing . . .[37]

At the time, this sort of thing was hailed as a new and radical form of theatre. Jerzy Gliksman, a Polish socialist who saw *Aristokraty* performed in Moscow in 1935, described the experience:

Instead of being in the usual place, the stage was built in the centre of the edifice, the audience sitting in a circle around it. The director's aim was to draw the audience closer to the action of the play, to bridge the gap between actor and spectator. There was no curtain, and the stage settings were exceedingly simple, almost as in the Elizabethan theatre . . . the topic – life in a labour camp – was thrilling in itself.[38]

Outside the camps, such literature had a dual function. On the one hand, it played a role in the continuing campaign to justify the rapid growth of prison camps to a sceptical foreign public. On the other hand, it probably also served to calm Soviet citizens, disquieted by the violence of collectivization and industrialization, by promising them a happy ending: even the victims of the Stalinist revolution would be given a chance to rebuild their lives in the labour camps.

The propaganda worked. After seeing *Aristokraty*, Gliksman asked to visit a real labour camp. Somewhat to his surprise, he was soon taken to the 'show' camp at Bolshevo, not far from Moscow. He later recalled 'nice white beds and bedding, fine washing rooms. Everything was spotlessly clean,' and met a group of younger prisoners who told the same uplifting personal stories that Pogodin and Gorky had described. He met a thief who was now studying to become an engineer. He met a hooligan who had seen the error of his ways and now ran the camp storeroom. 'How beautiful the world could be!' a French film director whispered into Gliksman's ear. Alas for Gliksman, five years later he found himself on the floor of a packed cattle car, heading for a camp that would bear no relationship to the model camp at Bolshevo, in the company of prisoners very different from those in Pogodin's play.[39]

Inside the camps, similar propaganda played a role as well. Camp publications and 'wall newspapers' – sheets posted on bulletin boards for prisoners to read – contained the same sorts of stories and poems told to outsiders, with some slight differences of emphasis. The newspaper *Perekovka* ('reforging'), written and produced by the inmates of the Moscow–Volga Canal, a project begun in the wake of the 'success' of the White Sea Canal, is typical. Filled with praise for shock-workers, and descriptions of their privileges ('They don't have to stand in line, they are given food straight at the table by waitresses!'), *Perekovka* spends less time than the authors of *Kanal imeni Stalina* singing hymns to the advantagess of spiritual transformation, and more time discussing the concrete privileges inmates might gain if they worked harder.

Nor is there quite so much pretence about the higher justice of the Soviet system. The issue of 18 January 1933 reprinted a speech made by Lazar Kogan, one of the camp bosses: 'We cannot judge whether someone was rightly or wrongly imprisoned. That's the business of the prosecutor . . . You are obliged to create something valuable to the state with your work, and we are obliged to make of you someone who is valuable to the state.'[40]

Also notable is *Perekovka*'s open and extremely candid 'complaints' department. Prisoners wrote in to complain about the 'squabbling and swearing' in the womens' barracks on the one hand, and the 'singing of hymns' on the other; about unfulfillable norms; about shortages of shoes or clean underwear; about the unnecessary beating of horses; about the black-market bazaar in the centre of Dmitrov, the headquarters of the camp; and about the misuse of machinery ('there are no bad machines, only bad managers'). This sort of openness about camp problems would disappear later, banished to the private correspondence between camp inspectors and their overlords in Moscow. In the early 1930s, however, such glasnost was quite common outside the camps as well as within them. It was a natural part of the urgent, frantic drive to improve conditions, improve work standards, and – above all – to keep pace with the feverish demands of the Stalinist leadership.[41]

Walking along the banks of the White Sea Canal today, it is hard to conjure up that near-hysterical atmosphere. I visited the site on a lazy day in August 1999, in the company of several local historians. We stopped, briefly, to look at the small monument to the victims of the canal in Povenets, which bears a brief inscription: 'To the innocents, who died while building the White Sea Canal, 1931–1933.' While we stood there, one of my companions insisted on ceremonially smoking a 'Belomor' cigarette. He explained that the 'Belomor' cigarette brand, once one of the Soviet Union's most popular, was for decades the only other monument to the canal's builders.

Near by stood an old *trudposelok*, or 'exile settlement', now virtually empty. The large, once-solid houses, made of wood in the Karelian style, were boarded up. Several had begun to sag. A local man, who came originally from Belorussia – he even spoke a little Polish – told us that he had tried to buy one of the houses a few years ago, but the local government would not sell it to him. 'Now it's all falling apart,' he said. In a little garden behind the house he grew squash and cucumbers and berries. He offered us home-made liqueur. With his garden and his 550-rouble pension – at the time, about $22 per month – he had enough, he said, to live on. Of course there was no work to be had on the canal.

And no wonder: along the canal itself, boys were swimming, throwing stones. Cows waded in the murky, shallow water, and weeds grew through the cracks of the concrete. Alongside one of the locks, in a small booth with pink curtains and the original Stalinist columns on the outside, the lone woman controlling the rise and fall of water told us that there were perhaps seven passing ships a day at the most, and often only three or four. That was more than Solzhenitsyn saw in 1966, when he spent a whole day beside the canal and saw two barges, both carrying firewood. Most goods by then, as nowadays, travel by rail – and, as a canal worker told him, the waterway is so shallow that 'not even submarines can pass through it under their own power; they have to be loaded on barges'.[42]

The shipping route from the Baltic to the White Sea had not, it seemed, proved so urgently necessary after all.

5

The Camps Expand

We go forward, and behind us
The whole brigade walks merrily along.
In front of us, the victory of the Stakhanovites
Opens a new path . . .

For the old path is no longer known to us,
From our dungeons we have risen to the call
Along the path of Stakhanovite triumph
Believing, we walk towards a life of freedom . . .

– from the journal *Kuznitsa*,
printed in Sazlag, 1936[1]

Politically, the White Sea Canal was the most important Gulag project of its era. Thanks to Stalin's personal involvement, no available resources were spared on its construction. Lavish propaganda also ensured that its successful completion was trumpeted far and wide. Yet the canal was not typical of the Gulag's new projects, of which it was neither the first nor the largest.

In fact, even before construction of the canal had begun, the OGPU had already started quietly deploying prison labour all over the country, with far less fuss and propaganda. By the middle of 1930, the Gulag system already had 300,000 inmates at its disposal, dispersed among a dozen or so camp complexes and a few smaller sites. It had put 15,000 people to work in Dallag, a new camp in the far east. More than 20,000 were building and operating chemical plants in Vishlag, a camp organized on the base of the Vishersky division of SLON, on the western side of the Ural mountains. In Siblag, in western Siberia, prisoners were building the northern railways, making bricks and cutting trees, while the 40,000 prisoners of SLON were at work building roads, cutting wood for export and packaging 40 per cent of the fish harvested in the White Sea.[2]

Unlike the White Sea Canal, these new camps were not for show. Although they were certainly of greater economic significance to the Soviet Union, no teams of writers set out to describe them. Their existence was not completely secret – not yet – but no one publicized them either: the 'real' achievements of the Gulag were not for foreign or even domestic consumption.

As the camps expanded, the nature of the OGPU changed too. As before, Soviet secret police continued to spy upon the regime's enemies, to interrogate suspected dissidents, and to ferret out 'plots' and 'conspiracies'. From 1929 onwards, the secret police also shouldered part of the responsibility for the Soviet Union's economic development. Over the next decade, they would even become pioneers of a sort, often organizing the exploration as well as the exploitation of the Soviet Union's natural resources. They planned and equipped geological expeditions which sought to identify the coal, oil, gold, nickel and other metals that lay beneath the frozen tundra of the Arctic and sub-Arctic regions of the Soviet far north. They decided which of the enormous stands of timber would be the next to be cut into valuable raw-wood exports. To move these resources into the Soviet Union's major cities and industrial centres, they set up a huge network of road and rail links, carving out a rudimentary transport system across thousands of kilometres of uninhabited wilderness. On occasion, they took part in these ventures themselves, marching across the tundra, clad in heavy fur coats and thick boots, telegraphing their discoveries back to Moscow.

Prisoners acquired new roles along with their captors. Although some continued to toil behind barbed wire, digging coal or ditches, throughout the first half of the 1930s prisoners also paddled canoes down rivers north of the Arctic Circle, carried the equipment needed for the geological surveys and broke the ground for new coal mines and oil wells. They built the barracks, unrolled the barbed wire and set up the watchtowers for new camps. They constructed the refineries needed to process the resources, pounded in the stakes for the railways and poured the cement for the roads. Eventually, they settled the newly opened territories too, populating the virgin wilderness.

Later, Soviet historians would lyrically call this episode in Soviet history the 'Opening Up of the Far North', and it is true that it did represent a real break with the past. Even in the last decades of tsarist rule, when a belated industrial revolution had finally exploded across Russia, no one had attempted to explore and settle the far northern regions of the country with this intensity. The climate was too harsh, the potential human suffering too great, Russian technology too primitive. The Soviet regime was less troubled by such concerns. Although its technology was not much better, it had little regard for the lives of the people it sent to do the 'opening up'. If some of them died – well, more could be found.

Tragedies were plentiful, particularly at the outset of this new era. Recently, the veracity of one particularly horrific incident, long a part of camp survivors' folklore, was confirmed by a document found in the archives in Novosibirsk. Signed by an instructor of the Party Committee in Narym, western Siberia, and sent for the personal attention of Stalin in May 1933, it precisely describes the arrival of a group of deported peasants – described as 'backward elements' – on the island of Nazino in the Ob River. The peasants were exiles, and as such were supposed to settle on the land, and presumably to farm it:

The first convoy contained 5,070 people, and the second 1,044; 6,114 in all. The transport conditions were appalling: the little food that was available was inedible and the deportees were cramped into nearly airtight spaces . . . The result was a daily mortality rate of 35–40 people. These living conditions, however, proved to be luxurious in comparison to what awaited the deportees on the island of Nazino . . . The island of Nazino is a totally uninhabited place, devoid of any settlements . . . There were no tools, no grain, and no food. That is how their new life began. The day after the arrival of the first convoy, on 19 May, snow began to fall again, and the wind picked up. Starving, emaciated from months of insufficient food, without shelter and without tools . . . they were trapped. They weren't even able to light fires to ward off the cold. More and more of them began to die . . .

On the first day, 295 people were buried. It was only on the fourth or fifth day after the convoy's arrival on the island that the authorities sent a bit of flour by boat, really no more than a few pounds per person. Once they had received their meagre ration, people ran to the edge of the water and tried to mix some of the flour with water in their hats, their trousers or their jackets. Most of them just tried to eat it straight off, and some of them even choked to death. These tiny amounts of flour were the only food that the deportees received during the entire period of their stay on the island . . .

By 20 August, three months later, the Party functionary went on to write, nearly 4,000 of the original 6,114 'settlers' were dead. The survivors had lived because they ate the flesh of those who had died. According to another inmate, who encountered some of these survivors in the Tomsk prison, they looked 'like walking corpses', and were all under arrest – accused of cannibalism.[3]

Even when the death toll was not quite so horrific, living conditions in many of the Gulag's best-known early projects could be very nearly as intolerable. BAMlag, a camp organized around the construction of a railway line from Baikal to Amur, in the Russian far east – part of the Trans-Siberian Express railway system – was one notable example of how badly things could go wrong through simple lack of planning. Like the White Sea Canal, the railway construction was carried out in great haste, with no advance preparation whatsoever. The camp's planners carried out the exploration of the terrain, the design of the railway and the building of the railway simultaneously; construction began before the surveys were complete. Even so, surveyors were forced to make their report of the 2,000-kilometre track in under four months, without adequate shoes, clothing and instruments. Existing maps were poor, as a result of which costly mistakes were made. According to one survivor, 'two workers' parties [each surveying a separate length of track] found they could not close ranks and finish work, because the two rivers along which they were walking came together only on maps, when in fact they were far apart'.[4]

Convoys began arriving at the camp's headquarters in the town of Svobodny (the name means 'Free') without any respite, as soon as the work had begun. Between January 1933 and January 1936 the numbers of prisoners rose from a few thousand to over 180,000. Many were already weak upon arrival, shoeless and badly clothed, suffering from scurvy, syphilis, dysentery, among them survivors of the famines that had swept the rural Soviet Union in the early 1930s. The camp was totally unprepared. One arriving convoy was put in cold, dark barracks upon arrival and given bread covered with dust. The BAMlag commanders were unable to deal with the chaos, as they admitted in reports they filed to Moscow, and were particularly ill-equipped to deal with weak prisoners. As a result, those too ill to work were simply put on disciplinary rations and left to starve. One convoy of twenty-nine people died within thirty-seven days of arrival.[5] Before the railway was completed, tens of thousands of prisoners may well have died.

Similar stories were repeated across the country. On the Gulag railway construction site of Sevlag, north-east of Arkhangelsk, engineers determined in 1929 that the number of prisoners assigned to their project would have to be increased sixfold. Between April and October of that year, convoys of prisoners duly began to arrive – to find nothing. One prisoner remembered: 'There were neither barracks, nor a village. There were tents, on the side, for the guards and for the equipment. There weren't many people, perhaps one and a half thousand. The majority were middle-aged peasants, former kulaks. And criminals. No visible intelligentsia . . .'[6]

Yet although all of the camp complexes founded in the early 1930s were disorganized to start out with – and all of them were unprepared to receive the emaciated prisoners coming in from the famine districts – not all of them descended into lethal disarray. Given the right set of circumstances – relatively favourable conditions on the ground, combined with strong support from Moscow – some found it possible to grow. With surprising speed, they developed more stable bureaucratic structures, built more permanent buildings, even spawned a local NKVD elite. A handful would eventually occupy whole swathes of territory, converting entire regions of the country into vast prisons. Of the camps founded at this time, two – the Ukhtinskaya Expedition and the Dalstroi Trust – eventually attained the size and status of industrial empires. Their origins deserve a closer look.

To the unobservant passenger, an automobile ride along the crumbling cement highway that leads from the city of Syktyvkar, the administrative capital of the Komi Republic, to the city of Ukhta, one of Komi's major industrial centres, would seem to offer little of interest. The 200-kilometre road, somewhat the worse for wear in a few places, leads through endless pine forests and across swampy fields. Although the road crosses a few rivers, the views are otherwise unremarkable: this is the taiga, the splendidly monotonous sub-Arctic landscape for which Komi (and indeed all of northern Russia) is best known.

Even though the views are not spectacular, closer examination reveals some oddities. If you know where to look, it is possible in certain places to see indentations in the ground, just alongside the road. These are the only remaining evidence of the camp that was once strung out along the length of the road, and of the teams of prisoners that built the road. Because the building sites were temporary, prisoners here were often housed not in barracks but in *zemlyanki*, earth dugouts: hence the marks in the ground.

On another section of the road lie the remains of a more substantial sort of camp, once attached to a small oilfield. Weeds and underbrush now cover the site, but they are easily pushed away to reveal rotting wooden boards – possibly preserved by the oil that came off the prisoners' boots – and bits of barbed wire. There is no memorial here, although there is one at Bograzdino, a transit camp further along the road, which held up to 25,000 people. No trace remains of Bograzdino whatsoever. In yet another place along the road – behind a modern petrol station, property of Lukoil, a present-day Russian company – stands an old wooden watchtower, surrounded by metal debris and bits of rusted wire.

Carry on to Ukhta in the company of someone who knows the city well, and its hidden history will be quickly revealed. All of the roads leading into town were once built by prisoners, as were all of central Ukhta's office blocks and apartment buildings. In the very heart of the city there is a park, planned and built by prisoner architects; a theatre in which prisoner actors performed; and sturdy wooden houses, where the camp commanders once lived. Today, the managers of Gazprom, another new Soviet company, inhabit modern buildings on the same leafy street.

Nor, in the Komi Republic, is Ukhta unique. Although difficult at first to see, traces of the Gulag are visible all over Komi, this vast region of taiga and tundra which lies to the north-east of St Petersburg and to the west of the Ural mountains. Prisoners planned and built all of the republic's major cities, not just Ukhta but also Syktyvkar, Pechora, Vorkuta and Inta. Prisoners built Komi's railways and roads, as well as its original industrial infrastructure. To the inmates who were sent there in the 1940s and 1950s, Komi seemed to be nothing but one vast camp – which it was. Many of its villages are still referred to locally by their Stalinist-era names: 'Chinatown', for example, where a group of Chinese prisoners were held; or 'Berlin', once inhabited by German prisoners of war.

The origins of this vast republic of prisons lay in one of the earliest OGPU expeditions, the Ukhtinskaya Expedition, which set out in 1929 to explore what was then an empty wilderness. By Soviet standards, the expedition was relatively well-prepared. It had a surfeit of specialists, most of whom were already prisoners in the Solovetsky system: in 1928 alone, sixty-eight mining engineers had been sent to SLON, victims of that year's campaigns against the 'wreckers' and 'saboteurs' who were supposedly holding back the Soviet Union's drive to industrialization.[7]

In November 1928, with mysteriously good timing, the OGPU also arrested N. Tikhonovich, a well-known geologist. After throwing him into Moscow's Butyrka prison, however, they did not carry out an ordinary interrogation. Instead, they brought him to a planning meeting. Wasting no time on preliminaries, Tikhonovich remembered later, a group of eight people – he was not told who they were – asked him, point-blank, how to prepare an expedition to Komi. What clothes would he take if he were going? How many provisions? Which tools? Which method of transport? Tikhonovich, who had first been to the region in 1900, proposed two routes. The geologists could go by land, trekking on foot and on horseback over the mud and forest of the uninhabited taiga to the village of Syktyvkar, then the largest in the region. Alternatively, they could take the water route: from the port of Arkhangelsk in the White Sea, along the northern coast to the mouth of the Pechora River, then continuing inland on the Pechora's tributaries. Tikhonovich recommended the latter route, pointing out that boats could carry more heavy equipment. On his recommendation, the expedition proceeded by sea. Tikhonovich, still a prisoner, became its chief geologist.

No time was wasted, and no expense was spared, for the Soviet leadership considered the expedition to be an urgent priority. In May, the Gulag administration in Moscow named two senior secret police bosses to lead the group: E. P. Skaya – the former chief of security at the Smolny Institute, Lenin's first headquarters during the Revolution, and later chief of security at the Kremlin itself – and S. F. Sidorov, the OGPU's top economic planner. At about the same time, the expedition bosses selected their 'workforce' – 139 of the stronger, healthier prisoners in the SLON transit camp in Kem, politicals, kulaks and criminals among them. After two more months of preparation, they were ready. On 5 July 1929, at seven o'clock in the morning, the prisoners began loading equipment on to SLON's steamer, the *Gleb Boky*. Less than twenty-four hours later, they set sail.

Not surprisingly, the floating expedition encountered many obstacles. Several of the guards appear to have got cold feet, and one actually ran away during a stopover in Arkhangelsk. Small groups of prisoners also managed to escape at various points along the route. When the expedition finally made it to the mouth of the Pechora River, local guides proved difficult to find. Even if paid, the indigenous Komi natives did not want anything to do with prisoners or the secret police, and they refused to help the ship navigate upstream. Nevertheless, after seven weeks the ship finally arrived. On

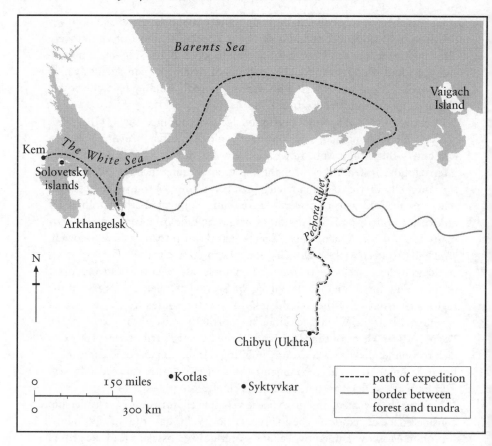

3 The route of the Ukhtinskaya Expedition, Komi Republic, 1929

21 August, they set up their base camp in the village of Chibyu – later to be renamed Ukhta.

After the tiring voyage, the general mood must have been exceptionally gloomy. They had travelled a long way – and where had they arrived? Chibyu offered little in the way of creature comforts. One of the prisoner specialists, a geographer named Kulevsky, remembered his first view of the place: 'The heart compressed at the sight of the wild, empty landscape: the absurdly large, black, solitary watch tower, the two poor huts, the taiga and the mud...'[8]

He would have had little time for further reflection. By late August, hints of autumn were already in the air. There was little time to spare. As soon as they arrived, the prisoners immediately began to work twelve hours a day, building their camp and their work sites. The geologists set out to find the best places to drill for oil. More specialists arrived later in the autumn. New

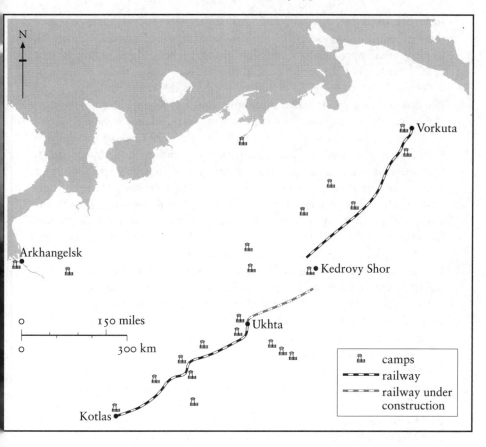

4 Ukhtpechlag, Komi Republic, 1937

prisoner convoys arrived too, first monthly and then weekly, throughout the 1930 'season'. By the end of the expedition's first year, the number of prisoners had grown to nearly a thousand.

Despite the advance planning, conditions in these early days, for both prisoners and exiles, were horrendous, as they were everywhere else. Most had to live in tents, as there were no barracks. Nor were there enough winter clothes and boots, or anywhere near enough food. Flour and meat arrived in smaller quantities than had been ordered, as did medicines. The number of sick and weakened prisoners rose, as the expedition's leaders admitted in a report they filed later. The isolation was no less difficult to bear. So far were these new camps from civilization – so far were they from roads, even, let alone railway lines – that no barbed wire was used in Komi until 1937. Escape was considered pointless.

Still, prisoners kept arriving – and supplementary expeditions continued to set out from the base camp at Ukhta. If they were successful, each one of these expeditions founded, in turn, a new base camp – a *lagpunkt* – sometimes in places that were almost impossibly remote, several days' or weeks' trek from Ukhta. They, in turn, founded further sub-camps, to build roads or collective farms to serve the prisoners' needs. In this manner, camps spread like fast-growing weeds across the empty forests of Komi.

Some of the expeditions proved to be temporary. Such was the fate of one of the first, which set out from Ukhta in the summer of 1930 for Vaigach Island, in the Arctic Sea. Earlier geological expeditions had already found lead and zinc deposits on the island, although the Vaigach Expedition, as it came to be called, was well provided with geologist prisoners as well. Some of these geologists performed in such an exemplary manner that the OGPU rewarded them: they were allowed to bring their wives and children to live with them on the island. So remote was the location that the camp commanders appear not to have worried about escape, and they allowed prisoners to walk anywhere they wished, in the company of other prisoners or free workers, without any special permissions or passes. To encourage 'shock-work in the Arctic', Matvei Berman, then the Gulag boss, granted prisoners on Vaigach Island two days off their sentence for every such day worked.[9] In 1934, however, the mine filled with water, and the OGPU moved both prisoners and equipment off the island the following year.[10]

Other expeditions would prove more permanent. In 1931, a team of twenty-three set off northwards from Ukhta by boat, up the inland waterways, intending to begin the excavation of an enormous coal deposit – the Vorkuta coal basin – discovered in the Arctic tundra of the northern part of Komi the previous year. As on all such expeditions, geologists led the way, prisoners manned the boats, and a small OGPU contingent commanded the operation, paddling and marching through the swarms of insects that inhabit the tundra in summer months. They spent their first nights in open fields, then somehow built a camp, survived the winter, and constructed a primitive mine the following spring: Rudnik No. 1. Using picks and shovels and wooden carts, and no mechanized equipment whatsoever, the prisoners began to dig coal. Within a mere six years, Rudnik No. 1 would grow into the city of Vorkuta and the headquarters of Vorkutlag, one of the largest and toughest camps in the entire Gulag system. By 1938, Vorkutlag contained 15,000 prisoners and had produced 188,206 tons of coal.[11]

Technically, not all of the new inhabitants of Komi were prisoners. From 1929, the authorities also began to send 'special exiles' to the region. At first these were almost all kulaks, who arrived with their wives and children and were expected to start living off the land. Yagoda himself had declared that the exiles were to be given 'free time' in which they were to plant gardens, raise pigs, go fishing, and build their own homes: 'first they will live on camp rations, then at their own cost'.[12] While all of that sounds rather rosy, in fact nearly 5,000 such exile families arrived in 1930 – over 16,000 people – to find, as usual, almost nothing. There were 268 barracks built by November of that year, although at least 700 were needed. Three or four families shared each room. There was not enough food, clothing or winter boots. The exile villages lacked baths, roads, a postal service and telephone cables.[13]

Although some died, and many tried to escape – 344 had attempted to escape by the end of July – the Komi exiles became a permanent adjunct to the Komi camp system. Later waves of repression brought more of them to the region, particularly Poles and Germans. Hence the local references to some of the Komi villages as 'Berlin'. Exiles did not live behind barbed wire, but did the same jobs as prisoners, sometimes in the same places. In 1940, a logging camp was changed into an exile village – proof that, in a certain sense, the groups were interchangeable. Many exiles also wound up working as guards or administrators in the camps.[14]

In time, this geographical growth was reflected in camp nomenclature. In 1931, the Ukhtinskaya Expedition was renamed the Ukhto-Pechorsky Corrective-Labour Camp, or Ukhtpechlag. Over the subsequent two decades, Ukhtpechlag itself would be renamed many more times – and reorganized and divided up – to reflect its changing geography, its expanding empire, and its growing bureaucracy. By the end of the decade, in fact, Ukhtpechlag would no longer be a single camp at all. Instead, it spawned a whole network of camps, two dozen in total, including: Ukhtpechlag and Ukhtizhemlag (oil and coal); Ustvymlag (forestry); Vorkuta and Inta (coal mining); and Sevzheldorlag (railways).[15]

In the course of the next several years, Ukhtpechlag and its descendants also became denser, acquiring new institutions and new buildings in accordance with their ever-expanding requirements. Needing hospitals, camp administrators built them, and introduced systems for training prisoner pharmacists and prisoner nurses. Needing food, they constructed their own collective farms, their own warehouses and their own distribution systems. Needing electricity, they built power plants. Needing building materials, they built brick factories.

Needing educated workers, they trained the ones that they had. Much of the ex-kulak workforce turned out to be illiterate or semiliterate, which caused enormous problems when dealing with projects of relative technical sophistication. The camp's administration therefore set up technical training schools, which required, in turn, more new buildings and new cadres: maths and physics teachers, as well as 'political instructors' to oversee their work.[16] By the 1940s, Vorkuta – a city built in the permafrost, where roads had to be resurfaced and pipes had to be repaired every year – had acquired a geological institute and a university, theatres, puppet theatres, swimming pools and nurseries.

Yet if the expansion of Ukhtpechlag was not much publicized, neither was it haphazard. Without a doubt the camp's commanders on the ground wanted their project to grow, and their prestige to grow along with it. Urgent necessity, not central planning, would have led to the creation of many new camp departments. Still, there was a neat symbiosis between the Soviet government's needs (a place to dump its enemies) and the regions' needs (more people to cut trees). When Moscow wrote offering to send exile settlers in 1930, for example, local leaders were delighted.[17] The camp's fate was discussed at the highest possible levels as well. It is worth noting that in November 1932, the Politburo – with Stalin present – dedicated most of an entire meeting to a discussion of the present state and future plans of Ukhtpechlag, discussing its prospects and its supplies in surprising detail. From the meeting's protocols, it seems as if the Politburo made all the decisions, or at least approved everything of any importance: which mines the camp should develop; which railways it should construct; how many tractors, cars and boats it required; how many exile families it could absorb. The Politburo also allocated money for the camp's construction: more than 26 million roubles.[18]

It can be no accident that during the three years following this decision, the number of prisoners nearly quadrupled, from 4,797 in mid-1932 to 17,852 in mid-1933.[19] At the very highest levels of the Soviet hierarchy, someone very much wanted Ukhtpechlag to grow. Given his power and prestige – that could only have been Stalin himself.

In the same way that Auschwitz has become, in popular memory, the camp which symbolizes all other Nazi camps, so too has the word 'Kolyma' come to signify the greatest hardships of the Gulag. 'Kolyma,' wrote one historian, 'is a river, a mountain range, a region, and a metaphor.'[20] Rich in minerals – and above all rich in gold – the vast Kolyma region in the far north-eastern corner of Siberia, on the Pacific coast, may well be the most inhospitable part of Russia. Kolyma is colder than Komi – temperatures there regularly fall to more than 45 degrees centigrade below zero in the winter – and even more remote.[21] To reach the camps of Kolyma, prisoners travelled by train across the entire length of the USSR – sometimes a three-month journey – to Vladivostok. They made the rest of the trip by boat, travelling northwards past Japan, through the Sea of Okhotsk, to the port of Magadan, the gateway to the Kolyma River valley.

Kolyma's first commander is one of the most flamboyant figures in the history of the Gulag. Eduard Berzin, an Old Bolshevik, had been commander of the First Latvian Rifle Division, which guarded the Kremlin in 1918. Later, he helped to crush the Social Revolutionaries, Lenin's socialist opponents, and to unmask Bruce Lockhart's 'British plot'.[22] In 1926, Stalin gave Berzin the task of organizing Vishlag, one of the very first large-scale camps. He took to the job with enormous enthusiasm, inspiring a historian of Vishlag to speak of his reign there as being the height of the Gulag's 'romantic period'.[23]

The OGPU built Vishlag at the same time as the White Sea Canal, and Berzin seems to have very much approved of (or, at least, enthusiastically paid lip service to) Gorky's ideas about prisoner reform. Glowing with paternalistic goodwill, Berzin provided his inmates with film theatres and discussion clubs, libraries and 'restaurant-style' dining halls. He planted gardens, complete with fountains and a small zoological park. He also paid prisoners regular salaries, and operated the same policy of 'early release for good work' as did the commanders of the White Sea Canal. Not everyone benefited from these amenities: prisoners who were deemed poor workers, or who were simply unlucky, might be sent to one of Vishlag's many small forestry lagpunkts in the taiga, where conditions were poor, death rates were higher, and prisoners were quietly tortured and even murdered.[24]

Still, Berzin's intention, at least, was that his camp appeared to be an honourable institution. All of which makes him seem, at first glance, an odd candidate to become the first boss of the Far Northern Construction Administration – Dalstroi – the 'trust', or pseudo-corporation, which would develop the Kolyma region. For there was nothing particularly romantic or idealistic about the founding of Dalstroi. Stalin's interest in the region dated from 1926, when he sent an envoy engineer to the United States to study mining techniques.[25] Later, between 20 August 1931 and 16 March 1932, the Politburo discussed the geology and geography of Kolyma no fewer than eleven times – with Stalin himself contributing frequently to the discussions. Like the Yanson commission's deliberations on the organization of the Gulag, the Politburo conducted these debates, in the words of the historian David Nordlander, 'not in the idealistic rhetoric of socialist construction, but rather in the practical language of investment priorities and financial returns'. Stalin devoted his subsequent correspondence with Berzin to questions about inmate productivity, quotas and output, never touching on the ideals of prisoner reform.[26]

On the other hand, Berzin's talent for creating rosy public images may have been precisely what the Soviet leadership wanted. For although Dalstroi would later be absorbed directly into the Gulag administration, in the beginning the trust was always referred to – in public – as if it were a separate entity, a sort of business conglomerate, which had nothing to do with the Gulag at all. Quietly, the authorities founded Sevvostlag, a Gulag camp which leased out convicts to the Dalstroi Trust. In practice, the two institutions never competed. The boss of Dalstroi was also the boss of Sevvostlag, and nobody had any doubt about that. On paper, however, they were kept separate, and in public they appeared to be distinct entities.[27]

There was a certain logic to this arrangement. For one, Dalstroi needed to attract volunteers, especially engineers and marriageable women (there were

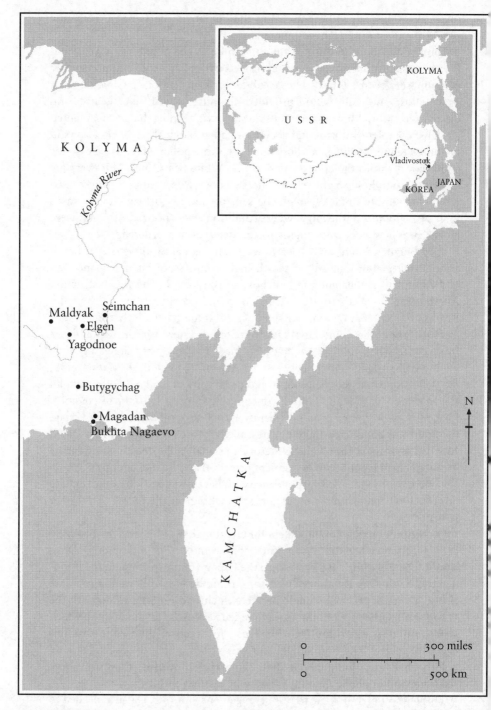

5 Kolyma, 1937

always shortages of both in Kolyma), and Berzin conducted many recruitment drives in an attempt to persuade 'free workers' to emigrate to the region, even setting up offices in Moscow, Leningrad, Odessa, Rostov and Novosibirsk.[28] For that reason alone, Stalin and Berzin may have wanted to avoid associating Kolyma too closely with the Gulag, fearing that the link might frighten away potential recruits. Although there is no direct proof, these machinations may also have been directed at the outside world. Like Soviet timber, Kolyma's gold would be sold directly to the West, exchanged for desperately needed technology and machinery. This may help explain why the Soviet leadership wanted to make the Kolyma gold fields seem as much like a 'normal' economic enterprise as possible. A boycott of Soviet gold would be far more damaging than a boycott of Soviet timber.

In any case, Stalin's personal involvement with Kolyma was extremely strong from the beginning. In 1932, he actually demanded daily reports on the gold industry, and, as already noted, interested himself in the details of Dalstroi's exploration projects and quota fulfilments. He sent out inspectors to examine the camps, and required Dalstroi's leaders to travel frequently to Moscow. When the Politburo allotted money to Dalstroi, it also issued precise instructions as to how the money was to be spent, as it did with Ukhtpechlag.[29]

Yet Dalstroi's 'independence' was not entirely fictitious either. Although he did answer to Stalin, Berzin also managed to leave his mark on Kolyma, so much so that the 'Berzin era' was later remembered with some nostalgia. Berzin appears to have understood his task in quite a straightforward manner: it was his job to get his prisoners to dig as much gold as possible. He was not interested in starving them or killing them or punishing them – only production figures mattered. Under Dalstroi's first boss, conditions were therefore not nearly as harsh as they became later, and prisoners were not nearly as hungry. Partly as a result, Kolyma's gold output increased eight times in the first two years of Dalstroi's operation.[30]

True, the first years were fraught with the same chaos and disorganization that prevailed elsewhere. By 1932, nearly 10,000 prisoners were at work in the region – among them the group of inmate engineers and specialists whose skills tallied so beautifully with the task in front of them – along with more than 3,000 voluntary 'free workers' – camp workers who were not prisoners.[31] The high numbers were accompanied by high death rates. Of the 16,000 prisoners who travelled to Kolyma in Berzin's first year, only 9,928 even reached Magadan alive.[32] The rest were thrown, underclothed and underprotected, into the winter storms: survivors of the first year would later claim that only half of their number had lived.[33]

Still, once the initial chaos had passed, the situation did gradually improve. Berzin worked hard to improve conditions, apparently believing, not irrationally, that prisoners needed to be warm and well fed in order to dig large quantities of gold. As a result, Thomas Sgovio, an American Kolyma survivor, wrote that camp 'old-timers' spoke of Berzin's reign warmly: 'when the frost dipped below minus 60 degrees, they were not sent to work. They were given three Rest Days a month. The food was adequate and nutritious. The *zeks* [prisoners] were given warm clothing – fur caps and felt boots . . .'[34] Varlam Shalamov, another Kolyma survivor – whose short stories, *Kolyma Tales*, are among the bitterest in the entire camp genre – also wrote of the Berzin period as a time of

excellent food, a workday of four to six hours in winter and ten in summer, and colossal salaries for convicts, which permitted them to return to the mainland as well-to-do men when their sentences were up . . . The cemeteries dating back to those days are so few in number that the early residents of Kolyma seemed immortal to those who came later.[35]

If living conditions were better than they would be later, the camp command also treated prisoners with a greater degree of humanity. At that time, the line between the volunteer free workers and the prisoners was blurred. The two groups associated normally; inmates were sometimes allowed to move out of their barracks to live in the free workers' villages, and could be promoted to become armed guards, as well as geologists and engineers.[36] Mariya Ioffe, an exile in Kolyma in the mid-1930s, was allowed to keep books and paper, and remembered that most exile families were allowed to stay together.[37]

Inmates were also allowed to participate, up to a point, in the political events of their time. Like the White Sea Canal, Kolyma promoted its own inmate shock-workers and Stakhanovites. One prisoner even became Dalstroi's 'instructor in the Stakhanovite methods of labour', and those inmates who performed well could receive a small badge, declaring them to be 'Kolyma shock-workers'.[38]

Like Ukhtpechlag, Kolyma's infrastructure quickly became more sophisticated. In the 1930s, prisoners built not only the mines, but also the docks and breakwaters for Magadan's port, as well as the region's single important road, the Kolyma Highway, which leads due north from Magadan. Most of Sevvostlag's *lagpunkts* were located along this road, and indeed they were often named according to their distance from Magadan ('Camp Forty-Seventh Kilometre', for example). Prisoners also built the city of Magadan itself, which contained 15,000 people by 1936, and would go on growing. Returning to the city in 1947, after serving seven years in the further-flung camps, Evgeniya Ginzburg 'nearly swooned with surprise and admiration' at the speed of Magadan's growth: 'It was only some weeks later that I noticed you could count the big buildings on your fingers. But at the time it really was a great metropolis for me.'[39]

In fact, Ginzburg was one of the few prisoners to notice a peculiar paradox. It was strange, but true: in Kolyma, as in Komi, the Gulag was slowly bringing 'civilization' – if that is what it can be called – to the remote wilderness. Roads were being built where there had been only forest, houses were appearing in the swamps. Native peoples were being pushed aside to make way for cities, factories and railways. Years later, a woman who had been the daughter of a camp cook in a far-flung outpost of Lokchimlag, one of the Komi logging camps, reminisced to me about what life had been like when the camp was still running. 'Oooh, there was a whole warehouse of vegetables, fields full of squash – it wasn't all barren like today.' She waved her arm in disgust at the tiny village which now stood on the site, at the former camp punishment cells, still inhabited. 'And there were real electric lights, and the bosses in their big cars drove in and out almost every day . . .'

Evgeniya Ginzburg made the same observation, more eloquently:

How strange is the heart of man! My whole soul cursed those who had thought up the idea of building a town in this permafrost, thawing out the ground with the blood and tears of innocent people. Yet at the same time I was aware of a sort of ridiculous pride . . . How it had grown, and how handsome it had become during my seven years' absence, our Magadan! Quite unrecognizable. I admired each street lamp, each section of asphalt, and even the poster announcing that the House of Culture was presenting the operetta *The Dollar Princess*. We treasure each fragment of our life, even the bitterest.[40]

By 1934, the expansion of the Gulag in Kolyma, in Komi, in Siberia, in Kazakhstan and elsewhere in the USSR had followed the same pattern as Solovetsky. In the early days, slovenliness, chaos and disorder caused many unnecessary deaths. Even without outright sadism, the unthinking cruelty of guards, who treated their prisoners as domestic animals, led to much misery.

Nevertheless, as time went on, the system seemed to be falling shakily into place. Death rates dropped from their high of 1933 as famine across the country receded and camps became better organized. By 1934, they were, according to the official statistics, hovering at around 4 per cent.[41] Ukhtpech-lag was producing oil, Kolyma was producing gold, the camps in the Arkhan-gelsk region were producing timber. Roads were being built across Siberia. Mistakes and mishaps abounded, but this was true everywhere in the USSR. The speed of industrialization, the lack of planning and the dearth of well-trained specialists made accidents and overspending inevitable, as the bosses of the big projects surely would have known.

Despite the setbacks, the OGPU was fast becoming one of the most important economic actors in the country. In 1934, Dmitlag, the camp that constructed the Moscow–Volga Canal, deployed nearly 200,000 prisoners, more than had been used for the White Sea Canal.[42] Siblag had grown too, boasting 63,000 prisoners in 1934, while Dallag had more than tripled in size in the four years since its founding, containing 50,000 in 1934. Other camps had been founded all across the Soviet Union: Sazlag, in Uzbekistan, where prisoners worked on collective farms; Svirlag, near Leningrad, where prisoners cut trees and prepared wood products for the city; and Karlag, in Kazakhstan, which deployed prisoners as farmers, factory workers and even fishermen.[43]

It was also in 1934 that the OGPU was reorganized and renamed once again, partly to reflect its new status and greater responsibilities. In that year, the secret police officially became the People's Commissariat of Internal Affairs – and became popularly known by a new acronym: NKVD. Under its new name, the NKVD now controlled the fate of more than a million prisoners.[44] But the relative calm was not to last. Abruptly, the system was about to turn itself inside out, in a revolution that would destroy masters and slaves alike.

6

The Great Terror and Its Aftermath

That was a time when only the dead
Could smile, delivered from their struggles,
And the sign, the soul of Leningrad
Dangled outside its prison house;
And the regiments of the condemned,
Herded in the railroad-yards
Shrank from the engine's whistle-song
Whose burden went, 'Away, pariahs!'
The star of death stood over us.
And Russia, guiltless, beloved, writhed
Under the crunch of bloodstained boots,
Under the wheels of Black Marias.

– Anna Akhmatova,
Requiem 1935–1940[1]

Objectively speaking, the years 1937 and 1938 – remembered as the years of the Great Terror – were not the deadliest in the history of the camps. Nor did they mark the camps' greatest expanse: the numbers of prisoners were far greater during the following decade, and peaked much later than is usually remembered, in 1952. Although available statistics are incomplete, it is still clear that death rates in the camps were higher both at the height of the rural famine in 1932 and 1933 and at the worst moment of the Second World War, in 1942 and 1943, when the total number of people assigned to forced-labour camps, prisons and POW camps hovered around four million.[2]

As a focus of historical interest, it is also arguable that the importance of 1937 and 1938 has been exaggerated. Even Solzhenitsyn complained that those who decried the abuses of Stalinism 'keep getting hung up on those years which are stuck in our throats, '37 and '38', and in one sense he is right.[3] The Great Terror, after all, followed two decades of repression. From 1918 onwards, there had been regular mass arrests and mass deportations, first of opposition politicians at the beginning of the 1920s, then of 'saboteurs' at the end of the 1920s, then of kulaks in the early 1930s. All of these episodes of mass arrest were accompanied by regular round-ups of those responsible for 'social disorder'.

The Great Terror was also followed, in turn, by even more arrests and deportations – of Poles, Ukrainians and Balts from territories invaded in 1939; of Red Army 'traitors' taken captive by the enemy; of ordinary people who found themselves on the wrong side of the front line after the Nazi invasion in 1941. Later, in 1948, there would be rearrests of former camp inmates, and later still, just before Stalin's death, mass arrests of Jews. Although the victims of 1937 and 1938 were perhaps better known, and although nothing as spectacular as the public 'show trials' of those years was ever repeated, the arrests of the Great Terror are therefore best described not as the zenith of repression, but rather as one of the more unusual waves of repression that washed over the country during Stalin's reign: it affected more of the elite – Old Bolsheviks, leading members of the army and the Party – encompassed in general a wider variety of people, and resulted in an unusually high number of executions.

In the history of the Gulag, however, 1937 does mark a genuine watershed. For it was in this year that the Soviet camps temporarily transformed themselves from indifferently managed prisons in which people died by accident, into genuinely deadly camps where prisoners were deliberately worked to death, or actually murdered, in far larger numbers than they had been in the past. Although the transformation was far from consistent, and although the deliberate deadliness of the camps did ease again by 1939 – death rates would subsequently rise and fall with the tides of war and ideology up until Stalin's death in 1953 – the Great Terror left its mark on the mentality of camp guards and prisoners alike.[4]

Like the rest of the country, the Gulag's inhabitants would have seen the early warning signs of the terror to come. Following the still-mysterious murder of the popular Leningrad Party leader, Sergei Kirov, in December 1934, Stalin pushed through a series of decrees giving the NKVD far greater powers to arrest, try and execute 'enemies of the people'. Within weeks, two leading Bolsheviks, Kamenev and Zinoviev – both past opponents of Stalin – had already fallen victim to the decrees, and were arrested along with thousands of their supporters and alleged supporters, many from Leningrad. Mass expulsions from the Communist Party followed, although they were not, to start with, much broader than expulsions that had taken place earlier in the decade.

Slowly, the purge became bloodier. Throughout the spring and summer of 1936, Stalin's interrogators worked on Kamenev and Zinoviev, along with a group of Leon Trotsky's former admirers, preparing them to 'confess' at a large public show trial, which duly took place in August. All were executed afterwards, along with many of their relatives. Other trials of leading Bolsheviks, among them the charismatic Nikolai Bukharin, followed in due course. Their families suffered too.

The mania for arrests and executions spread down the Party hierarchy, and throughout society. It was pushed from the top by Stalin, who used it to eliminate his enemies, create a new class of loyal leaders, terrorize the Soviet population – and fill his concentration camps. Starting in 1937, he signed orders which were sent to the regional NKVD bosses, listing quotas of people to be arrested (no cause was given) in particular regions. Some were to be sentenced to the 'first category' of punishment – death – and others to be given the 'second category' – confinement in concentration camps for a term ranging from eight to ten years. The most 'vicious' among the latter were to be placed in special political prisons, presumably in order to keep them from contaminating other camp inmates. Some scholars speculate that the NKVD assigned quotas to different parts of the country according to its perception of which regions had the greatest concentration of 'enemies'. On the other hand, they may also have had no significance at all.[5]

Reading them is very much like reading the orders of a bureaucrat designing the latest version of the Five-Year Plan. Here, for example, is one dated 30 July 1937:

	First Category	Second Category	Total
Azerbaijan SSR	1,500	3,750	5,250
Armenian SSR	500	1,000	1,500
Belorussian SSR	2,000	10,000	12,000
Georgian SSR	2,000	3,000	5,000
Kirgiz SSR	250	500	750
Tadzhik SSR	500	1,300	1,800
Turkmen SSR	500	1,500	2,000
Uzbek SSR	750	4,000	4,750
Bashkir ASSR	500	1,500	2,000
Buryat Mongolian ASSR	350	1,500	1,850
Dagestan ASSR	500	2,500	3,000
Karelian ASSR	300	700	1,000
Kabardino-Balkar ASSR	300	700	1,000
Crimean ASSR	300	1,200	1,500
Komi ASSR	100	300	400
Kalmyk ASSR	100	300	400
Mari ASSR	300	1,500	1,800
Etc.[6]			

Clearly, the purge was in no sense spontaneous: new camps for new prisoners were even prepared in advance. Nor did the purge encounter much resistance. The NKVD administration in Moscow expected their provincial subordinates to show enthusiam, and they eagerly complied. 'We ask permission to shoot an additional 700 people from the Dashnak bands, and other anti-Soviet elements,' the Armenian NKVD petitioned Moscow in September 1937. Stalin personally signed a similar request, just as he, or Molotov, signed many others: 'I raise the number of First Category prisoners in the Krasnoyarsk region to 6,600.' At a Politburo meeting in February 1938, the NKVD of Ukraine was given permission to arrest an additional 30,000 'kulaks and other anti-Soviet elements'.[7]

Some of the Soviet public approved of new arrests: the sudden revelation of the existence of enormous numbers of 'enemies', many within the highest reaches of the Party, surely explained why – despite Stalin's Great Turning Point, despite collectivization, despite the Five-Year Plan – the Soviet Union was still so poor and backward. Most, however, were too terrified and confused by the spectacle of famous revolutionaries confessing and neighbours disappearing in the night to express any opinions about what was happening at all.

In the Gulag, the purge first left its mark on the camp commanders – by eliminating many of them. If, throughout the rest of the country, 1937 was remembered as the year in which the Revolution devoured its children, in the camp system it would be remembered as the year in which the Gulag consumed its founders, beginning at the very top: Genrikh Yagoda, the secret police chief who bore the most responsibility for the expansion of the camp system, was tried and shot in 1938, after pleading for his life in a letter to the Supreme Soviet. 'It is hard to die,' wrote the man who had sent so many others to their deaths. 'I fall to my knees before the People and the Party, and ask them to pardon me, to save my life.'[8]

Yagoda's replacement, the dwarfish Nikolai Yezhov (he was only 5 feet tall), immediately began to dispose of Yagoda's friends and subordinates in the NKVD. He attacked Yagoda's family too – as he would attack the families of others – arresting his wife, parents, sisters, nephews and nieces. One of the latter recalled the reaction of her grandmother, Yagoda's mother, on the day she and the entire family were sent into exile.

'If only Gena [Yagoda] could see what they're doing to us,' someone quietly said.

Suddenly Grandmother, who never raised her voice, turned towards the empty apartment, and cried loudly, 'May he be damned!' She crossed the threshold and the door slammed shut. The sound reverberated in the stairwell like the echo of this maternal curse.[9]

Many of the camp bosses and administrators, groomed and promoted by Yagoda, shared his fate. Along with hundreds of thousands of other Soviet citizens, they were alleged to be implicated in vast conspiracies, arrested and interrogated in complex cases which could involve hundreds of people. One of the most prominent of these cases was organized around Matvei Berman, boss of the Gulag from 1932 to 1937. His years of service to the Party – he had joined in 1917 – did him no good. In December 1938, the NKVD accused Berman of having headed a 'Right-Trotskyist terrorist and sabotage organization' that had created 'privileged conditions' for prisoners in the camps, had deliberately weakened the 'military and political preparedness' of the camp guards (hence the large numbers of escapes), and had sabotaged the Gulag's construction projects (hence their slow progress).

Berman did not fall alone. All across the Soviet Union, Gulag camp commanders and top administrators were found to belong to the same 'Right-Trotskyist organization', and were sentenced in one fell swoop. The records of their cases have a surreal quality: it is as if all of the previous years' frustrations – the norms not met, the roads badly built, the prisoner-built factories which barely functioned – had come to some kind of insane climax.

Aleksandr Izrailev, for example, deputy boss of Ukhtpechlag, received a sentence for 'hindering the growth of coal mining'. Aleksandr Polisonov, a colonel who worked in the Gulag's division of armed guards, was accused of having created 'impossible conditions' for them. Mikhail Goskin, head of the Gulag's railway-building section, was described as having 'created unreal plans' for the Volochaevka–Komsomolets railway line. Isaak Ginzburg, head of the Gulag's medical division, was held responsible for the high death rates among prisoners, and accused of having created special conditions for other counter-revolutionary prisoners, enabling them to be released early on account of illness. Most of these men were condemned to death, although several had their sentences commuted to prison or camp, and a handful even survived to be rehabilitated in 1955.[10]

A striking number of the Gulag's very earliest administrators met the same fate. Fyodor Eichmanns, former boss of SLON, later head of the OGPU's Special Department, was shot in 1938. Lazar Kogan, the Gulag's second boss, was shot in 1939. Berman's successor as Gulag chief, Izrail Pliner, lasted only a year in the job and was also shot in 1939.[11] It was as if the system needed an explanation for why it worked so badly – as if it needed people to blame. Or perhaps 'the system' is a misleading expression: perhaps it was Stalin himself who needed to explain why his beautifully planned slave-labour projects progressed so slowly and with such mixed results.

There were some curious exceptions to the general destruction. For Stalin not only had control over who was arrested, but he also sometimes decided who would *not* be arrested. It is a curious fact that, despite the deaths of nearly all of his former colleagues, Naftaly Frenkel managed to evade the executioner's bullet. By 1937, he was the boss of BAMlag, the Baikal–Amur railway line, one of the most chaotic and lethal camps in the far east. Yet when forty-eight 'Trotskyites' were arrested in BAMlag in 1938, he was somehow not among them.

His absence from the list of arrestees is made stranger by the fact that the camp newspaper did attack him, openly accusing him of sabotage. Nevertheless, his case was mysteriously held up in Moscow. The local BAMlag prosecutor, who was conducting the investigation into Frenkel, found the delay incomprehensible. 'I don't understand why this investigation was placed under "special decree", or from whom this "special decree" has come,' he wrote to Andrei Vyshinsky, the Soviet Union's chief prosecutor: 'If we don't arrest Trotskyite-diversionist-spies, then whom should we be arresting?' Stalin, it seems, was still well able to protect his friends.[12]

Perhaps the most dramatic 1937 camp-boss saga was one that occurred towards the end of that year, in Magadan, and began with the arrest of Eduard Berzin, the Dalstroi boss. As Yagoda's direct subordinate, Berzin ought to have suspected that his career would soon be shortened. He ought also to have been suspicious when, in December, he received a whole new group of NKVD 'deputies', among them Major Pavlov, an NKVD officer who ranked higher than Berzin himself. Although Stalin often introduced soon-to-be-disgraced officials to their successors in this manner, Berzin showed no sign of suspecting anything. When the ominously named SS *Nikolai Yezhov* pulled into Nagaevo Bay, carrying his new team, Berzin organized a brass band to welcome them. He then spent several days showing his new 'staff' the ropes – although they virtually ignored him – before boarding the SS *Nikolai Yezhov* himself.

Upon reaching Vladivostok, he proceeded, quite normally, to take the Trans-Siberian Express for Moscow. But although Berzin left Vladivostok as a first-class passenger, he arrived a prisoner. Just 70 kilometres outside Moscow, in the town of Aleksandrov, his train ground to a halt. In the middle of the night of 19 December 1937, Berzin was arrested on the station platform – outside the capital, so as not to cause a fuss in central Moscow – and driven to Lubyanka, Moscow's central prison, for interrogation. He was quickly indicted for 'counter-revolutionary sabotage-wrecking activities'. The NKVD accused him of organizing a 'spy-diversionist Trotskyist organization in Kolyma', which was allegedly shipping gold to the Japanese government and plotting a Japanese takeover of the Russian far east. They also accused him of spying for England and Germany. Clearly, the Dalstroi boss had been a very busy man. He was shot in August 1938 in the basement of Lubyanka prison.

The absurdity of the charges did not detract from the deadliness of the case. By the end of December, Pavlov, working quickly, had arrested the majority of Berzin's subordinates. I. G. Filippov, the boss of the Sevvostlag camp, provided, under torture, an extensive confession which implicated virtually all of them. Confessing that he had 'recruited' Berzin in 1934, he admitted that their 'anti-Soviet organization' had planned to overthrow the Soviet government through the 'preparation of an armed uprising against Soviet power in Kolyma . . . the preparation and accomplishment of terrorist

acts against the leaders of the Communist Party and the Soviet government
... the encitement of the native population ... and the encouragement of
widespread wrecking', among other things. Berzin's chief deputy, Lev
Epshtein, subsequently confessed to 'gathering secret intelligence for France
and Japan while conducting sabotage, diversion and wrecking'. The chief
medical doctor at the Magadan polyclinic was accused of having 'connections
with alien elements and doubledealers'. By the time it was over, hundreds of
people who had been associated with Berzin, from geologists to bureaucrats
to engineers, were either dead or had themselves become prisoners.[13]

To put their experience in perspective, the Kolyma elite was not the only
powerful network to be eliminated in 1937 and 1938. By the end of that year,
Stalin had purged the Red Army of a whole host of notables, including Deputy
People's Commissar for Defence, Marshal Tukhachevsky, Army Commander
Ion Yakir, Army Commander Uborevich and others, along with their wives
and children, most of whom were shot, but some of whom wound up in
camps.[14] The Communist Party met a similar fate. The purge penetrated not
only Stalin's potential enemies in the Party leadership, but also the provincial
Party elite, the First Party Secretaries, the heads of local and regional councils,
and the leaders of important factories and institutions.

So thorough was the wave of arrests in certain places and among a certain
social class, later wrote Yelena Sidorkina – herself arrested in November
1937 – that 'Nobody knew what tomorrow would bring. People were afraid
to talk to one another or meet, especially families in which the father or
mother had already been "isolated". The rare individuals foolhardy enough
to stand up for those arrested would themselves be automatically nominated
for "isolation".'[15]

But not everyone died, and not every camp was wiped out. In fact, the
more obscure camp bosses even fared slightly better than the average NKVD
officer, as the case of V. A. Barabanov, a protégé of Yagoda, illustrates. In
1935, when he was the deputy commander of Dmitlag, Barabanov was
arrested along with a colleague for having arrived at the camp 'in a drunken
state'. As a result, he lost his job, received a light prison sentence, and was
working at a distant camp in the far north in 1938 when the mass arrests of
Yagoda's henchmen took place. In the chaos, his existence was forgotten. By
1954, his love of alcohol forgiven, he had risen through the ranks once again
to become the deputy commander of the entire Gulag system.[16]

But in the folk memory of the camps, 1937 was not only remembered as the
year of the Great Terror: it was also the year that propaganda about the
glories of criminal re-education finally ground to a halt, along with any
remaining lip service to the ideal. In part, this may have been due to
the deaths and arrests of those most closely associated with the campaign.
Yagoda, still linked in the public mind to the White Sea Canal, was gone.

Maxim Gorky had died suddenly in June 1936. I. L. Averbakh, Gorky's collaborator on *Kanal imeni Stalina* and author of *From Crime to Labour*, a subsequent tome dedicated to the Moscow–Volga Canal, was denounced as a Trotskyite and arrested in April 1937. So were many of the other writers who had taken part in Gorky's White Sea Canal collective.[17]

But the change had deeper origins as well. As the political rhetoric grew more radical, as the hunt for political criminals intensified, the status of the camps, where these dangerous politicals resided, changed as well. In a country gripped by paranoia and spy-mania, the very existence of camps for 'enemies' and 'wreckers' became, if not exactly a secret (prisoners working on roads and apartment blocks were to be a common sight in many major cities in the 1940s), then at least a subject never discussed in public. Nikolai Pogodin's play, *Aristokraty*, was banned in 1937, to be revived again, though only briefly, in 1956, well after Stalin's death.[18] Gorky's *Kanal imeni Stalina* was also placed on the list of forbidden books, for reasons that remain unclear. Perhaps the new NKVD bosses could no longer stomach the frothy praise for the disgraced Yagoda. Or perhaps its bright depiction of the successful re-education of 'enemies' no longer made sense in an era when new enemies were appearing all the time, and when hundreds of thousands of them were being executed, instead of reformed. Certainly its tales of smooth, all-knowing Chekists were hard to reconcile with the massive purges of the NKVD.

Not wanting to seem lax in their task of isolating the regime's enemies, the Gulag's commanders in Moscow issued new internal secrecy regulations too, entailing huge new costs. All correspondence now had to be sent by special courier. In 1940 alone, the NKVD's couriers had to transmit twenty-five million secret packages. Those writing letters to camps now wrote exclusively to post office boxes, as the locations of camps became a secret. The camps themselves disappeared from maps. Even internal NKVD correspondence referred to them euphemistically as 'special objects' (*spetsobekty*) or 'sub-sections' (*podrazdeleniya*) in order to conceal their real activity.[19]

For more specific references, both to camps and to the activities of their inhabitants, the NKVD devised an elaborate code which could be used in open telegrams. A document from 1940 listed these code-names, some bizarrely creative. Pregnant women were to be referred to as 'Books', and women with children as 'Receipts'. Men, on the other hand, were 'Accounts'. Exiles were 'Rubbish', and prisoners undergoing investigation were 'Envelopes'. A camp was a 'Trust', a camp division a 'Factory'. One camp was code-named 'Free'.[20]

Language used inside the camps changed too. Until the autumn of 1937, official documents and letters frequently referred to camp inmates by profession, referring to them simply as 'lumberjacks', for example. By 1940, an individual prisoner was no longer a lumberjack, but just a prisoner: a *zaklyuchennyi*, or *z/k*, in most documents – pronounced *zek*.[21] A group of prisoners became a *kontingent* ('contingent', or 'quota'), a bureaucratic, depersonalized term. Nor could prisoners earn the coveted title of Stakhanovite: one camp administrator sent an indignant letter to his subordinates ordering them to refer to hard-working prisoners as 'prisoners, working as shock-workers' or 'prisoners, working according to the Stakhanovite methods of labour'.

Any positive use of the term 'political prisoner' had, of course, long since disappeared. Privileges for the socialist politicals had ended with their transfer from Solovetsky in 1925. But now, the term 'political' went through a complete transformation. It included anyone sentenced according to the infamous Article 58 of the prison code, which included all 'counter-revolutionary' crimes – and it had thoroughly negative connotations. The politicals – sometimes called 'KRs' (counter-revolutionaries), *kontras* or *kontriki* – were more and more often referred to as *vragi naroda*: 'enemies of the people'.[22]

This term, a Jacobin epithet first used by Lenin in 1917, had been revived by Stalin in 1927 to describe Trotsky and his followers. It began to have a wider meaning in 1936 after a secret letter – 'of Stalin's authorship', in the view of Dmitri Volkogonov, Stalin's Russian biographer – went out from the Central Committee to the Party organizations in the regions and republics. The letter explained that while an enemy of the people 'appeared tame and inoffensive', he did everything possible to 'crawl stealthily into socialism', even though he 'secretly did not accept it'. Enemies, in other words, could no longer be identified by their openly professed views. A later NKVD boss, Lavrenty Beria, would also frequently quote Stalin, noting that 'an enemy of the people is not only one who commits sabotage, but one who doubts the rightness of the Party line'. Ergo, an 'enemy' could mean anybody who opposed Stalin's rule, for any reason, even if he did not openly profess to do so.[23]

In the camps, 'enemy of the people' now became an official term used in official documents. Women were arrested as 'wives of enemies of the people' after an NKVD decree of 1937 made such arrests possible, and the same applied to children. Officially they were sentenced as 'ChSVR': 'Member of the Family of an Enemy of the Revolution'.[24] Many of the 'wives' were incarcerated together in the Temnikovsky camp, also known as Temlag, in the republic of Mordovia, central Russia. Anna Larina, the wife of Bukharin, the disgraced Soviet leader, remembered that there, 'We had become equals in our troubles – Tukhachevskys and Yakirs, Bukharins and Radeks, Uboreviches and Gamarniks: "Misfortune shared is half misfortune!" '[25]

Another Temlag survivor, Galina Levinson, remembered that the camp's regime had been relatively liberal, perhaps because 'we didn't have sentences, we were just "wives"'. The majority of women in the camp, she noted, were people who until then had been 'absolutely Soviet people', and were still convinced that their arrests were due to the machinations of some secret, fascist organization within the Party. Several occupied themselves writing daily letters to Stalin and the Central Committee, complaining angrily about the plot being conducted against them.[26]

Aside from its official uses, 'enemy of the people' had also, by 1937, evolved into a term of abuse. From the time of Solovetsky, the camps' founders and planners had organized the system around the idea that prisoners were not human, but rather 'units of labour': even at the time of the building of the White Sea Canal, Maxim Gorky had described the kulaks as 'half-animals'.[27] Now, however, the propaganda described 'enemies' as something even lower than two-legged cattle. From the late 1930s, Stalin also began publicly to refer to 'enemies of the people' as 'vermin', 'pollution' and 'filth', or sometimes simply as 'weeds' which needed to be uprooted.[28]

The message was clear: zeks were no longer considered full citizens of the Soviet Union, if they were to be considered people at all. One prisoner observed that they were subject to 'a kind of excommunication from political life, and are allowed to take no part in its liturgies and sacred rites'.[29] After 1937, no guard used the word tovarishch, or 'comrade', to address prisoners, and prisoners could be beaten for using it to address guards, who they had to call grazhdanin, or 'citizen'. Photographs of Stalin and other leaders never appeared on the walls within the camps or in prisons. A relatively common sight of the mid-1930s – a train carrying prisoners, its wagons bedecked with portraits of Stalin and banners declaring the occupants to be Stakhanovites – became unthinkable after 1937. So did celebrations of the workers' holiday on the First of May, such as those once held at the Solovetsky kremlin.[30]

Many foreigners were surprised at the powerful effect that this 'excommunication' from Soviet society had on Soviet prisoners. One French prisoner, Jacques Rossi, author of The Gulag Handbook, an encyclopaedic guide to camp life, wrote that the word 'comrade' could electrify prisoners who had not heard it in a long time: 'A brigade that had just completed an eleven-and-a-half-hour shift agreed to stay and work the next shift only because the chief engineer . . . said to the prisoners: "I ask that you do this, comrades."'[31]

From the dehumanization of the 'politicals' there followed a very distinct, and in some places drastic, change in their living conditions. The Gulag of the 1930s had been generally disorganized, frequently cruel, and sometimes deadly. Nevertheless, in some places and at some times during the 1930s, even political prisoners had been offered the genuine possibility of redemption. The workers of the White Sea Canal could read the newspaper Perekovka, whose very name meant 'reforging'. The conclusion of Pogodin's Aristokraty featured the 'conversion' of an ex-saboteur. Flora Leipman – daughter of a Scotswoman who had married a Russian, moved to St Petersburg and quickly been arrested as a spy – visited her imprisoned mother in a northern logging camp in 1934, and found that 'there was also still an element of humanity between the guards and the prisoners as the KGB was not so sophist-icated and psychologically orientated as it was to become a few years later'.[32] Leipman knew what she was talking about, since she herself became a prisoner 'a few years later'. For after 1937, attitudes did change, particularly towards those arrested under Article 58 of the criminal code for 'counter-revolutionary' crimes.

In the camps, politicals were removed from the jobs they had held in planning or engineering, and forced to return to 'general work', meaning unskilled physical labour in mines or forests: 'enemies' could no longer be allowed to hold any position of importance, for fear they would engage in sabotage. Pavlov, the new head of Dalstroi, personally signed the order forcing one prisoner geologist, I. S. Davidenko, to be 'used as a common labourer and in no case allowed to conduct independent work. Davidenko's tasks should be carefully controlled and subject to daily observation.'[33] In a report filed in February 1939, the commander of Belbaltlag also claimed that he had 'chased away all workers not deserving of political trust', and in particular 'all former prisoners, sentenced for counter-revolutionary crimes'. From then on, he pledged, administrative and technical jobs would be reserved for 'Communists, Komsomol members [members of the Young Communist League] and trusted specialists'.[34] Clearly, economic productivity was no longer the camps' top priority.

Camp regimes across the system grew harsher for ordinary criminal pris-oners as well as politicals. Bread rations for 'general work' at the beginning of the 1930s could be as high as 1 kilogram per day, even for those who did not fulfil 100 per cent of the norm, and up to 2 kilograms for Stakhanovites. In the main *lagpunkts* of the White Sea Canal, meat was served twelve days a month.[35] By the end of the decade, the guaranteed ration had more than halved, falling to 400–450 grams of bread, while those who managed 100 per cent got an extra 200 grams. The punishment ration fell to 300 grams.[36] Speaking of that era in Kolyma, Shalamov wrote

In order for a healthy young man, beginning his career at the gold-face in the clean, cold air, to turn into a 'goner', he needed only a period of twenty to thirty days of sixteen-hour workdays, without days off, coupled with systematic starvation, tattered clothes, nights in 60 degrees below zero of cold in a canvas tent full of holes . . . out of entire brigades which began the gold-mining season, not a single person would survive, except the brigadier himself, the brigade orderly, and a few of the brigadier's personal friends.[37]

Conditions also worsened because the number of prisoners rose, in some places with astonishing rapidity. The Politburo had, it is true, tried to prepare in advance for the influx, instructing the Gulag in 1937 to begin the construc-tion of five new timber camps in the Komi region, as well as more 'in the remote areas of Kazakhstan'. To hasten construction, the Gulag had even received an 'advance of 10 million roubles' to organize these new camps. In addition, the People's Commissariats of Defence, Health and Forestry were ordered to find 240 commanding officers and political workers, 150 physicians, 400 medical attendants, 10 eminent forestry specialists and '50 graduates of the Leningrad Academy of Forest Technology' to work in the Gulag – immediately.[38]

Nevertheless, the existing camps once again overflowed with new recruits, and the overcrowding of the early 1930s repeated itself. At a *lagpunkt* built for 250–300 people in Siblag, the Siberian forestry camp, a survivor guessed that the actual number of prisoners in 1937 surpassed 17,000. Even if the real number were only a quarter of that, the overestimate indicates how crowded it must have felt to be there. Lacking barracks, prisoners built *zemlyanki*, dugouts in the earth; even those were so crowded that it was 'impossible to move, without stepping on someone's hand'. Prisoners refused to go outside, for fear of losing their place on the floor. There were no bowls, no spoons, and huge lines for food. A dysentery epidemic began, and prisoners died rapidly.

In a later Party meeting, even Siblag's camp administration solemnly remembered the 'terrible lessons of 1938', not least for the 'number of working days lost' in the crisis.[39] Throughout the camp system, the number of fatalities officially doubled from 1937 to 1938. Statistics are not everywhere available, but death rates are presumed to be much higher in those far northern camps – Kolyma, Vorkuta, Norilsk – where political prisoners were sent in large numbers.[40]

But prisoners did not die only from starvation and overwork. In the new atmosphere, the incarceration of enemies quickly began to seem insufficient: better that they cease to exist altogether. Thus, on 30 July 1937, the NKVD issued an order on the repression of 'former kulaks, thieves and other anti-Soviet elements' – an order that contained execution quotas for Gulag prisoners as well as others.[41] Thus, on 25 August 1937, Yezhov signed another order calling for executions of inmates being held in the high-security political prisons. The NKVD, he said, must 'finish within two months the operation for the repression of the most active counter-revolutionary elements ... those sentenced for spying, diversion, terrorism, revolutionary activity and banditry, as well as those sentenced for being members of anti-Soviet parties'.[42]

To the politicals, he added the 'bandits and criminal elements' operating in Solovetsky, which by that time had been converted into a high-security political prison as well. The quota for Solovetsky was stated: 1,200 inmates still imprisoned on Solovetsky were to be shot. A witness recalled the day some of them were called away:

Unexpectedly, they forced everyone from the open cells of the Kremlin to a general count. At the count, they read out an enormous list of names – several hundred of them – to be taken on transport. They were given two hours to prepare, and were then meant to reassemble in the same central square. A terrible confusion ensued. Some people ran to gather up their things, others to bid farewell to friends. In two hours, most of those to be transported stood in their places . . . columns of prisoners marched out with suitcases and knapsacks . . .[43]

Some were also apparently carrying knives, which they later used to attack those who shot them, near the village of Sandormokh in northern Karelia, injuring them badly. After that incident, the NKVD stripped all prisoners to their underwear before shooting them. Later, the NKVD man in charge of the operation was rewarded with what the archives describe only as a 'valuable present' for his valour in carrying out the task. A few months later, he was shot too.[44]

In Solovetsky, the selection of prisoners for murder appears to have been random. In some camps, however, the administration took advantage of the opportunity to rid themselves of particularly difficult prisoners. This may also have been the case in Vorkuta, where a large number of the selected prisoners actually were former Trotskyites – genuine followers of Trotsky, that is, some of whom had been involved in camp strikes and other rebellions. One eyewitness reckoned that by the beginning of the winter of 1937–8, the Vorkuta administration had interned about 1,200 prisoners, mostly the Trotskyites, as well as other politicals and a sprinkling of criminals, in an abandoned brick factory and a series of large, crowded ('overflowing') tents. No hot food was given to the prisoners at all: 'the daily ration consisted only of 400 grams of half-dried bread'.[45] There they remained until the end of March, when a new group of NKVD officers arrived from Moscow. The officers formed a 'special commission' and called out the prisoners in groups of forty. They were told they were going off on a transport. Each was given a piece of bread. The prisoners in the tent heard them being marched away – 'and then the sounds of shooting'.

The atmosphere inside the tents became hellish. One peasant, imprisoned for the crime of 'speculation' – he had sold his own piglet at a bazaar – lay on his bunk, eyes open, reacting to nothing. 'What do I have in common with you politicals?' he would periodically moan. 'You were fighting for power, for rank, and I just need my life.' Another man committed suicide, according to the eyewitness. Two went mad. Finally, when there were about 100 people left, the shooting stopped, as abruptly and as inexplicably as it began. The NKVD bosses had returned to Moscow. The remaining prisoners returned to the mines. Throughout the camp, about 2,000 prisoners had been killed.

Stalin and Yezhov did not always send outsiders from Moscow to carry out such jobs. To speed up the process across the country, the NKVD also organized troikas, operating inside the camps as well as outside them. A troika was just what it sounds like: three men, usually the regional NKVD chief, the Chief Party Secretary of the province, and a representative of the prosecutor's office or of the local government. Together, they had the right to pass a sentence on a prisoner *in absentia*, without benefit of judge, jury, lawyers or trial.[46]

Once in place, the troikas did move quickly. On 20 September 1937, a fairly typical day, the troika of the Karelian Republic sentenced 231 prisoners of the White Sea Canal camp, Belbaltlag. Assuming a ten-hour workday, with no breaks, less than three minutes would have been spent considering the fate of each prisoner. Most of those condemned had received their original sentences much earlier, at the beginning of the 1930s. Now, they were accused of new crimes, usually connected to bad behaviour or a poor attitude to life in the camps. Among them were former politicals – Mensheviks, Anarchists, Social Democrats – and a former nun who 'refused to work for the Soviet authorities', as well as a kulak who had worked as a cook in the camp. He was accused of inciting dissatisfaction among the Stakhanovite workers. He had, the authorities claimed, deliberately created 'long lines for them to stand in, having earlier given food to ordinary prisoners'.[47]

The hysteria did not last. In November 1938, the mass shootings came to an abrupt halt, both in the camps and in the rest of the country. Perhaps the purge had gone too far, even for Stalin's tastes. Perhaps it had simply achieved what it was meant to achieve. Or perhaps it was causing too much damage to the still-fragile economy. Whatever the reason, Stalin told the Communist Party Congress of March 1939 that the purge had been accompanied by 'more mistakes than might have been expected'.[48]

No one apologized or repented, and almost no one was ever punished. Just a few months earlier, Stalin had sent a circular to all of the NKVD bosses, complimenting them for 'inflicting a crushing defeat on espionage-subversive agents of foreign intelligence services' and for 'purging the country of subversive, insurrectionary, and espionage cadres'. Only then did he point out some of the 'deficiencies' in the operation, such as the 'simplified procedures for investigation', the lack of witnesses and corroborating evidence.[49]

Nor did the purge of the NKVD itself come to a complete halt. Stalin removed the alleged author of all these 'mistakes', Nikolai Yezhov, from office in November 1938 – and sentenced him to death. The execution took place in 1940, after Yezhov had pleaded for his life, just like Yagoda before him: 'Tell Stalin that I shall die with his name upon my lips.'[50]

Yezhov's protégés went down along with him, as had Yagoda's cronies a few years earlier. In her prison cell, Evgeniya Ginzburg noticed one day that the prison regulations pasted to the wall had been removed. When they were replaced, the space in the top left-hand corner, which had read 'Approved.

Yezhov, Commissar-General for State Security', had been pasted over with white paper. But the changes did not end there: 'First the name Weinstock [the prison commander] was painted over and Antonov substituted; then Antonov went, and in his place it read: Chief Prison Administration. "That'll save them from changing it again," we laughed.'[51]

The productivity of the camp system continued to spiral downwards. In Ukhtpechlag, the mass shooting, the increased number of sick and weak prisoners, and the loss of prisoner specialists had forced the camp's output to drop precipitously from 1936 to 1937. In July 1938, a special Gulag commission was called upon to discuss Ukhtpechlag's massive deficit.[52] The productivity of the Kolyma gold mines also fell. Even the huge influx of new prisoners failed to bring up the overall quantity of gold mined to levels comparable with those in the past. Before being deposed, Yezhov himself called for more money to be spent updating Dalstroi's old-fashioned mining technology – as if that were the real problem.[53]

Meanwhile, the commander of Belbaltlag – the one who had bragged so proudly of his success in ridding the camp's administrative staff of political prisoners – complained of the current 'urgent need for administrative and technical personnel'. The purge had certainly made the camp's technical staff politically 'healthier', he wrote carefully, but it had 'increased its deficiencies' as well. In his 14th camp division, for example, there were 12,500 prisoners, of which only 657 were non-politicals. Of these, however, most had very severe criminal sentences, which also disqualified them from work as specialists and administrators, while 184 were illiterate – leaving only 70 who could be used as clerks or as engineers.[54]

Overall, the turnover of the NKVD camps, according to official statistics, dropped from 3.5 billion roubles in 1936 to 2 billion roubles in 1937. The value of the camps' gross industrial production also dropped, from 1.1 billion roubles to 945 million roubles.[55]

The unprofitability and vast disorganization of most camps, as well as the increasing numbers of sick and dying prisoners, did not go unnoticed in Moscow, where extremely frank discussions of camp economics took place during meetings of the central Gulag administration's Communist Party cell. At a meeting in April 1938, one bureaucrat complained of the 'chaos and disorder' in the Komi camps. He also accused the Norilsk camp commanders of producing a 'badly designed' nickel factory, and of wasting a great deal of money in consequence. Given the amount of money that had been spent setting up new forestry camps, grumbled another administrator, 'We could have expected more. Our camps are organized unsystematically. Major buildings were constructed in the mud, and now have to be moved.'

By April 1939, the complaints worsened. At the northern camps, there was a 'particularly difficult situation with food supplies', which led to 'an enormous percentage of weak workers, an enormous percentage of prisoners who couldn't work at all, and a high death rate and illness rate'.[56] In that same year, the Council of People's Commissars acknowledged that up to 60 per cent of camp prisoners suffered from pellagra or other diseases of malnutrition.[57]

The Great Terror was not responsible for all of these problems, of course. As noted, even Frenkel's forestry camps, so admired by Stalin, had never actually made a profit.[58] Prison labour had always been – and would always be – far less productive than free labour. But this lesson had not yet been learned. When Yezhov was removed from power in November 1938, his replacement as NKVD chief, Lavrenty Beria, almost immediately set about altering camp regimes, changing the rules, streamlining the procedures, all in order to put the camps back where Stalin wanted them: at the heart of the Soviet economy.

Beria had not – yet – concluded that the camp system itself was unproductive and wasteful by its very nature. Instead, he seemed to believe that the people in charge of the camp system had been incompetent. Now he was determined to turn the camps into a genuinely profitable part of the Soviet economy, this time for real.

Beria did not, then or later, release large numbers of unjustly accused prisoners from camps (although the NKVD released some from gaols). The camps did not, then or later, become any more humane. The dehumanization of 'enemies' continued to permeate the language of the guards and camp administrators until Stalin's death. The mistreatment of political prisoners, indeed of all prisoners, continued: in 1939, under Beria's watchful eye, the first prisoners began working in Kolyma's uranium mines with virtually no protection against radiation.[59] Beria changed only one aspect of the system: he told camp commanders to keep more prisoners alive, and to make better use of them.

Although the policy was never clear, in practice Beria also lifted the ban on 'hiring' political prisoners with engineering, scientific or technical skills to work in technical positions in the camps. On the ground, camp commanders were still wary of using political prisoners as 'specialists', and would remain so until the Gulag's demise in the mid-1950s. As late as 1948, different branches of the security services would still be arguing about whether or not political prisoners should be forbidden from holding jobs as specialists, some arguing that it was too politically dangerous, others claiming the camps would be too difficult to run without them.[60] Although Beria never fully resolved this dilemma, he was too intent on making the NKVD into a productive part of the Soviet economy to allow *all* of the Gulag's most important scientists and engineers to lose their limbs to frostbite in the far north. In September 1938, he began organizing special workshops and laboratories for prisoner scientists, known by prisoners as *sharashki*. Solzhenitsyn, who worked in a *sharashka*, described one – a 'top-secret research establishment, officially referred to only by a code number' – in his novel, *The First Circle*:

A dozen prisoners were brought from the camps to this old country house on the outskirts of Moscow, which had been duly surrounded by barbed wire ... at that time, the prisoners did not know exactly what kind of research they had been brought to Mavrino to do. They were busy unpacking stacks of crates which two special goods trains had delivered, securing comfortable chairs and desks for themselves, and sorting equipment ...[61]

Initially, the *sharashki* were christened the 'Special Construction Bureaus'. Later, they were known collectively as the 'Fourth Special Department' of the NKVD, and about 1,000 scientists would eventually work in them. In some cases, Beria personally tracked down talented scientists, and ordered them brought back to Moscow. NKVD agents gave them baths, a haircut, a shave and a long rest – and sent them off to work in prison laboratories. Among Beria's most important 'finds' was the aviation engineer Tupolev, who arrived at his *sharashka* carrying a bag with a hunk of bread and a few pieces of sugar (he refused to give them up, even after being told the food would improve).

Tupolev, in turn, gave Beria a list of others to recall, among them Valentin Glushko, the Soviet Union's leading designer of rocket engines, and Sergei Korolev, later to be the father of the sputnik, the Soviet Union's first satellite – indeed the father of the entire Soviet space programme. Korolev returned to the Lubyanka after seventeen months in Kolyma, having lost many of his teeth to scurvy, looking 'famished and exhausted', in the words of his fellow prisoners.[62] Nevertheless, in a report prepared in August 1944, Beria would list twenty important new pieces of military technology invented in his *sharashki*, and elaborate on the many ways in which they had been of use to the defence industry during the Second World War.[63]

In some ways, Beria's reign would have seemed like an improvement to ordinary *zeks* too. Overall, the food situation did temporarily improve. As Beria pointed out in April 1938, the camp food norm of 2,000 calories per day had been set for people sitting in prisons, not for people working at manual labour. Because theft, cheating and punishment for poor work reduced even this low quantity of food by as much as 70 per cent, large numbers of prisoners were starving. This he regretted, not because he pitied them, but because higher death rates and higher levels of sickness prevented the NKVD from fulfilling its production plans for 1939. Beria requested the drawing up of new food norms, so that the 'physical capabilities of the camp workforce can be put to maximum use in any industry'.[64]

Although food norms were raised, Beria's regime hardly heralded a redis-covery of prisoners' humanity. On the contrary, the transformation of pris-oners from human beings into units of labour had progressed several steps

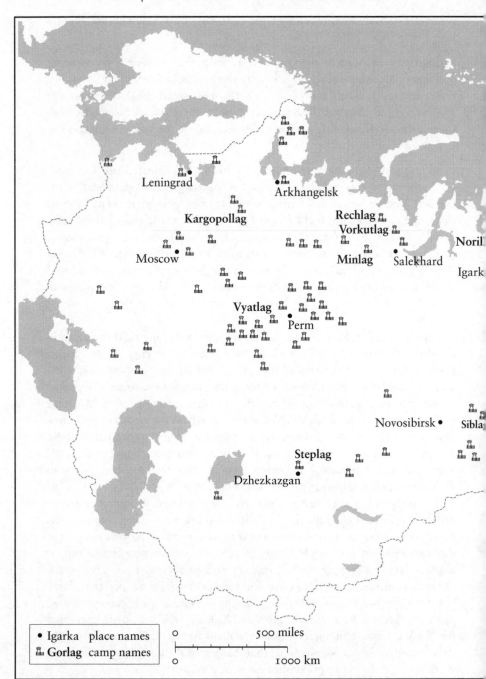

Leningrad

Arkhangelsk

Kargopollag

Rechlag
Vorkutlag

Noril

Moscow

Minlag   Salekhard

Igark

Vyatlag

Perm

Novosibirsk •   Sibla

Steplag

Dzhezkazgan

• Igarka   place names
Gorlag camp names

0   500 miles

0   1000 km

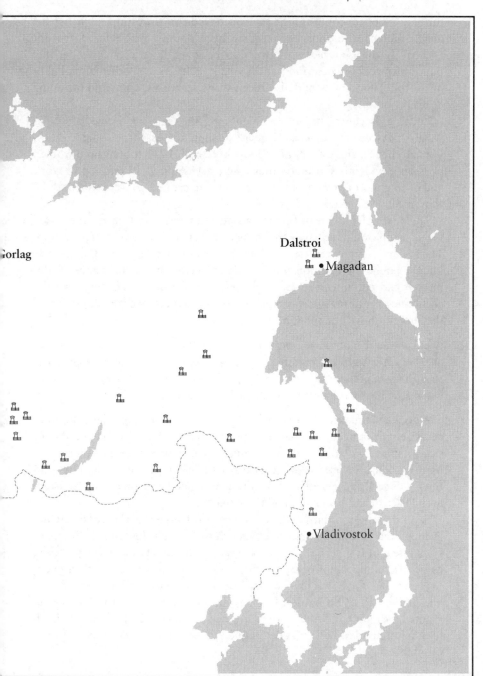

Gorlag

Dalstroi

•Magadan

•Vladivostok

6 The Gulag at its zenith, 1939–53

further. Prisoners could still be sentenced to die in the camps – but not for mere counter-revolutionary tendencies. Instead, those who refused to work or actively disorganized work were to be given 'a stricter camp regime, punishment cells, worse food and living conditions and other disciplinary measures'. 'Shirkers' would also receive new sentences, up to and including death.[65]

Local prosecutors began investigations into shirking immediately. In August 1939, for example, a prisoner was shot, not just for refusing to work, but for encouraging others not to work as well. In October, three women prisoners, evidently Orthodox nuns, were accused both of refusing to work and of singing counter-revolutionary hymns in camp: two were shot and the third received an extra sentence.[66]

The years of the Great Terror had also left their mark in another way. Never again would the Gulag treat prisoners as wholly worthy of redemption. The system of 'early release' for good behaviour was dismantled. In his one known public intervention into the daily operations of the camps, Stalin himself had put an end to early releases, on the grounds that they hurt the economic operations of the camps. Addressing a meeting of the Presidium of the Supreme Soviet in 1938, he asked,

Could we not think of some other form of reward for their work – medals, or such like? We are acting incorrectly, we are disturbing the work of the camp. Freeing these people may be necessary, but from the point of view of the national economy, it is a mistake . . . we will free the best people, and leave the worst.[67]

A decree to this effect was issued in June 1939. A few months later, another decree eliminated 'conditional early release' for invalids too. The number of sick prisoners would rise correspondingly. The main source of incentive for hard-working prisoners now was to be the improvement of 'supplies and food' – as well as the medals Stalin thought would be so appealing. By 1940, even Dalstroi had begun to hand them out.[68]

Several of these initiatives ran counter to the laws of the time, and actually encountered resistance. The chief prosecutor, Vyshinsky, and the People's Commissar of Justice, Richkov, both opposed the liquidation of early release, as well as the imposition of the death sentence for those accused of 'disorganizing camp life'. But Beria, like Yagoda before him, clearly had Stalin's support, and he won all of his battles. From 1 January 1940, the NKVD was even granted the right to take back some 130,000 prisoners who had been 'loaned' to other ministries. Beria was determined to make the Gulag really and truly profitable.[69]

With surprising speed, Beria's changes did make an impact. In the final months before the Second World War, the economic activity of the NKVD began, once again, to grow. In 1939, the NKVD's turnover was 4.2 billion roubles. In 1940, it was 4.5 billion roubles. As prisoners began to stream into the camps during the war years, those numbers would grow even more quickly.[70] According to official statistics, the number of deaths in camps also halved from 1938 to 1939, from 5 per cent back to 3 per cent, even as the number of prisoners continued to increase.[71]

There were also now far more camps than there had been, and they were much bigger than they had been at the beginning of the decade. The number of prisoners had nearly doubled between 1 January 1935 and 1 January 1938, from 950,000 to 1.8 million, with about another million people sentenced to exile.[72] Camps which had contained nothing more than a few huts and some barbed wire had become true industrial giants. Sevvostlag, the main Dalstroi camp, contained nearly 200,000 prisoners in 1940.[73] Vorkutlag, the mining camp that developed out of Ukhtpechlag's Rudnik No. 1, contained 15,000 prisoners in 1938; by 1951, it would contain over 70,000.

But there were new camps as well. Perhaps the grimmest of the new generation was Norillag, usually known as Norilsk. Located, like Vorkuta and Kolyma, north of the Arctic Circle, Norilsk sat right on top of an enormous nickel deposit, probably the largest in the world. The prisoners of Norilsk not only dug the nickel, but they also built the nickel-processing plant and the power stations alongside the mines. Then they built the city – Norilsk – to house the NKVD men who ran the mines and the factories. Like its predecessors, Norilsk grew quickly. The camp contained 1,200 prisoners in 1935; by 1940, it contained 19,500. At its largest, in 1952, 68,849 prisoners would be incarcerated there.[74]

In 1937, the NKVD also founded Kargopollag, in the Arkhangelsk region, followed, in 1938, by Vyatlag, in central Russia, and Kraslag, in the Krasno-yarsk district of northern Siberia. All were essentially forestry camps, which acquired side interests – brick factories, wood-processing plants, furniture-making workshops. All would double or triple in size in the 1940s, by which time they contained some 30,000 prisoners apiece.[75]

There were other camps too, opening and shutting and reorganizing them-selves so frequently that it is difficult to give precise numbers for a particular year. Some were quite small, built to serve the needs of a particular factory or industry or building project. Others were temporary, built for the purposes of road or railway construction, and abandoned afterwards. To manage their enormous numbers and complex problems, the Gulag administration eventually set up subdivisions: a Main Administration of Industrial Camps, a Main Administration of Road Building, a Main Administration of Forestry Work, and so on.

But it was not only their sizes that had changed. From the end of the 1930s, all new camps had a purely industrial character, without the fountains and 'gardens' of Vishlag, without the idealistic propaganda that accompanied the building of Kolyma, without the prisoner specialists at all levels of camp life.

Olga Vasileevna, an administrator who worked as an engineer and inspector on Gulag and other construction sites in the late 1930s and 1940s, remembered that in the earlier era 'there were fewer guards, fewer administrators, fewer employees . . . In the 1930s, prisoners were enlisted in all sorts of work, as clerks, barbers, guards.' In the 1940s, however, she recalled that all of that stopped: 'It all began to take on a mass character . . . things became harsher . . . as the camps grew bigger, the regime grew crueller.'[76]

It might be said, in fact, that by the end of the decade, the Soviet concentration camps had attained what was to be their permanent form. They had, by this time, penetrated nearly every region of the Soviet Union, all twelve of its time zones and most of its republics. From Aktyubinsk to Yakutsk, there was not a single major population centre that did not now have its own local camp or colony. Prison labour was used to build everything from children's toys to military aircraft. In the Soviet Union of the 1940s it would have been difficult, in many places, to go about your daily business and not run into prisoners.

More importantly, the camps had evolved. They were now no longer a group of idiosyncratically run work sites, but rather a full-fledged 'camp-industrial complex', with internal rules and habitual practices, special distribution systems and hierarchies.[77] A vast bureaucracy, also with its own particular culture, ruled the Gulag's far-flung empire from Moscow. The centre regularly sent out orders to local camps, governing everything from general policy to minor details. Although the local camps did not (or could not) always follow the letter of the law, the *ad hoc* nature of the Gulag's early days never returned.

The fortunes of prisoners would still fluctuate along with Soviet policy, economics and, most of all, the course of the Second World War. But the era of trials and experiments was over. The system was now in place. The group of procedures that prisoners called the 'meat-grinder' – the methods of arrest, of interrogation, of transport, of food and of work – were, at the start of the 1940s, set in stone. In essence, these would change very little until Stalin's death.

II

Life and Work in the Camps

7

Arrest

We never asked, on hearing about the latest arrest, 'What was he arrested for?' but we were exceptional. Most people, crazed by fear, asked this question just to give themselves a little hope; if others were arrested for some reason, then they wouldn't be arrested, because they hadn't done anything wrong. They vied with each other in thinking up ingenious reasons to justify each arrest: 'Well, she really is a smuggler, you know,' 'He really did go rather far,' or 'It was only to be expected, he's a terrible man,' 'I always thought there was something fishy about him,' 'He isn't one of us at all . . .'

This was why we had outlawed the question 'What was he arrested for?'

'*What for?*' Akhmatova would cry indignantly whenever, infected by the prevailing climate, anyone of our circle asked this question.

'What do you mean *what for*? It's time you understood that people are arrested *for nothing*!'

– Nadezhda Mandelstam, *Hope against Hope*[1]

Anna Akhmatova – the poet, quoted above by another poet's widow – was both right and wrong. On the one hand, from the middle of the 1920s – by the time the machinery of the Soviet repressive system was in place – the Soviet government no longer picked people up off the streets and threw them in gaol without giving any reason or explanation: there were arrests, investigations, trials and sentences. On the other hand, the 'crimes' for which people were arrested, tried and sentenced were nonsensical, and the procedures by which people were investigated and convicted were absurd, even surreal.

In retrospect, this is one of the unique aspects of the Soviet camp system: its inmates arrived, most of the time, via a legal system, if not always the ordinary judicial system. No one tried and sentenced the Jews in

Man entering his first prison cell: a drawing by Thomas Sgovio,
completed after his release

Nazi-occupied Europe, but the vast majority of inmates in Soviet camps had
been interrogated (however cursorily), tried (however farcically) and found
guilty (even if it took less than a minute). Undoubtedly, the conviction that
they were acting within the law was part of what motivated those working
within the security services, as well as the guards and administrators who
later controlled the prisoners' lives in the camps.

But I repeat: the fact that the repressive system was legal does not mean
that it was logical. On the contrary, it was no easier to predict with any
certainty who would be arrested in 1947 than it had been in 1917. True, it
became possible to guess who was *likely* to be arrested. During waves of
terror in particular, the regime appears to have chosen its victims in part
because they had for some reason come to the attention of the secret police –
a neighbour had heard them tell an unfortunate joke, a boss had seen them
engaging in 'suspicious' behaviour – and in larger part because they belonged
to whichever population category was at that moment under suspicion.

Some of these categories were relatively specific – engineers and specialists
in the late 1920s, kulaks in 1931, Poles or Balts in occupied territories during

the Second World War – and some were very vague indeed. Throughout the 1930s and 1940s, for example, 'foreigners' were always considered suspect. By 'foreigners', I mean people who actually were citizens of other countries, people who might have contacts abroad, or people who might have some link, imaginary or real, to a foreign country. No matter what they did they were always candidates for arrest – and foreigners who stood out in any way, for any reason, stood a particularly high chance. Robert Robinson, one of several black American communists who moved to Moscow in the 1930s, later wrote that 'Every single black I knew in the early 1930s who became a Soviet citizen disappeared from Moscow within seven years.'[2]

Diplomats were not exempt. Alexander Dolgun, for example, an American citizen and a junior employee of the American Embassy in Moscow, describes in his memoirs how he was picked up off the street in 1948 and accused, unjustly, of spying; suspicion fell upon him partly because of his youthful fondness for evading the 'tails' that the secret police set on him, and because he was skilled in persuading embassy chauffeurs to lend him cars, leading the Soviet secret police to suspect that he might be more important than his rank would indicate. He spent eight years in camps, returning to the United States only in 1971.

Foreign communists were frequently targets. In February 1937, Stalin ominously told Georgi Dmitrov, General Secretary of the Communist International – the Comintern, the organization dedicated to the fomenting of world revolution – that 'all of you there in the Comintern are working in the hands of the enemy'. Of the 394 members of the Executive Committee of the Communist International in January 1936, only 171 remained in April 1938. The rest had been shot or sent to camps, among them people of many nationalities: German, Austrian, Yugoslav, Italian, Bulgarian, Finnish, Baltic, even English and French. Jews appear to have suffered disproportionately. In the end, Stalin killed more members of the pre-1933 German Communist Party Politburo than did Hitler: of the 68 German communist leaders who fled to the Soviet Union after the Nazi seizure of power, 41 died, by execution or in camps. The Polish Communist Party may have been even more thoroughly decimated. According to one estimate, 5,000 Polish communists were executed in the spring and summer of 1937.[3]

But it was not necessary to be a member of a foreign communist Party: Stalin also targeted foreign fellow travellers, of whom the 25,000 'American Finns' were probably the most numerous. These were Finnish-speaking Finns, some had emigrated to America, some had been born there, all came to the Soviet Union during the 1930s, the years of the Great Depression in the United States. Most were factory workers, and most had been unemployed in the United States. Encouraged by Soviet propaganda – Soviet recruiters travelled around Finnish-speaking communities in the United States, speaking of the wonderful living conditions and work opportunities in the USSR –

they flocked to the Finnish-speaking Karelian Republic. Almost immediately, they caused problems for the authorities. Karelia was not, it turned out, much like America. Many loudly pointed this out to anyone who would listen, then tried to return – and wound up in the Gulag in the late 1930s instead.[4]

Soviet citizens with foreign connections were no less suspect. First in line were the 'diaspora nationalities', the Poles, Germans and Karelian Finns who had relatives and contacts across the border, as well as the Balts, Greeks, Iranians, Koreans, Afghans, Chinese and Romanians scattered across the USSR. According to their own archives, between July 1937 and November 1938 the NKVD convicted 335,513 people in these 'national' operations.[5] Similar operations would be repeated during and after the war, as we shall see.

But it was not even necessary to speak a foreign language in order to come under suspicion. Anyone with a foreign connection was suspected of spying: stamp collectors, Esperanto enthusiasts, anyone with a pen pal or with relatives abroad. The NKVD also arrested all Soviet citizens who had worked on the Chinese Eastern Railway, a railway line across Manchuria whose origins dated from the tsarist era, and accused them of having spied for Japan. In the camps, they were known as the 'Kharbintsy', after the city of Harbin, where many had lived.[6] Robert Conquest describes the arrests of an opera singer who had danced with the Japanese ambassador at an official ball, and of a veterinarian who attended to dogs belonging to foreigners.[7]

By the late 1930s, most ordinary Soviet citizens had worked out the pattern, and wanted no foreign contacts at all. Karlo Stajner, a Croatian communist with a Russian wife, remembered that 'Russians only rarely dared to have private dealings with foreigners ... My wife's relatives remained virtual strangers to me. None of them dared visit us. When her relatives learned of our plan to marry, Sonya was warned by all of them . . .'[8] Even as late as the mid-1980s – when I first visited the Soviet Union – many Russians remained wary of foreigners, ignoring them or refusing to make eye contact with them on the street.

And yet – not every foreigner was picked up by the police, and not everyone accused of having foreign connections actually did have foreign connections. It also happened that people were picked up for far more idiosyncratic reasons.[9] As a result, asking the question 'What for?' – the question Anna Akhmatova so disliked – produces a truly astonishing range of ostensible explanations.

Nadezhda Mandelstam's husband, Osip Mandelstam, for example, was arrested for his poetic attack on Stalin:

> We live, not feeling the land beneath us
> We speak, and ten steps away no one hears us
> But where there's even a whispered conversation

The Kremlin's mountaineer, murderer and peasant-slayer will be
 mentioned.
His fat fingers, like grubs, are greasy
His words, like lead weights, are final
His boot rims shine

And all around him, a gaggle of spineless leaders,
Half-humans, serve as his toys
One whinnies, one purrs, one whines
Only he shouts and points
Throwing decrees like horseshoes

Hitting a groin, a head, an eye –
Every death sentence tastes sweet
For the broad-chested Ossete.[10]

Although different reasons were officially stated, Tatyana Okunevskaya, one of the Soviet Union's best-loved film actresses, was arrested, she believed, for refusing to sleep with Viktor Abakumov, the wartime head of Soviet counter-intelligence. To make sure she understood that this was the true reason, she was (she claims) shown an arrest warrant with his signature on it.[11] The four Starostin brothers, all of them outstanding soccer players, were arrested in 1942. They always believed it was because their team, Spartak, had the misfortune to defeat Lavrenty Beria's favourite team, Dynamo, a touch too decisively.[12]

But it was not even necessary to be extraordinary. Lyudmila Khachatryan was arrested for marrying a foreigner, a Yugoslav soldier. Lev Razgon recounted the story of a peasant, Seryogin, who, on being told that someone had killed Kirov, replied, 'Damned if I care.' Seryogin had never heard of Kirov, and assumed he was someone who had died in a fight in the neighbouring village. For that mistake, he received a ten-year sentence.[13] By 1939, telling a joke, or hearing one, about Stalin; being late for work; having the misfortune to be named by a terrified friend or a jealous neighbour as a 'co-conspirator' in a non-existent plot; owning four cows in a village where most people owned one; stealing a pair of shoes; being a cousin of Stalin's wife; stealing a pen and some paper from one's office in order to give them to a schoolchild who had none: all of these could, under the right circumstances, lead to a sentence in a Soviet concentration camp. Relatives of a person who had illegally tried to cross the Soviet border were liable to arrest, according to a 1940 law, whether or not they had known about the attempted escape.[14] Wartime laws – on being late to work and forbidding job changes – would add more 'criminals' to the camps as well, as we shall see.

If the reasons for arrest were many and varied, so too were the methods. Some prisoners had ample warning. For several weeks prior to his arrest in the mid-1930s, an OGPU agent repeatedly called Alexander Weissberg in for questioning, asking him over and over again how he had come to be a 'spy': Who recruited you? Whom did you recruit? What foreign organization are you working for? 'He put exactly the same questions over and over again, and I always gave him the same answers.'[15]

At about the same time, Galina Serebryakova, the author of *The Young Marx* and the wife of a high functionary, was also 'invited' every evening to Lubyanka, kept waiting until two or three o'clock in the morning, interrogated, released at five in the morning and returned to her apartment. Agents surrounded her building and a black car followed her when she went outside. So convinced was she of her coming arrest that she tried to kill herself. Nevertheless, she endured several months of this sort of harassment before actually being arrested.[16]

During heavy waves of mass arrest – of kulaks in 1929 and 1930, of Party activists in 1937 and 1938, of former prisoners in 1948 – many knew their turn was coming simply because all those around them were being arrested. Elinor Lipper, a Dutch communist who had come to Moscow in the 1930s, was living in 1937 in the Hotel Lux, a special hotel for foreign revolutionaries: 'every night a few more persons vanished from the hotel ... in the morning, there would be large red seals pasted on the doors of a few more rooms'.[17]

In times of real terror, some even experienced the arrest itself as a sort of relief. Nikolai Starostin, one of the unlucky soccer stars, was trailed by agents for several weeks, and became so annoyed that he finally went up to one of them and demanded an explanation: 'If you want something from me, call me into your office.' As a result, at the moment of arrest he felt not 'shock and fear' but 'curiosity'.[18]

Still others were taken completely by surprise. The Polish writer Aleksander Wat, then living in occupied Lvov, was asked to a party at a restaurant with a group of other writers. He asked the host what the occasion was. 'You'll see,' he was told. A brawl was staged, and he was arrested there and then.[19] Alexander Dolgun, the American Embassy clerk, was hailed on the street by a man who turned out to be a secret policeman. When the man called out his name, Dolgun recalled, 'I was completely mystified. I wondered if it was some nut ...'[20] Okunevskaya, the actress, was in bed with a bad case of flu at the time of her arrest, and demanded that the police return another day. They showed her the arrest warrant (the one with Abakumov's signature on it) and dragged her down the stairs.[21] Solzhenitsyn repeats the possibly apocryphal tale of a woman taken out to the Bolshoi Theatre by her boyfriend, a professional interrogator, who took her straight from the theatre to Lubyanka.[22] The survivor and memoirist Nina Gagen-Torn recounts the tale of a woman who had been arrested while taking linen down from a clothes-line in a Leningrad courtyard; she was dressed in a bathrobe, and had left her baby alone in her apartment, assuming she would be back in a few minutes. She pleaded to be allowed to get him, to no avail.[23]

In fact, it seems as if the authorities deliberately varied their tactics, picking up some people at home and some at work, some on the street and some on trains. One memo to Stalin from Viktor Abakumov, dated 17 July 1947, confirms this suspicion, noting that prisoners were routinely 'surprised' by police in order to prevent escape, to prevent resistance, to prevent the suspect from warning others in his counter-revolutionary 'conspiracy'. In certain cases, the document continued, 'a secret arrest in the street is carried out'.[24]

The most common arrest, however, was one that took place at a person's home, in the middle of the night. In times of mass arrest, fear of the midnight 'knock on the door' became widespread. There is a very old Soviet joke about the terrible anxiety Ivan and his wife Masha experienced when the knock on the door came – and their relief when they learned it was only the neighbour come to tell them that the building was on fire. A Soviet proverb also has it that 'Thieves, prostitutes and the NKVD work mostly at night.'[25] Usually, these night-time arrests were accompanied by a search, although search tactics varied over time too. Osip Mandelstam was arrested twice, once in 1934 and then again in 1938, and his wife has described the differences between the two procedures:

In 1938 they wasted no time looking for papers and examining them – indeed, the police agents didn't even seem to know the occupation of the man they had come to arrest ... they simply turned over all the mattresses, swept his papers into a sack, poked around for a while and then disappeared, taking M. [Mandelstam] with them. The whole operation lasted no more than twenty minutes. But in 1934 they stayed all night until the early hours.

During the earlier raid, secret police, who clearly knew what they were looking for, had carefully gone through all of Mandelstam's papers, discarding old manuscripts, looking for new poetry. The first time around they also ensured that civilian 'witnesses' were present, as well as – in their case – a 'friend' in police pay, a literary critic known to the Mandelstams, presumably told to be there in order to ensure that the Mandelstams did not secretly start burning papers once they heard the knock at the door.[26] Later, they did not bother with such details.

Mass arrests of particular nationalities, such as those that took place in what had been eastern Poland and the Baltic States, the territories occupied by the Red Army in 1939–41, usually had an even more haphazard character. Janusz Bardach, a Jewish teenager in the Polish town of Wlodzimierz-Wolynski, was forced to act as a civilian 'witness' during one such mass arrest. He accompanied a group of drunken NKVD thugs who went from house to house on the night of 5 December 1939, rounding up people who were to be either arrested or deported. Sometimes they attacked the wealthier and better-connected citizens, whose names were marked on a list; sometimes they simply hauled in 'refugees' – usually Jews who had escaped to Soviet-occupied eastern Poland from Nazi-occupied western Poland – without bothering to write down their names at all. In one house, a group of refugees tried to defend themselves by pointing out that they had been members of the Bund, the Jewish socialist movement. Nevertheless, upon hearing that they came from Lublin, at that time on the other side of the border, Gennady, the leader of the NKVD patrol, began to shout:

'You filthy refugees! Nazi spies!' The children began to cry, which further irritated Gennady. 'Make them shut up! Or do you want me to take care of them?'

The mother pulled them close to her, but they couldn't stop crying. Gennady grabbed the little boy's hands, jerked him loose from his mother's arms, and threw him against the floor. 'Shut up, I said!' The mother screamed. The father tried to say something but could only gasp for air. Gennady picked up the boy and held him for a second, looking closely at his face, then threw him forcefully against the wall . . .

Later, the men destroyed the home of Bardach's childhood friends:

Off to the side was Dr Schechter's office. His dark mahogany desk stood in the middle, and Gennady walked straight to it. He ran his hand over the smooth wood and then, in a moment of unexpected rage, smashed it with a crowbar. 'Capitalist swine! Motherfucking parasites! We need to find these bourgeois exploiters!' He smashed harder and harder without pause, making several holes in the wood . . .

Unable to find the Schechters, the men raped and murdered the gardener's wife.

Those who conducted such operations, often members of the convoy guards – soldiers who manned the deportation trains – rather than the NKVD itself, had far less training than the secret police who conducted 'normal' arrests of 'normal' criminals. Violence was probably not officially mandated, but, since these were Soviet soldiers arresting 'capitalists' in the wealthier 'West', drunkenness, disorderliness and even rape seem to have been condoned, as they were later on, during the Red Army's march through Poland and Germany.[27]

Nevertheless, certain aspects of their behaviour were stringently dictated from above. The Main Administration of the Convoy Guards in Moscow decided in November 1940, for example, that guards doing the arresting should tell their arrestees to bring enough warm clothes and personal goods to last three years, as the Soviet Union was currently experiencing a shortage of such supplies. They hoped the arrestees would sell their belongings.[28] Earlier, soldiers had usually been instructed not to tell prisoners anything about where they were going, or for how long. The accepted formula was, 'Why worry? Why bring anything at all? We're only bringing you in for a short chat.' Sometimes they told deportees that they were only being moved to another area, further from the borders, 'for your own protection'.[29] The aim was to prevent arrestees from becoming frightened, from fighting back or from running away. The result was to deprive people of the basic tools they would need to live in a harsh and unfamiliar climate.

While Polish peasants encountering the Soviet regime for the first time might be excused their naivety in believing such lies, the very same formulas worked equally well on Moscow and Leningrad intellectuals and Party apparatchiks, possessed, as they often were, by the certainty of their own innocence. Evgeniya Ginzburg, at the time a Party worker in Kazan, was told, when arrested, that she would be gone 'forty minutes, perhaps an hour'. As a result, she did not take the opportunity to say goodbye to her children.[30] Yelena Sidorkina, an arrested Party member, walked down the street to prison with her arresting officer 'chatting peacefully', certain that she would be home soon.[31]

Sofia Aleksandrovna, the ex-wife of the Chekist Gleb Boky, was discouraged from taking a summer coat with her when the NKVD came to take her away ('it's warm tonight and we'll be back within an hour, at most'), prompting her son-in-law, the writer Lev Razgon, to ponder the strange cruelty of the system: 'What was the point of sending a middle-aged woman in not very good health to prison, without even the tiny bag of underclothes and washing things that an arrested person has always been allowed to take with him since the time of the Pharaohs?'[32]

At least the wife of the actor Georgi Zhenov had the sense to begin packing his spare clothes. When told he would be returning home soon, she snapped: 'Those who fall into your hands don't return quickly.'[33] Her view was close to the truth. Most of the time, when an arrestee walked through the heavy iron doors of a Soviet prison, it would be many years before he or she saw home again.

If the Soviet method of arrest seems to have been almost whimsical at times, the rituals that followed arrest were, by the 1940s, virtually immutable. However a prisoner had come to enter the gates of his local prison, once he arrived events followed a distinctly predictable course. As a rule, prisoners were registered, photographed and fingerprinted well before they were told why they had been arrested or what their fate would be. For the first few hours, and sometimes the first few days, they encountered no one more senior than ordinary prison wardens, who were completely indifferent to their fate, had no idea of the nature of their alleged crimes, and answered all questions with an indifferent shrug.

Many former prisoners believe that their first few hours in captivity were deliberately designed to shock them, to render them incapable of coherent thought. Inna Shikheeva-Gaister, arrested for being the daughter of an enemy of the people, felt this happening to her after only a few hours in Lubyanka, Moscow's central prison:

Here in Lubyanka, you are already not a person. And around you there are no people. They lead you down the corridor, photograph you, undress you, search you mechanically. Everything is done completely impersonally. You look for a human glance – I don't speak of a human voice, just a human glance – but you don't find it. You stand dishevelled in front of the photographer, try to somehow fix your clothes, and you are shown with a finger where to sit, an empty voice says 'face front' and 'profile'. They don't see you as a human being! You have become an object . . .[34]

If they were being taken into one of the main city prisons for interrogation (and not put, as exiles were, immediately on to trains), arrestees were thoroughly searched, in several stages. A 1937 document instructed prison wardens specifically not to forget that 'the enemy doesn't halt his struggle after his arrest', and might commit suicide in order to hide his criminal activity. As a result prisoners were deprived of buttons, belts, braces, shoelaces, garters, underwear elastic, whatever they could conceivably use to kill themselves.[35] Many felt humiliated by this edict. Nadezhda Joffe, daughter of a leading Bolshevik, was deprived of her belt, garters, shoelaces and hairpins:

I remember how I was struck by the degradation and absurdity of all this. What could a person do with hairpins? Even if the absurd idea popped into someone's head to hang himself by his shoelaces, then how could this actually be done? They simply had to place a person in a revolting and humiliating position, where one's skirt would fall down, stockings would slip and shoes would shuffle.[36]

The body search that followed was worse. In his novel *The First Circle*, Alexander Solzhenitsyn describes the arrest of Innokenty, a Soviet diplomat. Within hours of arrival at Lubyanka, a warder was examining every orifice of Innokenty's body:

Like a horse-dealer, his unwashed fingers prodding inside Innokenty's mouth, stretching one cheek, then the other, pulling down the lower eyelids, the warder convinced himself that there was nothing hidden in the eyes or mouth and tipped back the head so that the nostrils were lit up; then he checked both ears, pulling them back, told Innokenty to spread out his hands to show there was nothing between the fingers, and to swing his arms to show there was nothing under his armpits. In the same flat, irrefutable tone, he ordered:

'Take your penis in your hands. Turn back the foreskin. More. Right, that's enough. Move your penis up and right, up and left. Right, you can drop it. Turn your back to me. Straddle your legs. Wider. Bend down and touch the floor. Legs wider. Stretch your buttocks with your hands. Right. Now squat. Quickly! Once more!'

Thinking about his arrest before it happened, Innokenty had pictured to himself a duel of wits to the death. For this he was ready, prepared for a high-principled defence of his life and his convictions. Never had he imagined anything so simple, so dull, and so irresistible as this reality. The people who had received him were petty-minded, low-grade officials, as uninterested in his personality as in what he had done . . .[37]

The shock of such searches could be worse for women. One remembered that the gaoler performing the search 'took our brassieres, corset-belts which held our suspenders, and some other parts of our underwear essential to women. There followed a brief, disgusting, gynaecological examination. I kept silent, but felt as if I had been deprived of all human dignity.'[38]

While enduring a twelve-month stay in Aleksandrovsky Tsentral prison in 1941, the memoirist T. P. Milyutina was searched repeatedly. The women of her cells would be taken on to an unheated staircase, five at a time. They were then told to undress completely, put their clothes on the floor and their hands up. Hands were put 'in our hair, in our ears, under our tongues; also between our legs', both while standing up and sitting down. After the first such search, wrote Milyutina, 'many burst into tears, many were hysterical . . .'[39]

Following the search, some prisoners were isolated. 'The first hours of imprisonment,' continues Solzhenitsyn, 'are designed to break the prisoner down by isolating him from contact with other inmates, so that there is no one to keep his spirits up, so that the full force of the whole, vast, ramified apparatus is felt to be bearing down on him and him alone . . .'[40] The cell of Evgeny Gnedin, a Soviet diplomat and son of revolutionaries, contained only a small table, attached to the floor, and two stools, also attached to the floor. The folding bed, on which prisoners slept at night, was attached by a bolt to the wall. Everything, including the walls, stools, bed and ceiling, was painted light blue. 'It gave you the feeling of being inside the peculiar cabin of a ship,' Gnedin wrote in his memoirs.[41]

It was also quite common to be put, as was Alexander Dolgun, in a *boks* – a cell 'about four feet by nine feet. An empty box with a bench' – during the first hours following arrest, and held there for several hours or even a few days.[42] Isaac Vogelfanger, a Polish surgeon, was put in a cell with open windows in the middle of winter.[43] Others, like Lyubov Bershadskaya, a survivor who later helped lead a prisoners' strike in Vorkuta, were isolated during the entire period of their interrogation. Bershadskaya spent nine months in solitary, and wrote that she actually looked forward to being questioned, just to have someone to talk to.[44]

Yet to the newcomer, a crowded prison cell could be an even more horrifying place than a solitary one. Olga Adamova-Sliozberg's description of her first cell reads like a scene from Hieronymus Bosch:

The cell was huge. The arched walls were dripping. On either side, leaving only a narrow passage between them, were low continuous bed boards packed with bodies. Assorted rags were drying on lines overhead. The air was thick with the foul smoke of strong cheap tobacco, and loud with arguments, shouts and sobs.[45]

Another memoirist also tried to recapture his feeling of shock: 'It was such an awful sight, men with long hair, bearded, the smell of sweat, and nowhere even to sit down or rest. You must use your imagination to try to grasp the sort of place I was in.'[46]

Aino Kuusinen, the Finnish wife of Oleg Kuusinen, the leader of the Comintern, believed that on her first night she had been deliberately placed within earshot of prisoners under interrogation:

Even today, after thirty years, I can hardly describe the horror of that first night at Lefortovo. In my cell I could hear every noise from outside. Near by, as I later discovered, was the 'interrogation department', a separate structure which was in fact a torture chamber. All night long I heard inhuman screams and the repeated sound of the lash. A desperate and tormented animal could hardly have uttered such dreadful cries as the victims who were assaulted for hours on end with threats, blows and curses.[47]

But wherever they found themselves on their first night under arrest, whether in an old tsarist prison, a railway station lock-up, a converted church or monastery, all prisoners faced an urgent, immediate task: to recover from shock, to adjust to the peculiar rules of prison life – and to cope with interrogation. The speed with which they managed to do this would then help determine how well, or how badly, they emerged from the system and, ultimately, how they would fare in the camps.

Of all the stages that prisoners passed through on their road to the Gulag, the interrogation is perhaps the one that is most familiar to Westerners. Interrogations have been described not only in history books, but also in Western literature – Arthur Koestler's classic *Darkness at Noon*, for example – in war movies, and in other forms of high and low culture. The Gestapo were infamous interrogators, as were the agents of the Spanish Inquisition. The tactics of both are the stuff of popular legend. 'We have ways of making you talk . . .' is a phrase children still use when playing war games.

Interrogations of prisoners also take place, of course, in democratic, law-abiding societies, sometimes in accordance with the law, sometimes not. Psychological pressure, even torture, during interrogation is hardly unique to the USSR. The 'good cop, bad cop' technique – the nice, polite man asking questions, alternating with the angry inquisitor – has made its way not only as an idiom into other languages, but also into (now outdated) American police manuals as a recommended tactic. Prisoners have been pressured under questioning in many if not most countries at one time or another; indeed, it was evidence of such pressure that led the American Supreme Court to rule, in the *Miranda* v. *Arizona* case of 1966, that criminal suspects must be informed, among other things, of their right to remain silent, and of their right to contact a lawyer.[48]

Still, the 'investigations' conducted by the Soviet secret police were unique, if not in their methods, then in their mass character. In some eras, 'cases' routinely included hundreds of people, who were arrested all over the Soviet Union. Typical of its time was one report filed by the Orenburg regional department of the NKVD on 'Operational measures for the liquidation of clandestine groups of Trotskyites and Bukharinites, as well as other counter-revolutionary groups, carried out from 1 April to 18 September 1937.' According to the report, the Orenburg NKVD had arrested 420 members of a 'Trotskyite' conspiracy and 120 'right-wingers' – as well as more than 2,000 members of a 'right-wing military Japanese Cossack organization', more than 1,500 tsarist officers and civil servants exiled from St Petersburg in 1935, some 250 Poles indicted as part of the case against 'Polish spies', 95 people who had worked on the Harbin railway in China and were considered to be Japanese spies, 3,290 former kulaks and 1,399 'criminal elements'.

In all, the Orenburg NKVD arrested more than 7,500 people in a five-month period, which did not allow much time for careful examination of evidence. This hardly mattered, as the investigations into each one of these counter-revolutionary conspiracies had in fact been launched in Moscow. The local NKVD were merely doing their duty, filling in the numerical quotas that had been dictated from above.[49]

Because of the high volume of arrests, special procedures had to be put in place. These did not always entail extra cruelty. On the contrary, the large numbers of prisoners sometimes meant that the NKVD reduced actual investigations to a minimum. The accused was hurriedly questioned, and then equally hurriedly sentenced, sometimes with an extremely brief court hearing. General Gorbatov remembered that his hearing took 'four or five minutes', and consisted of a confirmation of his personal details, and one question: 'Why did you not admit to your crimes during the investigation?' Afterwards, he received a fifteen-year sentence.[50]

Still others had no trial at all: they were sentenced *in absentia*, either by an *osoboe soveshchanie* – a 'special commission' – or by a troika of three officials, rather than by a court. Such was the experience of Thomas Sgovio, whose investigation was completely perfunctory. Born in Buffalo, New York, Sgovio had arrived in the Soviet Union in 1935 as a political émigré, the son of an Italian American communist who had been forcibly deported to the Soviet Union from the United States for his political activities. During the three years he lived in Moscow, Sgovio gradually became disillusioned, and decided to reclaim his American passport – he had relinquished it upon entering the USSR – in order to return home. On 12 March 1938, he was arrested walking out of the American Embassy.

The record of Sgovio's subsequent investigation (which, decades later, he photocopied in a Moscow archive and donated to the Hoover Institution) is sparse, matching his own recollection of the same events. The evidence against him includes a list of what was found during his first body search: his trade union membership book, his telephone and address book, his library card, a sheet of paper ('with writing in a foreign language'), seven photographs, one penknife, and an envelope containing foreign postage stamps, among other things. There is a statement from Captain of State Security, Comrade Sorokin, testifying that the accused walked into the US Embassy on 12 March 1938. There is a statement from a witness, testifying that the accused left the US Embassy at 1.15 p.m. The file also includes the protocols of the initial investigation and the two brief interrogations, each page signed both by Sgovio and his interrogator. Sgovio's initial statement reads as follows: 'I wanted to regain my American citizenship. Three months ago I went to the American Embassy for the first time and applied to regain my citizenship. Today I returned . . . the clerk receptionist told me the American employee in charge of my case was out for lunch and for me to return in an hour or two.'[51]

During most of the subsequent interrogation, Sgovio was asked to repeat the details of his visit to the embassy over and over again. Only once was he asked, 'Tell us all about your espionage activities!' When he replied, 'You know I'm not a spy,' they appear not to have pushed him further, although the interrogator was fondling a rubber hose, of the sort normally used to beat prisoners, in a vaguely threatening manner.[52]

Although the NKVD were not much interested in the case, they never seem to have doubted its outcome. Some years later, after Sgovio demanded a review of his case, the prosecutor's office dutifully did so, summing up the facts as follows: 'Sgovio does not deny that he did make an application at the American Embassy. Therefore I believe there is no reason to review Sgovio's case.' Damned by the fact that he had confessed to entering the embassy – and had confessed to wanting to leave the USSR – Sgovio received a sentence from one of the 'special commissions' of five years' forced labour, condemned as a 'socially dangerous element'. His case had been treated as routine. In the crush of arrests at the time, the investigators had simply done the bare minimum required.[53]

Others were convicted on even less evidence, after even more cursory investigations. Because falling under suspicion was in itself considered a sign of guilt, prisoners were rarely released without serving at least a partial sentence. Lev Finkelstein, a Russian Jew arrested in the late 1940s, had the impression that although no one had managed to invent a particularly plausible case against him, he had been given a short camp sentence simply in order to prove that the arresting organs never made a mistake.[54] Another ex-prisoner, S. G. Durasova, even claims that he was specifically told, by one of his investigators, that 'we never arrest anyone who is not guilty. And even if you weren't guilty, we can't release you, because then people would say that we are picking up innocent people.'[55]

On the other hand, when the NKVD were more interested – and, it seems, when Stalin himself was more interested – the investigators' attitude to those picked up during periods of mass arrest could rapidly change from indifferent to sinister. In certain circumstances, the NKVD would even demand that investigators fabricate evidence on a massive scale – as happened, for example, during the 1937 investigation into what Nikolai Yezhov called the 'most powerful and probably the most important diversionist-espionage networks of Polish intelligence in the USSR'.[56] If Sgovio's interrogation represents one extreme of indifference, the mass operation against this alleged Polish spy ring represents the other: suspects were interrogated with the single-minded goal of making them confess.

The operation began with NKVD Order 00485, an order that set the pattern for later mass arrests. Operational Order 00485 clearly listed the sort of person who was to be arrested: all remaining Polish war prisoners from the 1920–21 Polish-Bolshevik war; all Polish refugees and emigrants to the Soviet Union; anyone who had been a member of a Polish political party; and all 'anti-Soviet activists' from Polish-speaking regions of the Soviet Union.[57] In practice, anyone of Polish background living in the Soviet Union – and there were many, particularly in the Ukrainian and Belorussian border regions – was under suspicion. The operation was so thorough that the Polish Consul in Kiev compiled a secret report describing what was happening, noting that in some villages 'anyone of Polish background and even anyone with a Polish-sounding name' had been arrested, whether a factory manager or a peasant.[58]

But the arrests were only the beginning. Since there was nothing to incriminate someone guilty of having a Polish surname, Order 00485 went on to urge regional NKVD chiefs to 'begin investigations simultaneously with arrests. The basic aim of investigation should be the complete unmasking of the organizers and leaders of the diversionist group, with the goal of revealing the diversionist network . . .'[59]

In practice, this meant – as it would in so many other cases – that the arrestees themselves would be forced to provide the evidence from which the case against them would be constructed. The system was simple. Polish arrestees were first questioned about their membership of the espionage ring. Then, when they claimed to know nothing about it, they were beaten or otherwise tortured until they 'remembered'. Because Yezhov was personally interested in the success of this particular case, he was even present at some of these torture sessions. If the prisoners lodged official complaints about their treatment, he ordered his men to ignore them and to 'continue in the same spirit'. Having confessed, the prisoners were then required to name others, their 'co-conspirators'. Then the cycle would begin again, as a result of which the 'spy network' grew and grew.

Within two years of its launch, the so-called 'Polish line of investigation' had resulted in the arrests of more than 140,000 people, by some accounts nearly 10 per cent of all of those repressed in the Great Terror. But the Polish operation also became so notorious for the indiscriminate use of torture and false confessions that in 1939, during the brief backlash against mass arrests, the NKVD itself launched an investigation into the 'mistakes' that had been made while it was being carried out. One officer involved remembered that 'it wasn't necessary to be delicate – no special permission was needed in order to beat people in the face, to beat without limitation'. Those with qualms, and apparently there were some, had explicitly been told that it was Stalin and the Politburo's decision to 'beat the Poles for all you are worth'.[60]

In fact, although Stalin later denounced the NKVD's 'simplified procedures for investigation', there is some evidence that he personally approved of these methods. In Viktor Abakumov's 1947 letter to Stalin, for example, he specifically notes that the primary task of an investigator is to try to get from the arrestee a 'true and open confession, with the goal not only of establishing the guilt of the arrestee, but also of uncovering those to whom he is linked, as well as those directing his criminal activity and their enemy plans'.[61] Abakumov skirts around the issue of physical torture and beatings, but does also write that investigators are enjoined to 'study the character of the arrestee', and on that basis to decide whether to give him a light prison regime or a strict one, and how best to make use of his 'religious convictions, family and personal ties, self-respect, vanity, etc. . . . Sometimes, in order to outwit the arrestee, and to create the impression that the organs of the MGB know everything about him, the investigator can remind the arrestee of separate, intimate details from his personal life, secrets that he hides from those around him, etc.'

Why the Soviet secret police were so obsessed with confession remains a matter for debate, and a wide variety of explanations has been proffered in the past. Some believe the policy came from the top. Roman Brackman, author of an unorthodox biography of Stalin, *The Secret File of Joseph Stalin*, believes the Soviet leader had a neurotic obsession with making others confess to crimes which he himself had committed: because he himself had been an agent of the tsarist secret police before the Revolution, he had a particular need to see people confess to having been traitors. Robert Conquest also believes that Stalin was interested in forcing at least those he knew personally to confess. 'Stalin wanted not merely to kill his old opponents, but to destroy them morally and politically,' although this, of course, applied only to a few out of the millions arrested.

But confession would also have been important to the NKVD agents carrying out the interrogations. Perhaps obtaining confessions helped them feel confident of the legitimacy of their actions: it made the madness of mass, arbitrary arrest seem more humane, or at least legal. As in the case of the 'Polish spies', confession also provided the evidence necessary to arrest others. The Soviet political and economic system was also obsessed with results – fulfilling the plan, completing the norm – and confessions were concrete 'proof' of a successful interrogation. As Conquest writes, 'the principle had become established that a confession was the best result obtainable. Those who could obtain it were to be considered successful operatives, and a poor NKVD operative had a short life expectancy.'[62]

Whatever the source of the NKVD's fixation on confession, police interrogators usually pursued them without either the deadly single-mindedness shown in the case of the 'Polish spies', or the indifference applied to Thomas Sgovio. Instead, prisoners generally experienced a mixture of the two. On the one hand, the NKVD demanded that they confess and incriminate themselves and others. On the other hand, the NKVD seemed to feel a slovenly lack of interest in the outcome altogether.

This somewhat surreal system was already in place by the 1920s, in the years before the Great Terror, and it remained in place long after the Great Terror had subsided. As early as 1931, the officer investigating Vladimir Tchernavin, a scientist accused of 'wrecking' and sabotage, threatened him with death if he refused to confess. At another point, he told him he would get a more 'lenient' camp sentence if he confessed. Eventually, he actually begged Tchernavin to give a false confession. 'We, the examining officers, are also often forced to lie, we also say things which cannot be entered into the record and to which we would never sign our names,' his interrogator told him, pleadingly.[63]

When the outcome mattered more to them, torture was deployed. Actual physical beatings seem to have been forbidden in the period before 1937. One former Gulag employee confirms that they were certainly illegal in the first half of the 1930s.[64] But as the pressure to get leading Party members to confess increased, physical torture came into use, probably in 1937, although it ended again in 1939. The Soviet leader Nikita Khrushchev publicly admitted this in 1956: 'How is it possible that a person confesses to crimes which he has not committed? Only in one way – because of applications of physical methods of pressuring him, tortures, bringing him to a state of unconsciousness, depriving him of his judgement, taking away his human dignity. In this manner were "confessions" acquired.'[65]

So widespread did the use of torture become during this period – and so frequently was it questioned – that in early 1939, Stalin himself sent out a memo to regional NKVD chiefs, confirming that 'from 1937 on in NKVD practice the use of physical pressure [on prisoners] was permitted by the Central Committee'. He explained that it was permitted

only with respect to such overt enemies of the people who take advantage of humane interrogation methods in order to shamelessly refuse to give away conspirators, who for months don't testify and try to impede the unmasking of those conspirators who are still free.

He did, he continued, consider this to be a 'totally correct and humane method', although he conceded that it might have occasionally been applied to 'accidentally arrested honest people'. What this notorious memo makes clear, of course, is that Stalin himself knew what sorts of methods had been used during interrogation, and had personally approved of them.[66]

Certainly it is true that during this period many, many prisoners record being beaten and kicked, their faces smashed in and their organs ruptured. Evgeny Gnedin describes being hit on the head simultaneously by two men, one on the left, one on the right, and then being beaten with a rubber club. This took place in Beria's private office, in Beria's presence, in the Sukhanovka prison.[67] The NKVD also practised methods of torture known to other secret police forces in other eras, such as hitting their victims in the stomach with sandbags, breaking their hands or feet, or tying their arms and legs behind their backs and hoisting them in the air.[68] One of the most sickening acounts of physical torture was penned by the theatre director Vsevelod Meyerhold, whose formal letter of complaint has been preserved in his file:

The investigators began to use force on me, a sick, 65-year-old man. I was made to lie face down and then beaten on the soles of my feet and my spine with a rubber strap. They sat me on a chair and beat my feet from above, with considerable force . . . For the next few days, when those parts of my legs were covered with extensive internal haemorrhaging, they again beat the red-blue-and-yellow bruises with the strap and the pain was so intense that it felt as if boiling hot water was being poured on these sensitive areas. I howled and wept from the pain. They beat my back with the same rubber strap and punched my face, swinging their fists from a great height . . .

One time my body was shaking so uncontrollably that the guard escorting me back from such an interrogation asked: 'Have you got malaria?' When I lay down on the cot and fell asleep, after eighteen hours of interrogation, in order to go back in an hour's time for more, I was woken up by my own groaning and because I was jerking about like a patient in the last stages of typhoid fever.[69]

Yet although this sort of beating was technically forbidden after 1939, the change of policy did not necessarily make the investigation process more humane. Throughout the 1920s, 1930s and 1940s many hundreds of thousands of prisoners were tormented not with actual beatings or physical attacks, but with psychological torture of the sort Abakumov alludes to in his letter to Stalin.

Those who remained stubborn and refused to confess could, for example, be slowly deprived of creature comforts, first walks, then packages or books, then food. They could be placed in a specially harsh punishment cell, very hot or very cold, as was the memoirist Hava Volovich, who was also being deprived of sleep by her interrogator at the time: 'I will never forget that first experience of prison cold. I can't describe it; I'm not capable of it. I was pulled one way by sleep, the other by cold. I would jump up and run around the cell, falling asleep on my feet, then collapse on the bed again, where the cold would soon force me up.'[70]

Others were confronted with 'witnesses', as was Evgeniya Ginzburg, who watched as her childhood friend Nalya 'recited like a parrot', accusing her of membership of the Trotskyite underground.[71] Still others were threatened with harm to family members, or were placed, after long periods of isolation, in cells with informers, to whom they were only too glad to open their hearts. Women were raped, or threatened with rape. One Polish memoirist told the following story:

Suddenly, for no apparent reason, my cross-examiner became extremely flirtatious. He got up from behind his desk, and came and sat beside me on the sofa. I stood up and went to drink some water. He followed me and stood behind me. I neatly evaded him and returned to the sofa. Down he sat himself again beside me. And once again I got up and went to drink water. Manoeuvres like these lasted for a couple of hours. I felt humiliated and helpless . . .[72]

There were also forms of physical torture less crude than beatings, and these were used regularly from the 1920s onwards. Tchernavin was early on given 'the standing test' – prisoners were told to stand, facing the wall, without moving – albeit briefly. Some of his other cell mates suffered worse:

One, Engraver P., over fifty years of age and heavily built, had stood for six and a half days. He was not given food or drink and was not allowed to sleep; he was taken to the toilet only once a day. But he did not 'confess'. After this ordeal he could not walk back to the cell and the guard had to drag him up the stairs . . . Another, Artisan B., about thirty-five years old, who had one leg amputated above the knee and replaced by an artificial one, had stood for four days and had not 'confessed'.[73]

Most commonly, however, prisoners were simply deprived of sleep: this deceptively simple form of torture – which seemed to require no special advance approval – was known to prisoners as being put 'on the conveyor', and it could last for many days, or even weeks. The method was simple: prisoners were interrogated all night, and afterwards forbidden from sleeping during the day. They were constantly awoken by guards, and threatened with punishment cells or worse if they failed to stay awake. One of the best accounts of the conveyor, and of its physical effects, is that given by the American Gulag inmate Alexander Dolgun. During his first month in Lefortovo, he was virtually deprived of any sleep at all, allowed an hour a day or less: 'Looking back it seems that an hour is too much, it may have been no more than a few minutes some nights.' As a result, his brain began to play tricks on him:

There would be periods when I suddenly knew that I had no recollection of what had happened in the last few minutes. Drop-outs in my mind. Total erasures . . .

Then, of course, later on, I began to experiment with sleeping upright, to see if my body could learn to hold itself erect. I thought if that would work I might escape detection in the cells for a few minutes at a time, because the guard at the peep-hole would not think I was asleep if I was sitting upright.

And so it would go, snatching ten minutes here, half an hour there, occasionally a little longer if Sidorov called it quits before six in the morning and the guards left me alone till the wake-up call. But it was too little. Too late. I could feel myself slipping, getting looser and less disciplined every day. I dreaded going crazy almost worse – no, really worse – than dying . . .

Dolgun did not confess for many months, a fact that provided him with something to be proud of throughout the rest of his imprisonment. Yet when, many months later, he was called back to Moscow from his camp in Dzhezkazgan and beaten up again, he did sign a confession, thinking, 'What the hell. They've got me anyway. Why didn't I do it a long time ago, and avoid all that pain?'[74]

Why not indeed? It was a question many others asked themselves, with varying answers. Some – a particularly high percentage of memoir writers, it would seem – held out either on principle, or in the mistaken belief that they would thereby avoid being sentenced. 'I'd rather die than defame myself,' General Gorbatov told his interrogator, even as he was being tortured (he does not specify how). Many also believed – as Solzhenitsyn, Gorbatov and others point out – that a ridiculously lengthy confession would create an atmosphere of absurdity which even the NKVD could not fail to notice. Gorbatov wrote with horror of his prison comrades:

They impressed me as being cultured and serious-minded people. I was all the more horrified to hear that during their interrogations every single one of them had written the most unmitigated rubbish, confessing to imaginary crimes and incriminating other people . . . Some even held the strange theory that the more people were gaoled the sooner it would be realized that all this was nonsense and harmful to the Party.[75]

Yet not everyone agreed that such people were to be blamed. Lev Razgon, in his own memoirs, replied to Gorbatov, whom he called 'arrogant and immoral':

It is wrong to shift the blame from the torturers to their victims. Gorbatov was lucky, that's all. Either his interrogator was lazy, or he had not been given a firm instruction to 'put pressure' on his charge. Doctors, psychologists, psychiatrists have not done enough research to say whether an individual can be tortured into giving false testimony against himself. But this century has provided a vast amount of evidence on the subject. Of course it can be done.[76]

There are also mixed views, in retrospect, about whether holding out actually mattered. Susanna Pechora, who was interrogated for more than a year in the early 1950s – she was a member of a tiny youth group which was founded, quixotically, to resist Stalin – said, looking back, that 'holding out' had not been worth it. Resisting confession simply prolonged the interrogation, she believes. Most were sentenced anyway, in the end.[77]

Nevertheless, the contents of Sgovio's file clearly illustrate that subsequent decisions – about early release, amnesty, and so on – were indeed taken on the basis of what was in a prisoner's file, including confession. If you had managed to hold out, in other words, you did stand a very, very slim chance of having your sentence reversed. Right up through the 1950s, all of these judicial procedures, however surreal, were taken seriously.

In the end, the interrogation's greatest importance was the psychological mark it left on prisoners. Even before they were subjected to the long transports east, even before they arrived in their first camps, they had been at some level 'prepared' for their new lives as slave labourers. They already knew that they had no ordinary human rights, no right to a fair trial or even a fair hearing. They already knew that the NKVD's power was absolute, and that the state could dispose of them as it wished. If they had confessed to a crime they had not committed, they already thought less of themselves. But even if they had not, they had been robbed of all semblance of hope, of any belief that the mistake of their arrest would soon be reversed.

8

Prison

A Gypsy read the cards – a distant road,
A distant road – and a prison house.
Maybe the old central prison,
It waits for me, a young man, once again . . .

– traditional Russian prisoners' song

Their arrests and interrogations wore prisoners down, shocked them into submission, confused them and disoriented them. But the Soviet prison system itself, where inmates were kept before, during and often for a very long time after their interrogations, had an enormous influence on their state of mind as well.

When looked at in an international context, there was nothing unusually cruel about Soviet prisons or the Soviet prison regime. Soviet prisons were certainly harsher than most Western prisons, and harsher than tsarist prisons had been too. On the other hand, prisons in China, or in other parts of the Third World in the mid-twentieth century, were extremely unpleasant as well. Nevertheless, elements of Soviet prison life remained peculiar to the Soviet Union. Some aspects of the daily prison regime, like the interrogation process itself, even seem to have been deliberately designed to prepare prisoners for their new life in the Gulag.

Certainly official attitudes to prisons reflect changes in the priorities of those running the camps. Genrikh Yagoda issued an order in August 1935, for example, just as arrests of political prisoners were beginning to pick up pace, making it clear that the most important 'point' of an arrest (if these arrests can be said to have had a 'point' in any normal sense of the word) was to feed the ever-more frenzied demand for confessions. Yagoda's order put not only the prisoners' 'privileges' but also their most basic living conditions directly into the hands of the NKVD officers investigating their cases. Provided a prisoner was co-operating – which usually meant confessing – he would be allowed letters, food parcels, newspapers and books, monthly meetings with relatives, and an hour of exercise daily. If not, he could be deprived of all these things, and lose his food ration as well.[1]

By contrast, in 1942 – after Beria had arrived, vowing to turn the Gulag into an efficient economic machine – Moscow's priorities had shifted. The camps were becoming an important factor in wartime production, and camp commanders had begun complaining about the large numbers of prisoners arriving at camp workplaces totally unfit to work. Starving, filthy and deprived of exercise, they simply could not dig coal or cut trees at the pace required. Beria therefore issued new interrogation orders in May of that year, demanding that prison bosses observe 'elementary health conditions', and limiting investigators' control over prisoners' daily life.

According to Beria's new order, prisoners were to have a daily walk of 'not less than one hour' (with the notable exception of those awaiting the death sentence, whose quality of health hardly mattered to the NKVD's production figures). Prison administrators also had to ensure that their prisons contained a yard specially built for the purpose: 'Not a single prisoner must stay in the cell during these walks . . . weak and aged prisoners must be helped by their cell mates.' Prison warders were told to ensure that inmates (except for those directly under interrogation) have eight hours of sleep, that those with diarrhoea receive extra vitamins and better food, and that the *parashi*, the buckets that served as prison toilets, be repaired if leaking. The last point was thought to be so crucial that the order even specified the ideal size of a *parasha*. In men's cells, they had to be 55–60 centimetres high, in women's cells 30–35 centimetres high – and they had to contain .75 litres of depth per person in the cell.[2]

Despite these ludicrously specific regulations, prisons continued to differ enormously. In part, they differed according to location. As a rule, provincial prisons were filthier and more lax, Moscow prisons cleaner and more deadly. But even the three main Moscow prisons had slightly different characters. The infamous Lubyanka, which still dominates a large square in central Moscow (and still serves as the headquarters for the FSB, the NKVD and KGB's successor), was used for the reception and interrogation of the most serious political criminals. There were relatively few cells – a 1956 document speaks of 118 – and 94 were very small, for one to four prisoners.[3] Once the offices of an insurance company, some of the cells of the Lubyanka building had parquet floors, which the prisoners had to wash every day. A. M. Garaseva, an Anarchist who later served as Solzhenitsyn's secretary, was imprisoned in Lubyanka in 1926, and remembered that food was still served by waitresses wearing uniforms.[4]

By contrast, Lefortovo, also used for interrogation, had been a nineteenth-century military prison. Its cells, never intended to hold large numbers of prisoners, were darker, dirtier and more crowded. Lefortovo is shaped like the letter K, and at its centre, recalled the memoirist Dmitri Panin, 'an attendant stands with a flag and directs the flow of prisoners being led to and from interrogation'.[5] In the late 1930s, Lefortovo became so overcrowded that the NKVD opened an 'annexe' in the Sukhanovsky monastery outside Moscow. Officially named 'Object 110', and known to prisoners as 'Sukhanovka', the annexe acquired a horrific reputation for torture: 'There were no rules of internal order, and no defined rules for the conduct of investigations either.'[6] Beria himself maintained an office there, and personally supervised torture sessions of the Sukhanovka prisoners.[7]

Butyrka prison, the oldest of the three, had been constructed in the eighteenth century, and was originally designed to be a palace, although it was quickly converted into a prison. Among its distinguished nineteenth-century inmates was Feliks Dzerzhinsky, along with other Polish and Russian revolutionaries.[8] Generally used to house prisoners who had finished interrogation and were awaiting transport, Butyrka was also crowded and dirty, but more relaxed. Garaseva records that whereas the Lubyanka guards forced prisoners to 'exercise' by walking in a tight circle, 'at Butyrka you could do what you wanted'. She, like others, also mentions the prison's excellent library, whose collection had been formed by generations of prisoners, all of whom left their books behind when they were transferred away.[9]

Prisons also differed from era to era. During the early 1930s, large numbers of prisoners were sentenced to months or even years of isolation. One Russian prisoner, Boris Chetverikov, kept sane for sixteen months in solitary by washing his clothes, the floor, the walls – and by singing all the opera arias and songs that he knew.[10] Alexander Dolgun was kept in solitary during his interrogation, too, and managed to keep his head by walking: he counted the steps in his cells, worked out how many there were to a kilometre, and started 'walking', first across Moscow to the American Embassy – 'I breathed in the clear, cold, imaginary air and hugged my coat around me' – then across Europe, and finally across the Atlantic, back home to the United States.[11]

Ginzburg spent nearly two years in the Yaroslavl isolator, deep in central Russia, much of that time completely alone: 'To this day, if I shut my eyes, I can see every bump and scratch on those walls, painted halfway up in the favourite prison colours, brownish-red and a dirty white above.' But eventually, even that 'special' prison began to fill up, and she was given a cell mate. Ultimately, most of the *tyurzeks*, the 'prison prisoners', were moved to camps. As Ginzburg writes, 'It was simply not practical to keep such multitudes in prison for ten or twenty years: it was inconsistent with the tempo of the age and with its economy.'[12]

In the 1940s, as the pace of arrests grew, it became far more difficult to isolate anyone, even new prisoners, even for a few hours. In 1947, Lev Finkelstein was initially thrown into the prison *vokzal* (literally, 'railway station'), a 'huge, common cell where all the arrested are thrown in first, without any facilities. Then they are sorted out, gradually, sent to the baths, and then to the cells.'[13] In fact, the experience of desperate overcrowding was far more common than that of solitary isolation. To choose a few random examples, the main Arkhangelsk city prison, which had a capacity of 740, held, in 1941, between 1,661 and 2,380 prisoners. The prison in Kotlas, in northern Russia, with a capacity of 300, held up to 460.[14]

Prisons in more distant provinces could be worse. In 1940, the prison of Stanislawow, in newly occupied eastern Poland, contained 1709 people, well above its capacity of 472, and possessed a mere 150 sets of sheets.[15] In February 1941, the prisons in the republic of Tartarstan, with a capacity for 2,710 prisoners, contained 6,353. In May 1942, the prisons of the central Asian republic of Tashkent, with a capacity for 960, contained 2,754.[16] These crowded conditions had a particularly harsh effect on those under interrogation, whose entire lives were being subject to intense, hostile questioning every night, and whose days nevertheless had to be spent in the company of others. One prisoner described the effects:

The whole process of the disintegration of personality took place before the eyes of everyone in the cell. A man could not hide himself here for an instant; even his bowels had to be moved on the open toilet, situated right in the room. He who wanted to weep, wept before everyone, and the feeling of shame increased his torment. He who wanted to kill himself – in the night, beneath the blanket, trying to cut the veins in his arm with his teeth – would be quickly discovered by one of the cell's insomniacs, and prevented from finishing the job.[17]

Margarete Buber-Neumann also wrote that the overcrowding turned prisoners against one another. When prisoners were awoken, at half-past four in the morning,

the effect on us was much as though an ant-heap had been turned over. Everyone grabbed her wash things in order to be first, if possible, because, of course, the washing accommodation was not remotely sufficient for all of us. In the room where we washed were five lavatories and ten water taps. I say 'lavatories' but they were in reality five holes in the ground and nothing else. Queues immediately formed in front of all five holes and all ten taps. Imagine if you can going to the lavatory in the morning with at least a dozen pairs of eyes watching you, and being shouted at and urged on by others impatiently waiting for their turn . . .[18]

Perhaps because they were aware of the crowding, prison authorities went to great lengths to break any semblance of prisoner solidarity. Yagoda's order of 1935 already forbade prisoners to talk, shout, sing, write on the walls of the cell, leave marks or signs anywhere in the prison, stand at the windows of the cell, or attempt to communicate with those in other cells in any way. Those breaking these rules could be punished by deprivation of exercise or letters, or even by being placed in a specially constructed punishment cell.[19]

Enforced silence is frequently mentioned by those imprisoned in the 1930s: 'No one spoke out loud and some of them made themselves understood by signs,' wrote Buber-Neumann of Butyrka, where 'the half-exposed bodies of most of the women were of a peculiar greyish-blue tinge from long confinement without light or air . . .'[20]

In some prisons, the rule of silence remained absolute well into the next decade, in others less so: one ex-prisoner writes of the 'complete silence' of Lubyanka in 1949, by comparison to which 'cell number 106 at Butyrka seemed like visiting a bazaar after a small shop'.[21] Another, in prison in the central Soviet republic of Kazan, remembers that when prisoners began whispering, 'the lid of the food hatch would open with a bang and someone would hiss, "Sssh!"'[22]

Many memoirists have also described how guards, when moving prisoners between cells or from a cell to interrogation, would jangle their keys, snap their fingers or make some other noise, to warn off those further down the corridor. In the case of an encounter, one of the prisoners would be quickly turned down another passageway, or placed into a special closet. V. K. Yasny, formerly a translator of Spanish literature, was once placed in a half-metre-square closet in Lubyanka for two hours.[23] Such closets seem to have been in wide use: the basement of the former NKVD headquarters in Budapest, now a museum, contains one. The object was to prevent prisoners from encountering others who might be involved in their particular 'case', as well as to keep them away from siblings or other relatives who might be under arrest.

The enforced silence made even the walk to the interrogation rooms unnerving. Alexander Dolgun recalls walking down the carpeted hallways of Lubyanka: 'The only sound as we moved along was the guard's clucking of his tongue . . . all those metal doors were grey, battleship grey, and the effect of the gloom and the silence and the grey doors repeating themselves down the corridors until they merged with the shadows was oppressive and discouraging.'[24]

To prevent prisoners in one cell from learning the names of those in other cells, prisoners were called out – for interrogation or for transfer – not by their names, but by a letter of the alphabet. The guard would shout 'G', for example, and all of the prisoners with surnames beginning with G would stand and give their first names and patronymics.[25]

Order was maintained – just as order is maintained in most prisons – through the rigid regulation of daily life. Zayara Vesyolaya, the daughter of a famous Russian writer and 'enemy', described in her memoirs a typical day in Lubyanka. It began with *opravka*, a trip to the toilets: 'Prepare for the toilet!' shouts the guard, and the women would silently line up, in pairs. Once in the toilets, they were given about ten minutes – not only to eliminate but also to wash themselves and whatever clothes they could. *Opravka* was then followed by breakfast: hot water, perhaps with something resembling tea or coffee mixed in, plus the daily bread ration, plus two or three pieces of sugar. Breakfast was followed by a visit from a guard, who took requests to see the doctor, and then by the 'central activity of the day', a twenty-minute walk in a 'small enclosed yard, walking single file in circles next to the wall'.

Only once was order broken. Although she was never told why, Vesyolaya was taken on to the Lubyanka roof one evening, after prisoners had already been told to sleep. As Lubyanka is in the centre of Moscow, that meant she could see, if not the city, then at least the city lights – which might as well have belonged to another country.[26]

Normally, however, the rest of the day was a repeat: lunch – prison soup, made of entrails or grain or rotten cabbage – and then the same soup for supper. There was another trip to the toilet in the evening. In between, prisoners whispered to one another, sat on their bunks, and sometimes read books. Vesyolaya recalls being allowed one book a week, but the rules varied from prison to prison, as did the quality of the prison libraries, which, as I say, were sometimes excellent. In some prisons, inmates were allowed to purchase food items from the 'commissary' if their relatives had sent them money.

But there were other tortures besides boredom and bad food. All prisoners were forbidden to sleep during the day – not just those undergoing interrogation. Warders kept constant vigil, peeping through the 'Judas hole', the peep-hole into the cell, to ensure this rule was kept. Lyubov Bershadskaya recalls that although 'we were woken at six, we were not allowed even to sit on the bed until eleven in the evening. We had either to walk, or to sit on the stool, not leaning against the wall.'[27]

Nights were no better. Sleep was made difficult, if not impossible, by the bright lights in the cells, which were never turned off, and by the rule forbidding prisoners to sleep with their hands under their blankets. Vesyolaya would start out trying to comply: 'It was awkward and uncomfortable, and made it hard for me to fall asleep . . . as soon as I dozed off, however, I would instinctively pull the blanket up to my chin. The key would grate in the lock, and the guard would shake my bed: 'Hands!'[28] Buber-Neumann wrote that 'until you got used to it, the night was worse than the day. Try to sleep at night under strong electric light – prisoners are not allowed to cover their faces – on bare planks without even a straw sack or a pillow, and perhaps without even a blanket, pressed against your fellow prisoners on either side.'

Perhaps the most effective tool for preventing prisoners from becoming too comfortable in their surroundings was the presence of informers – who were also to be found in all spheres of Soviet life. They would also play an important role in the camps, but in camps they would be easier to avoid. In prison, one could not walk away from them so easily, and they forced people to watch their words carefully. Buber-Neumann recalled that, with one exception, 'I never heard a word of criticism of the Soviet regime from a Russian prisoner the whole time I was in Butyrka.'[29]

Among the prisoners, the accepted wisdom was that there was at least one informer in every cell. When there were two people in a cell, both suspected the other. In larger cells the informer was often identified and shunned by the other inmates. When Olga Adamova-Sliozberg first arrived in Butyrka, she noyticed a free sleeping space beside the window. She was welcome to sleep there, she was told, 'but you won't have the best of neighbours'. The woman sleeping with no one around her was, it emerged, an informer who spent all her time 'writing statements denouncing everyone in the cell, so no one talks to her'.

Not all informers were so easily identified, and paranoia was so great that any unusual behaviour could spark hostility. Adamova-Sliozberg herself assumed that one of her fellow inmates was certainly a spy, having seen the 'foreign-looking sponge she washed with and the lacy underwear she wore'. Later, she came to look upon the woman as a friend.[30] The writer Varlam Shalamov also wrote that being transferred within a prison, between cells, 'is not a very pleasant experience. This always puts one's new cellmates on their guard and causes them to suspect that the transferred prisoner is an informer.'[31]

Without question, the system was rigid, inflexible and inhuman. And yet – if they could, prisoners fought back, against boredom, against the constant small humiliations, against the attempts to divide and atomize them. More than one former inmate has written of how prisoner solidarity was actually stronger in the gaols than it would be later, in the camps. Once prisoners were in camps, the authorities could divide and rule with greater ease. To alienate inmates from one another, they could tempt prisoners with the promise of a higher place in the camp hierarchy, better food or easier jobs.

In prison, by contrast, all were more or less equal. Although there were inducements to collaborate, these were fewer. For many prisoners, the days or months spent in gaol, prior to deportation, even provided a sort of introductory course in elementary survival techniques – and, despite all the authorities' efforts, their first experience of unity against authority.

Some prisoners simply learned from their fellow inmates elementary ways to preserve hygiene and dignity. In her prison cell, Inna Shikheeva-Gaister learned to make buttons from bits of chewed bread in order to hold her clothes up, to make needles from fish bones, to use stray threads for sewing up the holes ripped in her clothes during the search, as well as other sundry tasks which would also prove to be of use in the camps.[32] Dmitri Bystroletov – a former Soviet spy in the West – also learned to make 'thread' from old socks: the socks were pulled apart, and the ends of the threads were then sharpened with a bit of soap. Such thread, like the needles he learned to make from matches, could later be exchanged in the camp for food.[33] Susanna Pechora, the youthful anti-Stalinist, was taught 'how to sleep while they don't notice, how to sew with matchsticks, and how to walk without a belt'.[34]

The prisoners also maintained some control over their lives through the institution of the *starosta*, the cell's 'elder'. On the one hand, in prisons, in railway cars and in camp barracks, the *starosta* was an officially recognized figure, whose functions were described in official documents. On the other hand, the *starosta*'s many duties – ranging from keeping the cell clean to ensuring orderly marches to the toilet – meant that his authority had to be accepted by all.[35] Informers, and others favoured by the prison warders, were therefore not necessarily the best candidates. Alexander Weissberg wrote that in the larger cells, where there might be 200 prisoners or more, 'normal life was not possible without a cell senior to organize the distribution of food, the arrangements for exercise, and so on'. Yet because the secret police refused to recognize any form of prisoner organization ('its logic was simple: an organization of counter-revolutionaries was a counter-revolutionary organization') a classically Soviet solution was found, wrote Weissberg: 'the *starosta* was elected "illegally" by the prisoners. The prison governor heard about it through his spies and then officially appointed the prisoners' choice.'[36]

In the most overcrowded cells, the *starosta*'s main task was to greet new prisoners, and to ensure that everyone had a place to sleep. Almost universally, new prisoners were sent to sleep beside the *parasha*, the slop bucket, gradually progressing away from it and towards the window as they attained seniority. 'No exceptions,' noted Elinor Lipper, 'are made for sickness or age.'[37] The *starosta* also resolved fights, and generally kept order in the cell, a task that was far from easy. Kazimierz Zarod, a Polish arrestee, recalled that, while serving as cell *starosta*, 'the guards constantly threatened me with punishment if I did not keep the unruly element under some sort of control, particularly after 9 p.m., when there was a "no talking" rule after "Lights Out"'. Eventually, Zarod himself was put in a punishment cell for failing to keep control.[38] It seems from other accounts, however, as if the decisions of the *starosta* were usually respected.

Without a doubt, the prisoners' greatest ingenuity was applied to overcoming the most stringent rule: the strict prohibition of communication, both between cells and with the outside world. Despite the serious threat of punishment, prisoners left notes for other prisoners in toilets, or threw messages over walls. Lev Finkelstein tried to throw a piece of meat, a tomato and a piece of bread into another cell: 'when we were taken to the loo, I tried to open the window and push the food through'. He was caught, and put in a punishment cell.[39] Prisoners bribed guards to take messages, although they occasionally did so of their own accord. A warder at the Stavropol prison would occasionally transmit verbal communications from Lev Razgon to his wife.[40]

One former inmate, a prisoner for fourteen months in Vilnius after the Soviet occupation of the city – it had previously been under Polish rule – described in 1939, in testimony presented to the Polish government-in-exile, how the elements of the previous Polish prison regime had slowly broken down. One by one, prisoners lost their 'privileges' – the right to read and write letters, to use the prison library, to have paper and pencils, to receive parcels. New regulations, of the sort common to most Soviet prisons, were brought in: lights in the cells had to be kept on all night, and windows were blocked with sheets of tin. Unexpectedly, the latter created an opportunity for communication between cells: 'I opened the window, and, putting my head against the bars, spoke to my neighbours. Even if the sentry in the courtyard heard my conversation, he could not make out where the voice came from as, thanks to the tin sheet, it was impossible to detect an open window.'[41]

Perhaps the most elaborate form of forbidden communication, however, was the prisoners' Morse code, tapped on the walls of cells, or on the prison plumbing. The code had been devised in the tsarist era – Varlam Shalamov attributes it to one of the Decembrists.[42] Elinor Olitskaya had learned it from her Social Revolutionary colleagues long before she was imprisoned in 1924.[43] In fact, the Russian revolutionary Vera Figner had described the code in her memoirs, which is where Ginzburg had read about it. While under investigation, she remembered enough of of the code to use it to communicate with a neighbouring cell.[44] The code was relatively straightforward: the Russian alphabet was laid out in five rows of six letters:

А	Б	В	Г	Д	Е
Ж	З	И	К	Л	М
Н	О	П	Р	С	Т
У	Ф	Х	Ц	Ч	Ш
Щ	Ъ	Ы	Э	Ю	Я

Each letter was then designated by a pair of taps, the first signifying the row, the second the position in the row:

1,1	1,2	1,3	1,4	1,5	1,6
2,1	2,2	2,3	2,4	2,5	2,6
3,1	3,2	3,3	3,4	3,5	3,6
4,1	4,2	4,3	4,4	4,5	4,6
5,1	5,2	5,3	5,4	5,5	5,6

Even those who had not read about the code or learned it from others sometimes figured it out, as there were standard methods of teaching it. Those who knew it would sometimes tap out the alphabet, over and over again, together with one or two simple questions, in the hope that the unseen person on the other side of the wall would catch on. That was how Alexander Dolgun learned the code in Lefortovo, memorizing it with the help of matches. When he was finally able to 'talk' to the man in the next cell, and understood that the man was asking him 'Who are you?' he felt 'a rush of pure love for a man who has been asking me for three months who I am'.[45]

The code was not in widespread use at all times. By 1949, Zayara Vesyolaya 'could find no one who knew the "prison alphabet"' in Butyrka, and thought at first that the tradition must have died out. She later decided she was wrong, both because others told her they had used it at that time, and because a guard once burst into her cell when he heard a knocking sound, demanding to know the origins.[46] There were other variations. The Russian writer and poet Anatoly Zhigulin claims to have invented a code, also based on the alphabet, which he and a group of his friends (they were all arrested at once) used to communicate during the investigation of their case.[47]

In certain places and at certain times, prisoners' methods of self-organization took more elaborate forms. One in particular is described by Shalamov in his short story 'Committees for the Poor', and also mentioned by others.[48] Its origins lay in an unfair rule: at one point, during the late 1930s, the authorities suddenly decided that prisoners undergoing interrogation were to receive no packages from their relatives whatsoever, on the grounds that even 'two French rolls, five apples and a pair of old pants were enough to transmit any text into the prison'. Only money could be sent, and that only in round numbers, so that the sums could not be used to spell out 'messages'. Yet not all prisoners' families had money to send. Some were too poor, some too far away, while others may even have played a part in denouncing their relatives in the first place. That meant that although some prisoners had access once a week to the prison commissary – to butter, cheese, sausage, tobacco, white bread, cigarettes – others had to subsist on the poor prison diet, and, more importantly, would have felt 'out of place at the general holiday' that was 'commissary day'.

To solve this problem, the prisoners of Butyrka resurrected a phrase from the early days of the Revolution, and organized 'Committees of the Poor'. Each prisoner donated 10 per cent of his money to the committee. In turn, the committee purchased food items for prisoners who had none. This system went on for some years, until the authorities decided to eliminate the committees by promising some prisoners 'rewards' of various kinds for refusing to participate. The cells fought back, however, and ostracized the refusers. And who, asks Shalamov, 'would risk placing himself in opposition to the entire group, to people who are with you twenty-four hours a day, where only sleep can save you from the hostile glare of your fellow inmates?'

Curiously, this short story is one of the few in Shalamov's extensive repertoire to end on a positive note: 'Unlike the "free" world "outside", or the camps, society in prison is always united. In the committees this society found a way to make a positive statement as to the right of every man to live his own life.'[49]

This most pessimistic of writers had found, in this one organized form of prisoner solidarity, a shred of hope. The trauma of the transports, and the horror of the first bewildering days in the camps, soon shattered it.

9

Transport, Arrival, Selection

I remember Vanino port
And the clamour of the gloomy ship
As we walked along the gangway
Into the cold, murky hold.

The *zeks* suffered from the rolling of the surf
The deep sea howled all around them –
And in front of them lay Magadan
The capital of the land of Kolyma.

Not cries, but pitiful moans
Emerged from every breast
As they said goodbye to the mainland.
The ship rolled, strained, groaned . . .

– Soviet prisoners' song

In 1827, Princess Maria Volkonskaya, the wife of the Decembrist rebel Sergei Volkonsky, left her family, her child and her safe life in St Petersburg to join her husband in his Siberian exile. Her biographer described her journey, which was thought, at the time, to have been one of almost unendurable hardship:

Day after day, the sledge raced onwards into the endless horizon. Enclosed as if in a time capsule, Maria was in a state of feverish elation. There was a sense of unreality to the journey: lack of sleep and little food. She stopped only at an occasional relay for a glass of hot lemon tea from the ever-present brass samovar. The intoxicating speed of the sleigh, pulled by three plunging horses, devoured the empty distances at a gallop. 'Onward . . . forward!' shouted the drivers, dashing on as great plumes of snow rose from under the horses' hooves, and harness bells jingled relentlessly, warning of the approach of the vehicle . . .[1]

More than a century later Evgeniya Ginzburg's cell mate read a similar description of an aristocrat's journey across the Urals – and sighed with envy: 'And I always thought that the wives of the Decembrists endured the most frightful sufferings . . .'[2]

No horses and no sleighs drove twentieth-century prisoners with 'intoxicating speed' across the Siberian snow, and there were no glasses of hot lemon tea to be had from brass samovars at the relay stations. Princess Volkonskaya may have wept during her journey, but the prisoners who came after her could not even hear the word *etap* – prison jargon for 'transport' – without feeling a jolt of mouth-drying fear, even terror. Every journey was a wrenching leap into the unknown, a move away from familiar cell mates and familiar arrangements, however poor those might be. Worse, the process of moving prisoners from prison to transit prison, from transit prison to camp, and between camps within the system, was physically gruelling and openly cruel. In some senses, it was the most inexplicable aspect of life in the Gulag.

For those undergoing the ordeal for the first time, the event was pregnant with symbolism. Arrest and interrogation had been an initiation into the system, but the train journey across Russia represented a geographical break with the prisoners' former life, and the start of a new one. Emotions always ran high in the trains that left Moscow and Leningrad, headed north and east. Thomas Sgovio, the American who had failed to retrieve his passport, remembered what had happened when his train left for Kolyma: 'Our train left Moscow on the evening of June 24th. It was the beginning of an eastward journey which was to last a month. I can never forget the moment. Seventy men . . . began to cry.'[3]

Most of the time, long transports took place in stages. If they were being held in large city prisons, the *zeks* were first transported to the trains in trucks whose very design spoke of the NKVD's obsession with secrecy. From the outside, the 'Black Ravens', as they were nicknamed, appeared to be regular heavy-goods trucks. In the 1930s, they often had the word 'bread' painted on the sides, but later more elaborate ruses were used. One prisoner, arrested in 1948, remembered travelling in one truck marked 'Moscow Cutlets' and another labelled 'Vegetables/Fruits'.[4]

On the inside, the trucks were sometimes divided into 'two rows of tiny, pitch-black, airless cages', as one prisoner described them.[5] According to a design of 1951, others simply had two long benches, upon which prisoners squeezed beside one another.[6] Peasants, and those being transported at the start of the mass deportations from the Baltic States and eastern Poland, had a rougher time of it. They were often packed into ordinary goods trucks, as an elderly Lithuanian once described to me, 'like sardines': the first prisoner spread his legs, the second sat between the first's legs and spread his own legs – and so on, until the truck was full.[7] Such arrangements were particularly uncomfortable when there were many people to be collected, and a trip to the station could last all day. During the deportations that took place in the former Polish territories in the winter of February 1940, children froze to death before even reaching the trains, and adults suffered from severe frostbite, from which their arms and legs never recovered.[8]

In provincial cities, the secrecy rules were laxer and prisoners sometimes marched through towns to the train station, an experience which often provided their last glimpse of civilian life – and one of the civilians' few glimpses of prisoners. Janusz Bardach recalled his surprise at the reaction of townspeople in Petropavlovsk when they saw prisoners marching through the street:

Most in the entourage were women wrapped in shawls and long heavy coats made out of felt. To my amazement, they began shouting at the guards: 'Fascists ... Murderers ... Why don't you go and fight on the front ...' They began throwing snowballs at the guards. Several shots were fired into the air, and the women backed off several paces but continued cursing and following us. They tossed parcels, bread loaves and potatoes and bacon wrapped in cloth into the column. One woman removed her shawl and winter coat and gave them to a man who had none. I caught a pair of woollen mittens.[9]

Such reactions have a long tradition in Russia: Dostoevsky wrote of the housewives who sent 'fancy loaves made of the finest flour' to the inmates of tsarist prisons at Christmas time.[10] But by the 1940s, they were relatively rare. In many places – Magadan, famously, among them – the sight of prisoners in the street was so commonplace as to evoke no reaction at all.

Whether on foot or by truck, prisoners eventually reached the train stations. Sometimes these were ordinary stations, sometimes they were special stations – 'a piece of land surrounded by barbed wire', in the memory of Lev Finkelstein. He also remembered that prisoners were subjected to a series of special rituals before they were allowed to board:

There is a huge column of prisoners, you are counted, re-counted, re-counted. The train is there . . . then there is the travel order: 'On your knees!' During loading, it was a sensitive time, someone could start running. So they make sure that everybody is standing on their knees. But you better not get up, because at that point they are trigger-happy. Then they count, they put people on to the car, and lock them up. Then the train never moves – you just stand there for hours on end – then suddenly 'We're off!' and you start going.[11]

From the outside, the train cars often looked perfectly ordinary – except that they were better protected than most. Edward Buca, who had been arrested in Poland, surveyed his carriage with the careful eye of a man who hoped to escape. He recalled that 'each wagon was wound with several strands of barbed wire, there were wooden platforms outside for the guards, electric lights had been installed at the top and bottom of each wagon, and their small windows were protected by thick iron bars'. Later, Buca checked beneath the wagon to see if there were iron spikes along the bottom too. There were.[12] Finkelstein also remembered that 'every morning you hear this hammering – the guards have wooden hammers, and they always hammer up the trains, to make sure that nobody tried to break out, to make a hole'.[13]

Very rarely, exceptional arrangements were made for special prisoners. Anna Larina, the wife of the Soviet leader Nikolai Bukharin, did not travel with other prisoners, but was instead placed in the guards' compartment of the train.[14] But the vast majority of prisoners and exiles travelled together, in one of two types of train. The first were the *Stolypinki*, or 'Stolypin wagons' (named, ironically, after one of the more vigorous, reforming tsarist prime ministers of the early twentieth century, who is alleged to have introduced them). These were ordinary carriages that had been refitted for prisoners. They could be linked together in an enormous transport, or attached, one or two at a time, to ordinary trains. One former passenger described them:

A *Stolypinka* resembles an ordinary Russian third-class carriage except that it has a great many iron bars and grillwork. The windows are, of course, barred. The individual compartments are separated by steel netting instead of walls, like cages, and a long iron fence separates the compartments from the corridor. This arrangement enables the guards constantly to keep an eye on all prisoners in the car.[15]

The Stolypin wagons were also very, very crowded:

On each of the two top bunks two men lay head by foot. On the two middle ones were seven with their heads towards the door and one crosswise at their feet. Under each of the two bottom bunks there was one man, with fourteen more perched upon the bunks and on the bundles of belongings jammed in the floor space between the bunks and door. At night all those at the lower level somehow managed to lie down alongside one another.[16]

But there was another, more important disadvantage. Inside the Stolypin wagons, guards could watch the prisoners at all times, and were therefore able to control what prisoners ate, to hear their conversations – and to decide when and where they would be able to relieve themselves. As a result, virtually every memoirist who describes the trains mentions the horrors associated with urination and defecation. Once or sometimes twice a day, or sometimes not at all, the guards took prisoners to the toilet, or else stopped the train to let the passengers out: 'The worst happens when, after a long haggle with the guards, we are allowed off the cars and everybody looks for a spot somewhere under the boxcar to relieve himself or herself, not worrying about the audience watching from all directions.'[17]

However embarrassing such stops could be, the prisoners with stomach ailments or other medical problems were in a much worse position, as one remembered: 'Prisoners who could not hold themselves would whimperingly foul their pants and often also the prisoners next to them. Even in the community of hardship, it was difficult for some prisoners not to hate the unfortunates who did this.'[18]

It was for that reason that some prisoners actually preferred the other form of prisoner transport, the cattle wagons. These were what they sound like: empty wagons, not necessarily fitted out for human beings, sometimes with a small stove in the centre for heating, sometimes with bunks. Although more primitive than the Stolypin wagons, the cattle wagons were not divided into sections, and there was more room to move about. They also had 'toilets' – holes in the floor of the wagon – alleviating the prisoners' need to beg and plead with the guards.[19]

The open wagons had their special torments too, though. Sometimes, for example, the holes in the floor of the wagon became blocked. On Buca's train, the hole froze over. 'So what did we do? We pissed through a crack between the floor and the door and shat into a piece of cloth, making a small neat parcel and hoping that somewhere they would stop the train and open the door so that we could throw it out.'[20] On the trains full of deported exiles, in which men, women and children were all thrown together, the holes in the floor caused different problems. One former deportee, exiled as the daughter of a kulak in the early 1930s, remembered people being 'horribly embarrassed' at having to urinate in front of one another, and was thankful that she was able to do it 'behind my mother's skirts'.[21]

Yet the real torment was not the crowding or the toilets or the embarrassment, but the lack of food – and especially the lack of water. Sometimes, depending on the route and the type of train, prisoners were served hot food during the trip. Sometimes they were not. Usually, a prisoner's 'dry rations' for a transport consisted of bread, which could be distributed either in small chunks of 300 grams a day, or else in larger quantities – 2 kilograms or so – meant to last a 34-day journey.

Along with the bread, prisoners were usually given salted fish – the effect of which was to make them extremely thirsty.[22] Nevertheless, they were rarely given more than one mug of water per day, even in the summer. So prevalent was this practice that stories of the terrible thirst experienced by travelling prisoners appear again and again. 'Once, for three days we didn't get water, and on New Year's Eve of 1939, somewhere near Lake Baikal, we had to lick the black icicles which hung from the train carriages,' wrote one ex-*zek*.[23] In a 28-day trip, another remembers being given water three times, with the train occasionally stopping 'to take the corpses off'.[24]

Even those who did receive that one cup a day were tormented. Ginzburg recalled the excruciating decision prisoners had to make: whether to drink their whole cup in the morning, or try to save it. 'Those who took occasional sips and made it last all day never had a moment's peace. They watched their mugs like hawks from morning until night.'[25] If, that is, they were lucky enough to have mugs: one prisoner remembered to the end of her life the tragic moment when her teapot, which she had managed to keep with her, was stolen. The teapot had held water without spilling, enabling her to sip throughout the day. Without it she had nothing to hold water in at all, and was tormented by thirst.[26]

Worse were the recollections of Nina Gagen-Torn, who was on a transport train that stopped for three days outside of Novosibirsk in midsummer. The city's transit prison was full: 'It was July. Very hot. The roofs of the Stolypin wagons began to glow, and we lay on the bunks like buns in an oven.' Her car determined to go on a hunger strike, although the guards threatened them with new, longer sentences. 'We don't want to get dysentery,' the women shouted back at them. 'For four days we are lying in our own shit.' Reluctantly, the guards finally allowed them to drink a little bit, and to wash.[27]

A Polish prisoner also found herself on a train which had ground to a halt – but in the rain. Naturally, the prisoners tried to catch the water coming off the roof. But 'when we held our mugs between the bars of the windows, the guard who was sitting on the roof cried that he would shoot, for such behaviour was forbidden'.[28]

Winter journeys were not necessarily better. Another Polish deportee remembered having nothing but 'frozen bread and water in the form of ice' during her train journey east.[29] Summer or winter, other deportees experienced special torments. When one exile train stopped, unusually, at an ordinary station, the prisoners dashed out to buy food from local people. 'Our Jews made a dash for the eggs,' recalled a Polish passenger. 'They would rather starve than eat non-kosher food.'[30]

The very old and the very young suffered most. Barbara Armonas, a Lithuanian who had married an American, was deported along with a large group of Lithuanians, men, women and children. Among them was a woman who had given birth four hours earlier, as well as a paralysed 83-year-old who could not be kept clean – 'very soon everything around her was stinking and she was covered by open sores'. There were also three babies:

Their parents had great problems with diapers since it was impossible to wash them regularly. Sometimes when the train stopped after a rain the mothers would jump out to wash diapers in the ditches. There were fights over these water ditches because some wanted to wash dishes, some to wash their faces, while others wanted to wash dirty diapers, all at the same time ... the parents made every effort to keep their children clean. Used diapers were dried and shaken out. Sheets and shirts were torn up to improvise diapers and sometimes the men tied the wet diapers around their waists in an effort to dry them more quickly.

Small children fared no better:

Some days were very hot, and the heavy smell in the cars was unbearable and a number of people fell sick. In our car, one two-year-old boy ran a high fever and cried constantly because of pain. The only help his parents could get was a little aspirin which someone gave to them. He grew worse and worse and finally died. At the next stop in an unknown forest the soldiers took his body from the train and presumably buried him. The sorrow and helpless rage of his parents was heartbreaking. Under normal conditions and with medical attention he would not have died. Now, no one even knew for sure where he was buried.[31]

For arrested enemies, as opposed to deportees, special arrangements were sometimes made, which did not necessarily improve matters. Mariya Sandratskaya was arrested when her child was two months old, and was actually put on a transport train filled with nursing mothers. For eighteen days, sixty-five women and sixty-five infants travelled in two cattle cars, unheated except for two very small, very smoky stoves. There were no special rations, and no hot water to bathe the children or to wash the diapers, which subsequently turned 'green with filth'. Two of the women killed themselves, slitting their throats with glass. Another lost her mind. Their three babies were taken over by the other mothers. Sandratskaya herself 'adopted' one of them. To the end of her life, she remained convinced that breast milk alone had saved her own child, who contracted pneumonia. There had, of course, been no medicine available.

Upon arrival at the Tomsk transit prison, the situation hardly improved. More of the children grew ill. Two died. Two more mothers attempted suicide, but were prevented from doing so. Others went on hunger strike. On the fifth day of the strike, the women were visited by an NKVD commission: one of the women threw her baby at them. Only upon their arrival at Temlag – the women's camp, mostly for arrested 'wives' – did Sandratskaya manage to organize a children's nursery, eventually persuading relatives to come and take her child away.[32]

Bizarre and inhuman though her story may sound, Sandratskaya's experience was not unique. One former camp doctor has also described being sent along on a 'children's transport', along with fifteen nursing mothers and babies, plus twenty-five other children and two 'nannies'. All had been marched to the station under convoy, placed not on an ordinary train but in a Stolypin wagon with barred windows, and deprived of proper food.[33]

From time to time, all transport trains made stops, but these stops did not necessarily offer much respite. Prisoners were loaded off the trains, loaded back into trucks, and marched off to transit prisons. The regime in such places was similar to that in interrogation prisons, except that the gaolers had even less interest in the welfare of their charges, whom they were never likely to see again. As a result, the transport prison regime was wholly unpredictable.

Karol Harenczyk, a Pole who was transported from Western Ukraine to

Kolyma at the start of the Second World War, recorded the relative merits of the many transit prisons where he had stayed. In a questionnaire he filled out at the request of the Polish army, he noted that the Lvov prison had been dry, with 'good showers' and 'rather clean'. By contrast, the prison in Kiev was 'crowded, dirty beyond description', and filled with lice. In Kharkov, his 96-square-metre cell had been crammed with 387 people, and thousands of lice. In Artemovsk, the prison was 'almost completely dark', with no walks allowed: 'the cement floor is not cleaned, the remains of fish are on the floor. The dirt and smell and lack of air gives people headaches, dizziness,' so much so that prisoners went about on all fours. In Voroshilovgrad, the prison was again 'rather clean', and prisoners were allowed to relieve themselves outside of the cell, twice a day. In the transit camp at Starobelsk, prisoners were allowed walks only once a week, for half an hour.[34]

Probably the most primitive transit prisons were those on the Pacific coast, where prisoners stayed before being put on the boats to Kolyma. In the 1930s, there was only one: Vtoraya Rechka, near Vladivostok. So overcrowded was Vtoraya Rechka, however, that two more transit camps were built in 1938: Bukhta Nakhodka and Vanino. Even then there were not enough barracks for the thousands of inmates awaiting ships.[35] One prisoner found himself in Bukhta Nakhodka in late July 1947: 'Under the open sky they kept 20,000 people. Not a word was spoken about buildings – they sat, lay down, and lived, right there on the ground.'[36]

Nor was the water situation much improved from what it had been on the trains, despite the fact that the prisoners were still existing largely on salt fish, in high summer: 'All over the camp signs were posted, "Do not drink unboiled water." And two epidemics were raging amongst us – typhus and dysentery. And the prisoners did not heed the signs and drank water which trickled here and there on the grounds of the compound . . . anyone can understand how desperate we became for a drink of water to quench our thirst.'[37]

For prisoners who had been travelling for many weeks – and memoirists report train journeys to Bukhta Nakhodka of up to forty-seven days[38] – the conditions in the transit camps on the Pacific coast were almost unbearable. One records that by the time his transport arrived at Bukhta Nakhodka, 70 per cent of his comrades had night blindness, a side effect of scurvy, as well as diarrhoea.[39] Nor was much medical assistance available. With no drugs or proper care, the Russian poet Osip Mandelstam died in Vtoraya Rechka in October 1938, paranoid and raving.[40]

For those not too incapacitated, it was possible to earn a little bit of extra bread in the Pacific transit camps. Prisoners could carry cement buckets, unload goods wagons and dig latrines.[41] In fact, Bukhta Nakhodka is remembered by some as the 'only camp where prisoners begged to work'. One Polish woman remembered that 'They feed only those who work, but because there are more prisoners than work, some die of hunger . . . Prostitution flowers, like irises on Siberian meadows.'[42]

Still others, remembered Sgovio, survived by trading:

There was one large, open space called the bazaar. Prisoners gathered there and bartered . . . Currency was of no value. Greatest in demand were bread, tobacco, and bits of newspaper which we used for smoking. There were non-politicals serving time as maintenance and service men. They exchanged bread and tobacco for the clothes of fresh arrivees, then resold our clothes to citizens on the outside for roubles, thus accumulating a sum for the day they would be let out into the Soviet world. The bazaar was the most populated spot in the camp during the daytime. There, in that communist hell-hole, I witnessed what was in reality the crudest form of a free enterprise system.[43]

Yet for these prisoners, the horrors of the journey did not end with the trains and the transit camps. Their journey to Kolyma had to be completed by boat – just like the prisoners travelling up the Yenisei River, from Krasnoyarsk to Norilsk, or on barges, in the early days, across the White Sea from Arkhangelsk to Ukhta. It was a rare prisoner boarding the ships to Kolyma, in particular, who did not feel that he was undertaking a journey into the abyss, sailing across the Styx away from the known world. Many had never been on a boat before at all.[44]

The boats themselves were nothing out of the ordinary. Old Dutch, Swedish, English and American cargo steamers – boats never built to carry passengers – plied the route to Kolyma. The ships were redesigned to fit their new role, but the changes were largely cosmetic. The letters D.S. (for Dalstroi) were painted on their smokestacks, machine-gun nests were placed on the decks, and crude wooden bunks were constructed in the hold, sections of which were blocked off from one another with an iron grille. The largest of Dalstroi's fleet, originally designed to carry huge lengths of cable, was initially christened the *Nikolai Yezhov*. After Yezhov's fall from grace, it was renamed the *Feliks Dzerzhinsky* – an alteration which required a costly change in international shipping registration.[45]

Few other concessions were made to the ships' human cargo, who were forcibly kept below deck for the first part of the voyage, when the ships passed close to the coast of Japan. During these few days, the hatch leading from the deck to the hold would remain firmly shut, lest a stray Japanese fishing boat come into sight.[46] So secret were these voyages considered to be, in fact, that when the *Indigirka*, a Dalstroi ship containing 1,500 passengers – mostly prisoners returning to the mainland – hit a reef off the Japanese island of Hokkaido in 1939, the ship's crew chose to let most of the passengers die rather than seek aid. Of course, there were no life-saving devices aboard the ship, and the crew, still not wanting to reveal the true contents of their 'cargo boat', did not call upon other boats in the area to help, although many were available. A few Japanese fishermen came to assist the ship of their own accord, but to no avail: more than 1,000 people died in the disaster.[47]

But even when there was no catastrophe, prisoners suffered from the secrecy, which mandated forced confinement. The guards threw their food down into the hold, and they were left to scramble for it. They received their water in buckets, lowered down from the surface. Both food and water were therefore in short supply – as was air. Elinor Olitskaya, the Anarchist, remembered that people began to vomit immediately on embarking.[48] Descending into the hold, Ginzburg became instantly ill as well: 'If I remained on my feet it was only because there was no room to fall.' Once inside the hold, 'It was impossible to move, our legs grew numb, hunger and the sea air made us dizzy, and all of us were seasick . . . packed tightly in our hundreds we could hardly breathe; we sat or lay on the dirty floor or on one another, spreading out our legs to make room for the person in front.'[49]

Once past the Japanese coast, prisoners were sometimes allowed up on to the deck in order to use the ship's handful of toilets, which were hardly adequate for thousands of prisoners. Memoirists variously recall waiting '2 hours', '7 or 8 hours', and 'all day' for these toilets.[50] Thomas Sgovio described them:

A box-like makeshift contraption of boards was attached to the side of the ship . . . it was rather tricky to climb from the deck of the rolling ship over the railing, and into the box. The older prisoners and those who had never been at sea were afraid to enter. A prod from the guard and the necessity to relieve themselves finally made them overcome their reluctance. A long line was on the stairway day and night throughout the voyage. Only two men at a time were allowed in the box.[51]

Yet the physical torments of life on the ships were surpassed by the tortures invented by the prisoners themselves – or rather the criminal element among them. This was particularly true in the late 1930s and early 1940s, when the criminal influence in the camp system was at its height and the political and criminal prisoners were mixed indiscriminately. Some politicals had already encountered criminals on the trains. Aino Kuusinen remembered that 'the worst feature of the journey were the juveniles [young criminals] who were given the upper berths and perpetrated all kinds of indecencies – spitting, uttering obscene abuse and even urinating on the adult prisoners'.[52]

On the boats, the situation was worse. Elinor Lipper, who made the journey to Kolyma in the late 1930s, described how the politicals 'lay squeezed together on the tarred floor of the hold because the criminals had taken possession of the plank platform. If one of us dared to raise her head, she was greeted by a rain of fish heads and entrails from above. When any of the seasick criminals threw up, the vomit came straight down upon us.'[53]

Polish and Baltic prisoners, who had better clothes and more valuable possessions than their Soviet counterparts, were a particular target. On one occasion, a group of criminal prisoners turned out the ship's lights and attacked a group of Polish prisoners, killing some and robbing the rest. 'Those of the Poles who were there and remained alive,' wrote one survivor, 'would know for the rest of their lives that they had been in hell.'[54]

The consequences of the mixing of male and female prisoners could be far worse even than the mixing of criminals and politicals. Technically, this was forbidden: men and women were kept separately on the boats. In practice, guards could be bribed to let men into the women's hold, with drastic consequences. The 'Kolyma tram' – the shipboard gang rapes – were discussed throughout the camp system. Elena Glink, a survivor, described them:

They raped according to the command of the tram 'conductor' . . . then, on the command 'konchai bazar' ['stop the bazaar'], heaved off, reluctantly, giving up their place to the next man, who was standing in full readiness . . . dead women were pulled by their legs to the door, and stacked over the threshold. Those who remained were brought back to consciousness – water was thrown at them – and the line began again. In May 1951, on board the Minsk [famous throughout Kolyma for its 'big tram'] the corpses of women were thrown overboard. The guards didn't even write down the names of the dead . . .[55]

To Glink's knowledge, no one was ever punished for rape on board these ships. Janusz Bardach, a Polish teenager who found himself aboard a ship to Kolyma in 1942, concurred. He was present as a group of criminals planned a raid on the women's hold, and watched them chop a hole in the iron grille that separated the sexes:

As soon as the women appeared through the hole, the men tore off their clothing. Several men attacked each woman at once. I could see the victims' white bodies twisting, their legs kicking forcefully, their hands clawing the men's faces. The women bit, cried and wailed. The rapists smacked them back . . . when the rapists ran out of women, some of the bulkier men turned to the bed boards and hunted for young men. These adolescents were added to the carnage, lying still on their stomachs, bleeding and crying on the floor.

None of the other prisoners tried to stop the rapists: 'hundreds of men hung from the bed boards to view the scene, but not a single one tried to intervene'. The attack only ended, Bardach wrote, when the guards on the upper deck blasted the hold with water. A handful of dead and injured women were dragged out afterwards. No one was punished.[56]

'Anyone,' wrote one surviving prisoner, 'who has seen Dante's hell would say that it was nothing beside what went on in that ship.'[57]

There are many more stories of transports, some so tragic they hardly bear repeating. So horrific were these journeys, in fact, that they have become, in the collective memory of the survivors, a puzzle almost as hard to understand as the camps themselves. By applying more or less normal human psychology, it is possible to explain the cruelty of camp commanders, who were themselves under pressure to meet norms and fulfil plans, as we shall see. It is even possible to explain the actions of interrogators, whose lives depended on their success at extracting confessions, and who had sometimes been selected for their sadism. It is far more difficult, however, to explain why an ordinary convoy guard would refuse to give water to prisoners dying of thirst, to give aspirin to a child with fever, or to protect women from being gang-raped to death.

Certainly there is no evidence that convoy guards were explicitly instructed to torture prisoners being transported. On the contrary, there were elaborate rules about how to protect prisoner transports, and much official anger when these rules were frequently broken. A decree of December 1941, 'on improving the organization of the transport of prisoners', heatedly described the 'irresponsibility' and sometimes 'criminal' behaviour of some of the convoy guards and employees of the Gulag: 'This has resulted in prisoners arriving at the designated place in a state of starvation, as a result of which they cannot be put to work for some time.'[58]

An indignant official order, of 25 February 1940, complained not only that sick and incapacitated prisoners had been put on trains to the northern camps – which was in itself forbidden – but also that many more had not been fed or given water, had not been given clothes appropriate to the season *en route*, and had not been accompanied by their personal files, which had therefore gone missing. Prisoners arrived in camps, in other words, where no one knew their crime or their sentence. Out of 1,900 prisoners sent in one transport to the far north in 1939, 590 were of 'limited work capacity' upon arrival, being either too weak or too ill. Some had only a few months left to serve of their sentences, and some had finished them altogether. Most were without warm clothes and 'poorly shod'. In November 1939, another 272 prisoners, none of whom had winter coats, were driven a distance of 500 kilometres in open trucks, as a result of which many fell ill and some later died. All of these facts were reported with suitable outrage and anger, and negligent guards were punished.[59]

Numerous instructions regulated the affairs of the transit prisons as well. On 26 July 1940, for example, an order described the organization of transit prisons, explicitly demanding their commanders to construct baths, parasite disinfection systems and working kitchens.[60] No less important were the safety and security of Dalstroi's prison fleet. When, in December 1947, dynamite exploded on two of the ships moored in Magadan's harbour, resulting in 97 deaths and 224 hospitalizations, Moscow accused the port of 'criminally negligent behaviour'. Those held responsible were tried and received criminal sentences.[61]

The Gulag's bosses in Moscow were well aware of the horrors of prisoner boat travel. A report by the prosecutors' office inspectorate in Norilsk in 1943 complained that prisoners who arrived by boat – they came up the Yenisei River on barges – were 'frequently in poor physical condition . . . of the 14,125 prisoners who arrived in Norilsk in 1943, about 500 were hospitalized in Dudinka [the Norilsk port] on the first or second day after their arrival; up to 1,000 were temporarily unable to work, as they had been deprived of food'.[62]

Despite all of the bluster, the transport system changed very little over time. Orders were sent out, complaints were made. Yet on 24 December 1944, a convoy arrived at Komsomolsk station in the far east in what even the deputy prosecutor of the Gulag system thought was an execrable condition. His official account of the fate of 'echelon SK 950', a train composed of fifty-one wagons, must stand as some kind of low point, even in the nightmarish history of Gulag transport:

The prisoners arrived in unheated wagons which had not been prepared for prisoner transport. In each wagon, there were between 10–12 bunks, on which no more than 18 people could fit, yet there were up to 48 people in each wagon. The wagons were not supplied with enough canisters for water, as a result of which there were interruptions in water supply, sometimes for whole days and nights. The prisoners were given frozen bread, and for 10 days got none at all. The prisoners arrived dressed in summer uniforms, dirty, covered in lice, with obvious signs of frostbite . . . the sick prisoners had been rolled on to the wagon floors, without medical help, and had died there and then. Corpses were kept in the wagons for long periods . . .

Of the 1,402 people sent on echelon SK 950, 1,291 arrived: 53 had died *en route*, 66 had been left in hospitals along the way. On arrival, a further 335 were hospitalized with third- or fourth-degree frostbite, pneumonia and other diseases. The convoy had, it seemed, travelled for sixty days, twenty-four of which they had spent not moving, sitting on side tracks 'due to poor organization'. Yet in this extreme case, the leader of the echelon – one Comrade Khabarov – received nothing more than a 'censure with warnings'.[63]

Many survivors of similar transports have tried to explain this grotesque mistreatment of prisoners at the hands of young, inexperienced convoy guards, who were far from being the trained killers deployed in the prison system. Nina Gagen-Torn speculated that 'it wasn't evidence of evil, just the complete indifference of the convoy. They didn't look at us as people. We were living cargo.'[64] Antoni Ekart, a Pole arrested after the Soviet invasion of 1939, also thought that

the lack of water was not deliberately to torture us but because the escort had to put in extra work to bring it and would not do so without an order. The commander of the escort was not at all interested in this matter and the guards were unwilling to escort the prisoners several times a day to the wells or water taps at stations owing to the risk of escape.[65]

Yet some prisoners reported more than indifference: 'In the morning, the boss of the convoy came into the corridor . . . he stood with his face to the window, his back to us, and shouted insults, swear words: "I'm bored of you!"'[66]

Boredom – or, rather, boredom mixed with anger at having to carry out such a degrading job – was also Solzhenitsyn's explanation for this otherwise inexplicable phenomenon. He even tried to think himself into the minds of the convoy guards. Here they were, so busy and understaffed, and then to have 'to go carry water in pails – it has to be hauled a long way, too, and it's insulting: why should a Soviet soldier have to carry water like a donkey for enemies of the people?'. Worse, he went on,

It takes a long time to dole out that water. The *zeks* don't have their own mugs. Whoever did have one has had it taken away from him – so what it adds up to is that they have to be given the two government issue mugs to drink out of, and while they are drinking up you have to keep standing there and standing, and dipping it out and dipping it out some more and handing it to them . . .

But the convoy could have borne with all that, hauled the water, and doled it out, if only those pigs, after slurping up the water, didn't ask to go to the toilet. So here's the way it works out: if you don't give them water for a day, then they don't ask to go to the toilet. Give them water once, and they go to the toilet once; take pity on them and give them water twice – and they go to the toilet twice. So it's pure and simple common sense: just don't give them anything to drink.[67]

Whatever their motivation – indifference, boredom, anger, injured pride – the effect on the prisoners was devastating. As a rule, they arrived at their camps not only disoriented and degraded by their experience of prison and interrogation, but physically depleted – and ripe for the next stage of their journey into the Gulag system: entry into the camp.

If it was not dark, if they were not ill, and if they were interested enough to look up, the first thing the prisoners saw on arrival was their camp's gate. More often than not, the gate displayed a slogan. On the entrance into one of the Kolyma *lagpunkts* 'hung a plywood rainbow with a banner draped over it which read: "Labour in the USSR is a Matter of Honesty, Glory, Valour and Heroism!"'[68] Barbara Armonas was welcomed to a labour colony in the suburbs of Irkutsk with the banner: 'With Just Work I Will Pay My Debt to the Fatherland.'[69] Arriving in Solovetsky in 1933 – it had by then become a high-security prison – another prisoner saw a sign reading: 'With an Iron Fist, We Will Lead Humanity to Happiness!'[70] Yuri Chirkov, arrested at age fourteen, was also confronted with a sign at Solovetsky which read:

'Through Labour – Freedom!' – a slogan which is about as uncomfortably close as it is possible to get to the slogan that hung over the gates of Auschwitz: *Arbeit Macht Frei* – 'Work Makes You Free.'[71]

Like the arrival in prison, the arrival of a new *etap* in camp was also attended by rituals: prison inmates, exhausted by transport, now had to be turned into working *zeks*. 'On arrival at the camp,' remembered Karol Colonna-Czosnowski, a Polish prisoner,

We spent a long time being counted . . . That particular evening there seemed no end to it. Innumerable times we had to form five abreast and each row was told to advance three paces which several worried-looking NKVD officials would call aloud, '*odin, dva, tri* . . .' and laboriously write down each number on to their large clipboards. Presumably the number of those alive, added to the numbers of those who had been shot *en route*, did not produce the expected total.[72]

Following the count both men and women were taken to the baths and shaved – over their entire bodies. This procedure, carried out under official orders for the sake of hygiene[73] – it was assumed, usually correctly, that prisoners arriving from Soviet gaols would be covered with lice – nevertheless had an important ritual significance as well. Women describe it with particular horror and distaste, and no wonder. Often, they had to remove their clothes and then wait naked, under the full gaze of male soldiers, for their turn to be shaved. 'For the first time,' recalled Elinor Olitskaya, who was a participant in this ceremony on her arrival in Kolyma, 'I heard wails of protest: Women remain women . . .'[74] Olga Adamova-Sliozberg had suffered the same experience in a transit prison:

We undressed and handed over our clothes for treatment and were about to go upstairs to the washroom when we realized that the staircase was lined from top to bottom with guards. Blushing, we hung our heads and huddled together. Then I looked up, and my eyes met those of the officer in charge. He gave me a sullen look. 'Come on, come on,' he shouted. 'Get a move on!'

I suddenly felt relieved and the situation even seemed quite comic.

'To hell with them,' I thought. 'They're no more men to me than Vaska the bull who frightened me when I was a child.'[75]

Once washed and shaved, the second step in the process of turning men and women into anonymous *zeks* was the distribution of clothing. The rules changed, from era to era as well as from camp to camp, as to whether or not prisoners were allowed to wear their own clothes. The decision seems, in practice, to have been left to the whim of local camp officials: 'In one *lagpunkt* you could wear your own clothes, in another not,' remembered Galina Smirnova, a prisoner in Ozerlag in the early 1950s.[76] It did not always matter: by the time they reached the camp, many prisoners' own clothes were in rags, if they had not been stolen.

Those without clothes had to wear the camp-issue uniforms, which were invariably old, ripped, ill-made and ill-fitting. To some, particularly women, it sometimes seemed as if the clothes they were given were part of a deliberate attempt to humiliate them. Anna Andreevna, wife of the writer and spiritualist Danil Andreev, was at first sent to a camp where prisoners were allowed to wear their own clothes. Later, in 1948, she was moved into a camp where they were not. She found the change truly offensive: 'They had deprived us of everything, they deprived us of our names, of everything that is part of a person's personality, and dressed us, I can't even describe it, in a shapeless dress . . .'[77]

No effort was made to ensure that sizes matched the prisoners. 'Each of us received long underwear,' wrote Janusz Bardach, as well as 'a black tunic, quilted pants, a long quilted outer jacket, a felt hat with ear-flaps, rubber-soled boots, and fleece-lined mittens. These items were handed out indiscriminately, and it was up to us to find the right sizes. Everything I was given was much too big, and I spent hours trading for a better fit.'[78]

Equally scathing about camp fashions, another female prisoner wrote that they were given 'short padded coats, padded stockings up to our knees, and birch-bark shoes. We looked like uncanny monsters. We had scarcely anything of our own left. Everything had been sold to the convict women, or, more correctly, exchanged for bread. Silk stockings and scarves elicited such admiration that we were obliged to sell them. It would have been too dangerous to refuse.'[79]

Because the ripped clothes seemed designed to rob them of dignity, many prisoners would later go to great lengths to improve them. One woman prisoner recalled that she did not care, at first, about the 'very old and ruined' clothes she was given. Later, though, she began to sew up the holes, make pockets, and improve the clothes, 'as other women did', thus making herself feel less degraded.[80] In general, women who were able to sew or to quilt were able to earn extra bread rations, so coveted were even the slightest improvements to the standard uniform: the ability to distinguish oneself, to look slightly better than others, would become, as we shall see, associated with higher rank, better health, greater privilege. Varlam Shalamov well understood the significance of these minor changes:

In camp there is 'individual' and 'common' underwear; such are the verbal pearls found in official speech. 'Individual' underwear is newer and somewhat better and is reserved for 'trusties', convict foremen, and other privileged persons . . . 'common' underwear is underwear for anyone. It's handed out in the bathhouse right after bathing in exchange for dirty underwear, which is gathered and counted separately beforehand. There's no opportunity to select anything according to size. Clean underwear is a pure lottery, and I felt a strange and terrible pity at seeing adult men cry over the injustice of receiving worn-out clean underwear in exchange for dirty good underwear. Nothing can take the mind of a human being off the unpleasantnesses that comprise life . . .'[81]

Still, the shock of being washed, shaved and dressed as *zeks* was only the first stage in a long initiation. Immediately afterwards, the prisoners underwent one of the most critical procedures in their lives as inmates: selection – and segregation into categories of worker. This selection process would affect everything from a prisoner's status in camp, to the type of barrack he lived in, to the type of work he would be assigned to do. All of which might, in turn, determine whether he would live or die.

I have not, it must be noted, found any memoirs describing 'selections' of the sort that took place in German death camps. That is, I have not read of regular selections which ended in weak prisoners being taken aside and shot. Such atrocities surely took place – one Solovetsky memoirist claims to have survived one such occasion[82] – but the usual practice, at least by the end of the 1930s and the early 1940s, was different. Weak prisoners were not murdered upon arrival in some of the further-flung camps, but rather given a period of 'quarantine', both to ensure that any illnesses they were carrying would not spread, and to allow them to 'fatten up', to recover their health after long months in prison and terrible journeys. Camp bosses appear to have taken this practice seriously, and prisoners concur.[83]

Alexander Weissberg, for example, was given good food and allowed to rest before he was sent to the mines.[84] After a long transport to Ukhtizhemlag, Jerzy Gliksman – the Polish socialist who had once so enjoyed the performance of Pogodin's *Aristokraty* in Moscow – was given a three-day rest, during which he and his fellow new arrivals were treated as 'guests'.[85] Pyotr Yakir, the son of the Soviet general, was put in quarantine for fourteen days at Sevurallag.[86] Ginzburg remembered her first few days in Magadan, the main city of Kolyma, as a 'whirl of pain, blackouts of memory, and a dark abyss of unconsciousness'. She, like others, had been taken directly off the SS *Dzhurma* and placed in a hospital, where after two months she fully recovered her health. Some were sceptical. 'A lamb for the slaughter,' said Liza Sheveleva, another prisoner. 'Whom are you recovering for, may I ask? As soon as you get out of here, you'll go straight on to forced labour, and in a week you'll be the same sort of corpse that you were on board the *Dzhurma* . . .'[87]

Once the invalids had recovered, if they had been allowed to do so, and once dressed, if they had been allowed new clothes, the selection and segregation began in earnest. In principle, this was a heavily regulated process. As early as 1930, the Gulag issued very strict, complicated orders on the classification of prisoners. Theoretically, prisoners' work assignments were meant to reflect two sets of criteria: their 'social origin' and sentence, and their health. In these early days, prisoners were put into three categories: 'working-class' prisoners, not convicted of counter-revolutionary crimes, with sentences not longer than five years; 'working-class' prisoners, not convicted of counter-revolutionary crimes, with sentences above five years; and those sentenced for counter-revolutionary crimes.

Each of these three categories of workers was then assigned one of three categories of prison regime: privileged, light, and 'first-order', or heavy. Then they were meant to be examined by a medical commission, which determined whether they were able to carry out heavy work or light work. After taking into account all of these criteria, the camp administration would then assign each prisoner a job. According to how well they fulfilled the norms of that particular job, each prisoner would then be assigned one of four levels of food rations: basic, working, 'reinforced', or 'punishment'.[88] All of these categories would change many times. Beria's orders of 1939, for example, divided prisoners into 'heavy-work-capable', 'light-work-capable' and 'invalid' categories (sometimes called groups A, B and C), the numbers of which were regularly monitored by the central administration in Moscow, which heavily disapproved of camps which had too many 'invalid' prisoners.[89]

The process was far from orderly. It had both formal aspects – imposed by the camp commanders – and informal aspects, as prisoners made adjustments and bargained among themselves. For most, their first experience of the camp classification process was relatively crude. George Bien, a young Hungarian picked up in Budapest at the end of the Second World War, compared the selection process he went through in 1946 to a slave market:

Everyone was ordered to the courtyard and told to strip. When your name was called you appeared before a medical team for a health inspection. The exam consisted of pulling the skin of your buttocks to determine the amount of muscle. They determined your condition of strength by the muscle content, and if you passed you were accepted and your documents were put in a separate pile. This was done by women in white coats, and they had little choice from this group of living dead. They chose the younger prisoners, regardless of muscle.[90]

Jerzy Gliksman also used the expression 'slave market' to describe the segregation process that took place in Kotlas, the transit camp that supplied prisoners to the camps north of Arkhangelsk. There, guards awoke prisoners during the night and told them to assemble, with all of their belongings, on the following morning. Every prisoner was forced to attend, even the seriously ill. Then, all were marched out of the camp, into the forest. An hour later, they arrived at a large clearing, where they were formed into columns, sixteen men abreast:

All day long I noticed unknown officials, both uniformed and in civilian clothes, wandering among the prisoners, ordering some to remove their *fufaykas* [jackets], feeling their arms, their legs, looking over the palms, commanding others to bend over. Sometimes they would order a prisoner to open his mouth and peered at his teeth, like horse traders at a county fair ... some were looking for engineers and experienced locksmiths or lathe operators; others might require construction carpenters; and all were always in need of physically strong men for work as lumberjacks, in agriculture, in coalmining, and in the oil wells.

The most important consideration of those doing the inspecting, Gliksman realized, was 'not to let themselves be duped into inadvertently acquiring cripples, invalids, or the sick – in short, persons who were good only for eating up bread for nothing. This was the reason why special agents were dispatched from time to time to select the proper prisoner material.'[91]

Right from the start, it was also clear that rules were there to be broken. Nina Gagen-Torn went through a particularly humiliating selection at the Temnikovsky camp in 1947, which nevertheless had a positive result. Upon arriving in the camp, her convoy was immediately sent to the showers, their clothes put in the disinfection chamber. They were then marched into a room, still dripping wet and naked: there was to be 'a health inspection', they were told. 'Doctors' were going to examine them, and so they did – along with the camp production manager and guards:

The major walked along the line, quickly examining the bodies. He was choosing goods – to production, to the sewing factory! To the collective farm! To the zone! To the hospital! The production manager wrote down the surnames.

But when he heard her surname, the Major looked at her and asked,
– 'What relation are you to Professor Gagen-Torn?'
– 'Daughter.'
– 'Put her in the hospital, she has scabies, she has red marks on her stomach.'

As she did not have red marks on her stomach, Gagen-Torn assumed, correctly as it turned out, that the man had once known and admired her father, and was saving her, at least temporarily, from hard work.[92]

Prisoners' behaviour in the first few days of their camp life, during and after this selection process, could have a profound effect on their fate. During his three-day period of rest upon arrival at Kargopollag, for example, the Polish novelist Gustav Herling took stock of his situation and 'sold my high officer's boots for 900 grams of bread to an *urka* [a criminal prisoner] from the railway porters' brigade'. In recompense, the criminal prisoner used his connections in the camp administration to help Herling secure a job as a porter at the food supply centre. This was hard work, Herling was told, but at least he would be able to steal extra rations – as proved to be the case. And right away he was granted a 'privilege'. The camp commander told him to

report at the camp store to draw out a *bushlat* [a long-sleeved jerkin lined with wadding], a cap with ear-flaps, wadded trousers, waterproof gloves made of sail-cloth, and *valenki* [felt boots] of best quality, i.e., new or worn only a little – a full set of clothing such as is usually issued only to the best 'Stakhanovite' brigades of prisoners.[93]

Wheeling and dealing took other forms as well. Upon arriving at Ukhti-zhemlag, Gliksman immediately realized that the 'specialist' title he had been handed in the Kotlas transit camp – he was classified as a trained economist – had no meaning in the concentration camp itself. Meanwhile, he noticed that during the first few days in the camp, his savvier Russian acquaintances did not bother with official formalities:

Most of the 'specialists' utilized the three free days to visit the offices and bureaus of the camp, seeking old acquaintances wherever they went and conducting suspicious negotiations with some of the camp officials. They were all excited and preoccupied. Every one of them had secrets of his own and was fearful lest another spoil his chances and grab the more comfortable work each coveted. In no time at all the majority of these people knew where to go, at whose door to knock, and what to say.

As a result, a genuinely qualified Polish doctor was sent to cut trees in the forest, while a former pimp was given an office job as an accountant, 'although he had not the slightest notion of accounting and was altogether half illiterate'.[94]

Those prisoners who thus managed to avoid physical labour had indeed concocted the beginnings of a survival strategy – but only the beginnings. Now, they had to learn the strange rules that governed daily life in the camps.

10
Life in the Camps

The sound of a distant bell
Enters the cell with the dawn
I hear the bell calling out to me:
'Where are you? Where are you?'
'Here I am!' . . . Then tears of greeting,
Mean tears of captivity . . .
    Not for God,
    But for you, Russia.

– Simeon Vilensky, 1948[1]

According to the most accurate count to date, there were, between 1929 and 1953, 476 camp complexes in the realm of the Gulag.[2] But this number is misleading. In practice, each one of these camp complexes contained dozens, or even hundreds, of smaller camp units. These smaller units – *lagpunkts* – have not yet been counted, and probably cannot be, since some were temporary, some were permanent, and some were technically parts of different camps at different times. Nor can very much be said about the customs and practices of the *lagpunkts* that is guaranteed to apply to every single one. Even during Beria's reign over the system – which lasted, in effect, from 1939 until Stalin's death in 1953 – living and working conditions in the Gulag would continue to vary enormously, both from year to year and from place to place, even within the same camp complex.

'Every camp is its own world, a separate city, a separate country,' wrote the Soviet actress Tatyana Okunevskaya – and every camp had its own character.[3] Life in one of the mass industrial camps of the far north was very different from life on an agricultural farm camp in southern Russia. Life in any camp during the most intensive period of the Second World War, when one in four *zeks* died every year, was quite different from life in the early 1950s, when death rates were nearly the same as in the rest of the country. Life in a camp headed by a relatively liberal boss was not the same as life in a camp led by a sadist. *Lagpunkts* also ranged widely in size, from several thousand to several dozen prisoners, as well as in longevity. Some lasted from the 1920s to the 1980s, when they still functioned as criminal prisons. Others, such as those set up to build the roads and railways across Siberia, lasted only as long as a single summer.

Nevertheless, on the eve of the war, certain elements of life and of work were common to the vast majority of camps. The climate still varied from *lagpunkt* to *lagpunkt*, but the huge fluctuations in national policy that had characterized the 1930s had come to a halt. Instead, the same inert bureaucracy that would eventually lay its dead hand on virtually every aspect of life in the Soviet Union slowly took over the Gulag as well.

Striking, in this regard, are the differences between the sketchy and somewhat vague rules and regulations for the camps issued in 1930, and the more detailed rules issued in 1939, after Beria had taken control. This difference seems to reflect a changing relationship between the organs of central control – the Moscow Gulag administration itself – and the commanders of camps in the regions. During the Gulag's first, experimental decade, the order papers did not attempt to dictate what camps should look like, and barely touched on the behaviour of prisoners. They sketched out a general scheme, and left local commanders to fill in the blanks.

By contrast, the later orders were very specific and very detailed indeed, dictating virtually every aspect of camp life, from the method of construction of barracks to the prisoners' daily regime, in line with the Gulag's new sense of purpose.[4] From 1939, it seems that Beria – with, presumably, Stalin behind him – no longer explicitly intended the Gulag camps to be death camps, as some of them had been, in effect, in 1937 and 1938. Which is not to say, however, that their administrators were any more concerned with preserving human life, let alone respecting human dignity. From 1939 onwards, Moscow's central concerns were economic: prisoners were to be slotted into the camp's production plan like cogs in a machine.

Towards this end, the rules emanating from Moscow dictated strict control over the prisoners, to be obtained through the manipulation of their living conditions. In principle – as noted – the camp classified every *zek* according to his sentence, his profession and his *trudosposobnost*, or 'work capacity'. In principle, the camp assigned every *zek* a job, and a set of norms to fulfil. In principle, the camp allotted every *zek* the basic necessities of life – food, clothing, shelter, living space – according to how well, or how badly, he fulfilled these norms. In principle, every aspect of camp life was designed to improve production figures: even the camp 'cultural-educational' departments existed largely because the Gulag bosses believed they might convince prisoners to work harder. In principle, inspection teams existed in order to make sure that all of these aspects of camp life worked harmoniously. In principle, every *zek*, even, had the right to complain – to the camp boss, to Moscow, to Stalin – if the camps were not operating according to the rules.

And yet – in practice, things were very different. People are not machines, the camps were not clean, well-functioning factories, and the system never worked the way it was supposed to. Guards were corrupt, administrators stole, and the prisoners developed ways of fighting or subverting the camps' rules. Within the camps, prisoners were also able to form their own informal hierarchies which sometimes harmonized with, and sometimes conflicted with, the official hierarchy created by the camp administration. Despite regular visits from Moscow inspectors, often followed up by reprimands and angry letters from the centre, few camps lived up to the theoretical model. Despite the apparent seriousness with which prisoners' complaints were treated – whole commissions existed to examine them – they rarely resulted in actual change.[5]

This clash between what the Gulag administration in Moscow thought the camps were supposed to be, and what they actually were on the ground – the clash between the rules written on paper, and the procedures carried out in practice – was what gave life in the Gulag its peculiar, surreal flavour. In theory, the Gulag administration in Moscow dictated the smallest aspects of prisoners' lives. In practice, every aspect of life was also affected by the prisoners' relationships with those who controlled them, and with one another.

Zona
Within the Barbed Wire

By definition, the most fundamental tool at the disposal of the camp administrators was control over the space in which prisoners lived: this was the *zona*, or 'prison zone'. By law, a *zona* was laid out in either a square or a rectangle. 'In order to ensure better surveillance,' no organic or irregular shapes were permitted.[6] Within this square or rectangle, there was not much to interest the eye. Most of the buildings in a typical *lagpunkt* looked remarkably alike. Photographs of camp buildings once taken by Vorkuta administrators, and preserved in Moscow archives, show an array of primitive wooden buildings, otherwise indistinguishable except for the captions describing one as a 'punishment cell', another as a 'dining hall'. There was usually a large open space in the centre of the camp, near the gate, where the prisoners stood at attention twice a day to be counted. There were usually some guards' barracks and administrators' houses, also made of wood, just outside the main gate.

What distinguished the *zona* from any other workplace was, of course, the fence that surrounded it. Jacques Rossi, in *The Gulag Handbook*, wrote that the fence

is usually built of wooden posts with one-third of their length in the ground. They range from 2.5 to 6 meters (7.5 to 18 feet) high, depending on local conditions. Seven to fifteen rows of barbed wire are stretched horizontally between the posts, which are about 6 meters (18 feet) apart. Two strands of wire are stretched diagonally between each pair of posts.[8]

If the camp or colony was located near or within a city, the barbed-wire fence was usually replaced by a wall or fence made of bricks or wood, so that no one approaching the site would be able to see in from the outside. These barriers were well built: in Medvezhegorsk, for example, the headquarters of the White Sea Canal, a high wooden fence, built in the early 1930s to contain prisoners, was still standing when I visited the town in 1998.

To get through the fence, prisoners and guards alike had to travel through the *vakhta*, or 'guardhouse'. During the day, the guards of the *vakhta* monitored all of those who entered and left the camp, checking the passes of free workers coming into the camps, and of the convoy guards escorting prisoners on their way out. In the camp at Perm-36, which has been restored to its original state, the *vakhta* contains a passage blocked by two gates. A prisoner would walk through the first gate, then stop in the small space in between to be searched or checked. Only then would he be allowed to walk through the second gate. It was much the same system as one finds at the entrance to a Sicilian bank.

But barbed wire and walls alone did not define the *zona*'s boundaries. In most camps, armed guards observed the prisoners from high wooden watchtowers. Sometimes dogs also circled the camp, attached by chains to a metal wire which had been stretched all the way around the *zona*. The dogs, managed by special dog-handlers among the guards, were trained to bark at approaching prisoners and to follow the scent and chase anyone attempting escape. Prisoners were thus held in by barriers of sight, smell and sound, as well as by barbed wire and brick.

They were also held in by fear, which was sometimes enough to keep prisoners within a camp that had no fence at all. Margarete Buber-Neumann was kept in a low-security camp which allowed prisoners to 'move freely up to within half a mile of the camp perimeter; after that the guards shot without ceremony'.[9] This was unusual: in most camps, the guards would shoot 'without ceremony' much sooner than that. In his 1939 regulations, Beria ordered all camp commanders to line their fences with a no man's land, a strip of earth no less than 5 metres (15 feet) wide.[10] Guards regularly raked the no man's land in summer and deliberately left it covered with snow in winter, in order that the footprints of escaping prisoners might always be visible. The beginning of the no man's land was also marked, sometimes by barbed wire, sometimes by signs reading '*zapretnaya zona*', 'forbidden zone'. The no man's land was sometimes called the 'death zone', since guards were permitted to shoot anyone who entered it.[11]

And yet – the fences and walls and dogs and barricades that surrounded *lagpunkts* were not totally impenetrable. Whereas German concentration camps were completely self-contained – 'sealed off totally, hermetically', is how one expert puts it[12] – the Soviet system was in this sense different.

To begin with, the Soviet system classified prisoners as *konvoinyi* or *beskonvoinyi* – 'guarded' or 'unguarded' – and the small minority of unguarded prisoners were allowed to cross over the boundary without being watched, to run errands for the guards, to work during the day on an unguarded bit of railway, even to live in private apartments outside the *zona*. This latter privilege had been established early in the history of the camps, in the more chaotic years of the early 1930s.[13] Although it was explicitly forbidden several times after that, it persisted. One set of rules written in 1939 reminded camp commanders that 'all prisoners, without exception, are forbidden to live outside the zone in villages, private apartments, or houses belonging to the camp.' Theoretically, camps needed to get special permission even to let inmates live in a guarded accommodation, if it was outside the *zona*.[14] In practice, these rules were frequently disregarded. Despite the edict of 1939, inspectors' reports written long after that date list a wide variety of violations. In the city of Ordzhonikidze, one inspector complained, prisoners walked around the streets, went to bazaars, entered private apartments, drank and stole. In one Leningrad prison colony, a prisoner had been given use of a horse, on which he escaped. In work colony No. 14 in Voronezh, an armed guard left thirty-eight prisoners standing on the street while he went into a shop.[15]

The Moscow prosecutors' office wrote a letter to another camp, near the Siberian city of Komsomolsk, accusing commanders of allowing no fewer than 1,763 prisoners to attain the status of 'unguarded'. As a result, the prosecutors wrote angrily, 'it is always possible to meet prisoners in any part of the town, in any institution, and in private apartments'.[16] They also accused another camp of letting 150 prisoners live in private apartments, a violation of the regime, which had led to 'incidents of drunkenness, hooliganism and even robbery of the local population'.[17]

But within camps, prisoners were not deprived of all freedom of movement either. On the contrary, this is one of the quirks of the concentration camp, one of the ways in which it differs from a prison: when not working, and when not sleeping, most prisoners could walk in and out of the barracks at will. When not working, prisoners could also decide, within limits, how to spend their time. Only those prisoners subjected to the *katorga* regime, set up in 1943, or later those put in the 'special regime camps', created in 1948, were locked into their barracks at night, a circumstance they bitterly resented and later rebelled against.[18]

Arriving in the camps from claustrophobic Soviet prisons, inmates were often surprised and relieved by this change. One *zek* said of his arrival in Ukhtpechlag: 'Our mood was wonderful, once we got into the open air.'[19]

Olga Adamova-Sliozberg remembered talking 'from dawn to dusk about the advantages of camp over prison life' upon her arrival in Magadan:

The camp population (around a thousand women) seemed to us enormous: so many people, so many conversations to have, so many potential friends! Then there was nature. Within the compound, which was fenced with barbed wire, we could walk around freely, gaze at the sky and the faraway hills, go up to the stunted trees and stroke them with our hands. We breathed the moist sea air, felt the August drizzle on our faces, sat on the damp grass and let the earth run through our fingers. For four years we had lived without doing all this and discovered in doing so that it was essential to our being: without it you ceased to feel like a normal person.[20]

Lev Finkelstein concurs:

You were brought in, you got out of the prison van, and you are surprised by several things. First, that the prisoners are walking around, without guards – they were going somewhere on their duties, whatever. Second, they look completely different from you. The contrast was even greater felt when I was in the camp and they would deliver new prisoners. The new prisoners all have green faces – green faces because of the lack of fresh air, miserable food, and all that. The prisoners in the camps have more or less normal complexions. You find yourself among relatively free, relatively good-looking people.[21]

Over time, the apparent 'freedom' of this camp life usually palled. While in prison, wrote a Polish prisoner, Kazimierz Zarod, it was still possible to believe that a mistake had been made, that release would come soon. After all, 'we were still surrounded by the trappings of civilization – outside the walls of the prison there was a large town'. In the camp, however, he found himself milling freely about among a 'strange assortment of men ... all feelings of normality were suspended. As the days went by I was filled by a sort of panic which slowly turned into desperation. I tried to push the feeling down, back into the depths of consciousness, but slowly it began to dawn on me that I was caught up in a cynical act of injustice from which there appeared to be no escape ...'[22]

Worse, this freedom of movement could easily and quickly turn to anarchy. Guards and camp authorities were plentiful enough inside the *lagpunkt* during the day, but they often disappeared completely at night. One or two would remain within the *vakhta*, but the rest withdrew to the other side of the fence. Only when prisoners believed their lives were in danger did they sometimes turn to the guards in the *vakhta*. One memoirist recalls that in the aftermath of a brawl between political and criminal prisoners – a common phenomenon of the post-war period, as we shall see – the criminal losers 'ran to the *vakhta*', begging for help. They were sent away on a transport to another *lagpunkt* the following day, as the camp administration preferred to avoid mass murder.[23] Another woman, feeling herself in danger of rape and possibly murder at the hands of a criminal prisoner, 'turned herself in' to the *vakhta*, and asked to be placed in the camp punishment cell for the night for protection.[24]

The *vakhta* was not a reliable zone of safety, however. The guards residing within the guardhouse did not necessarily react to prisoners' requests. Informed of some outrage committed by one group of prisoners against the other, they were just as likely to laugh. There are records, in both official documents and memoirs, of armed guards ignoring or laughing off cases of murder, torture and rape among prisoners. Describing a gang rape that took place at one of the Kargopollag *lagpunkts* at night, Gustav Herling writes that the victim 'let out a short, throaty cry, full of tears and muffled by her skirt. A sleepy voice called from the watch-tower: "Come, come boys, what are you doing? Have you no shame?" The eight men pulled the girl behind the latrines, and continued.'[25]

In theory, the rules were strict: the prisoners were to stay inside the *zona*. In practice, the rules were broken. And behaviour that did not technically violate the rules, no matter how violent or harmful, was not necessarily punished.

Rezhim
Rules for Living

The *zona* controlled the prisoners' movement in space.[26] But it was the *rezhim* – or 'regime', as it is usually translated into English – that controlled their time. Put simply, the regime was the set of rules and procedures according to which the camp operated. If barbed wire limited a *zek*'s freedom of movement to the *zona*, a series of orders and sirens regulated the hours he spent there.

The regime differed in its severity from *lagpunkt* to *lagpunkt*, both according to shifting priorities and according to the type of prisoner being held in a particular camp. There were, at various times, light-regime camps for invalids, ordinary-regime camps, special-regime camps and punishment-regime camps. But the basic system remained the same. The regime determined when and how the prisoner should wake; how he should be marched to work; when and how he should receive food; when and for how long he should sleep.

In most camps, the prisoner's day officially began with the *razvod*: the procedure of organizing the prisoners into brigades and then marching them to work. A siren or other signal would awake them. A second siren warned them that breakfast was finished, and work was to begin. Prisoners then lined up in front of the camp gates for the morning count. Valery Frid, a scriptwriter for Soviet films and the author of an unusually lively memoir, has described the scene:

The brigades would organize themselves in front of the gate. The work-assigner would hold a narrow, smoothly planed signboard: on it would be written the number of the brigades, the number of workers (there were paper shortages, and the numbers could be scraped off the signboard with glass and rewritten the following day). The convoy guard and the work-assigner would check whether everyone was in place, and if they were – they would be taken off to work. If someone were missing, everyone would have to wait, while they searched for the shirker.[27]

According to instructions from Moscow, this wait was not meant to last more than fifteen minutes.[28] Of course, as Kazimierz Zarod writes, it often lasted much longer, bad weather notwithstanding:

By 3.30 a.m. we were supposed to be in the middle of the square, standing in ranks of five, waiting to be counted. The guards often made mistakes, and then there had to be a second count. On a morning when it was snowing this was a long, cold, agonizing process. If the guards were wide awake and concentrating, the count usually took about thirty minutes, but if they miscounted, we could stand for anything up to an hour.[29]

While this was happening, some camps took countermeasures to 'raise the prisoners' spirits'. Here is Frid again: 'Our *razvod* took place to the accompaniment of an accordion player. A prisoner, freed from all other work obligations, played cheerful melodies . . .'[30] Zarod also records the bizarre phenomenon of the morning band, composed of prisoner musicians, both professional and amateur:

Each morning, the 'band' stood near the gate playing military-style music and we were exhorted to march out 'strongly and happily' to our day's work. Having played until the end of the column had passed through the gate, the musicians abandoned their instruments and, tacking themselves on to the end of the column, joined the workers walking into the forest.[31]

From there, prisoners were marched to work. The guards shouted out the daily command – 'A step to the right, or a step to the left, will be considered an attempt to escape – The convoy will fire without warning – March!' – and the prisoners marched, still five abreast, to the workplace. If it was a great distance, they would be accompanied by guards and dogs. The procedure after the evening's return to camp was much the same. After an hour for supper, again prisoners were lined up in rows. And again, the guards counted (if the prisoners were lucky) and re-counted (if they were not). Moscow's instructions allotted more time for the evening count – thirty to forty minutes – presumably on the grounds that an escape from camp was more likely to have taken place from the work site.[32] Then another siren sounded, and it was time to sleep.

These rules and timetables were not written in stone. On the contrary, the regime changed over time, generally growing harsher. Jacques Rossi has written that 'the main trait of the Soviet penitentiary regime is its systematic intensification, gradual introduction of unadulterated, arbitrary sadism into the status of the law', and there is something to this.[33] Throughout the 1940s, the regime grew tighter, workdays grew longer, rest days became less frequent. In 1931, the prisoners of the Vaigach Expedition, a part of the Ukhtinskaya Expedition, worked six-hour days, in three shifts. Workers in the Kolyma region in the early 1930s also worked normal hours, fewer in winter and more in summer.[34] Within the decade, however, the working day had doubled in length. By the late 1930s, women at Elinor Olitskaya's sewing factory worked 'twelve hours in an unventilated hall', and the Kolyma workday had also been lengthened to twelve hours.[35] Later still, Olitskaya worked on a construction brigade: fourteen- to sixteen-hour days, with five-minute breaks at 10 a.m. and 4 p.m., and a one-hour lunch break at noon.[36]

Nor was she alone. In 1940, the Gulag's working day was officially extended to eleven hours, although even this was often violated.[37] In March 1942, the Moscow Gulag administration mailed a furious letter to all camp commanders, reminding them of the rule that 'prisoners must be allowed to sleep no less than eight hours'. Many camp commanders had ignored this rule, the letter explained, and had allowed their prisoners as little as four or five hours' sleep every night. As a result, the Gulag complained, 'prisoners are losing their ability to work, they are becoming "weak workers" and invalids'.[38]

Violations continued, particularly as production demands accelerated during the war years. In September 1942, after the German invasion, the Gulag's administration officially extended the working day for prisoners building airport facilities to twelve hours, with a one-hour break for lunch. The pattern was the same all over the USSR. Working days of sixteen hours were recorded in Vyatlag during the war.[39] Working days of twelve hours were recorded in Vorkuta in the summer of 1943, although these were reduced – probably because of the high rates of death and illness – to ten hours again in March 1944.[40] Sergei Bondarevsky, a prisoner in a wartime *sharashka*, one of the special laboratories for inmate scientists, also remembered working eleven-hour days, with breaks. On a typical day, he worked from 8 a.m. until 2 p.m., from 4 p.m. until 7 p.m., and then again from 8 p.m. until 10 p.m.[41]

In any case, the rules were often broken. One *zek*, assigned to a brigade panning gold in Kolyma, had to sift through 150 wheelbarrows a day. Those who had not finished that amount by the end of the workday simply remained until they had – sometimes as late as midnight. Afterwards they would go home, eat their soup, and be up at 5 a.m. to start work again.[42] The Norilsk camp administration applied a similar principle in the late 1940s, where another prisoner worked digging foundations for new buildings in the permafrost: 'At the end of twelve hours they would winch you out of the hole, but only if you had completed your work. If you hadn't, you were just left there.'[43]

Nor were many breaks usually granted during the day, as one wartime prisoner, assigned to work in a textile factory, later explained:

At six we had to be in the factory. At ten we had a five-minute break to smoke a cigarette, for which purpose we had to run to a cellar about two hundred yards away, the only place on the factory premises where this was permitted. Infringement of this regulation was punishable with two extra years' imprisonment. At one o'clock came a half-hour break for lunch. Small earthenware bowl in hand, one had to dash frantically to the canteen, stand in a long queue, receive some disgusting soya beans which disagreed with most people – and at all costs be back at the factory when the engines started working. After that, without leaving our places, we sat till seven in the evening.[44]

The number of days off work was also mandated by law. Ordinary prisoners were allowed to have one a week, those assigned to stricter regimes two per month. But these rules also varied in practice. As early as 1933, the Gulag administration in Moscow sent out an order reminding camp commanders of the importance of prisoners' rest days, many of which were being cancelled in the mad rush to fulfil the plan.[45] A decade later, hardly anything had changed. During the war, Kazimierz Zarod was given one day off out of ten.[46] Another recalled having one a month.[47] Gustav Herling remembered free days being even scarcer:

According to regulations, prisoners were entitled to one whole day's rest every ten days' work. But in practice, it transpired that even a monthly day off threatened to lower the camp's production output, and it had therefore become customary to announce ceremoniously the reward of a rest day whenever the camp had surpassed its production plan for the one particular quarter . . . Naturally we had no opportunity to inspect the output figures or the production plan, so that this convention was a fiction which in fact put us entirely at the mercy of the camp authorities.[48]

Even on their rare days off, it sometimes happened that prisoners were forced to do maintenance work within the camp, cleaning barracks, cleaning toilets, clearing snow in the winter.[49] All of which makes one order, issued by Lazar Kogan, the commander of Dmitlag, particularly poignant. Disturbed by the many reports of camp horses collapsing of exhaustion, Kogan began by noting that: 'The growing number of cases of illness and collapse of horses has several causes, including the overloading of horses, the difficult conditions of the roads, and the absence of full and complete rest time for horses to recover their strength.'

He then continued, issuing new instructions:

1. The workday of camp horses must not exceed ten hours, not counting the obligatory two-hour break for rest and food.
2. On average, horses must not walk more than 32 kilometres per day.

3. Horses must be allowed a regular rest day, every eighth day, and the rest on that day must be complete.[50]

Of the prisoners' need for a regular rest day every eighth day, there is, alas, no mention.

Baraki
Living Space

Most prisoners in most camps lived in barracks. Rare was the camp, however, whose barracks were constructed before the prisoners arrived. Those prisoners who had the bad luck to be sent to build a new camp lived in tents, or in nothing at all. As one prisoners' song put it:

> We drove quickly and fast across tundra
> When suddenly, the train came to a halt.
> Around us, only forest and mud –
> And here we will build the canal.[51]

Ivan Sulimov, a prisoner in Vorkuta in the 1930s, was dumped, along with a party of inmates, on 'a flat square of land in the polar tundra', and told to set up tents, build a bonfire, and begin construction of a 'fence of stone slabs, surrounded by barbed wire' as well as barracks.[52] Janusz Siemiński, a Polish prisoner in Kolyma after the war, was also once part of a team that constructed a new *lagpunkt* 'from zero', in the depths of winter. At night, prisoners slept on the ground. Many died, particularly those who lost the battle to sleep near the fire.[53] Prisoners arriving in the Prikaspiisky camp in Azerbaijan in December 1940 also slept, in the words of an annoyed NKVD inspector, 'beneath the open sky on damp ground'.[54] Nor were such situations necessarily temporary. As late as 1955, prisoners in some camps were still living in tents.[55]

If and when the prisoners did build barracks, they were invariably extremely simple buildings, made of wood. Moscow dictated their design and, as a result, descriptions of them are rather repetitive: prisoner after prisoner describes long, rectangular, wooden buildings, the walls unplastered, the cracks stopped up with mud, the inside space filled with rows and rows of equally poorly made bunk-beds. Sometimes there was a crude table, sometimes not. Sometimes there were benches to sit on, sometimes not.[56] In Kolyma, and in other regions where wood was scarce, the prisoners built barracks, equally cheaply and hastily, of stone. Where insulation was not available, older methods were used. Photographs of the barracks in Vorkuta, taken in the winter of 1945, make them look almost invisible: their roofs had been built at sharp angles but very low to the ground, so the snow accumulating around them would help insulate them from cold.[57]

Often, barracks were not proper buildings at all, but rather *zemlyanki*, or 'earth dugouts'. A. P. Evstonichev lived in one in Karelia, in the early 1940s:

A *zemlyanka* – it was a space cleaned of snow, with the upper layer of earth removed. The walls and roof were made of round, rough logs. The whole structure was covered with another layer of earth and snow. The entrance to the dugout was decked out with a canvas door. . . in one corner stood a barrel of water. In the middle stood a metal stove, complete with a metal pipe leading out through the roof, and a barrel of kerosene.[58]

In the temporary *lagpunkts* constructed alongside the building sites of roads and railways, *zemlyanki* were ubiquitous. As discussed in Chapter 5, their traces still line the prisoner-built roads of the far north today, as well as the river banks near the older sections of the city of Vorkuta. Sometimes prisoners lived in tents as well. One memoir of the early days of Vorkutlag describes the construction, in the course of three days, of 'fifteen tents with three-level bunk-beds' for 100 prisoners apiece, as well as a *zona* with four watchtowers and a barbed-wire fence.[59]

But the real barracks rarely lived up to the low standards that Moscow had set for them either. They were almost always terribly overcrowded, even after the chaos of the late 1930s had subsided. An inspection report of twenty-three camps, written in 1948, noted angrily that in most of them 'prisoners have no more than one to one and a half metres of living space per person', and even that was in an unsanitary condition: 'prisoners do not have their own places to sleep, or their own sheets and blankets'.[60] Sometimes there was even less space than that. Margarete Buber-Neumann records that on her arrival in camp, there was actually no sleeping space at all within the barracks, and she was forced to spend the first few nights on the floor of the washroom.[61]

Ordinary prisoners were meant to be given beds known as *vagonki*, a name taken from the beds found on the wagons of passenger trains. These were double-decker bunks, with room for two inmates at each level, four inmates in all. In many camps, prisoners slept on the even less sophisticated *sploshnye nary*. These were long wooden sleeping shelves, not even partitioned into separate bunks. Prisoners assigned to them simply lay down beside one another, in a long row. Because these communal beds were considered un-hygienic, camp inspectors constantly inveighed against them too. In 1948, the central Gulag administration issued a directive demanding that they all be replaced by *vagonki*.[62] Nevertheless, Anna Andreevna, a prisoner in Mordovia in the late 1940s and early 1950s, slept on *sploshnye nary*, and remembers that many prisoners still slept on the floor beneath them too.[63]

Bedding was also arbitrary, and varied greatly from camp to camp, despite further strict (and rather modest) rules issued in Moscow. Regulations stated that all prisoners should have a new towel every year, a pillowcase every four years, sheets every two years, and a blanket every five years.[64] In practice, 'a so-called straw mattress went with each prisoner's bed', wrote Elinor Lipper:

In the barracks: inmates listening to a prisoner musician – a drawing
by Beniamin Mkrtchyan, Ivdel, 1953

There was no straw in it and rarely hay, because there was not enough hay for the
cattle; instead it contained wood shavings or extra clothes, if a prisoner still owned
any extra clothes. In addition, there was a woollen blanket and pillowcase which you
could stuff with whatever you had, for there were no pillows.[65]

Others had nothing at all. As late as 1950, Isaak Filshtinsky, an Arabic
specialist arrested in 1948, was still sleeping beneath his coat in Kargopollag,
with spare rags for pillows.[66]

The 1948 directive also called for all earthen floors in barracks to be
replaced by wooden floors. But as late as the 1950s, Irena Arginskaya lived
in a barrack whose floor could not be cleaned properly as it was made of
clay.[67] Even if floors were wooden, they could often not be cleaned properly

for lack of brushes. Describing her experiences to a post-war commission, one Polish woman explained that in her camp, a group of prisoners were always put 'on duty' at night, cleaning up the barracks and lavatories while others slept: 'The mud on the barrack floor had to be scraped off with knives. The Russian women were frantic at our being unable to do it, and asked us how we had lived at home. It did not even occur to them that the dirtiest floor can be scrubbed with a brush.'[68]

Heating and light were often equally primitive, but again this varied greatly from camp to camp. One prisoner remembered the barracks being virtually dark: 'the electric lamps shone yellow-white, barely noticeable, and the kerosene lamps smoked and smelled rancid'.[69] Others complained of the opposite problem, that the lights were usually on all night.[70] Some prisoners in the camps of the Vorkuta region had no problem with heat, since they could bring lumps of coal home from the mines, but Susanna Pechora, in a *lagpunkt* near the coal mines of Inta, remembered that inside the barracks it was 'so cold in the winter that your hair freezes to the bed, the drinking water freezes in the cup'.[71] There was no running water in her barracks either, just water brought into the barracks in buckets by the *dezhurnaya* – an older woman, no longer capable of heavier work – who cleaned and looked after the barracks during the day.[72]

Worse, a 'terrible heavy smell' pervaded the barracks, thanks to the huge quantities of dirty and mildewed clothes drying along the edge of the bunks, the tables, anywhere it was possible to hang something. In those barracks in the special camps where the doors were closed at night and the windows barred, the stench made it 'almost impossible to breathe'.[73]

The air quality was not improved by the absence of toilets. In camps where prisoners were locked into their barracks at night, *zeks* had to make use of a *parasha*, or 'bucket', just as in prison. One prisoner wrote that in the morning the *parasha* was 'impossible to carry, so it was dragged along across the slippery floor. The contents invariably spilled out.'[74] Another, Galina Smirnova, arrested in the early 1950s, remembered that 'if it was something serious, you waited until morning, otherwise there was a terrible stench'.[75]

Otherwise, toilets were outhouses, and outhouses were outside the barracks, often some distance away, which was a serious hardship in the winter cold. 'There were wooden outdoor toilets,' said Smirnova of another camp, 'even when it was 30 or 40 degrees below zero.'[76] Thomas Sgovio wrote of the consequences:

Outside, in front of each barrack, they stuck a wooden pole and froze it to the ground. Another decree! We were forbidden to urinate anywhere on camp grounds other than the outhouses or on the pole with a white rag tied to the top. Anyone caught violating the decree would be sentenced to ten nights in the penal cell . . . The decree was issued because at night there were prisoners who, unwilling to walk the long distance to the outhouses, urinated instead all over the well-beaten snow paths. The grounds were littered with yellow spots. When the snow melted in late spring, there would be a terrible stench ... twice a month we chopped the frozen pyramids and carted the frozen pieces out of the zone ...'[77]

But filth and overcrowding were not merely aesthetic problems, or matters of relatively minor discomfort. The crowded bunks and the lack of space could also be lethal, particularly in camps that worked on a 24-hour schedule. In one such camp, where the prisoners worked three separate shifts, day and night, one memoirist wrote that 'people were asleep in the barracks at any time of the day. Fighting to be able to sleep was a fight for life. Arguing over sleep, people swore at one another, fought one another, even killed one another. The radio in the barracks was on at full strength at all times, and was much hated.'[78]

Precisely because the question of where one slept was so crucial, sleeping conditions were always an extremely important tool of prisoner control, and the camp administration consciously used them as such. In their central archives in Moscow, the Gulag's archivists carefully preserved photographs of different types of barracks, intended for different types of prisoners. The barracks of the *otlichniki* – the 'excellent ones' or 'shock-workers' – have single beds with mattresses and blankets, wooden floors and pictures on the walls. The prisoners are, if not exactly smiling for the photographers, then at least reading newspapers and looking well fed. The *rezhim* barracks, on the other hand – the punishment barracks for poor or unruly workers – have wooden planks on crude wooden pegs instead of beds. Even in these photographs, taken for propaganda purposes, the *rezhim* prisoners have no mattresses, and are shown sharing blankets.[79]

In some camps, the etiquette surrounding sleeping arrangements became quite elaborate. Space was at such a premium that the possession of space, and of privacy, were considered great privileges, accorded only to those who ranked among the camp's aristocracy. Higher-ranking prisoners – brigade leaders, norm-setters, and others – were often permitted to sleep in smaller barracks, with fewer people. Solzhenitsyn, initially assigned the job of 'works manager' upon his arrival at a camp in Moscow, was given a place in a barracks where

instead of multiple bunks there were ordinary cots and one bed table for every two persons, not for a whole brigade. During the day the door was locked and you could leave your things there. Last, there was a half-legal electric hot plate, and it was not necessary to go and crowd around the big common stove in the yard.[80]

This was all considered high luxury. Certain, more desirable jobs – that of a carpenter, or a tool repairman – also came with the much sought-after right to sleep in the workshop. Anna Rozina slept in the cobbler's workshop when she worked as a cobbler in the Temnikovsky camp, and had the 'right' to go to the baths more often as well, all of which counted as great privileges.[81]

In almost every camp, doctors, even prisoner doctors, were also allowed to sleep separately, a privilege which reflected their special status. Isaac Vogelfanger, a surgeon, felt himself privileged because he was allowed to sleep in a bunk-bed in a 'small room adjacent to the reception area' of his camp's infirmary: 'the moon seemed to be smiling upon me as I went to sleep'. Along with him slept the camp's *feldsher*, or 'medical assistant', who had the same privilege.[82]

Sometimes, special living conditions were arranged for invalids. The actress Tatyana Okunevskaya managed to get sent to an invalid's camp in Lithuania, where 'the barracks were long, with many windows, light, clean, and no upper bunks above your head'.[83] The prisoners sent to work on Beria's *sharashki* – the 'special bureaus' for talented engineers and technicians – received the best sleeping quarters of all. In Bolshevo, a *sharashka* just outside of Moscow, barracks were 'large, light, clean and heated by Dutch ovens' rather than metal stoves. The beds had linen and pillows, the light was turned off at night, and there was a private shower.[84] Prisoners who lived in these special quarters knew, of course, that they could easily be taken away, which enhanced their interest in working hard.

Informally, there was often another hierarchy at work within barracks as well. In most barracks, the critical decisions about who slept where were taken by those groups in the camps that were the strongest and most united. Until the late 1940s, when the big national groups – the Ukrainians, Balts, Chechens, Poles – grew stronger, the best-organized prisoners were usually the convicted criminals, as we shall see. As a rule, they therefore slept in the top bunks, where there was better air and more space, clubbing and kicking those who objected. Those who slept on the lower bunks had less clout. Those who slept on the floor – the lowest-ranking prisoners in the camp – suffered most, remembered one prisoner:

This level was called the '*kolkhoz* sector', and it was to this level that the thieves forced the *kolkhoznik* – various aged intellectuals and priests, that is, and even some of their own, who had broken the thieves' moral code. On to them fell not only things from the upper and lower bunks: the thieves also poured slops, water, yesterday's soup. And the *kolkhoz* sector had to tolerate all of this, for if they complained they would receive even more filth . . . people became sick, suffocated, lost consciousness, went crazy, died of typhus, dysentery, killed themselves.[85]

Prisoners, even political prisoners, could nevertheless better their circumstances. While working as a *feldsher*, an assistant doctor, Karol Colonna-Czosnowski, a Polish political prisoner, was picked out of an extremely crowded barrack by Grisha, the criminal 'boss' of the camp: 'He gave a majestic kick to one of his courtiers who took it for an order to make room for me and promptly abandoned his seat. I was embarrassed and protested that I would rather not sit so near the fire, but this was not in conformity with my host's wishes, as I discovered when one of Grisha's followers gave me a mighty push.' When he had regained his balance, he found himself sitting on the couch at Grisha's feet: 'This was, apparently, where he wanted me to remain . . .'[86] Colonna-Czosnowski did not argue. Even for a few hours, where one sat, or laid one's head, mattered intensely.

Banya
The Bath-House

Dirt, crowding and poor hygiene led to a plague of bedbugs and lice. In the 1930s, a 'humorous' cartoon in *Perekovka*, the newspaper of the Moscow–Volga Canal, featured a *zek* being handed new clothes. Beneath was the caption, 'They give you "clean" clothes, but they are full of lice.' Another was captioned 'And while you sleep in the barracks, the bedbugs bite like black crabs.'[87] Nor did the problem lessen over the years. One Polish prisoner records that, during the war, his camp acquaintance became obsessed with them: 'As a biologist, he was interested in how many lice could subsist on a certain space. Counting them on his shirt he found sixty, and an hour later another sixty.'[88]

By the 1940s, the Gulag's masters had long recognized the lethal danger of louse-borne typhus and, officially, conducted a constant battle against parasites. Baths were supposedly mandatory every ten days. All clothing was supposed to be boiled in disinfection units, both on entering the camp and then at regular intervals, to destroy all vermin.[89] As we have seen, camp barbers shaved the entire bodies of both men and women on entry into the camps, and their heads regularly thereafter. Soap, albeit tiny amounts of it, was regularly included in lists of products to be distributed to prisoners: in 1944, for example, this amounted to 200 grams per month, per prisoner. Women, prisoners' children and prisoners in hospitals were allotted an extra 50 grams, juveniles received an extra 100 grams, and prisoners working at 'especially dirty jobs' received an extra 200 grams. These tiny slivers were meant both for personal hygiene and for the washing of linen and clothes.[90] (Soap did not become any less scarce, inside or outside the camps. As late as 1991, Soviet coal-miners went on strike because, among other things, they had no soap.)

Nevertheless, not everyone was convinced of the efficacy of the camp's delousing procedures. In practice, wrote one prisoner, 'the baths seemed to increase the lice's sexual vigour'.[91] Varlam Shalamov went further: 'Not only was the delousing absolutely useless, no lice are killed by this disinfection chamber. It's only a formality and the apparatus has been created for the purpose of tormenting the convict still more.'[92]

Technically, Shalamov was wrong. The apparatus was not created for the purpose of tormenting convicts – as I say, the Gulag's central administration in Moscow really did write very strict directives, instructing camp commanders to do battle against parasites, and countless inspection reports inveigh against their failure to do so. A 1933 account of the conditions in Dmitlag angrily complains about the women's barracks, which were 'dirty, lacking sheets and blankets; the women complain of a massive quantity of bedbugs, which the Sanitation Division is not fighting against'.[93] A 1940 investigation into the conditions at one group of northern camps furiously described 'lice in the barracks, and bedbugs, which have a negative impact on the prisoners' ability to rest' at one *lagpunkt*, while the Novosibirsk corrective labour camp had '100 per cent lice infection among prisoners . . . as a result of poor sanitary conditions, there is a high level of skin diseases and stomach ailments . . . from this it is clear that the unsanitary conditions of the camp are very, very costly'.

Meanwhile, typhus had broken out twice at another *lagpunkt*, while in others, prisoners were 'black with dirt', the report continued with great agitation.[94] Complaints about lice, and angry orders to eliminate them, figure year in and year out in the inspection reports submitted by Gulag prosecutors.[95] After one typhus epidemic at Temlag in 1937, both the head of the *lagpunkt* and the deputy of the camp medical department were fired, accused of 'criminal negligence and inactivity', and put on trial.[96] Reward was used as well as punishment: in 1933, the inhabitants of one prisoners' barrack in Dmitlag received holidays from work as a prize for having cleared all of their beds of bedbugs.[97]

Prisoners' refusal to bathe was also taken very seriously. Irena Arginskaya, who was in a special camp for politicals at Kengir in the early 1950s, recalled a particular women's religious sect in the camp which refused, for reasons known only to itself, to bathe:

One day I had remained in the barracks because I was ill, and had been let off work. A guard came in, however, and told us that all of the sick prisoners would have to help wash the 'nuns'. The scene was as follows: a wagon pulled up to their section of the barracks, and we had to carry them out and put them on the wagon. They protested, kicked us and hit us, and so on. But when we finally got them on the wagon they lay quietly, and didn't try to escape. Then we pulled the wagon to the baths, where we took them off and carried them inside, undressed them – and then understood why the camp administration couldn't allow them not to bathe. As you took their clothes off, lice fell off them in handfuls. Then we put them under water, and washed them. Meanwhile, their clothes were boiled to kill the lice . . .[98]

Arginskaya also remembers that 'in principle it was possible to go to the baths as much as you wanted' in Kengir, where there were no restrictions on water. Similarly, Leonid Sitko, a former prisoner of war in Germany, reckoned that Soviet camps had fewer lice than German camps. He spent time in both Steplag and Minlag, where 'you could bathe as much as you wanted . . . you could even wash your clothes'.[99] Certain factories and work sites had their own showers, as Isaak Filshtinsky found in Kargopollag, where prisoners could use them during the day, even though other prisoners suffered from lack of water.[100]

Yet Shalamov was not entirely wrong either in his cynical description of the hygiene system. For even if they were instructed to take bathing seriously, it often happened that local camp administrators merely observed the rituals of delousing and bathing, without appearing to care much about the result. Either there was not enough coal to keep the disinfection apparatus hot enough; or those in charge could not be bothered to do it properly; or there were no soap rations issued for months on end; or the rations were stolen. At the Dizelny *lagpunkt* in Kolyma, on bath days they 'gave every prisoner a small sliver of soap and a large mug of warm water. They poured five or six of these mugs into a tub, and that sufficed for everyone, for the washing and rinsing of five or six people.' At the Sopka *lagpunkt*, 'water was brought there, like other freight, along the narrow railway and narrow road. In the winter they got it from snow, although there wasn't much snow there, the wind blew it away . . . Workers came back from the mine covered in dust, and there were no sinks to wash in.'[101]

Frequently, guards were bored by the process of bathing the prisoners, and allowed them only a few minutes in the baths, for formality's sake.[102] At a Siblag *lagpunkt* in 1941, an outraged inspector found that 'prisoners have not bathed for two months', thanks to the sheer disinterest of the guards.[103] And in the worst camps, open neglect of the prisoners' humanity did indeed make bathing a torture. Many describe the awfulness of bathing, but none quite so well as, again, Shalamov, who devotes an entire short story to the horrors of the baths of Kolyma. Despite their exhaustion, prisoners would have to wait for hours to take their turn: 'Bath-house sessions are arranged either before or after work. After many hours of work in the cold (and it's no easier in the summer) when all thoughts and hopes are concentrated on the desire to reach one's bunk and food so as to fall asleep as soon as possible, the bath-house delay is almost unendurable.'

First, the *zeks* would stand in lines, outside in the cold; then they would be herded into crowded dressing rooms, built for fifteen people and containing up to a hundred. All the while they knew that their barracks were being cleaned and searched. Their meagre possessions, including crockery and footrags, were being tossed into the snow:

It is characteristic of man, be he beggar or Nobel laureate, that he quickly acquires petty things. The same is true of the convict. He is, after all, a working man and needs a needle and material for patches, and an extra bowl perhaps. All this is cast out and then re-accumulated after each bath-house day, unless it is buried somewhere deep in the snow.

Once inside the baths themselves, there was often so little water that it was impossible to get clean. Prisoners were given 'a wooden basin with not very hot water . . . there is no extra water and no one can buy any'. Nor were the bath-houses heated: 'The feeling of cold is increased by a thousand draughts from under the doors, from the cracks. The baths were not fully heated; they had cracks in the walls.' Inside, there is also 'constant uproar accompanied by smoke, crowding, and shouting; there's even a common turn of speech: "to shout as in the bath-house" '.[104]

Thomas Sgovio also describes this hellish scene, writing that prisoners in Kolyma sometimes had to be beaten in order to make them go to the baths:

The waiting outside in the frost for those inside to come out – then came the changing room where it was cold – the compulsory disinfections and fumigating process where we tossed our rags in a heap – you never got your own back – the fighting and swearing, 'you son-of-a-bitch that's my jacket' – selecting the damp, collective underwear filled with lice eggs in the seams – the shaving of hairs on the body by the Camp Barber . . . then, when it was finally our turn to enter the washing room, we picked up a wooden tub, received a cup of hot water, a cup of cold water, and a small piece of black, evil-smelling soap . . .[105]

Then, after it was all over, the same humiliating process of handing out clothes began all over again, wrote Shalamov, ever-obsessive on the issue of underwear: 'Having washed themselves, the men gather at the window far in advance of the actual distribution of underwear. Over and over again they discuss in detail the underwear they received last time, the underwear received five years ago in Bamlag . . .'[106]

Inevitably, the right to bathe in relative comfort also became intimately intertwined with the system of privilege. In Temlag, for example, those employed in particular jobs had the right to bathe more often.[107] The very job of bath-house worker, which implied both proximity to clean water and the right to allow or deny others such proximity, was usually one of the most sought-after jobs in the camp. In the end, despite the strictest, severest and most drastic orders from Moscow, prisoners' comfort, hygiene and health were completely dependent on local whims and circumstances.

Thus was another aspect of ordinary life turned inside out, turned from a simple pleasure into what Shalamov calls 'a negative event, a burden in the convict's life . . . a testimony of that shift of values which is the main quality that the camp instils in its inmates . . .'[108]

Stolovaya
The Dining Hall

The vast Gulag literature contains many varied descriptions of camps, and reflects the experiences of a wide range of personalities. But one aspect of camp life remains consistent from camp to camp, from year to year, from memoir to memoir: the descriptions of the *balanda*, the soup that prisoners were served once or sometimes twice a day.

Universally, former prisoners agree that the taste of the daily or twice-daily half-litre of prison soup was revolting: its consistency was watery, and its contents were suspect. Galina Levinson wrote that it was made 'from spoiled cabbage and potatoes, sometimes with a piece of pig fat, sometimes with herring heads'.[109] Barbara Armonas remembered soup made from 'fish or animal lungs and a few potatoes'.[110] Leonid Sitko described the soup as 'never having any meat in it at all'.[111]

Another prisoner remembered soup made from dog meat, which one of his co-workers, a Frenchman, could not eat: 'a man from Western countries is not always able to cross a psychological barrier, even when he is starving', he concluded.[112] Even Lazar Kogan, the boss of Dmitlag, once complained that 'Some cooks act as if they were not preparing Soviet meals, but rather pig slops. Thanks to this attitude, the food they prepare is unsuitable, and often tasteless and bland.'[113]

Hunger was a powerful motivator nevertheless: the soup might have been inedible under normal circumstances, but in the camps, where most people were always hungry, prisoners ate it with relish. Nor was their hunger accidental: prisoners were kept hungry, because regulation of prisoners' food was, after regulation of prisoners' time and living space, the camp administration's most important tool of control.

For that reason, the distribution of food to prisoners in camps grew into quite an elaborate science. The exact norms for particular categories of prisoners and camp workers were set in Moscow, and frequently changed. The Gulag administration constantly fine-tuned its figures, calculating and recalculating the minimum quantity of food necessary for prisoners to continue working. New orders listing ration levels were issued to camp commanders with great frequency. These ultimately became long, complex documents, written in heavy, bureaucratic language.

Typical, for example, was the Gulag administration's order on rations, issued on 30 October 1944. The orders stipulated one 'guaranteed' or basic norm for most prisoners: 550 grams of bread per day, 8 grams of sugar, and a collection of other products theoretically intended for use in the *balanda*, the midday soup, and in the *kasha*, or 'porridge', served for breakfast and supper: 75 grams of buckwheat or noodles, 15 grams of meat

In the camp kitchen: prisoners lining up for soup – a drawing
by Ivan Sukhanov, Temirtau, 1935–7

or meat products, 55 grams of fish or fish products, 10 grams of fat, 500 grams of potato or vegetable, 15 grams of salt and 2 grams of 'surrogate tea'.

To this list of products, some notes were appended. Camp commanders were instructed to lower the bread ration of those prisoners meeting only 75 per cent of the norm by 50 grams, and for those meeting only 50 per cent of the norm by 100 grams. Those overfulfilling the plan, on the other hand, received an extra 50 grams of buckwheat, 25 grams of meat and 25 grams of fish, among other things.[114]

By comparison, camp guards in 1942 – a much hungrier year throughout the USSR – were meant to receive 700 grams of bread, nearly a kilo of fresh vegetables and 75 grams of meat, with special supplements for those living high above sea level.[115] Prisoners working in the *sharashki* during the war were even better fed, receiving, in theory, 800 grams of bread and 50 grams of meat as opposed to the 15 granted to normal prisoners. In addition, they received fifteen cigarettes per day, and matches.[116] Pregnant women, juvenile prisoners, prisoners of war, free workers and children resident in camp nurseries received slightly better rations.[117]

Some camps experimented with even finer tuning. In July 1933, Dmitlag issued an order listing different rations for prisoners who fulfilled up to 79 per cent of the norm; 80–89 per cent of the norm; 90–99 per cent of the norm; 100–109 per cent of the norm; 110–124 per cent of the norm; and 125 per cent and higher.[118]

As one might imagine, the need to distribute these precise amounts of food to the right people in the right quantities – quantities which sometimes varied daily – required a vast bureaucracy, and many camps found it difficult to cope. They had to keep whole files full of instructions on hand, enumerating which prisoners in which situation were to receive what. Even the smallest *lagpunkts* kept copious records, listing the daily norm-fulfilments of each prisoner, and the amount of food due as a result. In the small *lagpunkt* of Kedrovy Shor, for example – a collective farm division of Intlag – there were, in 1943, at least thirteen different food norms. The camp accountant – probably a prisoner – had to determine which norm each of the camp's 1,000 inmates should receive. On long sheets of paper, he first drew lines by hand, in pencil, and then added the names and numbers, in pen, covering page after page after page with his calculations.[119]

In larger camps, the bureaucracy was even worse. The Gulag's former chief accountant, A. S. Narinsky, has described how the administrators of one camp, engaged in building one of the far northern railway lines, hit on the idea of distributing food tickets to prisoners, in order to ensure that they received the correct rations every days. But even getting hold of tickets was difficult in a system plagued by chronic paper shortages. Unable to find a better solution, they decided to use bus tickets, which took three days to arrive. This problem 'constantly threatened to disorganize the entire feeding system'.[120]

Transporting food in winter to distant *lagpunkts* was also a problem, particularly for those camps without their own bakeries. 'Even bread which was still warm,' writes Narinsky, 'when transported in a goods car for 400 kilometres in 50 degrees of frost became so frozen that it was unusable not only for human consumption, but even for fuel.'[121] Despite the distribution of complex instructions for storing the scant vegetables and potatoes in the north during the winter, large quantities froze and became inedible. In the summer, by contrast, meat and fish went bad, and other foods spoiled. Badly managed warehouses burned to the ground, or filled with rats.[122]

Many camps founded their own *kolkhoz*, or 'collective farm', or dairy *lagpunkts*, but these too often worked badly. One report on a camp *kolkhoz* listed, among its other problems, the lack of technically trained personnel, the lack of spare parts for the tractor, the lack of a barn for the dairy cattle, and the lack of preparation for the harvest season.[123]

As a result, prisoners were almost always vitamin-deficient, even when they were not actually starving, a problem the camp officials took more or less seriously. In the absence of actual vitamin tablets, many forced prisoners to drink *khvoya*, a foul-tasting brew made out of pine needles and of dubious efficacy.[124] By way of comparison, the norms for 'officers of the armed forces' expressly stipulated vitamin C and dried fruit to compensate for the lack of vitamins in the regular rations. Generals and admirals were, in addition, officially able to receive cheese, caviar, canned fish and eggs.[125]

Even the very process of handing out soup, with or without vitamins, could be difficult in the cold of a far northern winter, particularly if it was being served at noon, at the work site. In 1939, a Kolyma doctor actually filed a formal complaint to the camp boss, pointing out that prisoners were being made to eat their food outdoors, and that it froze while it was being eaten.[126] Overcrowding was a problem for food distribution too: one prisoner remembered that in the *lagpunkt* adjacent to the Maldyak mine in Magadan, there was one serving window for more than 700 people.[127]

Food distribution could also be disrupted by events outside the camps: during the Second World War, for example, it often ceased altogether. The worst years were 1942 and 1943, when much of the western USSR was occupied by German troops, and much of the rest of the country was pre-occupied fighting them. Hunger was rife across the country – and the Gulag was not a high priority. Vladimir Petrov, a prisoner in Kolyma, recalls a period of five days without any food deliveries in his camp: 'real famine set in at the mine. Five thousand men did not have a piece of bread.'

Cutlery and crockery were constantly lacking too. Petrov, again, writes that 'soup still warm when received would become covered with ice during the period of time one man would wait for a spoon from another who had finished with one. This probably explained why the majority of the men preferred to eat without spoons.'[128] Another prisoner believed that she had remained alive because she 'traded bread for a half-litre enamel bowl . . . If you have your own bowl, you get the first portions – and the fat is all on the top. The others have to wait until your bowl is free. You eat, then give it to another, who gives it to another . . .'[129]

Other prisoners made their own bowls and cutlery out of wood. The small museum housed in the headquarters of Memorial in Moscow displays a number of these strangely moving items.[130] As ever, the central Gulag administration was fully aware of these shortages, and occasionally tried to do something about them: the authorities at one point complimented one camp for making clever use of its leftover tin cans for precisely this purpose.[131] But even when crockery and cutlery existed, there was often no way to clean it: one Dmitlag order 'categorically' forbade camp cooks from distributing food in dirty dishes.[132]

For all of these reasons, the food ration regulations issued in Moscow –

already calculated to the minimum level required for survival – are not a reliable guide to what prisoners actually ate. Nor do we need to rely solely on prisoners' memoirs to know that Soviet camp inmates were very hungry. The Gulag itself conducted periodic inspections of its camps, and kept records of what prisoners were actually eating, as opposed to what they were supposed to be eating. Again, the surreal gap between the neat lists of food rations drawn up in Moscow and the inspectors' reports is startling.

The investigation of the camp at Volgostroi in 1942, for example, noted that at one *lagpunkt*, there were eighty cases of pellagra, a disease of malnutrition: 'people are dying of starvation', the report noted bluntly. At Siblag, a large camp in western Siberia, a Soviet deputy prosecutor found that in the first quarter of 1941, food norms had been 'systematically violated: meat, fish and fats are distributed extremely rarely . . . sugar is not distributed at all'. In the Sverdlovsk region in 1942, the food in camps contained 'no fats, no fish or meat, and often no vegetables'. In Vyatlag in 1942, 'the food in July was poor, nearly inedible, and lacking in vitamins. This is because of the lack of fats, meat, fish, potatoes . . . all of the food is based on flour and grain products.'[133]

Some prisoners, it seems, were deprived of food because the camp had not received the right deliveries. This was a permanent problem: in Kedrovy Shor, the *lagpunkt* accountants kept a list of all food products which could be substituted for those that prisoners should have received but did not. These included not only cheese for milk, but also dried crackers for bread, wild mushrooms for meat, and wild berries for sugar.[134] It was hardly surprising that, as a result, the prisoners' diet looked quite different from how it did on paper in Moscow. An inspection of Birlag in 1940 determined that 'the entire lunch for working *zeks* consists of water, plus 130 grams of grain, and that the second course is black bread, about 100 grams. For breakfast and supper they reheat the same sort of soup.' In conversation with the camp cook, the inspector was also told that the 'theoretical norms are never fulfilled', that there were no deliveries of fish, meat, vegetables or fats. The camp, concluded the report, 'doesn't have money to buy food products or clothing . . . and without money not one supply organization wants to co-operate'. More than 500 cases of scurvy were reported as a result.[135]

Just as frequently, however, food arrived in a camp only to be stolen immediately. Thieving took place at just about every level. Usually, food was stolen while it was being prepared, by those working in the kitchen or food storage facilities. For that reason, prisoners sought out jobs which gave them access to food – cooking, dishwashing, work in storage warehouses – in order to be able to steal. Evgeniya Ginzburg was once 'saved' by a job washing dishes in the men's dining hall. Not only was she able to eat 'real meat broth and excellent dumplings fried in sunflower-seed oil', but she also found that other prisoners stood in awe of her. Speaking to her, one man's voice trembled, 'from a mixture of acute envy and humble adoration of anyone who occupied such an exalted position in life – "where the food is!"'.[136]

Even jobs harvesting crops on camp farms or peeling potatoes were very desirable, and prisoners paid bribes to obtain them, simply to be in a position to steal food. Later in her camp career, Ginzburg also worked tending the chickens that would be eaten by the camp bosses. She and her co-worker took full advantage of the situation: 'we smothered the camp semolina with cod-liver oil that we "borrowed" from the chickens. We boiled up oatmeal jelly. We also had three eggs daily between us – one in the soup, and one each to be eaten raw as a special gastronomic treat. (We took no more because we dared not lower the egg productivity index, by which our work was judged.).'[137]

Theft also took place on a much grander scale, particularly in the camp towns of the far north, where food shortages among free workers and camp guards as well as prisoners made it worth everybody's while to steal. Every camp filed reports every year of lost property. Those of the Kedrovy Shor *lagpunkt* show losses of goods and money of more than 20,000 roubles for the fourth quarter of 1944 alone.[138]

On a national scale, the numbers went much higher. A prosecutors' office report for 1947, for example, lists many cases of theft, among them one in Vyatlag, where twelve people, including the head of the camp warehouse, helped themselves to 170,000 roubles worth of food products and vegetables. Another report of that year calculated that in thirty-four camps investigated in the second quarter of 1946 alone, a total of 70,000 kilograms of bread had been stolen, along with 132,000 kilograms of potatoes and 17,000 kilograms of meat. The inspector writing the report concluded that 'the complicated system of feeding prisoners creates the conditions for the easy theft of bread and other products'. He also blamed the 'system of feeding free workers with ration cards', as well as the internal camp inspection teams, whose members were thoroughly corrupt too.[139]

In some cases the inspection system did make an impact: some camps, fearing trouble, made an effort to fulfil the letter if not the spirit of the law. One camp inmate, for example, received a half-glass of sugar at the end of each month, which he ate raw. This was how his camp's boss ensured he received the amount stipulated by the Moscow bureaucracy. He and his fellow prisoners celebrated the occasion as 'sugar day'.[140]

In the end, not everybody starved. For even if most food products disappeared before they made it into the soup, one staple food was usually available: bread. Like soup, the bread of the Gulag has been described many times. Sometimes it is remembered as badly baked: one prisoner remembered it being so hard it 'resembled a brick', and so small it could be eaten 'in two bites'.[141] Another wrote that it was 'literally "black" bread because the bran left in it coloured the bread black and made the texture coarse'.[142] He also noted that it was baked with a great deal of water, so that it was 'wet and weighed heavy, so that in actual fact we received less than our allotted 700 grams'.

Others recalled that prisoners fought over the drier, less watery ends of the loaves.[143] In Shalamov's short story 'Cherry Brandy', a fictive description of the death of Osip Mandelstam, the poet's approaching death is signalled by his loss of interest in such matters: 'He no longer watched for the heel of the loaf or cried when he didn't get it. He didn't stuff the bread into his mouth with trembling fingers.'[144]

In the hungrier camps, in the hungrier years, bread took on an almost sacred status, and a special etiquette grew up around its consumption. While camp thieves stole almost everything else with impunity, for example, the theft of bread was considered particularly heinous and unforgivable. Vladimir Petrov found on his long train journey to Kolyma that 'thieving was permitted and could be applied to anything within the thief's capacity and luck, but there was one exception – bread. Bread was sacred and inviolable, regardless of any distinctions in the population of the car.' Petrov had in fact been chosen as the *starosta* of the car, and in that capacity was charged with beating up a petty thief who had stolen bread. He duly did so.[145] Thomas Sgovio also wrote that the unwritten law of the camp criminals in Kolyma was: 'Steal anything – excepting the holy bread portion.' He too had 'seen more than one prisoner beaten to death for violating the sacred tradition'.[146] Similarly, Kazimierz Zarod remembered that

If a prisoner stole clothes, tobacco, or almost anything else and was discovered, he could expect a beating from his fellow prisoners, but the unwritten law of the camp – and I have heard from men from other camps that it was the same everywhere – was that a prisoner caught stealing another's bread earned a death sentence.[147]

In his memoirs, Dmitri Panin, a close friend of Solzhenitsyn, described exactly how such a death sentence might be carried out: 'An offender caught in the act of stealing bread would be tossed in the air by other prisoners and allowed to crash to the ground; this was repeated several times, damaging his kidneys. Then they would heave him out of the barracks like so much carrion.'

Panin, like many other camp survivors who lived through the hungry war years, also wrote eloquently about the individual rituals with which some prisoners ate their bread. If prisoners received bread only once a day, in the morning, they faced an agonizing decision: eat it all at once, or save some until the afternoon. To save the bread risked loss or theft of the precious quarter-loaf. On the other hand, a piece of bread was something to look forward to during the day. Panin's caution against the latter approach must stand as a unique testimony to the science of avoiding hunger:

When you get your ration you have an overwhelming desire to stretch out the pleasure of eating it, cutting your bread up evenly into tiny pieces, rolling the crumbs into little balls. From sticks and strings you improvise a pair of scales and weigh every piece. In such ways you try to prolong the business of eating by three hours or more. But this is tantamount to suicide!

Never on any account take more than a half-hour to consume your ration. Every bite of bread should be chewed thoroughly, to enable the stomach to digest it as easily as possible so that it gives up to one's organism a maximum amount of energy . . . if you always split your ration and put aside a part of it for the evening, you are finished. Eat it all at one sitting; if, on the other hand, you gobble it down too quickly, as famished people often do in normal circumstances, you will also shorten your days . . .[148]

Zeks were not the only inhabitants of the Soviet Union who became obsessed with bread and the many ways to eat it, however. To this day, a Russian acquaintance of mine will not eat brown bread of any kind, because, as a child during the war in Kazakhstan, he ate nothing else. And Susanna Pechora, a prisoner in Minlag in the 1950s, once overheard a conversation about camp bread between two Russian peasant women, also prisoners – women who had known what life was like *without* camp bread:

One of them was holding a piece of bread and stroking it. 'Oh my *khlebushka* [a nickname, 'little bread', such as one might give to a child],' she said, gratefully, 'they give you to us every day.' The other said, 'We could dry it, and send it to the children, they are hungry after all. But I don't think they'd allow us to send it . . .'[149]

After that, Pechora told me, she thought twice before complaining about the lack of food in the camps.

11

Work in the Camps

Those who are sick, no good,
Too weak for mining
Are lowered down, sent
To the camp below
To fell the trees of Kolyma.
It's very simple when
Written down on paper. But I cannot forget
The chain of sleds upon the snow
And people, harnessed.
Straining their sunken chests, they pull the carts.
They either stop to rest
Or falter on steep slopes . . .
The heavy weight rolls down
And any moment
It will trip them . . .

Who has not seen a horse that stumbles?
But we, we have seen people in a harness . . .

        – Elena Vladimirova, 'Kolyma'[1]

Rabochaya Zona
The Work Zone

Work was the central function of most Soviet camps. It was the main occupation of prisoners, and the main preoccupation of the administration. Daily life was organized around work, and the prisoners' well-being depended upon how successfully they worked. Nevertheless, it is difficult to generalize about what camp work was like: the image of the prisoner in the snowstorm, digging gold or coal with a pickaxe, is only a stereotype. There were many such prisoners – millions, as the figures for the camps of Kolyma and Vorkuta make clear – but there were also, we now know, camps in central Moscow where prisoners designed aeroplanes, camps in central Russia where prisoners built and ran nuclear power plants, fishing camps on the Pacific coast, collective farm camps in southern Uzbekistan. The archives of the Gulag in Moscow are chock-full of photographs of prisoners with their camels.[2]

Without a doubt, the range of economic activity within the Gulag was as wide as the range of economic activity within the USSR itself. A glance through the *Guide to the System of Corrective-Labour Camps in the USSR*, the most comprehensive listing of camps to date, reveals the existence of camps organized around gold mines, coal mines, nickel mines; highway and railway construction; arms factories, chemical factories, metal-processing plants, electricity plants; the building of airports, apartment blocks, sewage systems; the digging of peat, the cutting of trees and the canning of fish.[3] The Gulag administrators themselves preserved a photo album solely dedicated to the goods that inmates produced. Among other things, there are pictures of mines, missiles and other army equipment; car parts, door locks, buttons; logs floating down rivers; wooden furniture, including chairs, cabinets, telephone boxes and barrels; shoes, baskets and textiles (with samples attached); rugs, leather, fur hats, sheepskin coats; glass cups, lamps and jars; soap and candles; even toys – wooden tanks, tiny windmills and mechanical rabbits playing drums.[4]

Work varied within individual camps as well as between them. True, many prisoners in forestry camps did nothing but fell trees. Prisoners with sentences of three years or less worked in 'corrective-labour colonies', light-regime camps which were usually organized around a single factory or occupation. Larger Gulag camps, by contrast, might contain a number of industries: mines, a brick factory and a power plant, as well as housing or road construction sites. In such camps, prisoners unloaded the daily goods trains, drove trucks, picked vegetables, worked in kitchens, hospitals and children's nurseries. Unofficially, prisoners also worked as servants, nannies and tailors for the camp commanders, guards and their wives.

Prisoners with long sentences often held down a wide variety of jobs, changing work frequently as their luck rose and fell. In her nearly two-decade camp career, Evgeniya Ginzburg worked cutting trees, digging ditches, cleaning the camp guest-house, washing dishes, tending chickens, doing laundry for camp commanders' wives and caring for prisoners' children. Finally, she became a nurse.[5] During the eleven years he spent in camps, another political prisoner, Leonid Sitko, worked as a welder, as a stonemason in a quarry, as a construction worker on a building brigade, as a porter in a railway depot, as a miner in a coal mine and as a carpenter in a furniture factory, making tables and bookshelves.[6]

But although jobs could be as varied within the camp system as they were in the outside world, working prisoners usually broke down into two categories: those assigned to *obshchie raboty* – 'general work' – and the *pridurki*, a word usually translated into English as 'trusties'. The latter had, as we shall see, the status of a separate caste. General work, the lot of the vast majority of prisoners, was precisely what it sounds like: unskilled, physically demanding hard labour. 'The first camp winter of 1949–50 was especially difficult for me,' wrote Isaak Filshtinsky. 'I didn't have a profession which could be put to use in the camps, and I was forced to go from place to place, doing various kinds of general work, to saw, to carry, to pull, to push, and so on – to go, in other words, wherever it came into the head of the work-assigner to send me.'[7]

With the exception of those who had been lucky in the very first round of work assignments – usually those who were building engineers or members of other useful camp professions, or else had already established themselves as informers – the majority of *zeks* were assigned to general work as a matter of course after their week or so in quarantine had ended. They were also assigned to a brigade: a group of anywhere from four to 400 *zeks*, who not only worked together, but also ate together and generally slept in the same barracks. Each brigade was led by a brigadier, a trusted, high-status prisoner who was responsible for doling out jobs, overseeing the work – and ensuring that the team met the production norm.

The importance of the brigadier, whose status lay somewhere between that of prisoner and that of administrator, was not lost on camp authorities. In 1933, the boss of Dmitlag sent an order to all of his subordinates, reminding them of the need to 'find among our shock-workers the capable people who are so necessary to our work', since 'the brigadier is the most important, most significant person on the construction site'.[8]

From the individual prisoner's point of view, his relationship with the brigadier was more than merely important: it could determine his quality of life – even whether he lived or died, as one prisoner wrote:

The life of a person depends very much on his brigade and his brigadier, given that you spend all your days and nights in their company. At work, in the dining hall, and in your bunks – always the same faces. The brigade members can either work all together, in groups, or individually. They can help you survive, or help destroy you. Either sympathy and help, or hostility and indifference. The role of the brigadier is no less important. It also matters who he is, what he thinks his tasks and obligations are: to serve the bosses at your cost and his own benefit, to treat his brigade members like underlings, servants and lackeys – or to be your comrade in ill-fortune and to do everything possible to make life easier for the members of the brigade.[9]

Some brigadiers did indeed threaten and intimidate their workforce. On his first day in the Karaganda mines, Alexander Weissberg fainted from hunger and exhaustion: 'with the roars of a maddened bull the brigadier now turned on me, flinging every ounce of his powerful body on to me, kicking and punching and finally dealing me such a blow on the head that I fell to

Grave-digging: a drawing by Beniamin Mkrtchyan, Ivdel, 1953

the ground, half-stunned, covered in bruises and with blood streaming down my face . . .'[10]

In other cases, the brigadier allowed the brigade itself to function as an organized peer group, putting pressure on prisoners to work harder even if they were otherwise inclined. In the novel *One Day in the Life of Ivan Denisovich*, Solzhenitsyn's hero at one point muses that a camp brigade 'isn't like a work gang outside, where Ivan Ivanovich and Pyotr Petrovich each get a wage of his own. In the camps things are arranged so that the *zek* is kept up to the mark not by his bosses but by the others in his gang. Either everybody gets a bonus or else they all die together.'[11]

Vernon Kress, another Kolyma prisoner, was beaten and shouted at by his brigade comrades for being unable to keep up, and was ultimately forced into a 'weak' brigade, none of whose members ever received the full ration.[12] Yuri Zorin also had the experience of being part of a genuinely hard-working brigade, composed mostly of Lithuanians who would not tolerate shirkers in their ranks: 'You can't imagine how willingly and well they worked . . . if they thought you worked badly, you got kicked out of the Lithuanian brigade.'[13]

If you had the bad luck to end up in a 'bad' brigade, and you could not bribe or squirm your way out, you could starve. M. B. Mindlin, later one of the founders of the Memorial Society, was once assigned to a Kolyma brigade composed mostly of Georgians and led by a Georgian brigadier. He quickly realized not only that the brigade members were as afraid of their brigadier as they were of the camp guards, but also that as the 'only Jew in a brigade of Georgians', he would be shown no special favours. One day he worked particularly hard, in an attempt to be awarded the highest level of rations, 1,200 grams of bread. The brigadier refused to recognize this, however, and marked him down as deserving only 700 grams. With the aid of a bribe, Mindlin switched brigades, and found a completely different atmosphere: the new brigadier actually cared about his underlings, and even allowed him a few days of lighter work in the beginning, in order to get his strength back: 'Everyone who got into his brigade considered himself lucky, and was saved from death.' Later, he himself became a brigadier, and took it upon himself to dole out bribes, in order to ensure that all the members of his brigade got the best possible deal from the camp cooks, bread-cutters and other important people.[14]

The brigadier's attitude mattered because, for the most part, general work was not intended to be phoney or meaningless. Whereas in German camps, work was often designed, according to one prominent scholar, to be 'principally a means of torture and abuse', Soviet prisoners were meant to be fulfilling some aspect of the camp's production plan.[15] True, there were exceptions to this rule. At times, stupid or sadistic guards would actually set prisoners pointless tasks. Susanna Pechora recalled being assigned to carry buckets of clay back and forth, 'totally pointless work'. One of the 'bosses' in charge of her work site specifically told her, 'I don't need your work, I need your suffering,' a phrase which would have been familiar to the prisoners of Solovetsky in the 1920s.[16] By the 1940s, as we shall see, there also arose a system of punishment camps, whose purpose was not primarily economic but punitive. Even within them, however, prisoners were expected to produce something.

Most of the time, prisoners were not meant to suffer – or perhaps it is more accurate to say that no one cared if they did or not. Far more important was that they fit into a camp production plan and fulfil a work norm. A norm could be anything: a certain number of cubic metres of wood to be cut down, of ditches to be dug, of coal to be hauled. And these norms were taken deadly seriously. Camps were covered with posters exhorting prisoners to fulfil their norms. The entire 'cultural-educational' apparatus of the camps was devoted to the same message. The dining halls or central square of some camps featured enormous chalkboards, listing each brigade and its latest norm-fulfilment.[17]

Norms were calculated with great care and scientific reasoning by the norm-setter (*normirovshchik*), whose job was thought to require great skill. Jacques Rossi records, for example, that those shovelling snow were assigned different norms depending upon whether the snow was freshly fallen snow, light snow, lightly packed snow, packed snow (requiring pressure from the foot on the shovel), heavily packed snow or frozen snow (requiring work with picks). Even after all of that, 'a series of coefficients account for the distance and height of the shovelled snow, and so forth'.[18]

But although theoretically scientific, the process of establishing norms for work, and of determining who had achieved them, was fraught with corruption, irregularity and incongruity. To begin with, prisoners were usually assigned norms that corresponded with those assigned to free workers: they were meant to achieve the same as professional foresters or miners. By and large, however, prisoners were not professional foresters or miners, and often had little idea what they were meant to be doing. Nor, after long terms in gaol and harrowing journeys in unheated cattle cars, were they even in average physical condition.

The more inexperienced and exhausted the prisoner, the more he would suffer. Evgeniya Ginzburg wrote a classic description of two women, both intellectuals unaccustomed to hard labour, both weakened by years in prison, trying to cut down trees:

For three days, Galya and I struggled to achieve the impossible. Poor trees, how they must have suffered at being mangled by our inexpert hands. Half-dead ourselves, and completely unskilled, we were in no condition to tackle them. The axe would slip and send showers of chips in our faces. We sawed feverishly, jerkily, mentally accusing each other of clumsiness – we knew we could not afford the luxury of a quarrel. Time and again the saw got stuck. But the most terrifying moment was when the tree was at last on the point of falling, only we didn't know which way. Once Galya got hit on the head, but the medical orderly refused even to put iodine on the cut, saying, 'Aha! That's an old trick! Trying to get exempted on the first day, are you?'

At the end of the day, the brigadier declared Evgeniya and Galya had achieved 18 per cent of the norm, and 'paid' them for their poor showing: 'Receiving the scrap of bread which corresponded to our performance, we were led out next day literally staggering from weakness to our place of work.' Meanwhile, the brigadier kept repeating that he 'did not intend to throw away precious food on traitors who could not fulfil their norm'.[19]

In the camps of the far north – particularly the camps of the Kolyma region, as well as Vorkuta and Norilsk, all of which lie beyond the Arctic Circle – the climate and the terrain exacerbated the difficulties. Summer, contrary to popular belief, was often no more bearable in these Arctic regions than winter. Even there, temperatures can rise well above 30 degrees centigrade. When the snow melts, the surface of the tundra turns to mud, making walking difficult, and mosquitoes appear to travel in grey clouds, making so much noise it is impossible to hear anything else. One prisoner remembered them:

The mosquitoes crawled up our sleeves, under our trousers. One's face would blow up from the bites. At the work site, we were brought lunch, and it happened that as you were eating your soup, the mosquitoes would fill up the bowl like buckwheat porridge. They filled up your eyes, your nose and throat, and the taste of them was

1 Vasily Zhurid; Aleksandr Petlosy; Grigori Maifet; Arnold Karro; Valentina Orlova (*top to bottom, left to right*)

2a Prisoners arriving at Kem, the Solovetsky transit camp

2b Women harvesting peat, Solovetsky, 1928

3a Maxim Gorky (*centre*), wearing a cloth cap, coat and tie, visiting Solovetsky, 1929, with his son, daughter-in-law and camp commanders. Sekirka church – the punishment cell – is in the background

3b The Solovetsky monastery, as it appears today

3c Frenkel

4a Prisoners breaking rocks, with handmade tools

4b 'Everything was done by hand ... We dug earth by hand, and carried it out in wheelbarrows, we dug through the hills by hand as well ...'

5a 'The best shock-workers': this placard hung in a place of honour

5b Stalin and Yagoda, visiting the White Sea Canal to celebrate its completion

Gaolers

ИСКОРЕНИМ
ШПИОНОВ и ДИВЕРСАНТОВ,
ТРОЦКИСТСКО-БУХАРИНСКИХ АГЕНТОВ ФАШИЗМА!

6a 'We will eradicate Spies and Diversionists, Agents of the Trotskyite-Bukharinite Fascists!' – NKVD poster, 1937

6b *Arrest of an Enemy in the Workplace* – Soviet painting, 1937

7a Four camp commanders, Kolyma, 1950. The daughter of a prisoner
has written 'Killers!' across the photograph

7b Armed guards, with dogs

Exiles

8a (*left*) Beside a grandmother's grave

8b (*below*) In central Asia

8c Outside a *zemlyanka*, an earth dugout

sweet, like blood. The more you moved and waved them away, the more they attacked. The best method was to ignore them, to dress lighter and instead of an anti-mosquito hat, to wear a wreath of grass or birch bark.[20]

Winters, of course, were very, very cold. Temperatures could fall to 30, 40 or 50 degrees below zero. Memoirists, poets and novelists have all struggled to describe what it felt like to work in such frost. One wrote of it being so cold that 'the simplest sudden motion of a hand in the air caused a notable swishing sound'.[21] Another wrote that one Christmas Eve morning, he awoke to discover that he could not move his head.

My first waking thought was that it had somehow been tied to the planks of my bunk during the night, but as I tried to sit up, the piece of material I had tied around my head and over my ears before I went to sleep the night before had pulled away. Pulling myself up on one elbow, I tugged at the material and realized that it was frozen to the wooden plank. My breath and the breath of all the men in the hut hung in the air like smoke.[22]

Yet another wrote that 'It was dangerous to stop moving. During head count we jumped, ran in place, and slapped our bodies to keep warm. I perpetually kneaded my toes and curled my fingers into a fist . . . touching a metal tool with a bare hand could tear off the skin, and going to the bathroom was extremely dangerous. A bout of diarrhoea could land you in the snow for ever.' As a result, some prisoners simply soiled their trousers: 'Working next to them was unpleasant, and back in the tent, when we began to warm up, the stench was unbearable. Those who had soiled themselves were often beaten and thrown out.'[23]

Certain general-work jobs, from the point of view of the weather, were worse than others. In the coal mines of the Arctic, one inmate remembered, the underground air was warmer, but freezing water was constantly dripping on the miners: 'The miner becomes a sort of giant icicle, his organism begins to freeze for a long and stable period of time. After three or four months of such hellish work, prisoners begin to experience massive illnesses . . .'[24]

Isaak Filshtinsky also wound up assigned to one of the most unpleasant winter jobs in Kargopollag, sorting logs on their way to be processed. It meant standing in water all day, and although the water was warm – it was pumped from the electrical plant – the air was not:

Because in that winter the Arkhangelsk region maintained a stable frost of forty, forty-five degrees below zero, a thick fog hung at all times over the sorting basin. It was at the same time very wet, and very cold . . . the work was not very difficult, but after thirty to forty minutes your entire body was permeated and enveloped by damp, your chin, lips and eyelashes were covered in frost, and the frost had penetrated to your very bones, through the pathetic camp clothing.[25]

The worst winter jobs were in the forests. For not only was the taiga cold in winter but it was also periodically swept by severe, unpredictable winter storms – called *burany* or *purgai*. Dmitri Bystroletov, a prisoner in Siblag, was caught in one:

In that instant, the wind began a wild and terrifying howl, forcing us down to the ground. The snow swirled up into the air, and everything disappeared – the lights of the camp, the stars, the aurora borealis – and we were left alone in a white fog. Opening our arms wide, clumsily slipping and stumbling, falling and supporting one another, we tried as quickly as possible to find the road back. Suddenly, a thunderclap burst above our heads. I scarcely managed to hang on to my fellow climber, when a violent stream of ice, snow, and rocks began gushing towards our faces. The swirling snow made it impossible to breathe, impossible to see . . .[26]

Janusz Bardach was caught in a *buran* in Kolyma as well, while working in a quarry. Along with their guards, he and his fellow prisoners made their way back to camp following the watchdogs, attached to one another by rope:

I couldn't see anything beyond Yuri's back and clung to the rope as though it were a life preserver . . . With the familiar landmarks gone, I had no idea how much further we had to go and was sure we'd never make it back. My foot fell upon something soft – a prisoner who had let go of the rope. 'Stop!' I shouted. But there was no stopping. No one could hear my voice. I leaned down and pulled his arm towards the rope. 'Here!' I tried to link his hand with the rope. 'Hold on!' It was no use. The man's arm fell to the ground when I let go. Yuri's stern command to move on carried me forward . . .

When Bardach's brigade returned to the camp, three prisoners were missing. Usually, 'the bodies of prisoners who got lost weren't found until springtime, often within one hundred metres of the zone'.[27]

The regulation clothing allotted to prisoners gave them little protection from the weather. In 1943, for example, the central Gulag administration ordered that prisoners were to receive, among other things, one summer shirt (to last two seasons), a pair of summer trousers (to last two seasons), one padded-cotton winter jacket (to last two years), padded winter trousers (to last eighteen months), felt boots (to last two years) and underwear, intended for nine months.[28] In practice, there were never enough even of these paltry items. An inspection of twenty-three camps in 1948 reported that the supply of 'clothes, underclothes and shoes is unsatisfactory'. That appears to have been an understatement. In a camp at Krasnoyarsk, less than half of the prisoners had shoes. In Norilsk, in the far north, only 75 per cent had warm boots, and only 86 per cent had warm clothes. In Vorkuta, also in the far north, only 25–30 per cent of prisoners had underclothes, while only 48 per cent had warm boots.[29]

In the absence of shoes, prisoners improvised. They made boots out of birch bark, scraps of fabric, old rubber tyres. At best, these contraptions were clumsy and difficult to walk in, particularly in deep snow. At worst, they leaked, virtually guaranteeing frostbite.[30] Elinor Lipper described her home-made boots, which in her camp were nicknamed 'Che-Te-Ze', the abbreviation for the Chelyabinsk Tyre Factory:

They were made of lightly padded and quilted sacking with high, wide tops that reach to the knee, the shoe itself being strengthened by oil cloth or artificial leather at the toe and heel. The sole is made of three cross sections of rubber from worn-out automobile tyres. The whole thing is fastened to the foot with string and tied with string below the knee so that the snow does not get in . . . after a day's use they become all twisted, and the flabby soles turn every which way. They absorb moisture with incredible speed, especially when the sacks of which they are made were used for bagging salt . . .[31]

Another prisoner describes a similar improvisation: 'The sides were open so that the toes were exposed from the sides. The cloth to wrap up the feet could not be secured tightly, meaning that toes were thereby exposed to frost.' As a result of wearing these shoes, he did indeed get frostbite – which, he reckoned, saved his life, as he was no longer able to work.[32]

Different prisoners had different theories about how to cope with the cold. To recover from the frost at the end of the day, for example, some prisoners would rush into the barracks after work and crowd round the stove, so close that their clothes would sometimes burst into flames: 'The repulsive smell of burning rags would come up and bite into your nostrils.'[33] Others thought this unwise. Isaak Filshtinsky was told by more experienced inmates that crowding round the stove or the camp fire was dangerous, as the sudden change of temperature brought on pneumonia: 'The human organism is so constructed that no matter how cold it is, the body adjusts and gets used to it. I always followed this sage rule in camp and I never caught cold.'[34]

Camp authorities were supposed to make some concessions to the cold. According to the rules, prisoners in certain northern camps received extra rations. But these, according to documents of 1944, could amount to as little as 50 extra grams of bread a day – a few bites – which was hardly enough to compensate for extreme cold.[35] Theoretically, when it was too cold, or when a storm was pending, prisoners were not meant to work at all. Vladimir Petrov claimed that during the Berzin regime in Kolyma, prisoners had stopped working when temperatures reached 50 degrees centigrade below zero. In the winter of 1938–9, after Berzin had been deposed, temperatures had to fall to 60 degrees below zero before work stopped. Even this rule was not always adhered to, writes Petrov, since the only person at the gold field who had a thermometer was the camp commander. As a result, 'only three days during the winter of 1938–39 were declared non-working days because of low temperatures, as against fifteen days during the winter of 1937–38'.[36]

Another memoirist, Kazimierz Zarod, recorded that the cut-off temperature in his camp during the Second World War was 45 degrees below zero, and recalled one occasion when his logging brigade was told to return to camp during the day, because the thermometer had reached minus 47: 'How briskly we collected our equipment, formed ourselves into a column and began our journey back to camp.'[37] Bardach recalls that in Kolyma in the war years, the rule was minus 50 degrees, 'although the wind chill was never taken into account'.[38]

But weather was not the only obstacle to norm-fulfilment. In many camps, norms were set really impossibly high. In part this was a side effect of the logic of Soviet central planning, which decreed that enterprises had to increase their output every year. Elinor Olitskaya remembered her fellow inmates struggling to fulfil the norms in a camp sewing factory, wanting to keep their warm, indoor jobs. But because they did fulfil them, the camp administration kept raising them, as a result of which they became unattainable.[39]

Norms also grew tougher because prisoners and norm-setters alike lied, overestimating how much work had been and would be done. As a result, norms sometimes became astronomical over time. Alexander Weissberg recalled that even for the supposedly easier jobs, the norms seemed incredible: 'Everyone seemed to be faced with a virtually impossible task. The two men in charge of the laundry had to wash the clothes of 800 men in ten days.'[40]

Not that overfulfilling the norm necessarily brought the expected advantages. Antoni Ekart recalled an incident when ice on the river near his camp broke, and a flood threatened: 'Several brigades of the strongest prisoners, including all the "shock" men, worked like mad for two days, practically without a break. For what they had done they received one herring for every two men and a packet of *makhorka* [rough tobacco] for every four.'[41]

In such conditions – with long working days, few days off, and little rest during the day – accidents were frequent. In the early 1950s, a group of inexperienced women prisoners were ordered to put out a brush-fire near Ozerlag. On that occasion alone, recalled one of them, 'several people burned to death'.[42] Exhaustion and the weather often proved a lethal combination, as Alexander Dolgun testifies:

Cold, numbed fingers could not hold on to handles and levers and timbers and crates, and there were many accidents, often fatal. One man was crushed when we were rolling logs off a flat car, using two logs as a ramp. He was buried when twenty or more logs let loose at once and he was not fast enough. The guards shoved his body out of the way on the platform and the blood-stiffened mass was waiting for us to carry it home when night came.[43]

Moscow kept statistics on accidents, and these occasionally provoked irate exchanges between inspectors and camp commanders. One such compilation, for the year 1945, lists 7,124 accidents in the Vorkuta coal mines alone, including 482 that resulted in serious injury and 137 that resulted in death. The inspectors laid the blame on the shortage of miners' lamps, on electrical failures, and on the inexperience of workers and their frequent rotation. Angrily, the inspectors calculated the number of workdays lost due to accidents: 61,492.[44]

Absurdly bad organization and slovenly management also hampered work. Although it is important to note that ordinary Soviet workplaces were badly run too, the situation was worse within the Gulag, where the lives and health of workers were not held to be important, and where the regular arrival of spare parts was disrupted by weather and huge distances. Chaos had been the reigning spirit of the Gulag since the days of the White Sea Canal, and it continued into the 1950s, even after far more workplaces in the Soviet Union were mechanized. For those doing forestry work, 'there were no chain-saws, no timber-haulage tractors, and no mechanical loaders'.[45] Those working in textile factories were given 'working tools either too few or else inappropriate'. This meant, according to one prisoner, that 'all the seams had to be pressed with a huge iron weighing two kilograms. One had to iron 426 pairs of trousers during one session, one's hands got numb with lifting the weight and one's legs swollen and painful.'[46]

Machinery also broke down constantly, a factor not necessarily taken into account when norms were calculated. In the same textile factory, 'mechanics were constantly being summoned. These were mostly female convicts. The repairs went on for hours, for the women were not skilled. It became impossible to do the compulsory amount of work, and consequently we received no bread.'[47]

The theme of broken machinery and unskilled machine technicians comes up in the annals of the Gulag administration again and again. Regional camp administrators attending the Far Eastern Party Conference in Khabarovsk in 1934 complained that constant breakdowns in equipment supply and the poor qualifications of technicians meant they could not meet norms for gold production.[48] A 1938 letter addressed to the Deputy Minister of Internal Affairs in charge of the Gulag states that '40–50 per cent of tractors are broken'. But even more primitive working methods often failed to work too. A letter of a year earlier notes that of the 36,491 horses employed by the Gulag, 25 per cent were not fit to work.[49]

The Gulag's enterprises also felt very keenly the lack of engineers and administrators. Few skilled technicians voluntarily worked on Gulag projects, and those who did volunteer did not necessarily have the appropriate skills. Over the years, many efforts were made to attract free workers to the camps, and enormous incentives were offered. As early as the mid-1930s, recruiters from Dalstroi were agitating across the country, offering special privileges for anyone who signed a two-year labour contract. These included a wage 20 per cent higher than the Soviet average for the first two years, and 10 per cent higher for the following years, as well as paid vacations, access to special food products and supplies, and a generous pension.[50]

The camps of the far north were also portrayed with great fanfare and enthusiasm in the Soviet press. An example of this sort of propaganda appeared in English in a publication called *Sovietland*, written for the benefit of foreigners. In an April 1939 article devoted to Magadan, a classic of the genre, the magazine gushed about the city's magical appeal:

The sea of lights that is Magadan by night is a most stirring and alluring spectacle. This is a town which is alive and bustling every minute of the day and night. It swarms with people whose lives are regulated by a strict working schedule. Accuracy and promptness begets speed, and speed becomes easy and happy work . . .[51]

No mention is made of the fact that most of the people whose lives were 'regulated by a strict working schedule' were prisoners.

Not that it mattered: these efforts failed to attract the necessary calibre of specialists anyway, leaving the Gulag to rely upon prisoners who found themselves there by accident. One prisoner recalled having been sent, with a building brigade, 600 kilometres north of Magadan to build a bridge. Once they arrived, they realized that no one in the brigade had ever built a bridge before. One of the prisoners, an engineer, was put in charge of the project, although bridges were not his speciality. The bridge was built. It was also washed away in the first flood.[52]

This was a minor disaster, however, in comparison to some others. There were entire Gulag projects, employing thousands of people and enormous resources, which proved spectacularly wasteful and ill-conceived. Of these, perhaps the most famous was the attempted construction of a railway line from the Vorkuta region to the mouth of the Ob River on the Arctic Sea. The decision to start building was taken by the Soviet government in April 1947. A month later, exploration, surveying work and construction all began simultaneously. Prisoners also began building a new seaport at the Kamenny cape, where the Ob River widens out towards the sea.

As usual, there were complications: there were not enough tractors, so prisoners used old tanks instead. The planners made up for their lack of machines by overworking the prisoners. Eleven-hour days were normal, and even free workers sometimes stayed on the job from nine o'clock in the morning until midnight during the long summer days. By the end of the year, the complications had grown more serious. The surveying team had established that the Kamenny cape was a poor location for the port: the water was not deep enough for large ships and the land was too unstable for heavy industry. In January 1949, Stalin held a midnight meeting, where the Soviet leadership determined to move the site, and the railway too: the line would now connect the Ob not with the Vorkuta region to the west, but with the Yenisei River to the east. Two new camps were built – Construction Site

No. 501 and Construction Site No. 503. Each began to lay down railway track at the same time. The idea was to meet in the middle. The distance between them was 1,300 kilometres.

Work continued. At its height there were, according to one source, 80,000 people working on this railway; according to another, 120,000. The project became known as the 'Road of Death'. Construction proved nearly impossible in the Arctic tundra. As winter permafrost turned quickly into summer mud, track had to be constantly prevented from bending or sinking. Even so, wagons frequently came off the rails. Because of supply problems, the prisoners began using wood instead of steel in the railway construction, a decision which guaranteed the project's failure. At the time of Stalin's death in 1953, 500 kilometres had been built from one end of the railway, 200 kilometres from the other end. The port existed only on paper. Within weeks of Stalin's funeral, the entire project, which had cost 40 billion roubles and tens of thousands of lives, was abandoned for good.[53]

On a smaller scale, such stories were repeated every day, all across the Gulag. Yet despite weather, inexperience and mismanagement, pressure on camp administrators never slackened, nor did pressure on prisoners. The bosses were subject to endless inspections and verification programmes, and constantly harangued to do better. However fictitious, the results mattered. Ludicrous though it may have seemed to prisoners, who knew perfectly well how shoddily work was being done, this was, in fact, a deadly serious game. Many of them would not survive it.

KVCh
The Cultural-Educational Department

Were they not clearly marked as belonging to the NKVD archives, the casual observer could be forgiven for thinking that the photographs of Bogoslovlag, which appear in a carefully preserved album, dated 1945, were not of a camp at all. The pictures show carefully planted gardens, flowers, shrubs, a fountain and a gazebo in which prisoners can sit and rest. The entrance to the camp is marked by a red star, and a slogan: 'All of our strength for the future power of the Motherland!' The photographs of prisoners gracing another album, filed near by, are equally hard to reconcile with the popular image of the Gulag inmate. There is a happy man holding a pumpkin; cows pulling a plough; a smiling camp commander picking an apple. Beside the pictures are graphs. One shows the camp's planned production, the other the plan's fulfilment.[54]

All of these albums, neatly cut, pasted and labelled with the same conscientiousness that schoolchildren show when putting together a class project, were produced by the same institution: the Gulag's *Kulturno-vospitatelnaya chast*, the Cultural-Educational Department, or KVCh, as it was usually known to prisoners. The KVCh, or its equivalent, had been in existence since the Gulag began. In 1924, the very first edition of *SLON*, the journal of the Solovetsky prison, contained an article on the future of prisons in Russia: 'The corrective-labour policy of Russia must re-educate prisoners through accustoming them to participating in organized productive labour.'[55]

Most of the the time, however, the real goal of camp propaganda was higher production figures. This was even the case during the building of the White Sea Canal, when, as we have seen, the 're-education' propaganda was at its loudest and perhaps most sincere. At that time, the national cult of the shock-worker was at its height. Camp artists painted portraits of the canal's best workers, and camp actors and musicians put on special concerts for them. The shock-workers were even invited to huge assemblies, at which songs were sung and speeches were read out. One such assembly, held on 21 April 1933, was followed by a two-day 'work storm': for forty-eight hours, none of the 30,000 shock-workers left their workplaces at all.[56]

This sort of activity was unceremoniously abandoned in the late 1930s when prisoners became 'enemies' and could no longer be 'shock-workers' at the same time. Nevertheless, after Beria took control of the camps in 1939, propaganda did slowly return. While there would never again be a White Sea Canal – a Gulag project whose 'success' was trumpeted to the world – the language of re-education was brought back to the camps. By the 1940s, every camp theoretically had at least one KVCh instructor, as well as a small library and a KVCh 'club', where theatrical performances and concerts were put on, political lectures were given and political discussions were held. Thomas Sgovio remembered one such club: 'The main room, seating about thirty persons, had wooden, gaudily painted walls. There were a few tables, supposedly for reading purposes. However, there were no books, newspapers or periodicals. How could there be? Newspapers were worth their weight in gold. We used them for smoking.'[57]

From the 1930s onwards, the main 'clients' of the KVCh were supposed to be the criminal prisoners. Just as it was unclear whether politicals would be allowed to hold specialists' jobs, so too was it unclear whether it was worth anybody's time trying to re-educate them. A 1940 NKVD directive on the cultural-educational work of the camps stated explicitly that those who had committed counter-revolutionary crimes were not suitable targets for re-education. In the camps' theatrical productions, they were allowed to play musical instruments, but not to speak or sing.[58]

As was so often the case, these orders were ignored more frequently than they were obeyed. And – as was also often the case – the KVCh's actual function in camp life differed from what the Gulag's masters in Moscow had designed it to do. If Moscow intended the KVCh to force prisoners to work harder, the prisoners used the KVCh for their own purposes: for moral support – and for survival.

On the face of it, it appears as if the cultural-educational instructors inside the camps sought to propagate the value of work among prisoners much in the same way that Communist Party operatives sought to do so in the world outside the prison gates. In the larger camps, the KVCh produced camp newspapers. Sometimes these were full newspapers, with reports and long articles on the successes of the camp, as well as 'self-criticism' – comments about what was going wrong inside the camp – a standard feature of all the Soviet press. Aside from a brief period in the early 1930s, these newspapers were intended largely for the free workers and the camp administration.[59]

For prisoners, there were also 'wall newspapers', designed not for distribution (there were paper shortages, after all) but for display on special noticeboards. One prisoner described the wall newspapers as 'an attribute of the Soviet way of life, no one ever read them but they appeared regularly'. They often featured 'humour sections'. 'They assumed, obviously, that workers dying of hunger would read the material in this section, give a great belly laugh and finally hold up to shame those refusers and shirkers who didn't want to repay their guilt to the Motherland through honest work.'[60]

Ludicrous though they seemed to many, the central Gulag administration in Moscow took the wall newspapers very seriously. Wall newspapers, ordered one directive, should 'portray the best examples of work, popularize the shock-workers, condemn the shirkers'. No pictures of Stalin were allowed: these were, after all, still criminals, not 'comrades', and they were still excommunicated from Soviet life, forbidden even to gaze upon their leader. The often absurd atmosphere of secrecy which had descended upon the camps in 1937 remained in place throughout the 1940s as well: newspapers printed in the camps could not be taken out of the camps.[61]

Along with hanging up newspapers, the KVCh also showed films. Gustav Herling was shown an American musical, 'full of women in fitted bodices, men in tight jackets and frilly cravats', as well as a propaganda film which ended in 'the triumph of righteousness': 'The clumsy students came first in their socialist competition of work and with blazing eyes delivered a speech glorifying the State where manual labour had been raised to the highest position of honour.'[62]

Meanwhile, some criminal prisoners took advantage of the darkened rooms where the films were shown to carry out revenge killings and murders. 'I remember, at the end of one of these performances, seeing the body of a dead man carried past on a stretcher,' one prisoner told me.[63]

The KVCh also sponsored football matches, chess matches, concerts and performances referred to solemnly as 'self-taught creative activities'. One archival document lists the following repertoire of an NKVD singing and dancing ensemble, which was touring the camps:

1. The Ballad of Stalin
2. The Cossack Meditation on Stalin
3. The Song of Beria
4. The Song of the Motherland
5. The Fight for the Motherland
6. Everything for the Motherland
7. The Song of the NKVD Warriors
8. The Song of the Chekists
9. The Song of the Distant Frontier Post
10. The March of the Border Guards[64]

There were also some lighter numbers, such as 'Let's Smoke' and 'Song of the Dnieper', the latter celebrating a river at least, and not a secret police institution. The theatrical repertoire included some Chekhov plays as well. Nevertheless, the bulk of the artistic efforts were meant, at least in theory, for the prisoners' enlightenment, not their entertainment. As one 1940 order from Moscow declared, 'Every performance must educate the prisoners, teaching them greater consciousness of labour.'[65] As we shall see, the prisoners learned to use the performances to help them survive, as well.

But 'self-taught creative activity' was not the Cultural-Educational Department's only concern – nor was it the only path to a lighter workload. The KVCh was also responsible for collecting suggestions as to how to improve or 'rationalize' the prisoners' work, a task which it took grimly seriously. In its semi-annual report to Moscow, one camp in Nizhne-Amursk claimed, without irony, to have achieved 302 rationalizations, of which 157 were put into practice, thereby saving 812,332 roubles.[66]

Isaak Filshtinsky also notes, with a great deal of irony, that some prisoners became adept at twisting this policy to their own advantage. One, a former chauffeur, claimed that he knew how to construct a mechanism that would allow cars to run on oxygen. Excited by the prospect of discovering a really important 'rationalization', the camp bosses gave him a laboratory in which to work on the idea: 'I can't say whether they believed him or not. They were simply fulfilling instructions of the Gulag. In every camp, there should be people working as rationalizers and inventors . . . and who knows, maybe Vdovin would find something, and then they would all get the Stalin prize!' Vdovin's bluff was called, finally, when he returned one day from his lab with a giant construction made of scrap metal, the purpose of which he was incapable of explaining.[67]

As in the outside world, the camps also continued to hold 'socialist competitions', work contests in which prisoners were meant to compete against one another, the better to raise output. They also honoured the camp shock-workers, for their alleged ability to triple and quadruple the norms. I've described the first such campaigns in Chapter 4, which began in the 1930s, but they continued – with markedly less enthusiasm and markedly more absurd hyperbole – into the 1940s. Prisoners who participated could win many different sorts of awards. Some received bigger rations or better living conditions. Others received more intangible prizes. In 1942, for example, a reward for good performance could include a *knizhka otlichnika*, a booklet awarded to those who attained the status of 'excellent' workers. This contained a little calendar, with space for putting in daily percentages of norms fulfilled; a blank space for writing in suggestions for 'rationalizations'; a list of the rights of the booklet holder (to receive the best place in the barracks, to get the best uniforms, the unlimited right to receive parcels, etc.); and a quote from Stalin: 'The hard-working person feels himself a free citizen of his country, a social activist of a sort. And if he works hard, and gives society that which he can give, he is a hero of labour.'[68]

Not everybody would have taken such a prize terribly seriously. Antoni Ekart, a Polish prisoner, also described one such work campaign:

A plywood Board of Honour was put up on which were posted the results of the Socialist Workers' Contests when announced. Sometimes a crude portrait of the leading 'shock' man was exhibited, giving details of the records achieved. Almost unbelievable figures, showing outputs of five hundred per cent or even one thousand per cent of the normal, were shown. This referred to the digging up of the ground with spades. Even the most backward prisoner could understand that to excavate five to ten times more than the standard was impossible . . .[69]

But the KVCh instructors were also ultimately responsible for convincing 'refusers' that it was in their interest to work, not to sit in punishment cells, or to attempt to get by on small rations. Clearly, not many took their lectures seriously: there were too many other ways to persuade prisoners to work. But a few did, much to the delight of the Gulag's bosses in Moscow. In fact, they took this function terribly seriously, and even held periodic conferences of KVCh instructors, designed to discuss such questions as 'What are the basic motives of those who refuse to work?' and 'What are the practical results of eliminating the prisoners' day off?'

At one such meeting, held during the Second World War, the organizers compared notes. One acknowledged that some 'shirkers' could not work because they were too weak to live off the amount of food they were given. Still, he claimed, even starving people could be motivated: he had told one shirker that his behaviour was 'like a knife in the neck of his brother, who was at the front'. That was enough to persuade the man to ignore his hunger, and work harder. Another claimed he had shown some shirkers photographs of 'Leningrad in battle', after which they all went immediately to work. Yet another said that in his camp, the best brigades were allowed to decorate their own barracks, and the best workers were encouraged to plant flowers in their own individual plots. On the minutes from this meeting, preserved in the archives, someone has made a notation beside this latter comment: 'Khorosho!' 'Excellent!'[70]

This sharing of experiences was considered so important that at the height of the war, the Cultural-Educational Department of the Gulag in Moscow took the trouble to print a pamphlet on the subject. The title – with clear religious echoes – was *Return to Life*. The author, one Comrade Loginov, describes a series of relationships he had with prisoner 'shirkers'. Using clever psychological tactics, he converted every one of them to a belief in the value of hard work.

The stories are fairly predictable. In one of them, for example, Loginov explains to Ekaterina Sh., the educated wife of a man condemned to death for 'espionage' in 1937, that her ruined life can once again have meaning within the context of the Communist Party. To another prisoner, Samuel Goldshtein, Loginov recounts Hitler's 'racial theories' and explains to him what 'Hitler's new order' in Europe would mean for him. So inspired is Goldshtein by this surprising (in the USSR) appeal to his Jewishness, that he wants to leave immediately for the front. Loginov tells him that 'today, your weapon is your labour', and persuades him to work harder in the camp. 'Your life is needed by your fatherland, and so are you,' he tells yet another prisoner who, with tears in his eyes, returns to work upon hearing these words.[71]

Clearly, Comrade Loginov was proud of his work, and applied himself to it with great energy. His enthusiasm was real. The rewards he received for his work were real too: V. G. Nasedkin, then the boss of the entire Gulag system, was so pleased with his effort that he ordered the pamphlet sent to all of the camps in the system, and awarded Loginov a bonus of 1,000 roubles.

Whether Loginov and his shirkers actually believed in what he was doing is less clear. We do not know, for example, whether Loginov understood, at some level, that many of the people he was 'bringing back to life' were innocent of any crime. Nor do we know whether people like Ekaterina Sh. (if she existed) really reconverted to Soviet values, or whether she suddenly realized that by appearing to be so converted she might receive better food, better treatment or an easier job. The two possibilities are not even mutually exclusive. For people shocked and disoriented by their rapid transition from useful citizen to despised prisoner, the experience of 'seeing the light' and rejoining Soviet society may have helped them make a psychological recovery from their experiences, as well as providing them with the better conditions that saved their lives.

In fact, this question – 'Did they believe in what they were doing?' – is actually a small part of a much larger question, one which goes to the heart of the nature of the Soviet Union itself: did any of its leaders ever believe in what they were doing? The relationship between Soviet propaganda and

Soviet reality was always a strange one: the factory is barely functioning, in the shops there is nothing to buy, old ladies cannot afford to heat their apartments, yet in the streets outside, banners proclaim the 'triumph of socialism' and the 'heroic achievements of the Soviet motherland'.

These paradoxes were no different within the camps than outside them. In his history of the Stalinist industrial city Magnitogorsk, Stephen Kotkin points out that in the prison newspaper of the Magnitogorsk corrective-labour colony, the profiles of reformed convicts were written in 'language strikingly reminiscent of what could be heard from accomplished workers outside the colony: they were labouring, studying, making sacrifices and trying to better themselves'.[72]

Still, there was an extra level of strangeness in the camps. If, in the free world, the enormous gap between this sort of Soviet propaganda and Soviet reality already struck many as ludicrous, in the camps, the absurdity seemed to reach new heights. In the Gulag, where they were constantly addressed as 'enemies', explicitly forbidden to call one another 'comrade', and forbidden to gaze upon a portrait of Stalin, prisoners were nevertheless expected to work for the glory of the socialist motherland, just the same as those who were free – and to participate in 'self-taught creative activity' as if they were doing so out of the sheer love of art. The absurdity was perfectly clear to all. At one point in her camp career, Anna Andreevna became a camp 'artist', meaning that she was actually employed to paint those slogans. This job, very easy by camp standards, certainly saved her health and possibly her life. Yet interviewed years later, she claimed not even to be able to remember the slogans. She said, she supposed, that 'the Bosses thought them up. Something like, "We give all of our strength to work," something like that . . . I wrote them very quickly, and technically very well, but I absolutely forgot everything that I wrote. It was some kind of self-defence mechanism.'[73]

Leonid Trus, a prisoner in the early 1950s, was also struck by the point-lessness of the slogans which were plastered all over the camp buildings, and were repeated through the loudspeakers:

There was a camp radio system, which regularly transmitted information on our labour successes, and scolded those who worked badly. These transmissions were very crude, but they reminded me of transmissions I had heard in freedom. I became convinced that they were no different, except that in freedom the people were more talented, they knew how to describe it all in a prettier way . . . but in general [the camp] was the same as freedom – the same posters, the same slogans – except that in the camp the phrases all sounded more absurd. 'They took on the job, they finished the job,' for example. Or 'Labour in the USSR – it is a thing of honesty, of glory, of valour and heroism' – the words of Stalin. Or all of the other slogans, like 'We are for peace,' or 'We welcome peace in the whole world.'[74]

Foreigners, who were not used to the presence of slogans and banners, found the work of the 're-educators' even more bizarre. Antoni Ekart, a Pole, described a typical political indoctrination session:

The method employed was as follows. A man from the KVCh, a professional agitator with the mentality of a six-year-old child, would address the prisoners on the nobility of putting all their effort into work. He would tell them that noble people are patriots, that all patriots love Soviet Russia, the best country in the world for the working man, that Soviet citizens are proud to belong to such a country, etc. etc. for two solid hours – all this to an audience whose very skins bore witness to the absurdity and the hypocrisy of such statements. But the speaker is not upset by the cool reception and keeps on speaking. Finally he promises to all 'shock' workers better pay, increased rations and improved conditions. The effect on those who are undergoing the discipline of hunger may be imagined.[75]

A Polish deportee had the same reaction to a propaganda lecture he attended in a Siberian camp.

For hours and hours the lecturer went on, trying to prove that God did not exist, that He was nothing but some bourgeois invention. We should consider ourselves lucky to have found ourselves among the Soviets, the most perfect country in the world. Here in the camp we should learn how to work and at last become decent people. From time to time he attempted to give us some education: so he told us that the 'earth is round' and he was absolutely convinced we knew nothing about it, and that we were also ignorant of such things as for instance that Crete is 'peninsular', or that Roosevelt was some foreign minister. He imparted such truths as these with unshakeable confidence in our complete lack of knowledge, for how could we, brought up in a bourgeois state, expect to have the advantage of even the most elementary education . . . he stressed the point with satisfaction that we could not even dream of regaining our freedom, that Poland would never rise again . . .

Alas for the poor lecturer, continued the Pole, his work was for naught: 'The more he held forth about it, the more we rebelled inwardly, hoping against hope. Faces became set with determination.'[76]

Another Pole, Gustav Herling, described his camp's cultural activities as a 'vestigial reminder of the regulations drawn up in Moscow in the days when the camps really were intended to be corrective, educational institutions. Gogol would have appreciated this blind obedience to an official fiction despite the general practice of the camp – it was like the education of "dead souls".'[77]

These views are not unique: they are found in the vast majority of memoirs, most of which either fail to mention the KVCh, or deride it. For that reason, it is difficult, when writing about the function of propaganda in the camps, to know how to rate its importance to the central administration. On the one hand, it can be reasonably argued (and many do) that camp propaganda, like all Soviet propaganda, was pure farce, that no one believed it, that it was produced by the camp administration purely in order to fool the prisoners in a rather juvenile and transparent manner.

On the other hand, if the propaganda, the posters and the political indoctrination sessions were completely farcical – and if no one believed in them at all – then why was so much real time and real money wasted on them? Within the records of the Gulag administration alone, there are hundreds and hundreds of documents testifying to the intensive work of the Cultural-Educational Department. In the first quarter of 1943, for example, at the height of the war, frantic telegrams were sent back and forth from the camps to Moscow, as camp commanders desperately tried to procure musical instruments for their prisoners. Meanwhile, the camps held a contest on the theme 'The Great Motherland War of the Soviet People against the German Fascist Occupiers': fifty camp painters and eight sculptors participated. At this time of national labour shortages, the central organs also recommended that every camp employ a librarian, a film technician to show propaganda movies, and a *kultorganizator*, a prisoner assistant to the cultural instructor, who would help conduct the 'battle' for cleanliness, raise the cultural level of prisoners, organize artistic activity – and help teach the prisoners to 'correctly understand questions of contemporary politics'.[78]

The camp cultural instructors also filed semi-annual or quarterly reports on their work, often listing their achievements in great detail. The KVCh instructor of Vosturallag, at the time a camp for 13,000 prisoners, sent one such report, for example, also in 1943. The 21-page report begins with the admission that, in the first half of 1943, the camp's industrial plan was 'not fulfilled'. In the second half of that year, however, steps were taken. The Cultural-Educational Department had helped to 'mobilize prisoners to fulfil and overfulfil the production tasks set by Comrade Stalin', to 'return prisoners to health and prepare for winter' and to 'liquidate insufficiencies in cultural-educational work'.[79] The camp KVCh chief then went on to list the methods he deployed. He notes grandly that in the second half of that year, 762 political speeches were given, attended by 70,000 prisoners (presumably, many attended more than once). At the same time, the KVCh held 444 political information sessions, attended by 82,400 prisoners; it printed 5,046 'wall newspapers', read by 350,000 people; it put on 232 concerts and plays, showed 69 films and organized 38 theatrical groups. One of the latter even wrote a song, proudly quoted in the report:

> Our brigade is friendly
> Our duty calls
> Our building site waits
> The Front needs our work.[80]

One can attempt to come up with explanations for this enormous effort. Perhaps the Cultural-Educational Department functioned, within the Gulag bureaucracy, as the ultimate scapegoat: if the plan was not being fulfilled, it was not poor organization or malnutrition that was to blame, not stupidly cruel work policies or the lack of felt boots – but insufficient propaganda. Perhaps the system's rigid bureaucracy was at fault: once the centre had decreed there must be propaganda, everyone tried to fulfil the order without ever questioning its absurdity. Perhaps the Moscow leadership was so isolated from the camps that they really did believe that 444 political information sessions and 762 political speeches would make starving men and women work harder – although given the material also available to them in camp inspection reports, this seems unlikely.

Or perhaps there is no good explanation. Vladimir Bukovsky, the Soviet dissident who was later a prisoner himself, shrugged when I asked him about it. This paradox, he said, was what made the Gulag unique: 'In our camps, you were expected not only to be a slave labourer, but to sing and smile while you worked as well. They didn't just want to oppress us: they wanted us to thank them for it.'[81]

12

Punishment and Reward

He who has not been there will get his turn. He who has been
there will never forget it.   – Soviet proverb about prisons[1]

SHIZO
Punishment Cells

Very few Soviet concentration camps have survived intact into the present,
even in ruined form. Nevertheless, it is a curious fact that quite a number of
shtrafnye izolyatory – 'punishment isolaters' or (using the inevitable acronym)
SHIZO – are still standing. Nothing remains of *lagpunkt* No. 7, Ukhtpechlag
– except its punishment block, now the workshop of an Armenian car
mechanic. He has left the barred windows intact, hoping, he says, that
'Solzhenitsyn will buy my building'. Nothing remains of the farming *lagpunkt*
at Aizherom, Lokchimlag – except, again, its punishment block, now converted into a house inhabited by several families. One of the elderly women
who lives there praises the solidity of one of the doors. It still has a large
'Judas hole' in its centre, through which guards once peered at the prisoners,
and shoved them rations of bread.

The longevity of punishment blocks testifies to the sturdiness of their
construction. Often the only brick building in a wooden camp, the isolator
was the *zona* within the *zona*. Within its walls ruled the *rezhim* within the
rezhim. 'A gloomy stone building,' is how one prisoner described the isolator in his camp: 'external gates, internal gates, armed sentry posts all
around'.[2]

By the 1940s, Moscow had issued elaborate instructions, describing both
the construction of punishment blocks and the rules for those condemned to
live within them. Each *lagpunkt* – or group of *lagpunkts*, in the case of the
smaller ones – had a punishment block, normally just outside the *zona*, or, if
within it, 'surrounded by an impenetrable fence', at some distance from the
other camp buildings. According to one prisoner, this stricture may not have
been necessary, since many prisoners tried to avoid the *lagpunkt* punishment

cell by 'walking round it at a distance, not even looking in the direction of those grey stone walls, pierced by openings which seemed to breathe out a cold dark emptiness'.[3]

Each camp complex was also meant to have a central punishment block near its headquarters, be it Magadan or Vorkuta or Norilsk. The central block was in fact often a very large prison which, the rules stated, 'should be set up in the place which is furthest away from populated regions and from transport routes, should be well guarded, and guaranteed strict isolation. The guards should consist of only the most trusted, disciplined, and experienced riflemen, selected from among the free workers.' These central prisons contained both communal cells and solitary cells. The latter were to be housed in a separate, special building, and were reserved for the 'particularly malicious elements'. Prisoners kept in isolation were not taken out to work. In addition, they were forbidden any sort of exercise, tobacco, paper and matches. This was on top of the 'ordinary' restrictions applying to those being kept in the group cells: no letters, no packages, no meetings with relatives.[4]

On the face of it, the existence of punishment cells appears to contradict the general economic principles upon which the Gulag was founded. To maintain special buildings and extra guards was expensive. To keep prisoners away from work was wasteful. Yet from the camp administration's point of view, the cells were not a form of supplementary torture, but rather an integral part of the vast effort to make prisoners work harder. Along with reduced food norms, the punishment regime was designed to frighten *otkaz-chiki* – those who refused to work – as well as to punish those caught committing a camp crime, such as murder, or attempting escape.

Because these two types of crimes tended to be committed by different types of prisoners, the punishment cells had, in some camps, a peculiar atmosphere. On the one hand, they were full of professional thieves, who were more likely to be murderers and escapees. Over time, however, another category of prisoner also began to fill up the punishment cells: the male religious prisoners, as well as the *monashki*, the religious 'nuns', who also refused on principle to work for the Soviet Satan. Aino Kuusinen, for example, was in a Potma *lagpunkt* whose commander built a special punishment barracks for a group of deeply religious women who 'refused to work in the fields and spent their time praying aloud and singing hymns'. The women were not fed with the other prisoners, but instead received punishment rations in their own barracks. Armed guards escorted them twice daily to the latrine: 'From time to time the commandant would visit their quarters with a whip, and the hut resounded with shrieks of pain: the women were usually stripped before being beaten, but no cruelty could dissuade them from their habits of praying and fasting.' They were eventually taken away. Kuusinen believed they had been shot.[5]

Other sorts of chronic 'refusers' found their way into punishment cells as well. Indeed, the very existence of the cells presented prisoners with a choice. They could either work – or they could sit for a few days in the cells, getting by on short rations, suffering from the cold and the discomfort, but not exhausting themselves in the forests. Lev Razgon recounts the story of Count Tyszkiewicz, a Polish aristocrat who, finding himself in a Siberian logging camp, worked out that he would not survive on the rations supplied and simply refused to work. He reckoned he would thereby save his strength, even if he received only the punishment ration.

Every morning before the prisoners were marched out of the camp to work and the columns of *zeks* were lined up in the yard, two warders would fetch Tyszkiewicz from the punishment cell. Grey stubble covered his face and shaven head, and he was dressed in the remnants of an old overcoat and puttees. The camp security officer would begin his daily educational exercise, 'Well you f——g Count, you stupid f——g f—k, are you going to work or not?'

'No, sir, I cannot work,' the count would reply in an iron-firm voice.

'Oh so you can't, you f—k!' The security officer would publicly explain to the count what he thought of him and of his close and distant relations, and what he would do to him in the very near future. This daily spectacle was a source of general satisfaction to the camp's other inmates.[6]

But although Razgon tells the story with humour, there were high risks to such a strategy, for the punishment regime was not designed to be pleasant. Officially, the daily punishment rations for prisoners who had failed to fulfil the norm consisted of 300 grams of 'black rye bread', 5 grams of flour, 25 grams of buckwheat or macaroni, 27 grams of meat and 170 grams of potato. Although these are tiny amounts of food, those resident in punishment cells received even less: 300 grams of 'black rye bread' a day, with hot water, and 'hot liquid food' – soup, that is – only once every three days.[7]

For most prisoners though, the greatest unpleasantness of the punishment regime lay not in its physical hardship – the isolated building, the poor food – but in the extra torments added at the whim of the local camp command. The communal bunks might, for example, be replaced by a simple bench. Or the bread might be baked using unprocessed wheat. Or the 'hot liquid food' might be very thin indeed. Janusz Bardach was put in a punishment cell whose floor was covered with water, and whose walls were wet and mouldy:

My underwear and undershirt were already damp, and I was shivering. My neck and shoulders got stiff and cramped. The soggy raw wood was decaying, especially on the edges of the bench . . . the bench was so narrow I could not lie on my back, and when I lay on my side, my legs hung over the edge; I had to keep them bent all the time. It was difficult to decide which side to lie on – on one side my face was pressed up against the slimy wall; on the other, my back became damp.[8]

Damp was common, as was cold. Although the rules stated that the temperature in punishment cells should not be lower than 16 degrees centigrade, the heating was often neglected. Gustav Herling remembered that in his punishment isolator 'the windows in the small cells had neither glass nor even a board over them, so that the temperature was never higher than outside'. He describes other ways in which the cells were designed for discomfort:

My cell was so low that I could touch the ceiling with my hand . . . it was impossible to sit on the upper bunk without bending one's back against the ceiling, and the lower one could only be entered with the movement of a diver, head first, and left by pushing one's body away from the wood, like a swimmer in a sandbank. The distance between the edge of the bunk and the bucket by the door was less than half a normal step.[9]

Camp commanders could also decide whether to allow a prisoner to wear clothes in the cell – many were kept in their underwear – and whether or not to send him to work. If he did not work, then he would be kept in all day in the cold with no exercise. If he did work, then he would be very hungry. Nadezhda Ulyanovskaya was kept on punishment rations for a month, yet made to work. 'I constantly wanted to eat,' she wrote. 'I began talking only about food.'[10] Because of these often unexpected twists to the punishment regime, prisoners dreaded being sent to the cells. 'Prisoners there wept like children, promising good behaviour only to get out,' wrote Herling.[11]

Within the larger camp complexes, there were different sorts of torment: not just punishment cells, but punishment barracks and even entire punishment *lagpunkts*. Dmitlag, the camp which built the Moscow–Volga Canal, set up a 'strict-regime *lagpunkt*' in 1933 for 'work-refusers, escapers, thieves and so on'. To ensure security, the camp bosses dictated that the new *lagpunkt* should have two layers of barbed wire surrounding it instead of one; that extra convoy guards should lead prisoners to work; and that prisoners should do hard physical labour on work sites from which it was difficult to escape.[12]

At about the same time, Dalstroi set up a punishment *lagpunkt*, which became, by the late 1930s, one of the most notorious in the Gulag: Serpantinnaya – or Serpantinka – located on the northern slope of the hills just above Magadan. Carefully placed in order to receive very little sunlight, colder and darker than the rest of the camps in the valley (which were already cold and dark for much of the year), Dalstroi's punishment camp was more heavily fortified than other *lagpunkts*, and also served as an execution site in 1937 and 1938. Its very name was used to frighten prisoners, who equated a sentence to Serpantinka with a sentence to death.[13] One of the very few survivors of Serpantinka described the barracks as 'so overcrowded that prisoners took turns sitting on the floor while everyone else remained standing. In the mornings, the door would open, and the names of ten or twelve prisoners would be called. No one would answer. The first people that came to hand were then dragged out and shot.'[14]

In fact, little is known of Serpantinka, largely because so few people emerged to describe it. Even less is known about punishment *lagpunkts* set up in other camps, such as Iskitim, for example, the punishment *lagpunkt* of the Siblag complex, which was built round a limestone quarry. Prisoners worked there without machines or equipment, digging limestone by hand. Sooner or later, the dust killed many of them, through lung disease and other respiratory ailments.[15] Anna Larina, Bukharin's young wife, was briefly incarcerated there. Most of Iskitim's other prisoners – and Iskitim's dead – remain anonymous.[16]

They have not, however, been forgotten altogether. So powerfully did the suffering of the prisoners there work on the imagination of the local people of Iskitim that, many decades later, the appearance of a new fresh-water spring on a hill just outside the former camp was greeted as a miracle. Because the gully below the spring was, according to local legend, the site of mass prisoner executions, they believed the sacred water was God's way of remembering them. On a still, freezing day at the end of the Siberian winter, with a metre of snow still covering the ground, I watched parties of the faithful trooping up the hill to the spring, filling their plastic cups and bottles with the clean water, sipping it reverently – and occasionally glancing, solemnly, into the gully below.

Pochtovyi Yashchik
Post Office Box

The SHIZO was the ultimate punishment of the penal system. But the Gulag could also provide its inmates with rewards too: carrots as well as sticks. For along with a prisoner's food, his ability to sleep and his place of work, the camp also controlled his access to the outside world. Year in and year out, Gulag administrators in Moscow would send out instructions, dictating how many letters, packages and money transfers prisoners could receive, as well as when and how relatives could visit them from the outside.

Like the instructions on punishment cells, rules governing outside contacts also fluctuated over time. Or perhaps it is more precise to say that, generally speaking, outside contacts grew more limited over time. The instructions outlining the prison regime of 1930, for example, state simply that prisoners are allowed to write and receive an unlimited number of letters and packages. Meetings with relatives are also allowed, with no particular restrictions, although the number of them – not stated in the instructions – would depend upon the good behaviour of prisoners.[17]

By 1939, however, the instructions were far more detailed. They stated specifically that only those prisoners who fulfilled the production norm were allowed to meet with their relatives, and then only once every six months.

Those who overfulfilled the norm were allowed one meeting per month. Packages also became more limited: prisoners were allowed only one per month, and prisoners convicted of counter-revolutionary crimes could receive a package only once every three months.[18]

Indeed, by 1939, a whole raft of rules governing the sending and receiving of letters had also sprung into existence. Some political prisoners could receive letters once a month, others only once every three months. Camp censors also explicitly forbade prisoners to write about certain subjects: they could not mention the number of prisoners in their camp, discuss details of the camp regime, name the camp guards, or say what sort of work the camp carried out. Letters which included such details were not only confiscated by camp censors, but also carefully noted in the prisoner's file – presumably because they were evidence of 'spying'.[19]

All of these regulations were continually changed, amended and adapted to circumstances. During the war years, for example, all limitations on the number of food parcels were lifted: camp authorities seem to have hoped, simply, that relatives would help feed the prisoners, a task the NKVD found extremely difficult at that time. After the war, on the other hand, prisoners in special disciplinary camps for violent criminals, as well as those in the special camps for political prisoners, saw their rights to contact with the outside world shrink once again. They were allowed to write only four times a year, and could receive letters only from close family members, meaning parents, siblings, spouses and children.[20]

Precisely because the regulations were so varied and complicated, and because they changed with great frequency, contacts with the outside world were in reality left – once again – to the whim of the camp commanders. Letters and packages certainly never reached prisoners in punishment cells, punishment barracks or punishment *lagpunkts*. Nor did they reach prisoners whom the camp authorities disliked, for whatever reason. Moreover, there were camps which were simply too isolated, and therefore did not receive any mail.[21] There were camps so disorganized that they did not bother to distribute mail. Of one camp, a disgusted NKVD inspector wrote that 'packages, letters and money orders are not distributed to prisoners, but rather lie by the thousands in warehouses and outposts'.[22] In many camps, letters were received months late, if at all. Many prisoners realized only years later how many of their letters and packages had gone missing. Whether stolen or lost, no one could say. Conversely, prisoners who had been strictly forbidden from receiving letters sometimes received them anyway, despite the best efforts of the camp administration.[23]

On the other hand, some camp censors not only did their duty and distributed letters, they even allowed some missives to pass unopened. Dmitri Bystroletov remembered one – a 'young *komsomolka*', a member of the Young Communist League – who gave prisoners their letters unopened and uncensored: 'She risked not just a piece of bread, but freedom: for that, they would give her a ten-year sentence.'[24]

There were, of course, ways round both the censorship of letters and the restrictions on their numbers. Anna Rozina once received a letter from her husband which had been baked inside a cake: by the time it reached her, he had already been executed. She also saw letters sewn into the clothes of prisoners being freed from the camp, or smuggled to the outside world tucked into the soles of shoes.[25] In one light-regime camp, Barbara Armonas smuggled letters via prisoners who worked unguarded outside the *zona*.[26]

General Gorbatov also describes how he sent an uncensored letter to his wife from inside a transport train, using a method mentioned by many others. First, he bought a pencil stub from one of the criminal prisoners:

I gave the convict the tobacco, took the pencil from him and, as the train moved off again, wrote a letter on the cigarette paper, numbering each sheet. Next I made an envelope of the *makhorka* wrapper and stuck it down with moistened bread. So that my letter should not be carried by the wind into the bushes beside the railway, I weighted it with a crust of bread which I tied on with threads pulled from my towel. Between the envelope and the crust I slipped a rouble note and four cigarette papers each with the message: would the finder of this envelope please stick on a stamp and post it. I sidled up to the window of our truck just as we were going through a big station and let the letter drop . . .[27]

Not long afterwards, his wife received it.

Some limitations on letter-writing were not mentioned in the instructions. It was all very well to be allowed to write, for example – but it was not always so easy to find something to write with or to write on, as Bystroletov remembered: 'Paper in the camp is an object of great value, because it is badly needed by prisoners, but impossible to get: what does the cry "Today is a mail day! Hand in your letters!" mean if there is nothing on which to write, if only a few lucky ones can write, and the rest must lie gloomily on their bunks?'[28]

One prisoner recalled trading bread in exchange for two pages ripped out of *The Question of Leninism*, a book by Stalin. He wrote a letter to his family between the lines.[29] Even the camp administrators, in smaller *lagpunkts*, had to think up creative solutions. In Kedrovy Shor, one camp accountant used old wallpaper for official documents.[30]

The rules surrounding packages were even more complex. The instructions sent to every camp commander expressly stipulated that prisoners open all packages in the presence of a guard, who could then confiscate any forbidden item.[31] In fact, the receipt of a package was often accompanied by an entire ceremony. First, the prisoner was alerted of his good fortune. Then, guards escorted him into the storeroom, where the prisoners' personal belongings were kept under lock and key. After he opened the package, the guards would cut or prise open every single item – every onion, every sausage – to ensure that it did not contain secret messages, potential weapons or money. If everything passed the inspection, the prisoner would then be allowed to take something from the package. The rest would be left in the warehouse, pending his next permitted visit. Prisoners who were being held in the SHIZO or who were otherwise in disgrace would, of course, be forbidden access to the food products sent to them from home.

There were variations on this system. One prisoner soon realized that if he left his packages in the storeroom, bits of them would quickly disappear, stolen by the guards. He therefore found a way to hang a bottle full of butter from his belt, hiding it in his trousers: 'Warmed by my body, it was always liquid.' In the evening, he spread the butter on his bread.[32] Dmitri Bystroletov was in a *lagpunkt* which did not have a storeroom at all, and had to be even more creative:

I worked then in the tundra, on a factory construction site, and lived in a workers' barracks where it was impossible to leave anything, and impossible to take anything to the work site: the soldiers standing at the entrance to the camp would confiscate anything they found and eat it themselves, and anything left behind would be stolen and eaten by the *dnevalnyi* [the prisoner assigned to clean and guard the barracks]. Everything had to be eaten at once. I took a nail out of the barrack bunks, knocked two holes in a can of condensed milk, and underneath my blanket began to sip out of it. My exhaustion was so great, however, that I fell asleep, and the priceless liquid dripped uselessly on to the dirty straw mattress.[33]

There were also complicated moral issues surrounding packages, since not everybody received them. Should they be shared or not? And, if so, was it better to share only with friends, or with potential protectors? In prison, it had been possible to organize 'Committees of the Poor', but in camp this was impossible. Some gave to everybody, out of kindness or the desire to spread goodwill. Others gave only to small circles of friends. And sometimes, as one prisoner remembered, 'it happened that one ate sweet biscuits in bed at night, as it was unpleasant to eat in front of others'.[34]

During the hardest war years, in the most difficult northern camps, packages could determine the difference between life and death. One memoirist, the film director Georgi Zhenov, claims literally to have been saved by two packages. His mother mailed them from Leningrad in 1940, and he received them three years later, 'at the most critical moment, when I, hungry, having lost all hope, was slowly dying of scurvy . . .'

At that time, Zhenov was working in the camp bath-house in a Kolyma *lagpunkt*, being too weak to work in the forest. Upon hearing that he had received the two packages, he at first did not believe it. Then, convinced that it was true, he asked the chief bath attendant for permission to walk the 10 kilometres to the central camp administrative headquarters where the storeroom was located. After two and a half hours, he turned back: 'I had with difficulty travelled a kilometre.' Then, seeing a group of camp bosses on a sleigh, 'a fantastic thought crossed my mind: what if I asked to go with them?' They said yes – and what happened next was 'as if in a dream'. Zhenov got on the sleigh, rode the 10 kilometres, got off the sleigh with great difficulty, helped by the NKVD bosses, entered the storeroom, claimed his three-year-old packages, and opened them up:

Everything that had been put into the package: sugar, sausage, lard, sweets, onions, garlic, biscuits, crackers, cigarettes, chocolate, along with the wrapping paper in which each thing had been packed, during the three years of following me from address to address, had become mixed up, as if in a washing machine, turning finally into one hard mass with the sweet smell of decay, mould, tobacco and the perfume of sweets . . .

I went to the table, took a knife to a piece of it, and in front of everyone, almost not chewing, hastily gulped, not distinguishing taste or smell, fearing, in a word, that someone would interrupt or take it away from me . . .[35]

Dom Svidanii
The House of Meetings

Letters and packages did not, however, evoke the greatest emotion, or the greatest agony, among prisoners. Far more wrenching were a prisoner's actual meetings with his relatives, usually a spouse or mother. Only prisoners who had both fulfilled the norm and obediently followed the rules of the camp were allowed such meetings: official documents openly described them as a reward for 'good, conscientious, and high-tempo work'.[36] And the promise of a visit from a relative was indeed an extremely powerful motivation for good behaviour.

Not all prisoners were in a position to receive visitors, of course. For one, their families had to be mentally courageous enough to maintain contact with their 'enemy' relative. The journey to Kolyma, Vorkuta, Norilsk or Kazakhstan, even travelling as a free citizen, required physical bravery as well. Not only would a visitor have to suffer a long train journey to a distant, primitive city, he would then have to walk, or hitch a bumpy ride in the back of a truck, to the *lagpunkt*. After that, the visitor might have to wait for several days or longer, begging sneering camp commanders for permission to see their prisoner relative – permission which might well be refused, for no reason at all. Afterwards, they faced another long journey home, by the same tedious route.

Leaving aside the physical hardships, the psychological strain of these meetings could be terrible too. The wives arriving to see their husbands, wrote Herling, 'feel the boundless suffering of the prisoner, without fully understanding it, or being in any way able to help; the long years of separation have killed much of their feeling for their husbands . . . the camp, distant and barred off from the visitor, yet casts its shadowy menace upon them. They are not prisoners, but they are related to these enemies of the people . . .'[37]

Nor were wives alone in their mixed feelings. One prisoner tells the story of a woman who had brought her two-year-old daughter to see her father. Upon arrival, she told her to 'go and kiss Daddy'. The girl ran up to the guard and kissed him on the neck.[38] The daughter of the Soviet rocket scientist Sergei Korolev still remembers being taken to see her father while he was in a *sharashka*. She had been told he was away, fighting with the air force. Entering the prison, she was surprised at the small size of the prison yard. Where, she asked her mother, did Daddy's plane land?[39]

In prisons – and in certain camps as well – such meetings were invariably brief, and usually took place in the presence of a guard, a rule which also created enormous strain. 'I wanted to speak, to speak a great deal, to tell of everything that had happened that year,' remembered one prisoner of the single meeting he was granted with his mother. Not only was it hard to find words, but 'if one did begin to speak, to describe something, the watchful guard would interrupt you: "Not allowed!" '.[40]

More tragic still is the story told by Bystroletov, who was granted a series of meetings with his wife in 1941 – all with a guard present. She had come from Moscow to say goodbye: since his arrest, she had contracted tuberculosis, and was near death. Saying her final farewell, she reached up and touched him on the neck, which was technically not allowed. Visitors were forbidden physical contact with the prisoners. The guard roughly pushed her arm away, and she fell to the floor, coughing blood. Bystroletov writes that he 'lost his head' and began beating the guard, who began to bleed. He was saved from dire punishment by the war, which broke out that same day. In the ensuing chaos, his attack on the guard was forgotten. He never saw his wife again.[41]

Guards were not always present, however. Indeed, in the larger *lagpunkts*, in the bigger camps, prisoners were sometimes allowed meetings of several days' length, without guards present. By the 1940s, these meetings usually took place in a designated 'House of Meetings' – *dom svidanii* – a building specially constructed for that purpose on the edge of the camp. Herling describes one:

The house itself, seen from the road which led to the camp from the village, made a pleasant impression. It was built of rough pine beams, the gaps filled in with oakum, the roof was laid with good tiling . . . The door outside the zone, which could be used only by the free visitors, was reached by a few solid wooden steps; cotton curtains hung in the windows, and long window-boxes planted with flowers stood by the window sills. Every room was furnished with two neatly made beds, a large table, two benches, a basin and a water-jug, a clothes-cupboard and an iron stove; there was even a lampshade over the electric-light bulb. What more could a prisoner, who had lived for years on a common bunk in a dirty barrack, desire of this model petit bourgeois dwelling? Our dreams of life at liberty were based on that room.[42]

And yet – those who had anxiously anticipated that 'dream of liberty' often felt far worse when the meeting turned out badly, which it often did. Fearing they would remain behind barbed wire for life, some prisoners greeted their relatives by telling them not to come again. 'You forget about this place,' one told his brother, who had travelled for many days in freezing temperatures to meet him for twenty minutes: 'It is more important to me that everything should be all right with you.'[43] Men meeting their wives for the first time in years suddenly found themselves beset with sexual anxiety, as Herling recalls:

Years of heavy labour and hunger had undermined their virility, and now, before an intimate meeting with an almost strange woman, they felt, beside nervous excitement, helpless anger and despair. Several times I did hear men boasting of their prowess after a visit, but usually these matters were a cause for shame, and respected in silence by all prisoners . . .[44]

Visiting wives had their own troubles to discuss. Usually, they had suffered a great deal from their husbands' imprisonment. They could not find jobs, could not study, and often had to hide their marriages from inquisitive neighbours. Some arrived in order to announce their intention to divorce. In *The First Circle*, Solzhenitsyn recounts, with surprising sympathy, one such conversation, based on a real one he had with his own wife, Natasha. In the book, Nadya, the prisoner Gerasimovich's wife, is on the verge of losing her job, her place in a student hostel, and the possibility of completing her thesis, all because her husband is a prisoner. Divorce, she knows, is the only way to 'have a chance to live again':

Nadya lowered her eyes. 'I wanted to say – only you won't take it to heart, will you? – you once said we ought to get divorced.' She said it very quietly . . .

Yes, there was a time when he had insisted on this. But now he was startled. Only at this moment did he notice that her wedding ring, which she had always worn, was not on her finger.

'Yes, of course,' he agreed, with every appearance of alacrity.

'Then you won't be against it . . . if . . . I . . . have to . . . do it?' With a great effort she looked at him. Her eyes were very wide. The fine pinpoints of her grey pupils were alight with a plea for forgiveness and understanding. 'It would be . . . pseudo,' she added, breathing the word rather than speaking it.[45]

Such a meeting could be worse than no meeting at all. Izrail Mazus, arrested in the 1950s, recounts the story of one prisoner who made the mistake of announcing to his fellow inmates that his wife had arrived. As he endured the routines required of every prisoner due to encounter a visitor – he went to the baths, to the barber, to the storage room to retrieve some proper clothes – the other prisoners relentlessly winked at him and poked him, teasing him about the squeaky bed in the House of Meetings.[46] Yet in the end, he was not even allowed to be alone in the room with his wife. What sort of 'glimpse of liberty' was that?

Contacts with the outside world were always complicated – by expectations, by desires, by anticipation. Herling, again, writes that:

Whatever the reason for their disappointment – whether the freedom, realized for three days, had not lived up to its idealized expectation, whether it was too short, or whether, fading away like an interrupted dream, it had left only fresh emptiness in which they had nothing to wait for – the prisoners were invariably silent and irritable after visits, to say nothing of those whose visits had been transformed into the tragic formality of separation and divorce. Krestynski ... twice attempted to hang himself after an interview with his wife, who had asked him for a divorce and for his agreement to place their children in a municipal nursery.

Herling, who as a Polish foreigner 'never expected to see anyone' in the House of Meetings, nevertheless saw the significance of the place more clearly than many Soviet writers: 'I came to the conclusion that if hope can often be the only meaning left in life, then its realization may sometimes be an unbearable torment.'[47]

13

The Guards

To the Chekists

A great and responsible task
Was placed upon you by Ilyich,
The face of a Chekist is worn with cares
Which no one else can comprehend.

On the face of a Chekist is valour,
He is ready to fight, even today,
For the good of all, and their well-being,
He stands up for the working people.

Many, many in battle have fallen,
Many of our brothers' tombs have arisen.
But there still remain many,
Honest and vigorous fighters.

Tremble, tremble, enemies!
Soon, soon, your end will come!
You, Chekist, stand always on guard
And in battle you will lead the throng!

– Poem by Mikhail Panchenko, an inspector in the Soviet
prison system, preserved in the same personal file that
describes his expulsion from the Party and from
the NKVD[1]

Strange though it may sound, not all of the rules in the camps were written
by the camp commanders. There were also unwritten rules – about how to
attain status, how to gain privileges, how to live a little better than everyone
else – as well as an informal hierarchy. Those who mastered these unwritten
rules, and learned how to climb the hierarchy, found it much easier to survive.

At the top of the camp hierarchy were the commanders, the overseers, the
warders, the gaolers and the guards. I deliberately write 'at the top of' rather

than 'above' or 'outside' the camp hierarchy, for in the Gulag the administrators and guards were not a separate caste, apart and aloof from the prisoners. Unlike the SS guards in German concentration camps, they were not considered immutably, racially superior to the prisoners, whose ethnicity they often shared. There were, for example, many hundreds of thousands of Ukrainian prisoners in the camps after the Second World War. There were also, in the same time period, a notable number of Ukrainian guards.[2]

Nor did the guards and prisoners inhabit entirely separate social spheres. Some guards and administrators had elaborate black-market dealings with prisoners. Some got drunk with prisoners. Many 'co-habited' with prisoners, to use the Gulag's euphemism for sexual relations.[3] More to the point, many were former prisoners themselves. In the early 1930s, it was considered perfectly normal for well-behaved prisoners to 'graduate' to the status of camp guards – and some even went higher.[4] Naftaly Frenkel's career represented perhaps the most outstanding transformation, but there were others.

Yakov Kuperman's career was less exalted than Frenkel's, for example, but more typical. Kuperman – who later donated his unpublished memoirs to the Memorial Society in Moscow – was arrested in 1930 and given a ten-year sentence. He spent time in Kem, the Solovetsky transit prison, and then went to work in the planning division of the White Sea Canal. In 1932, his case was re-examined and his status was changed from prisoner to exile. Eventually, he was freed, and took up a job on the Baikal–Amur Railway – BAMlag – an experience he remembered 'with satisfaction' until the end of his life.[5] His decision was not an unusual one. In 1938, more than half of the administrators and nearly half of the armed guards in Belbaltlag, the camp that ran the White Sea Canal, were former or actual prisoners.[6]

Status could be lost as well as gained, however. Just as it was relatively easy for a prisoner to become a gaoler, so too was it relatively easy for a gaoler to become a prisoner. Gulag administrators and camp commanders figured among the thousands of NKVD men arrested in the purge years of 1937 and 1938. In later years, too, Gulag guards and Gulag employees were regularly arrested by their suspicious colleagues. In the isolated lagpunkts, gossip and backbiting were rife: whole files of the Gulag's archives are devoted to denunciations and counter-denunciations, furious letters about camp deficiencies, lack of support from the centre, poor working conditions – and subsequent calls for arrests of the guilty, or of the disliked.[7]

Armed guards and administrators were regularly arrested for desertion, drinking, stealing, losing their weapons, even for mistreating prisoners.[8] The records of the Vanino port transit camp, for example, contain descriptions of V. N. Sadovnikov, an armed guard who murdered a camp nurse, having meant to murder his wife; of I. M. Soboleev, who stole 300 roubles from a group of prisoners, and then got drunk and lost his Party membership card; of V. D. Suvorov, who organized a group drinking session and picked a fight with a group of officers – as well as others who 'drank themselves into unconsciousness', or who were too drunk to man their posts.[9] The personal papers of Georgi Malenkov, one of Stalin's henchmen, contain a report on the case of two camp administrators who murdered two colleagues in the course of a drunken binge, among them a woman doctor with two small children.[10] So boring was life in the more distant camp outposts, one camp administrator complained in a letter to Moscow that lack of entertainment 'pushes many of the boys into desertion, violations of discipline, drunkenness and card-playing – all of which regularly ends with a court sentence'.[11]

It was even possible, indeed rather common, for some to make the full circle: for NKVD officers to become prisoners, and then to become gaolers again, making second careers in the Gulag administration. Certainly many former prisoners have written of the speed with which disgraced NKVD officers would find their feet in the camps, and go on to obtain positions of real power. In his memoirs, Lev Razgon records an encounter with one Korabelnikov, a low-level NKVD employee whom he met during the journey from Moscow. Korabelnikov told Razgon he had been arrested because he 'blabbed to my best mate . . . about one of the bosses' women . . . got five years as a Socially Dangerous Element – and into a transport with the rest'. But he was not quite like the rest. Some months later, Razgon met him again. This time he was wearing a clean, well-made camp uniform. He had wormed his way into a 'good' job, running the punishment camp in Ustvymlag.[12]

Razgon's story reflects a reality which is recorded in archives. Many, many Gulag officers had criminal records, in fact. Indeed, it seems as if the Gulag administration openly functioned within the NKVD as a place of exile, a last resort for disgraced secret police.[13] Once sent to the outer reaches of the Gulag's empire, officers were rarely allowed to return to any other branch of the NKVD, let alone to Moscow. As a sign of their different status, the Gulag's employees wore distinct uniforms, and had a slightly altered system of badges and ranks.[14] At Party conferences, Gulag officers complained about their inferior status. 'The Gulag is seen as an administration from which everything can be demanded and nothing given in return,' griped one officer: 'This excessively modest way of thinking – that we are worse than everyone else – is wrong, and it allows inequities in pay, in housing, and so on, to continue.'[15] Later, in 1946, when the NKVD was divided and renamed once again, the Gulag fell under the control of the Ministry of Internal Affairs (MVD) while almost all of the NKVD's more exciting functions, particularly intelligence and counter-intelligence, were moved to the more prestigious Ministry of State Security (MGB, later KGB). The MVD, which ran the prison system until the end of the Soviet Union, would remain a less influential bureaucracy.[16]

In fact, camp commanders had had relatively low status right from the beginning. In a letter smuggled out of Solovetsky in the early 1920s, one prisoner wrote that the camp administration consisted entirely of disgraced Chekists who 'have been convicted of speculation or extortion or assault or some other offence against the ordinary penal code'.[17] In the 1930s and 1940s, the Gulag became the ultimate destination of NKVD officials whose biographies did not match requirements: those whose social origins were not proletariat enough, or whose Polish, Jewish or Baltic nationality made them suspect during eras when those ethnic groups were being actively repressed. The Gulag was also the last refuge for those who were simply stupid, incompetent or drunk. In 1937, the then-chief of the Gulag, Izrail Pliner, complained that

We get the leftovers from other sections; they send us people based on the principle 'You can take what we do not need.' The cream of the crop are the hopeless drunkards; once a man goes over to drink he's dumped on to the Gulag . . . From the point of view of the NKVD apparatus, if someone commits an offence, the greatest punishment is to send him to work in a camp.[18]

In 1939, another Gulag official described camp guards as 'not second-class but fourth-class people, the very dregs'.[19] In 1945, Vasily Chernyshev, at the time the Gulag boss, sent out a memorandum to all camp commanders and regional NKVD chiefs expressing horror at the low quality of the camp armed guards, among whom had been discovered high levels of 'suicide, desertion, loss and theft of weapons, drunkenness and other amoral acts', as well as frequent 'violation of revolutionary laws'.[20] As late as 1952, when corruption was discovered at the highest levels of the secret police, Stalin's first response was to 'exile' one of the main perpetrators, who promptly became deputy commander of the Bazhenovsky camp in the Urals.[21]

The Gulag's own archives also confirm the belief, delicately expressed by one former prisoner, that both guards and administrators were 'more often than not, very limited people'.[22] Of the eleven men who held the title 'Commander of the Gulag', for example – the administrator of the entire camp system – between 1930 and 1960, only five had had any kind of higher education, while three had never got any further than primary school. Those who held this job rarely did so for long: over a thirty-year period, only two men, Matvei Berman and Viktor Nasedkin, held it for longer than five years. Izrail Pliner lasted only a year (1937–8), while Gleb Filaretov lasted only three months (1938–9).[23]

On the bottom of the NKVD hierarchy, on the other hand, personal files of the employees of the prison service from the 1940s show that even the most elite gaolers – Party members and those applying for Party membership – came almost entirely from peasant backgrounds, having received minimal education. Few had completed even five years of school, and some had completed only three.[24] As of April 1945, nearly three-quarters of the

Gulag's administrators had received no education beyond primary school, a percentage nearly double that in the rest of the NKVD.[25]

The camp armed guards – the *voenizirovannaya okhrana*, usually known, thanks to the Soviet mania for acronyms, as VOKhR – were even less educated. These were the men who walked round the perimeter of the camps, who marched prisoners to work, who manned the trains taking them east, often with only the dimmest idea of why they were doing it. According to one report from Kargopollag, 'it appears that the guards don't know the names of members of the Politburo, or leaders of the Party'.[26] Another document lists a series of incidents involving guards who misused their weapons. One of them wounded three prisoners 'as the result of not knowing how his gun worked'. Another, 'at his post in a drunken state, wounded citizen Timofeev'.[27]

Division commanders complained at meetings that 'The guards do not know how to oil, clean and take care of their weapons . . . A female guard stands on duty with her rifle barrel stuffed with a rag . . . Some guards take other people's rifles out on duty, leaving their own back at home because they're too lazy to clean them each time.'[28] There were constant missives back and forth from Moscow to the camps urging local commanders to spend more time on 'cultural-educational work' among the guards.[29]

Yet even the 'leftovers' and 'hopeless drunkards' from other departments of the NKVD managed to fill the Gulag's demands for employees. Most Soviet institutions suffered from chronic lack of personnel, and the Gulag suffered particularly badly. Even the NKVD could not produce enough delinquent employees to fulfil the demand for an eighteenfold increase in staff between 1930 and 1939, or for the 150,000 people who had to be hired between 1939 and 1941, or for the enormous post-war expansion. In 1947, with 157,000 people serving just in the camp armed guards brigades, the Gulag still reckoned itself to be 40,000 guards short.[30]

Right up until the system was finally disbanded, this dilemma never ceased to plague the Gulag administration. With the exception of the very top jobs, work in the camps was not considered to be prestigious or attractive, and living conditions were hardly guaranteed to be comfortable, particularly in the smaller, more distant outposts of the far north. General food shortages meant that guards and administrators received rationed food in quantities distributed according to the rank of the recipient.[31] Returning from a tour of inspection of the northern camps of the Vorkuta region, one Gulag inspector complained about the poor living conditions of the armed guards, who worked fourteen to sixteen-hour days in 'difficult northern climatic conditions', did not always have proper shoes and clothes, and lived in dirty barracks. Some suffered from scurvy, pellagra and other vitamin-deficiency diseases, just as prisoners did.[32] Another wrote that in Kargopollag, twenty-six members of the VOKhR had been given criminal sentences, many for falling asleep at their posts. In the summer, they worked thirteen-hour days – and when they were not at work they had no forms of entertainment. Those with families were in particularly poor condition, as they often did not have apartments and were forced to live in barracks.[33]

Those who wanted to leave did not find it easy, even at the higher levels. The NKVD archives contain a plaintive letter from the prosecutor of Norilsk, begging to be removed from work in the 'Arctic zone', on the grounds of health and overwork: 'If it isn't possible to move me to a prosecutor's job in another corrective-labour camp, then I would like to be put in a territorial job or else removed from the procuracy altogether.' In response, he was offered a transfer to Krasnoyarsk, which he turned down, as the conditions there – Krasnoyarsk lies to the south of Norilsk, but is still in northern Siberia – were almost the same.[34]

Since the death of Stalin, former camp officials have often defended their past livelihoods by describing the difficulties and hardships of the work. When I met her, Olga Vasileevna, a former inspector of camps for the road-building division of the Gulag, regaled me with tales of the hard life of a Gulag employee. During our conversation – held at her unusually spacious Moscow apartment, the gift of a grateful Party – Vasileevna told me that once, when visiting a distant camp, she was invited to sleep in the home of a camp commander, in his son's bed. At night she became hot and itchy. Thinking perhaps she was ill, she switched on the light: 'His grey soldier's blanket was alive, swarming with lice. It wasn't only prisoners who had lice, the bosses had them too.' As a rule, when she returned home from an inspection trip, she would remove all of her clothes before entering the front door, to avoid bringing parasites into her house.

As Vasileevna saw it, the job of camp commander was extremely difficult: 'It isn't a joke, you are in charge of hundreds, thousands of prisoners, there were recidivists and murderers, those convicted of heavy crimes, from them you could expect anything. That meant you have to be on guard the whole time.' Commanders, although under pressure to work as efficiently as possible, found themselves needing to solve all kinds of other problems as well:

The head of a building project, he was also the head of a camp, and spent at least 60 per cent of his time not on the building works, making engineering decisions and solving building problems, but dealing with the camp. Someone was ill, an epidemic might have broken out, or some kind of accident had happened which means someone has to be taken to the hospital, someone needs a car or a horse and cart.

Vasileevna also said that the 'bosses' did not necessarily eat well in Moscow either, especially during the war. In the canteen at Gulag headquarters, there was cabbage, soup and *kasha*: 'I don't remember meat, I never saw any.' During Stalin's lifetime, employees of the Gulag in Moscow worked from nine o'clock in the morning until two or three o'clock the next morning, every day. She saw her child only on Sundays. After Stalin died, however, things improved. S. N. Kruglov, then the head of the NKVD, issued an order granting ordinary employees of the NKVD central administration a one-hour lunch break, and NKVD officers a two-hour lunch break. In 1963, Vasileevna and her husband also received a very large apartment in central Moscow, the same one she was living in when I met her in 1998.[35]

In Stalin's lifetime, though, work in the Gulag was less well-rewarded, leaving the central camp administration to address the problem of the job's essential unattractiveness in different ways. In 1930, when the system was still perceived as part of the economic expansion of the time, the OGPU conducted internal advertising campaigns, asking for enthusiasts to work in what were then the new camps of the far north:

> The enthusiasm and energy of Chekists created and strengthened the Solovetsky camps, playing a large, positive role in the industrial and cultural development of the far northern European part of our country. The new camps, like Solovetsky, must play a reforming role in the economy and culture of the outer regions. For this responsibility . . . we need especially tough Chekists, volunteers desiring hard work . . .

The volunteers were offered, among other things, up to 50 per cent extra pay, a two-month holiday every year, and a bonus, after three years, of three months' salary and a three-month holiday. In addition, the top administrators would receive monthly ration packages for free, and access to 'radio, sporting facilities and cultural facilities'.[36]

Later on, as any genuine enthusiasm disappeared altogether (if it had ever existed), the inducements became more systematic. Camps were ranked according to their distance and their harshness. The more distant and the more harsh, the more NKVD officers would be paid to work in them. Some made a point of organizing sporting and other activities for their employees. In addition, the NKVD built special sanitoriums by the Black Sea, in Sochi and Kislovodsk, so that the highest-ranking officers could spend their long vacations in comfort and warmth.[37]

The central administration also created schools where Gulag officers could improve their qualifications and their rank. One, for example, established in Kharkov, taught courses not only in the obligatory 'History of the Party' and 'History of the NKVD' but also criminal law, camp policies, administration, management, accounting and military subjects.[38] Those willing to work at Dalstroi, in distant Kolyma, could even have their children reclassified as 'children of workers': this qualified them for preferential acceptance at institutes of higher education, and proved a highly popular inducement.[39]

The money and benefits were certainly enough to attract some employees at the lowest levels too. Many simply saw the Gulag as the best of all possible bad options. In Stalin's Soviet Union – a country of war, famine, starvation –

employment as a prison guard or warder could signify an immeasurable social advance. Susanna Pechora, a prisoner in the early 1950s, recalled meeting one female warder who was working in a camp because it was the only way to escape from the dire poverty of the collective farm where she had been born: 'she fed her seven brothers and sisters on her camp salary'.[40] Another memoirist tells the story of Maria Ivanova, a young woman who came voluntarily to work in a camp in 1948. Hoping to escape life on a collective farm, and hoping even more to find a husband, Maria Ivanova instead became the mistress of a series of officials of ever-declining rank. She wound up living with her two illegitimate children and her mother in a single room.[41]

But even the prospects of high salaries, long vacations and social advance were still not always enough to bring workers into the system, particularly at the lower levels. At times of great demand, Soviet labour boards would simply send workers where they were needed, not even necessarily telling them where they were going. One former Gulag nurse, Zoya Eremenko, was sent straight from nursing school to work on what she had been told would be a construction site. When she arrived, she discovered that it was a prison camp, Krasnoyarsk-26. 'We were surprised, frightened, but when we got to know the place, we found that "there", the people were the same and the medical work was the same as what we had been led to expect from our studies,' she recalled.[42]

Particularly tragic were the cases of those forced to work in the camps after the Second World War. Thousands of ex-Red Army soldiers who had fought their way across Germany, as well as civilians who had lived 'abroad' during the war, as deportees or refugees, were effectively arrested upon crossing the border back into the Soviet Union, and confined to 'filtration camps', where they were carefully cross-examined. Those who were not arrested were sometimes immediately sent to work in the prison guard service. By the beginning of 1946, there were 31,000 such people, and in some camps they accounted for up to 80 per cent of the guard service.[43] Nor could they easily leave. Many had been deprived of their documents – passports, residence permits, military service certificates. Without them, they were unable to leave the camps, let alone search for new jobs. Between 300 and 400 every year committed suicide. One who attempted to do so, explained why: 'I've been in the service for a very long time now, and I still have not been given a residence permit, and nearly every day a policeman comes round with an order to vacate the apartment, and this leads to quarrels in my family every single day.'[44]

Others simply degenerated. Karlo Stajner, a Yugoslav communist and a prisoner in Norilsk during and after the war, remembered such guards as being 'notably different from those who hadn't fought in the war':

There were definite signs of demoralization, for one. You could see it in their willingness to be bribed by the female prisoners or to become clients of the prettier ones, or to allow criminals to leave the brigade in order to break into some apartment, and share the loot with them later. They weren't afraid of the severe punishments they would be subject to if their superiors found out about these misdeeds.[45]

A very, very few protested. The archives record, for example, the case of one unwilling recruit, Danilyuk, who categorically refused to serve in the armed guards service, on the grounds that 'I don't want to serve in the organs of the Ministry of Internal Affairs at all.' Danilyuk kept up this stance despite what the archives call 'processing sessions', undoubtedly long periods of browbeating, perhaps actual beatings. He was, in the end, released from service. At least in his case, consistent and persistent refusal to work for the Gulag found its reward.[46]

In the end, though, the system did reward its luckiest and most loyal members, some of whom received far more than a mere social advance or better rations: those who delivered large quantities of gold or timber to the state with their prisoner labourers would, eventually, receive their rewards. And while the average logging *lagpunkt* was never a nice place to live, even for those running it, the headquarters of some of the bigger camps did over time become very comfortable indeed.

By the 1940s, the cities that stood at the centre of the larger camp complexes – Magadan, Vorkuta, Norilsk, Ukhta – were large, bustling places, with shops, theatres and parks. The opportunities for living the good life had increased enormously since the Gulag's pioneering early days. Top commanders in the bigger camps got higher salaries, better bonuses and longer vacations than those in the ordinary working world. They had better access to food and to consumer goods that were in short supply elsewhere. 'Life in Norilsk was better than anywhere else in the Soviet Union,' remembered Andrei Cheburkin, a foreman in Norilsk and later a local bureaucrat:

In the first place, all the bosses had maids, prisoner maids. Then the food was amazing. There were all sorts of fish. You could go and catch it in the lakes. And if in the rest of the Union there were ration cards, here we lived virtually without cards. Meat. Butter. If you wanted champagne you had to take a crab as well, there were so many. Caviare . . . barrels of the stuff lay around. I'm talking about bosses, of course. I am not talking about the workers. But then the workers were prisoners . . .

The pay was good . . . say you were a brigadier, you'd get 6,000–8,000 roubles. In central Russia you would get no more than 1,200. I came to Norilsk to work as a work supervisor in a special directorate of the NKVD, which was looking for uranium. I was given a supervisor's salary: 2,100 roubles I received from the first, and then each six months I got a 10 per cent rise, about five times more than they got in normal civilian life.[47]

Cheburkin's first point – 'all the bosses had maids' – was a key one, for it applied, in fact, not just to the bosses but to everyone. Technically, the use of prisoners as domestics was forbidden. But it was very widespread, as the authorities well knew, and despite frequent attempts to stop the practice, it continued.[48] In Vorkuta, Konstantin Rokossovsky, a Red Army officer who later became a general, then a marshal, then Defence Minister of Stalinist Poland, worked as a servant to a 'loutish warder named Buchko, his duties consisting of fetching the man's meals, tidying and heating his cottage and so forth'.[49] In Magadan, Evgeniya Ginzburg worked, for a time, as a laundress for the wife of a camp administrator.[50]

Thomas Sgovio also worked as a personal orderly to a senior camp guard in Kolyma, preparing his food and trying to procure alcohol for him. The man came to trust him. 'Thomas, my boy,' he would say, 'remember one thing. Take care of my Party membership card. Whenever I'm drunk – see that I don't lose it. You're my servant – and if I ever lose it, I'll have to shoot you like a dog . . . and I don't want to do that.'[51]

But for the really big bosses, servants were only the beginning. Ivan Niki-shov, who became the boss of Dalstroi in 1939, in the wake of the purges, and held the post until 1948, became infamous for accumulating riches in the middle of desperate poverty. Nikishov was a different generation from his predecessor, Berzin – a generation far removed from the lean and more fervent years of the Revolution and the civil war. Perhaps as a result, Nikishov had no compunction about using his position to live well. He equipped himself with a 'large personal security force, luxury automobiles, sweeping offices and a magnificent dacha overlooking the Pacific Ocean'.[52] The latter, according to prisoner accounts, was said to be equipped with oriental carpets, bearskins and crystal chandeliers. In the luxurious dining room, he and his second wife – a young, ambitious camp commander named Gridasova – were said to dine on roast bear, wine from the Caucusus, fruits and berries flown in from the south, as well as fresh tomatoes and cucumbers from private greenhouses.[53]

Nikishov was not alone in enjoying a life of luxury either. Lev Razgon, in his unforgettable description of Colonel Tarasyuk, the wartime commander of Ustvymlag, records similar excesses:

He lived like a Roman who has been appointed governor of some barbarous newly conquered province. Vegetables and fruit, and flowers quite alien to the North, were grown for him in special hot-houses and orangeries. The best cabinet-makers were found to make his furniture. The most famous couturiers of the recent past dressed his capricious and wilful wife. When he felt unwell he was not examined by some freely hired little doctor who had sold himself to the Gulag as a medical student. No, Tarasyuk was treated by professors who had headed the biggest Moscow clinics and were now serving their long sentences in the medical barracks of remote forest camps.[54]

Often, prisoners were required to help indulge these whims. Isaac Vogel-fanger, a camp doctor, found himself constantly short of medicinal alcohol because his pharmacist used it to make brandy. The camp boss then used the brandy to entertain visiting dignitaries: 'The more alcohol they consume, the better their opinion of work in Sevurallag.' Vogelfanger also witnessed a camp cook prepare a 'banquet' for visitors, using things he had saved up for the occasion: 'caviare, smoked eel, hot rolls made from French dough with mushrooms, Arctic char in lemon aspic, baked goose and baked piglet'.[55]

It was also in this period, the 1940s, that bosses like Nikishov began to see themselves as more than mere gaolers. Some even began to compete with one another, in a fantastic version of keeping up with the Joneses. They vied to produce the best prisoner theatrical groups, the best prisoner orchestras, the best prisoner artists. Lev Kopelev was in Unzhlag in 1946, at a time when its commander would select, straight from prison, 'the best performers, musicians and artists, to whom he gave the best trusty jobs, working as cleaners and caretakers in the hospital'. The camp became known as an 'asylum for artists'.[56] Dalstroi also boasted an inmate troupe called the Sevvostlag Club, which performed in Magadan and in some of the outlying camps of the mining zone, benefiting from the many well-known singers and dancers incarcerated in Kolyma.[57] Lev Razgon describes too the commander of Ukhtizhemlag, who 'maintained a real opera troupe in Ukhta', directed by a famous Soviet actor. He also 'employed' a famous Bolshoi ballerina, as well as well-known singers and musicians:

Sometimes the head of Ukhtizhemlag would pay his neighbouring colleagues a visit. Although the official purpose was to 'share experience', this flat description belies the elaborate preparations and protocol which more resembled a visit by a foreign head of state. The bosses were accompanied by a large entourage of section heads, special hotel accommodation was prepared for them, routes were carefully planned and presents were brought in . . . The Ukhtizhemlag boss also brought his best performers with him so that his hosts could see that the arts were just as flourishing there, if not more so.[58]

To this day, the former Ukhtizhemlag theatre – a vast, white, columned building, with theatrical symbols on its pediment – is one of the most substantial buildings in the city of Ukhta. It stands within walking distance of the former camp commander's residence, a spacious wooden house on the edge of a park.

But it was not just those with artistic tastes who indulged their whims. Those who preferred sport also had an opportunity to try their hand at founding their own football teams, which competed with one another quite fiercely. Nikolai Starostin – the star player who was arrested because his team had the misfortune to beat Beria's – was also sent to Ukhta, where his transport was met right at the train station. He was taken to meet the local football manager, who addressed him politely and told him that the camp boss had specially requested his presence: 'the General's soul is in football. He was the one who got you here.' Starostin was to spend much of his camp career managing football teams for the NKVD, moving from place to place according to whichever commander wanted him as trainer.[59]

Occasionally, just occasionally, word of such excesses sparked alarm, or at least interest, in Moscow. Perhaps responding to complaints, Beria once commissioned a secret investigation into Nikishov's luxurious life-style. The resulting report confirms, among other things, that on one occasion Nikishov spent 15,000 roubles, a huge sum at that time, on a banquet given to commemorate the visit of the Khabarovsk Operetta Company.[60] The report also condemns the 'atmosphere of sycophancy' around Nikishov and his wife, Gridasova: 'The influence of Gridasova is so great, that even the deputies of Nikishov testify that they can work in their positions only so long as she looks kindly upon them.'[61] No steps were taken, however. Gridasova and Nikishov continued to reign in peace.

In recent years, it has become fashionable to point out that, contrary to their post-war protestations, few Germans were ever forced to work in concentration camps or killing squads. One scholar recently claimed that most had done so voluntarily – a view which has caused some controversy.[62] In the case of Russia and the other post-Soviet states, the issue has to be examined differently. Very often, camp employees – like most other Soviet citizens – had few options. A labour committee simply assigned them a place of work, and they had to go there. Lack of choice was built right into the Soviet economic system.

Nevertheless, it is not quite right to describe the NKVD officers and armed guards as 'no better off than the prisoners they commanded', or as victims of the same system, as some have tried to do. For although they might have preferred to work elsewhere, once they were inside the system, the employees of the Gulag did have choices, far more than their Nazi counterparts, whose work was more rigidly defined. They could choose to behave brutally, or they could choose to be kind. They could choose to work their prisoners to death, or they could choose to keep as many alive as possible. They could choose to sympathize with the prisoners whose fate they might have once shared, and might share again, or they could choose to take advantage of their temporary stretch of luck, and lord it over their former and future comrades in suffering.

Nothing in their past history necessarily indicated what path they would take, for both Gulag administrators and ordinary camp guards came from as many different ethnic and social backgrounds as did the prisoners. Indeed, when asked to describe the character of their guards, Gulag survivors almost always reply that they varied enormously. I put that question to Galina Smirnova, who remembered that 'they were, like everyone, all different'.[63] Anna Andreevna told me that 'there were sick sadists, and there were completely normal, good people'. Andreevna also recalled the day, soon after Stalin's death, when the chief accountant in her camp suddenly rushed into the accounting office where prisoners were working, cheered, hugged them and shouted, 'Take off your numbers, girls, they're giving you back your own clothes!'[64]

Irena Arginskaya also told me that her guards were not only 'very different sorts of people', but also people who changed over time. The conscript soldiers in particular acted 'like beasts' when they were new on the job, as they had been pumped full of propaganda, but 'after a time they began to understand – not all of them, but a large part – and they often changed'.[65]

True, the authorities exerted some pressure on both guards and administrators, discouraging them from showing prisoners any kindness. The archive of the Gulag's inspectorate records the case of Levin, the boss of the supply division for a section of Dmitlag in 1937, who was actively investigated for his lenience. His crime was to have allowed a prisoner to meet with his brother: normally, relatives within the prison system were kept far apart. Levin was also accused of being too friendly to *zeks* in general, and especially so to a group of *zeks* said to be Mensheviks. Levin – himself a former prisoner on the White Sea Canal – claimed, in return, that he had not known they *were* Mensheviks. Given that this was 1937, he was convicted anyway.[66]

Yet such strictures were not rigorously applied. Indeed, several top commanders actually became renowned for their kindness to prisoners. In *Let History Judge*, his denunciation of Stalinism, the dissident historian and publicist Roy Medvedev describes one camp commander, V. A. Kundush, who took seriously the demands for increased production during wartime. He placed the better-educated political prisoners in clerical jobs, and set about treating his prisoners well, even securing some of them early release. His enterprise received the 'Red Banner for Management' during the war. But when the war ended, he too was arrested, perhaps for the very humanity that had transformed his production.[67] Lev Razgon describes an unusual transit prison in Georgievsk, which both he and his second wife, Rika, passed through:

The cells were not only swept but washed, both the floors and the bed boards. The food was so filling that the constant hunger of prisoners in transit disappeared. You could really get clean in the bath-house. There was even a special and fully equipped room (and this amazed Rika more than anything else) where the women could primp and perk . . .[68]

And there were others. At one point during his camp career, Genrikh Gorchakov, a Russian Jew arrested in 1945, was assigned to an invalids' camp within the Siblag complex. The camp had recently been taken over by a new commander, a former front-line officer who could not find any other work after the war. Taking his job seriously, the commander built new barracks, saw to it that prisoners had mattresses and even sheets, and reorganized the work system, completely transforming the camp.[69]

Yet another ex-*zek*, Aleksei Pryadilov, arrested at sixteen, was sent to a farming camp in the Altai. There the camp boss 'ran the camp like an economic organization, and behaved towards prisoners not as if they were criminals and enemies, whom it was necessary to "re-educate", but as though they were workers. He was convinced that there was no point in trying to get good work out of hungry people.'[70] Even Gulag inspectors sometimes uncovered good commanders. One visited Birlag in 1942, and found that 'the prisoners of this factory worked excellently because their conditions were excellent'. Their barracks were clean, each prisoner had their own sheets and blankets, good clothes and shoes.[71]

There were also more direct forms of kindness. The memoirist Galina Levinson recalled one camp commander who talked a woman prisoner out of having an abortion. 'When you leave the camp you will be alone,' he told her. 'Think how good it will be to have a child.' To the end of her life, the woman was grateful to him.[72] Anatoly Zhigulin wrote too of a 'good' camp boss, who 'saved hundreds from death', called his charges 'comrade prisoners' in defiance of the rules, and ordered the cook to feed them better. Clearly, noted Zhigulin, he 'didn't know the rules yet'.[73] Mariya Sandratskaya, arrested for being the wife of an 'enemy', also describes a camp boss who paid special attention to the mothers in the camp, making sure the nursery was well run, that nursing women had enough to eat, and that mothers did not work too hard.[74]

In fact, kindness was possible: at all levels, there were always a few who resisted the propaganda describing all prisoners as enemies, a few who understood the true state of affairs. And a startling number of memoirists do note a single experience of kindness from a prison guard, or a single instance of consideration. 'I don't doubt,' wrote Evgeny Gnedin, 'that in the enormous army of camp administrators, there were honest workers who were distressed by their role as overseers to completely innocent people.'[75] Yet at the same time, most memoirists also marvel at how exceptional such understanding was. For despite the few counter-examples, clean prisons were not the norm, many camps were lethal – and the majority of guards treated their charges with indifference at best, outright cruelty at worst.

Nowhere, I repeat, was cruelty actually required. On the contrary: deliberate cruelty was officially frowned upon by the central administration. Camp guards and administrators who were unnecessarily harsh to prisoners could be punished, and often were. The archives of Vyatlag contain reports of guards punished for 'systematically beating up *zeks*', for stealing prisoners' belongings, and for raping women prisoners.[76] The archives of Dmitlag record the criminal sentences handed out to camp administrators accused of beating prisoners while drunk. The Gulag's central archives also record punishments for prison camp commanders who beat up prisoners, who tortured them during investigations, or who sent them on transports without proper winter clothes.[77]

Yet cruelty persisted. Sometimes it was genuinely sadistic. Viktor Bulgakov, a prisoner in the 1950s, recalled one of his guards, an illiterate Kazakh, who appeared to derive pleasure from forcing prisoners to stand, slowly freezing, in the snow, and another who liked to 'show off his strength and beat prisoners' for no particular reason.[78] The Gulag's archives also contain, among many other similar records, a description of the chief of one of the *lagpunkts* at Volgostroi during the war, Comrade Reshetov, who put *zeks* in freezing cold cells as punishment, and ordered sick prisoners to work in severe frost, as a result of which many died on the job.[79]

More often, cruelty was not so much sadism as self-interest. Guards who shot escaping prisoners received monetary rewards, and could even be granted a vacation at home. Guards were therefore tempted to encourage such 'escapes'. Zhigulin described the result:

The guard would shout at someone in the column, 'Hey, bring me that plank!'
  'But it's across the fence . . .'
  'Doesn't matter. Go!'
  The prisoner would go, and a line of machine-gun fire would follow him.[80]

Such incidents were common – as archives show. In 1938, four VOKhR guards working in Vyatlag were sentenced for killing two prisoners whom they had 'provoked' to escape. In the aftermath, it emerged that the division commander and his assistant had helped themselves to the prisoners' belongings as well.[81] The writer Boris Dyakov also mentions the practice of provoking escapes in his 'pro-Soviet' Gulag memoir, published in the USSR in 1964.[82]

As on the convoy trains, the cruelty in camps seemed, at times, to derive from anger or boredom at having to do a menial job. While working as a nurse in a Kolyma hospital, the Dutch communist Elinor Lipper sat up in the night beside a patient with pleurisy and high fever. He also had a carbuncle on his back which had burst, thanks to the guard who had brought him to the hospital:

In painful gasps, he told me that the guard had wanted to get the uncomfortable march over with as soon as possible, and so he had driven the sick, feverish prisoner on for hours with the blows of a club. At the end of the march he had threatened to break every bone in the prisoner's body if the man reported at the hospital that the guard had beaten him.

Frightened to the end, the man refused to repeat the story in the presence of non-prisoners. 'We let him die in peace,' wrote Lipper, 'and the guard went on beating prisoners undisturbed.'[83]

Most of the time, however, the cruelty of Soviet camp guards was unthinking, stupid, lazy cruelty, of the sort that might be shown to cattle or sheep. If guards were not explicitly told to mistreat prisoners, neither were they taught to consider prisoners, particularly political prisoners, as fully human either. On the contrary, great effort was put into cultivating hatred for prisoners, who were constantly described as 'dangerous criminals, as spies and saboteurs trying to destroy the Soviet people'. Such propaganda had an enormous effect on people who were already embittered by misfortune, by their unwanted jobs and by poor living conditions.[84] It also shaped the views of the camp's free workers – the local people working in the camp who were not NKVD employees – as much as the armed guards, as one prisoner remembered: 'Usually, from the free workers we were cut off by a wall of mutual distrust . . . Our grey shapes, being led under convoy and sometimes with dogs, was probably, for them, something very unpleasant, of which it was better not to think.'[85]

This was true as early as the 1920s, the era when Solovetsky guards were forcing freezing prisoners to jump into rivers at the cry of 'Dolphin!' It grew worse, of course, in the late 1930s, with the downgrading of political prisoners to 'enemies of the people', and the harshening of the camp regimes. In 1937, hearing that a large transport of Trotskyites were on their way to Kolyma, the boss of the camp, Eduard Berzin, told a group of co-workers that 'If these swine, who are now on their way here, committed sabotage on the mainland, let's make sure that here in Kolyma they work for the Soviet Union. We have the means to force them to work . . .'[86]

Even after the Great Terror ended, however, the propaganda never really let up. Throughout the 1940s and into the 1950s, prisoners were regularly referred to as war criminals and collaborators, traitors and spies. The Ukrainian nationalists who began pouring into the camps after the Second World War were variously called 'snake-like, slavish dogs of the Nazi hangmen', the 'Ukrainian German Fascists' or the 'agents of foreign intelligence services'. Nikita Khrushchev, then the leader of Ukraine, told a Central Committee plenum that the Ukrainian nationalists had 'killed themselves trying to please their master, Hitler, and to get only a small portion of the loot for their doggish service'.[87] During the war, guards called almost all political prisoners 'fascists' or 'Hitlerites' or 'Vlasovites' (followers of General Vlasov, who deserted the Red Army and supported Hitler).

This was especially galling for Jews, for veterans who had bravely fought the Germans, and for foreign communists who had fled fascism in their own countries.[88] 'We're not fascists, most of us are former Party members,' the Yugoslav communist Karlo Stajner indignantly told a group of jeering criminal prisoners, who had flung the 'fascist' insult at a brigade of politicals.[89] Margarete Buber-Neumann, a German communist who was released from the Gulag only to be transferred directly into a German concentration camp,

Ravensbruck, also wrote that she was repeatedly referred to as 'the German Fascist'.[90] And when one arrested NKVD officer, Mikhail Shreider, told his interrogator that as a Jew he could hardly be accused of collaborating with Hitler, he was told that he was not a Jew, but rather 'a German disguised as a Jew'.[91]

This name-calling was not just a pointless, juvenile exercise, however. By describing them as 'enemies' or as 'sub-human', guards reassured themselves of the legitimacy of their own actions. In fact, the rhetoric of 'enemies' was only a part of the ideology of the Gulag cadres. The other part – call it the rhetoric of 'state slavery' – constantly hammered home the importance of work, and of the ever-increasing production figures which were necessary for the continued existence of the Soviet Union. To put it bluntly: anything could be justified if it brought more gold out of the ground. This thesis was beautifully summed up by Aleksei Loginov, a retired former director of production and of prison camps in Norilsk, in an interview he gave to a British documentary film-maker:

From the beginning we knew perfectly well that the outside world would never leave our Soviet Revolution alone. Not only Stalin realized it – everyone, every ordinary communist, every ordinary person realized that we had not only to build, but to build in the full knowledge that soon we would be at war. So in my area, the search for all sources of raw materials, copper, nickel, aluminum and iron, and so on, was incredibly intense. We had always known of the huge resources in Norilsk – but how to develop them in the Arctic? So the whole venture was put in the hands of the NKVD, the Ministry of Internal Affairs. Who else could have done it? You know how many people had been arrested. And we needed tens of thousands up there . . .[92]

Loginov was speaking in the 1990s, nearly half a century after Norilsk ceased to be a vast prison complex. But his words echo those written in 1964 by Anna Zakharova, the wife of a camp commander, in a letter to the government newspaper *Izvestiya* which was never published – but did later appear in the underground press. Like Loginov, Zakharova also spoke of duty and of the sacrifices her husband had made for the greater glory of their country: 'His health has already been ruined working with the criminal world, because all the work here wears on your nerves. We would be happy to move on, because my husband has already served his time, but they won't let him go. He is a Communist and an officer, and he is bound by the duty of his position.'[93]

Similar views were put to me by a camp administrator who wanted to remain anonymous. With pride she told me of the work her prisoners had done on behalf of the USSR during the war: 'Absolutely every prisoner worked and paid his own way, and gave everything to the front that he could.'[94]

Within this larger framework of loyalty to the Soviet Union and its economic goals, cruelty carried out in the name of production figures seemed, to the perpetrators, downright admirable. More to the point, the true nature of the cruelty, like the true nature of the camps, could be hidden beneath the jargon of economics. After interviewing a former Karlag administrator in 1991, the American journalist Adam Hochschild complained that: 'From the colonel's words you would not have known that it was a prison. Instead, he talked almost entirely about Karlag's role in the Soviet economy. He sounded like a proud regional Party boss. "We had our own agricultural experiment station. Cattle breeding was also advanced. A special breed of cow, Red Steppe, was raised here, also Kazakh whiteheads . . ." '[95]

At the highest levels, administrators frequently described the prisoners as if they were machines or tools, necessary for completing the job and nothing else. They were openly thought of as convenient, cheap labour – a necessity, simply, just like supplies of cement or steel. Again, Loginov, the Norilsk commander, puts it best:

If we had sent civilians [to Norilsk] we would first have had to build houses for them to live in. And how could civilians live there? With prisoners it is easy – all you need is a barrack, an oven with a chimney, and they survive. And then maybe later somewhere to eat. In short, prisoners were, under the circumstances of that time, the only possible people you could use on such a large scale. If we had had time, we probably wouldn't have done it that way . . .[96]

At the same time, economic jargon enabled the camp leadership to justify anything, even death: all was for the greater good. At times, this argument was taken to real extremes. Lev Razgon, for example, gives an account of a conversation between Colonel Tarasyuk, then the commander of Ustvymlag, and a camp doctor, Kogan, who made the mistake of bragging to Tarasyuk about how many patients he had 'plucked from the grips of pellagra', a disease caused by starvation and protein deprivation. According to Razgon, the following dialogue ensued:

Tarasyuk: What are they getting?
Kogan: They are all receiving the anti-pellagra ration established by the Gulag Health and Sanitation Department (and he specified the quantity of proteins in calories).
Tarasyuk: How many of them will go out to work in the forest, and when?
Kogan: Well, none of them will ever go to work in the forest again, of course. But now they'll survive and it will be possible to use them for light work within the compound.
Tarasyuk: Stop giving them any anti-pellagra rations. Write this down: these rations are to be given to those working in the forest. The other prisoners are to get the disability rations.
Kogan: Comrade Colonel! Obviously I didn't explain clearly. These people will

only survive if they are given a special ration. A disabled prisoner receives 400 grams of bread. On that ration they'll be dead in ten days. We can't do that!

Tarasyuk looked at the upset doctor, and there was even a sign of interest on his face. 'What's the matter? Do your medical ethics prevent you from doing this?'

'Of course they do . . .'

'Well, I don't give a damn for your ethics,' said Tarasyuk calmly, and with no indication whatsoever of anger. 'Have you written that down? Let's move on . . .'

All 246 died within the month.[97]

Such conversations were not unique, nor apocryphal, as archives show. One inspector, reporting on the conditions of prisoners in Volgostroi during the war, complained that the camp's administration was 'exclusively interested in producing wood . . . and was not even slightly interested in the feeding or clothing of prisoners, sending them out to work without regard to physical fitness, never worrying about whether they were clothed, healthy and fed'.[98] Accounts also record the following comment, made at a meeting of Vyatlag officers in January 1943. Speaking in the purely neutral language of statistics, Comrade Avrutsky made the following proposal: 'We have 100 per cent of our workforce, but we cannot fulfil our programme, since Group B continues to grow. If the food which we gave to Group B were given to another contingent – then we wouldn't have Group B at all, and we would fulfil the programme . . .'[99] The phrase 'Group B', of course, referred to weaker prisoners, who would indeed cease to exist if they were not given any food.

If camp commanders had the luxury of making such decisions far removed from the people who would actually be affected, proximity did not necessarily make those lower down the hierarchy feel any more sympathy. One Polish prisoner, Kazimierz Zarod, was in a column of prisoners marching to a new camp site. Given virtually no food, prisoners began to weaken. Finally, one of them fell, and was unable to get up again. A guard raised a gun at him. A second guard threatened to shoot:

'For God's sake,' I heard the man groan, 'if you will only let me rest for a while I can catch up.'

'You walk, or die,' said the first guard . . .

I saw him lift his rifle and take aim – I could not believe that he would shoot. The men in the column behind me had by this time regrouped and my view of what was happening was obscured, but suddenly a shot rang out followed by a second, and I knew the man was dead.

But Zarod also records that not all of those who fell while marching were shot. If they were young, those too exhausted to walk further were picked up and thrown on to a cart, where they 'lay like sacks until they recovered . . . The reasoning, as far as I could see, being that the young would recover and have work left in them, while the old were not worth saving. Certainly those thrown like bundles of old clothes into the provisions carts were not there because of any humanitarian reason. The guards, although young men, had travelled this route before and were apparently devoid of any human feelings.'[100]

Although there are no memoirs to document it, this attitude surely affected even those who occupied the posts at the very top of the camp system. Throughout the preceding chapters, I have been regularly quoting from reports found in the files of the Gulag inspectorate, a part of the Soviet prosecutors' office. These reports, filed with great regularity and precision, are remarkable for their honesty. They refer to typhus epidemics, to food shortages, to clothing shortages. They report on camps where death rates are 'too high'. They angrily accuse particular camp commanders of providing unsuitable living conditions for prisoners. They estimate numbers of 'working days' lost to illness, accidents, death. Reading them, one can have no doubt that the Gulag bosses in Moscow knew – really and truly knew – what life was like in the camps: it is all there, in language no less frank than that used by Solzhenitsyn and Shalamov.[101]

Yet although changes were sometimes made, although commanders occasionally were sentenced, what is striking about the reports is their very repetitiveness: they call to mind the absurd culture of phoney inspection so beautifully described by the nineteenth-century Russian writer Nikolai Gogol. It is as if the forms were observed, the reports were filed, the ritual anger was expressed – and the real effects on human beings were ignored. Camp commanders were routinely reprimanded for failing to improve living standards, living standards continued to fail to improve, and there the discussion ended.

In the end, nobody forced guards to rescue the young and murder the old. Nobody forced camp commanders to kill off the sick. Nobody forced the Gulag bosses in Moscow to ignore the implications of inspectors' reports. Yet such decisions were made openly, every day, by guards and administrators apparently convinced they had the right to make them.

Nor was the ideology of state slavery exclusive to the Gulag's masters. Prisoners too were encouraged to co-operate – and some did.

14

The Prisoners

Man is a creature that can get used to anything, and I think that is the best definition of him.

– Fyodor Dostoevsky, *The House of the Dead*[1]

Urki
The Criminals

To the inexperienced political prisoner, to the young peasant girl arrested for stealing a loaf of bread, to the unprepared Polish deportee, a first encounter with the *urki*, the Soviet Union's professional criminal caste, would have been bewildering, shocking and unfathomable. Evgeniya Ginzburg met her first female criminals as she was boarding the boat to Kolyma:

They were the cream of the criminal world: murderers, sadists, adept at every kind of sexual perversion . . . without wasting any time they set about terrorizing and bullying the 'ladies', delighted to find that 'enemies of the people' were creatures even more despised and outcast than themselves . . . They seized our bits of bread, snatched the last of our rags with our bundles, pushed us out of the places we had managed to find . . .[2]

Travelling the same route, Aleksandr Gorbatov – General Gorbatov, a Soviet war hero, hardly a cowardly man – was robbed of his boots while in the hold of the SS *Dzhurma*, crossing the Sea of Okhotsk:

One of them hit me hard on the chest and then on the head and said with a leer: 'Look at him – sells me his boots days ago, pockets the cash, and then refused to hand them over!' Off they went with their loot, laughing for all they were worth and only stopping to beat me up again when, out of sheer despair, I followed them and asked for the boots back.[3]

Dozens of other memoirists describe similar scenes. The professional criminals would descend upon the other prisoners in what appeared to be a mad fury, throwing them off bunks in barracks or trains; stealing what remained of their clothing; howling, cursing and swearing. To ordinary people, their appearance and behaviour seemed bizarre in the extreme. Antoni Ekart, a Polish prisoner, was horrified by the 'complete lack of inhibition on the part of the *urkas*, who would openly carry out all natural functions, including onanism. This gave them a striking resemblance to monkeys, with whom they seemed to have much more in common than with men.'[4] Mariya Ioffe, the wife of a famous Bolshevik, also wrote that the thieves had sex openly, walked naked around the barracks, and had no feelings for one another: 'Only their bodies were alive.'[5]

Only after weeks or months in the camps did the uninitiated outsiders begin to understand that the criminal world was not uniform, that it had its own hierarchy, its own system of ranks; that, in fact, there were many different kinds of thieves. Lev Razgon explained: 'They were split up into castes and communities, each with its own iron discipline, with many rules and customs, and if these were infringed the punishment was harsh: at best the individual was expelled from that group, and, at worst, he was killed.'[6]

Karol Colonna-Czosnowski, a Polish prisoner who found himself the only political in an otherwise exclusively criminal northern logging camp, also observed these differences:

The Russian criminal was extremely class-conscious in those days. In fact, class to them was everything. In their hierarchy, big-time criminals, such as bank or train robbers, were members of the upper class. Grisha Tchorny, the head of the camp Mafia, was one of them. At the opposite end of the social scale were the petty crooks, like pickpockets. The big boys would use them as their valets and messengers and they received very little consideration. All other crimes formed the bulk of the middle class, but even there, there were distinctions.

In many ways this strange society was, in caricature, a replica of the 'normal' world. In it one could find the equivalent of every shade of human virtue or failing. For example, you could readily recognize the ambitious man on his way up, the snob, the social climber, the cheat as well as the honest and generous man . . .[7]

At the very top of this hierarchy, setting the rules for all the others, were the professional criminals. Known as *urki, blatnye* or, if they were among the criminal world's most exclusive elite, *vory v zakone* – the expression translates as 'thieves-in-law' – Russian professional criminals lived by a whole set of rules and customs which preceded the Gulag, and which outlasted it. They had nothing whatsoever to do with the vast majority of Gulag inmates who had 'criminal' sentences. The so-called 'ordinary' criminals – people convicted of petty theft, infringements of workplace regulations, or other non-political crimes – hated the thieves-in-law with the same passion as they hated political prisoners.

And no wonder: the thieves-in-law had a culture very different from that of the average Soviet citizen. Its origins lay deep in the criminal underground of tsarist Russia, in the thieves' and beggars' guilds which controlled petty crime in that era.[8] But it had grown far more widespread during the first decades of the Soviet regime, thanks to the hundreds of thousands of orphans – direct victims of revolution, civil war and collectivization – who had managed to survive, first as street children, then as thieves. By the late 1920s, when the camps began to expand on a mass scale, the professional criminals had become a totally separate community, complete with a strict code of behaviour which forbade them to have anything to do with the Soviet state. A true thief-in-law refused to work, refused to own a passport, and refused to co-operate in any way with the authorities unless it was in order to exploit them: the 'aristocrats' of Nikolai Pogodin's 1934 play *Aristokraty* are already identifiable as thieves-in-law who refuse, on principle, to do any work.[9]

For the most part, the indoctrination and re-education programmes of the early 1930s were in fact directed at thieves-in-law rather than political prisoners. Thieves, being 'socially close' (*sotsialno-blizkii*) – as opposed to politicals, who were 'socially dangerous' (*sotsialno-opasnyi*) – were assumed to be reformable. But by the late 1930s, the authorities appear to have given up on the idea of reforming the professional criminals. Instead, they resolved to use the thieves-in-law to control and intimidate other prisoners, 'counter-revolutionaries' in particular, whom the thieves naturally loathed.[10]

This was not a wholly new development. A century earlier, criminal convicts in Siberia already hated political prisoners. In *The House of the Dead*, his lightly fictionalized memoir of his five years in prison, Dostoevsky recounts the remarks of a fellow prisoner: 'No, they don't like gentlemen convicts, especially political ones; they wouldn't mind murdering them, and no wonder. To begin with, you're a different sort of people, not like them . . .'[11]

In the Soviet Union, the camp administration openly deployed small groups of professional criminals to control other prisoners from about 1937 until the end of the war. During that period the highest-ranking thieves-in-law did not work, but instead ensured that others did.[12] As Lev Razgon described it:

> They did not work but they were allocated a full ration; they levied a money tribute from all the 'peasants', those who did work; they took half of the food parcels and purchases from the camp commissary; and they brazenly cleaned out the new transports, taking all the best clothes from the newcomers. They were, in a word, racketeers, gangsters, and members of a small mafia. All the ordinary criminal inmates of the camp – and they made up the majority – hated them intensely.[13]

Some political prisoners found ways to get along with the thieves-in-law, particularly after the war. Some top criminal bosses liked to have politicals as mascots or sidekicks. Alexander Dolgun won the respect of the criminal boss in a transit camp by beating up a lower-ranking criminal.[14] Partly because he too had defeated a criminal in a fist fight, Marlen Korallov – a young political prisoner, later a founding member of Memorial – was noticed by Nikola, his camp's criminal boss, who allowed Korallov to sit near him in the barracks. The decision changed Korallov's status in the camp, where he was immediately regarded as 'protected' by Nikola, and given a much better sleeping arrangement: 'The camp understood: if I become part of the troika around Nikola, then I become part of the camp elite . . . all attitudes to me changed instantly.'[15]

For the most part, however, the thieves' rule over the politicals was absolute. Their superior status helps to explain why they felt, in the words of one criminologist, 'at home' in the camps: they lived better there than other prisoners, and had a degree of real power in camps that they did not enjoy on the outside.[16] Korallov explains, for example, that Nikola inhabited the 'only iron bed' in the barrack, which had been pushed into a corner. No one else slept on the bed, and a group of Nikola's sidekicks lurked around it to make sure this remained so. They also hung blankets on the sides of the beds around their leader, to prevent anyone from looking in. Access to the space around the leader was carefully controlled. Such prisoners even looked upon their long sentences with a form of macho pride. Korallov observed that

There were some young guys who, in order to heighten their authority, would make an attempt to escape, a hopeless attempt, and then they received an additional twenty-five years, maybe another twenty-five for sabotage. Then when they pitched up at a new camp, and told people they had 100-year sentences, that made them great figures according to camp morality.[17]

Their higher status made the thieves' world attractive to younger prisoners, who were sometimes inducted into the fraternity at elaborate initiation rituals. According to accounts put together by secret police officers and prison administrators in the 1950s, new members of the clan had to swear an oath promising to be a 'worthy thief' and to accept the strict rules of the thieves' life. Other thieves recommended the novice, perhaps praising him for 'defying camp discipline' and bestowing upon him a nickname. News of the 'coronation' would be passed throughout the camp system via the thieves' network of contacts, so that even if the new thief was transferred to another *lagpunkt*, his status would be maintained.[18]

That was the system that Nikolai Medvedev (no relation to the Moscow intellectuals) found in 1946. Arrested as a teenager for stealing grain from a collective farm, Medvedev was taken under the wing of one of the leading thieves-in-law while still on the transports, and gradually inducted into the thieves' world. Upon arrival in Magadan, Medvedev was put to work like other prisoners – he was assigned to clean the dining hall, hardly an onerous task, but his mentor shouted at him to stop: 'and so I didn't work, just like all the other thieves didn't work'. Instead, other prisoners did his work for him.[19]

As Medvedev explains it, the camp administration were not concerned about whether particular prisoners worked or not. 'For them only one thing mattered: that the mine produced gold, as much gold as possible, and that the camp stayed in order.' And, as he writes rather approvingly, the thieves did ensure that order prevailed. What the camps lost in prisoner work-hours, they gained in discipline. He explained that 'if someone offended someone else, they would go to the criminal "authorities" with their complaints', not to the camp authorities. This system, he claimed, kept down the level of violence and brawling, which would otherwise have been distractingly high.[20]

Nikolai Medvedev's positive account of the thieves' reign in the camps is unusual, partly because it describes the thieves' world from the inside – many of the *urki* were illiterate, and hardly any wrote memoirs – but mainly because it is sympathetic. Most of the Gulag's 'classic' chroniclers – witnesses to the terror, the robbery and the rape that the thieves inflicted on the other inhabitants of the camps – hated them with a passion. 'The criminals are not human,' wrote Shalamov, point-blank. 'The evil acts committed by criminals in camps are innumerable.'[21] Solzhenitsyn wrote that 'It was precisely this universally human world, *our* world, with its morals, customs, and mutual relationships, which was most hateful to the thieves, most subject to their ridicule, counterposed most sharply to their antisocial, anti-public *kubla* or clan.'[22] Zhigulin described, graphically, how the thieves' imposition of 'order' actually worked. One day, while sitting in a virtually empty dining hall, he heard two prisoners fighting over a spoon. Suddenly Dezemiya, the senior 'deputy' of the camp's senior thief-in-law, burst through the door:

'What's this noise, what's this quarrel? You're not allowed to disturb the peace in the dining hall!'

'Look, he took my spoon and changed it. I had a whole one, he gave me back a broken one . . .'

'I will punish you both, and reconcile you,' chortled Dezemiya. And he made two rapid movements towards the quarrellers with his pick; as quick as lightning he had knocked out one eye apiece.[23]

Certainly the thieves' influence over camp life was profound. Their slang, so distinct from ordinary Russian that it almost qualifies as a separate language, became the most important means of communication in the camps. Although famed for its huge vocabulary of elaborate curses, a list of criminal slang words collected in the 1980s (many still the same as those used in the 1940s) also includes hundreds of words for ordinary objects, including clothes, body parts and utensils, which are quite different from the usual Russian words. For objects of particular interest – money, prostitutes, theft and thieves – there were literally dozens of synonyms. As well as general terms for crime (among them *po muzike khodit*, literally 'move to the music') there were also many specific terms for stealing: stealing in a train station (*derzhat sadku*), stealing on a bus (*marku derzhat*), an unplanned theft (*idti na shalnuyu*), a daytime theft (*dennik*), a thief who stole from a church (*klyukvennik*), among others.[24]

Learning to speak *blatnoe slovo*, 'thieves' talk' – sometimes called *blatnaya muzyka*, literally 'thieves' music' – was an induction ritual that most prisoners endured, though not necessarily willingly. Some never got used to it. One female political later wrote that

The hardest thing to bear in such a camp is the constant vituperation and abuse ... the bad language which the women criminals use is so obscene that it is quite unbearable and they seem to be able to speak to each other only in the lowest and coarsest terms. When they started with this cursing and swearing we hated it so much that we used to say to each other, 'If she was dying beside me, I would not give her a drop of water.'[25]

Others tried to analyse it. As early as 1925, one Solovetsky prisoner speculated upon the origins of this rich vocabulary in an article he wrote for *Solovetskie Ostrova*, one of the camp magazines. Some of the words, he noted, simply reflected thieves' morality: language about women was half obscene, half sickly sentimental. Some of the words emerged from the context: thieves used the word for 'knocking' (*stukat*) in place of the word for 'speaking' (*govorit*), which made sense, since prisoners tapped on walls to communicate with one another.[26] Another ex-prisoner remarked on the fact that a number of the words – *shmon* for 'search'; *musor* for 'cop'; *fraier* for 'non-criminal' (also translatable as 'sucker') – seemed to come from Hebrew or Yiddish.[27] Perhaps this is a testament to the role that the largely Jewish port city of Odessa, once the smugglers' capital of Russia, played in the development of thieves' culture.

From time to time, the camp administration even tried to eliminate the slang. In 1933, the commander of Dmitlag ordered his subordinates to 'take appropriate measures' in order to get prisoners – as well as guards and camp administrators – to stop using the criminal language, which was now in 'general use, even in official letters and speeches'.[28] There is no evidence whatsoever that he succeeded.

The highest-ranking thieves not only sounded different, they also looked different from other prisoners. Perhaps even more than their slang, their clothing and bizarre fashion sense established them as a separate identifiable caste, which contributed further to the power of intimidation they exercised over other prisoners. In the 1940s, according to Shalamov, the Kolyma thieves-in-law all wore aluminium crosses around their necks, with no religious intent: 'It was a kind of symbol.' But fashions changed:

In the twenties, the thieves wore trade-school caps; still earlier, the military officer's cap was in fashion. In the forties, during the winter, they wore peakless leather caps, folded down the tops of their felt boots, and wore a cross around the neck. The cross was usually smooth but if an artist was around, he was forced to use a needle to paint it with the most diverse subjects: a heart, cards, a crucifixion, a naked woman . . .[29]

Georgi Feldgun, also in the camps in the 1940s, remembered that the thieves had a distinctive walk, 'with small steps, legs held slightly apart', and wore gold or silver crowns on their teeth which they had affixed as a sort of fashion: 'The *vor* of 1943 went around normally in a dark-blue three-piece outfit, with trousers tucked into boxcalf boots. Blouse under the waist-coat, tucked out. Also a cap, pulled over the eyes. Also tattoos, usually sentimental: "I'll never forget my beloved mother." "There is no happiness in life . . ."'[30]

These tattoos, mentioned by many others, also helped to distinguish members of the thieves' world from the criminal prisoners, and to identify each thief's role within that world. According to one camp historian, there were different tattoos for homosexuals, for addicts, for those convicted of rape and those convicted of murder.[31] Solzhenitsyn is more explicit:

They surrendered their bronze skin to tattooing and in this way gradually satisfied their artistic, their erotic, and even their moral needs: on one another's chests, stomachs and backs they could admire powerful eagles perched on cliffs or flying through the sky. Or the big hammer, the sun, with its rays shooting out in every direction; or women and men copulating; or the individual organs of their sexual enjoyment; and all of a sudden, next to their hearts were Lenin or Stalin or perhaps both . . . Sometimes they would laugh at a droll stoker hurling coal into their rear orifice, or a monkey engaged in masturbation. And they would read slogans on each other which, even if they were already familiar, they none the less dearly loved to repeat! '— all the girls in the mouth!' . . . Or else on a girl thief's stomach there might be 'I will die for a hot —!'[32]

As a professional artist, Thomas Sgovio was quickly sucked into the tattooing trade. Once, he was asked to draw Lenin's face on someone's chest: it was a common belief among thieves that no firing squad would ever shoot at a portrait of Lenin or Stalin.[33]

The thieves also distinguished themselves from other prisoners in their manner of entertainment. Elaborate rituals surrounded their card games, which involved huge risks, both from the games themselves, which had high stakes, and from the authorities, who punished anyone caught playing.[34] But the risks were probably part of their attraction for people accustomed to danger: Dmitri Likhachev, the literary critic imprisoned on Solovetsky, noted that many thieves 'compare their emotions during card games to the emotions they feel while carrying out a crime'.[35]

Indeed, the criminals outwitted all NKVD attempts to stop the games. Searches and confiscations were of no use. 'Experts' among the thieves specialized in the production of playing cards, a process which had become, by the 1940s, highly sophisticated. First, the 'expert' would cut squares of paper with a razor blade. To ensure the cards were sturdy enough, he then pasted five or six squares together using 'glue' made by rubbing a piece of damp bread against a handkerchief. After that, he put the cards under one of the bunks overnight to harden. When they were ready, he stamped the suits on to the card, using a stamp carved out of the bottom of a mug. He used black ash for the black cards. If the medicine streptomycin was available – if the camp or prison doctor had it, and could be threatened or bribed to give some away – he would make red cards as well.[36]

The card-playing rituals were another part of the terror that the thieves exerted over the political prisoners. When playing with one another, the thieves bet money, bread and clothes. When they had lost their own, they bet the money, bread and clothes of other prisoners. Gustav Herling first witnessed such an incident on a Stolypin wagon bound for Siberia. He was travelling with a fellow Pole, Shklovski. In the same car, three *urki*, among them a 'gorilla with a flat Mongolian face', were playing cards.

. . . the gorilla suddenly threw down his cards, jumped down from the bench and came up to Shklovski.

'Give me the coat,' he yelled, 'I've lost it at cards.'

Shklovski opened his eyes and, without moving from his seat, shrugged his shoulders.

'Give it to me,' the gorilla roared, enraged, 'give it, or – *glaza vykolu* – I'll poke your eyes out!' The colonel slowly got up and handed over the coat.

Only later, in the labour camp, I understood the meaning of this fantastic scene. To stake the possessions of other prisoners in their games of cards is one of the *urka*'s most popular distractions, and its chief attraction lies in the fact that the loser is obliged to force from the victim the item previously agreed upon.[37]

One female prisoner was the inhabitant of an entire women's barracks that had been 'lost' in a card game. After hearing the news, the women waited anxiously for several days, 'incredulous' – until, one night, the attack came: 'The uproar was terrific – the women yelled, screamed the skies down, until men came to our rescue . . . in the end nothing but a few bundles of clothes were stolen and the *starosta* was stabbed.'[38]

But cards could be no less dangerous for the professional criminals themselves. General Gorbatov encountered a thief in Kolyma who had only two fingers on his left hand. He explained:

I was playing cards and I lost. I had no cash so I staked a good suit, not mine of course, one that a political had on. I meant to take the suit during the night when the new prisoner had stripped for bed. I had to hand it over before eight in the morning, only they took the political away to another camp that very day. Our council of seniors met to hand out my punishment. The plaintiff wanted all my left hand fingers off. The seniors offered two. They bargained a bit and agreed on three. So I put my hand on the table and the man I'd lost to took a stick and with five strokes knocked off my three fingers . . .

The man concluded, almost proudly: 'We have our laws too, only tougher than yours. If you do your comrades down, you have to answer for it.'[39] Indeed, the thieves' judicial rituals were as elaborate as their initiation ceremonies, involving a 'court', a trial, and a sentence that could entail beating, humiliation, or even death. Colonna-Czosnowski witnessed a bitter, prolonged card game between two high-ranking thieves, which ended only when one of them had lost all of his possessions. Instead of an arm or a leg, the winner demanded a terrible humiliation as penalty: he commanded the barrack 'artist' to tattoo an enormous penis on the man's face, pointing at his mouth. Minutes later, the loser pressed a hot poker against his face, obliterating his tattoo, and scarring himself for life.[40] Anton Antonov-Ovseenko, the son of a leading Bolshevik, also claimed to have met a 'deaf-mute' in the camps, who had lost at cards and thereby forfeited the use of his voice for three years. Even as he was shipped from camp to camp, he dared not violate this penalty, as every local *urka* would know about it: 'Violations of this agreement would be punished by death. No one can evade the law of thieves.'[41]

The authorities knew of these rituals and occasionally tried to intervene, not always successfully. In one incident in 1951, a thieves' court sentenced a thief called Yurilkin to death. Camp authorities heard of the sentence, and transferred Yurilkin, first to another camp, then to a transit prison, then to a third camp in a completely different part of the country. Nevertheless, two thieves-in-law finally tracked him down there and murdered him – four years later. They were subsequently tried and executed for murder, but even such punishments were not necessarily a deterrent. In 1956, the Soviet prosecutors' office circulated a frustrated note complaining that 'this criminal formation exists in all Corrective-Labour Camps and often the decision of the group to murder one or another prisoner who is in a different camp is executed in that camp unquestioningly'.[42]

The thieves' courts could exact punishment on outsiders too, which perhaps explains why they inspired so much terror. Lev Finkelstein, a political prisoner in the early 1950s, remembered one such revenge murder:

I personally saw only one killing, but that was very spectacular. Do you know what a big metal file is? Such a file, sharpened at one end, is an absolutely murderous weapon . . .

We had a *naryadchik*, the man who assigned work to prisoners – what he was guilty of, I cannot tell. But the thieves-in-law decided he should be killed. It happened when we were standing at the count, before going to work. Every brigade was standing separate from the others. The *naryadchik* was standing in front. Kazakhov was his name, he was a heavy man with a heavy paunch. One of the thieves darted out of the formation, and thrust this file into his stomach, into his belly. It was probably a trained assassin. The man was caught immediately – but he had twenty-five years. He was of course retried, and given another twenty-five years. So his term was extended for a couple of years, so who cares . . .[43]

Nevertheless, it was relatively rare for the thieves to aim their 'justice' at those running the camps. By and large they were, if not exactly loyal Soviet citizens, then at least happy to co-operate in the one task that Soviet authorities set for them: they were perfectly happy, that is, to lord it over the politicals – that group which was, to quote Ginzburg again, 'even more despised and outcast than themselves'.

Kontriki and Bytovye
The Politicals and the Ordinary Prisoners

With their special slang, distinctive clothing and rigid culture, the professional criminals were easy to identify, and are easy to describe. It is far harder to make generalizations about the rest of the prisoners, the people who formed the raw material of the Gulag's workforce, since they came from every stratum of Soviet society. Indeed, for too long, our understanding of who exactly the majority of the camps' inmates were has been skewed by our forced reliance on memoirs, particularly memoirs published outside the Soviet Union. Their authors were usually intellectuals, often foreigners, and almost universally political prisoners.

Since Gorbachev's glasnost in 1989, however, a wider variety of memoir material has become available, along with some archival data. According to the latter, which must be treated with a great deal of caution, it now appears that the vast majority of prisoners were not intellectuals at all – not people, that is, from Russia's technical and academic intelligentsia, which was effectively a separate social class – but workers and peasants. Some figures for the 1930s, the years when the bulk of the Gulag's inmates were kulaks, are particularly revealing. In 1934, only .7 per cent of the camp population had higher education, while 39.1 per cent were classified as having only primary education. At the same time, 42.6 per cent were described as 'semi-literate', and 12 per cent were completely illiterate. Even in 1938, the year the Great Terror raged among Moscow and Leningrad intellectuals, those with higher education in the camps still numbered only 1.1 per cent, while over half had primary education and a third were semi-literate.[44]

Comparable figures on the social origins of prisoners do not seem to be available, but it is worth noting that in 1948, less than one quarter of prisoners

Draft portrait of two *zeks*: a drawing by Sergei Reikhenberg, Magadan,
date unknown

were politicals – those sentenced, according to Article 58 of the Criminal
Code, for 'counter-revolutionary' crimes. This follows an earlier pattern.
Politicals accounted for a mere 12 and 18 per cent of prisoners in the terror
years of 1937 and 1938; hovered around 30–40 per cent during the war; rose
in 1946 to nearly 60 per cent, as a result of the amnesty given to criminal
prisoners in the wake of victory; and then remained steady, accounting for
between a quarter and a third of all prisoners, throughout the rest of Stalin's
reign.[45] Given the higher turnover of non-political prisoners – they often had
shorter sentences and were more likely to meet requirements for early release
– it is safe to say that the vast majority of the inmates who passed through
the Gulag system in both the 1930s and 1940s were people with criminal
sentences, and therefore more likely to be workers and peasants.

Yet although these numbers may help to correct past impressions, they can
be misleading too. Looking at the new memoir material accumulated in
Russia since the collapse of the Soviet Union, it is also becoming clear that
many of the politicals were not really 'political prisoners' in the way we define
the term today. In the 1920s, the camps did indeed contain members of
anti-Bolshevik parties, who actually called themselves 'politicals'. There were
also, in the 1930s, a few genuine Trotskyites – people who really did support
Trotsky against Stalin. In the 1940s, following mass arrests in Ukraine, the
Baltic States and Poland, a wave of authentically anti-Soviet partisans and
activists also arrived in the camps. In the early 1950s, a handful of anti-
Stalinist students were arrested too.

Nevertheless, of the hundreds of thousands of people referred to in the camps as political prisoners, the vast majority were not dissidents, or priests saying mass in secret, or even Party bigwigs. They were ordinary people, swept up in mass arrests, who did not necessarily have strong political views of any kind. Olga Adamova-Sliozberg, once an employee of one of the industrial ministries in Moscow, wrote, 'Before my arrest, I led a very ordinary life, typical of a professional Soviet woman who didn't belong to the Party. I worked hard but took no particular part in politics or public affairs. My real interests lay with home and family.'[46]

If the politicals were not necessarily political, the vast majority of criminal prisoners were not necessarily criminals either. While there were some professional criminals and, during the war years, some genuine war criminals and Nazi collaborators in the camps, most of the others had been convicted of so-called 'ordinary' or non-political crimes that in other societies would not be considered crimes at all. The father of Aleksandr Lebed, the Russian general and politician, was twice ten minutes late to work for his factory job, for which he received a five-year camp sentence.[47] At the largely criminal Polyansky camp near Krasnoyarsk-26, home of one of the Soviet Union's nuclear reactors, archives record one 'criminal' prisoner with a six-year sentence for stealing a single rubber boot in a bazaar, another with ten years for stealing ten loaves of bread, and another – a truck driver raising two children alone – with seven years for stealing three bottles of the wine he was delivering. Yet another got five years for 'speculation', meaning he had bought cigarettes in one place and sold them in another.[48] Antoni Ekart tells the story of a woman who was arrested because she took a pencil from the office where she worked. It was for her son, who had been unable to do his schoolwork for lack of something to write with.[49] In the upside-down world of the Gulag, criminal prisoners were no more likely to be real criminals than political prisoners were likely to be active opponents of the regime.

In other words, criminals were not always people who had committed a real crime. And it was even rarer for a political to have committed a political offence. This did not stop the Soviet judicial system from classifying them with great care, however. As a group, the status of the counter-revolutionaries was lower than that of the criminals; as I say, they were considered to be 'socially dangerous', less compatible with Soviet society than the 'socially close' criminals. But the politicals were also ranked according to whatever section of Article 58 of the Criminal Code they had been indicted under. Evgeniya Ginzburg noted that among the political prisoners it was by far 'best' to have been sentenced under Section 10 of Article 58, for 'Anti-Soviet Agitation' (ASA). These were the 'babblers': they had told an unfortunate anti-Party joke, or had let slip some criticism of Stalin or the local Party boss (or had been accused by a jealous neighbour of having done so). Even the camp authorities tacitly recognized that the 'babblers' had committed no crime whatsoever, so those sentenced for ASA sometimes found it easier to get lighter work assignments.

Below them were those convicted for 'counter-revolutionary activity' (KRD). Lower still were those convicted of 'counter-revolutionary terrorist activity' (KRTD). The additional 'T' could mean, in some camps, that a prisoner was actually forbidden to be assigned to anything but the most difficult 'general work' – cutting trees, digging mines, building roads – particularly if the KRTD was accompanied by a sentence of ten or fifteen years or more.[50]

And it was possible to go lower still. Below KRTD was yet another category: KRTTD, not just terrorist activities, but 'Trotskyist terrorist activities'. 'I knew of cases,' wrote Lev Razgon, 'when the additional T would appear in a prisoner's camp documents because of a quarrel during a general head-count with the work distributor or the head of Distribution, who were both criminals.'[51] A minor change like that could mean the difference between life and death, since no foreman would assign a KRTTD prisoner to anything but the toughest physical labour.

These rules were not always clear-cut. In practice, prisoners constantly weighed the value of these different sentences, trying to work out what effect they would have on their lives. Varlam Shalamov records that after he had been selected to take a paramedical course, one which would enable him to become a *feldsher* – a doctor's assistant, one of the most prestigious and comfortable jobs in the camp – he was worried about the effect his sentence would have on his ability to complete the course: 'Would they accept political prisoners convicted under Article 58 of the Criminal Code? Only those who came under Section 10. And how about my neighbour in the rear of the truck? He too was ASA, anti-Soviet agitation.'[52]

Official sentences alone did not determine the politicals' place in the camp hierarchy. Although they did not have a rigid code of behaviour like the criminals, or a unifying language, they did eventually segregate themselves into distinct groups. These political clans hung together for comradeship, for self-protection, or because they shared a common world-view. They were not distinct – they overlapped with one another, and with the clans of non-political prisoners – and they did not exist in every camp. When they did, however, they could be vital to a prisoner's survival.

The most fundamental, and ultimately the most powerful, of the political clans were those formed around nationality or place of origin. These grew more important during and after the Second World War, when the numbers of foreign prisoners increased dramatically. Their derivation was natural enough. A new prisoner would arrive, and immediately search his barracks for fellow Estonians, fellow Ukrainians or, in a tiny number of cases, fellow Americans. Walter Warwick, one of the 'American Finns' who wound up in the camps in the late 1930s, has described, in a manuscript he wrote for his family, how the Finnish speakers in his camp banded together specifically in order to protect themselves from the thievery and banditry of the professional criminals: 'We came to the conclusion that if we wanted to have a little rest from them, we must have a gang. So we organized our own gang to help each other. There were six of us: two American Finns . . . two Finnish Finns . . . and two Leningrad District Finns . . .'[53]

Not every national clan had the same character. Opinions differ, for example, as to whether Jewish prisoners actually had their own network, or whether they melded into the general Russian population (or, in the case of the large numbers of Polish Jews, into the general Polish population). At different times, it seems, the answer was different, and much depended on individual attitudes. Many of the Jews arrested in the late 1930s, during the repressions against top nomenklatura and the army, appear to have considered themselves communists first and Jews second. As one prisoner put it, in the camps 'Everyone became Russian – Caucasians, Tartars, Jews.'[54]

Later, as more Jews arrived along with the Poles during the war, they seem to have formed recognizable ethnic networks. Ada Federolf, who wrote her memoirs together with Ariadna Efron, Marina Tsvetaeva's daughter, described one camp where the tailors' workshop – by camp standards a luxurious place to work – was run by a man called Lieberman. Whenever a new transport arrived, he would go through the crowd calling out, 'Any Jews, any Jews?' When he found Jews he arranged for them to work for him in his workshop, thereby saving them from general work in the forests. Lieberman also devised ingenious plans to save rabbis, who needed to pray all day. He built a special closet for one rabbi, hiding him inside it so that no one would know that he was not working. He also invented the job of 'quality controller' for another rabbi. This allowed the man to walk up and down the lines of sewing women all day long, smiling at them and praying under his breath.[55]

By the early 1950s, when official anti-Semitism in the Soviet Union began to grow stronger, buoyed by Stalin's obsession with the Jewish doctors he thought were trying to kill him, it became more difficult to be Jewish once again. Although even at this time, the degree of anti-Semitism seemed to vary from camp to camp. Ada Puryzhinskaya, a Jewish prisoner arrested at the height of the 'Doctors' Plot' (her brother had been tried and executed for 'conspiring to kill Stalin'), remembered 'no special problems because of being Jewish'.[56] But Leonid Trus, another Jewish prisoner arrested at that time, remembered differently. Once, he said, an older *zek* saved him from a raving anti-Semite, a man who had been arrested for trading in icons. The older *zek* shouted at the trader: he, a man who had 'bought and sold pictures of Christ', should be ashamed of himself.

Nevertheless, Trus did not try to hide the fact that he was Jewish: on the contrary, he painted a Star of David on his boots, largely to prevent anyone from stealing them. In his camp, 'Jews, like Russians, didn't organize them-selves into a group.' This left him without obvious companions: 'The worst for me . . . was loneliness, the sense of being a Jew among Russians, that everyone has friends from their region, whereas I am completely alone.'[57]

Because of their small numbers, the West Europeans and North Americans who found themselves in the camps also found it difficult to form strong networks. They were hardly in a position to help one another anyway: many were completely disoriented by camp life, did not speak Russian, found the food inedible and the living conditions intolerable. After watching a whole group of German women die in the Vladivostok transit prison, despite being allowed to drink boiled water, Nina Gagen-Torn, a Russian prisoner, wrote, only half tongue-in-cheek, that 'If the barracks are filled with Soviet citizens, accustomed to the food, they can tolerate the salted fish, even if it is spoiled. When a big transport consisting of arrested members of the Third Inter-national arrived, they all came down with severe dysentery.'[58] Lev Razgon also pitied foreigners, writing that 'they could neither understand nor assimi-late; they did not try to adapt and survive. They merely huddled together instinctively.'[59]

But the Westerners – a group which included Poles, Czechs and other East Europeans – had a few advantages too. They were the object of special fascination and interest, which sometimes paid off in contacts, in gifts of food, in kinder treatment. Antoni Ekart, a Pole educated in Switzerland, was given a place in a hospital thanks to an orderly named Ackerman, originally from Bessarabia: 'The fact that I came from the West simplified matters': everyone was interested in the Westerner, and had wanted to save him.[60] Flora Leipman, a Scottish woman whose Russian stepfather had talked her family into moving to the Soviet Union, deployed her 'Scottishness' to entertain her fellow prisoners:

I pulled up my skirt above the knees to look like a kilt and turned down my stockings to make them look knee high. In Scots fashion my blanket was thrown over my shoulder and I hung my hat in front of me like a sporran. My voice soared with pride, singing 'Annie-Laurie', 'Ye Banks and Braes o' Bonnie Doon', always finishing up with 'God Save the King' – without translation.[61]

Ekart also described what it felt like being an 'object of curiosity' for Russian intellectuals:

At specially organized, carefully hidden meetings with some of the more trusted among them, I told them of my life in Zurich, in Warsaw, in Vienna and other cities of the West. My sports coat from Geneva, my silk shirts, were most carefully examined, for they were the only material evidence of the high standard of living outside the world of communism. Some of them were visibly incredulous when I said that I could easily buy all these articles on my monthly salary as a junior engineer in a cement factory.

'How many suits did you have?' asked one of the agricultural experts.

'Six or seven.'

'You are a liar!' said one man of not more than 25, and then, turning to the others: 'Why should we tolerate such fantastic stories? Everything has its limits; we are not children.'

I had difficulty making it clear that in the West, an ordinary person, taking some care of his appearance, would aim at having several suits, because clothes keep better if one can change from time to time. For a member of the Russian intelligentsia, who seldom has more than one suit, this was difficult to grasp.[62]

John Noble, an American picked up in Dresden, also became a 'Vorkuta VIP' and regaled his camp mates with tales of American life they found incredible. 'Johnny,' one of them said to him, 'you would have us believe American workers drive their own cars.'[63]

But although their foreignness won them admiration, it also prevented them from making the closer contacts which sustained so many in the camps. Leipman wrote that 'even my new camp "friends" were frightened of me because I was a foreigner in their own eyes'.[64] Ekart suffered when he found himself the only non-Russian prisoner in a *lagpunkt*, both because Soviet citizens did not like him and because he did not like them: 'I was surrounded by an aroma of dislike if not hatred . . . they resented the fact that I was not like them. At every step I felt their mistrust and brutishness, their ill-will and their innate vulgarity. I had to spend many sleepless nights in defence of myself and my belongings.'[65]

Again, his feelings have an echo in an earlier era. Dostoevsky's descriptions of the relationship between Poles and Russian criminals in the nineteenth century suggest that Ekart's forebears had felt the same: 'The Poles (I speak only of the political offenders) behaved with a sort of refined, insulting politeness towards them, were extremely uncommunicative and could in no way conceal from the convicts the revulsion they felt for them; the convicts, for their part, understood this very well and repaid them in their own coin.'[66]

In an even weaker position still were the Muslim and other prisoners from central Asia and some of the Caucasian republics. They suffered the same kind of disorientation as Westerners, but usually were not able to entertain or interest the Russians either. Known as *natsmeny* (from the Russian for 'national minorities'), they had been part of camp life from the late 1920s. Large numbers had been arrested during the pacification – and Sovietization – of central Asia and the northern Caucasus, and sent to work on the White Sea Canal, where a contemporary wrote that 'Everything is hard for them to understand: the people who direct them, the canal which they are building, the food they are eating.'[67] From 1933 on many of them worked on the Moscow–Volga Canal as well, where the camp boss seems to have taken pity on them. At one point he ordered his subordinates to set up separate barracks and separate work brigades for them, so that they would at least be surrounded by fellow countrymen.[68] Later, Gustav Herling encountered them in a northern logging camp. He remembered seeing them every evening in the camp infirmary, waiting to see the camp doctor:

Even in the waiting-room they clasped their stomachs in pain, and the moment they entered behind the partition burst into a sorrowful whining, in which moans were mixed indistinguishably with their curious broken Russian. There was no remedy for their disease . . . they were dying simply of homesickness, of longing for their native country, of hunger, cold and the monotonous whiteness of snow. Their slanting eyes, unused to the northern landscape, were always watering and their eyelashes were stuck together by a thin yellow crust. On the rare days on which we were free from work, the Uzbeks, Turcomen and Kirghiz gathered in a corner of the barrack, dressed in their holiday clothes, long coloured silk robes and embroidered skullcaps. It was impossible to guess of what they talked with such great animation and excitement, gesticulating, shouting each other down and nodding their heads sadly, but I was certain that it was not of the camp.[69]

Life was not much better for the Koreans, usually Soviet citizens of Korean extraction, or the Japanese, a staggering 600,000 of whom arrived in the Gulag and the prisoner-of-war camp system at the end of the war. The Japanese suffered in particular from the food, which seemed not only scarce but strange and virtually inedible. As a result, they would hunt and eat things that seemed to their fellow prisoners equally inedible: wild herbs, insects, beetles, snakes and mushrooms that even Russians would not touch. Occasionally, these forays ended badly: there are records of Japanese prisoners dying from eating poisonous grasses or wild herbs.[70] A hint at how isolated the Japanese felt in the camps comes from the memoirs of a Russian prisoner who once, in a camp library, found a brochure – a speech by the Bolshevik Zhdanov – written in Japanese. He brought it to a Japanese acquaintance, a war prisoner: 'I saw him genuinely happy for the first time. Later he told me that he read it every day, just to have contact with his native language.'[71]

Some of the other Far Eastern nationalities adapted more rapidly. A number of memoirists mention the tight organization of the Chinese – some of whom were 'Soviet' ethnic Chinese born in the USSR, some of whom had been legal guest-workers in the 1920s, and some of whom were unlucky people who had accidentally or whimsically walked over the very long Chinese–Soviet border. One prisoner recalled being told by a Chinaman that he, like many others, had been arrested because he had swum across the Amur River to the Soviet Union, attracted by the views on the other side: 'The green and gold of the trees . . . the steppes looked so beautiful! And everyone who crossed the river from our area never came back. We thought this meant that life must be good over there, so we decided to cross. The minute we did we were arrested and charged under Article 58, Section 6, espionage. Ten years.'[72]

In the camps, remembered Dmitri Panin, one of Solzhenitsyn's camp companions, the Chinese 'communicated only among themselves. By way of reply to any question of ours, they put on a look of incomprehension.'[73] Karlo Stajner recalled that they were very good at procuring jobs for one another: 'All over Europe, the Chinese are famous as jugglers, but in the camps they were employed in the laundry. I cannot remember seeing any non-Chinese laundry workers in any of the camps I passed through.'[74]

By far the most influential ethnic groups in the camps were those formed by the Balts and West Ukrainians who had been swept *en masse* into the camps during and after the war (see Chapter 20). Fewer in numbers, but also influential, were the Poles, particularly the anti-communist Polish partisans who also appeared in the camps in the late 1940s – as well as the Chechens, whom Solzhenitsyn described as 'the one nation which would not give in, would not acquire the mental habits of submission', and who stood out, in a number of ways, from the other Caucasians.[75] The strength of these particular ethnic groups was in their sheer numbers, and in their clear opposition to the Soviet Union, whose invasion of their respective countries they regarded as illegal. The post-war Poles, Balts and Ukrainians also had military and partisan experience, and in some cases their partisan organizations were maintained in the camps. Just after the war, the general staff of UPA, the Ukrainian Rebel Army, one of several groups fighting for control of Ukraine at that time, issued a statement to all Ukrainians who had been deported into exile or sent to camps: 'Wherever you are, in the mines, the forest or the camps, always remain what you have formerly been, remain true Ukrainian, and continue our fight.'

In the camps, ex-partisans self-consciously helped one another, and watched over newcomers. Adam Galinski, a Pole who had fought with the anti-Soviet Polish Home Army, both during and after the war, wrote that: 'We took special care of the youth of the Home Army and kept up its morale, the highest in the degrading atmosphere of moral decline that prevailed among the different national groups imprisoned in Vorkuta.'[76]

In later years, when they acquired more power to influence the running of the camps, Poles, Balts and Ukrainians – like Georgians, Armenians and Chechens – also formed their own national brigades, slept separately in national barracks, and organized celebrations of national holidays. At times, these powerful groups co-operated with one another. The Polish writer Aleksander Wat wrote that Ukrainians and Poles, bitter wartime enemies whose partisan movements fought one another over every inch of Western Ukraine, related to one another in Soviet prisons 'with reserve but with incredible loyalty. "We are enemies, but not here." '[77]

At other times these ethnic groups competed, both with one another and with Russians. Lyudmila Khachatryan, herself arrested for falling in love with a Yugoslav soldier, remembered the Ukrainians in her camp refusing to work with the Russians.[78] The national resistance groups, wrote another observer, 'are characterized on the one hand by hostility to the regime, on the other by hostility to the Russians'. Edward Buca remembered a more generalized hostility – 'It was unusual for a prisoner to give any help to anyone of a different nationality'[79] – although Pavel Negretov, in Vorkuta at the same time as Buca, felt that most nationalities got along, except when they succumbed to the administrations 'provocations': 'they tried, through their informers . . . to get us to quarrel'.[80]

During the late 1940s, when the various ethnic groups took over the criminals' role as *de facto* policemen within the camps, they sometimes fought one another for control. Marlen Korallov recalled that 'they began to fight for power, and power meant a great deal: who controlled the dining hall, for instance, mattered a great deal, because the cook would work directly for its master'. According to Korallov, the balance between the various groups at that time was extremely delicate, and could be upset by the arrival of a new transport. When a group of Chechens arrived in his *lagpunkt*, for example, they entered the barracks and 'threw all of the belongings on the lower bunks on to the floor' – in that camp the lower bunks were the 'aristocratic' bunks – 'and moved in with their own possessions.'[81]

Leonid Sitko, a prisoner who spent time in a Nazi POW camp only to be arrested on his return to Russia, witnessed a far more serious battle between Chechens, Russians and Ukrainians in the late 1940s. The argument started with a personal dispute between brigade leaders and escalated: 'it became war, all out war'. The Chechens staged an attack on a Russian barracks, and many were wounded. Later, all of the ringleaders were put in a punishment cell. Although the disputes were over influence within the camp, they had their origin in deeper national feelings, Sitko explained: 'The Balts and Ukrainians considered Soviets and Russians to be one and the same thing. Although there were plenty of Russians in the camp, that didn't stop them from thinking of Russians as occupiers and thieves.'

Sitko himself was once approached in the middle of the night by a group of West Ukrainians:

'Your name is Ukrainian,' they said to me. 'Who are you, a traitor?'

I explained to them that I had grown up in the North Caucasus, in a family that spoke Russian, and that I didn't know why I had a Ukrainian name. They sat for a while, and then left. They could have killed me though – they had a knife.[82]

One woman prisoner, who otherwise remembered national differences as being 'no big deal', also joked that this was true for everyone except the Ukrainians, who simply 'hated everyone else'.[83]

Odd though it sounds, in most camps there was no clan for Russians, the ethnic group which formed the decided majority in the camps, according to the Gulag's own statistics, throughout their existence.[84] Russians did, it is true, attach themselves to one another according to what city or part of the country they came from. Muscovites found other Muscovites, Leningraders other Leningraders, and so on. Vladimir Petrov was helped, at one point, by a doctor who asked him,

'What were you, before?'

'A student in Leningrad.'

'Ah! So you are a countryman of mine – very good,' said the doctor, patting my shoulder.[85]

Often, the Muscovites were particularly powerful and organized. Leonid Trus, arrested while still a student, recalled the older Muscovites in his camp forming a tight network which left him out. Even when, on one occasion, he wanted to borrow a book from the camp library, he first had to convince the librarian, a member of this clan, that he could be trusted with it.[86]

More often, however, such links were weak, providing prisoners with nothing more than people who remembered the street where they had lived or knew the school they had attended. Whereas other ethnic groups formed whole networks of support, finding places in barracks for newcomers, helping them to get easier jobs, the Russians did not. Ariadna Efron wrote that upon arrival in Turukhansk, where she was exiled with other prisoners at the end of her camp sentence, her train was met by exiles already living there:

A Jewish man took aside the Jewish women in our group, gave them bread, explained to them how to comport themselves, what to do. Then a group of Georgian women were met by a Georgian – and, after a while, there were only us Russians left, perhaps ten to fifteen people. No one came to us, offered us bread, or gave us any advice.[87]

Still, there were some distinctions among the Russian inmates – distinctions based on ideology rather than ethnicity. Nina Gagen-Torn wrote that the 'definite majority of women in the camps understood their fate and their suffering as an accidental misfortune, not trying to look for reasons'. For those, however, who 'found for themselves some kind of explanation for what was happening, and believed in it, things were easier'.[88] Chief among those who had an explanation were the communists: those prisoners, that is, who continued to maintain their innocence, continued to profess loyalty to the Soviet Union, and continued to believe, against all of the evidence, that everyone else was a genuine enemy and should be avoided. Anna Andreevna remembered the communists searching one another out: 'They found one another and clung together, they were clean, Soviet people, and thought everyone else were criminals.'[89] Susanna Pechora described seeing them upon arrival in Minlag in the early 1950s, 'sitting in a corner and telling one another, "We are honest Soviet people, hurrah for Stalin, we aren't guilty and our state will free us from the company of all these enemies." '90

Both Pechora and Irena Arginskaya, a prisoner in Kengir at the same time, recall that most of the members of this group belonged to the class of high-ranking Party members arrested in 1937 and 1938. They were mostly older; Arginskaya remembered that they were often grouped in the invalid camps, which still contained many people arrested in that earlier era. Anna Larina, the wife of the Soviet leader Nikolai Bukharin, was one of those arrested at this time who remained faithful to the Revolution at first. While still in prison, she wrote a poem commemorating the anniversary of the October Revolution:

> Yet, though behind iron bars I stay,
> Feeling the anguish of the damned
> Still I celebrate this day
> Together with my happy land.
>
> Today I have a new belief
> I will enter life again,
> And stride again with my Komsomol
> Side by side across Red Square!

Later, Larina came to regard this poem 'as the ravings of a lunatic'. But at the time, she recited it to the imprisoned wives of the Old Bolsheviks, and 'they were moved to tears and applause'.91

Solzhenitsyn dedicated a chapter of The Gulag Archipelago to the communists, whom he referred to, not very charitably, as 'Goodthinkers'. He marvelled at their ability to explain away even their own arrest, torture and incarceration as, variously, 'the very cunning work of foreign intelligence services' or 'wrecking on an enormous scale' or 'a plot by the local NKVD' or 'treason'. Some came up with an even more magisterial explanation: 'These repressions are a historical necessity for the development of our society.'92

Later, a few of these loyalists also wrote memoirs, willingly published by the Soviet regime. Boris Dyakov's novella, A Story of Survival, was published in 1964 in the journal Oktyabr, for example, with the following introduction: 'The strength of Dyakov's story lies in the fact that it is about genuine Soviet people, about authentic communists. In difficult conditions, they never lost their humanity, they were true to their Party ideals, they were devoted to the Motherland.' One of Dyakov's heroes, Todorsky, describes how he helps an NKVD lieutenant write a speech on the history of the Party. On another occasion, he tells the camp security officer, Major Yakovlev, that despite his unfair conviction, he believes himself to be a true communist: 'I am guilty of no crime against Soviet authority. Therefore I was, and I remain, a communist.' The major advises him to keep quiet about it: 'Why shout about it? You think everyone in the camp loves communists?'[93]

Indeed they did not: open communists were often suspected of working, secretly or otherwise, for the camp authorities. Writing about Dyakov, Solzhenitsyn noted that his memoir appeared to leave some things out. '*In exchange for what*,' he asks, did security officer Sokovikov agree to secretly post Dyakov's letters for him, bypassing the camp censor? 'That kind of friendship – *whence came it*?'[94] In fact, archives now show that Dyakov had been a secret police agent all of his life – code-named 'Woodpecker' – and that he had continued to work as an informer in the camps.[95]

The only group that surpassed the communists in their absolute faith were the Orthodox believers, as well as the members of the various Russian Protestant religious sects who were also subject to political persecution: Baptists, Jehovah's Witnesses, and Russian variations thereof. They were a particularly strong presence in the women's camps, where they were colloquially known as *monashki*, or 'nuns'. In the late 1940s, in the women's camp in Mordovia, Anna Andreevna remembered that 'the majority of the prisoners were believers', who organized themselves so that 'on holidays the Catholics would work for the Orthodox and vice versa'.[96]

As previously noted, some of these sects refused to co-operate in any way with the Soviet Satan, and would neither work nor sign any official documents. Gagen-Torn describes one religious woman who was released on grounds of illness, but refused to leave the camps. 'I don't recognize your authority,' she told the guard who offered to give her the necessary documents and send her home. 'Your power is illegitimate, the Anti-Christ appears on your passports . . . If I go free, you'll arrest me again. There isn't any reason to leave.'[97] Aino Kuusinen was in a camp with a group of women prisoners who refused to wear numbered clothing, as a result of which 'the numbers were stamped on their bare flesh instead', and they were forced to attend morning and evening roll-calls stark naked.[98]

Solzhenitsyn tells the story, repeated in various forms by others, of a group of religious sectarians who were brought to Solovetsky in 1930. They rejected anything that came from the 'Anti-Christ', refusing to handle Soviet passports or money. As punishment, they were sent to a small island in the Solovetsky archipelago, where they were told they would receive food only if they agreed to sign for it. They refused. Within two months they had all starved to death. The next boat to the island, remembered one eyewitness, 'found only corpses which had been picked by the birds'.[99]

Even those sectarians who did work did not necessarily mix with other prisoners, and sometimes refused to speak to them at all. They would huddle together in one barrack, keeping absolutely silent, or else singing their prayers and their religious songs at the appointed times:

I sat behind the prison bars
Remembering how Christ
Humbly and mildly carried his heavy Cross
With penitence, to Golgotha.[100]

The more extreme believers tended to inspire mixed feelings on the part of other prisoners. Arginskaya, a decidedly secular prisoner, jokingly remembered that 'we all loathed them', particularly those who, for religious reasons, refused to bathe.[101] Gagen-Torn remembered other prisoners complaining about those who refused to work: 'We work and they don't! And they take bread too!'[102]

Yet in one sense, those men or women who arrived at a new camp and immediately joined a clan or a religious sect were lucky. For those who belonged to them, the criminal gangs, the more militant national groups, the true communists, and the religious sects provided instant communities, networks of support, and companionship. Most political prisoners, on the other hand, and most 'ordinary' criminals – the vast majority of the Gulag's inhabitants – did not fit in so easily with one or another of these groups. They found it more difficult to know how to live life in the camp, more difficult to cope with camp morality and the camp hierarchy. Without a strong network of contacts they would have to learn the rules of advancement by themselves.

15

Women and Children

. . . the prisoner who was our barrack orderly greeted me with
a cry: 'Run and see what's under your pillow!'

My heart leaped: perhaps I'd got my bread ration after all!

I ran to my bed and threw off the pillow. Under it lay three
letters from home, three whole letters! It was six months since
I'd received anything at all.

My first reaction on seeing them was acute disappointment.
And then – horror.

What had become of me if a piece of bread was worth more
to me now than letters from my mother, my father, my children
. . . I forgot all about the bread and wept.

– Olga Adamova-Sliozberg, *My Journey*[1]

They met the same work norms and they ate the same watery soup. They
lived in the same sort of barracks and travelled in the same cattle trains. Their
clothes were almost identical, their shoes equally inadequate. They were
treated no differently under interrogation. And yet – men's and women's
camp experiences were not quite the same.

Certainly many women survivors are convinced that there were great
advantages to being female within the camp system. Women were better at
taking care of themselves, better at keeping their clothes patched and their
hair clean. They seemed better able to subsist on low amounts of food, and
did not succumb so easily to pellagra and the other diseases of starvation.[2]
They formed powerful friendships, and helped one another in ways that male
prisoners did not. Margarete Buber-Neumann records that one of the women
arrested with her in Butyrka prison had been picked up in a light summer
dress which had turned to rags. The cell determined to make her a new dress:

They clubbed together and bought half-a-dozen towels of rough, unbleached Russian
linen. But how was the dress to be cut without a pair of scissors? A little ingenuity
solved the problem. The 'cut' was marked with the burnt ends of matches, the material

was folded along the marked lines, and a lighted match was run backwards and forwards for a moment or two along the fold. Then the material was unfolded again and the line was burnt through. The cotton for sewing was obtained by carefully withdrawing threads from other clothing . . .

The towel dress – it was made for a fat Lettish woman – went from hand to hand and was beautifully embroidered at the neck, the sleeves, and round the bottom of the skirt. When it was finally finished it was dampened down and carefully folded. The fortunate possessor slept on it at night. Believe it or not, but when it was produced in the morning, it was really delightful; it would not have disgraced the window of a fashionable dress shop.[3]

Nevertheless, among many male ex-prisoners the opposite point of view prevails: that women deteriorated, morally, more rapidly than men. Thanks to their sex they had special opportunities to obtain a better work classification, an easier job, and with it superior status in the camp. As a result, they became disoriented, losing their bearings in the harsh world of the camp. Gustav Herling writes, for example, of a 'black-haired singer of the Moscow Opera', who was arrested for 'espionage'. Because of the severity of her sentence, she was assigned immediately to work in the forest upon her arrival in Kargopollag:

Unfortunately for her, she was desired by Vanya, the short *urka* in charge of her brigade, and she was put to work clearing felled fir trees of bark with a huge axe she could hardly lift. Lagging several yards behind the hefty foresters, she arrived in the zone in the evening with hardly enough strength left to crawl to the kitchen and collect her 'first cauldron' [the lowest-level soup ration] . . . it was obvious that she had a high temperature, but the medical orderly was a friend of Vanya's and would not free her from work . . .

Eventually, she gave in, first to Vanya, then finally to 'some camp chief' who 'dragged her out by the hair from the rubbish heap and placed her behind a table in the camp accountant's office'.[4]

There were worse fates too, as Herling also describes. He gives, for example, an account of a young Polish girl, whom an 'informal jury of *urkas*' rated very highly. At first,

she walked out to work with her head raised proudly, and repulsed any man who ventured near her, with darting, angry looks. In the evenings she returned from work rather more humbly, but still untouchable and modestly haughty. She went straight from the guard-house to the kitchen for her portion of soup, and did not leave the women's barracks again during the night. Therefore it looked as if she would not quickly fall a victim to the night hunts of the camp zone.

But these early efforts were in vain. After weeks of being carefully watched by her supervisor, who forbade her to steal a single carrot or rotten potato from the food warehouse where she worked, the girl gave in. One evening, the man came into Herling's barracks and 'without a word threw a torn pair of knickers on my bunk'. It was the beginning of her transformation:

From that time the girl underwent a complete change. She never hurried to get her soup from the kitchen as before, but after her return from work wandered about the camp zone till late at night like a cat on heat. Whoever wanted to could have her, on a bunk, under the bunk, in the separate cubicles of the technical experts, or in the clothing store. Whenever she met me, she turned her head aside, and tightened her lips convulsively. Once, entering the potato store at the centre, I found her on a pile of potatoes with the brigadier of the 56th, the hunchbacked half-breed Levkovich; she burst into a spasmodic fit of weeping, and as she returned to the camp zone in the evening she held back her tears with two tiny fists . . .[5]

That is Herling's version of a frequently told story – one which, it must be said, always sounds somewhat different when told from the woman's point of view. Another version, for example, is recounted by Tamara Ruzhnevits, whose camp 'romance' began with a letter, a 'standard love letter, a pure camp letter', from Sasha, a young man whose cushy cobbler's job made him a part of the camp aristocracy. It was a short, blunt letter: 'Let's live together, and I'll help you.' A few days after sending it, Sasha pulled Ruzhnevits aside, wanting to know the answer. 'Will you live with me or not?' he asked. She said no. He beat her up with a metal stave. Then he carried her to the hospital (where his special cobbler's status gave him influence) and instructed the staff to take good care of her. There she remained, recovering from her wounds, for several days. Upon release, having had plenty of time to think about it, she then returned to Sasha. Otherwise, he would have beaten her up again.

'Thus began my family life,' wrote Ruzhnevits. The benefits were immediate: 'I got healthier, walked about in nice shoes, no longer wore the devil knows what kind of rags: I had a new jacket, new trousers . . . I even had a new hat.' Many decades later, Ruzhnevits described Sasha as 'my first, genuine true love'. Unfortunately, he was soon sent away to another camp, and she never saw him again. Worse, the man responsible for Sasha's transfer also desired her. As there was 'no way out', she began sleeping with him too. While she does not write of feeling any love for him, she does recall that there were benefits to this arrangement as well: she was given a pass to travel unguarded, and a horse of her own.[6] Ruzhnevits's story, like the one Herling tells, could be described as a tale of moral degradation. Alternatively, it could be called a story of survival.

From the administration's point of view, none of this was supposed to happen. In principle, men and women were not supposed to be held in camps together at all, and there are prisoners who speak of having not laid eyes on a member of the opposite sex for years and years. Nor did camp commanders

Hunger for love: male prisoners peering over the fence into the women's zone
– a drawing by Yula-Imar Sooster, Karaganda, 1950

particularly want women prisoners. Physically weaker, they were liable to become a drag on camp production output, as a result of which some camp administrators tried to turn them away. At one point, in February 1941, the Gulag administration even sent out a letter to the entire NKVD leadership and all camp commanders, sternly instructing them to accept convoys of women prisoners, and listing all the jobs which women could usefully do. The letter mentions light industry and textile factories; woodwork and metalwork; certain types of forestry jobs; loading and unloading freight.[7]

Perhaps because of the camp commanders' objections, the numbers of women who were actually sent to camps always remained relatively low (as did the number of women executed during the 1937–8 purge). According to the official statistics, for example, only about 13 per cent of Gulag prisoners in the year 1942 were women. This went up to 30 per cent in 1945, due in part to the enormous number of male prisoners drafted and sent to the front, and also to the laws forbidding workers to leave their factory – laws which led to the arrest of many young women.[8] In 1948 it was 22 per cent, falling again to 17 per cent in 1951 and 1952.[9] Still, even these numbers fail to reflect the true situation, as women were far more likely to be assigned to serve their sentences in the light-regime 'colonies'. In the large, industrial camps of the far north, they were even fewer, their presence even rarer.

Their low numbers meant, however, that women were – like food, clothing and other possessions – almost always in shortage. So although they might have had little value to those compiling the camp production statistics, they had another sort of value to the male prisoners, the guards and the camp free workers. In those camps where there were more or less open contacts between male and female prisoners – or where, in practice, certain men were allowed access to women's camps – they were frequently propositioned, accosted and, most commonly, offered food and easy work in exchange for sex. This was not, perhaps, a feature of life unique to the Gulag. A 1999 Amnesty International report on women prisoners in the United States, for example, uncovered cases of male guards and male prisoners raping female prisoners; of male inmates bribing guards for access to women prisoners; of women being strip-searched and frisked by male guards.[10] Nevertheless, the strange social hierarchies of the Soviet camp system meant that women were tortured and humiliated to an extent unusual even for a prison system.

From the start, a woman's fate depended greatly on her status and position within the various camp clans. Within the criminal world, women were subject to a system of elaborate rules and rituals, and received very little respect. According to Shalamov, 'A third- or fourth-generation criminal learns contempt for women from childhood . . . woman, an inferior being, has been created only to satisfy the criminal's animal craving, to be the butt of his crude jokes and the victim of public beatings when her thug decides to "whoop it up".' Women prostitutes effectively 'belonged' to leading male criminals, and could be traded or bartered, or even inherited by a brother or friend, if the man were transferred to a different camp or killed. When an exchange occurred, 'usually the parties concerned do not come to blows, and the prostitute submits to sleeping with her new master. There are no *ménages à trois* in the criminal world, with two men sharing one woman. Nor is it possible for a female thief to live with a non-criminal.'[11]

Women were not the only targets either. Among the professional criminals, homosexual sex appears to have been organized according to equally brutal rules. Some criminal bosses had young male homosexuals in their entourages, along with or instead of camp 'wives'. Thomas Sgovio writes of one brigadier who had a male 'wife' – a young man who received extra food in exchange for sexual favours.[12] It is hard to describe the rules governing male homosexuality in camps, however, because memoirists so rarely mention the subject. This may be because homosexuality remains, in Russian culture, partly taboo, and people prefer not to write about it. Male homosexuality in the camps also seems to have been largely confined to the criminal world – and criminals left few memoirs.

Nevertheless, we do know that by the 1970s and 1980s, Soviet criminals did develop extremely complicated rules of homosexual etiquette. 'Passive' male homosexuals were ostracized from the rest of prison society, ate at separate tables, and did not speak to the other men.[13] Although rarely described, similar rules seem to have existed in some quarters as early as the late 1930s, when Pyotr Yakir, aged fifteen, witnessed an analagous phenomenon in a cell for juvenile criminals. At first, he was shocked to hear the other boys speaking of their sexual experiences, and believed them to be embellished,

but I was mistaken. One of the kids had hung on to his bread ration until evening when he asked Mashka, who had had nothing to eat all day, 'Do you want a bite?'

'Yes,' Mashka replied.

'Then take your trousers down.'

It took place in a corner, into which it was difficult to see from the spyhole, but in full view of everybody in the cell. It surprised no one and I pretended not to be surprised by it. There were many other instances while I was in that cell; it was always the same boys who played the passive partner. They were treated like pariahs, were not allowed to drink from the common cup, and were the objects of humiliation.[14]

Curiously, lesbianism in the camps was more open, or at least it is more frequently described. Among the women criminals, it was also heavily ritualized. Lesbians were referred to by the Russian neuter pronoun, *ono*, and they divided themselves into more feminine 'mares' and more masculine 'husbands'. The former were sometimes 'genuine slaves', according to one account, cleaning and caring for their 'husbands'. The latter took on male nicknames, and almost always smoked.[15] They spoke openly about lesbianism, even sang songs about it:

> O thank you Stalin
> You've made of me a baroness
> I am both a cow and a bull
> A woman and a man.[16]

They also identified themselves by what they wore, and by their behaviour. One Polish woman wrote later that:

Pairs of such women are known to everybody, and they make no attempt to conceal their habits. Those who play the part of the man are generally dressed in men's clothes, their hair is short and they hold their hands in their pockets. When such a pair of lovers are suddenly seized by a wave of passion, they jump up from their seats, leave their sewing machines, and chase after each other, then amid frantic kisses they fall to the ground.[17]

Valery Frid writes of criminal women prisoners who, dressed as men, passed themselves off as hermaphrodites. One was 'short-haired, pretty, in officer's trousers'; another did seem to have a genuine genital deformation.[18]

Another prisoner described lesbian 'rape': she witnessed one lesbian pair chase a 'modest, quiet girl' beneath the bunks, where they broke her hymen.[19] In intellectual circles, lesbianism seems to have been less kindly regarded. One ex-political prisoner remembered it as 'a most revolting practice'.[20] Still, although it was usually more hidden among politicals, it did exist among them too, often occurring among women who had husbands and children in freedom. Susanna Pechora told me that in Minlag, a largely political camp, lesbian relationships 'helped some people to survive'.[21]

Whether voluntary or forced, homosexual or heterosexual, most sexual relationships in the camps shared in the generally brutal atmosphere. Of necessity, they were conducted with an openness that many prisoners found shocking. Couples would 'crawl under the barbed wire and make love next to the toilet, on the ground', one former prisoner told me.[22] 'A multiple bunk curtained off with rags from the neighbouring women was a classic camp scene,' wrote Solzhenitsyn.[23] Isaak Filshtinsky once awoke in the middle of the night and found a woman lying in the bed next to his. She had snuck over the wall to make love to the camp cook: 'Other than myself, no one had slept that night, but with rapt attention listened to the proceedings.'[24] Hava Volovich wrote that 'things that a free person might have thought about a hundred times before doing happened here as simply as they would between stray cats'.[25] Another prisoner remembered that love, particularly among the thieves, was 'animal-like'.[26]

Indeed, sex was so public that it was treated with a certain amount of apathy: rape and prostitution became, for some, part of a daily routine. Edward Buca was once working beside a women's brigade in a sawmill. A group of criminal prisoners arrived. They 'grabbed the women they wanted and laid them down in the snow, or had them up against a pile of logs. The women seemed used to it and offered no resistance. They had their own brigade-chief, but she didn't object to these interruptions, in fact, they almost seemed to be just another part of the job.'[27] Lev Razgon also tells the story of a very young, fair-haired girl whom he happened to encounter sweeping the courtyard of a camp medical unit. He was a free worker by then, visiting a doctor acquaintance, and although not hungry, was offered a generous lunch. He gave it to the girl, who 'ate quietly and neatly and one could tell that she had been brought up in a family'. She reminded Razgon, in fact, of his own daughter:

The girl finished eating, and neatly piled the plates on the wooden tray. Then she lifted her dress, pulled off her pants and, holding them in her hand, turned her unsmiling face in my direction.

'Lying down or what?' she asked.

At first not understanding, and then scared by my response, she said in self-justification, again without a smile, 'People don't feed me without it . . .'[28]

It also happened, in some camps, that certain women's barracks became little more than open brothels. Solzhenitsyn described one which was

incomparably filthy and rundown, and there was an oppressive smell in it, and the bunks were without bedding. There was an official prohibition against men entering it, but this prohibition was ignored and no one enforced it. Not only men went there, but juveniles too, boys from twelve to thirteen, who flocked in to learn . . . Everything took place very naturally, as in nature, in full view, and in several places at once. Obvious old age and obvious ugliness were the only defences for women there – nothing else.[29]

And yet – running directly counter to the tales of brutal sex and vulgarity, there are, in many memoirs, equally improbable tales of camp love, some of which began simply out of women's desire for self-protection. According to the idiosyncratic rules of camp life, women who adopted a 'camp husband' were usually left alone by other men, a system which Herling calls the 'peculiar *ius primae noctis* of the camp'.[30] These were not necessarily 'marriages' of equals: respectable women sometimes lived with thieves.[31] Nor, as Ruzhnevits described, were they necessarily freely chosen. Nevertheless, it would not be strictly correct to describe them as prostitution either. Rather, writes Valery Frid, they were '*braki po raschetu*' – 'calculated marriages' – 'which were also sometimes marriages for love'. Even if they had begun for purely practical reasons, prisoners took these relationships seriously. 'About his more or less permanent lover, a *zek* would say "my wife", ' wrote Frid, 'And she would say of him "my husband". It was not said in jest: camp relationships humanized our lives.'[32]

And, strange though it may sound, prisoners who were not too exhausted or emaciated really did look for love. Anatoly Zhigulin's memoirs include a description of a love affair he managed to conduct with a German woman, a political prisoner, the 'happy, good, grey-eyed, golden-haired Marta'. He later learned that she had a baby, whom she named Anatoly. (That was in the autumn of 1951, and, as Stalin's death was followed by a general amnesty for foreign prisoners, he supposed that 'Marta and the child, assuming no bad luck had occurred, returned home.'[33]) The memoirs of the camp doctor Isaac Vogelfanger at times read like a romantic novel, whose hero had to tread carefully between the perils of an affair with the wife of a camp boss, and the joys of real love.[34]

So desperately did people deprived of everything long for sentimental relationships that some become deeply involved in platonic love affairs, conducted by letter. This was particularly the case in the late 1940s, in the special camps for political prisoners, where male and female prisoners were kept strictly apart. In Minlag, one such camp, men and women prisoners sent notes to one another via their colleagues in the camp hospital, which was shared by both sexes. Prisoners also organized a secret 'mailbox' in the railway work zone where the women's brigades laboured. Every few days, a woman working on the railroad would pretend to have forgotten a coat, or other object, go to the mailbox, pick up what letters had been sent, and leave letters in return. One of the men would pick them up later.[35] There were other methods too: 'At a specific time, a chosen person in one of the zones would throw letters from men to women or women to men. This was the "postal service".'[36]

Such letters, remembered Leonid Sitko, were written on tiny pieces of paper, with tiny letters. Everyone signed them with false names: his was 'Hamlet', his girlfriend's was 'Marsianka'. They had been 'introduced' through other women, who had told him she was extremely depressed, having had her small baby taken away from her after her arrest. He began to write to her, and they even managed to meet once, inside an abandoned mine.[37]

Others developed even more surreal methods in their quest for some kind of intimacy. In the Kengir special camp, there were prisoners – almost all foreign politicals, deprived of all contact with their families, their friends and the wives and husbands they had left back home – who developed elaborate relationships with people they had never met.[38] Some actually married one another across the wall that divided the men's and women's camps, without ever meeting in person. The woman stood on one side, the man on the other; vows were said, and a prisoner priest recorded the ceremony on a piece of paper.

This kind of love persisted, even when the camp administration raised the wall, covered it with barbed wire, and forbade prisoners to go near it. In describing these blind marriages even Solzhenitsyn momentarily drops the cynicism he applies to almost all other camp relationships: 'In this marriage with an unknown person on the other side of a wall . . . I hear a choir of angels. It is like the unselfish, pure contemplation of heavenly bodies. It is too lofty for this age of self-interested calculation and hopping-up-and-down jazz . . .'[39]

If love, sex, rape and prostitution were a part of camp life, so too, it followed, were pregnancy and childbirth. Along with mines and construction sites, forestry brigades and punishment cells, barracks and cattle trains, there were maternity hospitals and maternity camps in the Gulag too – as well as nurseries for babies and small children.

Not all of the children who found their way into these institutions were born in the camps. Some were 'arrested' along with their mothers. Rules governing this practice were always unclear. The operational order of 1937, which mandated the arrests of wives and children of 'enemies of the people', explicitly forbade the arrest of pregnant women and women nursing babies.[40]

A 1940 order, on the other hand, said that children could stay with their mothers for a year and a half, 'until they cease to need mother's milk', at which point they had to be put in orphanages or given to relatives.[41]

In practice, both pregnant and nursing women were regularly arrested. Upon carrying out routine examinations of a newly arrived prisoner convoy, one camp doctor discovered a woman having labour contractions. She had been arrested in her seventh month of pregnancy.[42] Another woman, Natalya Zaporozhets, was sent on a transport when she was eight months pregnant: after being knocked around on trains and in the back of trucks, she gave birth to a dead baby.[43] The artist and memoirist Evfrosiniya Kersnovskaya helped deliver a baby who was actually born on a convoy train.[44]

Small children were 'arrested' along with their parents too. One woman prisoner, arrested in the 1920s, wrote an acid letter of complaint to Dzerzhinsky, thanking him for 'arresting' her three-year-old son: prison, she said, was preferable to a children's home, which she called a 'factory for making angels'.[45] Hundreds of thousands of children were effectively arrested, along with their parents, during the two great waves of deportation, the first of the kulaks in the early 1930s, the second of 'enemy' ethnic and national groups during and after the Second World War.

For these children, the shock of the new situation would remain with them all of their lives. One Polish prisoner remembered that a woman in her gaol cell had been accompanied by her three-year-old son: 'The child was well-behaved, but delicate and silent. We amused him as well as we could with stories and fairy tales, but he interrupted us from time to time, saying, "We're in prison, aren't we?" '[46]

Many years later, a child of deported kulaks recalled his ordeal on the cattle trains: 'People became wild . . . How many days we travelled, I have no idea. In the wagon, seven people died of hunger. We got to Tomsk and they took us out, several families. They also unloaded several corpses, children, young people and the elderly.'[47]

Despite the hardships, there were also women who deliberately, even cynically, became pregnant while in the camps. These were usually criminal women or those convicted of petty crimes who wanted to be pregnant so as to be excused from hard work, to receive slightly better food, and to benefit, possibly, from the periodic amnesties given to women with small children. Such amnesties – there was one in 1945, for example, and another in 1948 – did not usually apply to women sentenced for counter-revolutionary crimes.[48] 'You could ease your life by getting pregnant,' Lyudmila Khachatryan told me, as a way of explaining why women happily slept with their gaolers.[49]

Another woman recalled hearing a rumour that all women with babies – *mamki*, in prison slang – would be released. She deliberately became pregnant afterwards.[50] Nadezhda Joffe, a prisoner who had become pregnant after being allowed to meet with her husband, wrote that her fellow inmates at the Magadan 'wet nurse barracks' simply 'didn't have any maternal instincts', and left their babies behind as soon as they were able.[51]

Perhaps not surprisingly, not all of the women who found they had become pregnant while in a camp wanted to remain that way. The Gulag administration seemed to be ambivalent about whether women should be allowed to have abortions or not, sometimes permitting them, sometimes slapping second sentences on those who attempted them.[52] Nor is it at all clear how frequent they were, because they are so rarely described: in dozens of interviews and memoirs, I have read or heard only two accounts. In an interview, Anna Andreevna told me of a woman who 'stuffed nails into herself, sat down and began to work on her sewing machine. Eventually she began to bleed heavily.'[53] Another woman described how a camp doctor attempted to terminate her pregnancy:

Imagine the picture. It is night. It is dark . . . Andrei Andreevich is trying to cause me to abort, using his hands, covered in iodine, without instruments. But he is so nervous that nothing comes of it. I can't breathe from the pain, but I endure it without a sound, so that no one will hear. 'Stop!' I finally shout from unbearable pain, and the whole procedure is stopped for two days. In the end, everything came out – the foetus, with a great deal of blood. That is why I never became a mother.[54]

But there were women who wanted their children, and tragedy was often their lot too. Against everything that has been written about the selfishness, the venality of the women who bore children in the camps, stands the story of Hava Volovich. A political arrested in 1937, she was extremely lonely in the camps, and deliberately sought to give birth to a child. Although she had no special love for the father, Eleonora was born in 1942, in a camp without special facilities for mothers:

There were three mothers there, and we were given a tiny room to ourselves in the barracks. Bedbugs poured down like sand from the ceiling and walls; we spent the whole night brushing them off the children. During the daytime we had to go out to work and leave the infants with any old woman we could find who had been excused from work; these women would calmly help themselves to the food we had left for the children.

Nevertheless, wrote Volovich,

Every night for a whole year, I stood at my child's cot, picking off the bedbugs and praying. I prayed that God would prolong my torment for a hundred years if it meant that I wouldn't be parted from my daughter. I prayed that I might be released with her, even if only as a beggar or a cripple. I prayed that I might be able to raise her to adulthood, even if I had to grovel at people's feet and beg for alms to do it. But God did not answer my prayer. My baby had barely started walking, I had hardly heard her first words, the wonderful heartwarming word 'Mama', when we were dressed in rags despite the winter chill, bundled into a freight car, and transferred to the 'mothers' camp'. And here my pudgy little angel with the golden curls soon turned into a pale ghost with blue shadows under her eyes and sores all over her lips.

Volovich was put first into a forestry brigade, then sent to work at a sawmill. In the evenings, she took home a small bundle of firewood which she gave to the nurses in the children's home. In return she was sometimes allowed to see her daughter outside normal visiting hours.

I saw the nurses getting the children up in the mornings. They would force them out of their cold beds with shoves and kicks . . . pushing the children with their fists and swearing at them roughly, they took off their nightclothes and washed them in ice-cold water. The babies didn't even dare cry. They made little sniffing noises like old men and let out low hoots.

This awful hooting noise would come from the cots for days at a time. Children already old enough to be sitting up or crawling would lie on their backs, their knees pressed to their stomachs, making these strange noises, like the muffled cooing of pigeons.

One nurse was assigned to seventeen children, which meant she had barely enough time to keep all of the babies changed and fed, let alone cared for properly:

The nurse brought a steaming bowl of porridge from the kitchen, and portioned it out into separate dishes. She grabbed the nearest baby, forced its arms back, tied them in place with a towel, and began cramming spoonful after spoonful of hot porridge down its throat not leaving it enough time to swallow, exactly as if she were feeding a turkey chick.

Slowly, Eleonora began to fade.

On some of my visits I found bruises on her little body. I shall never forget how she grabbed my neck with her skinny hands and moaned, 'Mama, want home!' She had not forgotten the bug-ridden slum where she first saw the light of day, and where she'd been with her mother all of the time . . .

Little Eleonora, who was now fifteen months old, soon realized that her pleas for 'home' were in vain. She stopped reaching out for me when I visited her; she would turn away in silence. On the last day of her life, when I picked her up (they allowed me to breast-feed her) she stared wide-eyed somewhere off into the distance, then started to beat her weak little fists on my face, clawing at my breast, and biting it. Then she pointed down at her bed.

In the evening, when I came back with my bundle of firewood, her cot was empty. I found her lying naked in the morgue among the corpses of the adult prisoners. She had spent one year and four months in this world, and died on 3 March 1944 . . .

That is the story of how, in giving birth to my only child, I committed the worst crime there is.[55]

In the archives of the Gulag, photographs of the type of camp nursery Volovich described have been preserved. One such album begins with the following introduction:

The sun shines in their Stalinist fatherland. The nation is filled with love for the leaders and our wonderful children are happy just as the whole young country is happy. Here, in wide and warm beds, sleep the new citizens of our country. Having eaten, they sleep sweetly and are certainly dreaming happy dreams . . .

The accompanying photographs belie the captions. In one, a row of nursing mothers, white masks covering their faces – proof of the hygienic practices of the camp – sits solemn-eyed and unsmiling on a bench, holding their babies. In another, the children are all going for their evening walk. Lined up in a row, they look no more spontaneous than their mothers. In many pictures, the children have shaved heads, presumably to prevent lice, which has the effect of making them look like the tiny prisoners they were in fact considered to be.[56] 'The children's home was also part of the camp compound,' wrote Ginzburg. 'It had its own guardhouse, its own gates, its own huts and its own barbed wire.'[57]

At some level, the Gulag administration in Moscow must have known how terrible life in the camps was for children who lived in them. We know, at least, that the camp inspectors passed on the information: a 1949 report on the condition of women in the camps noted disapprovingly that of the 503,000 women then in the Gulag system, 9,300 were pregnant while another 23,790 had small children with them. 'Taking into account the negative influence on the health and education of children,' the report argued for their mothers' early release, as well as the early release of those women who had children at home, a total – when exceptions were made for recidivists and counter-revolutionary political prisoners – of about 70,000.[58]

From time to time such amnesties were carried out. But few improvements were made in the lives of those children who remained. On the contrary, because they contributed nothing to the productivity of the camp, their health and well-being ranked very low on most camp commanders' list of priorities, and they invariably lived in the poorest, coldest, oldest buildings. One inspector determined that the temperature in one camp children's home never rose higher than 11 degrees centigrade; another found a children's home with peeling paint and no light at all, not even kerosene lamps.[59] A 1933 report from Siblag said the camp lacked 800 pairs of children's shoes, 700 children's overcoats and 900 sets of cutlery.[60] Nor were those working in them necessarily qualified. On the contrary, nursery jobs were 'trusty' jobs, and as such usually went to professional criminals. Joffe writes that 'For hours on end, they would stand under the stairway with their "husbands", or they would simply leave, while the children, unfed and unattended, would get sick and begin dying."[61]

Nor were mothers, whose pregnancies had already cost the camp a great deal, usually allowed to make up for this neglect – assuming that they cared to do so. They were made to return to work as soon as possible, and only grudgingly allowed time off from work to breast-feed. Usually, they would simply be released from work every four hours, given fifteen minutes with the child – still wearing their dirty work clothes – and then sent back again, meaning that the children went hungry. Sometimes they were not allowed even that. One camp inspector cited the case of a woman who arrived a few minutes late to nurse her baby, thanks to work obligations, and was refused access to him.[62] In an interview, a former supervisor of a camp nursery told me – dismissively – that children who could not drink their fill in what she said was the half-hour allowed were given the rest out of a bottle by one of the nurses.

This same woman also confirmed prisoners' descriptions of another form of cruelty: once breast-feeding ended, women were often forbidden any further contact with their child. In her camp, she said, she had personally forbidden all mothers to go on walks with their children, on the grounds that convict mothers would harm their children. She claimed to have seen one mother giving her child sugar mixed with tobacco to eat, in order to poison him. Another, she said, had deliberately taken off her child's shoes in the snow. 'I was responsible for the death rates of children in the camps,' she told me, explaining why she had taken steps to keep the mothers away. 'These children were unnecessary to their mothers, and the mothers wanted to kill them.'[63] This same logic might have led other camp commanders to forbid mothers from seeing their children. It is equally possible, however, that such rules were another product of the unthinking cruelty of the camp administration: it was inconvenient to arrange for mothers to see children, so the practice was banned.

The consequences of separating parents from children at such a young age were predictable. Infant epidemics were legion. Infant death rates were extremely high – so high that they were, as the inspectors' reports also record, often deliberately covered up.[64] But even those children who survived infancy had little chance of a normal life inside the camp nurseries. Some might be lucky enough to be cared for by the kinder sort of female prisoner nurse. Some might not. Ginzburg herself worked in a camp nursery, and found, upon arrival, that even the older children could not yet speak:

Only certain of the four-year-olds could produce a few odd, unconnected words. Inarticulate howls, mimicry and blows were the main means of communication. 'How can they be expected to speak? Who was there to teach them?' explained Anya dispassionately. 'In the infants' group they spend their whole time just lying on their cots. Nobody will pick them up, even if they cry their lungs out. It's not allowed, except to change wet diapers – when there are dry ones available, of course.'

When Ginzburg tried to teach her new charges, she found that only one or two, those who had maintained some contact with their mothers, were able to learn anything. And even their experience was very limited:

'Look,' I said to Anastas, showing him the little house I had drawn. 'What's this?'

'Barrack,' the little boy replied quite distinctly.

With a few pencil strokes I put a cat alongside the house. But no one recognized it, not even Anastas. They had never seen this rare animal. Then I drew a traditional rustic fence round the house.

'And what's this?'

'*Zona!*' Vera cried out delightedly.[65]

Usually, children were transferred out of the camp nurseries and into regular orphanages at the age of two. Some mothers welcomed this, as a chance for the children to escape from the camp. Others protested, knowing that they might be deliberately or accidentally transferred to different camps, away from their children, whose names might then be changed or forgotten, making it impossible to establish a relationship or even contact.[66] This sometimes happened to children in ordinary children's homes. Valentina Yurganova, the daughter of Volga German kulaks, was put into a children's home where some of the wards were too small to remember their names, and the authorities were too disorganized to remember them. One child, she told me, was simply renamed 'Kashtanova' ('Chestnut') because there were so many chestnut trees in the park behind the orphanage.

Years later, another such child wrote a heartbreaking description of her unsuccessful, lifelong search to find the real names of her parents: there was no record of any child being born in her region under the surname that appeared on her passport, and she had been too small to know their real names. Nevertheless, she remembered fragments of her past: 'Mama at a sewing machine. Me asking her for a needle and thread . . . Myself in a garden.. . . Then later . . . The room is dark, the bed on the right is empty, something has happened. Somehow I am alone. I am terrified.'[67]

No wonder some mothers 'cried and screamed and some even went crazy and were locked in bunkers until they quieted down' when their children were taken away. Once they were gone, the chances of a reunion were slim.[68]

Outside, life for children born in camps did not necessarily improve. Instead, they joined the massed ranks of the children who had been transferred directly to children's homes following the arrests of their parents – another category of child victim. As a rule, state orphanages were vastly overcrowded, dirty, understaffed and often lethal. A former prisoner recalled the emotions and high hopes with which her camp sent a group of prisoners' children into a city orphanage – and the horror they felt on hearing that all eleven had died in an epidemic.[69] As early as 1931, at the height of collectivization, the heads of children's homes in the Urals wrote desperate letters to regional authorities, begging for help in caring for the thousands of newly orphaned kulak children:

In a room 12 square metres, there are 30 boys. For 38 children there are seven beds, on which the 'recidivists' sleep. Two eighteen-year-olds have destroyed the electrical installations, robbed the shop, and drink with the director . . . children sleep on the dirty floor, play cards which they have made from torn-up pictures of the 'Leader', smoke, break the bars on the windows and climb over the walls intending to escape.[70]

In another home for kulaks' children:

Children sleep on the floor, and don't have enough shoes . . . sometimes there is no water for several days. They eat badly; aside from water and potatoes, they have no lunch. There are no plates and bowls, they eat out of ladles. For 140 people there is one cup, and not enough spoons; they eat in turns, or by hand. There is no light, only one lamp for the whole home, and it has no kerosene.[71]

In 1933, a children's home near Smolensk sent the following telegram to the Moscow children's commission: 'Food supply of the home has been cut. One hundred children are starving. The organization refuses to give rations. There is no help. Take urgent measures.'[72]

Nor did much change over time. A 1938 NKVD order describes one children's home in which two eight-year-old girls were raped by some of the older boys, and another in which 212 children shared twelve spoons and twenty plates, and slept in their clothes and shoes for lack of nightclothes.[73] In 1940, Savelyeva Leonidovna was 'kidnapped' from her children's home – her parents had been arrested – and adopted by a family who wanted to use her as a house servant. She was thus separated from her sister, whom she never found again.[74]

Children of arrested politicals had a particularly hard time in such homes, and were often treated worse than the ordinary orphans they shared them with. They were told, as was Svetlana Kogteva, aged ten, to 'forget their parents, since they were enemies of the people'.[75] NKVD officers responsible for such homes were ordered to maintain special vigilance, and to single out the children of counter-revolutionaries, to ensure that they did not receive privileged treatment of any kind.[76] Thanks to this rule, Pyotr Yakir lasted precisely three days in one of these orphanages, following his parents' arrest. During that time, he 'managed to get a name as a ringleader of the "traitors'"' children' and was immediately arrested, aged fourteen. He was transferred into a prison, and eventually sent to a camp.[77]

More often, the children of politicals suffered teasing and exclusion. One remembered that upon arrival at the orphanage, children of 'enemies' had their fingerprints taken, like criminals. The teachers and caretakers were all afraid to show them too much affection, not wanting to be accused of having sympathy with 'enemies'.[78] The children of arrested parents were teased mercilessly about their 'enemy' status, according to Yurganova, who deliberately forgot the German language she had spoken in her youth as a result.[79]

In these surroundings, even the children of educated parents soon learned criminal habits. Vladimir Glebov, the son of the leading Bolshevik Lev Kamenev, was one such child. At the age of four, his father was arrested, and Glebov was 'exiled' to a special children's orphanage in western Siberia. About 40 per cent of the children there were children of 'enemies', about 40 per cent were juvenile delinquents, and about 20 per cent were Gypsy children, arrested for the crime of nomadism. As Glebov explained to the writer Adam Hochschild, there were advantages, even for the children of politicals, to having early contact with young criminals:

My buddy taught me some things which helped me a lot in later life, about protecting myself. Here I have one scar, and here another . . . when people are attacking you with a knife, you need to know how to fight back. The main principle is to respond in advance, not to let them hit you. That was our happy Soviet childhood![80]

Some children, however, were permanently damaged by their orphanage experiences. One mother returned from exile, and was reunited with her young daughter. The child, at the age of eight, could still barely talk, grabbed at food, and behaved like the wild animal that the orphanage had taught her to be.[81] Another mother, released after an eight-year sentence, went to get her children from the orphanage, only to find that they refused to go with her. They had been taught that their parents were 'enemies of the people' who deserved no love and no affection. They had been specifically instructed to refuse to leave, 'if your mother ever comes to get you', and they never wanted to live with their parents again.[82]

Not surprisingly, children ran away from such orphanages – in large numbers. Once they found themselves on the streets, they fell very quickly into the criminal netherworld. And once they were part of the criminal netherworld, the vicious cycle continued. Sooner or later, they would probably be arrested too.

At first glance, the 1944–5 annual NKVD report from one particular group of eight camps in Ukraine shows nothing out of the ordinary. The report lists which of the camps met the Five-Year Plan, and which did not. It praises inmate shock-workers. It notes sternly that in most of the camps the food was very poor and monotonous. It notes more approvingly that an epidemic had broken out in only one camp, during the time period surveyed – and that

that was after five inmates had been transferred there from the overcrowded Kharkov prison.

A few of the report's details, however, serve to illustrate the precise nature of these eight Ukrainian camps. An inspector complains, for example, that one of the camps is short of 'textbooks, pens, notebooks, pencils'. There is also a strict note about the propensity of certain inmates to gamble their food away, sometimes losing their bread rations for many months in advance: the younger denizens of the camp were, it seems, too inexperienced to play cards with the older ones.[83]

The eight camps in question were the eight children's colonies of Ukraine. For not all of the children who fell under the jurisdiction of the Gulag belonged to arrested parents. A portion of them found their way into the camp system by themselves. They committed crimes, were arrested, and were sent to special camps for juveniles. These were run by the same bureaucrats who ran the adult camps, and they resembled the adult camps in many ways.

Originally, these 'children's camps' were organized for the *besprizornye*, the orphans, waifs and dirty street children who had got lost or run away from their parents during the years of civil war, famine, collectivization and mass arrest. These street children had become, by the early 1930s, a common sight in the train stations and public parks of Soviet cities. The Russian writer Victor Serge described them:

I saw them in Leningrad and in Moscow, living in sewers, in billboard kiosks, in the vaults of cemeteries where they were the undisturbed masters; holding conferences at night in urinals; travelling on the roofs of trains or on the rods below. They would emerge, pestiferous, black with sweat, to ask a few kopecks from travellers and to lie in wait for the chance to steal a valise . . .[84]

So numerous and so problematic were these children that in 1934 the Gulag set up the first children's nurseries within the adult camps, in order to prevent the children of arrested parents from roaming the streets.[85] Slightly later, in 1935, the Gulag decided to set up special children's colonies as well. Children were picked up off the streets in mass raids, and sent to the colonies to be educated and prepared to join the workforce.

In 1935, the Soviet authorities also passed a notorious law making children as young as twelve liable to be charged as adults. Afterwards, peasant girls arrested for stealing a few grains of wheat, and children of 'enemies' suspected of collaborating with their parents, found their way into juvenile prison alongside the under-age prostitutes, young pickpockets, street children, and others.[86] According to an internal report, NKVD agents in the 1930s picked up a twelve-year-old Tartar girl who spoke no Russian and had been separated from her mother at a train station. They deported her, alone, to the far north.[87] So numerous were the Soviet Union's child criminals that the NKVD created children's homes with a 'special regime' in 1937, for children who systematically broke the rules in the ordinary children's homes. By 1939, mere orphans were no longer sent to the children's camps at all. Instead, these were now reserved for child criminals who had actually been sentenced by courts or by the *osoboe soveshchanie*, the 'special commission'.[88]

Despite the threat of harsher punishment, the number of juvenile delinquents continued to grow. The war produced not only orphans but runaways as well, unsupervised children whose fathers were at the front, and whose mothers were working twelve-hour days in factories, as well as whole new categories of child criminal: under-age workers who had run away from their factory jobs – sometimes after the factories had been evacuated, away from the children's families – thereby violating the wartime law 'On Unauthorized Departure from Work at Military Enterprises'.[89] According to the NKVD's own statistics, children's 'reception centres' collected an extraordinary 842,144 homeless children in the years 1943–5. Most were sent back to their parents, to children's homes or to trade schools. But a sizeable number – 52,830, according to the records – were assigned to 'labour-educational colonies'. The phrase 'labour-educational colony' was nothing more than a palatable description of a children's concentration camp.[90]

In many ways, the treatment of children in juvenile camps hardly differed from the treatment of their parents. Children were arrested and transported according to the same rules, with two exceptions: they were meant to be kept separately from adults, and were not to be shot in the case of attempted escape.[91] They were kept in the same kind of gaols as adults, in separate but equally poor cells. An inspector's description of one such cell is depressingly familiar: 'The walls are dirty; not all prisoners have bunks and mattresses. They don't have sheets, pillowcases, or blankets. In cell No. 5, the window is covered by a pillow, for lack of a windowpane, and in cell No. 14, one window does not close at all.'[92] Another report describes juvenile prisons as 'unacceptably unsanitary', with shortages of hot water and elementary necessities such as mugs, bowls and stools.[93]

Some younger prisoners were also interrogated like adults. After his arrest in an orphanage, fourteen-year-old Pyotr Yakir was first placed in an adult prison, and then subjected to a full adult interrogation. His interrogator accused him of 'organizing a band of Anarchist cavalry, whose aim it was to be active behind the lines of the Red Army', citing as evidence the fact that Yakir was a keen rider. Afterwards, Yakir was sentenced for the crime of being a 'Socially Dangerous Element'.[94] Jerzy Kmiecik, a sixteen-year-old Polish boy who was caught trying to cross the Soviet border into Hungary – this was in 1939, following the Soviet invasion of Poland – was also interrogated like an adult. Kmiecik was kept standing or sitting on a backless stool for hours on end, fed salty soup and denied water. Among other things, his questioners wanted to know, 'How much did Mr Churchill pay you for providing information?' Kmiecik did not know who Churchill was, and asked to have the question explained.[95]

Archives have also preserved the interrogation records of Vladimir Moroz, aged fifteen, who was accused of conducting 'counter-revolutionary activity' in his orphanage. Moroz's mother and his seventeen-year-old elder brother had already been arrested. His father had been shot. He had kept a diary, which the NKVD found, in which he decried the 'lies and slander' all around him: 'If someone had fallen into a deep sleep twelve years ago, and suddenly woken up now, he would be shocked by the changes which had taken place here in that time.' Although condemned to serve three years in camp, Moroz died in prison, in 1939.[96]

These were not isolated incidents. In 1939, when the Soviet press reported a few cases of NKVD officers arrested for extorting false confessions, a Siberian newspaper told the story of one case involving 160 children, mostly between the ages of twelve and fourteen, but some as young as ten. Four officers in the NKVD and the prosecutors' office received five- to ten-year sentences for interrogating these children. The historian Robert Conquest writes that their confessions were obtained 'with comparative ease': 'A ten-year-old broke down after a single night-long interrogation, and admitted to membership in a fascist organization from the age of seven.'[97]

Child prisoners were not exempt from the relentless demands of the slave labour system either. Although children's colonies were not, as a rule, located within the tougher northern forestry or mining camps, in the 1940s there was a children's *lagpunkt* in the far northern camp of Norilsk. Some of its 1,000 inmates were put to work in the Norilsk brick factory, while the others were put to work clearing snow. Among them were a few children of twelve, thirteen and fourteen, with the majority fifteen or sixteen, the older juvenile prisoners having already been transferred to the adult camp. Many inspectors complained about the conditions in the Norilsk children's camp and it was eventually moved to a more southerly part of the USSR – but not before many of its young prisoners fell victim to the same diseases of cold and malnutrition as their adult counterparts.[98]

More typical is the Ukrainian report, which explains that children in the Ukrainian children's labour colonies had been assigned jobs in woodwork, metalwork and sewing.[99] Kmiecik, who was in a children's colony near Zhitomir, in Ukraine, worked in a furniture factory.[100] Still, the colonies observed many of the same practices as the adult camps. There were production targets to be achieved, individual norms to meet, a regime to observe. One NKVD order of 1940 directed children between the ages of twelve and sixteen to work four-hour days, and to spend a further four hours on schoolwork. The same order required children aged sixteen to eighteen to work eight-hour days, with two hours devoted to schoolwork.[101] In the Norilsk camp, this regime was not observed, as there was no school at all.[102]

In Kmiecik's juvenile camp, there were only evening classes. Among other things, he was taught there that 'England is an island in Western Europe . . . It is ruled by lords wearing red robes with white collars. They own the workers who toil for them, paying them little money.'[103] Not that the children were there primarily to be educated: in 1944, Beria proudly informed Stalin that the Gulag's juvenile camps had contributed impressively to the war effort, producing mines, grenades and other goods worth a total of 150 million roubles.[104]

Children were also subjected to the same sort of camp propaganda as adults were. Camp newspapers of the mid-1930s feature child Stakhanovites, and gush with praise for the '35ers', the street children placed in camps according to the law of 1935, glorifying those who had seen the light and been reformed by physical work. The same newspapers also lambast those children who had not understood that 'they must abandon their past, that it is time to start a new life . . . Card games, drunkenness, hooliganism, refusal to work, thievery, etc., are all widespread among them.'[105] To combat this youthful 'parasitism', children were made to take part in the same sorts of cultural-educational concerts as adults, singing the same Stalinist songs.[106]

Finally, children were subject to the same psychological pressures as adults. Another NKVD directive of 1941 called for the organization of an *agenturno-operativnoe obsluzhivanie* – a 'network of informers' – within NKVD children's colonies and children's reception centres. Rumours had spread of counter-revolutionary sentiments among both the staff and the children in the camps, particularly the children of counter-revolutionaries. The children in one camp had even staged a mini-revolt. They took over the dining room, trashed it, and attacked the guards, wounding six of them.[107]

In only one sense were the children of the juvenile camps lucky: they had not been sent to ordinary camps, to be surrounded by ordinary adult prisoners, as other children were. Indeed, just like ubiquitous pregnant women, the endlessly expanding numbers of juveniles in adult camps provided a perennial headache for camp commanders. In October 1935, Genrikh Yagoda angrily wrote to all camp commanders that 'despite my instructions, under-aged prisoners are not being sent to work colonies for juveniles, but are being mixed up in prison with adults'. At last count, he stated, there had been 4,305 juveniles still in ordinary prisons.[108] Thirteen years later, in 1948, investigators from the prosecutors' office were still complaining that there were too many under-aged prisoners in adult camps, where they were being corrupted by adult criminals. Even camp authorities noticed when a camp's reigning criminal boss transformed one eighteen-year-old petty thief into a contract murderer.[109]

The *maloletki* – 'juveniles' – inspired little sympathy among their fellow inmates. 'Hunger and the horror of what had happened had deprived them of all defences,' wrote Lev Razgon, who observed that the juveniles gravitated naturally towards those who seemed the strongest. These were the professional criminals, who turned the boys into 'servants, mute slaves, jesters, hostages, and everything else', and both boys and girls into prostitutes.[110] Their horrifying experiences failed to inspire much pity, however; on the contrary, some of the harshest invective in camp memoir literature is reserved for them. Razgon wrote that whatever their background, child prisoners soon 'all displayed a frightening and incorrigibly vengeful cruelty, without restraint or responsibility'. Worse,

They feared nothing and no one. The guards and camp bosses were scared to enter the separate barracks where the juveniles lived. It was there that the vilest, most cynical and cruel acts that took place in the camps occurred. If one of the prisoners' criminal leaders was gambling, lost everything and had staked his life as well, the boys would kill him for a day's bread ration or simply 'for the fun of it'. The girls boasted that they could satisfy an entire team of tree-fellers. There was nothing human left in these children and it was impossible to imagine that they might return to the normal world and become ordinary human beings again.[111]

Solzhenitsyn felt the same:

In their consciousness there was no demarcation line between what was permissible and what was not permissible, and no concept of good and evil. For them, everything that they desired was good and everything that hindered them was bad. They acquired their brazen and insolent manner of behaviour because it was the most advantageous form of conduct in the camp . . .[112]

A Dutch prisoner, Johan Wigmans, also writes of the young people who 'probably did not really mind having to live in these camps. Officially they were supposed to work, but in practice that was the last thing they ever did. At the same time they had the benefit of regular means and ample opportunity of learning from their cronies.'[113]

There were exceptions. Aleksandr Klein tells the story of two thirteen-year-old boys, arrested as partisans, who had received twenty-year camp sentences. The two remained ten years in the camps, managing to stick together by declaring hunger strikes when anyone separated them. Because of their age, people took pity on them, gave easy work and extra food. Both managed to enrol in camp technical courses, becoming competent engineers before being let out in one of the amnesties that followed Stalin's death. If it had not been for the camps, wrote Klein, 'who would have helped half-literate country boys become educated people, good specialists?'[114]

Nevertheless, when, in the late 1990s, I began to look around for memoirs of people who had been juvenile prisoners, I found it very difficult to find any. With the exception of Yakir's, Kmiecik's and a handful of others collected by Memorial and other organizations, there are very few.[115] Yet there had been tens of thousands of such children, and many should still have been alive. I even suggested to a Russian friend that we advertise in a newspaper, in an attempt to find a few such survivors to interview. 'Don't,' she advised me. 'We all know what such people became.' Decades of propaganda, of posters draped across orphanage walls, thanking Stalin 'for our happy childhood', failed to convince the Soviet people that the children of the camps, the children of the streets, and the children of the orphanages had ever become anything but full-fledged members of the Soviet Union's large and all-embracing criminal class.

16

The Dying

What does it mean – exhaustion?
What does it mean – fatigue?
Every movement is terrifying,
Every movement of your painful arms and legs
Terrible hunger – Raving over bread
'Bread, bread,' the heart beats.
Far away in the gloomy sky,
The indifferent sun turns.
Your breath is a thin whistle
It's minus fifty degrees
What does it mean – dying?
The mountains look on, and remain silent.

– Nina Gagen-Torn, *Memoria*[1]

Throughout the Gulag's existence, the prisoners always reserved a place at the very bottom of the camp hierarchy for the dying – or rather, for the living dead. A whole sub-dialect of camp slang was invented to describe them. Sometimes, the dying were called *fitili*, or 'wicks', as in the wick of a candle, soon to be blown out. They were also known as *gavnoedy* ('shit-eaters') or *pomoechniki* ('slop-swillers'). Most often they were called *dokhodyagi*, from the Russian verb *dokhodit*, 'to reach' or 'to attain', a word usually translated as 'goners'. Jacques Rossi, in his *Gulag Handbook*, claims the expression was a sarcastic one: the dying were at last 'reaching socialism'.[2] Others, more prosaically, say the expression meant they were reaching not socialism, but the end of their lives.

Put simply, the *dokhodyagi* were starving to death, and they suffered from the diseases of starvation and vitamin deficiency: scurvy, pellagra, various forms of diarrhoea. In the early stages, these diseases manifested themselves in the form of loosened teeth and skin sores, symptoms which sometimes even afflicted the camp guards.[3] In later stages, prisoners would lose their ability to see in the dark. Gustav Herling remembered 'the sight of the

A dying *zek*: a portrait by Sergei Reikhenberg, Magadan, date unknown

night-blind, walking slowly through the zone in the early mornings and evenings, their hands fluttering in front of them'.[4]

The starving also experienced stomach problems, dizziness, and grotesque swelling of the legs. Thomas Sgovio, who came to the brink of starvation before recovering, woke up one morning to discover that one of his legs was 'purple, twice the size of the other leg. It itched. There were blotches all over it.' Soon, 'the blotches turned into huge boils. Blood and pus trickled from them. When I pressed a finger into the purple flesh – an indentation remained for a long time.' When Sgovio found his legs could not fit into his boots, he was told to slit the boots.[5]

In the final stages of starvation, the *dokhodyagi* took on a bizarre and inhuman appearance, becoming the physical fulfilment of the dehumanizing rhetoric used by the state: in their dying days, enemies of the people ceased, in other words, to be people at all. They became demented, often ranting and raving for hours. Their skin was loose and dry. Their eyes had a strange gleam. They ate anything they could get their hands on – birds, dogs, garbage. They moved slowly, and could not control their bowels or their bladders, as a result of which they emitted a terrible odour. Tamara Petkevich describes the first time she saw them:

There behind the barbed wire was a row of creatures, distantly reminiscent of human beings . . . there were ten of them, skeletons of various sizes covered with brown, parchment-like skin, all stripped to the waist, with shaved heads and pendulous withered breasts. Their only clothing was some pathetic dirty underpants, and their shinbones projected from concave circles of emptiness. Women! Hunger, heat and hard toil had transformed them into dried specimens that still, unaccountably, clung to the last vestiges of life.[6]

Varlam Shalamov has also left an unforgettable poetic description of the *dokhodyagi*, invoking their similarity to one another, their loss of identifying, humanizing characteristics, and their anonymity, which was part of the horror they inspired:

> I raise my glass to a road in the forest
> To those who fall on their way
> To those who can't drag themselves further
> But are forced to drag on
>
> To their bluish hard lips
> To their identical faces
> To their torn, frost-covered coats
> To their hands without gloves
>
> To the water they sip, from an old tin can
> To the scurvy which sticks to their teeth.
> To the teeth of fattened grey dogs
> Which awake them in the morning
>
> To the sullen sun,
> Which regards them without interest
> To the snow-white tombstones,
> The work of clever snowstorms
>
> To the ration of raw, sticky bread
> Swallowed quickly
> To the pale, too-high sky
> To the Ayan-Yuryakh river![7]

But the term *dokhodyaga*, as it was used in the Soviet camps, did not merely describe a physical state. The 'goners', as Sgovio has explained, were not just ill: they were prisoners who had reached a level of starvation so intense that they no longer looked after themselves. This deterioration usually progressed in stages, as prisoners stopped washing themselves, stopped controlling their bowels, stopped having normal human reactions to insults – until they became, quite literally, insane with hunger. Sgovio was deeply shocked the first time he met someone in this state, an American communist named Eisenstein, a man who had been an acquaintance in Moscow:

At first I did not recognize my friend. Eisenstein did not answer when I greeted him. His face wore the blank expression of the *dokhodyaga*. He looked through me as if I were not there. Eisenstein didn't seem to see anyone. There was no expression at all in his eyes. Gathering the empty plates from the mess tables, he scanned each one of them for leftover food particles. He ran his fingers around the inside of the plates and then licked them.

Eisenstein, wrote Sgovio, had become like the other 'wicks', in that he had lost all sense of personal dignity:

They neglected themselves, did not wash – even when they had the opportunity to do so. Nor did the wicks bother to search for and kill the lice that sucked their blood. The *dokhodyagas* did not wipe the dribble off the ends of their noses with the sleeves of their *bushlats* . . . the wick was oblivious to blows. When set upon by fellow *zeks*, he would cover his head to ward off the punches. He would fall to the floor and when left alone, his condition permitting, he would get up and go off whimpering as if nothing had happened. After work the *dokhodyaga* could be seen hanging around the kitchen begging for scraps. For amusement, the cook would throw a dipperful of soup in his face. On such occasions, the poor soul would hurriedly pass his fingers over his wet whiskers and lick them . . . The wicks stood around the tables, waiting for someone to leave some soup or gruel. When that happened, the nearest lunged for the leavings. In the ensuing scramble they often spilled the soup. And then, on hands and knees, they fought and scraped until the last bit of precious food was stuffed into their mouths.[8]

A few prisoners who became *dokhodyagi*, and who recovered and survived, have tried to explain, not wholly successfully, what it felt like to be one of the living dead. Janusz Bardach remembered that after eight months in Kolyma, 'I felt dizzy upon awakening, and my mind was foggy. It took more time and effort to pull myself together and go to the mess hall in the morning.'[9] Yakov Efrussi became a *dokhodyaga* after first having his glasses stolen – 'to anyone near-sighted it will be perfectly clear what life is like without glasses, everything around you seems to be in a cloud' – and then losing the fingers of his left hand to frostbite. He described his feelings like this:

Constant hunger destroys the human psyche. It is impossible to stop thinking about food, you think about food all of the time. To your physical incapability is added moral weakness, as constant hunger removes your sense of self-respect, your sense of self-worth. All of your thoughts run in one direction: how to get more food? That's why on the garbage pit, near the dining hall, at the entrance to the kitchen, the *dokhodyagi* were always milling about. They wait to see if someone won't possibly throw something edible out of the kitchen, for instance some scraps of cabbage.[10]

The attraction to the kitchen and the obsession with food blinded many to almost all other considerations, as Gustav Herling has also tried to describe:

There is no limit to the physical effects of hunger beyond which tottering human dignity might still keep its uncertain but independent balance. Many times I flattened my pale face against the frosted-glass pane of the kitchen window, to beg with a dumb look for another ladleful of thin soup from the Leningrad thief Fyedka who was in charge. And I remember that my best friend, the engineer Sadovski, once, on the empty platform by the kitchen, snatched from my hand a canful of soup and, running away with it, did not even wait until he reached the latrine but on the way there drank up the hot mess with feverish lips. If God exists, let him punish mercilessly those who break others with hunger.[11]

Yehoshua Gilboa, a Polish Zionist arrested in 1940, eloquently describes the deceptions which prisoners used to convince themselves that they were eating more than they were:

We attempted to deceive the stomach by crumbling the bread until it was almost like flour and mixing it with salt and large quantities of water. This delicacy was called 'bread sauce'. The salty water took on something of the colour and taste of bread. You drank it and the bread pap remained. You poured more water on it until the final drop of bread flavour was squeezed out of it. If you ate this bread sauce for dessert after you had filled up on bread water, as it were, it had no taste at all but you created an illusion for yourself by stretching several hundred grams.

Gilboa also writes that he soaked salt fish in water as well. The resulting liquid 'could be used for making bread sauce and then you really had a delicacy fit for a king'.[12]

Once a prisoner was spending all of his time hanging around the kitchen, picking up scraps, he was usually close to death, and could in fact die at any time: in bed at night, on the way to work, walking across the *zona*, eating his dinner. Janusz Bardach once saw a prisoner fall during roll-call at the end of the day:

A group formed around him. 'I get the hat,' one man said. Others grabbed the victim's boots, foot rags, coat and pants. A fight broke out over his undergarments.

No sooner had the fallen prisoner been stripped naked than he moved his head, raised his hand, and stated weakly but clearly, 'It's so cold.' But his head flopped back into the snow and a glazed look came over his eyes. The ring of scavengers turned away with whatever scraps they had, unaffected. In those few minutes after being stripped, he probably died of exposure.[13]

Starvation was not, however, the only way in which prisoners died. Many died at work, in the unsafe conditions of the mines and factories. Some, weakened by hunger, succumbed easily to other diseases and epidemics as well. I have mentioned the typhus epidemics already, but weak and hungry prisoners were susceptible to many other diseases. In Siblag, in the first quarter of 1941, for example, 8,029 people were hospitalized, 746 with tuberculosis, of which 109 died; 72 with pneumonia, of which 22 died; 36 with dysentery, of which 9 died; 177 with frostbite, of which 5 died; 302 with stomach ailments, of which 7 died; 210 who had accidents at work, of which 7 died; and 912 with circulation problems, of which 123 died.[14]

Although it is a curiously taboo subject, prisoners did also commit suicide. How many took this route it is difficult to say. There are no official statistics. Nor, strangely, is there much consensus among survivors about how many suicides there were. Nadezhda Mandelstam, wife of the poet, wrote that people in the camps did not commit suicide, so hard were they struggling to live, and her belief has been echoed by others.[15] Evgeny Gnedin wrote that although he thought of killing himself in prison, and later in exile, during his eight years in camps, 'the thought of suicide never came into my head. Every day was a fight for life: how, in such a battle, was it possible to think about leaving life? There was a goal – to get out of that suffering – and hope: to meet with the people one loved.'[16]

The historian Catherine Merridale puts forward a different theory. During her research, she met two Moscow-based psychologists who had studied or worked in the Gulag system. Like Mandelstam and Gnedin, they insisted that suicide and mental illness were rare: 'They were surprised – and modestly offended' when she cited evidence to the contrary. She attributes this curious insistence to the 'myth of stoicism' in Russia, but it may have other sources as well.[17] The literary critic Tzvetan Todorov guesses that witnesses write of the strange absence of suicide because they want to emphasize the uniqueness of their experience. It was so awful no one even took the 'normal' route of suicide: 'the survivor aims above all to convey the otherness of the camps'.[18]

In fact, the anecdotal evidence of suicide is great, and many memoirists remember them. One describes the suicide of a boy whose sexual favours were 'won' by a criminal prisoner in a card game.[19] Another tells of a suicide of a Soviet citizen of German origins, who left a note for Stalin: 'My death is a conscious act of protest against the violence and lawlessness directed against us, Soviet Germans, by the organs of the NKVD.'[20] One Kolyma survivor has written that in the 1930s, it became relatively common for prisoners to walk, quickly and purposefully, towards the 'death zone', the no man's land beside the camp fence, and then to stand there, waiting to be shot.[21]

Evgeniya Ginzburg herself cut the rope from which her friend Polina Melnikova hung, and wrote admiringly of her: 'She had asserted her rights to be a person by acting as she had, and she had made an efficient job of it.'[22] Todorov again also writes that many survivors of both the Gulag and of the Nazi camps saw suicide as an opportunity to exercise free will: 'By committing suicide, one alters the course of events – if only for the last time in one's life – instead of simply reacting to them. Suicides of this kind are acts of defiance, not desperation.'[23]

To the camp administration, it was all the same how prisoners died. What mattered to most was keeping the death rates secret, or at least semi-secret: *lagpunkt* commanders whose death rates were found to be 'too high' risked punishment. Although the rules were irregularly enforced, and although some did advocate the view that more prisoners ought to die, commanders of some particularly lethal camps did occasionally lose their jobs.[24] This was why, as some ex-prisoners have described, doctors were known to physically conceal corpses from camp inspectors, and why in some camps it was common practice to release dying prisoners early. That way, they did not appear in the camp's mortality statistics.[25]

Even when deaths were recorded, the records were not always honest. One way or another, camp commanders made sure that doctors writing out prisoner death certificates did not write 'starvation' as the primary cause of death. The surgeon Isaac Vogelfanger was, for example, explicitly ordered to write 'failure of the heart muscle' no matter what the real cause of a prisoner's death.[26] This could backfire: in one camp, the doctors listed so many cases of 'heart attack' that the inspectorate became suspicious. The prosecutors forced the doctors to dig up the corpses, establishing that they had, in fact, died of pellagra.[27] Not all such chaos was deliberate: in another camp, the records were in such disarray that an inspector complained that 'the dead are counted as living prisoners, escapees as imprisoned and vice versa'.[28]

Prisoners were often kept deliberately ignorant of the facts of death as well. Although death could not be hidden altogether – one prisoner spoke of corpses lying 'in a pile by the fence until the thaw'[29] – it could be shrouded in other ways. In many camps, corpses were removed at night, and taken to secret locations. It was only by accident that Edward Buca, forced to stay working late to meet his norm, saw what happened to corpses at Vorkuta:

After they had been stacked like timber in an open-sided shed until enough had accumulated for a mass burial in the camp cemetery, they were loaded, naked, on to sledges, heads on the outside, feet inside. Each body bore a wooden tag, a *birka*, tied to the big toe of the right foot, bearing its name and number. Before each sledge left the camp gate, the *nadziratel*, an NKVD officer, took a pickaxe and smashed in each head. This was to ensure that no one got out alive. Once outside the camp, the bodies were dumped into a *transheya*, one of several broad ditches dug during summer for this purpose. But as the number of dead mounted, the procedure for making certain they were really dead changed. Instead of smashing heads with a pickaxe, the guards used a *shompol*, a thick wire with a sharpened point, which they stuck into each body. Apparently this was easier than swinging the pick.[30]

Mass burials may have also been kept secret because they too were technically forbidden – which is not to say they were uncommon. Former camp sites all over Russia contain evidence of what were clearly mass graves, and from time to time, the graves even re-emerge: the far northern permafrost not only preserves bodies, sometimes in eerily pristine condition, but it also shifts and moves with the annual freezes and thaws, as Shalamov writes: 'The north resisted with all its strength this work of man, not accepting the corpses into its bowels . . . the earth opened, bearing its subterranean storerooms, for they contained not only gold and lead, tungsten and uranium, but also undecaying human bodies.'[31]

Nevertheless, they were not supposed to be there, and in 1946, the Gulag administration sent out an order to all camp commanders, instructing them to bury corpses separately, in funeral linen, and in graves which were no less than 1.5 metres deep. The location of the bodies was also meant to be marked not with a name, but with a number. Only the camp's record-keepers were supposed to know who was buried where.[32]

All of which sounds very civilized – except that another order gave camps permission to remove the dead prisoners' gold teeth. These removals were meant to take place under the aegis of a commission, containing representatives of the camp medical services, the camp administration, and the camp financial department. The gold was then supposed to be taken to the nearest state bank. It is hard to imagine, however, that such commissions met very frequently. The more straightforward theft of gold teeth was simply too easy to carry out, too easy to hide, in a world where there were too many corpses.[33]

For there *were* too many corpses – and this, finally, was the terrifying thing about a prison death, as Herling wrote:

Death in the camp possessed another terror: its anonymity. We had no idea where the dead were buried, or whether, after a prisoner's death, any kind of death certificate was ever written . . . The certainty that no one would ever learn of their death, that no one would ever know where they had been buried, was one of the prisoners' greatest psychological torments . . .

The barrack walls were covered with names of prisoners scratched in the plaster, and friends were asked to complete the data after their death by adding a cross and a date; every prisoner wrote to his family at strictly regular intervals, so that a sudden break in the correspondence would give them the approximate date of his death.[34]

Despite prisoners' efforts, many, many deaths went unmarked, unremembered and unrecorded. Forms were not filled out; relatives were not notified; wooden markers disintegrated. Walking around old camp sites in the far north, one sees the evidence of mass graves: the uneven, mottled ground, the young pine trees, the long grass covering burial pits half a century old. Sometimes, a local group has put up a monument. More often, there is no marking at all. The names, the lives, the individual stories, the family connections, the history – all were lost.

17
Strategies of Survival

I am poor, alone and naked,
I've no fire.
The lilac polar gloom
Is all around me . . .

I recite my poems
I shout them
The trees, bare and deaf,
Are frightened.

Only the echo from the distant mountains
Rings in the ears.
And with a deep sigh
I breathe easily again.

– Varlam Shalamov,
Neskolko moikh zhiznei[1]

In the end, prisoners survived. They survived even the worst camps, even the toughest conditions, even the war years, the famine years, the years of mass execution. Not only that, some survived psychologically intact enough to return home, to recover, and to live relatively normal lives. Janusz Bardach became a plastic surgeon in Iowa City. Isaak Filshtinsky went back to teaching Arabic literature. Lev Razgon went back to writing children's fiction. Anatoly Zhigulin went back to writing poetry. Evgeniya Ginzburg moved to Moscow, and for years was the heart and soul of a circle of survivors, who met regularly to eat, drink and argue around her kitchen table.

Ada Puryzhinskaya, imprisoned as a teenager, went on to marry and produce four children, some of whom became accomplished musicians. I met two of them over a generous, good-humoured family dinner, during which Puryzhinskaya served dish after dish of delicious cold food, and seemed disappointed when I could not eat more. Irena Arginskaya's home is also full of laughter, much of it coming from Irena herself. Forty years later, she was able to make fun of the clothes she had worn as a prisoner: 'I suppose you *could* call it a sort of *jacket*,' she said, trying to describe her shapeless camp overcoat. Her well-spoken, grown-up daughter laughed along with her.

Some even went on to lead extraordinary lives. Alexander Solzhenitsyn became one of the best-known, and best-selling, Russian writers in the world. General Gorbatov helped lead the Soviet assault on Berlin. After his terms in Kolyma and a wartime *sharashka*, Sergei Korolev went on to become the father of the Soviet Union's space programme. Gustav Herling left the camps, fought with the Polish army, and, although writing in Neapolitan exile, became one of the most revered men of letters in post-communist Poland. News of his death in July 2000 made the front pages of the Warsaw news- papers and an entire generation of Polish intellectuals paid tribute to his work – especially *A World Apart*, his Gulag memoir. In their ability to recover, these men and women were not alone. Isaac Vogelfanger, who himself became a professor of surgery at the University of Ottawa, wrote that 'wounds heal, and you can become whole again, a little stronger and more human than before . . .'[2]

Not all Gulag survivors' stories ended so well, of course, which one would not necessarily be able to tell from reading memoirs. Obviously, people who did not survive did not write. Those who were mentally or physically damaged by their camp experiences did not write either. Nor did those who had survived by doing things of which they were later ashamed write very often either – or, if they did, they did not necessarily tell the whole story. There are very, very few memoirs of informers – or of people who will confess to having been informers – and very few survivors who will admit to harming or killing fellow prisoners in order to stay alive.

For these reasons, some survivors question whether written memoirs have any validity at all. Yuri Zorin, an elderly and not very forthcoming survivor whom I interviewed in his home city, Arkhangelsk, waved away a question I asked him about philosophies of survival. There weren't any, he said. Although it might seem, from their memoirs, as if prisoners 'discussed every- thing, thought about everything', it was not like that, he told me: 'The whole task was to live through the next day, to stay alive, not to get sick, to work less, to eat more. And that was why philosophical discussions, as a rule, were not held . . . We were saved by youth, health, physical strength, because there we lived by Darwin's laws, the survival of the fittest.'[3]

The whole subject of who survived – and why they survived – must therefore be approached very carefully. In this matter, there are no archival documents to rely upon, and there is no real 'evidence'. We have to take the word of those who were willing to describe their experiences, either on paper or for an interviewer. Any one of them might have had reason to conceal aspects of their biographies from their readers.

With that caveat, it is still possible to identify patterns within the several hundred memoirs which have been published or placed in archives. For there were strategies for survival, and they were well-known at the time, although they varied a great deal, depending on a prisoner's particular circumstances. Surviving a labour colony in western Russia in the mid-1930s or even late 1940s, when most of the work was factory work and the food was regular if not plentiful, probably did not require any special mental adjustments. Surviving one of the far northern camps – Kolyma, Vorkuta, Norilsk – during the hungry war years, on the other hand, often required huge reserves of talent and willpower, or else an enormous capacity for evil, qualities that the prisoners, had they remained in freedom, might never have discovered within themselves.

Without a doubt, many such prisoners survived because they found ways to raise themselves above the other prisoners, to distinguish themselves from the swarming mass of starving *zeks*. Dozens of camp sayings and proverbs reflect the debilitating moral effects of this desperate competition. 'You can die today – I'll die tomorrow,' was one of them. 'Man is wolf to man' – the phrase Janusz Bardach used as the title of his memoir – was another.

Many ex-*zeks* speak of the struggle for survival as cruel, and many, like Zorin, speak of it as Darwinian. 'The camp was a great test of our moral strength, of our everyday morality, and 99 per cent of us failed it,' wrote Shalamov.[4] 'After only three weeks most of the prisoners were broken men, interested in nothing but eating. They behaved like animals, disliked and suspected everyone else, seeing in yesterday's friend a competitor in the struggle for survival,' wrote Edward Buca.[5]

Elinor Olitskaya, with her background in the pre-revolutionary social democratic movement, was particularly horrified by what she perceived as the amorality of the camps: while inmates in prisons had often co-operated, the strong helping the weak, in the Soviet camps every prisoner 'lived for herself', doing down the others in order to attain a slightly higher status in the camp hierarchy.[6] Galina Usakova described how she felt her personality had changed in the camps: 'I was a well-behaved girl, well brought up, from a family of intelligentsia. But with these characteristics you won't survive, you have to harden yourself, you learn to lie, to be hypocritical in various ways.'[7]

Gustav Herling elaborated further, describing how it is that the new prisoner slowly learns to live 'without pity':

At first he shares his bread with hunger-demented prisoners, leads the night-blind on the way home from work, shouts for help when his neighbour in the forest has chopped off two fingers, and surreptitiously carries cans of soup and herring-heads to the mortuary. After several weeks he realizes that his motives in all this are neither pure nor really disinterested, that he is following the egotistic injunctions of his brain and saving first of all himself. The camp, where prisoners live at the lowest level of

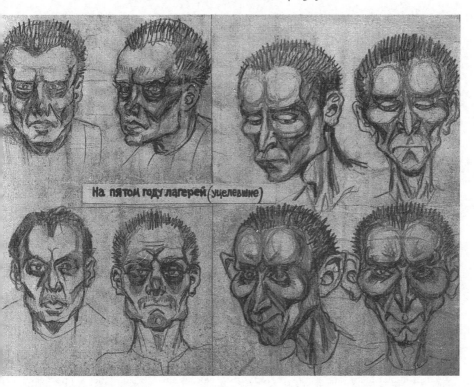

'In the fifth year of the camp (survivors)': prisoners' faces, transformed over time – a drawing by Aleksei Merekov, a prisoner, place and date unknown

humanity and follow their own brutal code of behaviour towards others, helps him to reach this conclusion. How could he have supposed, back in prison, that a man can be so degraded as to arouse not compassion but only loathing and repugnance in his fellow prisoners? How can he help the night-blind, when every day he sees them being jolted with rifle-butts because they are delaying the brigade's return to work, and then impatiently pushed off the paths by prisoners hurrying to the kitchen for their soup; how visit the mortuary and brave the constant darkness and stench of excrement; how share his bread with a hungry madman who on the very next day will greet him in the barrack with a demanding, persistent stare . . . He remembers and believes the words of his examining judge, who told him that the iron broom of Soviet justice sweeps only rubbish into its camps . . .[8]

Such sentiments are not unique to the survivors of Soviet camps. 'If one offers a position of privilege to a few individuals in a state of slavery,' wrote Primo Levi, an Auschwitz survivor, 'exacting in exchange the betrayal of a natural solidarity with their comrades, there will certainly be someone who will accept.'[9] Also writing of German camps, Bruno Bettelheim observed that older prisoners often came to 'accept SS values and behaviour as their own', in particular adopting their hatred of the weaker and lower-ranking inhabitants of the camps, especially the Jews.[10]

In the Soviet camps, as in the Nazi camps, the criminal prisoners also readily adopted the dehumanizing rhetoric of the NKVD, insulting political prisoners and 'enemies', and expressing disgust for the *dokhodyagi* among them. From his unusual position as the only political prisoner in a mostly criminal *lagpunkt*, Karol Colonna-Czosnowski was able to hear the criminal world's view of the politicals: 'The trouble is that there are just too many of them. They are weak, they are dirty, and they only want to eat. They produce nothing. Why the authorities bother, God only knows . . .' One criminal, Colonna-Czosnowski writes, said he had met a Westerner in a transit camp, a scientist and university professor. 'I caught him eating, yes, actually eating, the half-rotten tail fin of a Treska fish. I gave him hell, you can imagine. I asked him if he knew what he was doing. He just said he was hungry . . . So I gave him such a wallop in the neck that he started vomiting there and then. Makes me sick to think about it. I even reported him to the guards, but the filthy old man was dead the following morning. Serves him right!'[11]

Other prisoners watched, learned and imitated, as Varlam Shalamov wrote:

The young peasant who has become a prisoner sees that in this hell only the criminals live comparatively well, that they are important, that the all-powerful camp administration fear them. The criminals always have clothes and food, and they support each other . . . it begins to seem to him that the criminals possess the truth of camp life, that only by imitating them will he tread the path that will save his life . . . the intellectual convict is crushed by the camp. Everything he valued is ground into the dust while civilization and culture drop from him within weeks. The method of persuasion is the fist or the stick. The way to induce someone to do something is by means of a rifle butt, a punch in the teeth . . .[12]

And yet – it would be incorrect to say there was no morality in the camps at all, that no kindness or generosity was possible. Curiously, even the most pessimistic of memoirists often contradict themselves on this point. Shalamov himself, whose depiction of the barbarity of camp life surpasses all others, at one point wrote that 'I refused to seek the job of foreman, which provided a chance to remain alive, for the worst thing in a camp was the forcing of one's own or anyone else's will on another person who was a convict just like oneself.' In other words, Shalamov was an exception to his own rule.[13]

Most memoirs also make clear that the Gulag was not a black-and-white world, where the line between masters and slaves was clearly delineated, and the only way to survive was through cruelty. Not only did inmates, free workers and guards belong to a complex social network, but that network was also constantly in flux, as we have seen. Prisoners could move up and down the hierarchy, and many did. They could alter their fate not only through collaboration or defiance of the authorities, but also through clever wheeling and dealing, through contacts and relationships. Simple good luck and bad luck also determined the course of a typical camp career, which, if it was a long one, might well have 'happy' periods, when the prisoner was established in a good job, ate well and worked little, as well as periods when the same prisoner dropped into the nether world of the hospital, the mortuary and the society of the *dokhodyagi* who crowded around the garbage heap, looking for scraps of food.

In fact, the methods of survival were built in to the system. Most of the time, the camp administration was not trying to kill prisoners; they were just trying to fulfil impossibly high norms set by the central planners in Moscow. As a result, camp guards were more than willing to reward prisoners whom they found useful towards this end. The prisoners, naturally, took advantage of this willingness. The two groups had different goals – the guards wanted to dig more gold or cut more wood, and the prisoners wanted to survive – but sometimes they found shared means to meet these different ends. A handful of survival strategies in particular suited both prisoners and guards, and a list of them follows.

Tufta
Pretending to Work

To write a straightforward description of *tufta* – a word which translates, very imprecisely, as 'swindling the boss' – is not an easy task. For one, such practices were so deeply ingrained in the Soviet system that it is hardly fair to describe them as if they were somehow unique to the Gulag.[14] Nor were they unique to the USSR. The communist-era proverb, 'They pretend to pay us, and we pretend to work,' could once be heard in most of the languages of the old Warsaw Pact.

More to the point, *tufta* permeated virtually every aspect of work – work assignments, work organization, work accounting – and affected virtually every member of the camp community, from the Gulag bosses in Moscow, to the lowliest camp guards, to the most downtrodden prisoners. This was true from the very beginning of the Gulag until the very end. One much-repeated prisoners' rhyme dated from the days of the White Sea Canal:

> *Bez tufty i ammonala*
> *Ne postroili by kanala.*
> Without *tufta* and dynamite
> They would never have built the canal.[15]

In the years since this topic became the subject of debate, controversy has also surrounded the question of how hard prisoners did or did not work, and how much effort they did or did not put into evading work. Ever since the 1962 publication of Solzhenitsyn's *One Day in the Life of Ivan Denisovich* opened up a more or less public debate about the subject of the camps, the broader community of survivors, polemicists and camp historians has had notable difficulty in coming to a unanimous agreement about the morality of camp work. For much of Solzhenitsyn's ground-breaking novella was indeed dedicated to its hero's attempts to avoid work. During the course of Ivan Denisovich's day, he approaches a doctor, hoping for sick leave; fantasizes about becoming ill for a few weeks; gazes up at the camp thermometer, hoping it will prove too cold to go to the workplace; speaks admiringly of brigade leaders who can 'make it look as if the work's done, whether it is or not'; feels relieved when his brigade leader gets a 'good rate for the job', despite the fact that 'half the day was gone and they'd done nothing'; steals wood chips from the workplace to light the barracks fire; and steals extra gruel at dinner time. 'Work,' thinks Ivan at one point, 'is what horses die of.' He tries to avoid it.

In the years that followed the book's publication, this portrait of a typical *zek* was disputed by other survivors, both for ideological and personal reasons. On the one hand, those who believed in the Soviet system – and therefore also believed that the 'work' of the camps was valuable and necessary – found Denisovich's 'laziness' offensive. Many of the 'alternative', more 'pro-Soviet' accounts of camp life, published in the official Soviet press in the wake of *Ivan Denisovich*, even focused explicitly on the dedication to work shown by those who, despite the unfairness of their arrests, remained true believers. The Soviet writer (and lifelong informer) Boris Dyakov described an engineer employed on a Gulag construction project near Perm. The engineer had been so engrossed in the job, he told Dyakov's narrator, that he forgot he was a prisoner. 'For a while I enjoyed my work so much I forgot what I had become.' So conscientious was the engineer in Dyakov's story that he even secretly sent a letter to a local newspaper, complaining about the poor organization of the camp's transport and supply systems. Although admonished by the camp commander for this indiscretion – it was unheard of for a prisoner's name to appear in the newspaper – the engineer, as Dyakov tells it, remained pleased that 'after the article, things improved a little'.[16]

The views of those who ran the camps were even more extreme. Anonymously, a former camp administrator told me quite angrily that all of the stories of camp inmates living badly were simply untrue. Those who worked well lived extremely well, she said, much better than the general public: they could even purchase *condensed milk* – my italics – which ordinary people could not. 'It was only those who refused to work, they lived badly,' she told me.[17] Such views were generally not voiced in public, but there were some exceptions. Anna Zakharova, the wife of an NKVD officer, whose letter to *Izvestiya* circulated in the Russian underground press in the 1960s, was sharply critical of Solzhenitsyn. Zakharova wrote that she was 'angered to the depths of my soul' by *Ivan Denisovich*:

We can see why the hero of this story, having such an attitude to the Soviet people, hopes for nothing but the sick bay in order somehow to get out of redeeming his guilt, the wrong he did to his motherland, through toil . . . And why exactly should a person try to avoid physical labour and show scorn for it? After all, for us labour is the foundation of the Soviet system, and it is only in labour that man becomes cognizant of his true powers.[18]

Other, less ideological objections have also come from ordinary *zeks*. V. K. Yasny, a prisoner for five years in the early 1940s, wrote in his memoirs that 'We tried to work honestly, and not for fear of losing rations, or ending up in the isolator . . . hard work, and that was what it was in our brigade, helped you forget, helped chase away anxious thoughts.'[19] Nadezhda Ulyanovskaya, who was imprisoned along with her mother, wrote that her mother worked hard 'in order to prove that Jews and intelligentsia work no worse than others'. ('I worked because I was forced to do so,' she writes of herself, however, 'I fear that on this point, I did not hold up the honour of the Jewish people.')[20]

Prisoners who had worked enthusiastically on behalf of the Soviet regime all of their lives did not quickly change either. Aleksandr Borin, a political prisoner and aviation engineer, was assigned to a Gulag metalworking plant. In his memoirs, he proudly describes the technical innovations he made there, mostly worked out in his spare time.[21] Alla Shister, another political arrested in the late 1930s, told me in an interview that 'I always worked as if I were free. This is my personality trait, I cannot work badly. If a hole has to be dug, I'll keep on digging until it is finished.' After two years on general work, Shister became a brigade leader, because, she said, 'They saw that I work not like a prisoner works, but with all of my strength.' In that capacity, she then made every attempt to inspire those beneath her, although admittedly not by firing them up with love of the Soviet state. This is how she described her first encounter with the men who were to work for her:

I came to the quarry where they were digging. The guards offered to accompany me, but I said that was unnecessary, and I went alone. It was midnight. I came up to the team, and told them, 'I need to fulfil the plan, bricks are needed at the front.'

They said, 'Alla Borisovna, we don't care about the plan for bricks, give us our bread ration.'

I said, 'You'll get the ration, if you fulfil the plan.'

They said, 'We'll throw you in a hole now, dig you under and no one will find you.'

I stood there quietly, and said, 'You won't dig me under. I promise you that if today, by twelve noon, you fulfil the norm, I'll bring you some tobacco.' Tobacco there was worth more than gold or diamonds . . .

Shister had, she said, simply saved her own allotted tobacco rations, as she herself did not smoke, and happily handed them over to her charges.[22]

There were also those, of course, who recognized the material advantage to be gained in doing work. Some prisoners tried, simply, to do what was expected of them: to beat the norm, to attain the status of shock-worker, to receive better rations. Vladimir Petrov arrived at a Kolyma *lagpunkt* and immediately perceived that the inhabitants of the 'Stakhanovite tent', who worked harder than the other prisoners, possessed all of the attributes that the *dokhodyagi* did not:

They were incomparably cleaner. Even in the extremely harsh conditions of their life in camp they had managed to wash their faces every day, and when they could not get water they had used snow. They were better dressed, too ... [and] more self-possessed. They did not crowd about the stoves, but sat on their bunks either doing something or talking about their affairs. Even from the outside their tent looked different.

Petrov begged to join their brigade, whose members received 1 kilo of bread every day. Once in, however, he could not keep up with the pace of work. He was expelled from the brigade, which could tolerate no weakness.[23] Nor was his experience atypical, as Herling wrote:

The fascination of the norm was not the exclusive privilege of the free men who imposed it, but also the dominating instinct of the slaves who worked to it. In those brigades where the work was done by teams of men working together, the most conscientious and fervent foremen were the prisoners themselves, for there the norm was reckoned collectively by dividing the total output by the number of workers. Any feeling of mutual friendliness was completely abolished in favour of a race for percentages. An unqualified prisoner who found himself assigned to a coordinated team of experienced workers could not expect to have any consideration shown to him; after a short struggle he was forced to give up and transfer to a team in which he in his turn frequently had to watch over weaker comrades. There was in all this something inhuman, mercilessly breaking the only natural bond between prisoners – their solidarity in face of their persecutors.[24]

But hard work sometimes backfired. Lev Razgon described peasants who killed themselves trying to overfulfil the norm, earning themselves a 'big ration', 1.5 kilos of bread: 'It may have been raw and badly baked, but it was real bread. For peasants who had lived in semi-starvation for years this appeared an enormous quantity, even without any cooked food.' Yet even this 'enormous quantity' of food did not make up for the energy expended in doing the forestry work. The forest worker was thus condemned, Razgon wrote: 'quite literally, he would starve to death while eating one and a half kilos of bread a day'.[25] Shalamov has also described the 'myth of the big ration', and Solzhenitsyn wrote that 'the big ration is the one that kills. In one season of hauling timber the strongest slogger would end up a hopeless last-legger himself.'[26]

Nevertheless, the vast majority of memoirists (backed up, to a degree, by archival evidence) do indeed speak of avoiding work. Yet their primary motive was not usually mere sloth, or even the desire to 'show scorn' for the Soviet system: their primary motive was survival. Having been given poor clothing and insufficient food, having been ordered to work in extreme weather with broken machinery, many realized that avoiding work would save their lives.

The unpublished memoir of Zinaida Usova, one of the wives arrested in 1938, illustrates beautifully how prisoners came to this conclusion. Usova was first placed in Temlag, a camp which mostly contained women like herself, the wives of leading Party members and army bigwigs who had been shot. With a relatively easygoing camp boss and reasonable work schedule, everyone in Temlag worked enthusiastically. Not only were most still 'loyal Soviet citizens', convinced that their arrests had been part of a giant mistake, but they also believed that by working hard they would earn an early release. Usova herself 'went to sleep and woke up with thoughts of work, thinking through my designs. One of them was even taken into production.'

Later, however, Usova and a group of other wives moved to another camp, one which also contained criminals. There she found herself working in a furniture factory. Her new camp had much higher, much stricter norms – the 'unreasonable' norms spoken of by so many other prisoners. This system, wrote Usova, 'made people into slaves, with the psychology of slaves'. Only those who completed the whole norm received the full bread ration of 700 grams. Those who could not, or who were unable to work at all, got 300, barely enough to live on.

To compensate, the prisoners at her new camp tried as best they could to 'trick the bosses, to wriggle out of work, to do as little as possible'. With their relative enthusiasm for work, the newly arrived prisoners from Temlag found themselves pariahs. 'From the point of view of the older inhabitants, we were fools, or something like strike-breakers. They all hated us immediately.'[27] Soon, of course, the women from Temlag adopted the techniques of work-avoidance already mastered by everyone else. Thus did the system itself create *tufta*, and not vice versa.

Sometimes, prisoners thought up methods of *tufta* on their own. One Polish woman worked in a Kolyma fish-processing plant where the only people who fulfilled the impossible norms were those who cheated. The Stakhanovites were simply the 'cleverest cheaters': rather than packing all of the herring, they would put a few pieces into a jar and toss the rest out, doing it 'so cleverly that the foreman would never notice'.[28] While helping to build a camp bath-house, Valery Frid was shown a similar trick: how to hide cracks in the building with moss instead of filling them with concrete. He had only one regret about this labour-saving device: 'What if I would one day come to wash myself in that bath? After all, the moss would dry out, and then the cold wind would blow through the cracks.'[29]

Ginzburg has also described how she and her erstwhile logging partner, Galya, finally managed to fulfil their impossible tree-felling norm. Noticing that one of their colleagues always managed to reach the norm, 'despite working on her own with a one-handed saw', they asked her how she did it:

As we pressed her further, she looked around furtively and then explained:

'This forest is full of piles of timber cut by previous work gangs. No one ever counted how many there are.'

'Yes, but anyone can see that they're not freshly cut . . .'

'The only reason you can see is that the cross sections are dark in colour. If you saw off a small section at each end, it looks as if it has just been cut. Then you stack them up in another place, and there's your "norm".'

This trick, which we christened 'freshening up the sandwiches', saved our lives for the time being . . . I may add that we did not feel the slightest compunction . . .[30]

Thomas Sgovio also spent time in a Kolyma tree-felling brigade which, quite simply, did nothing at all:

During the first part of January, my partner Levin and I did not fell a single tree. Neither did any of the others in the lumber brigade. There were many log-piles in the forest. We selected one or two, cleaned off the snow and sat down by the fire. There was even no need to clean off the snow, because not once during the first month did the brigadier, foreman, or overseer come to check our work output.[31]

Others used connections and relationships to find their way around impossible work assignments. One prisoner in Kargopollag paid another – the payment took the form of a chunk of lard – to teach him how to cut trees more efficiently, thereby enabling him to fulfil the norm, and even to rest in the afternoons.[32] Another prisoner assigned to pan for gold in Kolyma paid a bribe to be given an easier job, standing on a slag heap instead of standing in the water.[33]

More frequently, *tufta* was organized at the level of work brigades, for brigadiers were able to disguise how much individual prisoners had worked. One ex-*zek* described how his brigadier allowed him to declare that he had fulfilled 60 per cent of the norm, when in fact he could barely do anything at all.[34] Yet another prisoner wrote of how his brigadier negotiated with the camp authorities to have his brigade's norms lowered, as all of his workers were dying off.[35] Still other brigadiers took bribes, as Yuri Zorin, who was himself a brigadier, acknowledged: 'There, in the camps, there are camp laws which may not be understood by those who live outside the zone,' was how he delicately put it.[36] Leonid Trus recalled that his Norilsk brigadiers simply 'decided which of his workers deserved better food and pay than others', without any regard to what they had actually achieved. Bribery, and clan loyalties, determined a prisoner's 'output'.

From the *zek*'s point of view, the best brigadiers were those who were capable of organizing *tufta* on a grand scale. Working in a quarry in the northern Urals in the late 1940s, Lev Finkelstein found himself in a brigade whose leader had worked out a highly complex system of cheating. In the mornings, the team would go down into the canyon. The guards would stay up on the rim, where they spent the day sitting around bonfires to keep warm. Ivan, the brigadier leader, would then organize the *tufta*:

We knew precisely which parts of the bottom of the canyon are visible from up there, and that was our swindle . . . in the visible part of the bottom, we were cutting very hard at the stone wall. We were working and it was a great deal of noise – the guards could both see and hear us work. Then, Ivan would walk along the row . . . and would say, 'One to the left' – and we would each make one step to the left. It was never noticed by the guards.

So we would step, one to the left, one to the left, until the last one would step into the invisible zone – we knew where it was, there was a chalk strip on the ground. Once we were in the invisible zone, we would relax, sit on the ground, take an axe and hit the ground next to us, in a relaxed way, just to produce the noise. Then someone else would join, someone else, and so on. Then Ivan would say – 'You: to the right!' – and the man would go and join the cycle again. None of us ever worked even half the shift.[37]

At another point in his camp career, Finkelstein also worked digging a canal. There, *tufta* was different, but no less sophisticated: 'The main thing was to show that the gang has fulfilled its norm.' Workers were asked to dig, but to leave untouched 'a little post, a pile, showing what height you dug on the shift, how deep you dug'. Although norms were very heavy, 'There were artists, real artists, who managed to extend this post, its height. It is unbelievable, it was cut out of earth, so it would be immediately visible if somebody tampered with it, and yet it was tampered with in a most artistic way. Then, of course the whole gang gets the Stakhanovite dinner.'[38]

Such special talents were not always necessary. At one point, Leonid Trus was assigned to unload goods wagons: 'We would simply write that we had carried the goods further than had actually been the case, say 300 metres, instead of 10 metres.' For that, they were given better food rations. '*Tufta* was constant,' he said of Norilsk, 'without it there would have been nothing at all.'

Tufta could also be organized higher up the administrative hierarchy, through careful negotiations between brigadiers and norm-setters, the camp functionaries whose job it was to determine how much a brigade should or should not be able to achieve in one day. Norm-setters, like brigadiers, were very prone to favouritism and bribery – as well as to whim. In Kolyma in the late 1930s, Olga Adamova-Sliozberg found herself appointed brigadier, head of a women's ditch-digging brigade composed mostly of political prisoners, all weakened by long gaol sentences. When, after three days' work, they had completed just 3 per cent of the norm, she went to the norm-setter and begged for an easier assignment. Upon hearing that the weak brigade was mostly composed of former Party members, his face darkened.

'Oh yes, former members of the Party, are they? Now, if you'd been prostitutes, I'd have been happy to let you wash windows and do three times the norm. When those Party members in 1929 decided to punish me for being a kulak, threw me and my six children out of our home, I said to them, "What've the children ever done?" and they told me, "That's the Soviet law." So there you are, you can stick to your Soviet law and dig nine cubic metres of mud a day.'[39]

Norm-setters were also aware of the need to conserve the workforce at certain times – if, for example, the camp had been criticized for its high mortality rates, or when the camp was one of those in the far north which could only get replacement workers once a season. In such circumstances, they might indeed lower the norm, or turn a blind eye when it was not fulfilled. This practice was known in the camps as 'norm-stretching', and to call it widespread is an understatement.[40] One prisoner worked in a mine which required prisoners to dig 5.5 tonnes of coal every day, an impossible task. Sensibly, the mine's chief engineer – a free worker – asked around to find out how many prisoners ought to be fulfilling the norm every day, and simply told his norm-setters to make their decisions about how much had actually been done on that basis, rotating the shock-worker distinction among all of the prisoners so that they all got more or less the same amount of food.[41]

Bribery also worked higher up the hierarchy, sometimes through an entire chain of people. Aleksandr Klein was in a camp in the late 1940s, at a time when small salaries were introduced to inspire *zeks* to work harder:

Having received his earned money (it wasn't much) the worker gave a bribe to the brigadier. This was obligatory: the brigadier then had to give a bribe to the foreman and the norm-setter, who determined what norm had been fulfilled by the brigade . . . aside from this, the foreman and the brigadiers had to give bribes to the *naryadchik*, the work-assigner. The cooks also paid bribes to the chief cook, and the bath-house workers to the director of the bath-house.

On average, wrote Klein, he gave away half of his 'salary'. The consequences for those who did not could be dire. Those inmates who failed to pay up were automatically put down as having achieved a lower percentage of the norm, and therefore received less food. Brigadiers who did not want to pay suffered worse. One, wrote Klein, was murdered in his bed. His head was bashed in with a rock – and those sleeping around him did not even wake up.[42]

Tufta also affected the keeping of statistics at all levels of camp life. Camp commanders and camp accountants frequently changed numbers to benefit themselves, according to the dozens of reports of larceny kept in the files of the inspectorate. Anyone with even a remote connection to a camp stole food, money, whatever there was to steal: in 1942, the sister of the former boss of the railways division of the camps in Dzhezkazgan, Kazakhstan, was accused of having 'unlawfully removed some food products', and being involved in speculation. At one *lagpunkt* in 1941, the camp commander and the chief accountant 'used their professional status' to set up a false bank account, enabling them to milk the camp accounts. The commander stole 25,000 roubles, the accountant 18,000, a fortune in Soviet terms. But the sums were not always large either: a thick file on Siblag, containing prosecutors' reports from 1942 to 1944, includes, among other things, a long series of letters reflecting a bitter dispute over a camp employee who supposedly stole two iron bowls, one enamel teapot, one blanket, one mattress, two sheets, two pillows and two pillowcases.[43]

From theft, it was hardly a great moral leap to telling fibs about production statistics. If *tufta* began at the brigade level, and was compounded at the *lagpunkt* level, by the time the accountants at the larger camps were calculating total production statistics, the numbers were already very far from reality – and would, as we shall see, give very misleading ideas about the camps' real productivity, which was in all probability extremely low.

In truth, it is almost impossible to know what to make of Gulag production figures, given the degree of lying and cheating that went on. For that reason, I am always mystified by the Gulag's carefully detailed annual reports, such as the one produced in March 1940. More than 124 pages, this striking document describes the production figures for dozens of camps, carefully listing each one by speciality: the forestry camps, the factory camps, the mines, the collective farms. The report is accompanied by extensive charts and calculations, and many different sorts of figures. In conclusion, the report's author confidently declared that the total value of Gulag production in 1940 was 2,659.5 million roubles – a figure which must, under the circumstances, be considered completely meaningless.[44]

Pridurki
Co-operation and Collaboration

Tufta was not the only method that prisoners used to bridge the gap between the impossible norms expected of them, and the impossible rations they were allotted. Nor was it the only tool the authorities used to meet their own impossible production targets. There were other ways of persuading prisoners to co-operate, as Isaak Filshtinsky brilliantly and memorably describes in the first chapter of his memoirs, *My shagaem pod konvoem* ('*We March under Convoy Guard*').

Filshtinsky begins his story on one of his first days in Kargopollag, the logging and construction camp which lay to the north of Arkhangelsk. Newly arrived himself, he met another newcomer, a young woman. She was part of a female contingent that had been temporarily attached to his brigade. Noticing her 'timid, frightened appearance' and her ragged camp clothes, he moved closer to her in the line of prisoners. Yes, she said, answering his query, 'I arrived yesterday on a transport from prison.' They began to talk. She had what Filshtinsky described as 'for that era, a rather banal personal history'. She was an artist, twenty-six years old. She was married, with a three-year-old son. She had been arrested because she had 'said something or other to an artist friend, and the friend had informed'. Because her father had also been arrested in 1937, she had been quickly convicted of promoting anti-Soviet propaganda.

As they talked, the woman, still looking around with a frightened gaze, held on to Filshtinsky's arm. Such contacts were forbidden, but fortunately the guards did not notice. As they arrived at the work site the men and women were divided, but on the way home the young artist found Filshtinsky again. For the next week and a half, they walked to and from the forest together, she telling him of her homesickness, of the husband who had abandoned her, of the child she might not see again. Then the women's brigade was separated from the men's brigade for good, and Filshtinsky lost track of his friend.

Three years passed. It was a hot day – a rarity in the far north – when Filshtinsky caught sight of the woman again. This time she was dressed in a 'new jacket, perfectly fitting her size and figure'. Instead of the average prisoners' tattered cap she wore a beret. Instead of prisoners' worn boots she wore shoes. Her face had grown fatter, her looks more vulgar. When she opened her mouth, she spoke in the foulest slang, her language 'testifying to long and durable links with the criminal world of the camp'. Catching sight of Filshtinsky, a look of horror came over her face. She turned and walked away, 'almost running'.

By the time Filshtinsky encountered her for the third and final time, the woman was dressed in what seemed to him to be 'the latest in city fashions'. She was sitting behind a boss's desk, and was no longer a prisoner at all. She was also now married to Major L., a camp administrator famous for his cruelty. She addressed Filshtinsky rudely, and was no longer embarrassed to speak to him. The metamorphosis was complete: she had changed from prisoner to collaborator, and then from collaborator to camp boss. She had adopted first the language of the criminal world, then its dress and its habits. Through that route she had, finally, attained the privileged status of the camp authorities. Filshtinsky felt he had 'nothing more to say to her' – although, as he left the room, he turned to look at her again. Their eyes met for an instant, and he thought he perceived in hers a flash of 'limitless melancholy' and a hint of tears.[45]

The fate of Filshtinsky's acquaintance is one that readers familiar with other camp systems will recognize. In describing the Nazi camps, the German sociologist Wolfgang Sofsky wrote that 'absolute power is a structure, not a possession'. By this, he meant that power in the German camps was not a simple matter of one person controlling the lives of others. Instead, 'by making a small number of victims into its accomplices, the regime blurred the boundary between personnel and inmates'.[46]

Although the brutality that reigned in the Gulag was different, in its organization and its effects, Nazi and Soviet camps were similar in this respect: the Soviet regime also made such use of prisoners, tempting some into collaboration with the repressive system, raising them above the others, and granting them privileges which allowed them, in turn, to help the authorities exert their power. It is no accident that Filshtinsky concentrated, in his story, on the ever-improving wardrobe of his female acquaintance: in the camps, where everything was in chronic shortage, tiny improvements in clothing or food or living conditions were enough to persuade prisoners to co-operate, to strive for advancement. Those prisoners who succeeded were the *pridurki*, or 'trusties'. And once they attained that status, their lives in the camps improved in a myriad small ways.

Solzhenitsyn, who returns to the subject of trusties again and again, describes their obsession with small privileges and favours in *The Gulag Archipelago*:

Because of the human race's customary narrow-minded attachment to caste, it very soon became inconvenient for trusties to sleep in the same barracks as ordinary sloggers, on the same multiple bunks, or even, for that matter, on any multiple bunk at all, or anywhere else except a bed, or to eat at the same table, to undress in the same bath, or to put on the same underwear in which the sloggers had sweated and which they had torn . . .

Although recognizing that 'all classifications in this world lack sharp boundaries', Solzhenitsyn did his best to describe the trusties' hierarchy. On the lowest rung, he explained, were the 'work trusties': the prisoner engineers, designers, mechanics and geologists. Ranked just above them were the prisoner foremen, planners, norm-setters, construction superintendents, technicians. Both of these groups had to line up and be counted in the morning, and marched to work under convoy. On the other hand, they did not do physical work and were therefore not 'utterly exhausted' at the end of the day; this made them more privileged than prisoners on general work.

'Compound trusties' were more privileged still. These were prisoners who never left the *zona* during the day. According to Solzhenitsyn,

A worker in the camp workshops lived much more easily and better than the slogger out on general work: he did not have to go out for line-up, and this meant he could rise and breakfast much later; he did not have to march under convoy to the work site and back; there were fewer severities, less cold, less strength spent; also, his workday ended earlier; either his work was in a warm place or else a place to warm up was always handy ... 'Tailor' in camp sounds and means something like 'Assistant Professor' out in freedom.[47]

The lowest in the compound trusty hierarchy actually did physical work: bath-house attendants, laundresses, dishwashers, stokers and orderlies, as well as those who worked in the camp workshops, repairing clothing, shoes and machinery. Ranked above these indoor workers were the 'genuine' compound trusties, who did no physical work at all: the cooks, bread-cutters, clerks, doctors, nurses, medical assistants, barbers, senior orderlies, work-assigners, accountants. In some camps, there were even prisoners employed as official food-tasters.[48] This latter group, writes Solzhenitsyn, were 'not only well fed, clad in clean clothes, and exempt from lifting heavy weights and from crooks in their backs, but they had great power over what was most needed by a human being, and consequently power over people'.[49] These were the trusties who had the power to decide what sort of work ordinary prisoners were to do, how much food they were going to receive, and whether they would receive medical treatment or not – whether, in short, they would live or die.

Unlike the privileged prisoners in the Nazi camps, the trusties of the Soviet camps did not have to belong to a particular racial category. In theory, anybody could rise to the status of trusty – just as anybody could become a prison guard – and there was a great deal of fluctuation between the two groups. Although in principle ordinary prisoners could become trusties, and in principle trusties could be demoted to the ranks of ordinary prisoners, there were complicated rules governing this process.

These rules differed greatly from camp to camp and from era to era, although there do seem to be a few conventions that held more or less true over time. Most importantly, it was easier to become a trusty if a prisoner was classified as a 'socially close' criminal prisoner, and not a 'socially dangerous' political. Because the twisted moral hierarchy of the Soviet camp system decreed the 'socially close' – not just the professional criminals, but the ordinary thieves, swindlers, murderers and rapists – more capable of being reformed into good Soviet citizens, they were automatically more likely to receive trusty status. And in a certain sense, the thieves, who had no fear of using brutality, made ideal trusties. 'Everywhere and at all times,' wrote one political bitterly, 'these convicts enjoyed almost unlimited confidence of the prison and camp administration, and were appointed to such soft jobs as working in offices, prison stores, canteens, bath-houses, barber shops and so on.'[50] As I've said, this was particularly the case during the late 1930s and throughout the war, the years when criminal gangs ruled supreme in the Soviet camps. Even afterwards – Filshtinsky was writing of the late 1940s – the 'culture' of the trusties was hardly distinguishable from the culture of the professional criminals.

But the criminal trusties also presented a problem for the camp authorities. They were not 'enemies' – but they were not educated either. In many cases they were not even literate, and did not want to become literate: even when camps set up literacy classes, criminals often did not bother to go to them.[51] That left camp bosses with no choice, wrote Lev Razgon, except to employ the politicals: 'The plan exerted an implacable pressure of its own which tolerated no excuses. Under its influence even the most zealous camp bosses who expressed the greatest hatred for the counter-revolutionary prisoners were obliged to put political prisoners to work.'[52]

In fact, after 1939, when Beria replaced Yezhov – and simultaneously set about trying to make the Gulag profitable – the rules were never clear one way or another. Beria's instructions of August 1939, while explicitly forbidding camp commanders to make use of political prisoners in any administrative capacity whatsoever, did, in fact, make exceptions. Qualified doctors were to be used in their professional capacity and, under special circumstances, so were prisoners sentenced according to some of the 'lesser' crimes of Article 58 – sections 7, 10, 12 and 14, which included 'Anti-Soviet Agitation' (telling anti-regime jokes, for example) and 'anti-Soviet propaganda'. Those sentenced for 'terrorism' or 'betrayal of the motherland', on the other hand, were theoretically not to be employed as anything except hard labourers.[53] When the war broke out, even this command was reversed. Stalin and Molotov sent out a special circular allowing Dalstroi, 'in view of the exceptional situation', to 'conclude individual agreements for a particular time period with engineers, technicians and administrative workers who have been sent to work in Kolyma'.[54]

Nevertheless camp administrators who had too many politicals in high-ranking jobs still risked censure, and a degree of ambivalence always remained. According to both Solzhenitsyn and Razgon, it sometimes therefore happened that political prisoners were given 'good' indoor jobs, accounting and bookkeeping – but only temporarily. Once every year, when the inspection teams from Moscow were due to arrive, they were fired again. Razgon developed a theory about this procedure:

A good camp boss would wait for the commission to arrive, let the commission do its work, remove anyone who had to be removed. It was not a time-consuming process and anyone not removed would remain for a long time – for a year, until the next

December, or for a half-year at least. A less capable camp boss, a more foolish one, would remove such persons in advance so as to report that everything was in order. The worst camp bosses, those who had the least experience, would conscientiously carry out the orders of their superiors and not permit persons condemned under Article 58 to work with any instrument other than the pick and the wheelbarrow, the saw and the axe. Such camp bosses were the least succesful. Such camp bosses were quickly fired.[55]

In practice, the rules were often simply nonsensical. As a political prisoner in Kargopollag, Filshtinsky was strictly forbidden from taking a prisoners' course in forestry technology. However, he was allowed to read the course books, and once he had passed the exam, studying on his own, he was allowed to work as a forestry specialist as well.[56] Meanwhile, V. K. Yasny, also a political prisoner in the late 1940s, worked as an engineer in Vorkuta without causing any controversy at all.[57] In the post-war years, as the stronger national groups began to make an impact in the camps, the reign of the criminals was frequently supplanted by that of the better-organized prisoners, often Ukrainians and Balts. Those in better jobs – the foreman and supervisors – could and did look after their own, and distributed other plum posts to political prisoners who happened to be their countrymen.

At no point did prisoners have full power to distribute trusty jobs, however. The camp administration had the ultimate say over who would become a trusty, and most camp commanders were inclined to give the cushier trusty jobs to those willing to collaborate more openly – in other words, to inform. Alas, it is difficult to say how many informers the system employed. Although the Russian state archives have opened up the rest of the Gulag administration archive, they have left closed the documents on the 'Third Division', the camp division responsible for informers. The Russian historian Viktor Berdinskikh, in his book on Vyatlag, cites some figures without naming a source: 'In the 1920s, the leadership of the OGPU set itself the task of having no less than 25 per cent informers among camp prisoners. In the 1930s and 1940s, this planned number was lowered to 10 per cent.' But Berdinskikh also agrees that a real assessment of the numbers is 'complicated' without better access to archives.[58]

Nor are there many memoirists who will admit openly to having been informers, although some admit that they were recruited. Clearly, prisoners who had served as informers in prison (or even before their arrests) would have arrived in the camp with a note of their willingness to co-operate already in their files. Others, it seemed, were approached just after their arrival in camp, when they were still extremely disoriented and afraid. On his second day in camp, Leonid Trus was taken to the operative commander – known in camp slang as the *kum*, the recruiter of informers – and asked to co-operate. Not really understanding what he was being asked, he refused. This, he thinks, is why he was initially given difficult physical work, a low-status job by camp standards. Berdinskikh also quotes from his own interviews and correspondence with former prisoners:

From the first day in the zone, the new arrivals were called to the *kum*. I was called to the *kum* as well. Flattering, slippery, smooth, he played on the fact that the car accident, for which I was sentenced (ten years in camp, plus three years without full legal rights) was not shameful (it was not robbery, murder or something similar) and he proposed that I inform – that I become a sneak. I politely refused and didn't sign the proposal of the *kum*.

Although the *kum* swore at him, this prisoner was not sent to the punishment cells. Upon returning to his barracks, he found no one would come near him: knowing that he had been asked to inform, seeing that he had not been beaten up or punished, the other prisoners assumed he had agreed.[59]

Perhaps the most famous exception to the near-universal refusal to admit to informing is, once again, Alexander Solzhenitsyn, who describes his flirtation with the camp authorities at length. He dates his initial moment of weakness to his early days in camp, when he was still struggling to accustom himself to his abrupt loss of status. When invited to speak to the operative commander, he was ushered into a 'small, cosily furnished room' where a radio was playing classical music. After politely asking him whether he was comfortable and adjusting to camp life, the commander asked him, 'Are you still a Soviet person?' After hemming and hawing, Solzhenitsyn agreed that he was.

But although confessing to being 'Soviet' was tantamount to confessing a desire to collaborate, Solzhenitsyn initially declined to inform. That was when the commander switched tactics. He turned off the music, and began to speak to Solzhenitsyn about the camp criminals, asking how he would feel if his wife in Moscow were attacked by some who managed to escape. Finally, Solzhenitsyn agreed that if he should hear any of them planning to escape, he would report it. He signed a pledge, promising to report news of any escapes to the authorities, and chose a conspiratorial pseudonym: Vetrov. 'Those six letters,' he writes, 'are branded in shameful grooves on my memory.'[60]

By his own account, Solzhenitsyn never did actually report on anything. When recruited again in 1956, he says he refused to sign anything at all. Nevertheless, his initial promise was enough to keep him, while in camp, in one of the trusty jobs, living in the trusties' special quarters, slightly better dressed and better fed than other prisoners. This experience 'filled me with shame', he wrote – and doubtless provoked his disdain for all trusties.

At the time of its publication, Solzhenitsyn's description of the camp trusties was controversial – and it still is. Like his description of inmate work habits, it also sparked a running debate in the world of camp survivors and historians, one which continues to this day. Virtually all of the classic, most widely read memoirists were trusties at one time or another: Evgeniya Ginzburg, Lev

Razgon, Varlam Shalamov, Solzhenitsyn. It may well be, as some claim, that the majority of *all* prisoners who survived long sentences were trusties at some point in their camp career. I once met a survivor who recounted to me a reunion of old camp friends he had once attended. The group had taken to reminiscing, and were laughing at old camp stories, when one of them looked around the room and realized what it was that held them together, what made it possible for them to laugh at the past instead of crying: 'All of us had been *pridurki*.'

There is no doubt that many people survived because they were able to get indoor trusty jobs, thereby escaping the horrors of general work. But did this always amount to active collaboration with the camp regime? Solzhenitsyn felt that it did. Even those trusties who were not informers could, he alleged, still be described as collaborators. 'What trusty position,' he asked, 'did not in fact involve playing up to the bosses and participating in the general system of compulsion?'

Sometimes the collaboration was indirect, Solzhenitsyn explained, but damaging none the less. The 'work trusties' – the norm-setters, bookkeepers, engineers – did not actually torture people, but they all participated in a system that forced prisoners to work to their deaths. The same was true of 'compound trusties': typists ran off orders for the camp command. Every bread-cutter who was able to steal an extra loaf for himself might be said to be depriving a *zek* working in the forest of his full portion, wrote Solzhenitsyn: 'Who short-weighed Ivan Denisovich's bread? Who stole his sugar by dampening it with water? Who kept fats, meat or good cereals from the common pot?'[61]

Others felt the same way. One ex-*zek* wrote that she had deliberately remained assigned to general work for nine years in order to avoid being caught up in the corrupt relationships which were needed to stay in a trusty job.[62] Dmitri Panin (who, as I've written, knew Solzhenitsyn in the camps and features in his novel *The First Circle*) also confessed that he was greatly embarrassed by the two weeks he had held a soft job in the camp kitchen: 'Even worse was the realization that I was stealing food from other prisoners. I tried to gain comfort from the thought that when a man has been reduced to the condition I was in then, he doesn't fret over niceties; but it did not lighten my sense of wrongdoing, and when they kicked me out of the kitchen, I was actually glad.'[63]

Bitterly opposed to Solzhenitsyn – as many others were and are – was Lev Razgon, a writer who became, in the 1990s, almost as great an authority on the Gulag inside Russia. While in the camps, Razgon had been a norm-setter, one of the top trusty jobs. Razgon argued that for him, and for many others, choosing to become a trusty was simply a matter of choosing to live. Particularly during the war years, 'it was impossible to survive if you were felling timber'. Only peasants survived: 'those who knew how to sharpen and set instruments, and those given familiar agricultural work to do who could make up their diet with a filched potato, radish, or any other kind of vegetable'.[64]

Razgon did not believe that it was immoral to choose life, nor that those who did so were 'no better than the people who arrested them'. He also disputed Solzhenitsyn's venal portrait of the trusties. Once they were in more comfortable jobs, many trusties routinely helped other prisoners:

It was not that they were indifferent to the Ivan Denisoviches who went out to fell timber or that they felt estranged from them. Simply, they could not help those who did not know how to do anything other than physical work. And even among the latter they sought and found people with the most unexpected skills: those who knew how to make shaft-bows and barrels were sent to the outpost where skis were produced; those who could weave baskets began to fashion basketwork armchairs, chairs and sofas for the bosses.[65]

Just as there were good guards and bad guards, Razgon argued, so too were there good trusties and bad trusties, people who helped other people, people who harmed them. And in the end, they were no more secure than the people who came below them in the hierarchy. If they were not being worked to death, they knew that they soon could be. At any moment, a distant camp boss could order a transfer to take them away to another camp, to another job, to another deadlier fate.

Sanchast
Hospitals and Doctors

Of the many absurdities found in camp life, perhaps the strangest was also one of the most mundane: the camp doctor. Every *lagpunkt* had one. If there were not enough trained doctors, then at the very least the *lagpunkt* would have a nurse or a *feldsher*, a medical assistant who may or may not have had medical training. Like guardian angels, medical personnel had the power to pluck inmates out of the cold, to deposit them in clean camp hospitals, where they might be fed and nursed back to life. Everyone else – the guards, the camp commander, the brigadiers – constantly told the *zeks* to work harder. The doctor alone was not obligated to do so. 'Only the doctor,' wrote Shalamov, 'has the authority to save the convict from going out into the white winter fog to the icy stone face of the mine for many hours a day.'[66]

Some inmates were quite literally saved thanks to a few words from a medical man. Burning with fever, reduced to a skeleton, tortured by hunger, one doctor diagnosed Lev Kopelev with pellagra, a bowel infection and a bad cold. 'I'm sending you to the hospital,' she declared. It was not an easy journey from the *lagpunkt* to the camp central hospital, the *sanchast*. Kopelev gave up all of his property – on the grounds that all camp belongings must stay in the camp – marched through 'deep, icy puddles' and crowded into a cattle car with other sick and dying prisoners. The journey was hellish. But when he awoke in his new surroundings, he found his life transformed:

In a blissful half-sleep, I sat in a bright, clean hospital room, on a bunk covered with an unbelievably clean sheet . . . The doctor was a small, round-faced man, whose grey moustache and thick eyeglasses added to his air of kindness and concern. 'In Moscow,' he asked, 'did you know a literary critic named Motylova?'

'Tamara Lazarevna Motylova? Of course!'

'She's my niece.'

Uncle Borya, as I came to know him, looked at the thermometer. 'Oho! Have him washed,' he told his assistant. 'Have his clothes boiled. Get him into bed.'

Upon awaking again, Kopelev discovered he had been brought six pieces of bread: 'Three pieces of black bread and – miraculous sight! Three pieces of white bread! I ate them greedily, my eyes filled with tears.' Better still, he was given anti-pellagra rations: turnips and carrots, as well as yeast and mustard to spread on bread. He was for the first time allowed to receive parcels and money from home, and was thus able to buy boiled potatoes, milk and *makhorka*, the cheapest form of tobacco. Having been, it seemed, condemned to a living death, he realized he was now destined to be saved.[67]

This was a common experience. 'Paradise' is what Evgeniya Ginzburg called the hospital where she worked in Kolyma.[68] 'We felt like kings,' wrote Thomas Sgovio of the 'recovery barracks' in the Srednikan *lagpunkt*, where he received a 'fresh, sweet roll in the morning'.[69] Others write with remembered awe of the clean sheets, of the kindness of nurses, of the lengths to which doctors went to save their patients. One prisoner tells the story of a doctor who, risking his own position, illegally left the camp to procure necessary medications.[70] Tatyana Okunevskaya wrote that her doctor 'brought the dead back to life'.[71] Vadim Aleksandrovich, who was himself a camp doctor, remembered that 'The doctor and his assistant in the camps are, if not gods, then demi-gods. Upon them hangs the possibility of a few days' freedom from killing work, even the possibility of being sent to a sanatorium.'[72]

Janos Rozsas, an eighteen-year-old Hungarian who found himself in the same camp as Alexander Solzhenitsyn after the war, wrote a book entitled *Sister Dusya*, named in honour of the camp nurse he believed had saved his life. Not only did she sit and talk to him, convincing him that it was impossible to die under her care, Sister Dusya even traded her own bread ration in order to procure milk for Rozsas, who could digest very little food. He remained grateful for the rest of his life: 'I conjured up in my head two beloved faces, the faraway face of my natural mother, and the face of Sister Dusya. They were amazingly similar . . . I told myself that if, in time, I were ever to forget my mother's face, I would only need to think of the face of Sister Dusya, and through her I would always see my mother.'[73]

Rozsas's gratitude to Sister Dusya eventually translated itself into a love of the Russian language and Russian culture. When I met Rozsas in Budapest half a century after his release, he still spoke elegant, fluent Russian, still maintained contact with Russian friends, and proudly told me where to find the references to his story in *The Gulag Archipelago* and in the memoirs of Solzhenitsyn's wife.[74]

Yet there was, as many also noticed, another paradox at work here. When a prisoner with mild scurvy was in the work brigade, no one was interested in his loose teeth or the boils on his legs. His complaints would bring derisive scorn from the guards, or worse. If he became a *dokhodyaga* dying on a camp bunk, he would be a figure of fun. But when his temperature finally reached the requisite level or his illness reached the critical moment – when he 'qualified' as sick, in other words – the same dying man would immediately be given 'scurvy rations' or 'pellagra rations', and would receive all the medical care that the Gulag could muster.

This paradox was built right into the system. From the beginning of the camps' existence, sick prisoners had been treated differently. Invalid brigades were set up, for prisoners who could no longer do hard physical work, as early as January 1931.[75] Later, there would be invalid barracks, and even whole invalid *lagpunkts*, devoted to nursing weak prisoners back to life. In 1933, Dmitlag organized 'recovery *lagpunkts*' designed to hold 3,600 prisoners.[76] Official Gulag documents carefully describe the extra rations for hospitalized prisoners: a few meat products, real tea (as opposed to the surrogate offered to ordinary prisoners), onions to ward off scurvy and, inexplicably, pepper and bay leaves. Even if, in practice, the extra food only amounted to 'a bit of potatoes or dried green peas (only half-cooked to retain the vitamins) or sauerkraut' it was, compared to ordinary rations, real luxury.[77]

So bizarre did Gustav Herling find this contrast between the murderous conditions of camp life, and the efforts which camp doctors invested in reviving the prisoners whose health had been duly destroyed, he concluded that a 'hospital cult' must exist in the Soviet Union:

There was something incomprehensible in the fact that the moment a prisoner left the hospital he became a prisoner again, but as long as he had been lying motionless in a clean bed all the rights of a human being, though always with the exception of freedom, had been accorded to him. For a man unaccustomed to the violent contrasts of Soviet life, camp hospitals seemed like churches which offer sanctuary from an all-powerful Inquisition.[78]

George Bien, a Hungarian prisoner who was sent to a well-stocked hospital in Magadan, also found it hard to understand: 'I asked myself why they were trying to save me when it had seemed that they only wanted my tortured death – but logic had left a long time ago.'[79]

Certainly the Gulag bosses in Moscow took the problems posed by the large numbers of invalid 'work-incapable' prisoners very seriously. Although their existence was hardly new, the problem became acute after Stalin and Beria's 1939 decision to eliminate the policy of 'conditional early release' for invalids: suddenly, the ill could no longer be easily shucked off the work rolls. This, if nothing else, would have forced camp commanders to turn their attention to camp hospitals. One inspector did a precise calculation of the time and money lost to illness: 'From October of 1940, to the first half of March 1941, there were 3,472 cases of frostbite, thanks to which 42,334 working days were lost. 2,400 prisoners became too weak to work.' Another inspector reported that in that same year, of 2,398 prisoners in the labour camps in the Crimea, 860 had only a limited ability to work, and 273 could not work at all. Some were in hospital beds, some, for lack of beds, were being kept in prison cells, producing a drag on the whole system.[80]

Yet, like everything else in the Gulag, there was nothing straightforward about the need to heal the sick. In some camps, it seems the special invalid *lagpunkts* were created largely to prevent the invalids from dragging down the camp production statistics. This was the case in Siblag, which counted 9,000 invalids and 15,000 'half-invalids' among its 63,000 prisoners in 1940 and 1941 – more than a third. When these weak prisoners were removed from the significant work sites and replaced with brigades of 'fresh' new workers, the camp's production figures magically rose much higher.[81]

Pressure to meet the plan forced many camp commanders into a dilemma. On the one hand, they genuinely wanted to cure the sick – so that they could be put back to work. On the other hand, they did not want to encourage the 'lazy'. In practice, this often meant that camp administrations set limits – sometimes very precise – on how many prisoners were allowed to be ill at any one time, and how many could be sent to recovery *lagpunkts*.[82] Whatever the actual number of suffering prisoners, in other words, they permitted doctors to grant rest days only to a small percentage. Aleksandrovich, the camp doctor, remembered that in his camp 'about 10 per cent of the *lagpunkt*', thirty or forty people, showed up every evening at the doctor's receiving hour. It was understood, however, that no more than 3–5 per cent could be freed from work: 'more than that, and an investigation would begin'.[83]

If more were ill, they would have to wait. Typical was the story of one prisoner in Ustvymlag, who stated several times that he was ill and could not work. According to the official report filed afterwards, 'The medical workers paid no attention to his protest, and he was sent to work. Not being in a condition to work, he refused to work, for which he was shut up in the punishment cell. There he was kept for four days, after which he was taken in very poor condition to the hospital, where he died.' In another camp, a tubercular patient was sent out to work and, according to the inspectors' report, 'was in such poor condition that he could not return to the camp without assistance'.[84]

The low numbers set on those 'allowed' to be sick meant that doctors were under terrible, conflicting pressures. They could be censured, or even sentenced, if too many sick prisoners died, having been refused access to the camp hospital.[85] They could also be threatened by the more violent and aggressive members of the camp criminal elite, who wanted release from work. If the camp doctor wanted to give rest days to genuinely sick prisoners, he had to resist these criminals' advances. Shalamov, again, described the fate of one Doctor Surovoy, sent to work in the largely criminal *lagpunkt* at the Spokoiny mine in Kolyma:

He was a young doctor, and – more important – he was a convict doctor. Surovoy's friend tried to persuade him not to go. He could have refused and been sent to a general work gang instead of taking on this patently dangerous work. Surovoy had come to the hospital from a general work gang; he was afraid to return to it and agreed to go to the mine and work at his profession. The camp authorities gave him instructions but no advice on how to conduct himself. He was categorically forbidden to send healthy thieves from the mine to the hospital. Within a month he was killed while admitting patients; on his body were fifty-two knife wounds.[86]

When he arrived to work as a *feldsher* in a criminal *lagpunkt*, Karol Colonna-Czosnowski was also warned that his predecessor had been 'hacked to death' by his patients. On his first night in camp, he was confronted with a man carrying an axe, demanding to be excused from the following day's work. Karol managed, he claims, to surprise him and throw him out of the *feldsher*'s hut. The next day he did a deal with Grisha, the camp criminal boss: in addition to the genuinely ill, Grisha would give him the names of two additional people a day who were to be freed from work.[87]

Alexander Dolgun also describes a similar experience. On one of his first days as a *feldsher*, a criminal prisoner presented himself to Dolgun, claiming to have a stomach ache – and demanding opium. 'He motioned me to come close. "Here!" he whispered fiercely, pulling back his shirt. His right hand was inside his shirt, holding a wicked carved knife like a miniature scimitar. "I want opium. I am always treated very well here. You're new. You might as well know that if I don't get my opium, you get the knife."' Dolgun managed to fend him off with a fake opium solution. Others were not so quick-witted, and could be kept in the criminals' power indefinitely.[88]

Even when a prisoner finally made it into the hospital, he often found that the quality of medical care varied widely. The larger camps had proper hospitals, with staff and medicines. The central Dalstroi hospital, in the city of Magadan, was known for having the latest equipment, as well as for being staffed by the best prisoner doctors, often Moscow specialists. While most of its patients were NKVD officers or camp employees, some of the more fortunate prisoners got treated by specialists as well, there and elsewhere: during his camp sentence, Lev Finkelstein was even allowed to visit a dentist.[89] Some of the invalid *lagpunkts* were also well-appointed, and seem to have been genuinely intended to nurse prisoners back to health. Tatyana Okunevskaya was sent to one, and marvelled at the open spaces, the generous barracks, the trees: 'I hadn't seen them in so many years! And it was springtime!'[90]

In the smaller *lagpunkt* hospitals, the situation was far grimmer. Usually, *lagpunkt* doctors found it impossible to maintain even minimal standards of sterility and cleanliness.[91] Hospitals were often no more than ordinary barracks in which the sick were simply dumped on ordinary beds – sometimes two to a bed – with only minimal supplies of medicine. An inspector reporting on one small camp complained that it had no designated hospital buildings, no sheets and underwear for patients, no medicine and no qualified medical personnel. Death rates, as a result, were extremely high.[92]

Eyewitnesses concur. In one small hospital, in a *lagpunkt* of Sevurallag, 'treatment and documentation were poor', according to Isaac Vogelfanger, once the camp's chief surgeon. Worse,

food rations were remarkably inadequate and very few drugs were available. Surgical cases such as fractures and major injuries to soft tissues were badly handled and neglected. Seldom, as I later discovered, were patients discharged to return to work. Having been admitted with advanced signs of malnutrition, the majority would die in the hospital.[93]

A Polish prisoner, Jerzy Gliksman, remembered that in one *lagpunkt* prisoners actually lay 'in a clutter' on the floor: 'All passages were crowded with lying bodies. Filth and wretchedness were everywhere. Many of the patients raved and shouted incoherently, while others lay motionless and pale.'[94]

Worse were the barracks, or rather mortuaries, for terminally ill patients. In one such barrack, set up for prisoners with dysentery, 'patients lay in bed for weeks. If they were lucky they recovered. More often they died. There was no treatment, no medicines . . . patients usually tried to conceal a death for three or four days in order to get the dead man's rations for themselves.'[95]

Conditions were worsened by Gulag bureaucracy. In 1940, a camp inspector complained that one camp simply did not have enough hospital beds for sick prisoners. Since a prisoner who was not actually lying down inside a hospital was not allowed to receive a hospital ration, this meant that ill prisoners outside the hospital were simply receiving the reduced 'shirkers' ration.[96]

Nor, although many camp doctors can be said to have saved the lives of many people, were they all necessarily inclined to be helpful. Some, from their privileged perspective, had come to sympathize more with the bosses than with the 'enemies' whom they were required to treat. Elinor Lipper described one doctor, the head of a hospital for 500 patients: 'She behaved like a *pomeshchitsa*, a great lady and landowner of tsarist times, and considered the entire staff of the hospital her personal serfs. With her fleshy hand, she once took hold of a neglectful orderly and pulled his hair until he screamed.'[97] In another camp, the wife of the camp commander, a doctor in the hospital section, was actually censured by the camp inspectorate because she 'allowed the seriously ill into the hospital far too late, didn't free the sick from work, was rude, and threw sick prisoners out of the infirmary'.[98]

In some cases, doctors knowingly mistreated prisoner patients. While working in a mining camp in the early 1950s, one of Leonid Trus's legs was crushed. The camp doctor bound the wound, but more was needed. Trus had already lost a great deal of blood, and was beginning to feel very cold. Because the camp did not have its own facilities for blood transfusions, the camp authorities sent him, in the back of a truck, to a local hospital. Half-conscious, he heard the doctor ask a nurse to begin a blood transfusion. The friend accompanying him gave his personal details: name, age, sex, place of work – after which the doctor halted the blood transfusion. Such help was not given to a prisoner. Trus recalls being given some glucose to drink – thanks to the friend, who paid a bribe for it – and some morphine. The following day, his leg was amputated:

The surgeon was so convinced I wouldn't live that he didn't even do the operation himself, but gave it to his wife, a therapist who was trying to re-qualify as a surgeon. Later they told me that she did everything well, that she knew what she was doing, except that she left out a few details. She hadn't forgotten them, but she didn't think I would live, and therefore it was immaterial whether these medical details were completed. And look, I remained alive![99]

Not that camp doctors, whether kind or indifferent, were necessarily qualified either. Those who carried the title ranged from top Moscow specialists serving out their prison sentences, to charlatans who knew nothing whatsoever about medicine, but were willing to fake knowledge in order to get a high-status job. As early as 1932, the OGPU had complained of the dearth of qualified medical personnel.[100] This meant that prisoners with medical degrees were the exception to every rule governing trusty jobs: whatever counter-revolutionary terrorist act they were alleged to have committed, they were almost always allowed to practise medicine.[101]

Shortages also meant that prisoners received training as nurses and *feldshers* – training which was often rudimentary. Evgeniya Ginzburg qualified as a nurse after spending 'several days' in a camp hospital, learning the art of 'cupping' and how to give an injection.[102] Alexander Dolgun, having been taught in one camp the basics of the *feldsher*'s job, was tested on his knowledge after being transferred to another camp. Told to do an autopsy by an officer suspicious of his qualifications, he 'put on the best show I could and acted as if I did this sort of thing all the time'.[103] In order to get his job as *feldsher*, Janusz Bardach also lied: he claimed to be a third-year medical student when, in fact, he had not yet entered university.[104]

The results were predictable. Upon arriving at his first posting as a convict doctor in Sevurallag, Isaac Vogelfanger, himself a qualified surgeon, was surprised to find the local *feldsher* treating scurvy boils – a condition caused by malnutrition, not infection – with iodine. Later, he witnessed a number of patients die because an unqualified doctor insisted upon injecting patients with a solution made of ordinary sugar.[105]

None of this would have come as a surprise to the Gulag bosses, one of whom complained, in a letter to his Moscow boss, of a doctor shortage: 'In several *lagpunkts*, medical help is given by self-taught nurses, prisoners without any medical qualification whatsover.' Another wrote of a camp medical system which defied 'all principles of the Soviet health service'.[106] The bosses knew they were flawed, the prisoners knew they were flawed – and yet the camp medical services went on functioning all the same.

Even with all of their faults – even when doctors were venal, wards were poorly equipped, medication was scarce – so attractive did life in the hospital or the infirmary seem to prisoners, that to get there they were willing not only to injure or threaten doctors, but to hurt themselves too. Like soldiers trying to avoid the battlefield, *zeks* also engaged in *samorub* ('self-mutilation') and *mastyrka* ('faking illness') in desperate attempts to save their lives. Some believed they would eventually receive an invalid's amnesty. So many believed this, in fact, that the Gulag on at least one occasion issued a declaration denying that invalids would be freed (although they were, occasionally).[107] Most, however, were simply glad to avoid work.

The punishment for self-mutilation was particularly high: an extra camp sentence. This reflected, perhaps, the fact that a disabled worker was a burden to the state and a drag on the production plan. 'Self-mutilation was punished viciously, like for sabotage,' wrote Zhigulin.[108] One prisoner tells the story of a thief who cut off four fingers of his left hand. Instead of being sent to an invalid camp, however, the invalid was made to sit in the snow and watch as others worked. Forbidden to move around, on pain of being shot for attempted escape, 'very soon he himself requested a shovel and, moving it like a crutch, with his surviving hand, poked at the frozen earth, crying and swearing'.[109]

Nevertheless, many prisoners thought the potential benefits made the risk worth taking. Some of the methods were crude. Criminals in particular were famous for simply cutting off their three middle fingers with an axe, so they could no longer cut trees or hold a wheelbarrow in the mines. Others cut off a foot, or a hand, or rubbed acid into their eyes. Still others, upon departing for work, wrapped a wet rag around one foot: in the evening they returned with third-degree frostbite. The same method could be applied to fingers. In the 1960s, Anatoly Marchenko watched a man nail his testicles to a prison bench.[110] Nor was he the first: Valery Frid describes a man who nailed his scrotum to a tree stump.[111]

But there were subtler methods used as well. The more daring criminal would steal a syringe and inject melted soap into his penis: the resulting ejaculation looked like venereal disease. Another prisoner found a way to fake silicosis, a lung disease. First, he filed a small quantity of silver dust from a silver ring which he had managed to keep among his personal belongings. He then mixed the silver dust with tobacco, and smoked it. Although he felt nothing, he then took himself to the hospital coughing in the way that he had seen silicosis victims cough. On the subsequent X-ray, a terrible shadow appeared on his lungs – enough to disqualify him from hard labour and get him sent to a camp for the incurably ill.[112]

Prisoners also attempted to create infections, or long-term illnesses. Vadim Aleksandrovich treated a patient who had infected himself with a dirty sewing needle.[113] Gustav Herling watched one prisoner thrust his arm in the fire, when he thought no one was looking; he did it once every day, the better to maintain a mysteriously persistent wound.[114] Anatoly Zhigulin made himself ill by drinking ice water and then breathing cold air. It gave him a temperature high enough to allow him to be excused from work: 'Oh happy ten days in the hospital!'[115]

Prisoners also faked insanity. Bardach, during his career as *feldsher*, worked for a time in the psychiatric ward of the central Magadan hospital. There, the primary method of unmasking fake schizophrenics was to put them on a ward with real schizophrenics: 'Within hours, many prisoners, even the most determined, knocked on the door to be let out.' If that failed, the prisoner was given a camphor injection, which induced a seizure. Those who survived rarely wanted the procedure repeated.[116]

There was even a standard procedure for prisoners who attempted to fake paralysis, according to Elinor Lipper. The patient was put on an operating table and given a slight anaesthetic. When he awoke, the doctors would place him on his feet. Inevitably, when they called his name, he would take a few steps before remembering to collapse to the floor.[117] Dmitri Bystroletov also witnessed a woman cured of 'deafness' by her own mother. The administration, suspicious of the woman's claim to be hard of hearing, invited the mother to visit her imprisoned daughter, but refused to let her in the barracks. Instead, she was made to stay outside the gates, where she stood, calling her daughter's name. Naturally, the daughter responded.[118]

But there were also doctors who helped patients find methods of self-mutilation. Alexander Dolgun, although very weak and suffering from uncontrollable diarrhoea, did not have a fever high enough to merit being excused from work. Nevertheless, when he told the camp doctor, an educated Latvian, that he was American, the man brightened. 'I've been dying to find someone to talk English with,' he said – and showed Dolgun how to infect his own cut. This produced an enormous purple boil on his arm, enough to impress the MVD guards inspecting the hospital with the seriousness of his illness.[119]

Once again, ordinary morality was reversed. In the free world, no doctor who deliberately made his patients ill would be considered a good man. In the camps, however, such a doctor was revered as a saint.

'Ordinary Virtues'

Not all of the strategies for survival in the camps necessarily derived from the system itself. Nor did they all involve collaboration, cruelty or self-mutilation. If some prisoners – perhaps the vast majority of prisoners – managed to stay alive through manipulating the rules of the camp to their advantage, there were also some who built upon what Tzvetan Todorov, in his book on concentration camp morality, has called the 'ordinary virtues': caring and friendship, dignity, and the life of the mind.[120]

Caring took many forms. There were prisoners, as we've seen, who built their own survival networks. Members of the ethnic groups which dominated some of the camps in the late 1940s – Ukrainians, Balts, Poles – created whole systems of mutual assistance. Others built up independent networks of acquaintances over years in the camps. Still others simply made one or two extremely close friends. Perhaps the best known of these Gulag friendships was that between Ariadna Efron, the daughter of the poet Marina Tsvetaeva, and her friend Ada Federolf. They exerted enormous efforts in order to remain together, both in camps and in exile, and later published their memoirs together in one volume. At one point in her half of the story, Federolf told of how they were reunited after a long separation when Efron was put on a different transport:

It was already summer. The first days after we arrived were horrible. They took us out to exercise once a day – the heat was intolerable. Then suddenly a new transport from Ryazan and – Alya. I gasped with happiness, pulled her on to the upper bunks, closer to the fresh air ... There it is, prisoners' happiness, the happiness of simply meeting a person.[121]

Others agreed. 'It is very important to have a friend, a trusted face, who will not leave if you are in trouble,' wrote Zoya Marchenko.[122] 'It was impossible to survive alone. People organized themselves into groups of two or three,' wrote another prisoner.[123] Dmitri Panin also attributes his ability to withstand the attacks of criminals to the self-defence pact he made with a group of other prisoners.[124] There were limits, of course. Janusz Bardach wrote of his best camp friend that 'neither one of us ever asked the other for food, nor did we offer it. We both knew that this sanctum could not be violated if we were to remain friends.'[125]

If respect for others helped some maintain their humanity, respect for themselves helped others. Many, particularly women, speak of the need to keep clean, or as clean as possible, as a way of preserving one's dignity. Olga Adamova-Sliozberg describes how a prison cell mate 'washed and dried her white collar and sewed it back on her blouse' every morning.[126] Japanese prisoners in Magadan set up a Japanese 'bath' – a large barrel, to which benches were attached – along the bay.[127] During sixteen months in Leningrad's Kresty prison, Boris Chetverikov washed his clothes over and over again, as well as the walls and the floors of his cell – before going through all of the opera arias he knew in his head.[128] Others practised exercise or hygienic routines. This is Bardach again:

... despite my fatigue and the cold, I kept the exercise routine I had followed at home and in the Red Army, washing my face and hands at the hand pump. I wanted to retain as much pride in myself as I could, separating myself from the many prisoners I had seen give up day by day. They'd stop caring first about their hygiene or appearance, then about their fellow prisoners, and finally about their own lives. If I had control over nothing else, I had control over this ritual which I believed would keep me from degradation and certain death.[129]

Still others practised intellectual disciplines. Many, many prisoners wrote or memorized poetry, repeating their verses and those of others to themselves over and over again, later repeating them to friends. In Moscow, in the 1960s, Ginzburg once met a writer who could not believe that in such conditions prisoners had really been able to repeat poems to themselves and derive mental relief from doing so. 'Yes, yes,' he told her: 'he knew I was not the first person to attest to this, but, well, it still seemed to him that the idea came to us after the event.' Ginzburg writes that the man did not understand her generation, the men and women who still belonged to an 'epoch of magnificent illusions ... we were flinging ourselves into Communism from the poetic heights'.[130]

Nina Gagen-Torn, herself an ethnographer, wrote poetry, often singing her own verses to herself:

In the camps I understood, at a practical level, why pre-literate cultures had always passed on texts in the form of song – otherwise you don't remember, you can't be sure of the exact words. Books appeared among us accidentally, they were given and then taken away. Writing was forbidden, as were study groups: the authorities feared they would lead to counter-revolution. Thus did everyone prepare for himself, as well as he could, food for the brain.[131]

Shalamov has written that poetry, among 'pretence and evil, decay' saved him from becoming completely callous. This is one verse he wrote, entitled 'To a Poet':

> I ate as a beast, growling over food
> A simple sheet of writing-paper
> Seemed a miracle
> Falling from the sky to the dark forest.
>
> I drank as a beast, lapping up water
> Soaking my long whiskers
> Measuring my life not by months or years
> But by hours.
>
> And every evening
> Surprised that I was still alive
> I repeated verses
> As if I heard your voice.
>
> And I whispered them as prayers,
> I honoured them as the water of life
> As an icon saved in battle
> As a guiding star.
>
> They were the only link with another life
> There, where the world choked us
> With everyday filth
> And death followed closely on our heels.[132]

Solzhenitsyn 'wrote' poetry in the camps, composing it in his head and then reciting it to himself with the aid of a collection of broken matchsticks, as his biographer Michael Scammell recounts:

He would lay out two rows of ten pieces of matchstick with his cigarette-case, one row representing tens and the other units. He then recited his verses silently to himself, moving one 'unit' for each line and one 'ten' for every ten lines. Every fiftieth and hundredth line was memorized with special care, and once a month he recited the whole poem once through. If a line was misplaced or forgotten, he would go through the whole thing again until he got it right.[133]

Perhaps for similar reasons, prayer helped some too. The memoir of one Baptist believer, sent to the post-Stalinist camps in the 1970s, consists almost entirely of accounts of when and where he prayed, and of where and how he hid his bibles.[134] Many memoirists have written of the importance of religious festivals. Easter could take place secretly, in a camp bakery – as it did one year in a Solovetsky transit prison – or it could take place openly, in transport trains: 'the wagon rocked, the songs were discordant and shrill, the guards banged on the wagon walls at every stop. Still, they kept singing.'[135] Christmas could take place in a barrack. Yuri Zorin, a Russian prisoner, recalled with amazement how well the Lithuanians in his camp had organized the celebration of Christmas, a feast which they had begun preparing for a year in advance: 'Can you imagine, in the barracks, a table laid with everything, vodka, ham, everything.' They had, he thought, brought the vodka in 'by thimblefuls' in their shoes.[136]

Lev Kopelev, himself an atheist, attended a secret Easter ceremony:

The beds were placed alongside the walls. There was a fragrant smell of incense. A little table covered by a blanket was the altar. Several home-made candles cast their glow on an icon. The priest, wearing vestments made of sheets, held up an iron cross. The candles flickered in the dark. We could hardly see the faces of the others in the room, but I felt sure that we were not the only unbelievers present. The priest chanted the service in an old man's quaver. Several women in white handkerchiefs joined in softly, their voices ardent and pure. A choir gave harmonious responses, softly, softly, in order not to be heard outside.[137]

Kazimierz Zarod was among fellow Poles who celebrated the Christmas Eve of 1940 in a labour camp, under the guidance of a priest who stole quietly around the camp that evening, saying Mass in each barracks:

Without benefit of Bible or prayer book, he began to speak the words of the Mass, the familiar Latin, spoken in a whisper barely audible and answered so quietly it was like a sigh –

'Kyrie eleison, Christe eleison – Lord have mercy on us. Christ have mercy on us. Gloria in excelsis Deo . . .'

The words washed over us and the atmosphere in the hut, usually so brutal and raw, changed imperceptibly, the faces turned towards the priest softening and relaxing as the men strained to hear the barely discernible whisper.

'All clear,' came the voice of the man sitting watching from the window.[138]

More broadly, involvement in some larger intellectual or artistic project kept many educated people alive, spiritually and physically – for those with gifts or talents often found practical uses for them. In a world of constant shortage, for example, where the most elementary possessions took on enormous significance, people who could supply something others needed were in constant demand. Thus did Prince Kirill Golitsyn learn to make needles of fishbone while still in Butyrka prison.[139] Thus did Alexander Dolgun, before he found his job as *feldsher*, look around for a way to 'make a few roubles or extra grams of bread':

I saw that there was a very good supply of aluminium in the cables that the arc welders used. I thought that if I could learn to melt it down, I might be able to mould some spoons. I did a little talking around to some prisoners who seemed to know what they were doing with metal, and picked up some ideas without giving my own away. I also found some good hiding places, where you could spend part of the day without being rousted out to work, and some other hiding places where you could conceal tools or bits of scrap aluminium wire.

I built two shallow boxes for my foundry, stole myself some scraps of aluminium wire, fashioned a rough crucible from some thin steel from the stove works, scrounged some good charcoal and diesel fuel to fire my forge, and was ready to go into business.

Soon, wrote Dolgun, he was able to 'turn out two spoons almost every day'. These he traded to other prisoners for a water flask, and for cooking oil to keep inside it. That way he had something in which to dip his bread.[140]

Not all of the objects that prisoners produced for one another were necessarily utilitarian. Anna Andreevna, an artist, received constant requests for her services – and not only from prisoners. She was asked by the camp authorities to decorate a tombstone during a funeral, to fix broken crockery and toys, and to make toys as well: 'We did everything for the bosses, whatever they needed or asked.'[141] Another prisoner carved small 'souvenirs' for other prisoners out of mammoth tusks: bracelets, small figurines with 'northern' themes, rings, medallions, buttons. Occasionally, he felt guilty for taking money from other prisoners: 'But so what? Everyone is free to think for themselves . . . for work it is not shameful to take money.'[142]

The museum of the Memorial Society in Moscow, set up by ex-prisoners and dedicated to telling the history of Stalin's repressions, is to this day full of such things: bits of embroidered lace, hand-carved trinkets, painted playing cards and even small works of art – paintings, drawings, sculptures – which prisoners preserved, brought home with them, and later donated.

The goods that prisoners learned to provide were not always tangible, either. Strange though it sounds, in the Gulag it was possible to sing – or dance, or act – for your life. This was true particularly for talented prisoners in the larger camps, with the flashier bosses, those who longed to show off their camp orchestras and theatrical troupes. If the commander of Ukhtizhemlag aspired to maintain a real opera troupe – as one of them did – that meant that the lives of dozens of singers and dancers would be saved. At the very least, they would get time off from work in the forests for rehearsals. More importantly, they might regain some feeling of humanity. 'When the actors were onstage, they forgot about their constant feeling of hunger, about their lack of rights, about the convoy waiting with guard dogs outside the gate,' wrote Aleksandr Klein.[143] While playing in the Dalstroi orchestra, the prisoner and violinist Georgi Feldgun felt 'as if I breathed the full air of freedom'.[144]

Sometimes the rewards were even greater. A document from Dmitlag describes the special clothing to be distributed to members of the camp orchestra – including highly coveted officers' boots – and orders a *lagpunkt* commander to supply them with special barracks as well.[145] Thomas Sgovio visited one such musicians' barrack in Magadan: 'Upon entering, to the right was a separate compartment with a small stove. Foot coverings and felt boots hung on wires stretched from wall to wall. Individual bunks were neatly covered by blankets. Mattresses and pillowcases were filled with straw. Instruments hung on the walls – a tuba, a french horn, a trombone, trumpet, etc. About half the musicians were criminals. All of them held soft jobs – the cook, the barber, the bath manager, the accountants, etc.'[146]

Better conditions were supplied for performers in smaller camps as well, however, and even in some prisons. Georgi Feldgun received extra food while in transit camp, after performing on his violin for a group of criminals. He found the experience very strange: 'Here we are on the edge of the world, in Vanino Port . . . and we are playing eternal music, written more than 200 years ago. We are playing Vivaldi for fifty gorillas.'[147]

Another prisoner found herself in a cell with a troupe of singers and actresses who were, thanks to their talents, not being sent out on the transports to the camps. Seeing their better treatment, she convinced them to let her appear with them, then sang off-key and made fun of herself. Throughout the rest of her camp career, her previously undiscovered comic talents won her extra food and help from her fellow prisoners.[148] Others used humour to survive as well. Dmitri Panin has written of a professional clown from Odessa who performed for his life, knowing that if he made the camp authorities laugh, he would save himself from being transferred to a punishment camp. 'The only incongruity in this gay dance came from the clown's large black eyes, which seemed to be begging for mercy. I have never seen such an emotional performance.'[149]

Out of all the many ways of surviving through collaboration with the authorities, 'saving oneself' through acting in the camp theatre or participating in other cultural activities was the method which seemed to prisoners the least morally problematic. This may have been because other prisoners derived some benefit too. Even for those who did not receive special treatment, the theatre provided tremendous moral support, something which was also necessary for survival. 'For the prisoners, the theatre was the source of happiness, it was loved, it was adored,' wrote one.[150] Gustav Herling remembered that for concerts 'the prisoners took their caps off at the door, shook the snow from their boots in the passage outside, and took their places on the benches with ceremonious anticipation and almost religious awe'.[151]

Perhaps that was why those whose artistic talent enabled them to live better inspired admiration, not envy and hatred. Tatyana Okunevskaya – the film star sent to the camps for her refusal to sleep with Abakumov, the head of Soviet counter-intelligence – was recognized everywhere, and helped by everyone. During one camp concert, she felt what seemed to be stones being thrown at her legs; she looked down and realized they were cans of Mexican pineapple, an unheard-of delicacy, which a group of thieves had acquired just for her.[152]

Nikolai Starostin, the football player, was also held in the highest respect by the *urki*, who, he wrote, passed the message to one another: don't touch Starostin. In the evenings, when he began to recount football stories, the 'card games ceased' as prisoners gathered around him. When he arrived at a new camp, he was usually offered a clean bed in the camp hospital. 'It was the first thing that was proposed to me, whenever I arrived, if, among the doctors or the bosses, there was a fan.'[153]

Only a very few were bothered by the more complex moral question of whether it was 'right' to sing and dance while in prison. Nadezhda Joffe was one of them: 'When I look back at my five years, I am not ashamed to recall them and I have nothing to blush about. There is only the question of the amateur theatre . . . Essentially there was nothing wrong with it, and yet . . . our distant ancestors, in approximately analogous conditions, hung up their lutes and said they wouldn't sing in bondage.'[154]

Some prisoners, particularly those of non-Soviet origin, also had their doubts about the productions. One Polish prisoner, arrested during the war, wrote that the camp theatre was 'designed to destroy your self-respect further . . . Sometimes there were "artistic" performances, or some sort of strange orchestra, but it was not done for the satisfaction of the soul. Rather, it was designed to show you their [Soviet] "culture", to unnerve you further.'[155]

Still, for those who felt uncomfortable, it was not necessary to participate in the official performances. A striking number of political prisoners who wrote memoirs – and this may explain *why* they wrote memoirs – attribute their survival to their ability to 'tell stories': to entertain criminal prisoners by recounting the plots of novels or of films. In the world of the camps and the prisons, where books were scarce and films were rare, a good storyteller was highly prized. Lev Finkelstein says that he will be 'forever grateful to a thief who, on my first prison day, recognized this potential in me, and said, "You've probably read a lot of books. Tell them to people, and you will be living very well." And indeed I was living better than the rest. I had some notoriety, some fame . . . I ran into people who said, "You are Levchik-Romanist [Levchik-the-storyteller], I heard about you in Taishet." ' Because of this skill, Finkelstein was invited, twice a day, into the brigadier leader's hut where he received a mug of hot water. In the quarry where he was then working, 'that meant life'. Finkelstein found, he said, that Russian and foreign classics worked best: he had far less success retelling the plots of more recent, Soviet novels.[156]

Others found the same. On her hot, stuffy train to Vladivostok, Ginzburg learned that 'there were material advantages in reciting poetry . . . For instance, after each act of Griboyedov's *The Misfortune of Being Clever*, I was given a drink of water out of someone else's mug as a reward for "services to the community".'[157]

Aleksander Wat retold Stendhal's *The Red and the Black* to a group of bandits while in prison.[158] Alexander Dolgun recounted the plot of *Les Misérables*.[159] Janusz Bardach told the story of *The Three Musketeers*: 'I felt my status rise with every twist of the plot.'[160] In response to the thieves who dismissed the starving politicals as 'vermin', Colonna-Czosnowski also defended himself by telling them 'my own version of a film, suitably embellished for maximum dramatic effect, which I had seen in Poland some years earlier. It was a "Cops and Robbers" story, taking place in Chicago, involving Al Capone. For good measure, I threw in Bugsy Malone, maybe even Bonnie and Clyde. I decided to include everything I could remember, plus some extra refinements which I invented on the spur of the moment.' The story impressed its listeners, and they asked the Pole to repeat it many times: 'Like children, they would listen intently. They didn't mind hearing the same stories over and over again. Like children, too, they liked me to use the same words every time. They also noticed the slightest change or the smallest omission ... within three weeks of my arrival I was a different man.'[161]

Yet an artistic gift did not need to earn a prisoner money or bread in order to save his life. Nina Gagen-Torn describes a musical historian, a lover of Wagner, who managed to write an opera while in the camps. Voluntarily, she chose to work cleaning camp sewers and outhouses, since this otherwise unpleasant job gave her enough freedom to think through her music.[162] Aleksei Smirnov, one of contemporary Russia's leading advocates of press freedom, tells the story of two literary scholars who, while in the camps, created a fictitious eighteenth-century French poet, and wrote pastiche eighteenth-century French verse.[163] Gustav Herling also derived enormous benefit from the 'lessons' in the history of literature which he received from a former professor: his teacher, he speculated, may have benefited even more.[164]

Irena Arginskaya was even helped by her aesthetic sensibility. Years after her release, she could still speak of the 'incredible beauty' of the far north, how at times the sunsets and the views of the open spaces and great forests left her breathless. It even once happened that her mother made the long, terrible journey to visit her in camp, only to discover upon arrival that her daughter had been taken away to hospital: the visit was in vain. Nevertheless, she spoke 'until the end of her life', as did her daughter, about the beauty of the taiga.[165]

And yet – beauty could not help everybody, and its perception was subjective. Surrounded by the same taiga, the same open air, the same sweeping landscapes, Nadezhda Ulyanovskaya found that the scenery made her feel only disgust: 'Almost against my will, I remember grandiose sunrises and sunsets, pine tree forests, bright flowers which for some reason had no scent.'[166]

So struck was I by this comment, that when I myself visited the far north in high summer, I looked with different eyes at the wide rivers and the endless forests of Siberia, at the empty moonscape that is the Arctic tundra. Just outside a coal mine, which stands on what used to be a Vorkuta *lagpunkt*, I even picked a handful of Arctic wild flowers to see if they had a scent. They do. Perhaps Ulyanovskaya had simply not wanted to detect it.

18

Rebellion and Escape

If I had heard the sound of the sledge dogs announcing the start of the patrol now, I think I might have been physically sick. We ran the few yards to the outer fence ... we were probably making little noise, but it seemed to me that the commotion was deafening ... In a final mad scramble we leapt and tumbled over the last lot of barbed wire at the foot of the outer fence, picked ourselves up, breathlessly inquired if everyone was all right, and, with one accord, started to run.

– Slavomir Rawicz, *The Long Walk*[1]

Among the many myths about the Gulag, the myth of the impossibility of escape looms among the largest. Escape from Stalin's camps, wrote Solzhenitsyn, was 'an enterprise for giants among men – but for doomed giants'.[2] According to Anatoly Zhigulin, 'Escape from Kolyma was impossible.'[3] Shalamov, with characteristic gloom, wrote that 'convicts who try to escape are almost always newcomers, serving their first year, men in whose hearts freedom and vanity had not yet been annhilated'.[4] Nikolai Abakumov, the former deputy commander of the Norilsk garrison, dismissed the idea of successful escape: 'Some people got out of the camps, but no one managed to reach the "mainland", – by which he meant central Russia.[5]

Gustav Herling recounts the story of a fellow inmate who tried to escape and failed: after months of careful planning, a successful break-out, and seven days of hungry wandering in the forest, he found himself only eight miles from the camp, and, starving, voluntarily turned himself in. 'Freedom isn't for us,' the man concluded, whenever he told the story of his escape attempt to his fellow prisoners. 'We're chained to this place for the rest of our lives, even though we aren't wearing chains. We can escape, we can wander about, but in the end we'll come back.'[6]

Camps were, of course, constructed to prevent break-outs: ultimately, that was what the walls, barbed wire, watchtowers and carefully raked no man's land were for. But in many camps, barbed wire was hardly necessary to keep prisoners inside. The weather worked against escape – ten months of the year, the temperature was below freezing – as did the geography, a fact it is impossible to appreciate until one has actually seen the location of some of the more distant camps for oneself.

It is, for example, fair to describe Vorkuta, the city which sprang up beside the coal mines of Vorkutlag, not only as isolated but also as virtually inaccessible. There is no road that leads to Vorkuta, which lies beyond the Arctic Circle: the city and its mines can only be reached by rail or by plane. In winter, anyone crossing the open, treeless tundra would be a moving target. In summer, the same landscape turns into an equally open, impenetrable swamp.

In the more southerly camps, distances were a problem too. Even if a prisoner did climb over the barbed wire, or slip away from his workplace in the forest – given the slovenliness of the guards, this was not so difficult – he then found himself miles from a road or a railway track, and sometimes miles from anything resembling a town or village. There was no food, no shelter, and sometimes very little water.

More to the point, there were sentries everywhere: the whole of the Kolyma region – hundreds and hundreds of square miles of taiga – was really a vast prison, after all, as were the entire Komi Republic, large swathes of the Kazakh desert and northern Siberia. In such places, there were few ordinary villages, and few ordinary inhabitants. Anyone walking alone without proper identity documents would have immediately been identified as a runaway, and either shot, or beaten up and returned to his camp. One prisoner decided against joining a group of escaping inmates for this reason: 'Where could I go without papers or money in a territory packed with concentration camps and therefore scattered with control points?'[7]

The escaping prisoner was not likely to find much help from those local people who were not guards or prisoners, either, even if he encountered any. In tsarist Siberia, there had been a tradition of sympathy for runaway convicts and serfs, for whom bowls of bread and milk were placed on doorsteps at night. An old, pre-revolutionary prisoners' song describes the attitude:

> The peasant women provided me milk
> The young lads supplied tobacco.[8]

In Stalin's Soviet Union, the mood was different. Most people would have been inclined to turn in an escaped 'enemy', and even more inclined to turn in a criminal 'recidivist'. This was not only because they believed, or half believed, the propaganda about the prisoners, but also because those who failed to turn in a runaway risked being given long prison sentences themselves.[9] Not that their fears needed to be specific, given the paranoid climate of daily life:

As for the local population, nobody saved us and hid us, the way others saved and hid those who escaped from the German concentration camps. It was because for so many years, all had lived in constant fear and suspicion, from minute to minute awaiting some new misfortune, even being afraid of each other . . . In a place where everyone, from the smallest to the most important, was terrified of spies, it was impossible to count on a successful escape.[10]

If ideology and fear did not impel the locals to turn in escaped prisoners, greed did. Fairly or unfairly, many memoirists believe that local tribal peoples – the Eskimos of the far north, the Kazakhs to the south – were constantly on the lookout for runaways. Some became professional bounty-hunters, searching for prisoners in return for a kilogram of tea or a bag of wheat.[11] In Kolyma, a local inhabitant who brought in the right hand of a runaway – or, by some accounts, the runaway's head – received a 250-rouble prize, and the prizes seem to have been similar elsewhere.[12] In one recorded case, a local man recognized an escaped prisoner masquerading as a free man, and reported his presence to the police. He received 250 roubles. His son, who had gone to the police station, received 150 as well. In another case, a man who reported the location of a runaway to a camp chief was given the princely sum of 300 roubles.[13]

For those who were caught, the punishments were extreme. Many were shot instantly. The bodies of dead runaways had their propaganda uses as well:

As we approached the gate, I thought for a moment that I must be having a bad dream: a naked corpse was suspended from the gatepost. Its hands and feet were bound with wire, its head was sunk to one side, the rigid eyes were half open. Above the head was a board with the inscription: 'This is the fate of all those who try to escape from Norilsk.'[14]

Zhigulin remembers the dead bodies of men who had attempted escape lying in the centre of his Kolyma *lagpunkt*, sometimes for as long as a month.[15] The practice was in fact an old one, dating back to Solovetsky. By the 1940s, it was nearly universal.[16]

And yet – prisoners did try to escape. Indeed, to judge by the official statistics, and by the angry correspondence on the subject in the Gulag archives, both attempted and successful escapes were more common than most memoirists concede. There are, for example, records of punishments meted out following successful escapes. In 1945, following several group escapes from the camps surrounding 'NKVD Construction Site 500' – a railroad across eastern Siberia – officers in the armed guards received five- or ten-day prison sentences, with their pay docked 50 per cent for every day behind bars. In other instances, guards were put on trial following prominent escapes, while camp bosses sometimes lost their jobs.[17]

There are also records of guards who foiled escapes. A 300-rouble prize was awarded to a prison guard who sounded the alarm after escaping prisoners had suffocated a night watchman. His boss received 200 roubles, as did another prison chief, and the soldiers involved received 100 roubles apiece.[18]

No camp was completely secure. Solovetsky, with its remote location, was thought to be impregnable. Yet a pair of White Guards, S. A. Malsagov and Yuri Bessonov, escaped from one of the SLON mainland camps in May 1925. After attacking their guards, they walked for thirty-five days to the Finnish border. Both later wrote books about their experiences, among the first about Solovetsky to appear in the West.[19] There was another famous break-out from Solovetsky in 1928, in which half a dozen prisoners attacked their guards and broke through the gates of the camp. Most got away, probably escaping over the Finnish border too.[20] Two particularly spectacular escapes, also from Solovetsky, occurred in 1934. One involved four 'spies'; the other concerned 'one spy and two bandits'. Both parties had managed to steal boats, and had escaped by water, presumably to Finland. As a result, the camp boss was fired, and others were reprimanded.[21]

As the SLON camps expanded on to the Karelian mainland in the late 1920s, opportunities for escape multiplied – and Vladimir Tchernavin took advantage of them. Tchernavin was a fisheries expert who had bravely tried to inject some realism into the Murmansk Fishing Trust's Five-Year Plan. His criticism of the project won him a conviction for 'wrecking'. He received a five-year sentence and was sent to Solovetsky. SLON eventually put him to work as a prisoner expert in northern Karelia, where he was meant to design new fishing enterprises.

Tchernavin bided his time. Over many months he won the trust of his superiors, who even granted permission for his wife and fifteen-year-old son, Andrei, to pay him a visit. One day during their visit, in the summer of 1933, the family headed off on a 'picnic' across the local bay. When they reached the western edge, Tchernavin and his wife told Andrei that they were leaving the USSR – on foot. 'Without compass or map, we walked over wild mountains, through forests and across swamps, to Finland and freedom,' wrote Tchernavin.[22] Decades later, Andrei remembered that his father had believed he could change the world's view of Soviet Russia if he wrote a book about his experiences. He did. It did not.[23]

But Tchernavin's experience may not have been unique: indeed, the period of the Gulag's early expansion might well have been the golden age of escape. The number of prisoners was multiplying rapidly, the number of guards was insufficient, the camps were relatively near to Finland. In 1930, 1,174 escaped convicts were captured on the Finnish border. By 1932, 7,202 had been found – and it may well be that the number of successful attempts also went up proportionately.[24] According to the Gulag's own statistics – which may not, of course, be accurate – in 1933, 45,755 people escaped from camps, of which only just over half – 28,370 – were captured.[25] The local population was reported to be terrorized by the huge number of convicts on the loose, and camp commanders submitted constant requests for reinforcements, as did the border guards and the local OGPU.[26]

In response, the OGPU instituted tighter controls. At about this time, the local population were actively recruited to help: one OGPU order called for the creation of a 25–30-kilometre belt around each camp, within which the local population would 'actively fight escapes'. Those in charge of trains and boats in the vicinity of camps were also enlisted. An order was also issued forbidding guards to take prisoners out of their cells after sundown.[27] Local officials begged for more resources, and especially for more guards to prevent escapes.[28] New laws mandated extra prison sentences for escapees. Guards knew that if they shot a prisoner in the course of an escape, they might even be rewarded.[29]

Nevertheless, the numbers did not fall so quickly. In 1930s Kolyma, group escapes were more common than they became later. Criminal prisoners, camping out in the forests, would organize themselves into bands, steal weapons, and even attack local residents, geological parties and native villages. After no fewer than twenty-two such incidents, a special camp division was set up for 1,500 'especially dangerous elements' – prisoners likely to escape – in 1936.[30] Later, in January 1938, at the height of the Great Terror, one of the deputy chiefs of the NKVD sent out a circular to all the camps across the Soviet Union, noting that 'despite a series of orders on conducting a decisive war against prisoners' escapes from camps . . . serious improvements in this matter have yet to be made'.[31]

In the early days of the Second World War, the number of escapes rose sharply again, thanks to opportunities created by the evacuation of camps in the western part of the country, and the general chaos.[32] In July 1941, fifteen prisoners escaped from Pechorlag, one of the more remote camps in the Komi Republic. In August of that same year, eight former sailors, led by a former senior lieutenant of the Northern Fleet, managed to get away from a distant outpost of Vorkuta itself.[33]

The numbers did start to go down later in the war, but they never vanished altogether. In 1947, when escapes reached their post-war height, 10,440 prisoners attempted escape, of whom only 2,894 were caught.[34] This is, perhaps, a small percentage of the millions who were in the camps at the time, but it nevertheless suggests that escapes were not as impossible as some remember. It may even be that their frequency helps to explain the harshening of camp regimes, and the higher levels of security, which characterized life in the Gulag during the last half-decade of its existence.

Generally, memoirists agree that the overwhelming majority of would-be runaways were professional criminals. Criminal slang reflects this, even referring to the coming of spring as the arrival of the 'green prosecutor' (as in

'Vasya was released by the green prosecutor') since spring was when summer escapes were most often contemplated: 'A trip through the taiga is possible only during the summer, when it is possible to eat grass, mushrooms, berries, roots, or pancakes baked from moss flour, to catch fieldmice, chipmunks, squirrels, jays, rabbits . . .'[35] In the very far north, the optimum time to escape was the winter, which criminals there referred to as the 'white prosecutor': only then would the swamps and mud of the tundra be passable.[36]

In fact, professional criminals were more successful at escaping because once they had gone 'under the wire' they stood a far better chance of surviving. If they made it to a major city, they could melt into the local criminal world, forge documents and find hiding places. With few aspirations to return to the 'free' world, criminals also escaped simply for the fun of it, just to be 'out' for a little while. If they were caught, and managed to survive, what was another ten-year sentence to someone who already had two 25-year sentences, or more? One ex-*zek* remembers a woman criminal who escaped merely to have a rendezvous with a man. She returned 'filled with delight', although she was immediately sentenced to the punishment cell.[37]

Political prisoners escaped much less often. Not only did they lack the network and the expertise, but they were also pursued with greater fervour. Tchernavin – who gave these issues much thought before escaping himself – explained the difference:

The guards did not take the escape of criminals very seriously and did not exert much effort in pursuing them: they would be caught when they came out to the railroad or reached a town. But for the pursuit of political prisoners, posses would be organized at once: sometimes all neighbouring villages would be mobilized and the frontier guards called to assist. The political prisoner always tried to escape abroad – in his motherland he had no refuge.[38]

Most runaways were men, but not all of them. Margarete Buber-Neumann was in a camp from which a Gypsy girl escaped, running away with the camp cook. An older Gypsy woman, hearing the story, nodded knowingly: 'She's got an idea there's a *tabor* [a Gypsy encampment] somewhere in the neighbourhood. If she can get to that, she's safe.'[39] Usually, escapes were planned in advance, but they could be spontaneous too: Solzhenitsyn tells the story of a prisoner who jumped over a barbed-wire fence during a dust storm in Kazakhstan.[40] Escape attempts were often launched from the more loosely guarded camp work sites, but that was not always the case either. In the randomly selected month of September 1945, for example, 51 per cent of recorded escape attempts took place in the working zone; 27 per cent took place from the living zone; and 11 per cent took place during transport.[41] Edward Buca planned an escape from a prisoner transport train bound for Siberia, along with a group of young Ukrainians:

With my hacksaw blade, we would try to cut through four or five planks, working only at night and concealing the marks with a mixture of bread and horse dung from the floor of the car. When the opening was ready, we would wait until the train stopped in the forest and then push out the planks and leap from the wagon – as many of us as possible, scattering in all directions to confuse the guard. Some of us would be shot at, but most of us could get away.[42]

They had to give up the plan when the escape attempt was suspected. Others did try to escape from the trains, however: in June 1940, two criminal prisoners actually got out through a hole in a wagon.[43] In that same year, Janusz Bardach slipped through some rotten boards in a wagon too. He neglected to fix them back in place, however, and was immediately caught, tracked down by dogs, and badly beaten – but allowed to live.[44]

Some escapes had their origins, as Solzhenitsyn puts it, 'not in despairing impulse but in technical calculations and the love of fine workmanship'.[45] False walls were built into railway boxcars; prisoners hammered themselves into boxes and had themselves shipped out of the camp.[46] Once, twenty-six criminal prisoners dug their way under a wall. All made it out, although – according to the officer who led the search – they were also all captured again within the year.[47]

Others, like Tchernavin, used their special positions within the camp to organize their escape. Archives record the story of a prisoner who deliberately caused an accident on a goods train and escaped amid the confusion.[48] In another recorded case, prisoners who had been assigned to bury bodies in the camp cemetery shot their convoy guard and placed him in the mass grave, so that his corpse would not be immediately noticed.[49] Escape was also easier for 'unguarded' prisoners who had passes allowing them to move about between camps.

Disguise was used as well. Shalamov tells the story of a prisoner who escaped and managed to spend two years in freedom, wandering through Siberia, pretending to be a geologist. At one point, regional authorities, proud to have such an expert in their midst, asked him very respectfully to give a lecture. 'Krivoshei smiled, quoted Shakespeare in English, sketched something on the blackboard and ran through dozens of foreign names.' He was caught, in the end, because he sent money to his wife.[50] His story might possibly be apocryphal – but the archives do record similar tales. In one such episode, a Kolyma prisoner stole some documents, smuggled himself on to a plane, and flew to Yakutsk. There he was found, comfortably installed in a hotel, with 200 grams of gold in his pocket.[51]

Not all escapes involved clever flights of fancy. Many – probably the majority – criminal escapes involved violence. Runaways attacked, shot and suffocated armed guards, as well as free workers and local residents.[52] They did not spare their fellow inmates either. One of the standard methods of criminal escape involved cannibalism. Pairs of criminals would agree in advance to escape along with a third man (the 'meat'), who was destined to become the sustenance for the other two on their journey. Buca also describes the trial of a professional thief and murderer, who, along with a colleague, escaped with the camp cook, their 'walking supply':

They weren't the first to get this idea. When you have a huge community of people who dream of nothing but escape, it is inevitable that every possible means of doing so will be discussed. A 'walking supply' is, in fact, a fat prisoner. If you have to, you can kill him and eat him. And until you need him, he is carrying the 'food' himself.

The two men did as planned – they killed and ate the cook – but they had not bargained on the length of the journey. They began to get hungry again:

Both knew in their hearts that the first to fall asleep would be killed by the other. So both pretended they weren't tired and spent the night telling stories, each watching the other closely. Their old friendship made it impossible for either to make an open attack on the other, or to confess their mutual suspicions.

Finally, one fell asleep. The other slit his throat. He was caught, Buca claims, two days later, with pieces of raw flesh still in his sack.[53]

Although there is no way of knowing how often this type of escape occurred, there are enough similar stories, told by a wide enough range of prisoners, from camps from the early 1930s to the late 1940s, to be certain that they did take place, at least from time to time.[54] Thomas Sgovio heard the death sentence pronounced on two such escapees – they had taken a boy prisoner, and salted his flesh after murdering him – when he was in Kolyma.[55] Vatslav Dvorzhetsky was told a similar story in Karelia, in the mid-1930s.[56]

There are also to be found, in the oral tradition of the Gulag, some truly extraordinary tales of escape and of escapers – many, again, quite possibly apocryphal. Solzhenitsyn relates the saga of Georgi Tenno, an Estonian political who escaped from camps over and over again, on one occasion travelling 500 kilometres by horse, boat and bicycle, very nearly making it to the central Siberian city of Omsk. While some of Tenno's stories are probably true – he later befriended another Gulag survivor and memoirist, Alexander Dolgun, whom he also introduced to Solzhenitsyn – some of his other, more spectacular tales of escape are harder to verify.[57] One English anthology contains the story of an Estonian, a preacher, who managed to escape from a camp, forge papers, and walk over the border to Afghanistan with his companions. The same anthology tells of a Spanish prisoner who escaped by pretending to be dead after an earthquake wrecked his camp. Later, he says, he slipped over the border to Iran.[58]

Finally, there is the curious case of Slavomir Rawicz, whose memoir, *The Long Walk*, contains the most spectacular and moving description of an escape in all of Gulag literature. According to his account, Rawicz was captured after the Soviet invasion of Poland, and deported to a camp in northern Siberia. He claims to have escaped, with the connivance of a camp commander's wife, in the company of six other prisoners, one of them an American. Along with a Polish girl, a deportee whom they picked up along the way, they made their way out of the Soviet Union.

During what would have been an extraordinary journey – if it ever took place – they walked round Lake Baikal, over the border into Mongolia, across the Gobi Desert, over the Himalayas and Tibet, and into India. Along the way, four of the prisoners died; the rest suffered extremes of privation. Unfortunately, several attempts to verify this story – which bears a distinct resemblance to a Rudyard Kipling short story, 'The Man Who Was' – have come to nothing.[59] *The Long Walk* is a superbly told story, even if it never happened. Its convincing realism may well serve as a lesson to all of us who try to write a factual history of escapes from the Gulag.

For, in fact, fantasy about escape played an important part in many prisoners' lives. Even for the many thousands of prisoners who never would attempt it, the thought of escape – the dream of escape – remained an important psychological prop. A Kolyma survivor told me that 'one of the most obvious forms of opposition to the regime was to escape'. Young male prisoners in particular planned, discussed and argued about the best ways of escape. For some, this discussion itself was a way of fighting the sensation of powerlessness, as Gustav Herling writes:

We would often meet in one of the barracks, an intimate group of Poles, to discuss the details of the plan; we collected scraps of metal found at work, old boxes and fragments of glass which we deluded ourselves could be made into an improvised compass; we gathered information about the surrounding countryside, and the distances, climatic conditions and geographical peculiarities of the north . . .

In the nightmare land to which we had been brought from the West on hundreds of goods trains, every grasp at our own private day-dreams gave us fresh life. After all, if membership of a non-existent terrorist organization can be a crime punished by ten years in a labour camp, then why should a sharpened nail not be a compass-needle, a piece of wood a ski, and a scrap of paper, covered with scribbled dots and lines, a map?

Herling suspects that everyone involved in these discussions believed, deep down, that their preparations were futile. Nevertheless, the exercise served its purpose:

I remember a junior officer of the Polish cavalry who, during the worst periods of hunger in the camp, found enough strength of will to cut a thin slice of bread from his daily ration, dry it over the fire, and save these scraps in a sack which he concealed in some mysterious hiding place in the barrack. Years later, we met again in the Iraqi desert, and as we recalled prison days over a bottle in an army tent, I made fun of his 'plan' of escape. But he answered gravely: 'You shouldn't laugh at that. I survived the camp thanks to hope of escape, and I survived the mortuary thanks to my store of bread. A man can't live if he doesn't know what he's living for.'[60]

If escapes from the camp were impossible in the folk memory of most survivors, rebellion was unthinkable. The caricature of the downtrodden, defeated and dehumanized zek, desperate to collaborate with the authorities, incapable even of thinking ill of the Soviet regime – let alone organizing against it – appears in many memoirs, not least those of two of the Russian survivor community's greatest literary figures: Solzhenitsyn and Shalamov. And it may well be that, throughout much of the Gulag's history, this image was not far off the mark. The system of internal spying and informers did make prisoners suspicious of one another. The grinding inevitability of the work and the dominance of the thieves-in-law did make it difficult for other prisoners to think of organized opposition. The humiliating experience of interrogation, prison and deportation had robbed many of the will to live, let alone the will to oppose the authorities. Herling, who organized a hunger strike with a group of other Polish prisoners, describes the reaction of his Russian friends:

They were excited and fascinated by the very fact that we had dared to lift a hand against the unalterable law of slavery, which had never before been disturbed by one gesture of rebellion. On the other hand, there was the instinctive fear, which they had retained from their former lives, that they might be involved in something dangerous, perhaps a case threatened by a war tribunal. Who was to know whether the hearings would not reveal the 'rebel's' conversations in the barracks immediately after committing the offence?[61]

Once again, however, archives tell a different story, revealing the existence of many minor camp protests and work stoppages. Criminal bosses in particular seemed to have conducted frequent, brief, apolitical workplace strikes if they wanted something from the camp authorities, who treated such incidents as nothing more than an annoyance. Particularly in the late 1930s and early 1940s, the professional criminals' privileged position would have made them less afraid of punishment, and would have given them more opportunities to organize these minor rebellions.[62]

Spontaneous criminal protests sometimes also occurred on the long train rides to the east, when there was no water available and no food except salted herring. To force the guards to give them water, the criminal prisoners would agree to 'set up a cry and clamour together', creating a noise that the guards hated, as one prisoner remembered: 'Once, the Roman legion wept at the sound of the ancient Germans' shriek, it was so terrifying. The same terror was felt by the sadists of the Gulag . . .'[63] This tradition lasted through the 1980s, when, as the poet and dissident Irina Ratushinskaya recalled, prisoners on a transport, if dissatisfied with their treatment, would carry the protest one step further:

'Hey, fellas! Start 'er rocking!' comes a male voice.

The prisoners bodily start to rock the carriage. All together, in unison, throwing themselves first against one wall of their enclosures, then against the opposite one. The carriage is so packed that the results can be felt immediately. In this manner, the carriage can be tipped off the tracks, derailing the whole train.[64]

Overcrowding and poor food could also produce protests of a sort best described as semi-organized outbreaks of hysteria. A witness described one such scene, led by a group of female criminals:

About 200 women, as if by command, suddenly undressed and ran completely naked into the yard. In rude poses, they crowded around the guards and shouted, screeched, laughed and swore, fell on the ground in terrifying convulsions, tore at their hair, scratched blood from their faces, fell again on the ground and again stood up and ran to the gate.

'A-a-a-a-a-a-a-gh!' howled the crowd.[65]

Aside from these moments of madness and spontaneity, there was another, older tradition of protest used, one whose goals and methods were inherited directly from the earliest politicals (who in turn had inherited them from pre-revolutionary Russia), the Social Democrats, Anarchists and Mensheviks who were imprisoned in the early 1920s. This group of prisoners kept up their tradition of hunger strikes after they were sent to isolator prisons, away from Solovetsky, in 1925. Aleksandr Fedodeev, one of the leaders of the Social Revolutionaries, went on conducting hunger strikes in Suzdal prison, demanding the right to correspond with his relatives, right up to the moment of his execution in 1937.[66]

But even after they had been moved on again, from the prisons back to camps, some still tried to keep the tradition going. In the mid-1930s, the social-ists were joined in their hunger strikes by some of the genuine Trotskyites. In October of 1936, hundreds of Trotskyites, Anarchists and other political prisoners in one Vorkuta *lagpunkt* began a hunger strike that was to last, according to records, 132 days. Without question, their purpose was political: the strikers demanded that they be separated from criminal prisoners, that their working day be limited to eight hours, that they should be fed regardless of their work – and that their sentences should be annulled. In another Vorkuta *lagpunkt*, an even larger strike – joined, in this case, by a handful of professional criminals – was to last 115 days. In March 1937, the Gulag administration decreed that the strikers' demands were to be met. By the end of 1938, however, most had been murdered in the mass executions of that year.[67]

At about the same time, another group of Trotskyites went on strike in the Vladivostok transit camp, while awaiting transit to Kolyma. While in the camp, they held organizational meetings and elected a leader. He demanded the right to examine the boat that they would be transported in. The request was refused. Still, as they got on the boat, they sang revolutionary songs and even – if the reports of the NKVD's informers are to be believed – unfurled posters with slogans such as 'Hooray for Trotsky, Revolutionary Genius!' and 'Down with Stalin!' When the steamer reached Kolyma, the prisoners again began making demands: everyone should receive work according to his speciality, everyone must be paid for his work, spouses must not be divided, all prisoners have a right to send and receive mail without restriction. In due course, they called a series of hunger strikes, one of which lasted 100 days. A contemporary observer wrote that 'The leadership of the Trotskyite prisoners at Kolyma had entered a fantasy realm, and ignored the real power relationships.' In due course, they too were all sentenced and shot.[68] Yet their suffering made an impact. Years later, a former Kolyma prosecutor remembered the events very well:

Everything that happened afterwards made such a strong impression on me and my comrades, that for several days I myself wandered around as if in a fog, and in front of me seemed to walk a row of sentenced Trotskyite fanatics, fearlessly departing this life with their slogans on their lips . . .[69]

In response, perhaps, to these incidents of rebellion, the NKVD began to treat political hunger strikes and work strikes with more seriousness. From the late 1930s onwards, perpetrators of such disruptions received additional prison sentences, even death sentences. Hunger strikes were taken seriously, but work refusals were taken most seriously of all: they ran counter to the entire ethos of the camp. The prisoner who would not work was not only a disciplinary problem, he was a serious obstacle to the camp's economic goals as well. After 1938 in particular, strikers were severely punished, as one ex-prisoner described:

Some of the prisoners refused to go out to work . . . something about the food being rotten. The administration of course acted with vigour. Fourteen of the ringleaders, twelve men and two women, were shot. The executions took place in the camp, with all the prisoners lined up to see the show. Then details from every barrack helped dig the graves, just outside the barbed-wire fence. Not much chance for another riot as long as the memory of this one remains fresh . . .[70]

But even the prospect of certain punishment – and the awareness of certain death – could not altogether eliminate every prisoner's urge to rebel, and later, following Stalin's death, some of them would do so *en masse*. Yet even during Stalin's lifetime, even during the toughest, most difficult war years, the spirit of rebellion lived on – as the remarkable story of the Ust-Usa uprising of January 1942 well illustrates.

*

In the annals of the Gulag, the Ust-Usa rebellion was, as far as we know, unique. If there were other mass break-outs while Stalin was alive, we do not yet know about them. About Ust-Usa we know quite a lot: garbled versions of the story have long been part of the Gulag's oral history, but in recent years it has been carefully documented as well.[71]

Oddly enough, this rebellion was led not by a prisoner, but by a free worker. Mark Retyunin was, at that time, the chief administrator of the Lesoreid *lagpunkt*, a small logging camp within the Vorkutlag complex. The *lagpunkt* held about 200 prisoners, more than half of whom were politicals. Retyunin had had much experience in the camp system by 1942: like many minor camp bosses, he was a former prisoner, having served ten years for alleged bank robbery. Nevertheless, he was trusted by the camp administration, one of whom described him as a man 'prepared to sacrifice his life for the productive interests of the camp'. Others have remembered him variously as a drinker and a card-player – testimony, perhaps, to his criminal origins. Still others describe him as a poetry-lover and as a 'strong character' with a tendency to boasting and brawling – testimony, perhaps, to the legend he left in his wake.

Retyunin's precise motives remain unclear. It seems that he was deeply shocked when, following the outbreak of war in June 1941, the NKVD passed an edict forbidding all political prisoners from leaving their camp, even those whose sentences had expired. Afanasy Yashkin, the only one of the original co-conspirators to survive the rebellion, told his NKVD interrogators that Retyunin had believed that all of the *lagpunkt*'s inhabitants, prisoners and non-prisoners alike, would be executed when the Germans began advancing deeper into the Soviet Union. 'What do we have to lose, even if they kill us,' he had urged them. 'What's the difference: we drop dead tomorrow, or we die today as rebels ... the camp authorities are going to shoot all of those with counter-revolutionary sentences, even us, the free workers who are being held here until the end of the war.' This was not a completely paranoid sentiment: having himself been an inmate of Vorkutlag in 1938, he would have known that mass murder was well within the capabilities of the NKVD. And despite his high status as boss of an entire *lagpunkt*, he had only recently been refused permission to return home on a holiday.

No other details of the preparations are known. Not surprisingly, Retyunin left behind no written documentation. Nevertheless, it is clear from the events themselves that the rebellion was carefully planned. The rebels made their first move on the afternoon of 24 January 1942. This was a Saturday, and the day on which the camp's armed guard planned to use the camp baths. They dutifully filed in. The camp bath attendant, a Chinese inmate named Lu Fa – who was in on the conspiracy – quickly locked the doors behind them. Immediately, the rest of the conspirators disarmed the remaining guards, who had been left standing sentry at the *vakhta*. Two of them fought back. One was killed, and the other wounded. All of their weapons fell into the hands of the rebels, twelve machine-guns and four revolvers in all.

Quickly, a group of the rebels opened the camp storerooms and began distributing high-quality clothing and boots to the prisoners. These had been specially stockpiled by Retyunin, who called on the prisoners to join his uprising. Not all of them did. Some were afraid, some saw the hopelessness of the situation, some even tried to talk the rebels out of continuing altogether. Others agreed. By about five o'clock that afternoon, an hour or so after the rebellion had begun, a group of 100 men were marching in a column towards Ust-Usa, the neighbouring town.

At first, the townspeople, thrown by the well-dressed appearance of the prisoners, did not understand what was happening. Then the rebels, by now split into two groups, attacked the town post office and the town gaol. Both attacks were successful. The rebels opened up the gaol cells, and twelve more prisoners joined their ranks. At the post office, they cut off communication links with the outside world. Ust-Usa had fallen under prisoner control.

At this point, the townspeople began to fight back. A few took up arms at the town militia building. Some rushed to defend the small airfield, where two small planes happened to be on the runway. Others sought help: one of the town policemen leaped on his horse and rode to the nearby *lagpunkt* of Polya-Kurya. There, panic broke out. The camp boss, convinced that the Germans had arrived, immediately ordered all prisoners to remove their shoes, so that they could not escape. Fifteen armed guards began marching from Polya-Kurya to Ust-Usa, thinking they were heading off to defend the motherland.

By this time, open fighting had broken out in the centre of Ust-Usa. The rebels had disarmed some of the town policemen, and had procured more weapons. They failed, however, to reckon with the spirited defenders of the militia building. The subsequent battle raged all night, and by early morning the rebels' losses were serious. Nine were dead, and one was wounded. Forty had been captured. Those who remained alive resolved upon a new tactic: they would leave Ust-Usa, and head for another town, Kozhva. They did not know, however, that the Ust-Usa authorities had already wired for help, using a hidden radio transmitter in the forest. All of the roads leading in every direction were slowly filling up with armed militiamen.

Still, they had some initial luck. Almost immediately, the rebels came upon a village where they met no real resistance. There, they harangued the local collective farmers in an unsuccessful attempt to persuade them to join them. At the post office, they listened in on an open line and realized that the militia were heading in their direction. They left the main road, and headed into the tundra, hiding, initially, at a reindeer farm. On the morning of 28 January they were discovered there: another battle broke out, with heavy casualties on both sides. By nightfall, however, the remaining rebels had escaped – about thirty were still alive – and holed up inside a hunters' shelter on a nearby mountain. Some determined to remain there and fight, although by now, having run out of ammunition, they had no chance. Others set off into the woods where, in the dead of winter, in open country, they stood no chance either.

The final showdown took place on 31 January, and lasted a day and a night. As the militia closed in, some of the rebels, including Retyunin, shot themselves. The NKVD hunted down the rest in the woods, picking them off one by one. The bodies were placed in a heap: the militia, in a frenzy of hatred, mutilated them, and then photographed them. The pictures, preserved in the regional archives, show tormented, twisted bodies, covered in snow and blood. There is no record of where the corpses were buried. Local legend has it that the militia men burned them on the spot.

In the aftermath, the rebels captured earlier were flown to Syktyvkar, the regional capital, and immediately put under investigation. After more than six months of questioning and torture, nineteen received new camp sentences, and forty-nine were executed on 9 August 1942.

The death toll among the defenders of Soviet order was high. But it was not just the loss of a few dozen guards and civilians that worried the NKVD. According to the recorded testimony, Yashkin also went on to 'confess' that Retyunin's ultimate goal was the overthrow of the regional authorities, the imposition of a fascist regime, and, naturally, an alliance with Nazi Germany. Knowing what we know about Soviet methods of interrogation, it is fairly safe to discount these motives.

Still, the rebellion was far more than a typical criminal rebellion: it was clearly politically motivated, and openly anti-Soviet. Nor did the participants fit the profile of the typical criminal runaway: the majority were political prisoners. Rumours of the rebellion would, the NKVD knew, travel quickly around the many nearby camps, which had an unusually high number of politicals during the war years. Some, then and later, suspected that the Germans knew about the Vorkuta camps, and planned to use them as a fifth column, should their march into Russia ever get that far. Rumours that German spies really did parachute into the region persist to this day.

Moscow feared a repeat performance, and took action. On 20 August 1942, all of the bosses of all of the camps in the system received a memorandum: 'On the Increase in Counter-Revolutionary Activities in NKVD Corrective-Labour Camps'. It demanded that they eliminate the 'counter-revolutionary and anti-Soviet element' in their camps within two weeks. The resulting series of investigations, carried out across the Soviet Union, 'uncovered' a massive number of alleged conspiracies, ranging from the 'Committee of People's Liberation' in Vorkuta, to the 'Russian Society for Vengeance Against the Bolsheviks' in Omsk. A report published in 1944 declared that 603 insurgency groups operating within the camps had been uncovered in the years 1941 to 1944, with a total of 4,640 participants.[72]

Doubtless, the vast majority of these groups were fictitious, created in order to prove that the camps' internal informer networks were actually doing something. Nevertheless, the authorities were right to be afraid: the Ust-Usa rebellion really would prove to be a harbinger of the future. Although it was defeated, it was not forgotten: neither were the sufferings of the executed socialists and Trotskyites. A decade later, a new generation of prisoners would re-invent the political strike, picking up where the rebels and the hunger strikers had left off, altering their tactics for a new era.

Properly speaking, however, their story belongs to subsequent chapters. They are not part of the history of life in the camps at the height of the Gulag's reign, but rather part of a later saga: the history of how the Gulag came to an end.

III

The Rise and Fall of the Camp-Industrial Complex, 1940–1986

19
The War Begins

I was a soldier, now I'm a convict
My soul is frozen, my tongue is silent.
What poet, what artist
Will depict my terrible captivity?

And the evil crows didn't know
What sort of sentence they gave us
When they tortured us, when they chased us
From prison to exile to camp.

But wonders occur! Above the quarry
A free star shines
Although my soul is frozen – it is not shattered
Although my tongue is silent – it will speak!

– Leonid Sitko, 1949[1]

Collective Western memory generally recognizes 1 September 1939, the date of the German invasion of western Poland, as the beginning of the Second World War. But in the Russian historical consciousness, neither that day, nor 15 September 1939 – the date of the Soviet invasion of eastern Poland – count as the start of the battle. Dramatic though it was, this joint invasion, arranged in advance through the negotiations that produced the Hitler-Stalin pact, did not directly affect most Soviet citizens.

By contrast, no Soviet citizen ever forgot 22 June 1941 – the day that Hitler launched Operation Barbarossa, his surprise attack on his Soviet allies. Karlo Stajner, then a prisoner in Norilsk, heard the news on the camp radio:

Suddenly the music was interrupted, and we heard Molotov's voice speaking of the Nazis' 'treacherous attack' on the Soviet Union. After a few words, the programme went off the air. There were about a hundred people in the barracks, but you could have heard a pin drop: we were all staring at one another. Vasily's neighbour said: 'It's all over for us now.'[2]

Accustomed to the idea that any major political event was bad for them, political prisoners absorbed the news of the invasion with particular horror. They were right to do so: 'enemies of the people' – now seen as a potential fifth column – were in some cases immediately singled out for increased repression. Some – a so-far unknown number – were executed. Stajner records that on the second day of the war, food supplies were cut: 'sugar was eliminated, and even our soap ration was cut in half'. On the third day of the war, all foreign prisoners were rounded up. Stajner, an Austrian citizen (although he considered himself a Yugoslav communist), was re-arrested, removed from his camp, and gaoled. The camp prosecutors reopened the investigation into his case.

The same pattern repeated itself across the camp system. In Ustvymlag, on the first day of the war, the camp command banned all letters, parcels and newspapers, and took down the camp's radio amplifiers.[3] The bosses of Kolyma removed political prisoners' right to read letters and newspapers, and cut off access to radios too. Everywhere, searches increased, morning counts grew longer. *Lagpunkt* commanders organized special maximum-security barracks for prisoners of German descent. 'All you Burgs, Bergs and Steins, fall out on the left. All you Hindenbergs and Ditgensteins and so forth,' the guards called out, indicating that Evgeniya Ginzburg should join them. She managed to dash into the Registration and Distribution office, and persuaded an inspector to look up her nationality and citizenship: 'This must have been the first time in the history of the world that being Jewish was an advantage.'[4]

The Karlag administration removed all prisoners of Finnish and German origin from the camp lumber factory, and sent them to cut timber. One Finnish-American prisoner remembered that 'After five days the factory stopped production because the Finns and the Germans were the only specialists who knew how to work . . . Without permission from Moscow, they took us back to the factory.'[5]

The most dramatic change, for those affected by it, was the order – also issued on 22 June 1941 – forbidding all prisoners convicted of 'betrayal of the Motherland, spying, terror, diversion, Trotskyism, rightish tendencies and banditry' (in other words, all politicals) from leaving the camps. The prisoners called this decree an 'extra term', although it was in fact an administrative order, not a new sentence. According to official records, 17,000 prisoners were immediately affected. Others would be included later.[6] Usually, there was no forewarning: on the day they were due to be released, those who fell under the terms of the order simply received a document instructing them to remain behind barbed wire 'for the duration of the war'.[7] Many assumed this meant they would remain in prison for ever. 'It was only then that I understood the whole tragedy of my situation,' one remembered.[8]

The tragedy hit women with children harder than anyone else. One Polish prisoner recounted the story of a woman who had been forced to leave her baby in a nursery outside the camp. Every day of her imprisonment, she thought of nothing but getting her child back. Then, when her release date came up, she was told she would not be set free because of the war: 'She threw her work aside and, falling on to the table, she began not to sob but to howl like a wild animal.'[9]

Olga Adamova-Sliozberg also tells the story of a woman, Nadya Fyodorovich, due to be released on 25 June 1941. Her son, then living in the home of distant relatives who wished to be rid of him, was waiting for her. She had been writing to him, telling him to be patient. When she learned she was not to be released, she wrote to him again. He did not answer:

At last, in the winter of 1942, she received a letter from a stranger. He had picked Borya up at some remote station in Siberia near Irkutsk, and found that the boy was suffering from pneumonia. He had taken him in and nursed him till he was better. He reproached Nadya for having forgotten about her son as soon as she was released; she was a bad mother; she had probably gone and gotten married and was doing nicely for herself while her fourteen-year-old son, hitching a free ride on a train all the way from Ryazan to Irkutsk, was dying of hunger.

Nadya tried to contact the stranger, but to no avail: the censors were no longer letting political prisoners' letters through, especially letters which referred to the indefinite extension of prisoners' sentences. Later, Nadya heard her son had joined a gang. In 1947, he too turned up in Kolyma, with a five-year criminal sentence.[10]

For everyone who remained behind barbed wire, life grew harsher as the war progressed. New laws established longer working days. A refusal to work was no longer just illegal, it became an act of treason. In January 1941, Vasily Chernyshev, then the commander of the central Gulag administration, sent a letter to the bosses of all of the camps and colonies, describing the fate of twenty-six prisoners. The camp court system had tried them, found them guilty of refusing to work, and granted five of them an additional ten-year camp sentence. The court sentenced the remaining twenty-one to death. Curtly, Chernyshev told his underlings to 'inform the prisoners of all camps and corrective-labour colonies' of these sentences.[11]

The message trickled down very quickly. All prisoners, wrote Herling, knew well that 'among the gravest offences which could be committed in the camp after 22 June 1941 were the spreading of defeatism and refusal to work, which, under the new defence regulations, was included in the category of "sabotage of the war effort"'.[12]

The results of all of these policies, coupled with the massive food shortages, were dramatic. Although mass executions were not as common as they had been in 1937 and 1938, prisoner mortality rates for 1942 and 1943 are nevertheless the highest in the Gulag's history. According to the official statistics, which are almost certainly an underestimate, 352,560 prisoners died in 1942, or one in four. One in five, or 267,826, died in 1943.[13] The number of sick prisoners, while officially calculated at 22 per cent in 1943 and 18 per cent in 1944, was probably much higher than that, as typhus, dysentery and other epidemics swept through the camps.[14]

By January 1943, the situation had become so dramatic that the Soviet government created a special food 'fund' for the Gulag: prisoners might be 'enemies', but they were still needed for war production. The food situation did improve as the tide of the war turned in the Soviet Union's favour, but even with these extra rations, the food norms at the end of the war contained a third less calories than those issued in the late 1930s.[15] In all, well over two million people died in the camps and colonies of the Gulag during the war years, not taking into account those who died in exile and other forms of imprisonment. More than 10,000 of these were shot, for treason or sabotage, on the orders of camp prosecutors.[16]

To put these figures and these changes in context, it must also be said that the free population of the Soviet Union also suffered during the war, and that stricter regimes and tighter rules affected workers outside the camps as well as within them. As early as 1940, in the wake of the Soviet invasion of Poland and the Baltic States, the Supreme Soviet established an eight-hour working day and a seven-day working week for all factories and institutions. Even more drastically, the regime forbade all workers from leaving their place of work. To do so became a crime, punishable with a camp sentence. The production of 'poor quality' goods ('sabotage') became a crime too, and sentences for other offences grew harsher. Workers accused of filching spare parts, tools, paper or writing instruments from their workplaces could be sentenced to spend a year in a camp – or more.[17]

People also starved outside the camps almost as frequently as they starved within them. During the German blockade of Leningrad, bread rations fell to 4 ounces a day, which was not enough to survive on, and heating oil was unavailable, turning the far northern winter into a torment. People caught birds and rats, stole food from dying children, ate corpses, and committed murder to get hold of ration cards. 'In their apartments people battled for life, like perishing polar explorers,' remembered one survivor.[18]

Nor was Leningrad the only starving city. NKVD reports written in April 1945 describe famine and mass starvation right across central Asia, in Uzbekistan, Mongolia and the Tartar Republic. Families of front-line soldiers, lacking their breadwinner, suffered the most. Famine hit Ukraine as well: as late as 1947, cases of cannibalism were still being reported.[19] In all, the Soviet Union claimed to have lost twenty million of its citizens during the war. Between 1941 and 1945, the Gulag was not the Soviet Union's only source of mass graves.

*

If greater regimentation and stricter rules immediately followed the declaration of war, so did chaos. The German invasion proceeded with shocking speed. In the first four weeks of Barbarossa, nearly all of the 319 Soviet units committed to battle were destroyed.[20] By the autumn, Nazi forces had occupied Kiev, besieged Leningrad, and appeared to be on the verge of capturing Moscow too.

The western outposts of the Gulag were overwhelmed in the very first days of the war. The authorities had closed the remaining barracks on the Solovetsky islands in 1939, and had transferred all prisoners to mainland prisons: they considered the camp to be too close to the Finnish border.[21] (In the course of the evacuation and the later Finnish occupation, the camp's archive disappeared. It was probably destroyed, according to standard procedures, but rumours, never substantiated, claim that all of the papers were stolen by the Finnish army and are still hidden in a top-secret government vault in Helsinki.)[22] The authorities also instructed Belbaltlag, the camp which ran the White Sea Canal, to evacuate its prisoners in July 1941, but to leave its horses and cattle behind for the Red Army. There is no record of whether the Red Army managed to make use of them before the Germans got there.[23]

Elsewhere, the NKVD simply panicked, and nowhere more so than in the recently occupied territories of eastern Poland and the Baltic States, where the gaols were overflowing with political prisoners. The NKVD had no time to evacuate them, yet could hardly leave 'anti-Soviet terrorists' in German hands either. On 22 June, the very day of the German invasion, the NKVD began to shoot the inmates in the prisons of Lwów, the Polish-Ukrainian city near the German-Soviet front line. While they were carrying out the operation, however, a Ukrainian-led uprising engulfed the city, forcing the NKVD to abandon the prisons altogether. Emboldened by the sudden absence of guards and the sound of nearby artillery fire, a group of inmates in Brygidka prison, in the Lwów city centre, smashed their way out. Others refused to leave, fearing the guards might be waiting outside the gates, hoping for just such an excuse to kill them.

Those who remained paid for their mistake. On 25 June, the NKVD, reinforced by border guards, returned to Brygidka, freed the 'ordinary' criminal prisoners – and machine-gunned the remaining political prisoners in their underground cells. The cars and trucks on the street above drowned out the noise of the shooting. The inmates of the city's other prisons met a similar fate. Altogether, the NKVD killed about 4,000 prisoners in Lwów, and left them in mass graves which they barely had time to cover with a light layer of sand.[24]

Similar atrocities took place all across the border regions. In the wake of the Soviet withdrawal, the NKVD left about 21,000 prisoners behind and freed another 7,000. In a final burst of violence, however, departing NKVD troops and Red Army soldiers murdered nearly 10,000 prisoners in dozens of Polish and Baltic towns and villages – Wilno (Vilnius), Drohobycz, Pińsk.[25] They shot them in their cells, in the courtyards of their gaols, in nearby forests. As they retreated, NKVD troops also burned down buildings and shot civilians, sometimes murdering the owners of the houses in which their own troops had been quartered.[26]

Further from the border, where there was more time to prepare, the Gulag attempted to organize proper prisoner evacuations. Three years later, in his long and pompous summation of the Gulag's war effort, the Gulag's wartime boss, Viktor Nasedkin, described these evacuations as 'orderly'. The plans had been 'worked out by the Gulag in co-ordination with the relocation of industry', he declared, although 'in connection with the well-known difficulties of transport, a significant proportion of the prisoners were evacuated on foot'.[27]

In fact, there had been no plans, and the evacuations were conducted in a panicked frenzy, often while German bombs were falling all around. The 'well-known difficulties of transport' meant that people suffocated to death in overcrowded train cars, or that falling bombs destroyed them before they reached their destination. One Polish inmate, Janusz Puchiński, arrested and deported on 19 June, escaped from a burning train full of prisoners, along with his mother and siblings:

At a certain moment, there was a strong explosion and the train stopped. People began escaping from the wagons . . . I saw that the train stood in a deep ravine. I thought I would never get out of there. Aeroplanes were screaming over my head, my legs seemed to be made of cotton. Somehow I climbed out, and began running to the woods, about 200–250 metres from the tracks. When I'd made it, I turned around, and saw that behind me, in the open space, there were crowds of people. At that moment, the next group of planes arrived and began shooting into the crowds . . .[28]

Bombs also hit a train carrying the inmates of Kołomyja prison, killing some of the prisoners but allowing nearly 300 to escape. Convoy guards captured 150 of them, but later set them free again. As they themselves explained, they had nothing to feed the prisoners and nowhere to keep them. All of the gaols in the area had been evacuated.[29]

The experience of being on a prisoner train during an air raid was relatively unusual, however – if only because prisoners were rarely allowed on the evacuation trains at all. On the train leaving one camp, the families and the baggage of camp guards and administrators took up so much space that there was no room for any prisoners.[30] Elsewhere, industrial equipment took priority over people, both for practical and propaganda reasons. Crushed in the west, the Soviet leadership promised to rebuild itself east of the Urals.[31] As a result, that 'significant proportion' of prisoners – in fact, the overwhelming majority – who Nasedkin had said were 'evacuated on foot' endured long forced marches, descriptions of which sound hauntingly similar to the marches undertaken by the prisoners of the Nazi concentration camps four years later: ' "We have no transport," one guard told an echelon of prisoners, as bombs fell around them. "Those who can walk will walk. Protest or not – all will walk. Those who can't walk – we will shoot. We will leave no one for the Germans . . . you decide your own fate." '[32]

Walk they did – although the journeys of many were cut short. The rapid advance of the Germans made the NKVD nervous, and when they became nervous, they started shooting. On 2 July, the 954 prisoners of the Czortków gaol, in West Ukraine, began their march to the east. Along the way, the officer who wrote the subsequent report identified 123 of them as Ukrainian nationalists and shot them for 'attempted rebellion and escape'. After walking for more than two weeks, with the German army within 20–30 kilometres, he shot those still alive.[33]

Evacuees who were not killed were sometimes hardly better off. Nasedkin wrote that 'the apparat of the Gulag in the front-line regions was mobilized to ensure that evacuating echelons and transports of prisoners had medical-sanitary services and nourishment'.[34] Alternatively, here is how M. Shteinberg, a political prisoner arrested for the second time in 1941, described her evacuation from Kirovograd prison:

Everything was bathed in blinding sunlight. At midday, it became unbearable. This was Ukraine, in the month of August. It was about 35 degrees [centigrade] every day. An enormous quantity of people were walking, and on top of this crowd hung a hazy cloud of dust. There was nothing to breathe, it was impossible to breathe . . .

Everyone had a bundle in their arms. I had one too. I had even brought a coat with me, since without a coat it is hard to survive imprisonment. It's a pillow, a blanket, a cover – everything. In most prisons, there are no beds, no mattresses, no linen. But after we had traversed 30 kilometres in that heat, I quietly left my bundle by the side of the road. I knew that I would not be able to carry it. The vast majority of the women did the same. Those who didn't leave their bundles after the first 30 kilometres left them after 130. No one carried them to the end. When we had gone another 20 kilometres, I took off my shoes and left them too . . .

When we passed Adzhamka I dragged behind me my cell mate, Sokolovskaya, for 30 kilometres. She was an old woman, more than seventy years old, completely grey-haired . . . it was very difficult for her to walk. She clung to me, and kept talking about her fifteen-year-old grandson, with whom she had lived. The last terror in Sokolovskaya's life was the terror that he would be arrested too. It was difficult for me to drag her, and I began to falter myself. She told me to 'rest awhile, I'll go alone'. And she immediately fell back by 2 metres. We were the last in the convoy. When I felt that she had fallen behind, I turned back, wanting to get her – and I saw them kill her. They stabbed her with a bayonet. In the back. She didn't even see it happen. Clearly, they knew how to stab. She didn't even move. Later, I realized that hers had been an easy death, easier than that of others. She didn't see that bayonet. She didn't have time to be afraid . . .[35]

In all, the NKVD evacuated 750,000 prisoners from 27 camps and 210 labour colonies.[36] Another 140,000 were evacuated from 272 prisons, and sent to new prisons in the east.[37] A significant proportion of them – though we still do not know the real numbers – never arrived.

20

'Strangers'

Willows are willows everywhere

Alma-Ata willow, how beautiful you are, draped in glowing
white frost.
But should I forget you, my withered willow in Warsaw's
Rozbrat Street,
Let my hand wither as well!

Mountains are mountains everywhere

Tian Shan, before my eyes, sails upwards into a purple sky . . .
But should I forget you, the Tatra peaks I left so far behind,
The Biały brook, where my son and I daydreamed colourful sea
voyages . . .
Let me turn into Tian Shan stone.

If I forget you
If I forget my hometown . . .

– Aleksander Wat, 'Willow Trees in Alma-Ata', January 1942[1]

From the Gulag's inception, its camps had always contained a notable number
of foreign prisoners. These were, for the most part, Western communists and
Comintern members, although there were also a handful of British or French
wives of Soviet citizens, as well as the odd expatriate businessman. They were
treated as rarities, as curiosities, yet nevertheless their communist origins and
their previous experience of Soviet life seemed to help them fit in with other
prisoners. As Lev Razgon wrote:

They were all 'ours' because they had either been born or grown up in the country or
else come to live there of their own free will. Even when they spoke Russian very badly
or did not speak it at all, they were ours. And in the melting pot of the camps they
quickly ceased to stand out or appear in any way different. Those of them who

survived the first year or two of camp life could thereafter only be distinguished among 'us' by their poor Russian.[2]

Quite different were the foreigners who appeared after 1939. With no warning, the NKVD had plucked these newcomers – Poles, Balts, Ukrainians, Belorussians and Moldavians – out of their bourgeois or peasant worlds after the Soviet invasion of multi-ethnic eastern Poland, Bessarabia and the Baltic States, and then dumped them, in large numbers, into the Gulag and the exile villages. Contrasting them with 'our' foreigners, Razgon called them 'strangers'. Having been 'swept from their own country to the far north of Russia by an alien and hostile historical force which they could not comprehend', they were instantly recognizable by the quality of their possessions: 'We were always alerted to their arrival in Ustvymlag by the appearance of exotic items of clothing among our criminal inmates: the shaggy tall hats and coloured sashes of Moldavia and, from Bukovina, embroidered fur waistcoats and fashionable close-fitting jackets with high, padded shoulders.'[3]

Arrests in the newly occupied territories had begun immediately after the Soviet invasion of eastern Poland, in September 1939, and continued after the subsequent invasions of Romania and the Baltic States. The NKVD's goal was both security – they wanted to prevent rebellion and the emergence of fifth columns – and Sovietization, and they therefore targeted people whom they thought most likely to oppose the Soviet regime. This included not only members of the former Polish administration, but also traders and merchants, poets and writers, wealthy peasants and farmers – anyone whose arrest seemed likely to contribute to the psychological breakdown of the inhabitants of eastern Poland.[4] They also targeted refugees from German-occupied western Poland, among them thousands of Jews fleeing Hitler.

Later, the criteria for arrest became more precise, or at least, as precise as any Soviet criteria for arrest ever became. One document of May 1941, concerning the expulsion of 'socially foreign' elements from the Baltic States, occupied Romania and occupied Poland, demanded, among other things, the arrest of 'active members of counter-revolutionary organizations' – meaning political parties; former members of the police or the prison service; important capitalists and bourgeoisie; former officers of the national armies; family members of all of the above; anyone repatriated from Germany; refugees from 'former Poland'; as well as thieves and prostitutes.[5]

Another set of instructions, issued by the commissar of newly Sovietized Lithuania in November 1940, said deportees should include, along with the categories above,

those frequently travelling abroad, involved in overseas correspondence or coming into contact with representatives of foreign states; Esperantists; philatelists; those working with the Red Cross; refugees; smugglers; those expelled from the Communist

Party; priests and active members of religious congregations; the nobility, landowners, wealthy merchants, bankers, industrialists, hotel and restaurant owners.[6]

Anyone who broke Soviet law, including the laws prohibiting 'speculation' – any form of trade – could be arrested, as could anyone who attempted to cross the Soviet border to escape into Hungary or Romania.

Because of the scale of arrests, the Soviet occupation authorities quickly had to suspend even the fiction of legality. Very few of those seized by the NKVD in the new western territories were actually put on trial, gaoled or sentenced. Instead, the war once again brought about a revival of 'administrative deportation' – the same procedure, instigated by the tsars, that had been used against the kulaks. 'Administrative deportation' is a fancy name for a simple procedure. It meant that NKVD troops or convoy guards arrived at a household and told its inhabitants to leave. Sometimes they had a day to prepare, sometimes a few minutes. Then trucks arrived, took them to train stations, and off they went. There was no arrest, no trial, no formal procedure at all.

The numbers involved were enormous. The historian Aleksandr Guryanov estimates that 108,000 people in the territories of eastern Poland were arrested and sent to the camps of the Gulag, while 320,000 were deported to exile villages – some of which had been founded by kulaks – in the far north and Kazakhstan.[7] To this must be added the 96,000 prisoners arrested and the 160,000 deported from the Baltic States, as well as 36,000 Moldavians.[8] The combined effect of the deportations and the war on the demographics of the Baltic States was shocking: between 1939 and 1945, the Estonian population declined by 25 per cent.[9]

The history of these deportations, like the history of the deportations of the kulaks, is distinct from the history of the Gulag itself, and, as I have said, the full story of this wholesale movement of families cannot be told in the context of this book. Yet it is not completely separate either. Why the NKVD chose to deport one person, sending him to live in an exile village, and why they chose to arrest another person, sending him to live in a camp, is often difficult to understand, as the backgrounds of the deportees and the arrestees were interchangeable. Sometimes, if a man was sent to a camp, then his wife and children were deported. Or if a son was arrested, then his parents were deported. Some arrestees served camp sentences, and afterwards went to live in an exile village, sometimes with their previously deported family members.

Aside from their punitive function, the deportations fitted neatly into Stalin's grand plan to populate the northern regions of Russia. Like the Gulag, the exile villages were deliberately placed in remote areas, and they appeared to be permanent. Certainly NKVD officers told many of the exiles that they would never return, even making speeches as the exiles boarded the trains, congratulating the 'new citizens' on their permanent emigration to the Soviet

Union.[10] In the exile villages, local commandants frequently reminded the new arrivals that Poland, now divided between Germany and the Soviet Union, would never exist again. One Russian teacher told a Polish schoolgirl that Poland's revival was about as likely 'as it is that hair will grow out of your hands'.[11] Meanwhile, in the cities and villages they had left, the new Soviet officials confiscated and redistributed the exiles' property. They converted their houses into public buildings – schools, hospitals, maternity homes – and gave their household goods (whatever had not been stolen by the neighbours or the NKVD) to children's homes and nurseries.[12]

The deportees suffered just as much as their countrymen who had been sent to labour camps, if not more so. At least those in camps had a daily bread ration and a place to sleep. Exiles often had neither. Instead, the authorities dumped them in virgin forest or in tiny villages – in northern Russia, in Kazakhstan and in central Asia – and left them to fend for themselves, sometimes without the means to do so. In the first wave of deportations, convoy guards forbade many to take anything with them, no kitchen goods, no clothes, no tools. Only in November 1940 did the administrative body of the Soviet convoy guards meet and reverse this decision: even the Soviet authorities realized that the deportees' lack of possessions was leading to high death rates, and they ordered guards to warn deportees, as noted earlier, to take enough warm clothes to last for three years.[13]

Even so, many of the deportees were mentally and physically unprepared for lives as foresters or *kolkhoz* farmers. The landscape itself seemed alien and terrifying. One woman described it in her diary, as she first saw it from the train: 'We are being carried through this endless space; such a flat and huge land with only a few scattered human settlements here and there. Invariably, we see squalid mud huts with thatched roofs and small windows, dirty and dilapidated, with no fences and no trees . . .'[14]

Upon arrival, the situation usually worsened. Many of the exiles had been lawyers, doctors, shopkeepers and merchants, accustomed to living in cities or towns of relative sophistication. By contrast, an archival report, dated December 1941, describes exiles from the 'new' western territories living in overcrowded barracks: 'The buildings are dirty, as a result of which there is a high incidence of disease and death, especially among children . . . most exiles have no warm clothes and are unused to cold weather.'[15]

The suffering, in the months and years that followed, only grew, as one unusual set of records testifies. After the war, what was then the Polish government-in-exile commissioned and preserved a collection of children's 'memoirs' of the deportations. They illustrate, better than any adult account could, both the culture shock and the physical deprivation experienced by the deportees. One Polish boy, aged thirteen at the time of his 'arrest', wrote the following account of his months in deportation:

There was nothing to eat. People ate nettle and swelled up from it and they left for the other world. They rushed us to the Russian school compulsively because they didn't give bread when you didn't go to school. They taught us not to pray to God that there is no God and when after the lesson was over we all got up and started praying, then the commander of the settlement locked me up in the *tyurma* [prison].[16]

Other children's stories reflect their parents' trauma. 'Mama wanted to take her own life and ours so as not to live in such torment, but when I told Mama that I want to see Dad and I want to return to Poland, Mama's spirit rose again,' wrote another boy, aged eight at the time of his arrest.[17] But not all women's spirits did rise again. Another child, aged fourteen at the time of his deportation, described his mother's attempted suicide:

Mommy came to the barracks, took a rope, a little bread, and went into the woods. I held my Mommy back in her grief she hit me with the rope and went away. A few hours later they found Mommy on a spruce tree, Mommy had a rope around her neck. Under the tree stood some girls, Mommy thought it was my sisters and wanted to say something but the girls raised up a rumpus to the commandant who had taken an axe in his belt and he chopped down the spruce . . . Mommy already crazy grabbed the commandant's axe and struck him in the back, the commandant fell to the floor . . .

On the next day they took Mommy to a gaol 300 kilometres away from me. I understood that I had to work and I continued to haul timber. I had a horse that was falling over together with me. I hauled timber for one month and then I got sick and could not work. The commandant notified the seller than he should not give us bread but the seller had an understanding for children and he gave us bread secretly . . . soon Mommy came from jail her feet frozen her face wrinkled . . .[18]

But not all mothers survived either – as another child wrote:

We came to the settlement and on the second day they drove us to work we had to work from dawn to night. When payday came for 15 days 10 roubles was the top pay so that in two days it was not even enough for bread. People were dying from hunger. They ate dead horses. This is how my mommy worked and got a cold because she had no warm clothing she got pneumonia and was sick for 5 months she got sick December 3. April 3 she went to the hospital. In the hospital they did not treat her at all if she had not gone to the hospital maybe she would still be alive she came to the barracks at the settlement and died there was nothing to eat and so she died of hunger April 30, 1941. My mommy was dying and I and my sister were at home. Daddy was not there he was at work and my mommy died when Daddy came home from work then mommy died and so my Mommy died of hunger. And then the amnesty came and we got out of that hell.[19]

Bruno Bettelheim, commenting upon this particular collection of stories, unusual in the number and their nature, tried to describe the special despair that they convey:

Since they were written soon after the children had reached freedom and security, it would seem reasonable for them to have spoken of their hope for liberation, if they had any. The absence of such statements suggests that they had none. These children were robbed of the freedom to vent deep and normal feelings, forced to repress them in order to survive for barely another day. A child who has been deprived of any hope for the future is a child dwelling in hell . . .[20]

No less cruel was the fate of another group of exiles, who were to join the Poles and the Balts during the course of the war. These were the Soviet minority groups, whom Stalin either targeted early in the war as a potential fifth column, or else fingered as German 'collaborators' later on. The 'fifth columnists' were the Volga Germans, people whose German ancestors had been invited to live in Russia at the time of Catherine the Great (another Russian ruler who cared deeply about populating her nation's great empty spaces), and the Finnish-speaking minority who had inhabited the Soviet republic of Karelia. Although not all of the Volga Germans even spoke German any more, nor all of the Karelian Finns Finnish, they did live in distinct communities, and had different customs from their Russian neighbours. That was enough, in the context of war with Finland and Germany, to make them figures of suspicion. In a leap of reasoning which was convoluted even by Soviet standards, the entire Volga German people were condemned, in September 1941, on a charge of 'concealing enemies':

According to trustworthy information received by the military authorities, there are, among the German population living in the Volga area, thousands and tens of thousands of diversionists and spies who, on a signal being given from Germany, are to carry out sabotage in the area inhabited by the Germans of the Volga . . . [However] none of the Germans of the Volga area have reported to the Soviet authorities the existence of such a large number of diversionists and spies among the Volga Germans; consequently the German population of the Volga area conceals enemies of the Soviet people and of Soviet authority in its midst.[21]

The Soviet authorities had 'trustworthy information' that there were thousands of spies, yet no spies had been reported. *Ergo*, everybody was guilty of hiding the enemy.

The 'collaborators' included several small Caucasian nations – the Karachai, the Balkars, the Kalmyks, the Chechens and the Ingush – as well as the Crimean Tartars and some other small minority groups: Meskhetian Turks, Kurds and Khemshils, as well as even smaller groups of Greeks, Bulgarians and Armenians.[22] Of these, only the Chechen and Tartar deportations were ever made public in Stalin's lifetime. Their exile, although actually carried out in 1944, was announced in the newspaper *Izvestiya* as having taken place in June 1946:

During the Great Patriotic War, when the peoples of the USSR were heroically defending the honour and independence of the Motherland in the struggle against the German-Fascist invaders, many Chechen and Crimean Tartars, at the instigation of German agents, joined volunteer units organized by the Germans. . . . In connection with this, the Chechens and Crimean Tartars were resettled in other regions of the USSR.[23]

In fact, there is no evidence of massive Chechen or Tartar collaboration, although the Germans did actively recruit Chechens and Tartars, whereas they did not actively recruit Russians. German forces stopped to the west of Grozny, the capital of Chechnya, and no more than a few hundred Chechens crossed the front line.[24] An NKVD report from the time speaks of only 335 'bandits' in the republic.[25] Similarly, although the Germans did occupy Crimea, did co-opt Tartars into the occupation regime, and did draft Tartars into the Wehrmacht – just as they drafted the French and the Dutch – there is no evidence that Tartars collaborated any more or less than other occupied regions of the Soviet Union (or of Europe), or that the Tartars participated in the murder of Crimea's Jews. One historian has pointed out, in fact, that more Tartars fought against Nazi Germany in the Red Army than fought with the Wehrmacht.[26]

In fact, Stalin's aim, at least in deporting the Caucasians and the Tartars, was probably not revenge for collaboration. He seems, rather, to have used the war as a form of cover story, as an excuse to carry out long-planned ethnic-cleansing operations. The tsars had dreamed of a Crimea free of the Tartars ever since Catherine the Great had incorporated the Crimean peninsula into the Russian Empire. The Chechens had also plagued Russia's tsars, and had caused even worse trouble for the Soviet Union as well. A series of anti-Russian and anti-Soviet uprisings had taken place in Chechnya, some following the Revolution, others after collectivization in 1929. Another rebellion had occurred as recently as 1940. All the evidence seems to indicate that Stalin simply wanted to wipe his hands of this troublesome, deeply anti-Soviet people.[27]

Like the deportations from Poland, the Volga German, Caucasian and Crimean deportations were very large. There were, by the war's end, 1.2 million deported Soviet Germans, 90,000 Kalmyks, 70,000 Karachai, 390,000 Chechens, 90,000 Ingush, 40,000 Balkars and 180,000 Crimean Tartars as well as 9,000 Finns and others.[28]

Given the numbers, the speed of these deportations was remarkable, surpassing even the rapidity of the Polish and Baltic deportations. Perhaps this was because the NKVD had, by now, a great deal of experience: this time around, there was no indecisiveness about who should be allowed to take what, who should be arrested, or what the procedure should be. In May 1944, 31,000 NKVD officers, soldiers and operatives completed the entire deportation of 200,000 Tartars in three days, using 100 jeeps, 250 trucks and 67 trains. Special orders, prepared in advance, limited the amount of baggage families could bring with them. As they were allowed only fifteen to twenty minutes to pack, most did not take even half of that. The vast majority of the Tartars were packed on trains and sent to Uzbekistan – men, women, children and old people. Between 6,000 and 8,000 died before arriving.[29]

If anything, the Chechen operation was crueller still. Many observers remember that the NKVD used American-made Studebakers in the Chechen deportations, recently purchased through the Lend-Lease programme, and shipped over the border from Iran. Many have also described how the Chechens were taken off the Studebakers, and placed into sealed trains: they were not only deprived of water, like 'ordinary' prisoners, but also of food. Up to 78,000 Chechens may have died on the transport trains alone.[30]

Upon their arrival in their designated place of exile – Kazakhstan, central Asia, northern Russia – those deportees who had not been arrested separately and sent to the Gulag were placed in special villages – just like those that the Poles and the Balts had settled, and were told that an escape attempt would bring a twenty-year camp sentence. Their experiences were similar too. Disoriented, removed from their tribal and village societies, many failed to adjust. Usually despised by the local population, frequently unemployed, they rapidly grew weak and sick. Perhaps the shock of the new climate was greater: 'When we arrived in Kazakhstan,' one Chechen deportee remembered, 'the ground was frozen hard, and we thought we would all die.'[31] By 1949, hundreds of thousands of the Caucasians, and between a third and a half of the Crimean Tartars, were dead.[32]

But from Moscow's point of view, there was one important difference between the wartime waves of arrest and deportation, and those that had happened earlier: the choice of target was new. For the first time, Stalin had decided to eliminate not just members of particular, suspect nationalities, or categories of political 'enemies', but entire nations – men, women, children, grandparents – and wipe them off the map.

Perhaps 'genocide' is not the proper term for these deportations, since there were no mass executions. In later years, Stalin would also seek collaborators and allies among these 'enemy' groups, so his hatred was not purely racial. 'Cultural genocide', however, is not inappropriate. After they had gone, the names of all of the deported peoples were eliminated from official documents – even from the *Great Soviet Encyclopaedia*. The authorities wiped their homelands off the map, abolishing the Chechen-Ingush Autonomous Republic, the Volga-German Autonomous Republic, the Kabardino-Balkar Autonomous Republic and the Karachai Autonomous Province. The Crimean Autonomous Republic was also liquidated, and Crimea simply became another Soviet province. Regional authorities destroyed cemeteries,

9a Kolyma landscape

9b Entrance to a Vorkuta *lagpunkt* (the sign reads: 'Work in the USSR is a matter of Honour and Glory …')

Work

10a Sawing logs

10b Hauling timber

11a Digging the Fergana Canal

11b Digging coal

12a 'If you have your own bowl, you get the first portions.'

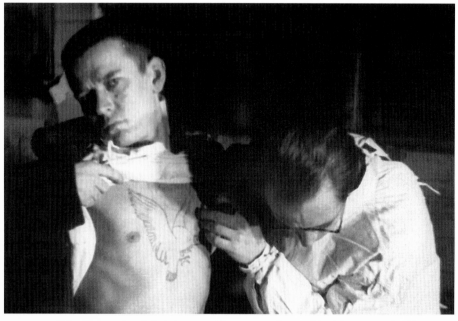

12b 'They surrendered their bronze skin to tattooing and in this way gradually satisfied their artistic, their erotic, and even their moral needs.'

13a 'We picked up a wooden tub, received a cup of hot water, a cup of cold water, and a small piece of black, evil-smelling soap ...'

13b 'Having been admitted with advanced signs of malnutrition, the majority would die in hospital ...'

14a&b Polish children, photographed just after amnesty, 1941

Women and Children

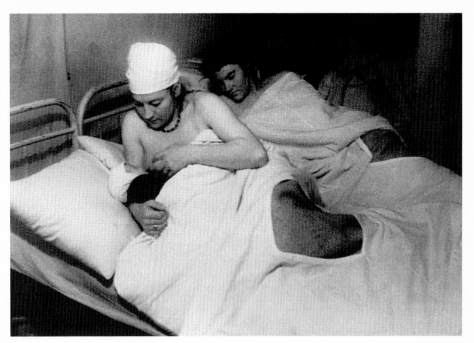

15a Camp maternity ward: a prisoner nursing her newborn

15b Camp nursery: decorating a holiday tree

16a A crowded barracks ...

16b ... a punishment isolator

renamed towns and villages, and removed the former inhabitants from the history books.[33]

In their new homes, all of the Muslim deportees – Chechen, Ingush, Balkar, Karachai and Tartar – were forced to send their children to Russian-language primary schools. All of them were discouraged from using their own languages, from practising their religions, from remembering their past. Without a doubt, the Chechens, the Tartars, the Volga Germans, the smaller Caucasian nations – and, over a longer period, the Balts and the Poles – were meant to vanish, to be absorbed into the Russian-speaking Soviet world. In the end, these nations did 'reappear' after the death of Stalin, albeit slowly. Although the Chechens were allowed to return home in 1957, the Tartars could not do so until the Gorbachev era. They received their Crimean 'citizenship' – their legal right to residence – only in 1994.

Given the climate of the time, the cruelty of the war and the presence, a few thousand kilometres to the west, of another planned genocide, some have wondered why Stalin did not simply murder the ethnic groups he so despised. My guess is that the destruction of the cultures, but not of the peoples, suited his purposes better. The operation rid the USSR of what he thought of as 'enemy' social structures: bourgeois, religious and national institutions that might resist him; educated people who might oppose him. At the same time, it also preserved more 'units of labour' for future use.

But the story of the foreigners in the camps does not end with the Chechens and the Poles. There were other ways for outsiders to end up in the Soviet camp system – and by far the largest numbers entered as prisoners of war.

Technically, the Red Army set up the first Soviet POW camps in 1939, following the occupation of eastern Poland. The first wartime decree on prisoner-of-war camps was issued on 19 September of that year, four days after Soviet tanks rolled across the border.[34] By the end of September, the Red Army held 230,000 Polish soldiers and officers in captivity.[35] Many were released, particularly younger soldiers of lower rank, although some – those considered potential partisans – eventually made their way either into the Gulag, or into one of the hundred or so POW camps deeper in the USSR. Following the German invasion, these camps were evacuated, along with other prisons, to camps in the east.[36]

Infamously, not all of the Polish POWs even made it to these eastern camps. In April 1940, the NKVD secretly murdered more than 20,000 of the captured Polish officers, shooting each one in the back of the head, following Stalin's direct orders.[37] Stalin murdered the officers for the same reason he had ordered the arrests of Polish priests and schoolteachers – his intention was to eliminate the Polish elite – and then he covered it up. Despite enormous efforts, the Polish government-in-exile was unable to discover what had become of the officers – until the Germans found them. In the spring of

1943, the German occupying regime uncovered 4,000 of the bodies in Katyń forest.[38] Although the Soviet Union denied responsibility for the Katyń massacre, as it later came to be known, and although the Allies sided with this interpretation – even citing the Katyń massacre as a German crime in the indictment at the Nuremberg Tribunal – the Poles knew from their own sources that the NKVD was responsible. The affair would undermine the Polish–Soviet 'alliance' not only during the war, but also for the subsequent fifty years. The Russian President, Boris Yeltsin, admitted Soviet responsibility for the massacre only in 1991.[39]

Although Polish war prisoners continued to turn up in forced-labour battalions and in Gulag camps throughout the war, the first labour camps built on a truly massive scale were not constructed for the Poles. As the Soviet Union's war fortunes began to turn, the Red Army quite suddenly, and seemingly unexpectedly, began to capture large numbers of German and Axis prisoners. The authorities were utterly, tragically unprepared. In the wake of the German surrender following the Battle of Stalingrad – often remembered as the turning point of the war – the Red Army captured 91,000 enemy soldiers, for whom no facilities and no rations were provided whatsoever. After three or four days, the food that did arrive was hardly sufficient: 'a loaf of bread between ten men, plus some soup made from water with a few millet seeds and salted fish'.[40]

Conditions in the first few weeks of captivity were hardly much better, and not just for the survivors of Stalingrad. As the Red Army advanced to the west, captured soldiers were routinely herded into open fields and left there with minimal food and no medicine, when they were not shot outright. Lacking shelter, prisoners slept in one another's arms, huddled in the snow, and awoke to find themselves clutching corpses.[41] In the first few months of 1943, death rates among captured POWs hovered near to 60 per cent, and about 570,000 are officially listed as having died in captivity, of hunger, disease and untreated wounds.[42] The real totals may be even higher, as many prisoners must have died before anyone even managed to count them. Similar death rates prevailed among Soviet soldiers in German captivity: the Nazi–Soviet war was truly a fight to the death.

From March 1944, however, the NKVD undertook to 'improve' the situation, and set up a new department of forced-labour camps, specially designed for the POWs. Although they were under the jurisdiction of the secret police, these new camps were not technically part of the Gulag, but rather belonged first to the NKVD's Administration of War Prisoners (UPV) and, after 1945, to its Main Administration of War Prisoners and Internees (GUPVI).[43]

The new bureaucracy did not necessarily bring better treatment. Japanese authorities, for example, reckon that the winter of 1945–6 – after the war had ended – was the hardest for Japanese prisoners, one in ten of whom died in Soviet captivity. Although they were hardly in a position to pass on useful military information, harsh restrictions on their letters to relatives remained firmly in place: prisoners of war were allowed to write home only after 1946, and then using special forms marked 'letter of a POW'. Special censor offices, staffed by censors with foreign-language training, were set up to read their mail.[44]

Nor did overcrowding cease. Throughout the last year of the war, and even afterwards, the numbers of people in these new camps continued to grow, reaching staggering levels. According to official statistics, the Soviet Union took 2,388,000 German prisoners of war between 1941 and 1945. Another 1,097,000 other European soldiers fighting for the Axis also fell into Soviet hands – mostly Italians, Hungarians, Romanians and Austrians, as well as some French, Dutch and Belgians – and about 600,000 Japanese, a stunning number, considering that the Soviet Union was at war with Japan relatively briefly. By the time of the armistice, the total number of captured soldiers had surpassed four million.[45]

This figure, large as it is, does not include all the foreigners swept into Soviet camps during the Red Army's march across Europe. The NKVD, trailing in the army's wake, were also looking for other types of prisoners: anyone accused of war crimes, anyone thought to be a spy (even for an Allied government), anyone thought to be anti-Soviet for any reason, anyone to whom any secret police took a personal dislike. Their scope ranged particularly wide in those central European countries where they intended to remain after the war's end. In Budapest, for example, they quickly picked up some 75,000 Hungarian civilians, sending them first to temporary camps in Hungary, and then to the Gulag – along with the hundreds of thousands of Hungarian war prisoners who were already there.[46]

Just about anyone could be arrested. Among the Hungarians picked up in Budapest, for example, was George Bien, aged sixteen. He was arrested, along with his father, because they owned a radio.[47] At the other end of the social spectrum, NKVD officers also arrested Raul Wallenberg, a Swedish diplomat who had singlehandedly saved thousands of Hungarian Jews from deportation to Nazi concentration camps. In the course of his negotiations Wallenberg had had many dealings with both fascist authorities and Western leaders. He also came from a prominent, and wealthy, Swedish family. For the NKVD, those were sufficient reasons for suspicion. They arrested him in Budapest in January 1945, along with his chauffeur. Both men disappeared into Soviet prisons – Wallenberg was registered there as a 'prisoner of war' – and were never heard from again. Throughout the 1990s, the Swedish government searched for clues as to Wallenberg's ultimate fate, to no avail. It is now widely assumed that he died under interrogation, or was executed soon after his arrest.[48]

In Poland, the NKVD set its sights on the remaining leaders of the Polish

Home Army. This partisan army which had, up until 1944, actually fought alongside Soviet troops against the Germans. As soon as the Red Army crossed the old Polish border, however, NKVD troops captured and disarmed Home Army partisan units, and arrested Home Army leaders. Some hid in Poland's forests, and continued fighting until the mid-1940s. Others were executed. The rest were deported. Thus did tens of thousands of Polish citizens, both partisans and suspect civilians, wind up in the Gulag and the exile villages *after* the war.[49]

But no occupied country was exempt. The Baltic States and Ukraine were, as I've said, subjected to vast post-war repressions, as were Czechoslovakia, Bulgaria, Romania and, most of all, Germany and Austria. The NKVD hauled everyone who was discovered in Hitler's bunker at the time of the Red Army's advance on Berlin back to Moscow for interrogation. They picked up several of Hitler's distant relations in Austria too. Among them were a cousin, Maria Koopensteiner, to whom Hitler had once sent some money, as well as her husband, her brothers, and one of the brother's sons. None, not even Maria, had laid eyes on Hitler since 1906. They were all to die in the USSR.[50]

In Dresden, the NKVD also picked up an American citizen, John Noble, who had been stranded in Nazi Germany and kept under house arrest during the war, along with his German-born father, a naturalized American. Noble finally returned to the United States more than nine years later, having spent much of the interim in Vorkuta, where his fellow prisoners nicknamed him 'Amerikanets'.[51]

The vast majority of those swept up in the mêlée eventually found their way into camps, either in the POW labour camps or the Gulag itself. The distinction between the two types of camps was never clear. Although they technically belonged to different bureaucracies, the administration of the prisoner-of-war camps soon came to approximate those of the forced-labour camps – so much so that in tracing the history of the POW camps and the history of the Gulag, it becomes difficult to keep the two separate. Sometimes, Gulag camps set up special *lagpunkts* just for POWs, and the two types of prisoner worked side by side.[52] For no clearly discernible reason, the NKVD also sometimes sent POWs directly into the Gulag system.[53]

By the end of the war, the food rations of war prisoners and criminal prisoners were nearly the same, as were the barracks they inhabited and the work they did. Like *zeks*, POWs worked in construction, in mines, in manufacturing, in road and railway building.[54] Like *zeks*, some of the better-educated POWs found their way into the *sharashki*, where they designed new military aircraft for the Red Army.[55] To this day, residents of certain districts of Moscow speak with pride of the apartment blocks they inhabit, supposedly finished to a higher standard by meticulous German prisoners of war.

Also like *zeks*, the war prisoners eventually became the recipients of a Soviet-style 'political education'. In 1943, the NKVD began organizing 'anti-fascist' schools and courses in the POW camps. The courses were intended to persuade the participants to 'conduct the battle for the "democratic" reconstruction of their countries and uproot the remains of fascism' on returning home to Germany, Romania or Hungary – and, of course, to prepare the way for Soviet domination.[56] Many former German POWs did indeed wind up working in the new police force of communist East Germany.[57]

But even for those who demonstrated their new loyalty, the return home would not come quickly. Although the USSR repatriated a group of 225,000 prisoners, mostly sick or injured privates, as early as June 1945, and although others continued steadily to return home after that, complete repatriation of the Soviet Union's POWs took more than a decade: 20,000 remained in the USSR in 1953, when Stalin died.[58] Stalin, still convinced of the efficacy of state slavery, looked upon the prisoners' labour as a form of reparation, and considered their long captivity to be wholly justified. Throughout the 1940s and 1950s – and indeed afterwards, as the Wallenberg case illustrates – Soviet authorities continued to cloak the issue of captive foreigners in confusion, propaganda and counter-propaganda, releasing people when it suited them, denying all knowledge of their existence when it did not. In October 1945, for example, Beria wrote to Stalin asking him to authorize the release of Hungarian war prisoners in the run-up to Hungarian elections: the Americans and British had released their war prisoners, he added, implying that the Soviet Union looked bad for not having done so.[59]

The fog persisted for decades. In the first few years following the war, envoys from all over the world kept pressing Moscow with lists of their citizens who had disappeared during the Red Army's occupation of Europe, or had, for one reason or another, fallen into POW or Gulag camps. Answers were not always easy to come by, since the NKVD itself did not necessarily know of these prisoners' whereabouts. Eventually, the Soviet authorities set up special commissions to find out how many foreigners were still in captivity in the USSR, and to examine the case for releasing them.[60]

Complex cases could take years to resolve. Jacques Rossi, a French communist born in Lyon, sent to the camps after a few years of teaching in Moscow, was still trying to get home in 1958. At first refused an exit visa to France, he tried to get one to Poland, where, he told the authorities, his brother and sister lived. That too was refused.[61] On the other hand, the authorities did also sometimes abruptly lift all of their objections, and unexpectedly allowed foreigners to go home. At one point in 1947, at the height of the post-war famine, the NKVD unexpectedly released several hundred thousand war prisoners. There was no political explanation: the Soviet leadership reckoned, simply, that it did not have enough food to keep them all alive.[62]

*

Repatriation did not flow in only one direction. If large numbers of West Europeans found themselves in Russia at the end of the war, equally large numbers of Russians found themselves in Western Europe. In the spring of 1945, more than 5.5 million Soviet citizens were outside the borders of the Soviet Union. Some of them were soldiers, captured and imprisoned in Nazi POW camps. Others had been drafted into slave-labour camps in Germany and Austria. A few had collaborated during the German occupation of their country, and had retreated with the German army. Up to 150,000 were 'Vlasovites', Soviet soldiers who had fought – or, more often, had been forced to fight – against the Red Army under the command of General Andrei Vlasov, a captured Russian officer who had turned against Stalin and fought with Hitler, or in other pro-Hitler, anti-Stalin Wehrmacht brigades. Some, strange though it sounds, were not Soviet citizens at all. Scattered throughout Europe, most notably in Yugoslavia, there were also anti-communist émigrés: White Russians, that is, who had lost their fight against the Bolsheviks and settled in the West. Stalin wanted them back too: no one was to be allowed to escape Bolshevik retribution.

In the end, he got them. Among the many controversial decisions they took at the Yalta Conference in February 1945, Roosevelt, Churchill and Stalin agreed that all Soviet citizens, whatever their individual history, must be returned to the Soviet Union. Although the protocols signed at Yalta did not explicitly command the Allies to return Soviet citizens against their will, that, in effect, is what happened.

Some wanted to return home. Leonid Sitko, a Red Army soldier who had spent time in a Nazi prison camp, and was later to spend more time in a Soviet camp, remembered making the choice to go home. Later, he put his feelings about his decision into verse:

> There were four roads – there were four countries.
> In three of them were peace and comfort.
> In the fourth, I knew, they destroy poets' lyres
> And me, most likely, they will kill.
>
> And what happened? To the three countries I said: to hell with you!
> And I chose my Fatherland.[63]

Others, frightened by what might await them, were nevertheless convinced to return by the NKVD officers who travelled to the POW and displaced-persons camps scattered all over Europe. The officers trawled the camps, looking for Russians, offering them smiling visions of a bright future. All would be forgiven, they claimed: 'You are now considered by us as true Soviet citizens, regardless of the fact that you were forced to join the German army . . .'[64]

Some, particularly those who had fallen on the wrong side of Soviet justice before, naturally did not want to go back at all. 'There is enough room in the Motherland for everyone,' the Soviet military attaché in Britain told a group of Soviet soldiers living in Yorkshire POW camps. 'We know what sort of room there will be for us,' one prisoner replied.[65] Allied officers were nevertheless under orders to send them – and so they did. In Fort Dix, New Jersey, 145 Soviet prisoners, captured wearing German uniforms, barricaded themselves inside their barracks to avoid being sent home. When American soldiers threw tear gas into the building, those who had not already committed suicide rushed out with kitchen knives and clubs, injuring some of the Americans. Afterwards, they said they had wanted to incite the Americans to shoot them.[66]

Worse were the incidents that involved women and children. In May 1945, British troops, under what they were told were direct orders from Churchill, undertook to repatriate more than 20,000 Cossacks, then living in Austria. These were former anti-Bolshevik partisans, some of whom had joined Hitler as a way of fighting Stalin, many of whom had left the USSR after the Revolution, and most of whom no longer held Soviet passports. After many days of promising them good treatment, the British tricked them. They invited the Cossack officers to a 'conference', handed them over to Soviet troops, and rounded up their families the following day. In one particularly ugly incident at a camp near Lienz, Austria, British soldiers used bayonets and rifle butts to force thousands of women and children on to trains which would take them to the USSR. Rather than go back, women threw their babies over bridges, and then jumped themselves. One man killed his wife and his children, laid their bodies neatly on the grass, and then killed himself. The Cossacks knew, of course, what would await them upon their return to the Soviet Union: firing squads – or the Gulag.[67]

Even those who returned home of their own accord could fall under suspicion. Whether they had left the Soviet Union voluntarily or by force, whether they had collaborated or been captured, whether they had returned willingly or been forced on to cattle cars, all were asked, at the border, to fill out a form which asked whether they had collaborated. Those who confessed (and some did) and those who seemed suspicious – including many Soviet POWs, despite the torments they had suffered in German camps – were kept for further questioning in filtration camps. These camps looked, and felt, similar to Gulag camps. Ringed by barbed wire, those inside were forced labourers in all but name.

In fact, the NKVD deliberately set up many of the filtration camps near industrial centres, so that the 'suspects' could contribute free labour to the Soviet Union while the authorities investigated their cases.[68] Between 27 December 1941 and 1 October 1944, the NKVD investigated 421,199 detainees in filtration camps. In May 1945, more than 160,000 detainees were still living in them, engaged in forced labour. More than half were digging coal.[69] In January 1946, the NKVD abolished the camps and repatriated another 228,000 to the USSR for further investigation.[70] Many, it is assumed, wound up in the Gulag.

Even among the POWs, however, there were special cases. Perhaps because the NKVD was handing out sentences to Soviet slave labourers and POWS – people who had, in fact, committed no crime whatsoever – the authorities invented a new kind of sentence for actual war criminals: people who had allegedly committed *real* crimes. As early as April 1943, the Supreme Soviet declared that the Red Army, in the course of liberating Soviet territory, had uncovered 'acts of unheard beastliness and horrific violence, carried out by German, Italian, Romanian, Hungarian and Finnish fascist monsters, Hitlerite agents, as well as by spies and traitors among Soviet citizens'.[71] In response, the NKVD declared that sentenced war criminals would receive fifteen-, twenty- or even twenty-five-year sentences, to be spent in specially designed *lagpunkts*. The *lagpunkts* were duly built in Norilsk, Vorkuta and Kolyma, the three harshest northern camps.[72]

With a curious linguistic flourish, and an ironic sense of history that may well reflect the involvement of Stalin himself, the NKVD named these *lagpunkts* using a term taken from the penal history of tsarist Russia: *katorga*. The choice of this word would not have been accidental. Its resurrection, which echoed the resurrection of tsarist terminology in other spheres of Soviet life (military schools for officers' children, for example), must have been intended to distinguish a new sort of punishment for a new sort of unreformable, dangerous prisoner. Unlike the ordinary criminals condemned to ordinary punishment in the corrective-labour camps of the Gulag, *katorga* prisoners could never hope to be reformed or redeemed, even in theory.

The revival of the word certainly seems to have caused some consternation. The Bolsheviks had fought against *katorga*, but now they were reinstating it – like the pigs in George Orwell's *Animal Farm*, who forbade animals to drink alcohol, and then began drinking whisky themselves. *Katorga* was also reinvented just as the world was beginning to discover the truth about the Nazi concentration camps. The use of the word eerily suggested that Soviet camps resembled 'capitalist' camps a bit more than the Soviet authorities let on.

Perhaps this is why General Nasedkin, the Gulag's wartime boss, commissioned, at this time, a history of tsarist *katorga*, and passed it on to Beria, at his request. Among other 'explanatory notes', the history painstakingly attempts to explain the difference between Bolshevik *katorga*, tsarist *katorga*, and other forms of punishment in the West:

in the conditions of the Soviet Socialist state, *katorga* – exile with forced labour – as a punishment method is based on a different principle than it was in the past. In tsarist

Russia and in bourgeois countries this harsh criminal punishment was inflicted upon the most progressive elements in the society . . . in our conditions, *katorga* allows us to cut down on the high number of death sentences, and focuses on especially dangerous enemies . . .[73]

Reading the instructions issued to describe the new regime, one wonders whether some of those assigned to *katorga* might not have preferred the death sentence after all. *Katorga* convicts were separated from other prisoners by high fences. They received distinct, striped uniforms, with numbers sewn on to the back. They were locked into their barracks at night, and the windows of the barracks were barred. They worked longer hours than ordinary prisoners, had fewer rest days, and were forbidden from carrying out any sort of work other than hard labour, at least for the first two years of imprisonment. They were carefully guarded: each group of ten prisoners was assigned two convoy guards, and each camp was told to deploy a minimum of five dogs. *Katorga* prisoners could not even be moved from one camp to another without the specific agreement of the Gulag administration in Moscow.[74]

Katorga prisoners also seem to have become the mainstay of a brand-new Soviet industry. In 1944, the NKVD claimed, in a list of its economic achievements, to have produced 100 per cent of the Soviet Union's uranium. 'It is not difficult,' writes the historian Galina Ivanova, 'to deduce who it was that mined and processed the radioactive ore.'[75] Prisoners and soldiers would also build the first Soviet nuclear reactor in Chelyabinsk, after the war. 'At that time, the whole building site was a camp of sorts,' remembered one worker. On the site, special 'Finnish' cottages would be built for the German specialists who were also drafted to work on the project.[76]

Without a doubt, the *katorga* prisoners included many genuine Nazi collaborators and war criminals, including those responsible for the murder of hundreds of thousands of Soviet Jews. With such people in mind, Simeon Vilensky, a Kolyma survivor, once warned me not to be too convinced of the innocence of everyone who was in the Gulag: 'These were people who would have been in prison, should have been in prison, under any regime.' As a rule, other prisoners shunned convicted war criminals, and were even known to attack and beat them.[77]

Nevertheless, of the 60,000 prisoners condemned to *katorga* by 1947, quite a few had been sentenced on more ambiguous grounds.[78] Among them, for example, were thousands of Polish, Baltic and Ukrainian anti-Soviet partisans, many of whom had fought against the Nazis before turning around to fight against the Red Army. By doing so, all of them believed they were fighting for their own national liberation. According to a document on under-age *katorga* prisoners, sent to Beria in 1945, these partisans included Andrei Levchuk, accused of joining the Organization of Ukrainian Nationalists (OUN), one of the two main anti-Soviet partisan groupings in Ukraine.

While in their service he allegedly 'took part in the murder of innocent citizens and the disarming of Red Army soldiers and the appropriation of their possessions'. At the time of his arrest in 1945, Levchuk was fifteen years old.

Yaroslava Krutigolova was another such 'war criminal'. Also a member of an OUN partisan group – she served as a nurse – she had been arrested at the age of sixteen.[79] The NKVD also picked up a woman of German origin who had worked as a German translator for Soviet partisans. Hearing that she had been arrested for 'aiding and abetting the enemy', the leader of her partisan brigade made a special journey, away from the front lines, to testify on her behalf. Thanks to him, she received a ten-year *katorga* instead of twenty-five.[80]

Finally, the ranks of *katorga* prisoners included Aleksandr Klein, a Red Army officer who was captured by the Germans, yet managed to escape and make his way back to a Soviet division. Upon his return, he was interrogated, as he later recounted:

Suddenly the Major raised himself sharply, and asked, 'Can you prove that you are Jewish?'

I smiled, embarrassed, and said that I could – by taking off my trousers.

The Major looked at Sorokin, and then again turned to me.

'And you are saying that the Germans didn't know that you are a Jew?'

'If they had known, believe me, I wouldn't be standing here.'

'Ach, you *yid* mug!' exclaimed the dandy, and kicked me in the lower stomach so hard that I suddenly gasped hard for breath and fell.

'What are these lies? Tell us, you motherfucker, with what mission were you sent here? Who are you involved with? When did you sell yourself? For how much? How much did you give yourself for, you creature for sale? What is your code name?'

As a result of this interrogation, Klein was first sentenced to death. He was then reprieved – and given a twenty-year *katorga*.[81]

'There were all kinds of people in the camps, especially after the war,' wrote Hava Volovich later. 'But we were all tormented just the same: the good, the bad, the guilty, and the innocent.'[82]

If, during the war years, millions of foreigners entered the Gulag against their will, at least one foreigner arrived voluntarily. The war may have provoked new paroxysms of anti-foreigner paranoia among the Soviet leadership; but it was also thanks to the war that a senior American politician visited the Gulag, for the first and only time. Henry Wallace, Vice-President of the United States, made a trip to Kolyma in May 1944 – and never even knew that he was visiting a prison.

Wallace's visit took place at the height of Soviet–American wartime friendship, the warmest moment of the alliance, when the American press was wont to describe Stalin as 'Uncle Joe'. Perhaps for that reason, Wallace was inclined to look kindly upon the Soviet Union even before he arrived. In Kolyma, he saw all of his prejudices confirmed. As soon as he arrived, he saw the many parallels between Russia and the United States: both were great 'new' countries, carrying none of the aristocratic baggage of the European past. He believed, as he told his hosts, that 'Soviet Asia' was in fact the 'Wild West of Russia'. He thought that there were 'no other two countries more alike than the Soviet Union and the United States': 'The vast expanses of your country, her virgin forests, wide rivers and large lakes, all kinds of climate – from tropical to polar – her inexhaustible wealth, remind me of my homeland.'[83]

If the landscape pleased him, so too did what he took to be the nation's industrial strength. Nikishov, the notoriously corrupt, high-living Dalstroi boss, escorted Wallace around Magadan, the main city of Kolyma. Wallace, in turn, imagined Nikishov, a senior NKVD officer, to be the rough equivalent of an American capitalist: 'He runs everything around here. With Dalstroi's resources at his command, he's a millionaire.' Wallace enjoyed the company of his new friend 'Ivan', and watched as he 'gamboled about' in the taiga, 'enjoying the wonderful air immensely'. He also listened closely to 'Ivan's' account of Dalstroi's origins: 'We had to dig hard to get this place going. Twelve years ago the first settlers arrived and put up eight pre-fabricated houses. Today Magadan has 40,000 inhabitants and all are well-housed.'

Nikishov failed to mention, of course, that the 'first settlers' were prisoners, and that most of the 40,000 inhabitants were exiles, forbidden to leave. Wallace was equally ignorant of the status of the contemporary workers – nearly all prisoners – and went on to write approvingly of the Kolyma gold miners. They were, he recalled, 'big, husky young men', free workers who were far harder-working than the political prisoners whom he supposed had inhabited the far north in tsarist times: 'The people of Siberia are a hardy, vigorous race, but not because they are whipped into submission.'[84]

This, of course, is precisely what the Dalstroi bosses wanted Wallace to think. According to the report which Nikishov himself later wrote for Beria, Wallace did ask to see a prison camp, but was kept away. Nikishov also assured his bosses that the only workers Wallace encountered were free workers rather than prisoners. Many of them may have even been members of the Komsomol, the Communist Youth League, who had been handed miners' clothing and rubber boots only minutes before Wallace's arrival, and would know what to say if asked questions. 'I spoke with some of them,' Wallace noted later. 'They were keen on winning the war.'[85]

Later, Wallace did encounter real prisoners, although he did not know it: these were the singers and musicians, many of them arrested opera performers from Moscow and Leningrad, who performed for him in the Magadan theatre. Told they were members of a 'non-professional Red Army choir' stationed in the city, he marvelled that amateurs could achieve such artistic heights. In fact, each one had been warned that 'one word or sign that we were prisoners would be considered an act of treason'.[86]

Wallace also saw some prisoner handiwork, although again he did not know that either. Nikishov took him to an exhibition of embroidery, and told him the works on display had been made by a group of 'local women who gathered regularly during the severe winter to study needlework'. Prisoners, of course, had done the work, in preparation for Wallace's visit. When Wallace stopped before one of the works, in clear admiration, Nikishov took it off the wall and handed it to him. Much to his (pleasurable) surprise, Nikishov's wife, the much-feared Gridasova, modestly let it be known that she herself was the artist. Later, a prisoner, Vera Ustieva, learned that her picture was one of two which had been given to the Vice-President as a memento of his trip. 'Our boss received a letter from the wife of the Vice-President, thanking her for the present and saying that the pictures hung in her hall,' she wrote later.[87] In his memoirs Wallace also described the gifts: 'These two wall paintings now convey to my visitors at my home in Washington rich impressions of the beauty of Russia's rural landscape.'[88]

Wallace's visit coincided, approximately, with the arrival of the 'American gifts' in Kolyma. The American Lend-Lease programme, which was meant to send weapons and military equipment to assist US Allies in their defence against Germany, brought American tractors, trucks, steam shovels and tools to Kolyma, which was not quite the American government's intention. It also brought a breath of air from the outside world. Machine parts arrived wrapped in old newspapers, and from them, Thomas Sgovio learned of the existence of the war in the Pacific. Until then, he, like most prisoners, had thought that the Soviet army was doing all of the fighting, with America providing nothing but supplies.[89] Wallace himself had noticed that Kolyma miners (or the Kolyma Komsomol members pretending to be miners) were wearing American boots, also the fruits of Lend-Lease. When he asked about this – Lend-Lease gifts were not meant to be used in the operation of gold mines – his hosts claimed to have purchased the boots with cash.[90]

The vast majority of the clothing sent by the United States wound up on the backs of the camp administration and their wives, although some of the clothing did end up being used by camp theatrical productions, and some of the canned pork did make its way to the prisoners. They ate it with relish: many had never seen canned meat before. Better still, they used the empty cans to make drinking cups, oil lamps, pots, pans, stove-pipes, and even buttons – hardly imagining the surprise such ingenuity would have occasioned in the country where the cans had originated.[91]

Before Wallace left, Nikishov gave an elaborate banquet in his honour. Extravagant dishes, their ingredients carved out of prisoners' rations, were served; toasts were made to Roosevelt, Churchill and Stalin. Wallace himself made a speech, which included the following memorable words:

Both the Russians and the Americans, in their different ways, are groping for a way of life that will enable the common man everywhere in the world to get the most good out of modern technology. There is nothing irreconcilable in our aims and purposes. Those who so proclaim are wittingly or unwittingly looking for war – and that, in my opinion, is criminal.[92]

21

Amnesty – and Afterwards

Today I bid farewell to the camp with a cheerful smile,
To the wires that for a year kept freedom away . . .
Will nothing be left of me here,
Will nothing restrain my hurried steps today?

Oh no! Behind the wire I leave a Golgotha of pain
Still trying to pull me to the outer ends of misery.
Behind I leave graves of anguish and the remains of yearning
And secretly shed tears, the beads of our rosary . . .

All that now seems to have floated away, like a leaf blown off
   a tree
At long last we have broken our ties of bondage.
And my heart is no longer filled with hate
For today rainbows break through the clouds in my eyes!

– Janusz Wedów, 'Goodbye to the Camp'[1]

Many of the metaphors that have been used to describe the Soviet repressive system – the 'meat-grinder', the 'conveyor belt' – make it sound relentless, inexorable, uncompromising. Yet at the same time, the system was not static: it kept turning, churning, producing new surprises. If it is true that the years from 1941 to 1943 brought death, illness and tragedy to millions of Soviet prisoners, it is equally true that for millions of others the war brought freedom.

Amnesties for healthy men, of fighting age, began only days after the war broke out. As early as 12 July 1941, the Supreme Soviet ordered the Gulag to free certain categories of prisoners directly into the Red Army: 'those sentenced for missing work, for ordinary and insignificant administrative and economic crimes'. The order was repeated several more times. In all, the NKVD released 975,000 prisoners during the first three years of the war, along with several hundred thousand ex-kulak special exiles. More amnesties continued up to, and during, the final assault on Berlin.[2] On 21 February

1945, three months before the end of the war, more orders were issued to release prisoners: the Gulag was told to have them ready for induction into the army by 15 March.[3]

The size of these amnesties had an enormous impact on the demography of the camps during the war, and, consequently, on the lives of those who remained behind. New prisoners poured into the camps, mass amnesties freed others, and millions died, making statistics for the war years extremely deceptive. Figures for the year 1943 show an apparent decline in the prisoner population, from 1.5 million to 1.2 million. In that year, however, another figure indicates that 2,421,000 prisoners passed through the Gulag, some newly arrested, some newly released, some transferred between camps, and many dead.[4] Still, despite the hundreds of thousands of new prisoners arriving every month, the total number of Gulag inmates most definitely declined between June 1941 and July 1944. Several forestry camps, hurriedly set up to accommodate the glut of new prisoners in 1938, were just as rapidly eliminated.[5] Remaining prisoners worked longer and longer workdays, yet even so, labour shortages were endemic. In Kolyma, during the war years, even free citizens were expected to help pan for gold in their free hours after work.[6]

Not that all prisoners were allowed to go: the amnesty orders explicitly excluded 'criminal recidivists' – meaning the professional criminals – as well as the political prisoners. Exceptions were made for a very few. Recognizing, perhaps, the damage done to the Red Army by the arrests of leading officers in the late 1930s, a few officers with political sentences had been quietly released after the Soviet invasion of Poland. Among them was General Aleksandr Gorbatov, who was recalled to Moscow from a distant *lagpunkt* of Kolyma in the winter of 1940. Upon seeing Gorbatov, the interrogator assigned to reinvestigate his case looked again at a photograph taken before his arrest, and immediately began asking questions. He was trying to establish whether the skeleton in front of him could really be one of the army's most talented young officers: 'My quilt trousers were patched, my legs were wrapped in cloths and I wore miner's ankle boots. I also had a padded jerkin which was smooth and shiny with dirt. I wore a tattered, filthy cap with earflaps . . .'[7] Gorbatov was ultimately released in March 1941, just before the German offensive. In the spring of 1945, he led one of the assaults on Berlin.

For ordinary soldiers, amnesty did not guarantee survival. Many speculate – although the archives have not yet confirmed this – that the prisoners released from the Gulag into the Red Army were assigned to 'penal battalions' and sent directly to the most dangerous sections of the front. The Red Army was notorious for its willingness to sacrifice men, and it is not hard to imagine that commanders were even more willing to sacrifice former prisoners. One ex-prisoner, the dissident Avraham Shifrin, claimed to have been put into a penal battalion because he was the son of an 'enemy of the people'. According to his account, he and his comrades were sent directly to the front despite a shortage of weapons: 500 men were given 100 rifles. 'Your weapons are in the hands of the Nazis,' the officers told them. 'Go get them.' Shifrin survived, although he was wounded twice.[8]

Nevertheless, Soviet prisoners who joined the Red Army often distinguished themselves. Perhaps surprisingly, few seem to have objected to fighting for Stalin either. At least from the way he tells it, General Gorbatov never had a moment's hesitation about rejoining the Soviet army, or about fighting on behalf of a Communist Party which had arrested him without cause. Upon hearing of the German invasion, his first thought was of how fortunate he was to have been freed: he could use his regained strength for the benefit of the motherland. He also writes with pride of the 'Soviet arms' that his soldiers were able to use, 'thanks to the industrialization of our country', with no comment about how that industrialization was achieved. True, on a number of occasions he showers scorn upon the Red Army's 'political officers' – the military secret police – for meddling too much with the work of the soldiers, and he was once or twice mistreated by NKVD officers, who murmured darkly that he 'hadn't learned much in Kolyma'. But the sincerity of his patriotism is hard to doubt.[9]

This also appears to have been true of many other released prisoners, at least from the evidence contained in NKVD files. In May 1945, the Gulag's boss, Viktor Nasedkin, composed an elaborate, almost gushing report on the patriotism and the fighting spirit shown by former prisoners who had entered the Red Army, quoting extensively from letters they sent back to their former camps. 'First of all, I inform you that I am in a hospital in Kharkov, wounded,' wrote one. 'I defended my beloved Motherland, disregarding my own life. I too was sentenced for working badly, but our beloved Party gave me the chance to pay back my debts to society by achieving victory on the front line. By my own calculations, I killed 53 fascists with my steel bullets.'

Another wrote to express his thanks:

First of all, I write to thank you sincerely for re-educating me. In the past, I was a recidivist, considered dangerous to society, and therefore was placed more than once in a prison, where I learned to work. Now, the Red Army has put even more trust in me, it has taught me to be a good commander, and trusted me with fighting comrades. With them, I go bravely into battle, they respect me for the care I take of them, and for the correctness with which we fulfil the military tasks we are set.

Occasionally, officers wrote back to camp commanders too. 'During the storming of Chernigov, Comrade Kolesnichenko commanded a company,' wrote one captain. 'The former prisoner matured into a cultured, steadfast, and militant commander.'

With the exception of five ex-*zeks* who became Heroes of the Soviet Union, receiving the highest military distinction in the Red Army, there do not appear to be separate records of how many other ex-prisoners won medals. But the records of the more than 1,000 *zeks* who wrote back to their camps are instructive: 85 had become officers, 34 had been inducted into the Communist Party, and 261 had won medals.[10]

While this was probably not a typical sampling of ex-prisoners, there is no reason to think that it was very unusual either. The war produced a surge of patriotism across the Soviet Union, and former prisoners were allowed to take part in it.[11]

Perhaps more surprisingly, prisoners still serving out their sentences in camps were sometimes swept up by patriotic feelings as well. Even harsh new rules and cuts in food supplies did not necessarily turn all of the Gulag's *zeks* into hardened opponents of the Soviet regime. On the contrary, many later wrote that the worst thing about having been in a concentration camp in June 1941 was being unable to go to the front and fight. The war was raging, their comrades were fighting – and they were far in the rear, burning with patriotism. They instantly snubbed all the German prisoners as fascists, insulted the guards for not being at the front, and constantly exchanged gossip and rumours about the war. As Evgeniya Ginzburg remembered, 'We were ready to forgive and forget now that the whole nation was suffering, ready to write off the injustice done to us . . .'[12]

On a few occasions, prisoners in camps close to the front line had the opportunity to put their patriotism into practice. In a report he intended as a contribution to the history of the Great Motherland War, Pokrovsky, a former employee of Soroklag, a camp in the Karelian Republic, near the Finnish border, described an incident which took place during the camp's hasty evacuation:

The column of tanks was growing closer, the situation was becoming critical, when one of the prisoners . . . jumped up into the cabin of a truck, and began driving as fast as possible towards the tank. Slamming into the tank, the prisoner-hero was destroyed, along with the truck – but the tank also stopped and burst into flames. The road was blocked, the other tanks turned round in the opposite direction. It saved the situation, and made possible the evacuation of the rest of the colony.

Pokrovsky also described how a group of more than 600 freed prisoners, stranded in the camp by the lack of trains, voluntarily threw themselves into the work of building the defences of the city of Belomorsk:

All of them agreed with one voice, and immediately formed themselves into working brigades, delegating brigadiers and foremen. This group of freed prisoners worked on the defences for more than a week, with exceptional zeal, from early morning until late evening, 13–14 hours every day. The only thing they demanded in return was that someone conduct political talks with them, and give them information about the situation on the front line. I fulfilled this task conscientiously.[13]

Camp propaganda encouraged such patriotism, and generally gathered pace during the war. As elsewhere in the Soviet Union, there were poster campaigns, war films and lectures. Prisoners were told 'we would now have to work even harder, since every gram of gold we dug out would be a blow against fascism'.[14] Of course, it is impossible to know whether this sort of propaganda worked, just as it is impossible to know whether any propaganda ever works. But the Gulag administration did perhaps take this message more seriously when the Gulag's production capacity suddenly became vital to the Soviet war effort. In his pamphlet on re-education, 'Return to Life', the KVCh officer Loginov wrote that the slogan 'All for the Front, all for Victory' found a 'warm echo' in the hearts of those working behind the front lines in the camps of the Gulag: 'The prisoners, temporarily isolated from society, doubled and tripled the pace of their work. Selflessly working in factories, building sites, woodlands and fields, they threw all of their highly productive work into speeding up the defeat of the enemy at the front.'[15]

Without a doubt, the Gulag did make an industrial contribution to the war effort. In the first eighteen months of the war, thirty-five Gulag 'colonies' were converted to the production of ammunition. Many of the timber camps were put to work producing ammunition cases. At least twenty camps made Red Army uniforms, while others made field telephones, more than 1.7 million gas masks and 24,000 mortar stands. Over one million inmates were put to work on the construction of railways, roads and airfields. Whenever there was a sudden, urgent need for construction workers – when a pipeline gave way or a new rail route had to be constructed – the Gulag was usually called in to do it. As in the past, Dalstroi produced virtually all of the Soviet Union's gold.[16]

But, as in peacetime, this data, and the efficiency it appears to suggest, is deceptive. 'From the first days of the war, the Gulag organized its industries in order to meet the needs of those fighting at the front,' wrote Nasedkin. Might those needs not have been better met by free workers? Elsewhere, he records that production of certain types of ammunition quadrupled.[17] How much more ammunition might have been made if patriotic prisoners had been allowed to work in ordinary factories? Thousands of soldiers who might have been at the front were kept behind the lines, guarding the imprisoned workforce. Thousands of NKVD men were deployed arresting and then releasing the Poles. They too might have been better used. Thus did the Gulag contribute to the war effort – and probably help to undermine it as well.

Alongside General Gorbatov and a few other military men, there was another, much larger exception to the general rule against political amnesties. Despite what the NKVD had told them, the exile of the Poles to the outer edges of the USSR was not, in the end, destined to be permanent. On 30 July 1941, a month after the launch of Barbarossa, General Sikorski, the leader of the

Polish government-in-exile in London, and Ambassador Maisky, the Soviet envoy to Great Britain, signed a truce. The Sikorski-Maisky Pact, as the treaty was called, re-established a Polish state – its borders still to be determined – and granted an amnesty to 'all Polish citizens who are at present deprived of their freedom on the territory of the USSR'.

Both Gulag prisoners and deported exiles were officially freed, and allowed to join a new division of the Polish army, to be formed on Soviet soil. In Moscow, General Władysław Anders, a Polish officer who had been imprisoned in Lubyanka for the previous twenty months, learned that he had been named commander of the new army during a surprise meeting with Beria himself. After the meeting, General Anders left the prison in a chauffeured NKVD car, wearing a shirt and trousers, but no shoes.[18]

On the Polish side, many objected to the Soviet Union's use of the word 'amnesty' to describe the freeing of innocent people, but this was not the time to quibble: relations between the two new 'allies' were shaky. The Soviet authorities refused to take any moral responsibility for the 'soldiers' of the new army – all in a terrible state of health – and would not give General Anders any food or supplies. 'You are Poles – let Poland feed you,' the army's officers were told.[19] Some camp commanders even refused to let their Polish prisoners out at all. Gustav Herling, still imprisoned in November 1941, realized that he would 'not survive until spring' if he were not released, and had to conduct a hunger strike before he was finally let go.[20]

The Soviet authorities complicated matters further by stating, a few months into the amnesty, that its terms applied not to all former Polish citizens, but only to ethnic Poles: ethnic Ukrainians, Belorussians and Jews were to remain in the USSR. Terrible tensions erupted as a result. Many of the minorities tried to pass themselves off as Poles, only to be unmasked by genuine Poles, who feared rearrest themselves if the identity of their 'false' comrades was revealed. Later, the passengers on one Polish evacuation train, bound for Iran, tried to evict a group of Jews: they feared the train would not be allowed out of the USSR with 'non-Polish' passengers.[21]

Other Polish prisoners were released from camps or exile settlements, but not given any money or told where to go. One ex-prisoner recalled that 'The Soviet authorities in Omsk didn't want to help us, explaining that they knew nothing about any Polish army, and instead proposed that we find work near Omsk.'[22] An NKVD officer gave Gustav Herling a list of places where he could get a residence permit, but denied all knowledge of a Polish army.[23] Following rumours, the released Polish prisoners hitch-hiked and rode trains around the Soviet Union, looking for the Polish army.

Stefan Waydenfeld's family, exiled to northern Russia, were not told of the existence of the Polish army at all, nor offered any means of transport whatsoever: they were simply told they could go. In order to get away from their remote exile village, they built a raft, and floated down their local river towards 'civilization' – a town which had a railway station. Months later, they were finally rescued from their wanderings when, in a café in the town of Chimkent, southern Kazakhstan, Stefan recognized a classmate from his school in Poland. She told them, finally, where to find the Polish army.[24]

Nevertheless, the ex-*zeks* and their deported wives and children did slowly make their way to Kuibyshev, the Polish army's base camp, and to the army's other outposts around the country. Upon arrival, many were overwhelmed by the experience of finding 'Poland' again, as Kazimierz Zarod wrote: 'All around us in every direction, Polish speech, familiar Polish faces! I myself met several old acquaintances, and there were scenes of jubilation and exultation as men and women greeted each other with hugs and kisses.'[25] On the day of General Anders's arrival, another ex-*zek*, Janusz Wedów, composed a poem, entitled 'A Welcome to the Leader':

> Ach, my heart! Again you beat so strongly, so happily
> I had thought you had grown hard, died inside me . . .[26]

Within a few months, however, the optimism had diminished. The army lacked food, medicine, equipment – everything. Its soldiers were mostly sick, tired, half-starved men, who needed professional help and medical care. One officer recalled the horror he felt when he realized that 'A vast tide of human beings who had left the places to which they had been exiled or deported . . . were now flowing down into the starving districts of Uzbekistan, to surge round an army organization which was itself undernourished and decimated by disease.'[27]

In addition, relations with the Soviet authorities remained poor. Employees of the Polish Embassy, deployed around the country, were still subject to unexplained arrest. Fearing the situation might worsen, General Anders changed his plan in March 1942. Instead of marching his army west, towards the front line, he won permission to evacuate his troops out of the Soviet Union altogether. It was a vast operation: 74,000 Polish troops, and another 41,000 civilians, including many children, were put on trains and sent to Iran.

In his haste to leave, General Anders left thousands more Poles behind, along with their Jewish, Ukrainian and Belorussian former fellow citizens. Some eventually joined the Kościuszko division, a Polish division of the Red Army. Others had to wait for the war to end to be repatriated. Still others never left at all. To this day, some of their descendants still live in ethnic Polish communities in Kazakhstan and northern Russia.

Those who left kept fighting. After recovering in Iran, Anders's army did manage to join the Allied forces in Europe. Travelling via Palestine – and in some cases via South Africa – they later fought for the liberation of Italy at the Battle of Montecassino. While the war continued, the Polish civilians were parcelled out to various parts of the British Empire. Polish children wound up in orphanages in India, Palestine, even East Africa. Most would never return to Soviet-occupied, post-war Poland. The Polish clubs, Polish historical societies and Polish restaurants still found in west London are testimony to their post-war exile.[28]

After they had left the USSR, the departed Poles performed an invaluable service for their less fortunate ex-fellow inmates. In Iran and Palestine, the army and the Polish government-in-exile conducted several surveys of the soldiers and their families in order to determine exactly what had happened to the Poles deported to the Soviet Union. Because the Anders evacuation was the only large group of prisoners ever allowed to leave the USSR, the material produced by these questionnaires and somewhat rushed historical inquiries remained the only substantial evidence of the Gulag's existence for half a century. And, within limits, it was surprisingly accurate: although they had no real understanding of the Gulag's history, the Polish prisoners did manage to convey the camp system's staggering size, its geographical extent – all they had to do was list the wide variety of places they had been sent to – and its horrific wartime living conditions.

After the war, the Poles' descriptions of their experiences formed the basis for reports on Soviet forced-labour camps produced by the Library of Congress and the American Federation of Labor. Their straightforward accounts of the Soviet slave-labour system came as a shock to many Americans, whose awareness of the camps had dimmed since the days of the Soviet timber boycotts in the 1920s. These reports circulated widely, and in 1949, in an attempt to persuade the United Nations to investigate the practices of forced labour in its member states, the AFL presented the UN with a thick body of evidence of its existence in the Soviet Union:

Less than four years ago the workers of the world won their first victory, the victory against Nazi totalitarianism, after a war which was waged with the greatest sacrifices – waged against the Nazis' policy of enslavement of all people whose countries they had invaded . . .

However, in spite of the Allied victory, the world is perturbed to a very high degree by communications which seem to indicate that the evils we have fought to eradicate, and for whose defeat so many have died, are still rampant in various parts of the world . . .[29]

The Cold War, now three years old, was intensifying.

Life within the camp system often mirrored and echoed life in the greater Soviet Union – and this was never more true than during the final years of the Second World War. As Germany crumbled, Stalin's thoughts turned to a post-war settlement. His plans to draw central Europe into the Soviet sphere of influence solidified. Not coincidentally, the NKVD also entered what might be described as its own expansive, 'internationalist' phase. 'This war is not as in the past,' Stalin remarked in a conversation with Tito, recorded by the Yugoslav communist Milovan Djilas. 'Whoever occupies a territory also imposes on it his own social system. Everyone imposes his own social system as far as his army can reach.'[30] Concentration camps were a fundamental part of the Soviet 'social system', and as the war drew to a close, the Soviet secret police began to export their methods and personnel to Soviet-occupied Europe, teaching their new foreign clients the camp regimes and methods they had now perfected at home.

Of the camps created in what was to become the 'Soviet bloc' of Eastern Europe, those set up in eastern Germany were perhaps the most brutal. As the Red Army marched across Germany in 1945, the Soviet Military Administration immediately began to construct them, eventually setting up eleven of these 'special' concentration camps – *spetslagerya* – in all. Two of them, Sachsenhausen and Buchenwald, were located on the site of former Nazi concentration camps. All of them were under the direct control of the NKVD, which organized and ran them in the same manner as it ran the camps of the Gulag back at home, with work norms, minimal rations and overcrowded barracks. In the famine-wracked post-war years, these German camps seem to have been even more lethal than their Soviet counterparts. Nearly 240,000 mostly political prisoners passed through them during the five years of their existence. Of these, 95,000 – more than a third – are thought to have died. If the lives of Soviet prisoners were never particularly important to the Soviet authorities, the lives of German 'fascists' mattered even less.

For the most part, the inmates of the East German camps were not high-ranking Nazis or proven war criminals. That sort of prisoner was usually taken back to Moscow, interrogated, and put directly into the Soviet POW camps or the Gulag. The *spetslagerya* were meant instead to serve the same function as the Polish and Baltic deportations: they were designed to break the back of the German bourgeoisie. As a result, they contained not leading Nazis or war criminals but judges, lawyers, entrepreneurs, businessmen, doctors and journalists. Among them were even some of the very few German opponents of Hitler, whom the Soviet Union – paradoxically – also feared. Anyone who had dared to fight the Nazis, after all, might also dare to fight the Red Army.[31]

The NKVD interned a similar sort of person in the Hungarian and Czecho-slovakian prison camps, set up by the local secret police services, on Soviet advice, after the Communist Party consolidated power in Prague in 1948, and in Budapest in 1949. Arrests were carried out with what has been described as a 'caricature' of Soviet logic: a Hungarian weatherman was arrested after reporting 'an influx of icy air coming from the north-eastern direction, from the Soviet Union' on the day that a Soviet division arrived in Hungary; a Czech businessman wound up in a camp after his neighbour accused him of referring to 'that imbecile, Stalin'.[32]

Yet the camps themselves were no caricature. In his memoir of Reczk, the most notorious Hungarian camp, the Hungarian poet Gyorgy Faludy sketches a portrait of a system which seems almost an exact copy of the Gulag, right down to the practice of *tufta* and the starving Hungarian prisoners searching for wild berries and mushrooms in the woods.[33] The Czech system also had a special feature: a set of eighteen *lagpunkts*, grouped around the uranium mines of Yachimov. In retrospect, it is clear that political prisoners with long sentences – the equivalent of the Soviet *katorga* inmates – were sent to these mining camps in order to die. Although they worked extracting uranium for the new Soviet atomic bomb project, they were not given special clothing or any form of protection at all. The death rates are known to have been high – though how high, exactly, is still unknown.[34]

In Poland, the situation was more complicated. By the end of the war, a significant proportion of the Polish population were living in a camp of some kind, whether a displaced persons' camp (Jews, Ukrainians, former Nazi slave labourers), a detention camp (Germans and *Volksdeutsch*, Poles who had claimed German ancestry) or a prison camp. The Red Army set up some of its POW camps in Poland, filling them not only with German prisoners but also with members of the Polish Home Army on their way to Soviet deportation. In 1954, 84,200 political prisoners were still incarcerated in Poland as well.[35]

There were also camps in Romania, in Bulgaria and – despite his 'anti-Soviet' reputation – in Tito's Yugoslavia. Like the central European camps, these Balkan camps began by resembling the Gulag, but over time began to differ. Most had been set up by local police, with Soviet advice and guidance of some kind. The Romanian secret police, the *Securitate*, seem to have been working under the direct orders of their Soviet counterparts. Perhaps for that reason, the Romanian camps most closely resemble the Gulag, even to the extent that they carried out absurd, overambitious projects of the sort Stalin himself favoured in the Soviet Union. The most famous of these, the Danube–Black Sea Canal, appears to have served no real economic function at all. To this day, it is every bit as empty and deserted as the White Sea Canal which it so eerily resembles. A propaganda slogan declared that the 'Danube–Black Sea Canal is the tomb of the Romanian bourgeoisie!' Given that up to 200,000 people may have died building it, that may have indeed been the canal's real purpose.[36]

The Bulgarian and Yugoslav camps had a different ethos. Bulgarian police appear to have been less concerned with the fulfilment of a plan and more interested in punishing the inmates. A Bulgarian actress who survived one of the camps later described being beaten nearly to death after collapsing from the heat:

They covered me with old rags and left me alone. The next day everyone went to work, while I was locked up for the entire day with no food or water or medication. I was too weak to get up, due to my bruises and all that I had endured the day before. I'd been brutally beaten. I was in a coma for fourteen hours, and survived by a miracle.[37]

She also witnessed a father and son being beaten to death in front of one another, merely to satisfy the sadistic pleasures of those doing the beating. Other survivors of Bulgarian camps describe being tormented by heat, cold, hunger and physical abuse.[38] The location of these more southerly camps also brought other sorts of suffering: among the most infamous Yugoslav camps was one built on the Adriatic island of Saint-Gregoire, where water was scarce and the main torment was thirst.[39]

Unlike the Gulag, the majority of these camps did not last, and many had closed even before Stalin's death. The East German *spetslagerya* were in fact disbanded in 1950, mostly because they contributed to the deep unpopularity of the East German Communist Party. To improve the new regime's image – and to prevent more Germans from escaping to the West, which was then still possible – the East German secret police actually nursed prisoners back to health before their release, and provided them with new clothes. Not all were let go: those deemed the most serious political opponents of the new order were, like the Poles arrested in this era, deported to the Soviet Union. Members of the *spetslager* burial battalions appear to have been deported as well. Otherwise, they might have exposed the existence of the camps' mass graves, which were not located and exhumed until the 1990s.[40]

The Czech camps did not last either: they reached their peak in 1949, and began shrinking after that, before vanishing altogether. The Hungarian leader Imre Nagy liquidated his country's camps immediately following Stalin's death, in July 1953. The Bulgarian communists, on the other hand, maintained several hard-labour camps well into the 1970s, long after the mass system of Soviet camps had been disbanded. Lovech, one of the cruellest camps in the Bulgarian system, operated from 1959 until 1962.[41]

Perhaps unexpectedly, the Gulag's export policy had its most enduring impact outside of Europe. In the early 1950s, at the height of the era of Sino-Soviet collaboration, Soviet 'experts' helped set up several Chinese camps, and organized forced-labour brigades at a coal mine near Fushun. The Chinese camps – *laogai* – still exist, although they scarcely resemble the Stalinist camps they were set up to emulate. They are still labour camps – and a sentence in one of them is often followed by a period of exile, just as in Stalin's system – but the camp commanders seem to be less obsessed with the norms and central work plans. Instead, they concentrate on a rigid form of 're-education'. Prisoners' atonement, and prisoners' ritual abasement before the Party, seem to matter to the authorities as much as, if not more than, the goods that the prisoners managed to produce.[42]

In the end, the details of daily life in the camps of the Soviet satellite states and allies – what they were used for, how long they lasted, how rigid or disorganized they became, how cruel or liberal they remained – all depended on the particular country and its particular culture. It was, it turned out, relatively easy for other nations to alter the Soviet model to meet their own needs. Or perhaps I should say it *is* relatively easy. The following quotation, from a collection published in 1998, describes an even more recent experience in a concentration camp, in the last remaining communist country on the Eurasian landmass:

On my very first day – at the age of nine – I received a quota. The first work I had to carry out was to walk to the mountain and collect firewood and bring back a large load to the school. I was told to repeat it ten times. It took two or three hours for a round trip from the mountain to the school with a load of wood. Unless you finish it you can't go home. I worked through the night and by the time I had finished it was after midnight and I fell to the ground. Of course, other children who had been there longer could do it faster . . .

Other types of work included collecting gold from sand, using a net in the river (shaking and washing it in the river). This was much easier, sometimes you would be lucky and meet the quota earlier, and then you could play just a little, rather than tell your teacher you had already met the quota . . .[43]

The writer Chul Hwan Kong defected from North Korea in 1992. He had previously spent ten years, along with his entire family, in Yodok punishment camp. One Seoul human rights group estimates that about 200,000 North Koreans are still being held in similar prison camps, for 'crimes' such as reading a foreign newspaper, listening to a foreign radio station, speaking to a foreigner, or in any way 'insulting the authority' of North Korea's leadership. About 400,000 are thought to have died as prisoners in such camps.[44]

Nor are the North Korean camps confined to North Korea. In 2001, the *Moscow Times* reported that the North Korean government was paying off its debts to Russia by sending labour teams to work in heavily guarded mining and logging camps across isolated parts of Siberia. The camps – 'a state within a state' – contain their own internal food distribution networks, their own internal prisons and their own guards. Some 6,000 workers were thought to be involved. Whether they were being paid or not was unclear – but they were certainly not free to leave.[45]

Not only was the idea of the concentration camp general enough to export, in other words, but it was also enduring enough to last to the present day.

22
The Zenith of the Camp-Industrial Complex

At seventeen – we loved to study.
At twenty – we learned to die.
To know that if we are allowed to live
That means nothing has happened, just yet.

At twenty-five – we learned to exchange
Life for dried fish, firewood and potatoes . . .

What was left to learn at forty?
We have skipped so many pages
Perhaps we've learned that life is short –
But then, we already knew that at twenty . . .
– Mikhail Frolovsky, 'My Generation'[1]

Meanwhile, 1949, twin brother of 1937, was advancing on our land, on the whole of Eastern Europe, and, before all else, on the places of prison and exile . . .

– Evgeniya Ginzburg, *Within the Whirlwind*[2]

With the end of the war came victory parades, tearful reunions – and the widespread conviction that life would, and should, grow easier. Millions of men and women had endured terrible privations in order to win the war. Now they wanted to live easier lives. In the countryside, rumours of the abolition of the collective farms spread rapidly. In cities, people openly complained about the high prices charged for rationed food. The war had also exposed millions of Soviet citizens, both soldiers and slave labourers, to the relative luxuries of life in the West, and the Soviet regime could no longer plausibly claim, as it had once done, that the Western working man was far poorer than his Soviet equivalent.[3]

Even many in power now felt it was time to reorient Soviet production away from armaments and towards the consumer goods that people desperately needed. In a private telephone conversation, taped and recorded for posterity by the secret police, one Soviet general told another that 'Absolutely everyone says openly how everyone is discontented with life. On the trains, in fact everywhere, it's what everyone is saying.'[4] Surely, the general speculated, Stalin must have known this too, and would soon have to take action.

By the spring of 1945, hopes were high among prisoners as well. In January of that year, the authorities had declared another general amnesty for women who were pregnant or had small children, and large numbers – 734,785 by 7 July, to be precise – were being released.[5] Wartime restrictions had been eased, and prisoners were allowed to receive food and clothing from home again. For the most part, it was not compassion that had dictated these new rules. The amnesty for women – which excluded political prisoners as a matter of course – did not represent a change of heart, but was rather a response to the shocking increase in the numbers of orphans, and the consequent problems of homeless children, hooliganism and children's criminal gangs all across the USSR: grudgingly, the authorities recognized that mothers were part of the solution. The lifting of restrictions on packages was not a kindness either, but an attempt to muffle the impact of the post-war famines: the camps could not feed the prisoners, so why not let their families help. One central directive declared sternly that 'in the matter of prisoners' food and clothing, packages and money orders must be treated as an important supplement'.[6] Nevertheless, many drew hope from these decrees, interpreting them as harbingers of a new, more relaxed era.

It was not to be. Within a year of victory, the Cold War had begun. The American atomic bombs dropped on Hiroshima and Nagasaki persuaded the Soviet leadership that the Soviet economy must devote itself wholeheartedly to military and industrial production, and not to the manufacture of refrigerators and children's shoes. Despite the devastation wreaked by five and a half years of fighting, Soviet planners tried harder than ever to cut corners, to build quickly – and to make as much use of forced labour as possible.[7]

As it happened, the emergence of a new threat to the Soviet Union suited Stalin's purposes: it was precisely the excuse he needed to tighten, once again, his control over his people, exposed as they had been to the corrupting influence of the outside world. He therefore ordered his subordinates to 'deliver a strong blow' to any talk of democracy, even before any such talk had become widespread.[8] He also strengthened and reorganized the NKVD, which was split into two bureaucracies in March 1946. The Ministry of Internal Affairs – or MVD – continued to control the Gulag and the exile villages, effectively becoming the ministry of forced labour. The other, more glamorous bureaucracy – the MGB, later called the KGB – would control counter-intelligence and foreign intelligence, border guards, and ultimately the surveillance of the regime's opponents as well.[9]

Finally, instead of relaxing repression after the war, the Soviet leadership embarked on a new series of arrests, again attacking the army, as well as select ethnic minorities, including Soviet Jews. One by one, the secret police 'discovered' anti-Stalinist youth conspiracies in nearly every city in the country.[10] In 1947, new laws prohibited marriages – and, in effect, all romantic relationships – between Soviet citizens and foreigners. Soviet academics who shared scientific information with colleagues abroad could be subject to criminal prosecution too. In 1948, the authorities rounded up some 23,000 collective farmers. All were accused of failing to work the obligatory number of days in the previous year, and were exiled to remote areas, without trial or investigation.[11]

Anecdotal evidence exists of some more unusual arrests made at the end of the 1940s. According to a recently declassified intelligence debriefing of a German POW, two American airmen may have found their way into the post-war Gulag as well. In 1954, the German ex-prisoner told American investigators that he had encountered two members of the US Air Force in his POW camp in the Komi region, near Ukhta, in 1949. They were the pilots of a plane that had crashed near Kharkov, in Ukraine. They had been accused of spying, and put in what sounds, from the German's description, like a *katorga* brigade. One allegedly died in the camp, murdered by one of the camp criminals. The other was taken away at a later date, supposedly to Moscow.[12]

Fainter, even more tantalizing rumours float around the Komi region as well. According to a local legend, another group of Englishmen, or at least English speakers, were also incarcerated in another *lagpunkt* – Sedvozh, also near Ukhta – in the 1940s. As one local man tells the story, the Englishmen were spies, parachuted into Germany at the end of the war. The Red Army captured them, interrogated them, and deported them to the Gulag in great secrecy, since Britain and the USSR had, after all, been wartime allies. Evidence of their presence is slim: a *lagpunkt* locally nicknamed 'Angliiskaya Koloniya', the 'English Colony', and a single reference in the Moscow military archive to 'ten Scotsmen', whatever that may mean, in a prisoner-of-war camp in the area.[13]

Thanks to all of these new additions, the Gulag did not contract after the war. On the contrary, it expanded – reaching its highest level in the early 1950s. According to official statistics, on 1 January 1950, the Gulag contained 2,561,351 prisoners in the camps and colonies of its system – a million more than there had been five years earlier, in 1945.[14] The number of special exiles also grew, due to the major deportation operations in the Baltic States, Moldavia and Ukraine, deliberately designed to complete the 'Sovietization' of those populations. And at about the same time, the NKVD resolved, once and for all, the thorny question of the exiles' future, decreeing that all deportees had been exiled 'in perpetuity' – along with their children. By the 1950s, the number of exiles roughly matched the number of prisoners in camps.[15]

The second half of 1948 and the first half of 1949 brought yet another unexpected tragedy to the Gulag's former inmates: a series of arrests, or rather rearrests, of former prisoners, mostly those who had originally been arrested in 1937 and 1938, given ten-year sentences and only recently released. The rearrests were systematic, thorough, and strangely bloodless. New investigations were rare, and most of the prisoners received only perfunctory interrogations.[16] The exile community in Magadan and the Kolyma valley knew something was wrong when they heard of the arrests of former 'politicals' whose names all began with the first three letters of the Russian alphabet: the secret police, they realized, were rearresting people in alphabetical order.[17] No one could decide if this was funny or tragic. Evgeniya Ginzburg wrote that whereas 'in '37 evil had assumed a monumental tragic appearance . . . in '49, the Georgian Serpent, yawning with repletion, was drawing up at leisure an alphabetical list of those to be exterminated . . .'[18]

Overwhelmingly, the rearrested describe feelings of indifference. The first arrest had been a shock, but also a learning experience: many had been forced to confront the truth about their political system for the first time. The second arrest brought no such new knowledge. 'By '49 I already knew that suffering can only cleanse one up to a point. When it drags on for decades and becomes a matter of routine, it no longer cleanses; it simply dulls all sensation,' wrote Ginzburg: 'after my second arrest I would surely turn into a thing of wood.'[19]

When the police came for her the second time, Olga Adamova-Sliozberg went to her cupboard to pack, then stopped. 'Why should I bother to take anything with me? The children can make better use of my things than I,' she thought. 'Obviously I won't survive this time; how could I possibly stand it?'[20] Lev Razgon's wife was rearrested, and he demanded to know why. When told she had been sentenced again for the same crimes as before, he demanded further explanations:

'She's already served her time. Does the law really permit you to punish a person twice for the same offence?'

The procurator looked at me in amazement.

'Of course not. But what's the law got to do with it?'[21]

The majority of those rearrested were not sent back to camps, but instead into exile, usually in particularly remote and underpopulated regions of the country: Kolyma, Krasnoyarsk, Novosibirsk, Kazakhstan.[22] There, most would live lives of unrelenting tedium. Shunned by the local communities as 'enemies', they found it difficult to find living space, difficult to work. No one wanted to be associated with a spy or a saboteur.

To the victims, Stalin's plans seemed clear enough: no one who had received a sentence for spying, sabotage, or any form of political opposition was ever to be allowed to return home. If released, they would be given 'wolves' passports', which forbade them from living anywhere near a major city, and would be constantly subject to rearrest.[23] The Gulag, and the exile system which supplemented it, were no longer temporary punishments. For those condemned to them, they had become a way of life.

Yet the war did have a lasting impact on the camp system, albeit one which is hard to quantify. Camp rules and regulations were not liberalized following victory – but the prisoners themselves had changed, and the politicals in particular.

To begin with, there were more of them. The demographic upheaval of the war years, and the amnesties which had pointedly excluded the political prisoners, had left a much higher percentage of political prisoners in the camps. As of 1 July 1946, more than 35 per cent of the prisoners in the entire system had been sentenced for 'counter-revolutionary' crimes. In certain camps that number was far higher, well above half.[24]

Although the overall figure would drop again, the position of the politicals had changed too. This was a new generation of political prisoners, with a different set of experiences. The politicals arrested in the 1930s – and particularly those arrested in 1937 and 1938 – had been intellectuals, Party members and ordinary workers. Most were shocked by their arrests, psychologically unprepared for prison life, and physically unprepared for forced labour. In the immediate post-war years, however, the politicals included former Red Army soldiers, Polish Home Army officers, Ukrainian and Baltic partisans, German and Japanese prisoners of war. These men and women had fought in trenches, conducted conspiracies, commanded troops. Some had survived German prison camps, others had led partisan bands. Many were openly anti-Soviet or anti-communist, and were not in the least surprised to find themselves behind barbed wire, as one prisoner remembered: 'Having looked death in the eyes, having passed through the fires and hell of war, having survived hunger and much tragedy, they were a completely different generation from the inmates of the pre-war period.'[25]

Almost as soon as they started appearing in the camps towards the end of the war, this new sort of prisoner began creating trouble for the authorities. By 1947, the professional criminals no longer found it so easy to dominate them. Among the various national and criminal tribes who dominated camp life, a new clan appeared: the *krasnye shapochki* or 'red hats'. These were usually ex-soldiers or ex-partisans who had banded together to fight against the dominance of the thieves – and, by extension, against the administration that tolerated them. Such groups operated well into the next decade, despite efforts to break them apart. In the winter of 1954–5, Viktor Bulgakov, then a prisoner in Inta, a far northern mining camp in the Vorkuta region, witnessed an administrative attempt to 'break' a group of politicals by importing a contingent of sixty thieves into their camp. The thieves armed themselves, and prepared to start attacking the politicals:

They suddenly got hold of 'cold weapons' [knives], just as one would expect in that sort of situation . . . we learned that they had stolen the money and possessions of an older man. We asked them to give the things back, but they weren't accustomed to giving things back. So at about two o'clock in the morning, just as it was turning light, we surrounded their barrack from all sides, and began attacking it. We started to beat them, and we beat them until they couldn't get up. One jumped through the window . . . ran to the *vakhta*, and collapsed on the threshold. But by the time the guards arrived, no one was there . . . They took the thieves out of the zone.[26]

A similar incident took place in Norilsk, as one prisoner recalled:

A party of thieves arrived at one *lagpunkt*, where all of the prisoners were politicals, and set about trying to set up their own system. The prisoners, all former Red Army officers, took them to pieces, even though they had no weapons. With wild screams the remaining thieves ran to the guards and the officers, begging for help.[27]

Even women had changed. Tired of being intimidated, a woman political told a group of female thieves that if they did not return some money they had stolen, 'we will throw all of you and your rags outside and you can sleep outdoors tonight'. The criminal women returned the money.[28]

The thieves did not always lose, of course. In one incident in Vyatlag, a struggle between the criminal and political prisoners ended with the deaths of nine politicals. The thieves had demanded a 25-rouble bribe from every prisoner, and had simply murdered those who refused to pay.[29]

But the authorities took note. If political prisoners could band together to fight thieves, they could also band together to fight the camp administration. In 1948, anticipating rebellion, the Gulag's Moscow bosses ordered all of the 'most dangerous' politicals into a new group of 'special camps' (*osobye lagerya*). Specifically designed for 'spies, diversionists, terrorists, Trotskyites, right-wingers, Mensheviks, Social Revolutionaries, Anarchists, nationalists, White emigrants and participants in other anti-Soviet organizations', the special camps were really an extension of the *katorga* regime, and contained many of the same features: the striped uniforms, the numbers on their foreheads, backs and chests; the barred windows; and the locking of the barracks at night. Prisoners were permitted only minimal contact with the outside world, in some cases one or two letters a year. Correspondence with anyone other than family members was strictly forbidden. The working day was set at ten hours, and prisoners were forbidden to work at anything except manual labour. Medical facilities were kept to a minimum: no 'invalid camps' were set up within the special camp complexes.[30]

Like the *katorga lagpunkts*, with which they soon overlapped, the special camps were also set up exclusively in the harshest regions of the country, in Inta, Vorkuta, Norilsk and Kolyma – all mining camps near or above the Arctic Circle – as well as in the Kazakh desert, and the bleak forests of

Mordovia. In effect, they were camps within camps, as most were placed within existing forced-labour complexes. Only one thing distinguished them. With a surprisingly poetic touch, the Gulag authorities gave them all names derived from the landscape: Mineral, Mountain, Oak, Steppe, Seashore, River, Lake, Sand and Meadow, among others. The point was presumably conspiratorial – to hide the nature of the camps – since there were no oak trees at Oak camp, and certainly no seashore at Seashore camp. Very soon, of course, the names were shortened, as was the Soviet custom, to Minlag, Gorlag, Dubravlag, Steplag, and so on. By the beginning of 1953, the ten special camps contained 210,000 people.[31]

But the isolation of the 'most dangerous' political prisoners did not make them more docile. On the contrary, the special camps freed the politicals from their constant conflicts with the criminals, and from the mitigating influence of other prisoners. Left to themselves, their opposition to the system only grew: this was 1948, not 1937. Ultimately, they would embark on a lengthy, determined and unprecedented struggle with the authorities.

As the repressive mechanisms started to tighten again, political prisoners were not the only ones caught in the noose. Now that profits mattered more than ever, the Gulag's bosses began to re-examine their attitudes to the professional criminals. Their corruption, laziness and threatening behaviour towards the guards harmed the productivity of the camps. Now that they no longer controlled the political prisoners, they brought no corresponding benefits either. Although criminals would never attract the same enmity as the politicals, and although they would never receive the same hateful treatment from camp guards, the Gulag's post-war leadership nevertheless resolved to put an end to the criminals' rule of the camps – and to eliminate for ever the thieves-in-law who refused to work.

In practice, the Gulag's war on the thieves took both straightforward and covert forms. To begin with, the most dangerous, dedicated criminals were simply separated from other inmates, and given longer sentences – ten, fifteen, twenty-five years.[32] In the winter of 1948, the Gulag also called for the creation of a group of strict-regime criminal *lagpunkts* for criminal recidivists. According to instructions issued in Moscow, only the most disciplined and 'physically healthiest' of the camp guards were allowed to work in them, and they were to be surrounded by particularly high, reinforced fences. Separate instructions laid out the specifications. The Gulag called for the creation of twenty-seven such camps immediately, with space for more than 115,000 prisoners.[33]

Unfortunately, very little is known about daily life in these punishment *lagpunkts*, or even whether all of them were created: if they survived, these criminals were even less likely to write their memoirs than criminals in ordinary camps. In practice, though, most camps did have some form of separate incarceration for serious criminals and, thanks to an extremely bad twist of luck, Evgeniya Ginzburg found herself, briefly, in one of them: Izvestkovaya, a punishment *lagpunkt* in Kolyma. She was the lone political prisoner among a group of criminal women.

During her sojourn in Izvestkovaya, Ginzburg spent her days working in a limestone quarry, where she was unable to meet the norm and therefore received no food whatsoever. During her first few evenings she sat 'bolt upright' in the corner of the barrack, since there was no space on the bunks, watching the mostly naked women drink ersatz alcohol in the vastly overheated cell. Later, one of the women, a syphilitic in the final stages of the disease, made way for Ginzburg and allowed her to lie down, but that was little comfort. 'The overpowering stench of putrefaction' coming from the woman's disintegrated nose nearly stifled her. 'In Izvestkovaya, as in the most real of hells, there was not only no day and no night, there was not even an intermediate temperature to make existence bearable. It was either the glacial cold of the lime quarry or the infernal cauldron of the hut.'

At this camp, Ginzburg barely avoided rape. One night, the camp guards, who were 'a long, long way from their bosses', burst into the barracks and began attacking the women. Another time, one of them thrust an unexpected loaf of bread at her. The camp management, expecting an inspection team, was worried she might die: 'What with the total isolation, the gluttony, the alcohol, and their constant skirmishes with the girls, our soldiers had completely lost their bearings and hardly knew what they might get it in the neck for. At any rate a death certificate was something they could do without if the management arrived.'[34]

But she escaped. With the help of friends, Ginzburg managed to get transferred to a different camp, using the influence of the house-cleaner of the boss of Sevvostlag, no less. Others would not have been so lucky.

Stricter regimes and longer sentences were not, however, the administration's only weapon against the criminal leadership. All across central Europe, the Soviet Union's great strength as an occupying power was its ability to corrupt local elites, to turn them into collaborators who willingly oppressed their own people. Precisely the same techniques were used to control the criminal elites in the camps. The method was straightforward: privileges and special treatment were offered to those professional criminals – the thieves-in-law – who would abandon their 'law' and collaborate with the authorities. Those who agreed received complete freedom to abuse their former comrades, even to torture and murder them, while the camp guards looked away. These thoroughly corrupted criminal collaborators became known as *suki*, or 'bitches', and the violent battles which erupted between them and the remaining professional criminals became known as the 'war between the bitches and the thieves'.

Like the politicals' own fight for survival, the thieves' war was one of the defining elements of post-war camp life. Although conflicts between criminal groups had occurred before, none had been so vicious, nor so clearly and so openly provoked: separate battles broke out simultaneously, all across the camp system, in 1948, leaving little doubt as to the authorities' role.[35] Many, many memoirists have recorded aspects of this struggle, although, again, most of those who wrote about it were not a part of it themselves. They watched instead, as horrified observers and sometimes as victims.

'Thieves and bitches fought one another to the death,' wrote Anatoly Zhigulin:

Thieves finding themselves in a bitches' *lagpunkt*, if they hadn't managed to hide in a punishment barrack, would often find themselves facing a dilemma: die, or become a bitch. Likewise, if a large group of thieves arrived at a *lagpunkt* all of the bitches would hide in the punishment barracks, as the power had shifted . . . when the regime changed, there were often bloody results.[36]

One thief told a prisoner that all bitches are 'already dead men, sentenced by the rest of us, and at the first opportunity some *blatnoi* [thief-in-law] will kill him'.[37] Another witnessed the aftermath of one of their battles:

After an hour and a half, the thieves from our group were carried back and thrown on the ground. They were unrecognizable. All of their good clothes had been ripped off and removed. In exchange, they had received ragged camp jackets, and instead of boots they had foot coverings. They had been beaten like animals, many had lost teeth. One couldn't lift his arm: it had been broken with an iron pipe.[38]

Leonid Sitko witnessed the start of one particularly vicious battle:

A guard ran down the corridor and shouted 'War! War!' – whereupon all of the thieves, who were less numerous than the bitches, ran to hide in the camp punishment cell. The bitches followed them there, and murdered several. The guards then helped the remainder to hide, not wanting them all to die, and then smuggled them out of the camp the next day.[39]

Non-criminal prisoners sometimes became involved in the battles too, particularly when camp commanders granted broad powers to the bitches. Although 'it isn't worth romanticizing the thieves and the laws, which is what they do in their lives and folklore', Zhigulin continued:

The bitches in prisons and camps were indeed truly terrible for ordinary prisoners. They faithfully served the prison directors, worked as foremen, commandants, brigade leaders. They behaved like beasts towards ordinary workers, fleeced them of their possessions, took their clothes down to the last thread. Bitches were not only informers: they would also carry out murder in accordance with the camp directors. The lives of prisoners living in camps run by bitches was very difficult indeed.

Yet this was the post-war era, and the politicals were no longer defenceless in the face of such harassment. In Zhigulin's camp, a group of ex-Red Army soldiers managed first to beat up the retinue of the much-hated bitch leader of the *lagpunkt*, and then to kill the leader himself, by attaching him to one of the woodcutting machines. When the rest of the bitches locked themselves up in the barracks, the politicals sent them a message: decapitate the man's deputy, show us his head through the window, and then we won't kill the rest of you. They did it. 'Obviously their lives were more important to them than the head of their leader.'[40]

The open warfare became so nasty that even the authorities eventually grew tired of it. In 1954 the MVD proposed that camp commanders designate 'separate camps for the incarceration of recidivists of specific types', and ensure the 'separate incarceration of prisoners' under threat from others. The 'isolation of hostile groups from one another' was the only way to avoid widespread bloodshed. The war had been started because the authorities wanted to gain control over the thieves – and it was brought to an end because the authorities lost control of the war.[41]

By the early 1950s, the Gulag's masters found themselves faced with a paradoxical situation. They had wanted to crack down on the criminal recidivists, the better to increase production and ensure the smooth functioning of camp enterprises. They had wanted to isolate counter-revolutionaries, in order to prevent them from infecting other prisoners with their dangerous views. By tightening the repressive noose, however, they had made their task more difficult. The rebelliousness of the politicals and the wars of the criminals hastened the onset of an even deeper crisis: finally, it was becoming clear to the authorities that the camps were wasteful, corrupt and, above all, unprofitable.

Or, rather, it was becoming clear to everyone except Stalin. Once again, Stalin's mania for repression and his dedication to the economics of slave labour dovetailed so neatly that it was hard for contemporary observers to say whether he raised the number of arrests in order to build more camps, or built more camps in order to accommodate the number of arrestees.[42] Throughout the 1940s, Stalin insisted upon giving even more economic power to the MVD – so much so that by 1952, the year before Stalin's death, the MVD controlled 9 per cent of the capital investment in Russia, more than any other ministry. The Five-Year Plan written for the years 1951–5 called for this investment to more than double.[43]

Once again, Stalin launched a series of spectacular, attention-grabbing Gulag construction projects, reminiscent of those he had supported in the 1930s. At Stalin's personal insistence, the MVD constructed a new asbestos production plant, a project that required a high degree of technological specialization, precisely the sort of thing the Gulag was bad at providing.

Stalin also personally advocated the construction of another railway line across the Arctic tundra, from Salekhard to Igarka – a project that became known as the 'Road of Death'.[44] The late 1940s were also the era of the Volga–Don, the Volga–Baltic and the Great Turkmen Canals, as well as the Stalingrad and Kuibyshev hydroelectric power stations, the latter the largest in the world. In 1950, the MVD also began the construction of a tunnel, and a railway line, to the island of Sakhalin, a project which would require many tens of thousands of prisoners.[45]

This time, there was no Gorky to sing the praises of the new Stalinist constructions. On the contrary, the new projects were widely considered wasteful and grandiose. Although there were no open objections to these projects in Stalin's lifetime, several, including the 'Road of Death' and the tunnel to Sakhalin, were aborted within days of his death. The sheer pointlessness of these feats of crude manpower had been well understood, as the Gulag's own files prove. One inspection carried out in 1951 showed that an entire 83 kilometres of far northern railway track, constructed at great expense and at the cost of many lives, had not been used for three years. Another 370 kilometres of similarly costly highway had not been used for eighteen months.[46]

In 1953, yet another inspection, carried out on the orders of the Central Committee, showed that the cost of maintaining the camps far exceeded any profits made from prison labour. In 1952, in fact, the state had subsidized the Gulag to the tune of 2.3 billion roubles, more than 16 per cent of the state's entire budgetary allocation.[47] One Russian historian has noted that MVD memos to Stalin concerning expansion of the camps often began with the phrase 'in accordance with Your wishes', as if to emphasize the writer's subtle objections.[48]

The Gulag's Moscow bosses were well aware of the spread of dissatisfaction and unrest within the camps too. By 1951, mass work refusals, carried out by both criminal and political prisoners, had reached crisis levels: in that year, the MVD calculated that it had lost more than a million workdays due to strikes and protests. In 1952, that number doubled. According to the Gulag's own statistics, 32 per cent of prisoners in the year 1952 had not fulfilled their work norms.[49] The list of major strike and protest actions in the years 1950–52, kept by the authorities themselves, is surprisingly long. Among others, there was an armed uprising in Kolyma in the winter of 1949–50; an armed escape from Kraslag in March 1951; mass hunger strikes in Ukhtizhemlag and Ekibastuzlag, in Karaganda, in 1951; and a strike in Ozerlag in 1952.[50]

So bad had the situation become that in January 1952, the commander of Norilsk sent a letter to General Ivan Dolgikh, then the Gulag's commander-in-chief, listing the steps he had taken to prevent rebellion. He suggested abandoning large production zones where prisoners could not receive enough supervision, doubling the number of guards (which he conceded would be difficult), and isolating the various prisoner factions from one another. This too would be difficult, he wrote: 'given the great number of prisoners who belong to one or other of the rival factions, we would be lucky if we could simply isolate the leaders'. He also proposed to isolate free workers from prisoners at production sites – and added, finally, that it would be quite useful to release 15,000 prisoners outright, since they would be more productive as free labourers. Needless to say, this suggestion implicitly threw the entire logic of forced labour into doubt.[51]

Higher up the Soviet hierarchy, others agreed. 'Now we have need of first-class technology,' conceded Kruglov, then boss of the MVD: clearly, the third-class technology found in the Gulag was no longer considered sufficient. A Central Committee meeting of 25 August 1949 even dedicated itself to the discussion of a letter received from an educated prisoner, identified as Zhdanov. 'The most important deficit of the camp system is the fact that it relies upon forced labour,' Zhdanov wrote. 'The real productivity of prison labour is extremely low. In different working conditions, half as many people could do double the work that prisoners do now.'[52]

In response to this letter, Kruglov promised to raise prisoner productivity, chiefly by bringing back wages for high-performing prisoners, and reinstating the policy of reducing sentences for good work performance. No one seems to have pointed out that both these forms of 'stimulation' had been eliminated in the late 1930s – the latter by Stalin himself – precisely on the grounds that they reduced the profitability of the camps.

It hardly mattered, since the changes made little difference. Very little of the prisoners' money actually reached their pockets: an investigation carried out after Stalin's death showed that the Gulag and other institutions had illegally confiscated 126 million roubles from prisoners' personal accounts.[53] Even those tiny amounts of money which did come into the prisoners' possession were probably more disruptive than helpful. In many camps, criminal bosses set up collection and protection systems, forcing prisoners further down the hierarchy to pay for the privilege of not being beaten or murdered. It became possible to 'purchase' easier trusty jobs with cash as well.[54] In political camps, prisoners used their new wages to bribe guards. Money also brought vodka into the camps, and later drugs as well.[55]

The promise of shorter sentences for harder work may have helped increase worker enthusiasm a bit more. Certainly the MVD keenly supported this policy, and in 1952 even proposed to free large groups of prisoners from three of the largest northern enterprises – the Vorkuta coal mine, the Inta coal mine, and the Ukhtinsky oil refinery – and to employ them as free workers. It seems that even MVD enterprise managers preferred, simply, to deal with free men rather than prisoners.[56]

So great were concerns about the economics of the camps that Beria, in the autumn of 1950, ordered Kruglov to survey the Gulag and uncover the truth. Kruglov's subsequent report claimed that the prisoners 'employed' by the MVD were no less productive than ordinary workers. He did concede, however, that the price of maintaining prisoners – the cost of food, clothing, barracks and above all guards, now needed in more numbers than ever – far exceeded the costs of paying ordinary free workers.[57]

In other words, the camps were unprofitable, and many people now knew it. Yet no one, not even Beria, dared take any action during Stalin's lifetime, which is perhaps not surprising. To anyone in Stalin's immediate entourage, the years between 1950 and 1952 would have seemed a particularly dangerous time to tell the dictator that his pet projects were economic failures. Although sick and dying, Stalin was not mellowing with age. On the contrary, he was growing ever more paranoid, and was now inclined to see conspirators and plotters all around him. In June 1951, he unexpectedly ordered the arrest of Abakumov, the head of Soviet counter-intelligence. In the autumn of that year, without prior consultation, he personally dictated a Central Committee resolution describing a 'Mingrelian nationalist conspiracy'. The Mingrelians were an ethnic group in Georgia, whose most prominent member was none other than Beria himself. All through 1952, a wave of arrests, firings and executions rolled through the Georgian communist elite, touching many of Beria's close associates and protégés. Stalin almost certainly intended Beria himself to be the purge's ultimate target.[58]

He would not have been the only victim of Stalin's final madness, however. By 1952, Stalin had become interested in prosecuting yet another ethnic group. In November 1952, the Czech Communist Party, now in control of Czechoslovakia, put fourteen of its leaders on trial – eleven Jews among them – and denounced them as 'Zionist adventurers'. A month later, Stalin told a party meeting that 'every Jew is a nationalist and an agent of American intelligence'. Then, on 13 January 1953, *Pravda*, the Communist Party newspaper, revealed the existence of the Doctors' Plot: 'Terrorist groups of doctors,' it was claimed, had 'made it their aim to cut short the lives of active public figures in the Soviet Union by means of sabotaged medical treatment.' Six of the nine 'terrorist doctors' were Jews. All were denounced for their supposed links to the Jewish Anti-Fascist Committee, whose wartime leadership – prominent Jewish intellectuals and writers – had been sentenced a few months earlier for the crime of promoting 'cosmopolitanism'.[59]

The Doctors' Plot was a terrible and tragic irony. Only ten years before, hundreds of thousands of Soviet Jews living in the western part of the country had been murdered by Hitler. Hundreds of thousands more had deliberately fled from Poland to the Soviet Union, looking for refuge from the Nazis. Nevertheless, Stalin spent his final, dying years planning another series of show trials, another wave of mass executions, and another wave of deportations. He may even have planned, ultimately, to deport all Jews resident in the Soviet Union's major cities to central Asia and Siberia.[60]

Fear and paranoia swept across the country once again. Terrified Jewish intellectuals signed a petition, condemning the doctors. Hundreds more Jewish doctors were arrested. Other Jews lost their jobs, as a wave of bitter anti-Semitism swept across the country. In her far-away Karaganda exile, Olga Adamova-Sliozberg heard local women gossip about packages sent to the post office by people with Jewish names. Allegedly, they had been found to contain cotton balls, riddled with typhus-bearing lice.[61] In Kargopollag, in his camp north of Arkhangelsk, Isaak Filshtinsky also heard rumours that Jewish prisoners were to be sent to special camps in the far north.[62]

Then, just as the Doctors' Plot looked set to send tens of thousands of new prisoners into camps and into exile, just as the noose was tightening around Beria and his henchmen, and just as the Gulag had entered what appeared to be an insurmountable economic crisis – Stalin died.

23

The Death of Stalin

For the last twelve hours the lack of oxygen became acute. His face and lips blackened as he suffered slow strangulation. The death agony was terrible. He literally choked to death as we watched. At what seemed to be the very last moment, he opened his eyes and cast a glance over everyone in the room. It was a terrible glance, insane or perhaps angry, and full of fear of death . . .

– Stalin's daughter, Svetlana,
describing her father's final moments[1]

If, in the 1930s, many Soviet prisoners believed the Gulag was a great mistake, a vast error which had somehow been hidden from the kind gaze of Comrade Stalin, by the 1950s few harboured such illusions. The attitude, remembered one camp doctor, was straightforward: 'The vast majority knew and understood what the man was made of. They understood that he was a tyrant, that he held a great country under the tip of his finger, and that the fate of every prisoner was somehow linked to the fate of Stalin.'[2]

Throughout the last years of his life, political prisoners hoped and prayed for Stalin's demise, discussing his death constantly, if subtly, so as not to attract the attention of informers. People would sigh and say, 'Ah, Georgians live a long time,' which managed to convey a wish for his death without actually committing treason. Even when he grew sick, they were still cautious. Maya Ulyanovskaya heard the news of what was to be his final illness from a woman she knew to be an informer. She responded carefully: 'So? Anyone can get sick. His doctors are good, they will cure him.'[3]

When his death was finally announced, on 5 March 1953, some maintained their caution. In Mordovia, the politicals studiously hid their excitement, which they feared might earn them a second sentence.[4] In Kolyma, women 'diligently wailed for the deceased'.[5] In one Vorkuta *lagpunkt*, Pavel Negretov heard the announcement read aloud in the camp dining hall. Neither the commander who read out the notice of death, nor any of the prisoners, said a word. 'The news was greeted with a tomb-like silence. Nobody said a thing.'[6]

In a Norilsk *lagpunkt*, prisoners assembled in the courtyard, and solemnly heard the news of the death of the 'great leader of the Soviet people and of free human beings everywhere'. A long pause followed. Then a prisoner raised his hand: 'Citizen Commander, my wife sent me some money, it's in my account. I have no use for it here, so I would like to spend it on a bouquet for our beloved leader. Can I do that?'[7]

But others openly rejoiced. In Steplag, there were wild cries and yells of celebration. In Vyatlag, prisoners threw their caps in the air and shouted 'Hurrah!'[8] On the streets of Magadan, one prisoner greeted another: 'I wish you great joy on this day of resurrection!'[9] He was not the only one overwhelmed by religious sentiment: 'There was a light frost, and it was very, very quiet. Soon the sky would be turning blue. Yuri Nikolaevich held up his arms and with passion declared, "To Holy Russia let the cocks crow! Soon it will be daylight in Holy Russia!"'[10]

Whatever they felt, and whether they dared to show their feelings or not, most prisoners and exiles were immediately convinced that things would change. In exile in Karaganda, Olga Adamova-Sliozberg heard the news, began to tremble, and put her hands over her face so that her suspicious workmates could not see her joy. 'It's now or never. Everything's got to change. Now or never.'[11]

In another Vorkuta *lagpunkt*, Bernhard Roeder heard the announcement on the camp radio while putting on his mining gear:

There were exchanges of furtive glances, hatred flaring up triumphantly, words stealthily whispered, excited movement – soon the hall was empty. Everyone rushed to pass on the good news . . . No work was done in Vorkuta that day. People stood together in groups, chatting excitedly . . . we heard the guards on the watchtowers phoning one another agitatedly, and, soon afterwards, the first drunks brawling.[12]

Among the camp administrators, the confusion was profound. Olga Vasileevna, then working in the Gulag headquarters in Moscow, remembers weeping openly: 'I cried and pretty much everyone cried, women and men too, they openly cried.'[13] Just like millions of their countrymen, the Gulag's employees were crying not only for their dead leader, but also out of fear for themselves and their careers. Khrushchev himself wrote later that 'I wasn't just weeping for Stalin. I was terribly worried about the future of the country. I already sensed that Beria would start bossing everyone around and that this could be the beginning of the end.'[14]

By 'the end', of course, he meant the end for himself: surely the death of Stalin would bring on a new round of bloodletting. Fearing the same, many Gulag bigwigs reportedly had heart attacks, bouts of high blood pressure and severe cases of fever and flu. Their distress, and their state of complete emotional confusion, had made them genuinely ill. They were literally sick with fear.[15]

If prison guards were confused, the new occupants of the Kremlin were not much clearer about what lay in the future. As Khrushchev had feared, Beria, who was barely able to contain his glee at the sight of Stalin's corpse, did indeed take power, and began making changes with astonishing speed. On 6 March, before Stalin had even been buried, Beria announced a reorganization of the secret police. He instructed its boss to hand over responsibility for the Gulag to the Ministry of Justice, keeping only the special camps for politicals within the jurisdiction of the MVD. He transferred many of the Gulag's enterprises over to other ministries, whether forestry, mining or manufacturing.[16] On 12 March, Beria also aborted more than twenty of the Gulag's flagship projects, on the grounds that they did not 'meet the needs of the national economy'. Work on the Great Turkmen Canal ground to a halt, as did work on the Volga–Ural Canal, the Volga–Baltic Canal, the dam on the lower Don, the port at Donetsk, and the tunnel to Sakhalin. The Road of Death, the Salekhard–Igarka Railway, was abandoned too, never to be finished.[17]

Two weeks later, Beria wrote a memo to the Presidium of the Central Committee, outlining the state of the labour camps with astonishing clarity. He informed them that there were 2,526,402 inmates, of whom only 221,435 were actually 'dangerous state criminals', and he argued in favour of releasing many of those remaining:

Among the prisoners, 438,788 are women, of which 6,286 are pregnant and 35,505 are accompanied by children under the age of two. Many women have children under the age of ten, who are being raised by relatives or in children's homes.

Among the prisoners, 238,000 are elderly – men and women above fifty years of age – and 31,181 are juveniles below the age of eighteen, mostly sentenced for petty theft and hooliganism.

About 198,000 prisoners living in camps suffer from serious, incurable illnesses, and are completely incapable of work.

It is well known that prisoners in camps . . . leave their relatives and intimates in very difficult situations, frequently breaking up their families, with seriously negative effects, lasting for the rest of their lives.[18]

On these humane-sounding grounds, Beria requested that an amnesty be extended to all prisoners with sentences of five years or less, to all pregnant women, to all women with young children, and to everyone under eighteen – a million people in all. The amnesty was announced on 27 March. Releases began immediately.[19]

A week later, on 4 April, Beria also called off the investigation into the Doctors' Plot. This was the first of the changes visible to the general public. The announcement appeared, again, in *Pravda*: 'The persons accused of incorrect conduct of the investigation have been arrested and brought to criminal responsibility.'[20]

The implications were clear: Stalinist justice had been found wanting. Secretly, Beria made other changes as well. He forbade all secret police cadres from using physical force against arrestees – effectively ending torture.[21] He attempted to liberalize policy towards West Ukraine, the Baltic States, even East Germany, reversing the policies of Sovietization and Russification which, in the case of Ukraine, had been put in place by Nikita Khrushchev himself.[22] As far as the Gulag was concerned, on 16 June he laid all of his cards on the table, openly declaring his intention to 'liquidate the system of forced labour, on the grounds of economic ineffectiveness and lack of perspective'.[23]

To this day, Beria's motives for making these rapid changes remain mysterious. Some have tried to paint him as a secret liberal, chafing under the Stalinist system, longing for reform. His party colleagues suspected he was trying to garner more power for the secret police, at the expense of the Communist Party itself: ridding the MVD of the cumbersome, expensive burden of the camps was simply a way of strengthening the institution. Beria also might have been trying to make himself popular, among the general public as well as among the many former secret police who would now return from distant camps. In the late 1940s, he had made a practice of rehiring such ex-prisoners – virtually guaranteeing their loyalty. But the most likely explanation for Beria's behaviour lies in his superior knowledge: perhaps more than anyone else in the USSR, Beria really did know how uneconomic the camps were, and how innocent most of the prisoners were. After all, he had been supervising the former, and arresting the latter, for much of the previous decade.[24]

Whatever his motives, Beria moved too quickly. His reforms disturbed and unsettled his colleagues. Khrushchev – whom Beria vastly underestimated – was the most shaken, possibly because Khrushchev may have helped organize the investigations into the Doctors' Plot in the first place, possibly because of his strong feelings about Ukraine. Khrushchev may also have feared that he would sooner or later figure on Beria's new list of enemies. Slowly, through use of an intensive whispering campaign, he turned the other Party leaders against Beria. By the end of June, he had won them all over. At a Party meeting, he surrounded the building with loyal troops. The surprise succeeded. Shocked, stuttering and stammering, the man who had been the second most powerful person in the USSR was arrested and removed to prison.

Beria would remain in prison for the few months left of his life. Like Yagoda and Yezhov before him, he occupied himself by writing letters, pleading for mercy. His trial was held in December. Whether he was executed then or earlier is unknown – but by the end of 1953 he was dead.[25]

The Soviet Union's leaders abandoned some of Beria's policies as quickly as they had been adopted. But neither Khrushchev nor anyone else ever revived the large Gulag construction projects. Nor did they reverse Beria's amnesty. The releases continued – proof that doubts about the Gulag's efficiency had not been limited to Beria, disgraced though he might be. The new Soviet leadership knew perfectly well that the camps were a drag on the economy, just as they knew that millions of the prisoners in them were innocent. The clock was now ticking: the Gulag's era was coming to an end.

Perhaps taking their cue from the rumours emanating from Moscow, the Gulag's administrators and guards adjusted to the new situation too. Once they got over their fears and their illnesses, many guards changed their behaviour almost overnight, relaxing the rules even before they had been ordered to do so. One of the commanders of Alexander Dolgun's Kolyma *lagpunkt* began shaking prisoners' hands and calling them 'comrade' as soon as news broke of Stalin's illness, even before the dictator had been officially declared dead.[26] 'The camp regime weakened, became more human,' recalled one prisoner.[27] Another put it somewhat differently: 'The guards didn't show the sort of patriotism they had shown when Stalin was alive.'[28] Prisoners who refused to do a particularly strenuous, unpleasant or unfair task were no longer punished. Prisoners who refused to work on Sundays were no longer punished.[29] Spontaneous protests broke out – and the protesters were not punished, either, as Barbara Armonas remembered:

Somehow this amnesty changed the basic discipline of the camp . . . One day we came from the fields in a rainstorm; we were completely soaked. The administration sent us to the baths without letting us first go to our rooms. We disliked this for we wanted to be able to exchange our wet clothing for dry things. The long line of prisoners began to protest by screaming and shouting insults, calling the administration 'chekists' and 'fascists'. Then we simply refused to move. Neither persuasion nor threats had any effect. After an hour of silent battle the administration gave in and we went to our rooms to pick up dry clothes.[30]

The change affected the prisons too. During the months following Stalin's death, Susanna Pechora was in a solitary prison cell, undergoing a second interrogation: as a Jewish 'counter-revolutionary', she had been recalled to Moscow from her camp in connection with the Doctors' Plot. Then, quite suddenly, her investigation stopped. Her interrogator summoned her to a meeting. 'You understand, I am not guilty of wronging you, I never beat you, I haven't hurt you,' he told her. He sent her to a new cell, and there, for the first time, she heard one of the women speaking of Stalin's death. 'What's happened?' she asked. Her cell mates fell silent: since everyone knew Stalin had died, they assumed she must be an informer who was trying to gauge their opinions. It took her a whole day to convince them of her genuine ignorance. After that, recalled Pechora, the situation began to change dramatically.

The guards were afraid of us, we did what we wanted, we shouted during exercise periods, made speeches, crawled through windows. We would refuse to stand up when they came into our cells and told us not to lie on our beds. We would have been shot for doing such things half a year earlier.[31]

Not everything changed. Leonid Trus was also under interrogation in March 1953. While Stalin's death may have saved him from execution, he still received a 25-year sentence. One of his cell mates got ten years for saying something untactful about Stalin's death.[32] Nor was everybody freed. The amnesty had been limited, after all, to the very young, the very old, women with children, and prisoners with sentences of five years or less. Overwhelmingly, those with short sentences were criminal prisoners, or politicals with unusually thin cases. That still left well over a million prisoners in the Gulag, including hundreds of thousands of politicals with long sentences.

In some camps, those due to be released were showered with gifts, attention, and letters to take back to friends and families.[33] Just as often, terrible rivalries broke out between prisoners who were due to be released and those who were not. Forty years later, one prisoner who was not released in the initial amnesty still recalled it bitterly as an 'amnesty for pickpockets', a freedom for petty thieves: 'the criminals were happy, they were all freed'.[34] In one camp, a gang of women prisoners with long sentences beat up a woman with a short sentence, out of spite. Those due to be released also provoked anger, holding themselves apart, looking down on the other 'criminals' who would remain behind.[35]

Other kinds of violence broke out as well. Some with long sentences approached camp doctors, demanding to be given the coveted 'invalid' certificate which would mandate their immediate release. Doctors who refused were threatened or beaten. In Pechorlag, there were six such incidents: doctors were 'systematically terrorized', beaten, even knifed. In Yuzhkuzbasslag, four prisoners threatened the camp doctor with death. In other camps, the number of prisoners released as 'invalids' exceeded the number of invalids previously recorded in the camps.[36]

But one particular group of prisoners, in one particular set of camps, experienced quite a different set of emotions. The prisoners of the 'special camps' were indeed a special case: overwhelmingly, their inmates had ten-, fifteen- or twenty-five-year sentences, and no hope of release under Beria's amnesty. Only minor changes had been made to their regime in the first few months following Stalin's death. Prisoners were now allowed to receive packages, for example, but only one per year. Grudgingly, the administration allowed camp football teams to play against one another. But they still wore numbered uniforms, the windows of their barracks were still barred, and the barracks remained locked at night. All contact with the outside world was kept to a minimum.[37]

It was a recipe for rebellion. By 1953, the inhabitants of the special camps had been kept separate from criminal and 'ordinary' prisoners since 1948, more than five years. Left to themselves, they had evolved systems of internal organization and resistance which had no parallel in the earlier years of the Gulag. For years, they had been on the brink of organized uprising, plotting and planning, restrained only by the hope that Stalin's death would bring their release. When Stalin's death changed nothing, hope vanished – and was replaced by anger.

24

The *Zeks'* Revolution

I cannot sleep. Blizzards are howling
For some unknown, forgotten time
And the coloured tents of Tamburlaine
Are out there on the steppe . . . blazing bonfires, blazing bonfires

I shall become a Mongol princess
Galloping deep into the past
And lash to the tale of my horse
My loved ones, and my enemies . . .

And then, at one of the battles
In an unthinkable orgy of blood
At the moment of utter defeat
I will throw myself on my own sword . . .

– Anna Barkova, 'In the Prison Camp Barracks'[1]

In the wake of Stalin's death, the special camps, like the rest of the country, were awash with rumours. Beria would take over; Beria was dead. Marshal Zhukov and Admiral Kuznetsov had marched into Moscow and were attacking the Kremlin with tanks; Khrushchev and Molotov had been murdered. All prisoners would be freed; all prisoners would be executed; the camps had been surrounded by armed MVD troops, ready to put down any sign of rebellion. Prisoners repeated these stories in whispers and shouts, hoping and speculating.[2]

At the same time, the national organizations in the special camps were growing stronger, the links between them steadier. Typical of this era are the experiences of Viktor Bulgakov, who was arrested in the spring of 1953 – on the night of Stalin's death, in fact – and accused of participating in an anti-Stalinist student political circle. Soon afterwards, he arrived in Minlag, the special camp in the coal-mining Inta complex, north of the Arctic Circle.

Bulgakov's description of the atmosphere in Minlag contrasts sharply with the memoirs of prisoners of an earlier era. A teenager at the time of his arrest, he walked into a well-organized, anti-Stalinist, anti-Soviet community. Strikes and protests occurred 'with regularity'. The prisoners had sorted themselves into several very distinct national groupings, each with its own character. The Balts had a 'tight organization, but without a well-run hierarchy'. The Ukrainians, mostly ex-partisans, were 'extremely well-organized, as their leaders had been partisan leaders prior to captivity, they all knew each other, and their structure appeared almost automatically'.

The camp also contained prisoners who believed in communism, although they had sorted themselves into two groups: those who merely toed the Party line; and those who considered themselves communists out of faith or conviction – and believed in the reform of the Soviet Union. Finally, it had become possible to be an anti-Soviet Marxist, something unthinkable in earlier years. Bulgakov himself belonged to the People's Workers' Union – the *Narodno-Trudovoi Soyuz*, or NTS – an anti-Stalinist opposition movement, which would gain a great deal of notoriety a decade or two later, as the paranoid authorities began to see signs of its influence everywhere.[3]

Bulgakov's preoccupations in camp would have stunned an earlier generation of prisoners too. In Minlag, the prisoners managed to put out a secret underground newspaper, written by hand and distributed around the camps. They intimidated the *pridurki*, who 'became afraid of the prisoners' as a result. They kept tabs on camp informers too – as did other prisoners in special camps. Dmitri Panin has also described the increasingly deadly war against informers:

Retribution was carried out systematically. During the course of eight months forty-five informers were done away with. Operations against them were directed from a clandestine centre . . . We saw how a number of stoolie prisoners, unable to stand the threat of liquidation that hung over them, sought to escape their fate by getting themselves put in the camp gaol – the only place they could hide from certain retaliation. They were all kept in the same cell, which was dubbed the 'funk hole'.[4]

One camp historian has written that murders of informers became 'such an ordinary occurrence that no one was surprised or interested', and notes that the informers 'died out quickly'.[5] Once again, life inside the camps mirrored and amplified life on the outside. The anti-Soviet partisan organizations in West Ukraine had also tried intensely to destroy informers, and their leaders brought the obsession with them to the camps.[6] Perhaps cognizant of this, the authorities in Panin's camp separated the Ukrainian prisoners from the others, since the Ukrainians were thought to be responsible for the deaths of informers. This only increased their solidarity and their anger.[7]

By 1953, Bulgakov's comrades in Minlag were also making a systematic attempt to keep track of their own numbers and living conditions, and to transmit this information to the West, using co-operative guards and other techniques that would be perfected in the dissident camps of the 1970s and

1980s, as we shall see. Bulgakov himself took on responsibility for hiding these documents, as well as copies of songs and poetry composed by the prisoners. Leonid Sitko did the same job in Steplag, using the basement of a building that camp workers were constructing as a place to hide documents. Among them were 'short descriptions of individual lives, the letters of dead inmates, a short document signed by a doctor, Galina Mishkina, on the inhuman conditions in the camps (including statistics on deaths, levels of starvation, and so on), an account of the organization and growth of the camps of Kazakhstan, a more detailed account of the history of Steplag – and poems'.[8]

Both Sitko and Bulgakov believed, simply, that some day the camps would be shut, the barracks would be burned down, and that the information could be retrieved again. Twenty years earlier, no one had dared to think such a thing, let alone act upon it.

Very quickly, the tactics and strategy of conspiracy spread throughout the special camp system, thanks to the Gulag administration itself. In the past, prisoners who were suspected of hatching conspiracies had simply been split up. The central authorities had moved prisoners from camp to camp, destroying rebel networks before they began. Within the more specific climate of the special camps, however, this tactic backfired. Instead, the frequent movements of prisoners became an excellent means of spreading rebellion.[9]

North of the Arctic Circle, the summers are very short, and very hot. Towards the end of May, the ice on the rivers begins to break up. The days grow longer, until night vanishes altogether. At some point in June – in some years as late as July – the sun suddenly begins to shine with real ferocity, sometimes for a month, sometimes two. From one day to the next, the Arctic wild flowers suddenly begin to bloom, and for a few short weeks, the tundra is awash with colour. For human beings, who have been locked inside for nine months, the summer brings an overwhelming desire to go outdoors, to be free. During the few hot summer days that I spent in Vorkuta, the inhabitants of the city seemed to spend virtually all of their days and all of their white nights outside, strolling the streets, sitting in the parks, talking to one another on the doorsteps of their houses. It is no accident that springtime was the season for prisoners to attempt escape. Nor is it an accident that the Gulag's three most important, most dangerous, and most famous uprisings all took place in northern camps in the spring.

In Gorlag, the special camp in the Norilsk complex, the mood was particularly angry in the spring of 1953. The previous autumn, a large group of prisoners, about 1,200 in all, had been transferred to Gorlag from Karaganda, where many seem to have been involved in the armed escape attempts and protests that had taken place there a few months earlier. All had been imprisoned for 'revolutionary activity in the West Ukraine and

Baltic States'. They had, according to the MVD's records, started organizing a 'revolutionary committee' even while still in transit to Norilsk.

According to prisoners' accounts, they also murdered four camp informers – with pickaxes – within a few days of their arrival.[10] By the spring of 1953, deeply angered by the amnesty which had passed them by, this group had created what the MVD described as an 'anti-Soviet organization' in the camp, which probably means that they had strengthened the national organizations already in place.

Unrest percolated throughout the month of May. On 25 May, convoy guards shot a prisoner on his way to work. On the following morning, two of the camp's divisions went on strike in protest. A few days later, guards opened fire on prisoners who were throwing messages over the wall that separated the male and the female camps. Some were wounded. Then, on 4 June, a group of prisoners broke down the wooden barrier which divided their camp's punishment barrack from the rest of the zona, and freed twenty-four prisoners. They also captured a member of the camp administration, took him into the zona, and made him hostage. The guards opened fire, killing five prisoners and wounding fourteen others. Four more camp divisions joined the protest. By 5 June, 16,379 prisoners were on strike. Soldiers surrounded the camps, and all of the exits were blocked.[11]

At about the same time, a similar process was taking place in Rechlag, the special camp in the Vorkuta coal-mining complex. Prisoners had attempted to organize mass strikes in Rechlag as early as 1951, and the administration would later claim to have uncovered no fewer than five 'revolutionary organ-izations' in the camp in 1951 and 1952.[12] When Stalin died, the prisoners of Rechlag were also particularly well-equipped to follow world events. Not only were they organized into national groups, as in Minlag and elsewhere, but they had also designated particular prisoners to follow Western radio transmissions on stolen or borrowed radios, and to write up the news in the form of bulletins, with commentary, which they carefully distributed among other prisoners. Thus did they learn not only of Stalin's death and Beria's arrest, but also of the mass strikes in East Berlin, which took place on 17 June 1953, and were put down by Soviet tanks.[13]

This piece of news appears to have galvanized the prisoners: if the Berliners could strike, so could they. John Noble, the American arrested in Dresden just after the war, recalled that 'their spirit inspired us and we discussed nothing else for days afterwards ... The next month we were cocky slaves. The long summer sun had melted the snow and its warmth was renewing our energy and courage. We discussed the chance of striking for our freedom, but no one knew what to do.'[14]

By 30 June, the inmates of the Kapitalnaya mine were distributing leaflets, calling on prisoners to 'Stop delivery of coal.' On the same day, someone wrote a slogan on the walls of mine No. 40: 'No deliveries of coal until there's an amnesty.' The trucks themselves were empty: the prisoners had stopped digging coal.[15] On 17 July, the authorities at Kapitalnaya mine had even greater cause for alarm: on that day, a group of prisoners beat up one of the foremen, allegedly because he had told them to 'stop the sabotage'. When it came time for the second shift to begin, the next foreman refused to go down the mine shaft.

Just as the prisoners of Rechlag were absorbing news of these events, a large contingent of prisoners arrived – again from Karaganda. All had been promised better living conditions and a re-examination of their cases. When they arrived at work in Vorkuta's mine No. 7, they found not an improvement, but the harshest conditions in the entire camp system. On the following day – 19 July – 350 of them went on strike.[16]

Other strikes followed – thanks, in part, to the geography of Vorkuta itself. Vorkutlag lies at the centre of a vast coal basin – one of the largest in the world. To exploit the coal, a series of mines were set up in a wide circle around the basin. Between the mines lay other enterprises – electric power stations, brick and cement factories – each one connected to a camp, as well as the city of Vorkuta and the smaller settlement of Yur-Shor. A railway line ran between all of these sites. The trains, like everything else in Vorkuta, were run by prisoners – which is how the rebellion spread: along with the coal and other supplies that they carried from one *lagpunkt* to the next, the prisoners manning the engines passed on news of the strike in camp No. 7. As the trains travelled round the great circle, thousands of prisoners heard the whispered accounts, thousands more saw the slogans painted on the trains' sides: 'To hell with your coal. We want freedom.'[17] One camp after another joined the strike until, by 29 July 1953, six of the seventeen divisions of Rechlag – 15,604 people – were on strike.[18]

Within most of the striking Vorkuta and Norilsk *lagpunkts*, strike committees took charge of what was clearly a dangerous situation. Terrified administrators had vacated the camps, and the potential for anarchy was great. In some cases, these committees found themselves organizing the prisoners' food. In others, they tried to persuade inmates not to take out their aggression on the now completely defenceless informers. In the case of both Rechlag and Gorlag, memoirs and archives agree that those in charge (to the extent that anyone was in charge) were almost always West Ukrainians, Poles and Balts. The MVD later fingered a Ukrainian named Herman Stepanyuk as the leader in Norilsk, and a Pole named Kendzerski – a 'former captain in the Polish army' – as one of the leaders in Vorkuta. In his account of the rebellion, Edward Buca, another Pole, also claimed to have led the strike in Vorkuta's mine No. 29. Although he was clearly in that camp at the time, there are reasons to doubt his account, not least because so many of the real strike leaders were later shot.[19]

Years afterwards, Ukrainian nationalists would claim that all of the major Gulag strikes had been planned and executed by their secret organizations, which hid behind multinational strike committees: 'The average prisoner, and we are referring in particular to the prisoners from the West and to the Russian prisoners, was unable either to participate in the decisions or to comprehend the mechanism of the movement.' As evidence, they cited the two 'Karaganda *etaps*', the contingents of Ukrainians who arrived in both camps, just in advance of the strikes.[20]

The same evidence has led others to conclude that the strikes were provoked by elements within the MVD itself. Perhaps members of the security services feared that Khrushchev was about to shut down the camps altogether – and dismiss all of the camp authorities. As a result, they fomented rebellions in order to put them down, and thereby to prove how very necessary they all still were. Simeon Vilensky, an ex-*zek* and publisher, who subsequently organized two conferences on the subject of opposition in the camps, puts it best: 'Who was running the camps? Thousands of people, who don't have a civilian profession, people who are used to complete lawlessness, used to owning the prisoners, being able to do what they want with them. These are people who, compared with other working citizens, get paid rather well.'

Vilensky remains convinced that he witnessed a provocation in his special camp in Kolyma, in 1953. Suddenly, he says, a group of newcomers arrived in the camp. One of them began openly to organize the younger people in the camp into a rebellious group. They spoke of strikes, wrote leaflets, drew in other prisoners. They even used the camp metal workshop to make knives. Their behaviour was so open and so provocative that Vilensky found it suspect: the camp administration could not be tolerating such activity by accident. He led the opposition to the newcomers until, finally, he was moved to another camp.[21]

In principle, these theses are compatible. It is possible that elements within the MVD brought rebellious Ukrainians into the camps in order to cause trouble of some kind. It is also possible that the Ukrainian strike leaders believed themselves to be acting of their own volition. From both official and eyewitness accounts, however, it seems more likely that the strikes gained momentum only thanks to the co-operation among the different national groups. Where the national groups competed more openly with one another, or did not have warm relationships – as in Minlag – strikes were much harder to organize.[22]

Outside the camps, the strikes received no support to speak of. The Gorlag strikers, whose camps lay very close to the city of Norilsk, did try to attract attention to their cause with a banner: 'Comrades, inhabitants of Norilsk! Help us in our struggle.'[23] As most of Norilsk's population were former prisoners, they were almost certainly too afraid to respond. Despite their bureaucratic language, the MVD reports written a few weeks after the events convey very well the terror that the strikes generated among prisoners and free workers alike. One of Gorlag's accountants swore to the MVD that 'if the strikers get out of the *zona*, we will fight against them, as we would fight against enemies'.

Another free worker told the MVD about his accidental meeting with the strikers: 'I had stayed past the end of the shift, in order to finish drilling at the coalface. A group of prisoners came up to me. Grabbing my electric drill, they ordered me to stop working, threatening punishment. I took fright, and stopped working . . .' Fortunately for him, the prisoners shone a lantern on his face, recognized him as a free worker, and left him in peace.[24] Alone, in the dark of the mine, surrounded by hostile, angry, coal-stained strikers, he must have been very frightened indeed.

Local camp bosses were intimidated too. Sensing this, strikers in both Gorlag and Rechlag demanded meetings with representatives from the Soviet government and the Communist Party – from Moscow. They argued that local commanders could not decide anything without Moscow's permission anyway, which was perfectly true.

And Moscow came. That is, on several occasions, representatives of 'Moscow commissions' met with committees of prisoners in Gorlag and Rechlag, to listen, and to discuss, their demands. I could describe these meetings as a break with precedent, but that hardly conveys the extent of their novelty. Never before had prisoners' demands been met with anything other than brute force. In this new, post-Stalinist era, however, Khrushchev seemed willing to try, at least, to win the prisoners over with genuine concessions.

He, or rather his representatives, did not succeed. Four days into the Vorkuta strike, a Moscow commission, led by a senior officer, General I. I. Maslennikov, presented the prisoners with a new list of privileges: a nine-hour working day, the removal of numbers from uniforms, permission to have meetings with relatives, permission to receive letters and money from home. As the official report puts it, many of the strike leaders received this news with 'hostility', and remained on strike. The same reaction had followed a similar offer in Gorlag. The prisoners, it seems, wanted amnesty, not just an improvement in their living conditions.

Although this was not 1938, it was not 1989 either. Stalin was dead, but his legacy lived on. The first step might have been negotiations – but the second step was brute force.

In Norilsk, the authorities first promised that they would 'look into the prisoners' demands'. Instead, as the MVD report explains, 'the commission of the MVD of the USSR decided to liquidate the strikes'. This decision, almost certainly taken by Khrushchev himself, had immediate, dramatic effects on the ground. Soldiers surrounded the striking camps. *Lagpunkt* by *lagpunkt*, they emptied the camps, arrested the strike leaders, and sent the other prisoners away on transports.

In a few cases, this 'liquidation' went relatively smoothly. Arriving at the first camp division, troops caught the prisoners by surprise. Over the camp loudspeaker, the Norilsk chief prosecutor, Babilov, told the prisoners to leave the *zona*, assuring them that those who walked away peacefully would not be punished for their part in the 'sabotage'. According to the official report, most of the prisoners did leave. Seeing that they were isolated, the ringleaders left as well. Out in the taiga, soldiers and camp bosses sorted the prisoners into groups. Trucks were waiting to take away those suspected of instigating the strike, and the 'innocent' were allowed to return to the camp.

Some of the subsequent 'liquidations' went less smoothly. When the authorities followed the same procedure on the following day in another *lagpunkt*, the strike leaders first threatened those wanting to leave – and then locked themselves into one of the barracks, from which they had to be forcibly removed. In the women's camp, the prisoners formed a human circle and hung a black flag – a symbol of unjustly murdered comrades – in the centre, and began to scream and shout slogans. After five hours of this, the guards began spraying them with powerful hoses. Only then did the circle break up sufficiently for the guards to drag the women out of the camp.

In *lagpunkt* No. 5, as many as 1,400 prisoners, mostly Ukrainians and Balts, refused to leave the *zona*. Instead, they hung black flags from their barracks, conducting themselves, in the words of an MVD bureaucrat, with 'extreme aggression'. Then, when the camp guards, assisted by forty soldiers, attempted to rope off the barracks and protect the camp's food supplies, a crowd of 500 prisoners attacked. They shouted curses and cheers, threw rocks, hit the soldiers with clubs and picks, tried to knock their guns out of their arms. The official report describes what happened next: 'At the most critical moment of their attack on the guards, the soldiers opened fire on the prisoners. After the conclusion of the shooting, the prisoners were forced to lie on the ground. After this, the prisoners began to fulfil all of the orders of the guards and of the camp administration.'[25]

According to the same report, twenty-three prisoners died that day. According to eyewitnesses, several hundred prisoners died over several days in Norilsk, in a series of similar incidents.

The authorities put down the Vorkuta strike in a like manner. *Lagpunkt* by *lagpunkt*, soldiers and police troops forced the prisoners out of the camps, sorted them into groups of 100, and put them through a 'filtration' process, separating the presumed strike leaders from the other prisoners. In order to get the prisoners to leave peacefully, the Moscow commission also loudly promised all of the prisoners that their cases would be reviewed, and that the strike leaders would not be shot. The ruse worked: thanks to General Maslennikov's 'fatherly' attitude, 'we believed him', one of the participants later explained.[26]

In one camp, however – the *lagpunkt* beside mine No. 29 – the prisoners did not believe the general – and when Maslennikov told them to return to work, they refused. Soldiers arrived, bringing a fire engine with them, intending to use water hoses to break up the crowd:

But before the hoses could be unwound and turned on us, Ripetsky waved the prisoners forward and a wall of them advanced, turning the vehicle out of the gate as if it had been a toy . . . There was a salvo of shots from the guards, straight into the mass of prisoners. But we were standing with our arms linked, and at first no one fell, though many were dead and wounded. Only Ihnatowicz, a little in front of the line, was standing alone. He seemed to stand for a moment in astonishment, then turned round to face us. His lips moved, but no words came out. He stretched out an arm, then fell.

As he fell, there came a second salvo, then a third, and a fourth. Then the heavy machine-guns opened fire.

Again, the estimates of those killed in mine No. 29 vary widely. The official documents speak of 42 dead and 135 wounded. Eyewitnesses again speak of 'hundreds' of casualties.[27]

The strikes were over. But neither camp was ever truly pacified. Throughout the rest of 1953 and 1954, protests broke out sporadically in Vorkuta and Norilsk, in the other special camps, and in the ordinary camps as well. 'A triumphant spirit, buoyed up by the wage increase we had won, was the strike's heritage,' wrote Noble. When he was transferred into mine No. 29, scene of the massacre, prisoners who had survived proudly showed him their scars from that day.[28]

As the prisoners grew bolder, practically no camp was unaffected. In November 1953, for example, 530 prisoners refused to work in Vyatlag. They demanded better pay, and an end to 'abnormalities' in clothing distribution and living conditions. The camp administration agreed to meet their demands, but the following day the prisoners went on strike again. This time, they demanded to be included in Beria's amnesty. The strike ended when the organizers were arrested and imprisoned.[29] In March 1954, a group of 'bandits' took over one *lagpunkt* of Kargopollag, threatening to riot unless they were given better food – and vodka.[30] In July 1954, 900 prisoners in Minlag staged a week-long hunger strike, protesting over the death of a prisoner who had been burned alive when a punishment block caught fire. The prisoners distributed leaflets around the camp and in the nearby village, explaining the reasons for the strike, stopping only when a Moscow commission arrived and met their demands for better treatment. Elsewhere in Minlag, strikes became a permanent part of life, sometimes carried out by individual brigades, sometimes by whole mines.[31]

More unrest was planned, as the authorities knew. In June 1954, the MVD sent an informer's report directly to Kruglov, the Interior Minister. The report contained an account of a conversation between a group of Ukrainian prisoners whom the informer had met in Sverdlovsk transit prison. The prisoners were from Gorlag, and had taken part in the strike there. Now they were being transported elsewhere – but they were preparing for next time:

Everyone in the cell was made to explain to Pavlishin and Stepanyuk what they did during the strike, including myself . . . In my presence, Morushko reported to Stepan-yuk about an incident on the barge from Norilsk to Krasnoyarsk. On this barge he conducted a filtration of prisoners, and those who were not useful, he destroyed. Stepanyuk told Pavlishin, 'The mission you were given has been fulfilled, now our deeds will be part of the history of Ukraine.' He then hugged Morushko, and said,

'Pan Morushko, you have done great service to our organization . . . for this you will receive a medal, and after the collapse of Soviet power you will occupy an important post.'[32]

Although it is perfectly possible that the informer who filed this report did hear a conversation somewhat like this one, he elaborated as well: later in his report, he went on to accuse the Ukrainians of organizing a most unlikely plot to kill Khrushchev. Still, the fact that such dubious information was sent straight to Kruglov itself indicates how seriously the authorities now took the threat of further rebellion. Both of the commissions sent to investigate the situation in Rechlag and Gorlag had concluded that it was necessary to increase the number of guards, to toughen the regime, and above all to increase the number of informers.[33]

As it turned out, they were right to worry. The most dangerous uprising was still to come.

Like its two predecessors, the uprising that Solzhenitsyn christened 'The Forty Days of Kengir' was not abrupt or unexpected.[34] It emerged slowly, in the spring of 1954, out of a series of incidents at the Steplag special camp, which was located beside the village of Kengir, in Kazakhstan.

Like their counterparts in Rechlag and Gorlag, the commanders of Steplag were, in the wake of Stalin's death, unable to cope with their prisoners. One of the historians of the strike, having studied the camp's archives from the year 1953, concludes that the administration had 'totally lost control'. In the run-up to the strike, Steplag's commanders periodically sent reports to Moscow, describing the underground organizations in the camp, the incidents of unrest, and the 'crisis' afflicting the system of informers, by now almost completely incapacitated. Moscow wrote back, ordering the camp to isolate the Ukrainians and Balts from the other prisoners. But the administration either would not or could not do so. At that time, nearly half of the 20,000 prisoners in the camp were Ukrainians, and a quarter were Balts and Poles; perhaps the facilities to separate them did not exist. As a result, the prisoners kept on breaking the rules, staging intermittent strikes and protests.[35]

Unable to cow the prisoners with threats of punishments, the guards resorted to actual violence. Some – including Solzhenitsyn – believe that these incidents also were provocations, designed to spark the revolt that followed. Whether or not this is true – and there are so far no records either way – camp guards did several times open fire on uncooperative prisoners during the winter of 1953 and the spring of 1954, killing several people.

Then, perhaps in a desperate attempt to reassert control, the camp administration shipped a group of criminals into the camps, and openly instructed them to provoke fights with the politicals in *lagpunkt* No. 3 – the most rebellious of the Steplag *lagpunkts*. The plan backfired. 'And here,' writes Solzhenitsyn, 'we see how unpredictable is the course of human emotions and of social movements! Injecting in Kengir no. 3 a mammoth dose of tested ptomaine, the bosses obtained not a pacified camp but the biggest mutiny in the history of the Gulag Archipelago.'[36] Instead of fighting, the two groups agreed to co-operate.

As in other camps, the prisoners of Steplag were organized by nationality. Steplag's Ukrainians, however, appear to have taken their organization a few steps further into conspiracy. Instead of openly choosing leaders, the Ukrainians formed a conspiratorial 'Centre', a secret group whose membership never became publicly known, and probably contained representatives of all of the camp's nationalities. By the time the thieves arrived in the camp, the Centre had already started to produce weapons – makeshift knives, clubs and picks – in the camp workshops, and were in contact with the prisoners of the two neighbouring *lagpunkts*, No. 1 – a *zona* for women – and No. 2. Perhaps these tough politicals impressed the thieves with their handiwork, or perhaps they terrified them. In any case, all agree that at a midnight meeting, representatives of both groups, criminal and political, shook hands and agreed to unite.

On 16 May, this co-operation bore its first fruit. That afternoon, a large group of prisoners in *lagpunkt* No. 3 began to destroy the stone wall which separated their camp from the other two neighbouring camps, and from the service yard, which contained both the camp workshops and the warehouses. In an earlier era, their aim would have been rape. Now, with Ukrainian nationalist partisans, male and female, on both sides of the wall, the men believed themselves to be coming to the aid of their women – their relatives, friends, or even spouses.

The destruction of the wall continued through the night. In response, the camp guards opened fire, killing thirteen prisoners and wounding forty-three, and beat up other prisoners, including women. The following day, infuriated by the killings, the prisoners of *lagpunkt* No. 3 staged a massive protest, and wrote anti-Soviet slogans on the walls of their dining hall. That night, groups of prisoners broke into the punishment isolator – literally taking it apart with their hands – and freed the 252 prisoners locked inside. They took full control of the camp warehouses, the camp kitchen and bakery, and the camp workshops, which they immediately turned over to the production of knives and clubs. By the morning of 19 May, most of the prisoners were on strike.

Neither Moscow nor the local camp leadership seemed to know what to do next. The camp commander promptly informed Kruglov, the MVD boss, of what had happened. Equally promptly, Kruglov ordered Gubin, the head of the Kazakh MVD, to investigate. Gubin then turned around and asked the Gulag to send a commission from Moscow. A commission arrived. Negotiations ensued – and the commission, playing for time, promised the prisoners it would investigate the unlawful shootings, leave open the walls between the camps, and even speed up the process of re-examining prisoners' cases.

The prisoners believed them. On 23 May, they returned to work. When the day shift returned home, however, they saw that at least one of the promises had been broken: the walls between the *lagpunkts* had been rebuilt. By 25 May, the boss of Kengir, V. M. Bochkov, was again telegramming frantically for permission to impose a 'strict regime' on the prisoners: no letters, no meetings, no money orders, no re-examinations of cases. In addition, he removed about 420 criminal prisoners from the camp, and sent them to another *lagpunkt*, where they went on striking.

The result: within forty-eight hours, the prisoners had chased all of the camp authorities out of the *zona*, having threatened them with their newly produced weapons. Although the authorities had guns, they were out-numbered. More than 5,000 prisoners lived in the three camp divisions, and most of them had joined the uprising. Those who had not joined were too intimidated to protest. Those who felt neutral were soon caught up in the spirit of the forty-day uprising. On the first morning of the strike, remembered one prisoner with wonder, 'we weren't woken up by the guards, we weren't greeted by shouts and cries'.

The camp authorities seem, at first, to have expected the strike to fall apart of its own accord. Sooner or later, they reckoned, the thieves and the politicals would fall out. The prisoners would wallow in anarchy and debauchery, the women would be raped, the food would be stolen. But although the prisoners' behaviour during the strike should not be idealized, it is true to say that nearly the opposite occurred: the camp began to run itself with a surprising degree of harmony.

Very quickly, the prisoners chose a strike committee, charged with the task of negotiations, as well as the organization of the daily life of the camp. Accounts of the origins of this committee differ radically. The official record of events claims that the authorities were holding general negotations with groups of prisoners, when suddenly a group of people claiming to be the strike committee burst in on the scene, and denied anyone else the right to speak. A number of witnesses, however, have said that it was the authorities themselves who suggested to the prisoners that they form a strike committee, which was subsequently chosen by democratic vote.

The true relationship of the strike committee to the 'real' leadership of the uprising also remains hazy, as it probably was at the time. Even if they had not exactly planned it step by step, the Ukrainian-led Centre was clearly the motivating force behind the strike, and played a decisive role in the 'democratic' election of the strike committee. The Ukrainians seem to have insisted on a multinational committee: they did not want the strike to seem too anti-Russian or anti-Soviet, and they wanted the strike to have a Russian leader.

That Russian was Colonel Kapiton Kuznetsov, who stands out, even in the murky tale of Kengir, as a notably ambiguous figure. An ex-Red Army officer, Kuznetsov had been captured by the Nazis during the war, and placed in a POW camp. In 1948, he was arrested and accused of having collaborated with the Nazi administration of the POW camp, and even accused of joining the battle against Soviet partisans. If these accusations are true, they help explain his behaviour during the strike. Having played the part of turncoat once, he would have been well prepared to play a double role once again.

Apparently, the Ukrainians chose Kuznetsov in the hope that he would give a 'Soviet' face to the uprising, depriving the authorities of an excuse to crush the prisoners. This he certainly did – perhaps going to extremes. At Kuznetsov's urging, the striking prisoners hung banners around the camp: 'Long live the Soviet constitution!' 'Long live the Soviet regime!' 'Down with the murdering Beriaites!' He harangued the prisoners, arguing that they should stop writing leaflets, that 'counter-revolutionary' agitation would only harm their cause. He assiduously courted the 'Soviet' prisoners, the inmates who had maintained their faith in the Party, and persuaded them to help keep order.

And although the Ukrainians had helped elect him, Kuznetsov certainly did not repay their faith. In the long, carefully detailed, written confession that he composed after the strike had come to its inevitable bloody end, Kuznetsov claimed he had always considered the Centre to be illegitimate, and had fought against its secret edicts throughout the strike. But the Ukrainians never really trusted Kuznetsov either. Throughout the strike, two armed Ukrainian guards followed him everywhere. Ostensibly, this was for his protection. In reality, it was probably to ensure that he did not slip out of the camp at night, betraying the cause.

The Ukrainians may have been right to fear Kuznetsov's escape, for another member of the strike committee, Aleksei Makeev, eventually did leave the camp, slipping out a few weeks into the strike. Later, Makeev read speeches over the camp radio, urging the prisoners to return to work. Perhaps he had understood early on that the strike was doomed to failure – or perhaps he had been a tool of the administration from the beginning.

Yet not all of the strike committee were people of doubtful commitment. Kuznetsov himself would later claim that at least three committee members – 'Gleb' Sluchenkov, Gersh Keller and Yuri Knopmus – were in fact representatives of the secret Centre. Camp authorities also later described one of them, Gersh Keller, as a representative of the secret Ukrainian conspiracy, and indeed his biography would seem to match this picture. Listed in the camp records as a Jew, Keller was in fact an ethnic Ukrainian – his real surname was Pendrak – who had managed to conceal his ethnicity from the MVD during his arrest. Keller put himself in charge of the strike's 'military' division, organizing the prisoners to fight back in case the guards attacked the camp. It was he who had begun the mass production of weapons – knives, staves, picks, clubs – in the camp workshops, and he who had set up a 'laboratory' to build makeshift grenades, Molotov cocktails, and other 'hot' weapons. Keller also supervised the building of barricades, and arranged for every barrack to keep a barrel of ground glass by its door – to be thrown in the eyes of the soldiers, if and when they should arrive.

If Keller represented the Ukrainians, Gleb Sluchenkov was linked, rather, to the camp's criminals. Kuznetsov himself described him as a 'representative of the criminal world', and Ukrainian nationalist sources also describe Sluchenkov as the leader of the thieves. During the uprising, Sluchenkov ran the strike committee's 'counter-intelligence' operation. He had his own 'police', who patrolled the camp, kept the peace, and imprisoned potential turncoats and informers. Sluchenkov organized all the camps into divisions, and put a 'commander' in charge of each one. Later, Kuznetsov would complain that the names of these commanders were kept secret, and were known only to Sluchenkov and Keller.

Kuznetsov was less vitriolic about Knopmus, an ethnic German born in St Petersburg, who ran the uprising's 'propaganda' division. Yet in retrospect, Knopmus's activities during the uprising were the most revolutionary, and the most anti-Soviet, of all. Knopmus's 'propaganda' included the production of leaflets – distributed to the local population outside the camp – the printing of a camp 'wall newspaper' for the benefit of striking prisoners, and, most extraordinarily, the building of a makeshift radio station.

Given that the authorities had cut off the camp's electricity in the first days of the strike, this radio station was not just a piece of bravado, but a great technical achievement. First, the zeks put together a 'hydroelectric' power station – using a water tap. A motor was converted into a generator, and enough electricity was made to power the camp telephone system, as well as the radio. The radio, in turn, was put together using parts from the camp's portable film projectors.

Within days, the camp had news announcers and regular news programmes, designed for the prisoners as well as the local population outside the camp, including the guards and soldiers. Camp stenographers recorded the text of one of the radio addresses, made after the uprising had lasted a month, when food supplies were beginning to run out. Directed at the soldiers who now stood on guard outside the camp, the stenograph made its way into the MVD files:

Comrade Soldiers! We are not afraid of you and we ask you not to come into our *zona*. Don't shoot at us, don't buckle under the will of the Beriaites. We are not afraid of them, just as we are not afraid of death. We would rather die of hunger in this camp, than give up to the Beriaite band. Don't soil your hands with the same dirty blood which your officers have on their hands . . .[37]

Kuznetsov, meanwhile, organized the distribution of food, which was prepared and cooked by the camp women. Each prisoner received the same ration – there were no extra portions for *pridurki* – which slowly grew smaller, as the weeks went by and the stores decreased. Voluntary details also cleaned the barracks, washed clothes and stood guard. One inmate remembered that 'order and cleanliness' reigned in the dining hall, which had often been filthy and chaotic in the past. The camp baths worked as usual, as did the hospital, although the camp authorities refused to hand over necessary medicines and supplies.

Prisoners organized their own 'entertainments' as well. According to one memoir, a Polish aristocrat named Count Bobrinski opened a 'café' in the camp, where he served 'coffee': 'He threw something in the water, boiled it, and prisoners in the middle of a hot day sipped this drink with satisfaction, laughing.' The count himself sat in the corner of the café, played his guitar and sang old romantic songs.[38] Other prisoners organized lecture series, as well as concerts. A group of self-motivated thespians rehearsed and performed a play. One of the religious sects, its male and female members reunited by the destruction of the walls, claimed that their prophet had predicted they would now all be taken to heaven, alive. For several days, they sat on their mattresses in the main square, in the centre of the *zona*, waiting to be taken to heaven. Alas, nothing happened.

Large numbers of newlyweds also appeared, united by the many prisoner priests who had been arrested along with their Baltic or Ukrainian flocks. Among them were some of those who had been married while standing on opposite sides of the camp walls, and were now meeting face to face for the first time. But although men and women mingled freely, all descriptions of the strike agree that women were never molested, and certainly not attacked or raped, as they were so often in ordinary camps.

Songs were written, of course. Someone composed a Ukrainian hymn, which at times all 13,500 striking prisoners would sing at once. The refrain went like this:

> We will not, we will not be slaves
> We will not carry the yoke any longer . . .

Another verse spoke of:

> Brothers in blood, of Vorkuta and Norilsk, of Kolyma and Kengir . . .

'It was a wonderful time,' remembered Irena Arginskaya, forty-five years later. 'I had not before then, and have not since, felt such a sense of freedom as I did then.' Others felt more foreboding. Lyuba Bershadskaya recalls that we 'did everything without any awareness: none of us knew or even thought about what was waiting for us'.

Negotiations with the authorities continued. By 27 May, the MVD commission delegated to deal with the strike had held its first meeting with the prisoners. Among what Solzhenitsyn calls the 'golden-epauletted personages' on the commission were Sergei Yegorov, the deputy chief of the MVD; Ivan Dolgikh, then the commander of the Gulag system; and Vavilov, the deputy state prosecutor responsible for overseeing the Gulag. They were met by a gathering of 2,000 prisoners, led by Kuznetsov, who presented them with a list of demands.

By the time the strike was in full swing, these demands would include both the imposition of criminal charges on guards who had shot prisoners – which the prisoners had demanded from the beginning – as well as more clearly political demands. Among these were the reduction of all 25-year sentences; the review of all political prisoners' cases; the liquidation of the punishment cells and punishment barracks; more freedom for prisoners to communicate with relatives; the removal of the requirement of forced eternal exile for freed prisoners; easier living conditions for women prisoners; and a permanent reuniting of the men's and women's camps.

The prisoners also demanded a meeting with a member of the Communist Party Central Committee. They continued to make this demand until the very end, on the grounds that they could not trust either the Steplag authorities or the MVD to abide by any promises made. 'And who could have inspired in you such hatred for the MVD?' the MVD deputy chief Yegorov reportedly asked them in response.

Had the strike taken place a few years earlier, there would, of course, have been no negotiations at all. But by 1954, the re-examination of politicals' cases had in fact begun, albeit slowly. During the course of the strike, it even happened that individual prisoners were summoned to leave the camp in order to attend meetings of the tribunal reinvestigating their cases. Knowing that many prisoners had already died, and apparently wanting a peaceful and rapid conclusion to events, Dolgikh almost immediately began to concede to some of the prisoners' minor demands, calling for bars to be removed from barrack windows, for the establishment of an eight-hour workday, even for the transfer of certain particularly hated camp guards and officials out of Kengir. Under direct orders from Moscow, Dolgikh at first refrained from using force. He did try to break the prisoners' resistance, however, actively urging them to leave the camp, and forbidding any new shipments of food or medicine.

As time went on, however, Moscow lost patience. In a telegram sent on 15 June, Kruglov lashed out at his deputy, Yegorov, for filling his reports with pointless statistics – such as how many pigeons had been released from the camp carrying leaflets – and informed him that an echelon of troops, accompanied by five T-34 tanks, were on their way.

The last ten days of the strike were very tense indeed. The MVD commission issued stern warnings via the camp loudspeaker system. In response, the prisoners broadcast messages from their makeshift radio station, telling the world that they were starving to death. Kuznetsov made a speech, in which he spoke of the fate of his family, which had been destroyed by his arrest. 'Many of us had also lost relatives, and listening to him we strengthened our resolve, deciding to stick it out until the end,' one prisoner remembered.

Just before dawn, at half past three on the morning of 26 June, the MVD struck. The previous evening, Kruglov had telegrammed Yegorov, advising him to use 'all possible resources', and he complied: no fewer than 1,700 soldiers, ninety-eight dogs, and the five T-34 tanks surrounded the camp. At first, the soldiers sent flares soaring into the sky above the barracks, and fired blanks. Urgent warnings began to sound over the camp loudspeakers: 'Soldiers are entering the camps. Prisoners who want to co-operate are asked to leave the camp quietly. Prisoners who resist will be shot . . .'

As the disoriented prisoners rushed around the camp, the tanks entered the gates. Armed troops, dressed in full battle gear, followed behind them. By some accounts, both the soldiers driving the tanks and those on the ground were drunk. While this may be a legend which grew up in the wake of the raid, it is true that both the Red Army and the secret police traditionally gave vodka to soldiers who were being asked to do dirty work: empty bottles are almost always found inside mass graves.

Drunk or not, the tank drivers had no qualms about running straight over those prisoners who advanced to meet them. 'I stood in the middle,' recalled Lyubov Bershadskaya, 'and all around me tanks crushed living people.' They ran straight over a group of women, who had locked arms together and stood in their path, not believing that the tanks would dare kill them. They ran over one newlywed couple who, holding on to one another tightly, deliberately threw themselves in their path. They destroyed barracks, with people sleeping inside. They resisted the home-made grenades, the stones, the picks and other metal objects that the prisoners threw at them. Surprisingly quickly – within an hour and a half, according to the report filed later – the soldiers had pacified the camp, removed those prisoners who had agreed to go quietly, and put the rest in handcuffs.

According to the official documents, thirty-seven prisoners died outright that day. Nine more died later of their wounds. Another 106 were wounded, along with forty soldiers. Again, all of these numbers are much lower than those recorded by the prisoners themselves. Bershadskaya, who helped the camp doctor, Julian Fuster, take care of the wounded, writes of 500 dead:

Fuster told me to put on a white cap and a surgeon's gauze mask (which I keep to this day) and asked me to stand by the operating table and write down the names of those who could still give their names. Unfortunately, almost nobody could. Most of the wounded died on the table, and, looking at us with departing eyes, said, 'Write to my mother . . . to my husband . . . to my children,' and so on.

When it became too hot and stuffy to bear, I took off the cap and looked at myself in the mirror. I had a completely white head. At first, I thought that there must have been powder inside the cap for some reason. I didn't realize that while standing in the centre of that unbelievable slaughter, observing all that took place, all of my hair had turned grey within fifteen minutes.

Fuster stood for thirteen hours on his feet, saving whoever he could. Finally, that resilient, talented surgeon couldn't take it any more himself. He lost consciousness, fell into a faint, and the operations finished . . .[39]

In the wake of the battle, all of the living who were not in hospital were marched out of the camp, and led out into the taiga. Soldiers with machine-guns made them lie face down, arms spread to the side – as if crucified – for many hours. Working from the photographs they had taken at the public meetings and from what few informers' reports they had, the camp authorities picked through the prisoners and arrested 436 people, including all of the members of the strike commission. Six of them would be executed, including Keller, Sluchenkov and Knopmus. Kuznetsov, who presented the authorities with a long, elaborate, written confession within forty-eight hours of his arrest, was sentenced to death – and then spared. He was moved to Karlag, and released in 1960. Another thousand prisoners – 500 men and 500 women – were accused of supporting the rebellion, and were shipped off to other camps, to Ozerlag and Kolyma. They, too, it seems, were mostly released by the end of the decade.

During the uprising, the authorities appear to have had no idea that there was any organizing force within the camp other than the official strike committee. Afterwards, they began to piece together the whole story, probably thanks to Kuznetsov's elaborate account. They identified five representatives of the Centre – the Lithuanian Kondratas; the Ukrainians Keller, Sunichuk and Vakhaev; and the thief known by the underworld pseudonym 'Moustache'. They even made a chart, showing the lines of command flowing out from the Centre, through the strike committee, towards the departments of propaganda, defence and counter-intelligence. They knew about the brigades that had been organized to defend each barrack, about the radio station and the makeshift generator.

But they never did identify all of the members of the Centre, the real organizers of the uprising. According to one account, many of the 'true activists' remained in the camp, quietly serving out their sentences, awaiting amnesty. Their names are unknown – and will probably remain so.

25

Thaw – and Release

Let's not beat around the bush,
No more nonsense.
We are the children of the cult.
We are its flesh and blood

We have been raised in the fog
Ambiguous indeed,
Inside gigantomania
And scarcity of mind . . .

– Andrei Voznesensky,
'Children of the Cult', 1967[1]

Although they lost their battle, the Kengir strikers won the war. In the aftermath of the Steplag rebellion, the leadership of the Soviet Union really did lose its appetite for forced-labour camps – and with striking speed.

By the summer of 1954, the unprofitability of the camps was widely recognized. Another survey of the Gulag's finances, carried out in June 1954, had again shown that they were heavily subsidized, and that the costs of guards in particular made them unprofitable.[2] At a meeting of camp commanders and top Gulag personnel held soon after Kengir, many administrators complained openly about the poor organization of food supplies for camps, about the out-of-control bureaucracy – by this time there were seventeen separate food norms – and about the poor organization of camps. Some camps were still open, but with very few prisoners. Strikes and unrest continued. In 1955, prisoners organized another general strike in Vorkuta.[3] The incentive to change was now overwhelming – and change came.

On 10 July 1954, the Central Committee issued a resolution, bringing back the eight-hour workday, simplifying the camp regimes, and making it easier for prisoners to earn early release through hard work. The special camps were dissolved. Prisoners were allowed to write letters and receive packages, often without restriction. In some camps, prisoners were allowed to get married, even to live with their spouses. The barking dogs and convoy guards became things of the past. New items became available for the prisoners to purchase: clothing, which had been unavailable before, and oranges.[4] The inmates of Ozerlag were even allowed to plant flowers.[5]

By this time, the upper echelons of the Soviet elite had also begun to conduct a wider debate about Stalinist justice. In early 1954, Khrushchev had ordered, and received, a report detailing how many prisoners had been accused of counter-revolutionary crimes since 1921, as well as an account of how many were still imprisoned. The numbers were by definition incomplete, since they did not include the millions sent into exile, those unjustly accused of technically non-political crimes, those tried in ordinary courts, and those never tried at all. Still, given that these figures represent numbers of people who had been killed or sent to prison for no reason at all, they are shockingly high. By the MVD's own count, 3,777,380 people had been found 'guilty' of fomenting counter-revolution by the OGPU collegiums, the NKVD troikas, the Special Commissions, and all of the military collegiums and tribunals that had mass-produced sentences throughout the previous three decades. Of these, 2,369,220 had been sent to camps, 765,180 had been sent into exile, and 642,980 had been executed.[6]

A few days later, the Central Committee undertook to re-examine all of these cases – as well as the cases of the 'repeaters', those prisoners who had been sentenced to a second term of exile in 1948. Khrushchev set up a national committee, led by the chief prosecutor of the Soviet Union, to oversee the task. He also set up local committees in every republic and region of the country to review prisoners' sentences. Some politicals were released at this time, although their original sentences were not yet annulled: real rehabilitation – the state's admission that a mistake had been made – would come later.[7]

Releases began, although for the next year and a half they would proceed at an excruciatingly slow pace. Those who had completed two-thirds of their sentences were sometimes let go, without explanation or rehabilitation. Others were kept inside the camps, for no reason at all. Despite everything they knew about the camps' unprofitability, Gulag officials were unwilling to close them. They needed, it seemed, an extra jolt from above.

Then, in February 1956, the jolt arrived, when Khrushchev gave what came to be known as his 'secret speech', delivering it to a closed session of the Twentieth Party Congress of the Communist Party. For the first time, Khrushchev openly attacked Stalin and the 'cult of personality' that had surrounded him:

It is impermissible, and foreign to the spirit of Marxism-Leninism, to elevate one person, to transform him into a superman possessing supernatural characteristics, akin to those of a god. Such a man supposedly knows everything, sees everything, thinks for everyone, can do anything, is infallible in his behaviour. Such a belief about a man, and specifically about Stalin, was cultivated among us for many years.[8]

Much of the rest of the speech was tendentious. Listing Stalin's crimes, Khrushchev focused almost exclusively on the victims of 1937 and 1938, singling out the ninety-eight Central Committee members who were shot, as well as a handful of Old Bolsheviks. 'The wave of mass arrests began to recede in 1939,' he declared – which was a patent falsehood, as in fact the numbers of prisoners increased in the 1940s. He did mention the Chechen and the Balkan deportations, perhaps because he had no hand in them. He did not mention collectivization, or the Ukrainian famine, or the mass repressions in West Ukraine and the Baltic States, perhaps because he had himself been involved in these operations. He spoke of 7,679 rehabilitations, and although those in the hall applauded him, this was in fact quite a small percentage of the millions whom Khrushchev knew had been falsely arrested.[9]

Flawed though it might have been, the speech – soon transmitted, also in secrecy, to Party cells all over the country – shook the Soviet Union to its core. Never before had the Soviet leadership confessed to any crimes, let alone such a broad range of them. Even Khrushchev was uncertain what the reaction would be. 'We were just coming out of a state of shock,' he wrote later. 'People were still in prisons and in the camps, and we didn't know how to explain what had happened to them or what to do with them once they were free.'[10]

The speech galvanized the MVD, the KGB, and the administrators of the camps. Within weeks, the atmosphere in the camps lightened further, and the process of release and rehabilitation finally began to speed up. If 7,000-odd people had been rehabilitated in the three years preceding the secret speech, 617,000 were rehabilitated in the ten months that followed it. New mechanisms were created to speed the process further. Ironically, many of the prisoners who had been sentenced by troikas were now released by troikas as well. Commissions composed of three people – a prosecutor, a Central Committee member, and a rehabilitated Party member, often an ex-prisoner – travelled to camps and places of exile all over the country. They were empowered to conduct fast investigations into individual cases, to conduct interviews with prisoners, and to release them on the spot.[11]

In the months that followed the secret speech, the MVD also prepared to make much deeper changes to the structure of the camps themselves. In April, the new Interior Minister, N. P. Dudorov, sent a proposal for the reorganization of the camps to the Central Committee. The situation in the camps and colonies, he wrote, 'has been abysmal for many years now'. They should be closed, he argued, and instead the most dangerous criminals should be sent to special, isolated prisons, in distant regions of the country, specifically naming the building site of the unfinished Salekhard–Igarka Railway as one such possibility. Minor criminals, on the other hand, should remain in their native regions, serving out their sentences in prison 'colonies', doing light industrial labour and working on collective farms. None should be required to work as lumberjacks, miners or builders, or indeed to carry out any other type of unskilled, hard labour.[12]

Dudorov's choice of language was more important than his specific suggestions. He was not merely proposing the creation of a smaller camp system, he was proposing to create a qualitatively different one, to return to a 'normal' prison system, or at least to a prison system which would be recognizable as such in other European countries. The new prison colonies would stop pretending to be financially self-sufficient. Prisoners would work in order to learn useful skills, not in order to enrich the state. The aim of prisoners' work would be rehabilitation, not profit.[13]

There were surprisingly angry objections to these suggestions. Although the representatives of economic ministries signalled their support, I. A. Serov, the KGB boss, lashed out at the Interior Minister's proposals, calling them 'incorrect' and 'unacceptable', not to mention expensive. He opposed the construction of new prison colonies, on the grounds that such a policy would 'create the impression of the presence in the USSR of a huge number of places of incarceration'. He opposed the liquidation of the camps, and could not understand why zeks should not work as foresters or miners. After all, hard labour would help 're-educate them in the spirit of honest working life of Soviet society'.[14]

The result of this clash between the two branches of the security services was a very mixed reform. On the one hand, the Gulag itself – the *Glavnoe upravlenie lagerei*, the Main Camp Administration – was dissolved. In 1957, both Dalstroi and Norilsk, two of the biggest and most powerful camp complexes, were dismantled. Other camps followed suit. The appropriate ministries – of mining, machine-building, forestry or road-building – took over large swathes of what had been the camp-industrial complex.[15] Slave labour would never again be an important part of the economy in the Soviet Union.

Yet at the same time, the judicial system remained unreformed. The judges were just as politicized, just as biased, just as unfair. The prison system also remained virtually untouched. The same gaolers continued to enforce the same regimes in the same unpainted, unaltered cells. When, with time, the prison system began to expand once again, even the rehabilitation and re-education programmes, the focus of so much concern and interest, would remain just as flimsy and as fictitious as they had in the past.

The surprisingly vitriolic debate between the MVD chief, Dudorov, and the KGB chief, Serov, also prefigured other, larger debates to come. Following what they took to be Khrushchev's lead, liberals wanted to make fast changes to almost every sphere of Soviet life. At the same time, defenders of the old system wanted to stop, reverse, or alter these changes, particularly when they affected the livelihoods of powerful groups of people. The result of this clash was predictable: not only unchanged prison cells, but also half-baked reforms, new privileges which were quickly revoked, and public discussions which were immediately hushed up. The era which came to be called the 'Thaw' was indeed an era of change, but change of a particular kind: reforms took two steps forward, and then one step – or sometimes three steps – back.

Release, whether it came in 1926 or 1956, had always left prisoners with mixed feelings. Gennady Andreev-Khomiakov, a prisoner released in the 1930s, was surprised by his own reaction:

I imagined that I would be dancing instead of walking, that when I finally got my freedom I'd be drunk with it. But when I was actually released, I felt none of this. I walked through the gates and past the last guard, experiencing no happiness or sense of uplift . . . There, along the sun-drenched platform ran two young girls in light dresses, merrily laughing about something. I looked at them in astonishment. How could they laugh? How could all these people walk around conversing and laughing as if nothing unusual was happening in the world, as if nothing nightmarish and unforgettable stood in their midst . . .[16]

After Stalin's death and Khrushchev's speech, the releases came more rapidly, and reactions became even more confused. Prisoners who had expected to spend another decade behind barbed wire were let go on a day's notice. One group of exiles was summoned during working hours to the offices of their mine, and simply told to go home. As one remembered, *Spetskomandant* Lieutenant Isaev 'opened a safe, pulled out our documents, and distributed them. . . .'[17] Prisoners who had filed petition after petition, demanding a re-examination of their cases, suddenly found that further letters were unnecessary – they could simply walk away.

Prisoners who had thought of nothing else except freedom were strangely reluctant to experience it: 'Although I could hardly believe it myself, I was weeping as I walked out to freedom . . . I felt as though I had torn my heart away from what was dearest and most precious to it, from my comrades in misfortune. The gates closed – and it was all finished.'[18]

Many were simply not ready. Yuri Zorin, riding a crowded prisoners' train south from Kotlas in 1954, made it past only two stations. 'Why am I going to Moscow?' he asked himself – and then turned around and headed back to his old camp, where his ex-commander helped him get a job as a free worker. There he remained, for another sixteen years.[19] Evgeniya Ginzburg knew a woman who actually did not want to leave her barracks: 'The thing is that I – I can't face living outside. I want to stay in camp,' she told her friends.[20] Another wrote in his diary that 'I really don't want freedom. What is drawing me to freedom? It seems to me that out there . . . there are lies, hypocrisy, thoughtlessness. Out there, everything is fantastically unreal, and here, every-thing is real.'[21] Many did not trust Khrushchev, expected the situation to worsen again, and took jobs as free workers in Vorkuta or Norilsk. They preferred not to experience the emotions and undergo the hassle of return, if they were ultimately to be rearrested anyway.

But even those who wanted to return home often found it nearly impossible to do so. They had no money, and very little food. Camps released prisoners with the equivalent of 500 grams of bread for every day they were expected to be on the road – a starvation ration.[22] Even that was insufficient, since they were often on the road much longer than expected, as it proved almost impossible to obtain tickets on the few planes and trains leading south. Arriving at the station in Krasnoyarsk, Ariadna Efron found 'such a crowd, that to leave was impossible, simply impossible. People from all of the camps were there, from all of Norilsk.' She was finally given a ticket out of the blue by an 'angel', a woman who by chance had two. Otherwise, she might have waited for months.[23]

Facing a similarly crowded train, Galina Usakova, like many others, solved the problem by riding home on a baggage rack.[24] Still others did not make it at all: it was not uncommon for prisoners to die on the difficult journey home, or within weeks or months of arrival. Weakened by their years of hard labour, tired out by exhausting journeys, the emotions surrounding their return overwhelmed them, resulting in heart attacks and strokes. 'How many people died from this freedom!' one prisoner marvelled.[25]

Some wound up back in prison. The MVD itself produced a report revealing that freed prisoners coming out of Vorkuta, Pechora and Inta camps could not buy clothes, shoes or bedding, as 'the towns above the Arctic Circle have no markets'. In desperation, some committed minor crimes in order to be rearrested. At least in prison they were guaranteed a bread ration.[26] Not that those in charge of the camps necessarily minded this: facing an employment crisis, the Vorkuta administration disobeyed orders from above and actually tried to prevent certain categories of prisoners from leaving the mines.[27]

If they did manage to return to Moscow, Leningrad, or whatever village they had originally come from, former camp inmates often found their lives no easier. Mere release, it turned out, was not sufficient to re-establish a 'normal' life. Without the documents testifying to actual rehabilitation – documents which annulled the prisoners' original sentence – former politicals were still suspect.

True, a few years earlier, they would have been handed the dreaded 'wolves' passports', which forbade ex-political prisoners from living in or near any of the Soviet Union's major cities. Others would have been sent directly into exile. Now the 'wolves' passports' had been abolished, but it was still difficult to find places to live, to find work, and, in Moscow, to get permission to remain in the capital. Prisoners returned to find their homes had long ago been requisitioned, their possessions disbursed. Many of their relatives, also 'enemies' by association, were dead, or impoverished: long after they had been released, familes of 'enemies' remained stigmatized, subject to official forms of discrimination and forbidden from working in certain kinds of jobs. Local authorities were still suspicious of former prisoners. Thomas Sgovio spent a year 'petitioning and hassling' before he was allowed to become a legal resident of his mother's apartment.[28] Older prisoners found it impossible to get a proper pension.[29]

These personal difficulties, coupled with their sense of injured justice, persuaded many to seek full rehabilitation – but this was not a simple or straightforward process either. For many, the option was not even available. The MVD categorically refused to review the case of anyone sentenced before 1935, for example.[30] Those who had gained an extra sentence in a camp, whether for insubordination, dissidence or theft, were never given the coveted rehabilitation certificates either.[31] The cases of the highest-ranking Bolsheviks – Bukharin, Kamenev, Zinoviev – remained taboo, and those condemned in the same investigations as those leaders were not rehabilitated until the 1980s.

For those who could attempt it, the rehabilitation process was a long one. Appeals for rehabilitation had to come from prisoners or their families, who often had to write two, three, or many more letters before their appeals were granted. Even after they succeeded, the arduous process sometimes went backwards: Anton Antonov-Ovseenko received a posthumous rehabilitation certificate for his father, which was then revoked in 1963.[32] Many former prisoners also remained wary of applying. Those who received a summons to appear at a meeting of a rehabilitation commission, usually held within the offices of the MVD or the Justice Ministry, would often turn up in layers of clothes, gripping food parcels, accompanied by weeping relatives, certain they were about to be sent away again.[33]

At the highest levels, many feared the rehabilitation process could go too fast and too far. 'We were scared, really scared,' wrote Khrushchev later. 'We were afraid the thaw might unleash a flood, which we wouldn't be able to control and which could drown us.'[34] One former senior KGB investigator, Anatoly Spragovsky, later recalled that between 1955 and 1960 he had travelled throughout the Tomsk region, interviewing witnesses and visiting the scenes of alleged crimes. He learned, among other things, that ex-prisoners had been accused of plotting to blow up factories or bridges that never existed. Yet when Spragovsky wrote to Khrushchev, proposing to streamline the rehabilitation process and speed it up, he was rebuffed: in Moscow, it seemed, officials did not want the errors of the Stalin years to seem too broad, or too absurd, and they did not want the investigation of old cases to proceed too quickly. Anastas Mikoyan, a Stalinist Politburo member who survived into the Khrushchev era, at one point explained why it was impossible to rehabilitate people too quickly. If they were all declared innocent at once, 'it would be clear that the country was not being run by a legal government, but by a group of gangsters'.[35]

The Communist Party was also wary of admitting too much error. Although it reviewed more than 70,000 petitions from ex-members, demanding to have their Party membership reinstated, less than half the petitions were granted.[36] As a result, full social rehabilitation – with the complete reinstatement of job, apartment and pension – remained very rare.

Far more common than full rehabilitation was the mixed experience, and the mixed feelings, of Olga Adamova-Sliozberg, who filed for her rehabilitation and that of her husband in 1954. She waited for two years. Then, after Khrushchev's secret speech in 1956, she received her certificate. It declared that her case had been reviewed, and closed for lack of evidence. 'I had been arrested on 27 April 1936. So I had paid for this mistake with twenty years and forty-one days of my life.' In compensation, the certificate stated, Adamova-Sliozberg was entitled to two months' pay for herself and her dead husband, and a further 11 roubles and 50 kopeks to compensate for the money that had been in her husband's possession at the time of his death. That was all.

As she stood in the waiting room outside an office of the Supreme Court building in Moscow, absorbing this news, she became aware of someone shouting. It was an elderly Ukrainian woman, who had just been handed a similar piece of news:

The old Ukrainian woman started yelling: 'I don't need your money for my son's blood; keep it yourself!' She tore up the certificates and threw them on the floor.

The soldier who had been handing out the certificates came up to her: 'Calm down, citizen,' he began.

But the old woman started shouting again and choked in a paroxysm of rage.

Everyone was silent, overwhelmed. Here and there I heard stifled sobs and tears.

I went back to my apartment, from which no policeman could evict me now. There was no one home, and finally I was able to weep freely.

To weep for my husand, who perished in the cellars of the Lubyanka, when he was thirty-seven years old, at the height of his powers and talent; for my children, who grew up orphans, stigmatized as the children of enemies of the people; for my parents, who died of grief; for Nikolai, who was tortured in the camps; and for all of my friends who never lived to be rehabilitated but lie beneath the frozen earth of Kolyma.[37]

Although often ignored in standard histories of the Soviet Union, the return home of millions of people from camps and exile must have stunned the millions of other Soviet citizens they encountered upon their arrival. Khrushchev's secret speech had been a shock, but it was a remote event, directed at the Party hierarchy. By contrast, the reappearance of people long considered dead brought home the message of the speech in a far more direct way, to a far wider range of people. Stalin's era had been one of secret torture and hidden violence. Suddenly, the camp veterans were on hand to provide living evidence of what had happened.

They were also on hand to bring news, both good and bad, of the vanished. By the 1950s, it had become customary for released prisoners to pay visits to the homes of both their dead and living comrades, to transmit oral messages or to repeat last words. M. S. Rotfort went back to Kharkov via Chita and Irkutsk, in order to see the families of his friends.[38] Gustav Herling paid an awkward visit to the family of his camp mate General Kruglov, whose wife pleaded with him not to tell their daughter about her father's new camp sentence, checked her watch repeatedly, and begged him to leave quickly.[39]

The returning prisoners were also a source of terror – to the bosses, the colleagues, the people who had sent them to prison in the first place. Anna Andreevna remembered that all of the trains to Moscow from Karaganda and Potma were filled with former prisoners in the summer of 1956. 'Everything was full of joy and its opposite, because people were meeting the people who had condemned them, who had condemned others. It was happy, and tragic, and all of Moscow would soon be filled with this.'[40] In his novel *Cancer Ward*, Solzhenitsyn imagines the reaction of a Party boss, ill with cancer, after his wife had told him that a former friend – a man he had personally denounced in order to take possession of his apartment – was due to be rehabilitated:

A weakness gripped his whole body – his hips, his shoulders; his arms had grown weak too, and the tumour seemed to wrench his head sideways. 'Why did you tell me that?' he moaned in a miserable, feeble voice. 'Haven't I had enough misfortune?' And twice his head and chest shuddered with tearless sobs . . .

'What right have they to let these people out now? Have they no pity? How dare they cause such traumas!'[41]

Feelings of guilt could be unbearable. After Khrushchev's secret speech, Aleksandr Fadeev, a committed Stalinist and much-feared literary bureaucrat, went on an alcoholic binge. While drunk, he confessed to a friend that as head of the Writers' Union, he had sanctioned the arrests of many writers he knew to be innocent. Fadeev killed himself the following day. He allegedly left a one-sentence suicide letter, addressed to the Central Committee: 'The bullet fired was meant for Stalin's policies, for Zhdanov's aesthetics, for Lysenko's genetics.'[42]

Others went mad. Olga Mishakova, an employee of the Komsomol, had denounced the youth organization's leader, Kosarev. After 1956, Kosarev was rehabilitated, and the Komsomol Central Committee expelled Mishakova. Nevertheless, for a year afterwards, she continued to come to the Komsomol building, to sit all day in her empty office, even to take a break for lunch. After the Komsomol confiscated her pass, she kept coming, standing by the entrance during her old office hours. When her husband was transferred to a job in Ryazan, she still got on the Moscow train every morning at four o'clock, and spent the day in front of her former office, returning in the evening. She was eventually placed in a mental institution.[43]

Even when the result was not insanity or suicide, the awkward encounters which plagued Moscow social life, post-1956, could be excruciating. 'Two Russias are eyeball to eyeball,' wrote Anna Akhmatova, 'those who were in prison, and those who put them there.' Many of the country's leaders, including Khrushchev, personally knew many returnees.[44] According to Antonov-Ovseenko, one such 'old friend' turned up on Khrushchev's doorstep in 1956, and persuaded him to speed up the rehabilitation process.[45] Worse were the encounters between former prisoners and the men who had actually been their gaolers or interrogators. A pseudonymous memoir published in Roy Medvedev's underground political journal in 1964 described a man's encounter with his former interrogator, who begged him for money for a drink: 'I gave him everything I had left from my trip, and it was a lot. I gave it to him so that he would leave quickly. I was afraid I wouldn't hold out. I felt an overpowering desire to let loose my hatred, pent up for so long, against him and his kind.'[46]

It could also be extremely uncomfortable to meet one's former friends, now thriving Soviet citizens. Lev Razgon encountered a close friend in 1968, more than a decade after his return: 'He met me . . . as though we had only parted the evening before. He expressed his condolences, of course, about Oksana's death, and asked after Yelena. But all of this was conveyed in a rapid, business-like way . . . and that was that.'[47] Yuri Dombrovksy put his feelings about a friend who offered his condolences too late into verse, in a poem entitled 'To a Famous Poet':

> Even our children didn't feel sorry for us
> Even our wives didn't want us
> Only a sentry shot at us, skilfully
> Using our numbers as targets . . .
>
> You were just drifting in restaurants
> And scattering jokes over glasses,
> You understood everything and welcomed everybody
> But didn't notice that we had died.
>
> So please explain to me now, why
> As they are reviewing the order of battle
> And I appear from a Northern grave
> You approach me as if I were a hero?
> Women were licking your hands –
> Was that for your courage? For the tortures you suffered?[48]

Lev Kopelev has written that after returning, he could no longer bear to be in the company of successful people at all, preferring the company of failures.[49]

How to talk about the camps – and how much to talk about the camps – with one's friends and family was another source of torment for former prisoners. Many tried to protect their children from the truth. The daughter of the rocket designer Sergei Korolev was not told her father had been in prison until her late teens, when she had to fill out a form which asked whether any of her relatives had ever been arrested.[50] Many prisoners were asked, upon leaving their camps, to sign documents forbidding them to say anything about them. This frightened some into speechlessness, although others were not cowed. Susanna Pechora refused outright to sign these papers upon leaving her camp and has, in her own words, 'been talking about it ever since'.[51]

Others found that their friends and family, if not exactly uninterested, did not want to know in any great detail where they had been or what had happened to them. They were too afraid – not just of the ever-present secret police, but of what they might learn about the people they loved. The novelist Vasily Aksyonov – Evgeniya Ginzburg's son – penned a tragic but horribly plausible scene in his trilogy, *The Generations of Winter*, describing what happened when a man and his wife encounter one another after both have spent years in concentration camps. He immediately notices that she looks too healthy: 'First tell me how you managed not to become ugly . . . you haven't even lost weight!' he says, knowing too well all of the ways in which it was possible for women to survive in the Gulag. That night, they lie in bed far apart, unable to speak: 'Melancholy and grief had burned them to the ground.'[52]

The writer and folk poet Bulat Okudzhava has also written a story describing a man's encounter with his mother who has spent ten years in camps. The man anticipated his mother's return with pleasure, believing he would pick her up at the train station, take her home for dinner after a tearful but joyful reunion, tell her of his life, maybe even go and see a film. Instead, he found a woman with dry eyes and a detached expression: 'She looked at me but didn't see me, her face was hardened, frozen.' He had expected her to be physically frail, but was totally unprepared for emotional damage – an experience that millions must have shared.[53]

True stories were often as bleak. Nadezhda Kapralova wrote of meeting her mother after thirteen years, having been separated from her at the age of eight: 'We were the closest possible of people, mother and daughter, and yet we were strangers, we spoke of irrelevancies, mostly crying and remaining silent.'[54] Another prisoner, Evgeny Gagen, was reunited with his wife after fourteen years, but found they had nothing in common. He had, he felt, 'grown' in those years, whereas she had remained the same.[55] Olga Adamova-Sliozberg had to tread carefully when she was reunited with her son in 1948:

'I was afraid to tell him anything of what I had learned "on the other side".
No doubt I could have convinced him that there was a great deal wrong with
our country, that Stalin, his idol, was actually far from perfect, but my son
was only seventeen. I was afraid to be completely frank with him.'[56]

Yet not everyone felt at odds with Soviet society either. Perhaps surprisingly, many of the returnees came back eager to rejoin the Communist Party,
not merely for the sake of privileges and status but in order to feel, once
again, full members of the Communist project, as it were. 'Allegiance to a
belief system can have deep, non-rational roots,' is how the historian Nanci
Adler tries to explain the feelings of one prisoner when he was reinstated in
the Party:

The most important factor that secured my survival in those harsh conditions was
my unflinching, ineradicable belief in our Leninist Party, in its humanist principles. It
was the Party that imparted the physical strength to withstand their trials . . . Reinstatement in the ranks of my native Communist Party was the greatest happiness of my
entire life.[57]

The historian Catherine Merridale goes a step further, arguing that the
Party, and the collective ideology of the Soviet Union, actually helped people
to recover from whatever trauma they had suffered: 'Russians really do seem
to have lived with their histories of unspeakable loss by working, singing,
waving the red flag. Some laugh about it now, but almost everyone is nostalgic
for a collectivism and a common purpose that have been lost. Up to a point,
totalitarianism worked.'[58]

Even though at some level they knew this struggle to be a false one; even
though they knew the nation was not as glorious as its leaders claimed; even
though they knew that whole Soviet cities had been built on the bones of
people unjustly condemned to forced labour – even then, some camp victims
still felt better when they were part of the collective effort, and no longer
excluded from it.

Either way, the enormous tension between those who had been 'there' and
those who had stayed home could not remain confined in bedrooms and
locked behind doors for ever. Those responsible for what had happened were
still alive. Finally, at the Twenty-Second Party Congress in October 1961,
Khrushchev, now fighting for influence within the Party, began naming them.
He announced that Molotov, Kaganovich, Voroshilov and Malenkov were
all 'guilty of illegal mass repressions against many Party, Soviet, military
and Komsomol officials and bear direct responsibility for their physical
destruction'. More ominously, he also hinted darkly at the 'documents in our
possession' which would prove this guilt.[59]

Yet Khrushchev did not, in the end, publish any such documents in the
course of his struggle against the Stalinists who opposed his reforms. Perhaps
he was not really powerful enough to do so – or perhaps such documents

would have revealed his own role in Stalinist repressions as well. Instead, Khrushchev deployed a new tactic: he widened the public discussion of Stalinism even further, broadening it beyond internal Party debates – spreading it to the literary world. Although Khrushchev probably was not much interested in Soviet poets and novelists for their own sake, he had seen, by the early 1960s, that they could play a role in his bid for power. Slowly, vanished names began to reappear in official publications, without explanation of why they had gone and why they were being allowed back. Characters hitherto unacceptable in Soviet fiction – greedy bureaucrats, returning camp inmates – began to appear in published novels.[60]

Khrushchev saw that such publications could conduct his propaganda for him: literary writers could discredit his enemies by tarring them with the crimes of the past. That, at any rate, appears to have been the reasoning behind his decision to allow the publication of Alexander Solzhenitsyn's *One Day in the Life of Ivan Denisovich*, the most famous of all Gulag novels.

For his literary significance, as well as for the role he played in publicizing the existence of the Gulag in the West, Alexander Solzhenitsyn would certainly deserve special mention in any history of the Soviet camp system. But his brief career as a famous, widely published, 'official' Soviet author is also worth telling because it marks an important moment of transition. When *Ivan Denisovich* first appeared in print, in 1962, the Thaw was at its height, political prisoners were few, and the Gulag seemed a thing of the past. By the summer of 1965, when a Party journal described *Ivan Denisovich* as 'an undoubtedly controversial work, both ideologically and artistically', Khrushchev had been ousted, the backlash had begun, and the number of political prisoners was rising with ominous speed. By 1974, when *The Gulag Archipelago* – Solzhenitsyn's massive, three-volume history of the camp system – had appeared in English, Solzhenitsyn had been expelled from the country, and his books could only be published abroad. The institution of the Soviet prison camp had been firmly re-established, and the dissident movement was in full swing.[61]

Solzhenitsyn's prison career had begun in a manner typical for *zeks* of his generation. After entering officers' training school in 1941, he fought across the Western front throughout the autumn and winter of 1943, penned some poorly disguised criticism of Stalin in a letter to a friend in 1945 – and was arrested soon afterwards. Hitherto a more or less true communist believer, the young officer was stunned by the brutality and crudity with which he was treated. Later, he would be even more shocked by the harsh treatment meted out to Red Army soldiers who had fallen into Nazi captivity. These, he felt, were men who should have returned home as heroes.

His subsequent camp career was perhaps slightly less than typical, only because – thanks to some undergraduate maths and physics – he served some of his time in a *sharashka*, an experience he later recorded in his novel *The First Circle*. Other than that, it is fair to say that he served in a series of unremarkable *lagpunkts*, including one in Moscow and one in a special camp complex in Karaganda. He was also an unremarkable prisoner. He flirted with the authorities, served as an informer before seeing the light, and wound up working as a bricklayer. Bricklaying was the career he later gave to Ivan Denisovich, the *zek* 'Everyman' who was the hero of his first novel. After his release, he went to teach at a school in Ryazan, and began to write about his experiences. That too was not unusual: the many hundreds of Gulag memoirs that have been published since the 1980s are ample testimony to the eloquence and talent of Soviet ex-prisoners, many of whom wrote in secret for years. What made Solzhenitsyn truly unique, in the end, was the simple fact that his work appeared in print, in the Soviet Union, while Khrushchev was still in power.

Many legends surround the publication of *One Day in the Life of Ivan Denisovich*, so many that Michael Scammell, Solzhenitsyn's biographer, has written that the tale 'has acquired such embellishments along the way that it is sometimes hard to disentangle fact from fiction'. The book's route to literary fame was a slow one. Before it became famous, the manuscript of *Ivan Denisovich* passed through the hands of Lev Kopelev – a Moscow literary figure, and one of Solzhenitsyn's camp comrades – and a copy-editor at *Novyi Mir*. Excited by her find, the copy-editor passed it to Alexander Tvardovsky, the editor-in-chief of *Novyi Mir*.

Tvardovsky, so the story goes, began reading *Ivan Denisovich* while lying in bed. After a few pages, however, he was so impressed by the manuscript that he felt he had to get up, get dressed and read the story sitting upright. He spent an entire night reading it, and then rushed into his office as soon as dawn broke, howling for the typists to make up extra copies so that he could distribute the book to his friends, all the while hailing the birth of a new literary genius. Whether or not all of this really happened, Tvardovsky certainly told people it had. Later, Solzhenitsyn wrote to him of how happy he had felt when he learned that Tvardovsky found *Ivan Denisovich* 'worth a sleepless night'.[62]

The novel itself was straightforward enough: it recorded a single day in the life of an ordinary prisoner. Reading it now, it can, in fact, be hard for contemporary readers, even contemporary readers in Russia, to understand why it created such a furore in the Soviet literary world. But to those who read it in 1962, the novel came as a revelation. Instead of speaking vaguely about 'returnees' and 'repressions', as some other books did at the time, *Ivan Denisovich* directly described life in the camps, a subject which had not, until then, been discussed in public.

At the same time, Solzhenitsyn's style – particularly his use of camp slang – and his descriptions of the dullness and unpleasantness of prison life, made a stunning contrast to the usual empty, phoney fiction then being published. The official Soviet literary creed of that time, 'socialist realism', was not realism at all, but rather the literary version of Stalinist political doctrine. Prison literature, such as it was, had not changed since Gorky's day. If there was a thief in a Soviet novel, he saw the light and converted to the true Soviet faith. The hero might suffer, but in the end the Party showed him the light. The heroine might shed tears, but once she had learned the value of Work, she would find her proper role in society.

Ivan Denisovich, by contrast, was genuinely realistic: it was not optimistic, and it was not a morality tale. The sufferings of its heroes were pointless. The work they did was exhausting and draining, and they tried to avoid it. The Party did not triumph in the end, and communism did not emerge the victor. This honesty, so unusual for a Soviet writer, was precisely what Tvardovsky admired: he told Solzhenitsyn's friend Kopelev that the story had 'not a drop of falsehood in it'. Which was precisely what would upset many readers, particularly those in the Soviet establishment. Even one of *Novyi Mir*'s editors found the story's frankness disturbing. In his comments on the novel he wrote that 'it shows life too one-sidedly, involuntarily twisting and up-setting the proportions'. For people used to simplistic conclusions, the novel seemed horrifyingly open-ended and amoral.

Tvardovsky wanted to publish it, but knew that if he simply had the story typeset and sent off to the censors, they would ban it immediately. Instead, he offered *Ivan Denisovich* to Khrushchev, to be used as a weapon against his enemies. According to Michael Scammell, Tvardovsky wrote a Preface that presented the story's usefulness in precisely this light, and then began giving it to people who he hoped would hand it to Khrushchev himself.[63]

After much back and forth, much debate, and a few changes to the manu-script – Solzhenitsyn was persuaded to add at least one 'positive hero', and to include a token condemnation of Ukrainian nationalism – the novel did finally reach Khrushchev. He approved. He even praised the book for having been written 'in the spirit of the Twenty-Second Party Congress', which presumably meant that he thought it would annoy his enemies. Finally, in the November 1962 issue of *Novyi Mir*, it appeared in print. 'The bird is free! The bird is free!' Tvardovsky is alleged to have shouted as he held the first proof copy in his hands.

At first, the critical praise was fulsome, not least because the story matched the official line of the moment. *Pravda*'s literary critic hoped that the 'fight against the personality cult' would from now on 'continue to facilitate the appearance of works of art outstanding for their ever-increasing artistic value'. *Izvestiya*'s literary critic said Solzhenitsyn had 'shown himself a true helper of the Party in a sacred and vital cause – the struggle against the personality cult and its consequences'.[64]

Those were not quite the reactions of the ordinary readers, however, who flooded Solzhenitsyn with mail in the months that followed the *Novyi Mir* publication. The story's close parallels to the new Party line did not impress the former camp inmates who wrote to him from all over the country. Instead, they were overjoyed to read something which actually reflected their own feelings and experience. People afraid to breathe a word of their experiences to their closest friends suddenly felt a sense of release. One woman wrote to describe her reaction: 'My face was smothered in tears. I didn't wipe them away because all this, packed into a small number of pages of the magazine, was mine, intimately mine, for every day of the fifteen years I spent in the camps.'

Another letter addressed Solzhenitsyn, 'Dear friend, comrade and brother,' before continuing: 'Reading your story I remembered Sivaya Maska and Vorkuta . . . the frosts and blizzards, the insults and humiliations . . . I wept as I read – they were all familiar characters, as if from my own brigade . . . Thank you once more! Please carry on in the same spirit – write, write . . .'[65]

Most powerful of all were the reactions of people still in prison. Leonid Sitko, then serving his second sentence, heard of the publication in distant Dubravlag. When the camp library's copy of *Novyi Mir* arrived, the camp commanders kept it for themselves for a whole two months. Finally, the *zeks* got hold of a copy and held a group reading. Sitko remembered that prisoners listened 'without breathing':

After they read the last word, there was a deathly silence. Then, after two, three minutes, the room detonated. Everyone had lived the story in his own, painful way . . . in the cloud of tobacco smoke, they discussed endlessly . . .

And frequently, more and more frequently, they asked: 'Why did they publish it?'[66]

Why indeed? It seems the Party bosses themselves began to wonder. Perhaps Solzhenitsyn's honest portrayal of camp life was too much for them: it represented too momentous a change, its appearance came about too swiftly for the tastes of men who still feared their own heads might roll next. Or perhaps they were tired of Khrushchev already, feared he had gone too far, and used Solzhenitsyn's novel as an excuse. Indeed, Khrushchev was deposed soon afterwards, in October 1964. His replacement, Leonid Brezhnev, was the leader of the Party's reactionary, anti-change, anti-Thaw neo-Stalinists.

In either case, it is clear that in the aftermath of the novel's publication, the conservatives rallied, and with amazing speed. *Ivan Denisovich* appeared in November. In December – a few days after Khrushchev met Solzhenitsyn and personally congratulated him – Leonid Ilyichev, the chairman of the Central Committee's new Ideological Commission, lectured a group of 400 writers and artists gathered at the Writers' Union. Soviet society, he told them, must not be 'shaken and weakened under the pretext of the struggle against the cult of the individual . . .'[67]

The rapidity of the change reflected the Soviet Union's ambivalent attitude towards its own history – an ambivalence which has never been resolved, even today. If the Soviet Union's elite were to accept that the portrait of Ivan Denisovich was authentic, that meant admitting that innocent people had endured pointless suffering. If the camps had really been stupid and wasteful and tragic, that meant that the Soviet Union was stupid and wasteful and tragic too. It was difficult, and it would remain difficult, for any Soviet citizen, whether a member of the elite or a simple peasant, to accept that their lives had been governed by a set of lies.

After a period of wavering – a few arguments for, a few arguments against – the attacks on Solzhenitsyn started coming thick and fast. In earlier chapters, I have already described the angry reactions, of both prisoners and guards, to Ivan Denisovich's many efforts to evade hard work. But there were more elevated criticisms too. Lydia Fomenko, the critic of *Literaturnaya Rossiya*, accused Solzhenitsyn of failing to 'disclose the full dialectic of that time'. Solzhenitsyn had condemned the 'cult of personality', in other words, but had failed to point the way to the optimistic future, and had failed to include 'good' communist characters who would triumph in the end. This kind of criticism was echoed by others, and some even tried to correct Solzhenitsyn's mistakes in literary form. Boris Dyakov's 'A Story of Survival', the 'loyal' camp novel published in 1964, explicitly featured descriptions of hard-working, loyal Soviet prisoners.[68]

As Solzhenitsyn's novel was being considered for the Lenin Prize, the Soviet Union's highest literary award, the insults grew worse. In the end – using tactics that would be repeated in later years – the establishment resorted to personal insults. At the Lenin Prize Committee meeting, the head of the Komsomol, Sergei Pavlov, stood up and accused Solzhenitsyn of having surrendered to the Germans during the war, and of having been convicted on criminal charges after that. Tvardovsky got Solzhenitsyn to produce his rehabilitation certificate, but it was too late. The Lenin Prize went to *The Sheep Bell*, a book best described as well forgotten, and Solzhenitsyn's official literary career was at an end.

He kept writing, but none of his subsequent novels appeared in print in the Soviet Union – or at least not legally – until 1989. In 1974, he was expelled from the Soviet Union, and eventually took up residence in Vermont. Until the Gorbachev era, only a tiny group of Soviet citizens – those who had access to underground, illegal typescripts or smuggled foreign copies – had read *The Gulag Archipelago*, his history of the camp system, put together from the flood of letters and memoirs he received after the publication of *Ivan Denisovich*.

Yet Solzhenitsyn was not the only victim of this conservative backlash. For just as the debate about *Ivan Denisovich* was growing angrier, another literary drama was also unfolding: on 18 February 1964, the young poet Joseph Brodsky was put on trial for 'parasitism'. The era of the dissidents was about to begin.

26
The Era of the Dissidents

Do not rejoice too early
And let some oracle proclaim
That wounds do not reopen
That evil crowds don't rise again.
And that I risk seeming retarded;
Let him orate. I firmly know that
Stalin is not dead.

As if the dead alone had mattered
And those who vanished nameless in the North.
The evil he implanted in our hearts,
Had it not truly done the damage?
As long as poverty divides from wealth
As long as we don't stop the lies
And don't unlearn to fear
Stalin is not dead.

– Boris Chichibabin,
'Stalin is Not Dead', 1967[1]

The death of Stalin really did signal the end of the era of massive slave labour in the Soviet Union. Although the Soviet Union's repressive policies were to take some very harsh forms over the subsequent forty years, nobody ever again proposed to revive concentration camps on a large scale. Nobody ever again tried to make them a central part of the economy, or used them to incarcerate millions of people. The secret police never again controlled such a large slice of the nation's productive capacity, and camp commanders never again found themselves acting as the bosses of enormous industrial enterprises. Even the Lubyanka building, the post-war KGB headquarters, ceased to be a prison: Gary Powers, the American U-2 pilot whose spy plane was shot down over the USSR in 1960, was the last person to be incarcerated in its cells.[2]

Yet the camps did not disappear altogether. Nor did Soviet prisons become part of an 'ordinary' penal system, organized for criminals alone. Instead, they evolved.

To begin with, the nature of the political prisoners evolved. In Stalin's era, the repressive system had resembled a vast game of roulette: anyone could be arrested, for any reason, at any time – peasants, workers and Party bureaucrats alike. After Khrushchev, the secret police still occasionally arrested people 'for nothing', as Anna Akhmatova had once put it. But most of the time, Brezhnev's KGB arrested people for *something* – if not for a genuine criminal act, then for their literary, religious or political opposition to the Soviet system. Usually called 'dissidents', or sometimes 'prisoners of conscience', this new generation of politicals knew why they had been arrested, identified themselves as political prisoners, and were treated as such. They were kept separate from criminal prisoners, given different uniforms, and were subjected to different regimes. They would also be marked as dissidents for the rest of their lives, subjected to discrimination at work, and mistrusted by their relatives and neighbours.

There were also far fewer political prisoners than there had been in Stalin's time. In the middle of the 1970s, Amnesty International estimated that no more than 10,000 of the Soviet Union's one million prisoners had political sentences, and most of them were incarcerated in the two 'political' camp complexes, one in Mordovia, south of Moscow, and one in Perm, on the western edge of the Urals.[3] In a given year, there were probably no more than a few thousand openly political arrests. Although this would have been a high number in any other country, it was certainly low by the standards of Stalin's Soviet Union.

According to former prisoners' accounts, this new sort of prisoner began appearing in the camps as early as 1957, in the wake of the Hungarian revolution of October 1956, following the arrests of Soviet soldiers and citizens who had sympathized with the rebellion.[4] At about this time, the first tiny wave of 'refuseniks', Jews who were refused the right to emigrate to Israel, also appeared in Soviet prisons. In 1958, Bym Gindler, a Polish Jew who had been left on the Soviet side of the border after the war, was refused the right to be repatriated to Poland, on the grounds that he would take the opportunity to emigrate to Israel.[5]

The late 1950s also saw the arrests of the first groups of Soviet Baptists, who would quickly become the largest single dissident group behind barbed wire, as well as members of other religious sects. In 1960, the dissident Avraham Shifrin even encountered a group of Old Believers, followers of the older rites of the Orthodox Church, in a punishment cell in the political camp at Potma. Their community had emigrated to the virgin forests of the northern Urals in 1919, and had lived there in complete secrecy, until a KGB helicopter discovered them fifty years later. When Shifrin met them, they had become permanent residents of the camp punishment cells, having refused categorically to work for the Soviet anti-Christ.[6]

Shifrin himself also represented a new category of prisoner: the sons and daughters of 'enemies of the people', who found themselves, in the late 1950s, unable to slot easily into the routines of Soviet life. In subsequent years, a striking number of the members of the dissident generation, particularly the human rights activists, would turn out to be children or relatives of Stalin's victims. The twin Medvedev brothers, Zhores and Roy, are among the most famous examples. Roy, a historian, became one of the best-known underground publicists in the Soviet Union; Zhores was a dissident scientist, who would be locked up in a psychiatric hospital as a result. Both were the sons of an 'enemy of the people': their father had been arrested when they were children.[7]

There were others. In 1967, forty-three children of communists, all repressed by Stalin, sent an open letter to the Central Committee, warning of the threat of neo-Stalinism. The letter, one of the first of many open protest letters to the authorities, contained several names of underground publishers and dissident leaders, many of whom would soon be in prison themselves: Pyotr Yakir, the son of General Yakir; Anton Antonov-Ovseenko, son of the Bolshevik revolutionary; and Larisa Bogoraz, whose father was arrested for Trotskyite activities in 1936. A family's experience of the camps could be enough, it seemed, to radicalize its younger members.[8]

If the prisoners had changed, so too had some aspects of the legal system. In 1960 – the year usually remembered as the height of the Thaw – a new criminal code was established. Without question, the new code was more liberal. It specifically abolished night-time interrogations, and limited the powers of the KGB (who conducted political investigations) and the MVD (who ran the prison system). It mandated the greater independence of prosecutors and, most of all, abolished the hated Article 58.[9]

Some of these changes were rightly dismissed as mere camouflage, linguistic change instead of real change. 'You are mistaken,' the novelist Yuli Daniel wrote a few years later, in a letter from prison smuggled out to a friend. 'You are mistaken if you thought I was sitting in prison. I was being "held in an investigative isolator", whence I was not thrown in the cooler, but was "installed in a punishment isolator". And this was done not by gaolers but by "controllers", and this letter is not being sent from a concentration camp but from an "institution".'[10]

Daniel was also right in another sense: if the state authorities wanted to arrest someone on suspicion of thinking differently, they still could. In place of Article 58, the code created Article 70, on 'Anti-Soviet Agitation and Propaganda', and Article 72, on 'Organizational Activity of Especially Dangerous Crimes Against the State and Also Participation in Anti-Soviet Organizations'. In addition, the authorities added Article 142, on 'Violation of Law on Separation of Church and State'. If the KGB wanted to arrest someone for his religion, in other words, they still could.[11]

Yet not everything was exactly the same either. In the post-Stalin era, the authorities – prosecutors, prisoners, camp guards, warders – were far more sensitive about appearances, and really did try to adhere to a semblance of legality. When, for example, the language of Article 70 proved too loose to convict everyone whom the authorities felt it necessary to put behind bars, they added Article 190-1 to the criminal code, which forbade the 'dissemination by word of mouth of deliberate fabrications discrediting the Soviet political and social system'. The judicial system had to look like a judicial system, even if everyone knew it was a sham.[12]

In what was also a clear reaction against the old system of troikas and special commissions, the new law stipulated that arrestees must be tried in a court of justice. This, it turned out, would inconvenience the Soviet authorities far more than they could have anticipated.

Although he had not been condemned under any of the new, anti-dissident laws, the trial of Joseph Brodsky was in many ways a harbinger of the new era to come. The fact that it was held at all was a novelty: in the past, people who irritated the state had not been tried in public except in pre-arranged show trials, if they were tried at all. More importantly, Brodsky's behaviour at the trial was enough to prove that he already belonged to a different generation from Solzhenitsyn, and from the political prisoners of the recent past.

Brodsky once wrote that his generation was 'spared' the experience of indoctrination endured by those just a few years older. 'We emerged from under the post-war rubble when the state was too busy patching its own skin and couldn't look after us very well. We entered schools, and whatever elevated rubbish we were taught there, the suffering and the poverty were visible all around. You cannot cover a ruin with a page of *Pravda*.'[13]

If they were Russians, Brodsky's generation typically arrived at their critique of the Soviet status quo via their literary or artistic tastes, which could not be expressed in Brezhnev's Soviet Union. If they were Balts, Caucasians or Ukrainians, they were more likely to have got there through nationalist sentiments, inherited from their parents. Brodsky was a classic Leningrad dissident. He rejected Soviet propaganda from a very early age, and dropped out of school at fifteen. He worked in a series of temporary jobs, and began to write poetry. By his early twenties he was well known in the Leningrad literary world. The ageing Akhmatova made him her protégé. His poems were circulated among friends, and read aloud at secret literary gatherings, another new feature of this era.

Predictably, all of that unofficial activity brought Brodsky to the attention of the secret police. Brodsky was first harassed, then arrested. The charge was 'parasitism': since Brodsky was not a poet licensed by the Writers' Union, he qualified as a vagrant. At his trial in February 1964, the state produced witnesses, mostly unknown to Brodsky, who testified that he was 'morally depraved, a draft-dodger, and a writer of anti-Soviet verses'. In his defence, there were letters and speeches from famous poets and writers, including Akhmatova. To all of this, the prosecution witnesses responded angrily:

This is nothing but his fancy friends ringing all the bells and demanding, 'Save the young man!' But he should be treated with forced labour, and no one will help him, no fancy friends. I do not know him personally, I know about him from the news-papers. And I am acquainted with the certificates. I'm suspicious about the certificates which deferred him from service in the army. I'm not a doctor, but I'm suspicious about it.[14]

Clearly, the trial was directed not just against Brodsky, but against the remnants of the independent intellectual class, with their connections, their suspected opposition to Soviet authority, and their scorn for 'labour'. And, in a certain sense, those who organized the trial had hit an accurate target: Brodsky did oppose Soviet authority; he did feel scorn for pointless, fruitless labour; and he did represent an alienated class, a group of people deeply frustrated by the clampdown which followed the Thaw. Knowing this per-fectly well, Brodsky was not astonished or surprised by his arrest, and was not flummoxed by his trial. Instead, he sparred with the judge:

JUDGE: What is your occupation?
BRODSKY: I am a poet.
JUDGE: Who recognized you as a poet? Who gave you the authority to call yourself a poet?
BRODSKY: No one. Who gave me the authority to enter the human race?
JUDGE: Have you studied for it?
BRODSKY: For what?
JUDGE: To become a poet. Why didn't you take further education at a school where they prepare you, where you can learn?
BRODSKY: I didn't think poetry was a matter of learning.
JUDGE: What is it then?
BRODSKY: I think it is . . . a gift from God.

Later, asked if he had any petitions to make to the court, Brodsky said, 'I would like to know why I am arrested.' The judge responded, 'That's a question, not a petition.' Said Brodsky, 'In that case I have no petitions.'[15]

Technically, Brodsky lost the argument: the judge condemned him to five years' hard labour in a prison colony near Arkhangelsk, on the grounds that he had 'systematically failed to fulfil the obligations of a Soviet citizen, failed to produce anything of material value, failed to provide for his own upkeep, as is evident from his frequent change of jobs'. Citing statements made by the

'Commission for Work with Young Poets', the judge also declared that Brodsky – who would later win the Nobel Prize for Literature – was 'not a poet'.[16]

Yet, in another sense, Brodsky 'won' in a way that previous generations of Russian prisoners could not have done. Not only did he publicly challenge the logic of the Soviet legal system, but his challenge was also recorded for posterity. A journalist took surreptitious notes at the trial, which were ultimately smuggled to the West. Thanks to this, Brodsky immediately became famous, in Russia and abroad. His behaviour at his trial not only became a model for others to follow, it also inspired both Russian and foreign writers to petition the government for his release. After two years, release was granted, and he was eventually expelled from the USSR.

Nothing like this had happened while Stalin was alive. 'People are as ever thrown behind bars and as ever transported to the East,' wrote Valentyn Moroz, a Ukrainian dissident historian, shortly afterwards: 'But this time, they have not sunk into the unknown.'[17] And that, in the end, was to be the greatest difference between Stalin's prisoners and the prisoners of Brezhnev and Andropov: the outside world knew about them, cared about them, and above all could affect their fate. Nevertheless, the Soviet regime was not growing more liberal – and events moved quickly in the wake of the Brodsky trial.

In the same way that 1937 stands out as a special year of persecution for the Stalinist-era intelligentsia, so too does 1966 stand out as a special year for the generation of the Thaw. By 1966, it was clear that the neo-Stalinists had triumphed. Stalin's reputation as a flawed but still admirable leader had been officially restored. Joseph Brodsky was in a labour camp. Solzhenitsyn was a banned author. Khrushchev had been ousted and replaced by Leonid Brezhnev, who openly made statements designed to refurbish Stalin's reputation.[18] Within a year, Yuri Andropov, who had just been appointed Chairman of the KGB, would make a speech to mark the fiftieth anniversary of the founding of the Cheka. He would praise the Soviet secret police, among other things, for its 'implacable struggle against state enemies'.[19]

In February 1966, Andrei Sinyavsky and Yuli Daniel also went on trial. Both were well-known writers, both had published their work abroad, and both were found guilty, under the terms of Article 70, of 'Anti-Soviet Agitation and Propaganda'. Sinyavsky received seven years' hard labour, Daniel received five.[20] This was the first time anyone had been put on trial not just for vagrancy, but because of the actual content of their literary work. A month later, in significantly greater secrecy, more than two dozen Ukrainian intellectuals went on trial in Kiev. One was accused, among other things, of owning a copy of a poem by the nineteenth-century Ukrainian poet Taras Shevchenko, after whom streets are named in Moscow and Kiev. Because the poem had been printed without the author's name, Soviet 'experts' classified it as an anti-Soviet poem by an unknown author.[21]

In a pattern that would soon become familiar, these trials spawned other trials, as other outraged intellectuals began to use the language of the Soviet legal system and the Soviet constitution to criticize the Soviet judiciary and the Soviet police. The case of Sinyavsky and Daniel, for example, made a great impression on another young Muscovite, Aleksandr Ginzburg, already active in 'unofficial' cultural circles. He compiled a transcript of the Sinyavsky–Daniel trial, the 'White Book', which he distributed around Moscow. He and three alleged collaborators were arrested soon afterwards.[22]

At about the same time, the Kiev trials made a great impression on a young Ukrainian lawyer, Vyacheslav Chornovil. He compiled a dossier on the Ukrainian judicial system, pointing out its internal contradictions and establishing the illegality and absurdity of the Ukrainian arrests.[23] Afterwards, he was quickly arrested.[24] In this manner, an intellectual and cultural movement, begun by writers and poets, became a human rights movement.

To put the Soviet human rights movement in context, it is important to note that Soviet dissidents never started a mass organization, as did their Polish counterparts, and they cannot receive full credit for bringing down the Soviet regime: the arms race, the war in Afghanistan, and the economic disaster wrought by Soviet central planning must receive equal credit. Nor did they ever manage more than a handful of public demonstrations. One of the most famous – staged on 25 August 1968 to protest against the Soviet invasion of Czechoslovakia – involved only seven people. At noon, the seven gathered in front of St Basil's Cathedral on Red Square, and unrolled Czech flags and banners marked with slogans: 'Long live free and independent Czechoslovakia', 'Hands off Czechoslovakia, for your freedom and ours'. Within minutes, a whistle blew and plain-clothes KGB rushed at the demonstrators, whom they seem to have been expecting, shouting, 'They're all Jews!' and 'Beat the anti-Sovietists!' They tore down the banners, beat up the demonstrators and took all but one – she was with her three-month-old son – straight to prison.[25]

But small though they were, these efforts caused a great deal of trouble for the Soviet leadership, particularly given its continued commitment to spreading world revolution and its consequent, obsessive concern about the USSR's international image. In Stalin's era, repression on a massive scale could be kept secret even from a visiting American Vice-President. In the 1960s and 1970s, news of a single arrest could travel around the world overnight.

In part, this was thanks to improvements in mass communication, the Voice of America, Radio Liberty, and television. In part, it was also because Soviet citizens found new ways to transmit news as well. For 1966 also marked another milestone: the birth of the term 'samizdat'. An acronym which deliberately echoed the term *Gosizdat*, or 'State Publishing House', samizdat literally means 'self-publishing house', and figuratively refers to the underground press. The concept was not new. In Russia, samizdat was nearly as old as the written word. Pushkin himself had privately distributed manuscripts of his more politically charged poetry in the 1820s. Even in Stalin's time, the circulation of stories and poems among friends was not entirely unknown.

But after 1966, samizdat grew into a national pastime. The Thaw had given many Soviet citizens a taste for a freer sort of literature, and at first samizdat was a largely literary phenomenon.[26] Very quickly, samizdat came to have a more political character. A KGB report which circulated among Central Committee members in January 1971 analysed the changes over the previous five years, noting that it had discovered

more than 400 studies and articles on economic, political and philosophical questions, which criticize from various angles the historical experience of socialist construction in the Soviet Union, revise the internal and external politics of the Communist Party, and advance various programmes of opposition activity.[27]

The report concluded that the KGB would have to work on the 'neutralization and denunciation of the anti-Soviet tendencies presented in samizdat'. But it was too late to put the genie back in the bottle, and samizdat continued to expand, taking many forms: typed poems, passed from friend to friend and retyped at every opportunity; handwritten newsletters and bulletins; transcripts of Voice of America broadcasts; and, much later, books and journals professionally produced on underground typesetting machines, more often than not located in communist Poland. Poetry, and poem-songs composed by Russian bards – Aleksandr Galich, Bulat Okudzhava, Vladimir Vysotsky – also spread quickly through the use of what was then a new form of technology, the cassette tape recorder.

Throughout the 1960s, 1970s and 1980s, one of the most important themes of samizdat was the history of Stalinism – including the history of the Gulag. Samizdat networks continued to print and distribute copies of the works of Solzhenitsyn, which were by now banned in the USSR. Varlam Shalamov's poems and stories also began circulating in the underground, as did Evgeniya Ginzburg's memoirs. Both writers began to attract large groups of admirers. Ginzburg became the centre of a circle of Gulag survivors and literary figures in Moscow.

The other important theme of samizdat was the persecution of the dissidents. Indeed, it was thanks to samizdat – and particularly to its distribution abroad – that the human rights advocates would gain, in the 1970s, a far wider international forum. In particular, the dissidents learned to use samizdat not only to underline the inconsistencies between the USSR's legal system and the KGB's methods, but also to point out, loudly and frequently, the gap between the human rights treaties that the USSR had signed and actual

Soviet practice. Their preferred texts were the UN Declaration on Human Rights, and the Helsinki Final Act. The former was signed by the USSR in 1948 and contained, among other things, a clause known as Article 19:

Everyone has the right to freedom of opinion and expression; this right includes freedom to hold opinions without interference and to seek, receive and impart information and ideas through any media and regardless of frontiers.[28]

The latter was the end result of a Europe-wide negotiation process, which had settled a number of political questions left open since the end of the Second World War. Although they were hardly noticed at the time of its 1976 signing, the Helsinki Treaty also contained some agreements on human rights – part of the so-called 'Basket Three' of the negotiations – which all of the participating nations signed. Among other things, the treaty recognized the 'freedom of thought, conscience and belief':

The participating States recognize the universal significance of human rights and fundamental freedoms ... they will constantly respect these rights and freedoms in their mutual relations and will endeavour jointly and separately, including in co-operation with the United Nations, to promote the universal and effective respect for them.

Both within the USSR and outside it, most of the information about the dissidents' efforts to promote the language of these treaties came from the house journal of the Soviet samizdat networks: the *Chronicle of Current Events*. This newsletter, dedicated to a neutral recording of otherwise unpublicized news events – human rights abuses, arrests, trials, demonstrations, new samizdat publications – was founded by a small group of acquaintances in Moscow, including Sinyavsky, Daniel, Ginzburg and two dissidents who would become famous later, Pavel Litvinov and Vladimir Bukovsky. The tale of the *Chronicle*'s further evolution and development is itself worthy of a book the length of this one. In the 1970s, the secret police conducted a virtual war against the *Chronicle*, organizing coordinated searches of the homes of anyone who was suspected of being connected with the journal: on one memorable occasion, an editor plunged a set of papers into a pot of boiling soup while the KGB searched her apartment. The *Chronicle* survived the arrests of its editors, however, and managed to reach the West as well. Eventually, Amnesty International would publish regular translations.[29]

The *Chronicle* played a special role in the history of the camp system too. Very quickly, it became the main source of information about life in the post-Stalinist Soviet camps. It published a regular feature, 'Inside the Prisons and Camps' – and, later, 'Inside the Punishment Cells' as well – which recorded news from the camps, and published interviews with prisoners. These startlingly accurate reports of events in the camps – the illnesses of various dissidents, the changes in regime, the organized protests – drove the authorities wild: they found it impossible to understand how the information got out. Years later, one of the editors explained:

Some [information] is carried when a fellow is released from the camps. There would be contact somewhere along the line after he left. Or you could bribe prison guards so that when you met with relatives, you could pass written information and verbal information. Then the relatives might stop in Moscow and pass on what you said. You could bribe guards, for example, in Mordovia. These [the Mordovian political camps] were all new camps, organized in 1972, and there were all new guards. They would pass notes sometimes when they became sympathetic to our situation. There was a mass hunger strike in the camps in 1974, and when they saw that, the guards were sympathetic.

You can also corrupt guards. They don't earn much. They don't have much. They come from provincial areas. You might, for example, get something from Moscow – a cigarette lighter – and bribe a guard. Or he would give you an address. The bribe – the goods or the money – would be sent there in exchange for passing information . . .[30]

There were also methods of concealment. One ex-prisoner described one of them:

In minute letters, I write out my latest poems on four centimetre-wide strips of cigarette paper . . . These strips of cigarette paper are then tightly rolled into a small tube (less than the thickness of your finger) sealed and made moisture proof by a method of our own devising, and handed on when a suitable opportunity presents itself.[31]

However they did it – by concealment, bribery or flattery – the information that the *Chronicle* managed to extract from the camps remains significant today. At the time of the writing of this book, post-Stalinist MVD and KGB files remain largely closed to researchers. Thanks to the *Chronicle*, however, to other samizdat and human rights publications, and to the many, many memoirs which describe the camps of the 1960s, the 1970s and the 1980s, it is nevertheless possible to reconstruct a consistent picture of what life in the Soviet camps was like in the years after Stalin.

'Today's camps for political prisoners are just as horrific as in Stalin's time. A few things are better, a few things are worse . . .'

So began Anatoly Marchenko's memoir of his years in prison, a document which, when it first began to circulate in Moscow in the late 1960s, deeply shocked the city's intelligentsia, who believed the Soviet labour camps had closed for good. The working-class son of illiterate parents, Marchenko's first prison conviction was for hooliganism. His second conviction was for treason: he had tried to escape the Soviet Union by crossing the border into Iran. He was condemned to serve his political term in Dubravlag, Mordovia, one of two notorious, strict-regime political camps.

Many elements of Marchenko's prison experience would have been familiar to people used to hearing stories of Stalin's camps. Just like his predecessors, Marchenko rode to Mordovia in a Stolypin wagon. Just like his predecessors, he received a loaf of bread, 1.5 ounces of sugar, and a salted herring to last him the trip. Just like his predecessors, he found that his access to water depended upon which soldier was in charge of the train: 'If he's a good one he'll bring you two or three kettles, but if he can't be bothered to fetch and carry for you, then you can sit there until you die of thirst.'[32]

Upon arriving in camp, Marchenko found the same generalized hunger, if not the starvation, that there would have been in the past. His daily food norm contained 2,400 calories: 25 ounces of bread, 1 pound of usually rotten vegetables, 3 ounces of usually spoiled cod, 2 ounces of meat. By contrast, the dogs guarding the prisoners got a pound of meat. As in the past, not all of Marchenko's ration actually ended up in his food, and there were few extras. 'During the six years in camp and gaol I had bread with butter twice, when I received visits. I also ate two cucumbers – one in 1964 and another in 1966. Not once did I eat a tomato or an apple.'[33]

Work still mattered to some extent, although it was a different type of work. Marchenko worked as a loader and as a carpenter. Leonid Sitko, also in Dubravlag at this time, built furniture.[34] Prisoners in the Mordovian women's camps worked in factories, often with sewing machines.[35] The prisoners in the other set of political camps, near the city of Perm, in the foothills of the Urals, also worked with wood. Those confined to isolation cells, as many were by the 1980s, sewed gloves or uniforms.[36]

Over time, Marchenko also found that conditions slowly deteriorated. By the mid-1960s, there were at least three categories of prisoner: privileged, ordinary and strict regime. Very soon, strict-regime prisoners – which included all of the most 'serious' political dissidents – were once again wearing black cotton uniforms instead of their own clothes. Although they could receive unlimited letters, as well as printed materials – if they were of Soviet origin – they could send only two letters per month. If they were on strict regime, they could receive no food or cigarettes.

Marchenko had served time both as an ordinary criminal and as a political prisoner, and his descriptions of the criminal world have a familiar ring. If anything, criminal culture had degraded even further since Stalin's death. In the wake of the thieves' war of the late 1940s, the professional criminals had split into further factions. Zhenya Fedorov, a former prisoner arrested in 1967 for theft, describes several groups, not only 'bitches' and 'thieves' but also *svoyaki*, whom he explains were apprentice thieves, and 'red caps', thieves who followed their own law, probably the intellectual descendants of the 'red caps' who emerged in the camps after the war. Other prisoners also grouped themselves into 'families' for self-protection and other tasks: 'When someone had to be murdered, "families" would decide who would do it,' said Fedorov.[37]

The violent culture of homosexual rape and domination – evident earlier in some descriptions of conditions in juvenile prisons – also now played a far greater role in criminal life. Unwritten rules now divided criminal prisoners into two groups: those who played the 'female' role, and those who played the 'male' role. 'The former were universally despised, while the latter went about like heroes, boasting of their masculine strength and their "conquests", not only to each other but to the guards,' wrote Marchenko.[38] According to Fedorov, the authorities played along, keeping the 'unclean' prisoners in separate cells. Anyone could wind up there: 'if you lost at cards, you could be forced to "do it" like a woman'.[39] In the women's camps, lesbianism was equally widespread, and sometimes no less violent. One political prisoner wrote later of a prisoner who had refused a visit from her husband and small child, so greatly did she fear reprisals from her prison lesbian lover.[40]

The 1960s were the beginning of the plague of tuberculosis in Russian prisons, a scourge which continues today. Fedorov described the situation like this: 'If there were eighty people in a barrack, then fifteen had tuberculosis. No one tried to cure them, there was just one kind of tablet, for headaches, whatever. The doctors were some kind of SS men, they never talked to you, didn't look at you, you were nobody.'[41]

To worsen matters, many of the thieves were now addicted to *chifir*, an extremely strong form of tea that produced a narcotic high. Others went to greater lengths than ever to get hold of alcohol. Those who worked outside the camp, as some did, developed a special method of smuggling it back in, past the guards:

A condom is hermetically attached to a long piece of thin plastic tubing. The *zek* then swallows it, leaving one end of the tube in his mouth. To avoid swallowing by accident, he wedges it in the gap between two teeth: there are not likely to be any *zeks* in existence with a full set of 32 teeth. Then, with the help of a syringe, up to three litres of spirit are pumped into the condom via the plastic tubing – and the *zek* goes back to his zone. If the bonding has been badly done, or if the condom happens to burst in the *zek*'s stomach, that means certain and painful death. Despite it, they run the risk: three litres of spirit makes seven litres of vodka. When the 'hero' returns to the zone . . . he is hung head-down from a beam under the barrack roof and the end of the plastic tubing is held over a dish until every drop has been retrieved. Then the empty condom is hauled out . . .

The practice of self-mutilation was equally widespread, except that now it took even more extreme forms. Once, in a prison cell, Marchenko watched two thieves swallow first the handles of their spoon, and then, after stamping on them to make them flat, the bowls of the spoons as well. After that, they broke a pane of glass and began swallowing pieces of it, before the warders managed to drag them away.[42] Edward Kuznetsov, condemned for having taken part in an infamous attempt to hijack an aircraft at Leningrad's Smolny airport, described dozens of methods of self-mutilation:

I have seen convicts swallow huge numbers of nails and barbed wire; I have seen them swallow mercury thermometers, pewter tureens (after first breaking them up into 'edible' proportions), chess pieces, dominoes, needles, ground glass, spoons, knives and many other similar objects. I have seen convicts sew up their mouths and eyes with thread or wire, sew rows of buttons to their bodies; or nail their testicles to the bed . . . I have seen convicts cut open the skin on their arms and legs and peel it off as if it were a stocking; or cut out lumps of flesh (from their stomach or their legs), roast them and eat them; or let the blood drip from a slit vein into a tureen, crumble bread crumbs into it, and then gulp it down like a bowl of soup; or cover themselves with paper and set fire to themselves; or cut off their fingers, or their nose, or ears, or penis . . .

Kuznetsov wrote that the convicts did such things to themselves not in protest, but for no particular reason at all, or just 'to get into the hospital where the nurses swing their hips, where you get your hospital ration and you're not forced to work, where you can get drugs, diets, postcards'. Many of the mutilators were masochists as well, 'in a permanent state of depression from one blood-letting to the next'.[43]

Indisputably, the relationships between the criminals and the political prisoners had changed greatly since Stalin's time too. Criminals did sometimes torment or beat up politicals: the Ukrainian dissident Valentyn Moroz was incarcerated in a cell with criminals who kept him awake at night, and finally attacked him, cutting his stomach with a sharpened spoon.[44] But there were also criminals who respected the politicals, if only for their resistance to the authorities, as Vladimir Bukovsky wrote: 'They used to ask us to tell them what we were in gaol for and what we wanted . . . the only thing they couldn't believe was that we did all this for nothing, and not for money.'[45]

There were even criminals who aspired to join their ranks. Believing that the political prisons were 'easier', some professional thieves attempted to get political sentences. They would write a denunciation of Khrushchev or the Party, sprinkled with obscenities, or make 'American flags' out of rags and wave them out of windows. By the late 1970s, it was very common to see criminals with slogans tattooed on their foreheads: 'Communists drink the blood of the people', 'Slave of the Communist Party', 'Bolsheviks give me bread'.[46]

The change in the relationship between the new generation of politicals and the authorities was even more profound. In the post-Stalin era, the politicals were prisoners who knew why they were in prison, who expected to be in prison, and who had already decided how they would act in prison: with organized defiance. As early as February 1968, a group of prisoners in Potma – Yuli Daniel among them – went on a hunger strike. They demanded an easing of the prison regime; an end to compulsory labour; the removal of restrictions on correspondence; and, in an echo of the early 1920s, recognition of their special status as political prisoners.[47]

The authorities made concessions – and then slowly withdrew them. Nevertheless, the politicals' demand to be kept separate from criminal prisoners would eventually be met, not least because the camp administrators wanted to keep this new generation of politicals, with their constant demands and their penchant for hunger strikes, as far away from ordinary criminals as possible.

These strikes were frequent and widespread, so much so that the *Chronicle*, from 1969 onwards, contains a record of almost constant protest. In that year, for example, prisoners went on strike to demand the reinstatement of concessions made a year earlier; to protest at being forbidden visits from relatives; to protest after one of their number was placed in a punishment cell; to protest after another was forbidden from receiving a parcel from relatives; to protest against the transfer of still others from camp to prison; and even to mark International Human Rights Day on 10 December.[48] Nor was 1969 an unusual year. Over the next decade, hunger strikes, work strikes and other protests became a regular feature of life in both Mordovia and Perm.

Hunger strikes, which took the form of short, one-day protests, as well as agonizing, drawn-out bouts with the authorities, even developed a wearisome pattern, as Marchenko wrote:

For the first few days, no one takes a blind bit of notice. Then, after several days – sometimes as many as ten or twelve – they transfer you to a special cell set aside for such people, and start to feed you artificially, through a pipe. It is useless to resist, for whatever you do they twist your arms behind your back and handcuff you. This procedure is usually carried out in the camps even more brutally than in remand prison – by the time you've been force-fed once or twice you are often minus your teeth . . .[49]

By the mid-1970s, some of the 'worst' politicals had been removed from Mordovia and Perm, and placed in special high-security prisons – most notably Vladimir, a central Russian prison of tsarist origins – where they occupied themselves almost exclusively with their struggle against the authorities. The game was dangerous, and it developed highly complex rules. The aim of the prisoners was to ease their conditions, and to score points, which could be reported, via the samizdat networks, to the West. The aim of the authorities was to break the prisoners: to get them to inform, to collaborate, and above all to publish public recantations of their views, which could appear in the Soviet press and be repeated abroad. Although their methods bore some resemblance to the torture carried out in the Stalinist interrogation cells of the past, they usually involved psychological pressure rather than physical pain. Natan Sharansky (born Anatoly Shcharansky), one of the most active prison protesters of the late 1970s and early 1980s – now an Israeli politician – described the procedure:

They will invite you for a talk. You think nothing depends on you? On the contrary: they will explain that everything depends on you. Do you like tea, coffee, meat? Would you like to go with me to a restaurant? Why not? We'll dress you in civilian clothes and we'll go. If we see you're on the road to rehabilitation, that you're prepared to help us – what, you don't want to squeal on your friends? But what does it mean to squeal? This Russian (or Jew, or Ukrainian, depending on the situation) who's serving time with you, don't you realize what kind of nationalist he is? Don't you know how much he hates you Ukrainians (or Russians, or Jews)?[50]

As in the past, the authorities could grant or withdraw privileges, and exact punishments, usually a term in a punishment cell. They could regulate a prisoner's living conditions by making minute but critical changes to the prisoner's daily life, shifting him between ordinary and strict regimes – always, of course, in rigid accord with regulations. As Marchenko wrote, 'The differences between these regimes might seem infinitesimal to someone who hasn't experienced them on his own back, but for a prisoner it is enormous. On normal regime there's a radio, on strict regime not; on normal regime you get an hour's exercise a day, on strict regime half an hour, with nothing at all on Sundays.'[51]

By the end of the 1970s, the number of food norms had grown from a handful to eighteen, from 1A to 9B, each with a specific number of calories (from 2,200 to 900) and its own selection of foods. Prisoners would be assigned one or another according to minor changes in their behaviour. The contents of the lowest food norm, 9B, given to prisoners in the punishment cells, consisted of a small piece of bread, a spoonful of *kasha*, and soup which theoretically contained 200 grams of potato and 200 grams of cabbage, but often did not.[52]

Prisoners could also be thrown in punishment cells – the 'cooler' – a form of punishment which was ideal, from the authorities' point of view. It was completely legal, and could not technically be described as torture. Its effects on prisoners were slow and cumulative, but since no one was rushing to complete a road across the tundra, that did not worry the prison authorities. These cells were comparable to anything invented by Stalin's NKVD. A 1976 document, published by the Moscow Helsinki group, described with great precision the punishment cells of Vladimir prison, of which there were about fifty. The walls of the cells were covered with cement 'fur', bumps and spikes. The floors were dirty and wet. In one cell, the window had been broken and replaced with newspapers, in others, the windows were blocked with bricks. The only thing to sit on was a cylinder of cement, about 25 centimetres across, ringed with iron. At night, a wooden bunk was brought in, but without sheets or pillows. The prisoner was expected to lie on bare boards and iron. Cells were kept so cold that prisoners found it difficult to sleep, even to lie down. In some cells, the 'ventilation' brought in air from the sewers.[53]

Worst of all, for people accustomed to active lives, was the boredom, described by Yuli Daniel:

Week after week
Dissolves in smoke from cigarettes
In this curious establishment
Everything's dream or else delirium . . .

In here the light doesn't go off at night
In here the light isn't too strong by day
In here silence, the managing director,
Has taken me over.

You can choke with nothing to do,
Or beat your head against the wall,
Week after week
Dissolves in blue smoke . . .[54]

Punishment-cell terms could last indefinitely. Technically, prisoners could only be confined for fifteen-day periods, but the authorities got round this by putting prisoners in, letting them out for a day, and then throwing them back in again. Marchenko was once kept in a cell for forty-eight days. Each time the fifteen-day limit was reached, his guards let him out for a few minutes – long enough to be read a directive confining him, again, to a punishment cell.[55] In the camp Perm-35, one prisoner was held for nearly two months before being taken to hospital, while another was held for forty-five days, after refusing to work in any job except his speciality, which was metalworking.[56]

Many of those sent to the cells were being punished for crimes even more insubstantial than that: when the authorities truly wanted to break someone, they deliberately doled out harsh punishments for very minor infractions. In 1973 and 1974, in the Perm camps, two prisoners were deprived of the right to relatives' visits for 'sitting on beds in daytime'. Another was punished because some jam in a parcel he received was found to have been cooked with alcohol as a flavouring. Other prisoners were punished or reprimanded for walking too slowly, or for not wearing socks.[57]

Sometimes, the prolonged pressure succeeded. Aleksei Dobrovolsky, one of the co-defendants in the trial of Aleksandr Ginzburg, 'broke' very early on, requesting in writing that he be allowed to testify on the radio and tell the whole story of his 'criminal' dissident activity, the better to caution young people against following his own dangerous path.[58] Pyotr Yakir also broke down under investigation, and 'confessed' to having invented what he wrote.[59]

Others died. Yuri Galanskov, another of Ginzburg's co-defendants, died in 1972. He had developed ulcers in prison. They went untreated, and eventually killed him.[60] Marchenko also died, in 1986, probably from drugs he was given while on hunger strike.[61] Several more prisoners died – one killed himself – during a month-long hunger strike in Perm-35 in 1974.[62] Later, Vasil Stus, a Ukrainian poet and human rights activist, died in Perm in 1985.[63]

But prisoners also fought back. In 1977, the political prisoners of Perm-35 described their form of defiance:

We often go on hunger strike. In the punishment cells, in transport wagons. On ordinary, insignificant days, on the days of the death of our comrades. On days of unusual activities in the *zona*, on the 8th of March and the 10th of December, on the 1st of August and the 8th of May, on the 5th of September. We go on hunger strike too often. Diplomats, civil servants sign new agreements on human rights, on the freedom of information, on the banning of torture – and we go on hunger strike, since in the USSR these things are not observed.[64]

Thanks to their efforts, knowledge of the dissident movement was growing all the time in the West – and protests were growing louder. As a result, the treatment of some prisoners took on a new form.

Although I have noted that few archival documents from the 1970s and the 1980s have appeared in public, there are, in fact, some exceptions. In 1991, Vladimir Bukovsky was invited back to Russia from Britain, where he had been living ever since he had been expelled from the country (in exchange for an imprisoned Chilean communist) fifteen years earlier. Bukovsky had been designated a 'court expert' in the 'trial' of the Communist Party, which took place after the Party had challenged President Yeltsin's attempt to ban it. He arrived at the Constitutional Court building in Moscow carrying a laptop computer with a hand scanner. Confident that no one in Russia had ever seen either machine before, he sat down and calmly began copying all of the documents that had been brought as evidence. Only as he approached the end of his task did those around him suddenly realize what he was doing. Someone said aloud, 'He's going to publish them, *there*!' The room fell silent. At that point – 'like in a film', Bukovsky said later – he simply closed his computer, walked to the exit, went straight to the airport, and flew out of Russia.[65]

Thanks to Bukovsky's efforts, we know, among other things, what happened at the 1967 Politburo meeting which took place just before his own arrest. Bukovsky in particular was struck by how many of those present felt that bringing criminal charges against him would 'cause a certain reaction inside the country and abroad'. It would be a mistake, they concluded, simply to arrest Bukovsky – so they proposed to put him in a psychiatric hospital instead.[66] The era of the *psikhushka* – the 'special mental hospital' – had begun.

The use of psychiatric hospitals for the imprisonment of dissidents had a prehistory. Returning from Western Europe to St Petersburg in 1836, the Russian philosopher Pyotr Chadaev wrote an essay critical of the regime of

Tsar Nicholas I: 'Contrary to all the laws of the human community,' he declared, at the height of the Russian imperial regime, 'Russia moves only in the direction of her own enslavement and the enslavement of all neighbouring peoples.' In response, Nicholas had Chadaev detained in his home. The Tsar was certain, he declared, that once the Russians learned that their compatriot 'suffers from derangement and insanity', they would forgive him.[67]

In the aftermath of the Thaw, the authorities began once again to use psychiatric hospitals to incarcerate dissidents – a policy which had many advantages for the KGB. Above all, it helped discredit the dissidents, both in the West and in the USSR, and deflected attention away from them. If these were not serious political opponents of the regime, but merely crazy people, who could object to their hospitalization?

With great enthusiasm, the Soviet psychiatric establishment participated in the farce. To explain the phenomenon of dissidence, they came up with the definition of 'sluggish schizophrenia' or 'creeping schizophrenia'. This, scientists explained, was a form of schizophrenia which left no mark on the intellect or outward behaviour, yet could encompass nearly any form of behaviour deemed asocial or abnormal. 'Most frequently, ideas about a "struggle for truth and justice" are formed by personalities with a paranoid structure,' wrote two Soviet professors, both of the Serbsky Institute:

A characteristic feature of overvalued ideas is the patient's conviction of his own rectitude, an obsession with asserting his trampled 'rights', and the significance of these feelings for the patient's personality. They tend to exploit judicial proceedings as a platform for making speeches and appeals.[68]

And, by this definition, just about all of the dissidents qualified as crazy. The writer and scientist Zhores Medvedev was diagnosed with 'sluggish schizophrenia' accompanied by 'paranoid delusions of reforming society'. His symptoms included that of a 'split personality' – meaning he worked both as a scientist and as a writer. Natalya Gorbanevskaya, the first editor of the *Chronicle*, was diagnosed with sluggish schizophrenia with 'no clear symptoms', but which resulted in 'abnormal changes in emotions, wills and thought patterns'. The dissident Red Army General Pyotr Grigorenko was diagnosed with a psychological condition 'characterized by the presence of reformist ideas, in particular for the reorganization of the state apparatus; and this was linked with ideas of overestimation of his own personality that reached messianic proportions'.[69] In one report sent up to the Central Committee, a local KGB commander also complained that he had on his hands a group of citizens with a very particular form of mental illness: they 'try to found new "parties", organizations, and councils, preparing and distributing plans for new laws and programmes'.[70]

Depending on the circumstances of their arrest – or non-arrest – prisoners deemed mentally ill could be sent to a variety of institutions. Some were assessed by prison doctors, others by clinics. In a category of its own was the Serbsky Institute, whose special diagnostic section, headed in the 1960s and 1970s by Doctor Danil Lunts, was responsible for assessing political offenders. Dr Lunts personally examined Sinyavsky, Bukovsky, Gorbanevskaya, Grigorenko and Viktor Nekipelov, among many others, and clearly had high status.[71] Nekipelov reported that he wore a blue uniform with two stars, 'the insignia of a general in the MVD troops'.[72] Some Soviet émigré psychiatrists would claim that Lunts, and the others at the institute, were sincere in their belief that their patients were mentally ill. Most of the political prisoners who met him, however, have characterized him as an opportunist, carrying out the work of his MVD bosses, 'no better than the criminal doctors who performed inhuman experiments on the prisoners in Nazi concentration camps'.[73]

If diagnosed as mentally ill, patients were condemned to a term in a hospital, sometimes for a few months, sometimes for many years. The luckier ones were sent on to one of the several hundred ordinary Soviet psychiatric hospitals. These were unhygienic and overcrowded, and often staffed by drunks and sadists. Still, the drunks and sadists were civilians, and the ordinary hospitals were generally less secretive than prisons and camps. Patients were allowed to write letters with greater freedom, and could receive visits from people other than relatives.

Those deemed 'especially dangerous', on the other hand, were sent to the 'special psychiatric hospitals', of which there were only a handful. These were run directly by the MVD. The doctors in them had, like Lunts, MVD ranks. They looked and felt like prisons, and were surrounded by watchtowers, barbed wire, guards and dogs. A photograph of the Oryol special psychiatric hospital taken in the 1970s shows patients exercising in an internal courtyard, indistinguishable from a prison exercise yard.[74]

In both the ordinary and the special hospitals, the doctors aimed, again, at recantation.[75] Patients who agreed to renounce their convictions, who admitted that mental illness had caused them to criticize the Soviet system, could be declared healthy and set free. Those who did not recant were considered still ill, and could be given 'treatment'. As Soviet psychiatrists did not believe in psychoanalysis, this treatment consisted largely of drugs, electric shocks and various forms of restraint. Drugs abandoned by the West in the 1930s were administered routinely, forcing patients' body temperatures above 40 degrees centigrade, causing pain and discomfort. Prison doctors also prescribed tranquillizers which caused a range of side effects, including physical rigidity, slowness and involuntary tics and movements, not to mention apathy and indifference.[76]

Other treatments included straightforward beating; the injection of insulin, which sends non-diabetics into hypoglycaemic shock; and a punishment called the 'roll-up', which Bukovsky described in a 1976 interview: 'It involved the use of wet canvas – long pieces of it – in which the patient is rolled up from head to foot, so tightly that it was difficult for him to breathe, and as the canvas began to dry out it would get tighter and tighter and make the patient feel even worse.'[77] Another treatment, which Nekipelov witnessed at the Serbsky Institute, was the 'lumbar puncture', the thrusting of a needle into the patient's spine. Those who returned from a lumbar puncture were put on their sides, where they lay, immobile, their backs smeared with iodine, for several days.[78]

Many people were affected. In 1977, the year Peter Reddaway and Sidney Bloch published their extensive survey of Soviet psychiatric abuse, at least 365 sane people were known to have undergone treatment for politically defined madness, and there were surely hundreds more.[79]

Nevertheless, the incarceration of dissidents in hospitals did not, in the end, achieve everything that the Soviet regime had hoped it would. Most of all, it did not deflect the attention of the West. For one, the horrors of psychiatric abuse probably inflamed Western imaginations far more than had more familiar tales of camps and prisons. Anyone who had seen the film *One Flew Over the Cuckoo's Nest* could imagine a Soviet psychiatric hospital all too well. More importantly, though, the issue of psychiatric abuse had a direct appeal to a defined, articulate group that had a professional interest in the subject: Western psychiatrists. From 1971, the year that Bukovsky smuggled out over 150 pages documenting such abuse in the USSR, the issue became a perennial topic for bodies such as the World Psychiatric Association, the Royal College of Psychiatrists in Britain, and other national and international psychiatric associations. The braver groups issued statements. Others did not, but were then condemned for their cowardice, generating more bad publicity for the USSR.[80]

Eventually, the issue galvanized scientists in the Soviet Union. When Zhores Medvedev was condemned to a psychiatric hospital, many of them wrote letters of protest to the Soviet Academy of Scientists. Andrei Sakharov, the nuclear physicist who was, by the late 1960s, emerging as the moral leader of the dissident movement, made a public statement on Medvedev's behalf at an international symposium at the Institute of Genetics. Solzhenitsyn, by now in the West, wrote an open letter to the Soviet authorities protesting Medvedev's incarceration. 'After all,' he wrote, 'it is time to think clearly: the incarceration of free-thinking healthy people is SPIRITUAL MURDER.'[81]

The international attention probably played a part in persuading the authorities to release a number of prisoners, among them Medvedev, who was then expelled from the country. But some in the upper echelons of the Soviet elite felt this had been the wrong response. In 1976, Yuri Andropov, then the chief of the KGB, wrote a secret memo, describing fairly accurately (if you ignore the snide tone and the anti-Semitism) the international origins of the 'anti-Soviet campaign':

Recent data testify to the fact that the campaign has the character of a carefully planned anti-Soviet action . . . at the present time, the initiators of the campaign are trying to draw in international and national psychiatric organizations as well as specialists of good reputation, to create a 'committee' designed to monitor the activity of psychiatrists in various countries, above all in the USSR . . . An active role in building up the anti-Soviet mood is being played by the Royal College of Psychiatrists in Great Britain, which is under the influence of Zionist elements.[82]

Andropov carefully described the efforts to get the World Psychiatric Association to denounce the USSR, and revealed quite extensive knowledge of which international seminars had condemned Soviet psychiatry. In response to his memo, the Soviet Ministry of Health proposed to launch a massive propaganda campaign in advance of the upcoming congress of the World Psychiatric Association. They also proposed to prepare scientific documents denying the charges, and to identify 'progressive' psychiatrists in the West who would back them up. These 'progressives' would, in turn, be rewarded with invitations to the USSR, where they would be taken on tours of specially designated psychiatric hospitals. They even named a few who might come.[83]

Rather than retreating from the political abuse of psychiatry, in other words, Andropov proposed to brazen it out. It was not in his nature to concede that any aspect of Soviet policy might be wrong.

27

The 1980s: Smashing Statues

The statue's sundered plinth is being smashed,
The steel of drills is sending up a howl.
The special hardest mixture of cement
Was calculated to endure millennia . . .

All handmade things in the world we live in
Can be reduced to scrap by hands of men.
But the main point is this:
Stone in its essence can
Be never either good or bad.

– Alexander Tvardovsky,
'The Statue's Sundered Plinth'[1]

By the time Yuri Andropov took over as the General Secretary of the Soviet Communist Party in 1982, his 'crackdown' on the asocial elements in the Soviet Union was in fact well under way. Unlike some of his predecessors, Andropov had always believed that the dissidents, despite their small numbers, should be treated as a serious threat to Soviet power. Having been Soviet Ambassador to Budapest in 1956, he had seen how quickly an intellectual movement could turn into a popular revolution. He also believed that all of the Soviet Union's many problems – political, economic, social – could be solved through the application of greater discipline: stricter camps and prisons, heavier surveillance and more harassment.[2]

These were the methods Andropov had advocated while head of the KGB, from 1979 onwards, and these were the methods he continued to pursue during his short reign as the Soviet Union's leader. Thanks to Andropov, the first half of the 1980s is remembered as the most repressive era in post-Stalinist Soviet history. It was as if the pressure within the system had to reach boiling point, just before the system itself broke down altogether.

Certainly, from the late 1970s, Andropov's KGB had made large numbers of arrests and rearrests: under his direction, recalcitrant activists often received new sentences right at the end of their old ones, as had happened in Stalin's time. Membership of one of the Helsinki monitoring groups – dissident organizations which tried to monitor the Soviet Union's observation of the Helsinki Treaty – became a surefire route to prison. Twenty-three members of the Moscow group were arrested between 1977 and 1979, and seven were expelled abroad. Yuri Orlov, leader of the Moscow Helsinki group, remained in prison throughout the first half of the 1980s.[3]

Nor was arrest Andropov's only weapon. Because his aim was to frighten people away from joining dissident movements in the first place, the scope of repression became much wider. Those even suspected of sympathizing with the human rights, religious or nationalist movements stood to lose everything. Suspects and their spouses could be deprived not only of their jobs, but also of their professional status and qualifications. Their children could be denied the right to attend university. Their telephones could be cut off, their residence permits revoked, their travel restricted.[4]

By the end of the 1970s, Andropov's multi-layered 'disciplinary measures' had succeeded in dividing both the dissident movement and its foreign supporters into small, hardened, and sometimes mutually suspicious interest groups. There were human rights activists, whose fate was closely monitored by groups like Amnesty International. There were Baptist dissidents, whose cause was supported by the international Baptist Church. There were nationalist dissidents – Ukrainians, Lithuanians, Latvians, Georgians – who were supported by their compatriots in exile. There were Meskhetians and Crimean Tartars, deported in Stalin's time, who wanted the right to return home.

In the West, probably the most prominent group of dissidents were the refuseniks, Soviet Jews who had been refused the right to emigrate to Israel. Raised to prominence by Congress's 1975 Jackson-Vanik amendment, which had linked US/Soviet trade to the emigration issue, the refuseniks remained a central concern for Washington right up to the end of the Soviet Union. In the autumn of 1986, at his meeting with Gorbachev in Reykjavik, President Reagan personally presented the Soviet leader with a list of 1,200 Soviet Jews who wanted to emigrate.[5]

Now kept firmly apart from the criminals, all of these groups were well represented within Soviet camps and prisons, where they organized themselves, like the politicals of eras past, according to their common causes.[6] By this time, it might even be said that the camps served as a sort of networking facility, almost a school of dissent, where political prisoners could meet others with similar ideas. At times, they celebrated one another's national holidays, Lithuanian and Latvian, Georgian and Armenian, and argued lightly over whose country would be the first to free itself from the Soviet Union.[7] Contacts were cross-generational too: Balts and Ukrainians had the opportunity to meet a previous generation of nationalists, the anti-Soviet partisans who had been given 25-year sentences and never released. Of the latter, Bukovsky wrote that because 'their lives had come to a halt when they were about twenty', the camps had somehow preserved them. 'On summer Sundays they would crawl out in the sun with their accordions and play tunes that had long since been forgotten in their native regions. Truly, being in the camps was like having entered a land beyond the grave.'[8]

The older generation often had trouble understanding their younger compatriots. Men and women who had fought with guns in the forest could not understand dissidents fighting with bits of paper.[9] But the old were still able to inspire the young with their example. Such encounters helped to form people who would, later in the decade, organize the nationalist movements that ultimately helped to destroy the Soviet Union itself. Looking back on the experience, David Berdzenishvili, a Georgian activist, told me he was glad that he had spent two years in a 1980s labour camp rather than two years in the 1980s Soviet army.

If the personal networks had hardened, so too had the links with the outside world. An edition of the *Chronicle* published in 1979 illustrates this perfectly, as it contains, among other things, a day-by-day account of life in the Perm 36 punishment cells:

13 September: Zhukauskas found a white worm in his soup.

26 September: He found a black insect 1.5 cm long in his bowl. The discovery was immediately reported to Captain Nelipovich.

27 September: In punishment cell No. 6 the temperature was officially measured as 12 degrees centigrade.

28 September: The morning temperature in the cells was 12 degrees. Second blankets and padded trousers were issued. Heaters were placed in the rooms of the duty guards. In the evening the temperature in the cells was 11 degrees.

1 October: 11.5 degrees.

2 October: A 500-watt heater was put in cell No. 6 (Zhukauskas, Gluzman, Marmus). The temperature, both morning and evening, was 12 degrees.

Zhukauskas was asked to sign a document in which his output was stated to be ten times lower than it was. He refused . . .

10 October: Balkhanov refused to attend voluntarily a meeting of the camp Education Commission. On the orders of Nikomarov he was taken by force.

And so on.

The authorities seemed powerless to stop this sort of information from flowing – or to prevent it from instantly appearing on Western radio stations, broadcasting in the USSR. The 1983 arrest of Berdzenishvili was announced on the BBC within two hours of its occurrence.[10] Ratushinskaya and her barrack mates in the women's camp in Mordovia sent Reagan a congratulatory message after he won the US elections. Within two days he had received it. The KGB, she wrote gleefully, were 'beside themselves'.[11]

To most sensible outsiders peering through the looking-glass at the strange world of the Soviet Union, such cleverness seemed somewhat beside the point. For all practical purposes, Andropov appeared to have won the game. A decade's worth of harassment, imprisonment and forced exile had kept the dissident movement small and weak.[12] Most of the better-known dissidents had been silenced: in the middle of the 1980s, Solzhenitsyn was in exile abroad, and Sakharov was in internal exile in the city of Gorky. KGB policemen sat outside Roy Medvedev's door, monitoring all of his movements. No one in the USSR seemed to notice their struggle. Peter Reddaway, probably the leading Western academic specialist on Soviet dissent at the time, wrote in 1983 that dissident groups 'have made little or no headway among the mass of ordinary people in the Russian heartland'.[13]

The goons and the warders, the crooked doctors and the secret police, all seemed safe and secure in their chosen professions. But the ground was moving beneath their feet. As it turned out, Andropov's strict refusal to tolerate dissent would not last. When he died in 1984, that policy died with him.

Appointed General Secretary of the Soviet Communist Party in March 1985, the character of the new Soviet leader, Mikhail Gorbachev, at first appeared mysterious, to foreigners and countrymen alike. He seemed as slick and as smooth as other Soviet bureaucrats – yet there were hints of something different. During the summer after his appointment, I met a group of Leningrad refuseniks who laughed at the West's naïvety: How could we believe that Gorbachev's alleged preference for whisky over vodka, and his wife's admiration for Western clothes, meant he was more liberal than his predecessors?

They were wrong: he was different. Few knew, at the time, that Gorbachev came from a family of 'enemies'. One of his grandfathers, a peasant, had been arrested and sent to a labour camp in 1933. His other grandfather had been arrested in 1938 and tortured in prison by an investigator who broke both of his arms. The impact on young Mikhail had been enormous, as he later wrote in his memoirs: 'Our neighbours began shunning our house as if it were plague-stricken. Only at night would some close relative venture to drop by. Even the boys from the neighbourhood avoided me . . . all of this was a great shock to me and has remained engraved on my memory ever since.'[14]

Nevertheless, the refuseniks' suspicions were not wholly ill-founded, for the early months of the Gorbachev era were disappointing. He threw himself into an anti-alcohol campaign, which angered people, destroyed the ancient vineyards of Georgia and Moldavia, and might even have provoked the economic crash that followed some years later: some believe that the collapse in the sales of vodka destroyed the country's delicate financial balance for good. Only in April 1986, after the explosion at the Chernobyl nuclear complex in Ukraine, was Gorbachev ready to make genuine changes. Convinced that the Soviet Union needed to speak openly about its troubles, he came up with another reform proposal: glasnost, or 'openness'.

At first, glasnost, like the anti-alcohol campaign, was essentially an economic policy. Apparently, Gorbachev hoped that open discussion of the Soviet Union's very real economic, ecological and social crises would lead to quick resolutions, to the restructuring – the perestroika – he had begun talking about in his speeches. Within an amazingly short period of time, however, glasnost began to be about Soviet history.

Indeed, when describing what happened to public debate in the Soviet Union in the late 1980s, one is always tempted to use flood metaphors: it was as if a dam had broken, or a dyke had burst, or a water main had given way. In January 1987, Gorbachev told an intrigued group of journalists that the 'blank spots' in the Soviet Union's history would have to be filled in. By November, so much had changed that Gorbachev became the second Party leader in Soviet history to refer openly to the 'blank spots' in a speech:

... the lack of proper democratization of Soviet society was precisely what made possible both the cult of personality and the violations of the law, arbitrariness, and repressions of the 1930s – to be blunt, crimes based on the abuse of power. Many thousands of members of the Party and non-members were subjected to mass repressions. That, comrades, is the bitter truth.[15]

Gorbachev was actually less eloquent than Khrushchev had been – but his impact on the broad Soviet public was probably greater. Khrushchev's speech had, after all, been made to a closed meeting. Gorbachev had spoken on national television.

Gorbachev also followed up on his speech with far more enthusiasm than Khrushchev had ever shown. In its wake, new 'revelations' began appearing in the Soviet press every week. Finally, the Soviet public had the chance to read Osip Mandelstam and Joseph Brodsky, Anna Akhmatova's *Requiem*, Boris Pasternak's *Doctor Zhivago*, even Vladimir Nabokov's *Lolita*. After a struggle, *Novyi Mir*, now under new editorship, began publishing instalments of Solzhenitsyn's *Gulag Archipelago*.[16] *One Day in the Life of Ivan Denisovich* would soon sell millions of copies, and authors whose works had previously circulated only in samizdat, if at all, sold hundreds of thousands of copies of their Gulag memoirs too. Some became household names in the process: Evgeniya Ginzburg, Lev Razgon, Anatoly Zhigulin, Varlam Shalamov, Dmitri Likhachev and Anna Larina.

The rehabilitation process resumed as well. Between 1964 and 1987, only twenty-four people had been rehabilitated. Now – partly in response to spontaneous press revelations – the process began again. This time, those who had been overlooked in the past were included: Bukharin, along with nineteen other Bolshevik leaders convicted at the 1938 purge trials, was first among them. 'The facts had been falsified,' a government spokesman announced solemnly.[17] Now the truth would be told.

The new literature was accompanied by new revelations from the Soviet archives. These came both from Soviet historians who had (they claimed) seen the light, as well as from the Memorial Society. Memorial was founded by a group of young historians, some of whom had been collecting oral histories of camp survivors for many years. Among them was Arseny Roginsky, founder of the journal *Pamyat* (*Memory*), which first began to appear in samizdat, and then in emigration, as early as the 1970s. Already, the group around Roginsky had begun to compile a database of the repressed. Later, Memorial would also lead the battle to identify the corpses buried in mass graves outside Moscow and Leningrad, and to build monuments and memorials to the Stalinist era. After a brief, failed attempt to turn itself into a political movement, Memorial would finally emerge, in the 1990s, as the most important centre for the study of Soviet history, as well as for the defence of human rights, in the Russian federation. Roginsky remained its leader, and one of its star historians. Memorial's historical publications were soon known to Soviet scholars around the world for their accuracy, their fidelity to facts, and their careful, judicious archives.[18]

Yet although the change in the quality of public debate had come about with astonishing rapidity, the situation was still not quite as straightforward as it seemed to those on the outside. Even as he was introducing the changes which would soon lead to the collapse of the Soviet Union, even as 'Gorbymania' swept through Germany and the United States, Gorbachev remained, like Khrushchev, a deep believer in the Soviet regime. He never intended to challenge the basic principles of Soviet Marxism, or the achievements of Lenin. His intention was always to reform and modernize the Soviet Union, not to destroy it. Perhaps because of his own family experience, he had come to believe that it was important to tell the truth about the past. Yet he did not, at first, appear to see the connection between the past and the present.

For that reason, the publication of a slew of articles about Stalinist camps, prisons and mass murders of the past was not immediately accompanied by mass releases of the still-imprisoned dissidents. At the end of 1986 – although Gorbachev was preparing to start talking about 'blank spots', although Memorial had begun openly to agitate for the construction of a monument to repression, although the rest of the world was beginning to talk with excitement about the new leadership of the USSR – Amnesty International knew the names of 600 prisoners of conscience still in Soviet camps, and suspected the existence of many more.[19]

One of them was Anatoly Marchenko, who died during a hunger strike in Khristopol prison in December of that year.[20] His wife, Larisa Bogoraz, arrived at the prison to find three soldiers standing guard over his body, which had been taken apart in an autopsy. She was not allowed to meet anyone at the prison – no doctors, no other prisoners, no administrators – except for a political officer, Churbanov, who treated her rudely. He refused to tell her how Marchenko had died, and would not give her a death certificate, a burial certificate, a medical case history, or even Marchenko's letters and diaries. With a group of friends, and the three-man prison 'escort', she took Marchenko to be buried in the town cemetery:

It was deserted there, and a strong wind blew, and there was nobody else around apart from us and Tolya's escort. They had everything necessary ready to hand, but they understood that we would not let them approach the grave, and they stood to one side 'until the end of the operation' as one of them put it. Tolya's friends spoke some words of farewell over the grave. Then we started to fill in the grave with earth – first with our hands and then with spades . . .

We erected a white pinewood cross – I hope that it had been made by the other prisoners. On the cross I wrote in ball-point pen 'Anatoly Marchenko 23.1.1938–8.12.1986 . . .'[21]

Although the authorities surrounded Marchenko's death with mystery, Bogoraz said later, they could not conceal that 'Anatoly Marchenko died in struggle. His struggle had lasted twenty-five years, and he had never hoisted the white flag of surrender.'[22]

But Marchenko's tragic death was not entirely in vain. Possibly spurred on by the wave of bad publicity surrounding his death – Bogoraz's statements were broadcast around the world – Gorbachev finally decided, at the end of 1986, to grant a general pardon to all Soviet political prisoners.

There were many strange things about the amnesty that shut down the political prisons of the Soviet Union for good. Nothing was stranger, however, than the scarce amount of attention it attracted. This, after all, was the end of the Gulag, the end of the camp system that had once contained millions of people. This was the triumph of the human rights movement, which had been the focus of so much diplomatic attention for the past two decades. This was a real moment of historical transformation – yet almost nobody noticed.

Moscow-based journalists sometimes dashed off the odd article but, with one or two exceptions, very few of those who wrote books about the era of Gorbachev and Yeltsin mentioned the last days of the concentration camps at all. Even the best of the many talented writers and journalists who lived in Moscow at the end of the 1980s were too preoccupied with the other events of that time: the bungled attempts at economic reform, the first free elections, the transformation of foreign policy, the end of the Soviet Empire in Eastern Europe, the end of the Soviet Union itself.[23]

Distracted by those same issues, nobody in Russia much noticed either. Dissidents whose names had been famous in the underground returned – and found themselves famous no longer. Most of them were old, and by now out of sync with the times. They had, in the words of a Western journalist who was in Russia at the time, 'made their careers in private, tapping out petitions on ancient typewriters at their dachas, defying the authorities while sipping absurdly sweet tea, dressed in their bathrobes. They weren't made for battles in parliament or on TV, and they seemed profoundly confused by how dramatically their country had changed while they were away.'[24]

Most of those former dissidents who remained in the public eye were no longer solely focused on the fate of the Soviet Union's remaining concentration camps. Andrei Sakharov, released from internal exile in December 1986, elected to the Congress of People's Deputies in 1989, quickly began agitating for the reform of property ownership.[25] Two years after his release, the Armenian prisoner Levon Ter-Petrossian was elected president of his country. A host of Ukrainians and Balts moved straight from camps in Perm and Mordovia into their respective countries' political madhouse, agitating loudly for independence.[26]

The KGB noticed that its political prisons were closing, of course – yet even they seemed scarcely able to understand the significance. Reading the few available official documents from the second half of the 1980s, it is striking how little the language of the secret police had changed, even relatively late in the game. In February 1986, Viktor Chebrikov, then the head of the KGB, proudly told a Party Congress that the KGB had carried out a major counter-intelligence operation. It had been necessary, he said, because 'the West spreads lies about human rights violations to spread anti-Soviet aspirations among such renegades'.[27]

Later that same year, Chebrikov sent a report to the Central Committee describing his organization's continued battle against the 'activities of the imperialist spy agencies, and the Soviet enemy elements who are linked to them'. He also bragged that the KGB had effectively 'paralysed' the activities of various groups, among them the Helsinki monitoring committees, and had even, in the period from 1982 to 1986, forced 'more than 100 people to resign from the conduct of illegal activity, and to return to the path of justice'. Some of them – he named nine – had even 'made public declarations on television and in the newspapers, unmasking the Western spies and those who think like them'.

Nevertheless, a few sentences later, Chebrikov acknowledged that things might have changed. One has to read closely to understand how dramatic the change actually was: 'The current conditions of the democratization of all aspects of society, and the strengthening of the unity of the Party and of society, make possible a re-examination of the question of amnesty.'[28]

What he meant, in fact, was that the dissidents were so weak they could not do much harm any more – and in any case they would be watched, as he had said at a previous Politburo meeting, 'to be certain that they don't persist in their hostile activity'.[29] In a separate statement he added, almost as an afterthought, that by the KGB's calculation, ninety-six people were being held unnecessarily in special psychiatric hospitals. He suggested that those among them who 'do not present a danger to society' should be released as well.[30] The Central Committee agreed, and in February 1987 it pardoned 200 prisoners convicted either of Article 70 or of Article 190-1. More were released from camps a few months later to mark the Millennium of Russian Christianity. Over 2,000 (a good deal more than ninety-six) would be released from psychiatric hospitals in the coming two years.[31]

Yet even then – perhaps out of habit, perhaps because it saw its own power waning along with the prison population – the KGB seemed strangely reluctant to let the politicals go. Because they were formally pardoned, not amnestied, the politicals released in 1986 and 1987 were at first asked to sign a piece of paper disassociating themselves from anti-Soviet activity. Most were allowed to invent their own formulas, evading apology: 'Thanks to worsening health I won't engage in further anti-Soviet activity,' or 'I was never an anti-Soviet, I was an anti-communist, and there are no laws prohibiting anti-communism.' One dissident, Lev Timofeev, wrote that 'I ask to be freed. I do not intend to harm the Soviet state, not that I have ever had such an intention before.'[32]

Others, however, were asked, once again, to renounce their beliefs, or ordered to emigrate.[33] One Ukrainian prisoner was released, but sent directly into exile, where he was held to a curfew and made to report to a militia station once a week.[34] One Georgian dissident remained for an extra six months in his labour camp, simply because he refused to put his pen to any formula the KGB could invent.[35] Another refused to ask formally for his pardon, 'on the grounds that he had committed no crime'.[36]

Symptomatic of the time was the plight of Bohdan Klymchak, a technician from Ukraine, arrested for trying to leave the USSR. In 1978, fearing arrest on charges of Ukrainian nationalism, he had walked over the Soviet border into Iran, and had asked for political asylum. The Iranians sent him back. In April 1990, he was still being held in the political prison at Perm. A group of American congressmen managed to visit him there, and discovered that conditions in Perm were virtually unchanged. The prisoners still complained of extreme cold, and were still sent to the punishment cells for crimes such as the refusal to button the top buttons of their uniforms.[37]

Nevertheless, creaking and cranking, groaning and complaining, the repressive regime was finally grinding to a halt – as was the entire system. Indeed, by the time the Perm political camps were finally closed for good, in February 1992, the Soviet Union itself had ceased to exist. All of the former Soviet republics had become independent countries. Some of them – Armenia, Ukraine, Lithuania – were led by former prisoners. Some were led by former communists whose beliefs had crumbled in the 1980s, when they saw for the first time evidence of the past terror.[38] The KGB and the MVD, if not quite disbanded, had been replaced by other, different organizations. Secret police agents started looking for new jobs in the private sector. Prison warders saw the light, and discreetly moved into local government. The new Russian parliament passed, in November 1991, a 'Declaration on Rights and Freedoms of the Individual', guaranteeing, among other things, freedom to travel, freedom of religion, and the freedom to disagree with the government.[39] Sadly, the new Russia was not destined to become a paradigm of ethnic, religious and political tolerance, but that is another, separate story.

The changes took place with bewildering speed – and no one seemed more bewildered by them than the man who had launched the Soviet Union's disintegration. For this, in the end, was Gorbachev's greatest blind spot: Khrushchev knew it, Brezhnev knew it – but Gorbachev, grandson of 'enemies' and author of glasnost, failed to realize that a full and honest discussion of the Soviet past would ultimately undermine the legitimacy of Soviet rule. 'We now visualize our goal more clearly,' he said, on New Year's Eve, 1989. 'It is a humane and democratic socialism, a society of freedom and social justice.'[40] He was unable, even then, to see that 'socialism', in its Soviet form, was about to disappear altogether.

Nor could he see, years later, the link between the press revelations of the glasnost era and the collapse of Soviet communism. Gorbachev did not realize, simply, that once the truth had been told about the Stalinist past, the myth of Soviet greatness would be impossible to sustain. There had been too much cruelty, too much bloodshed, and too many lies about both.

But if Gorbachev did not understand his own country, plenty of others did. Twenty years earlier, Solzhenitsyn's publisher, Alexander Tvardovsky, had felt the power of the hidden past, had known what revived memories could do to the Soviet system. He described his feelings in a poem:

> They're wrong to think that memory
> Hasn't an increasing value
> Or that the weeds of time grow over
> Any real past event or pain.
>
> That on and on the planet rolls,
> Measuring off the days and years . . .
>
> No. Duty commands that everything now
> That hasn't been said be said in full . . .[41]

Epilogue: Memory

And the killers? The killers live on . . .

– Lev Razgon,
Nepridumannoe, 1989[1]

In the early autumn of 1998, I took a boat across the White Sea, from the city of Arkhangelsk to the Solovetsky islands. It was the last cruise of the summer: after the middle of September, when the Arctic nights start to lengthen, boats stop travelling that route. The sea becomes too rough, the water too icy for an overnight tourist expedition.

Perhaps the knowledge that it was the end of the season imparted a touch of added gaiety to the trip. Or perhaps the passengers were simply excited to be out on the open sea. Whatever the reason, the ship's dining room buzzed with good cheer. There were many toasts, many jokes, and hearty applause for the ship's captain. My assigned dining companions, two middle-aged couples from a naval base down the coast, seemed determined to have a good time.

At first, my presence only added to their general merriment. It is not every day one meets a real American on a rickety ferry boat in the middle of the White Sea, and the oddity amused them. They wanted to know why I spoke Russian, what I thought of Russia, how it differs from the United States. When I told them what I was doing in Russia, however, they grew less cheerful. An American on a pleasure cruise, visiting the Solovetsky islands to see the scenery and the beautiful old monastery – that was one thing. An American visiting the Solovetsky islands to see the remains of the concentration camp – that was something else.

One of the men turned hostile. 'Why do you foreigners only care about the ugly things in our history?' he wanted to know. 'Why write about the Gulag? Why not write about our achievements? We were the first country to put a man into space!' By 'we' he meant 'we Soviets'. The Soviet Union had ceased to exist seven years earlier, but he still identified himself as a Soviet citizen, not as a Russian.

His wife attacked me as well. 'The Gulag isn't relevant any more,' she told me. 'We have other troubles here. We have unemployment, we have crime. Why don't you write about our real problems, instead of things that happened a long time ago?'

While this unpleasant conversation continued, the other couple kept silent, and the man never did offer his opinion on the subject of the Soviet past. At one point, however, his wife expressed her support. 'I understand why you want to know about the camps,' she said softly. 'It is interesting to know what happened. I wish I knew more.'

In my subsequent travels around Russia, I encountered these four attitudes to my project again and again. 'It's none of your business,' and 'It's irrelevant' were both common reactions. Silence – or an absence of opinion, as evinced by a shrug of the shoulders – was probably the most frequent reaction. But there were also people who understood why it was important to know about the past, and who wished it were easier to find out more.

In fact, with some effort, one can learn a great deal about the past in contemporary Russia. Not all Russian archives are closed, and not all Russian historians are preoccupied with other things: this book itself is testimony to the abundance of newly available information. The story of the Gulag has also become part of public debate in some of the ex-Soviet republics and ex-Soviet satellites. In a few nations – as a rule, those who remember them-selves as victims rather than perpetrators of terror – the memorials and the debates are very prominent indeed. The Lithuanians have converted the former KGB headquarters in Vilnius into a museum of the victims of geno-cide. The Latvians have turned an old Soviet museum, once dedicated to Latvia's 'Red Sharpshooters', into a museum of Latvian occupation.

In February 2002, I attended the opening of a new Hungarian museum, located in a building which was both the headquarters of the Hungarian fascist movement between 1940 and 1945, and the headquarters of the Hungarian communist secret police between 1945 and 1956. In the first exhibition room, a bank of television screens beamed fascist propaganda from one wall. Another bank of television screens beamed communist propaganda from the other wall. The effect was immediate and emotional, as it was intended to be, and the rest of museum continued in that vein. Using photographs, sound, video and very few words, the museum's organizers are unapologetically aiming its exhibits at people who are too young to remember either regime.

In Belarus, by contrast, the lack of a monument has become a major political issue: in the summer of 2002, the dictatorial president, Aleksandr Lukashenka, was still loudly proclaiming his intention to build a highway over the site of a mass murder that took place outside Minsk, the capital city, in 1937. His rhetoric galvanized the opposition, and sparked a greater discussion of the past.

Dotted around Russia itself, there are also a handful of informal, semi-official and private monuments, erected by a wide variety of people and organizations. The headquarters of Memorial in Moscow contains an archive of oral and written memoirs, as well as a small museum which houses, among other things, an outstanding collection of prisoners' art. The Andrei Sakharov Museum, also in Moscow, has exhibits and displays about the Stalinist era as well. On the outskirts of many cities – Moscow, St Petersburg, Tomsk, Kiev, Petrozavodsk – local Memorial chapters and other organizations have put up monuments to mark mass burial grounds, the sites of the mass murders of 1937 and 1938.

There are also larger efforts. The ring of coal mines around Vorkuta, each one a former *lagpunkt*, is dotted with crosses, statues and other memorials, erected by Lithuanian, Polish and German victims of the Vorkuta camps. The local historical museum in the city of Magadan contains several rooms devoted to Gulag history, including a camp watchtower; on a hill overlooking the city, a well-known Russian sculptor has built a monument to Kolyma's dead, featuring symbols of all of the many faiths they practised. A room tucked inside the walls of the Solovetsky monastery, itself now a museum, displays prisoners' letters, photographs and scraps from the archives; outside, an alley of trees has been planted in commemoration of the Solovetsky dead. In the centre of Syktyvkar, the capital of the Komi Republic, local leaders, and the local chapter of Memorial, have constructed a small chapel. A handful of prisoners' names are listed on the inside, deliberately chosen to illustrate the many nationalities of the Gulag: Lithuanian, Korean, Jewish, Chinese, Georgian, Spanish.

Strange, surprising, individual monuments can sometimes be found in out-of-the-way places. An iron cross has been placed on a barren hill outside the city of Ukhta, the old headquarters of Ukhtpechlag, commemorating the site of a mass murder of prisoners. To see it, I had to drive down an almost impassable muddy road, walk behind a building site and clamber over a railway track. Even then I was too far away to read the actual inscription. Still, the local activists who had erected the cross beamed with pride.

A few hours north of Petrozavodsk, another *ad hoc* memorial has been set up outside the village of Sandormokh. Or perhaps, in this case, 'memorial' is the wrong word. Although there is a commemorative plaque, as well as several stone crosses put up by Poles, Germans and others, Sandormokh – where prisoners from the Solovetsky islands were shot in 1937, the priest Pavel Florensky among them – is memorable for its strangely moving hand-made crosses and personal monuments. Because there are no records stating who is buried where, each family has chosen, at random, to commemorate a particular pile of bones. Families of victims have pasted photographs of their relatives, long dead, on wooden stakes, and some have carved epitaphs into the sides. Ribbons, plastic flowers and other funerary bric-à-brac are strewn throughout the pine forest which has grown up over the killing field. On the sunny August day that I visited – it was the anniversary of the murder, and a delegation had come from St Petersburg – an elderly woman stood up to speak of her parents, both buried there, both shot when she was seven years old. A whole lifetime had passed before she had been able to visit their graves.

Another larger project has taken shape outside the city of Perm. On the site of Perm-36, once a Stalinist-era *lagpunkt*, later one of the harshest political camps of the 1970s and 1980s, a group of local historians has constructed a full-scale museum, the only one actually located inside the barracks of a former camp. With their own resources the historians rebuilt the camp, barracks, walls, barbed-wire fences and all. They even went so far as to set up a small logging business, using the camp's own rusted and discarded machines, to pay for their project. Although they did not have much support from the local government, they attracted West European and American funding. Ambitiously, they now hope to restore twenty-five buildings, using four of them to house a larger Museum of Repression.

And yet – in Russia, a country accustomed to grandiose war memorials and vast, solemn state funerals, these local efforts and private initiatives seem meagre, scattered and incomplete. The majority of Russians are probably not even aware of them. And no wonder: ten years after the collapse of the Soviet Union, Russia, the country that has inherited the Soviet Union's diplomatic and foreign policies, its embassies, its debts and its seat at the United Nations, continues to act as if it has not inherited the Soviet Union's history. Russia does not have a national museum dedicated to the history of repression. Nor does Russia have a national place of mourning, a monument which officially recognizes the suffering of victims and their families. Throughout the 1980s, competitions were held to design such a monument, but they came to nothing. Memorial succeeded only in dragging a stone from the Solovetsky islands – where the Gulag began – and placing it in the centre of Dzerzhinsky Square, across from Lubyanka.[2]

More notable than the missing monuments, however, is the missing public awareness. Sometimes, it seems as if the enormous emotions and passions raised by the wide-ranging discussions of the Gorbachev era simply vanished, along with the Soviet Union itself. The bitter debate about justice for the victims disappeared just as abruptly. Although there was much talk about it at the end of the 1980s, the Russian government never did examine or try the perpetrators of torture or mass murder, even those who were identifiable. In the early 1990s, one of the men who carried out the Katyń massacres of Polish officers was still alive. Before he died, the KGB conducted an interview with him, asking him to explain – from a technical point of view – how the murders were carried out. As a gesture of goodwill, a tape of the interview was handed to the Polish cultural attaché in Moscow. No one suggested at any time that the man be put on trial, in Moscow, Warsaw, or anywhere else.

It is true, of course, that trials may not always be the best way to come to terms with the past. In the years after the Second World War, West Germany brought 85,000 Nazis to trial, but obtained fewer than 7,000 convictions. The tribunals were notoriously corrupt, and easily swayed by personal jealousies and disputes. The Nuremberg Trial itself was an example of 'victors' justice' marred by dubious legality and oddities, not the least of which was the presence of Soviet judges who knew perfectly well that their own side was responsible for mass murder too.

But there are other methods, aside from trials, of doing public justice to the crimes of the past. There are truth commissions, for example, of the sort implemented in South Africa, which allow victims to tell their stories in an official, public place, and make the crimes of the past a part of the public debate. There are official investigations, like the British Parliament's 2002 inquiry into the Northern Irish 'Bloody Sunday' massacre, which had taken place thirty years earlier. There are government inquiries, government commissions, public apologies – yet the Russian government has never considered any of these options. Other than the brief, inconclusive 'trial' of the Communist Party, there have in fact been no public truth-telling sessions in Russia, no parliamentary hearings, no official investigations of any kind into the murders or the massacres or the camps of the USSR.

The result: half a century after the war's end, the Germans still conduct regular public disputes about victims' compensation, about memorials, about new interpretations of Nazi history, even about whether a younger generation of Germans ought to go on shouldering the burden of guilt about the crimes of the Nazis. Half a century after Stalin's death, there were no equivalent arguments taking place in Russia, because the memory of the past was not a living part of public discourse.

The rehabilitation process did continue, very quietly, throughout the 1990s. By the end of 2001, about 4.5 million political prisoners had been rehabilitated in Russia, and the national rehabilitation commission reckoned it had a further half-million cases to examine. Those victims – hundreds of thousands, perhaps millions more – who were never sentenced will of course be exempt from the process.[3] But while the commission itself is serious and well-intentioned, and while it is composed of camp survivors as well as bureaucrats, no one associated with it really feels that the politicians who created it were motivated by a real drive for 'truth and reconciliation', in the words of the British historian Catherine Merridale. Rather, the goal has been to end discussion of the past, to pacify the victims by throwing them a few extra roubles and free bus tickets, and to avoid any deeper examination of the causes of Stalinism or of its legacy.

*

There are some good, or at least some forgivable, explanations for this public silence. Most Russians really do spend all of their time coping with the complete transformation of their economy and society. The Stalinist era was a long time ago, and a great deal has happened since it ended. Post-communist Russia is not post-war Germany, where the memories of the worst atrocities were still fresh in people's minds. In the early twenty-first century, the events of the middle of the twentieth century seem like ancient history to much of the population.

Perhaps more to the point, many Russians also feel that they have had their discussion of the past already, and that it produced very little. When one asks older Russians, at least, why the subject of the Gulag is so rarely mentioned nowadays, they wave away the issue: 'In 1990 that was all we could talk about, now we don't need to talk about it any more.' To further complicate things, talk of the Gulag and of Stalinist repression has become confused, in the minds of many, with the 'democratic reformers' who originally promoted the debate about the Soviet past. Because that generation of political leaders is now seen to have failed – their rule is remembered for corruption and chaos – all talk of the Gulag is somehow tainted by association.

The question of remembering or commemorating political repression is also confused – as I noted in the Introduction to this book – by the presence of so many other victims of so many other Soviet tragedies. 'To make matters more complicated,' writes Catherine Merridale, 'a great many people suffered repeatedly; they can describe themselves as war veterans, victims of repression, the children of the repressed and even as survivors of famine with equal facility.'[4] There are plenty of memorials to the wartime dead, some Russians seem to feel: Will that not suffice?

But there are other reasons, less forgivable, for the profound silence. Many Russians experienced the collapse of the Soviet Union as a profound blow to their personal pride. Perhaps the old system was bad, they now feel – but at least we were powerful. And now that we are not powerful, we do not want to hear that it was bad. It is too painful, like speaking ill of the dead.

Some – still – also fear what they might find out about the past, if they were to inquire too closely. In 1998, the Russian American journalist Masha Gessen described what it felt like to discover that one of her grandmothers, a nice old Jewish lady, had been a censor, responsible for altering the reports of foreign correspondents based in Moscow. She also discovered that her other grandmother, another nice old Jewish lady, had once applied for a job with the secret police. Both had made their choices out of desperation, not conviction. Now, she wrote, she knows why her generation had refrained from condemning their grandparents' generation too harshly: 'We did not expose them, we did not try them, we did not judge them . . . merely by asking such questions each one of us risks betraying someone we love.'[5]

Aleksandr Yakovlev, chairman of the Russian rehabilitation commission, put this problem somewhat more bluntly. 'Society is indifferent to the crimes of the past,' he told me, 'because so many people participated in them.'[6] The Soviet system dragged millions and millions of its citizens into many forms of collaboration and compromise. Although many willingly participated, otherwise decent people were also forced to do terrible things. They, their children, and their grandchildren do not always want to remember that now.

But the most important explanation for the lack of public debate does not involve the fears of the younger generation, or the inferiority complexes and leftover guilt of their parents. The most important issue is rather the power and prestige of those now ruling not only Russia, but also most of the other ex-Soviet states and satellite states. In December 2001, on the tenth anniversary of the dissolution of the Soviet Union, thirteen of the fifteen former Soviet republics were run by former communists, as were many of the former satellite states, including Poland, the country which supplied so many hundreds of thousands of prisoners for Soviet camps and exile villages. Even in those countries not actually run by the direct ideological descendants of the Communist Party, former communists and their children or fellow travellers also continued to figure largely in the intellectual, media and business elites. The President of Russia, Vladimir Putin, was a former KGB agent, who proudly identified himself as a 'Chekist'. Earlier, when serving as the Russian Prime Minister, Putin had made a point of visiting the KGB headquarters at Lubyanka, on the anniversary of the Cheka's founding, where he dedicated a plaque to the memory of Yuri Andropov.[7]

The dominance of former communists and the insufficient discussion of the past in the post-communist world is not coincidental. To put it bluntly, former communists have a clear interest in concealing the past: it tarnishes them, undermines them, hurts their claims to be carrying out 'reforms', even when they personally had nothing to do with past crimes. In Hungary, the ex-Communist Party, renamed the Socialist Party, fought bitterly against opening the museum to the victims of terror. When the ex-Communist Party, renamed the Social Democrats, was elected to power in Poland in 2001, it immediately cut the budget of the Polish Institute of National Memory, set up by its centre-right predecessors. Many, many excuses have been given for Russia's failure to build a national monument to its millions of victims, but Aleksandr Yakovlev, again, gave me the most succinct explanation. 'The monument will be built,' he said, 'when we – the older generation – are all dead.'

This matters: the failure to acknowledge or repent or discuss the history of the communist past weighs like a stone on many of the nations of post-communist Europe. Whispered rumours about the contents of old 'secret files' continue to disrupt contemporary politics, destabilizing at least one Polish and one Hungarian prime minister. Deals done in the past, between fraternal communist parties, continue to have ramifications in the present. In many places, the secret police apparatus – the cadres, the equipment, the offices – remains virtually unchanged. The occasional discovery of fresh caches of bones can suddenly spark controversy and anger.[8]

This past weighs on Russia most heavily of all. Russia inherited the trappings of Soviet power – and also the Soviet Union's great power complex, its military establishment and its imperial goals. As a result, the political consequences of absent memory in Russia have been much more damaging than they have in other former communist countries. Acting in the name of the Soviet motherland, Stalin deported the Chechen nation to the wastes of Kazakhstan, where half of them died and the rest were meant to disappear, along with their language and culture. Fifty years later, in a repeat performance, the Russian federation obliterated the Chechen capital, Grozny, and murdered tens of thousands of Chechen civilians in the course of two wars. If the Russian people and the Russian elite remembered – viscerally, emotionally remembered – what Stalin did to the Chechens, they could not have invaded Chechnya in the 1990s, not once and not twice. To do so was the moral equivalent of post-war Germany invading western Poland. Very few Russians saw it that way – which is itself evidence of how little they know about their own history.

There have also been consequences for the formation of Russian civil society, and for the development of the rule of law. To put it bluntly, if scoundrels of the old regime go unpunished, good will in no way have been seen to triumph over evil. This may sound apocalyptic, but it is not politically irrelevant. The police do not need to catch all the criminals all of the time for most people to submit to public order, but they need to catch a significant proportion. Nothing encourages lawlessness more than the sight of villains getting away with it, living off their spoils, and laughing in the public's face. The secret police kept their apartments, their dachas and their large pensions. Their victims remained poor and marginal. To most Russians, it now seems as if the more you collaborated in the past, the wiser you were. By analogy, the more you cheat and lie in the present, the wiser you are.

In a very deep sense, some of the ideology of the Gulag also survives in the attitudes and world-view of the new Russian elite. I once happened to listen in on a classic, late-night Russian kitchen-table conversation, which took place in the home of some Moscow friends. At a certain point very late in the evening, two of the participants – successful entrepreneurs – began to argue: Just how stupid, and just how gullible, are the Russian people? And just how much more intelligent are we? The old Stalinist division between categories of humanity, between the all-powerful elite and the worthless 'enemies' lives on in the new Russian elite's arrogant contempt for its fellow citizens. Unless that elite soon comes to recognize the value and the importance of all of Russia's citizens, to honour both their civil and their human rights, Russia is ultimately fated to become the Zaire of the north, a land populated by impoverished peasants and billionaire politicians who keep their assets in Swiss bank vaults and their private jets on runways, engines running.

Tragically, Russia's lack of interest in its past has deprived the Russians of heroes, as well as victims. The names of those who secretly opposed Stalin, however ineffectively – the students like Susanna Pechora, Viktor Bulgakov and Anatoly Zhigulin; the leaders of the Gulag rebellions and uprisings; the dissidents, from Sakharov to Bukovsky to Orlov – ought to be as widely known in Russia as are, in Germany, the names of the participants in the plot to kill Hitler. The incredibly rich body of Russian survivors' literature – tales of people whose humanity triumphed over the horrifying conditions of the Soviet concentration camps – should be better read, better known, more frequently quoted. If schoolchildren knew these heroes and their stories better, they would find something to be proud of even in Russia's Soviet past, aside from imperial and military triumphs.

Yet the failure to remember has more mundane, practical consequences too. It can be argued, for example, that Russia's failure to delve properly into the past also explains its insensitivity to certain kinds of censorship, and to the continued, heavy presence of secret police, now renamed the *Federalnaya sluzhba bezopasnosti*, or FSB. Most Russians are not especially bothered by the FSB's ability to open mail, tap telephones and enter private residences without a court order. Nor are they much interested, for example, in the FSB's long prosecution of Aleksandr Nikitin, an ecologist who wrote about the damage Russia's Northern Fleet is doing to the Baltic Sea.[9]

Insensitivity to the past also helps explain the absence of judicial and prison reform. In 1998, I paid a visit to the central prison in the city of Arkhangelsk. Once one of the capital cities of the Gulag, Arkhangelsk lay directly on the route to Solovetsky, to Kotlas, to Kargopollag and to other northern camp complexes. The city prison, which dated back to before Stalin's time, seemed hardly to have changed since then. I entered it in the company of Galina Dudina, a woman who qualifies as a genuine post-Soviet rarity, a prisoners' rights advocate. As we walked the halls of the stone building, accompanied by a silent warder, it seemed if we had stepped back into the past.

The corridors were narrow and dark, with damp, slimy walls. When the warder opened the door to a men's cell, I caught a glimpse of naked bodies stretched out on bunks, covered in tattoos. Seeing the men were undressed, he quickly closed the door and allowed them to compose themselves. Opening it again, I walked in to see about twenty men standing in a row, not at all pleased to have been interrupted. They offered mumbled, monosyllabic answers to the questions put to them by Galina, and mostly stared hard at the cement floor of their cell. They had, it seemed, been playing cards; the warder led us quickly away.

We spent more time in the women's cell. In the corner, there stood a toilet. Other than that, the scene could have been drawn straight from the pages of a 1930s memoir. Women's underwear hung from a rope strung across the ceiling; the air was thick and close, very hot, and heavy with the smell of perspiration, bad food, damp, and human waste. The women, also half-dressed, sat on bunks around the room and showered insults on the warder, shrieking their demands and complaints. It was as if I had walked into the cell that Olga Adamova-Sliozberg had entered in 1938. I repeat, again, her description:

The arched walls were dripping. On either side, leaving only a narrow passage between them, were low continuous bed boards packed with bodies. Assorted rags were drying on lines overhead. The air was thick with the foul smoke of strong cheap tobacco, and loud with arguments, shouts and sobs.[10]

Next door, in the juvenile cell, there were fewer prisoners but sadder faces. Galina handed a handkerchief to a sobbing fifteen-year-old girl who had been accused of stealing the rouble equivalent of $10. 'There now,' she said, 'you keep working on your algebra, and you'll be out of here soon.' Or so she hoped: Galina met many people who had been imprisoned for months without a trial, and this girl had only been in gaol for a week.

Afterwards, we spoke to the prison boss, who shrugged when asked about the girl in the juvenile cell, about the prisoner who had been on death row for many years yet claimed to be innocent, about the foul air in the prison and the lack of sanitation. It all came down to money, he said. There just was not enough money. The prison warders were badly paid. The electricity bills were mounting, which explained the dark corridors. No money was available for repairs, no money was spent on prosecutors or judges or trials. Prisoners just had to wait their turn, he said, until the money started flowing.

I was not convinced. Money is a problem, but it is not the whole story. If Russia's prisons look like a scene from Adamova-Sliozberg's memoirs, if Russia's courts and criminal investigations are a sham, that is partly because the Soviet legacy does not hang like a bad conscience upon the shoulders of those who run Russia's criminal justice system. The past does not haunt Russia's secret police, Russia's judges, Russia's politicians or Russia's business elite.

But then, very few people in contemporary Russia feel the past to be a burden, or as an obligation, at all. The past is a bad dream to be forgotten, or a whispered rumour to be ignored. Like a great, unopened Pandora's box, it lies in wait for the next generation.

Our failure in the West to understand the magnitude of what happened in the Soviet Union and central Europe does not, of course, have the same profound implications for our way of life as it does for theirs. Our tolerance for the odd 'Gulag denier' in our universities will not destroy the moral fabric of our society. The Cold War is over, after all, and there is no real intellectual or political force left in the communist parties of the West.

Nevertheless, if we do not start trying harder to remember, there will be consequences for us too. For one, our understanding of what is happening now in the former Soviet Union will go on being distorted by our misunderstanding of history. Again, if we really knew what Stalin did to the Chechens, and if we felt that it was a terrible crime against the Chechen nation, it is not only Vladimir Putin who would be unable to do the same things to them now, but we also would be unable to sit back and watch with any equanimity. Nor did the Soviet Union's collapse inspire the same mobilization of Western forces as the end of the Second World War. When Nazi Germany finally fell, the rest of the West created both NATO and the European Community – in part to prevent Germany from ever breaking away from civilized 'normality' again. By contrast, it was not until 11 September 2001 that the nations of the West seriously began rethinking their post-Cold War security policies, and then there were other motivations stronger than the need to bring Russia back into the civilization of the West.

But in the end, the foreign-policy consequences are not the most important. For if we forget the Gulag, sooner or later we will find it hard to understand our own history too. Why did we fight the Cold War, after all? Was it because crazed right-wing politicians, in cahoots with the military-industrial complex and the CIA, invented the whole thing and forced two generations of Americans and West Europeans to go along with it? Or was there something more important happening? Confusion is already rife. In 2002, an article in the conservative British *Spectator* magazine opined that the Cold War was 'one of the most unnecessary conflicts of all time'.[11] The American writer Gore Vidal has also described the battles of the Cold War as 'forty years of mindless wars which created a debt of $5 trillion'.[12]

Already, we are forgetting what it was that mobilized us, what inspired us, what held the civilization of 'the West' together for so long: we are forgetting what it was that we were fighting against. If we do not try harder to remember the history of the other half of the European continent, the history of the other twentieth-century totalitarian regime, in the end it is we in the West who will not understand our past, we who will not know how our world came to be the way it is.

And not only our own particular past. For if we go on forgetting half of Europe's history, some of what we know about mankind itself will be distorted. Every one of the twentieth-century's mass tragedies was unique: the Gulag, the Holocaust, the Armenian massacre, the Nanking massacre, the Cultural Revolution, the Cambodian revolution, the Bosnian wars, among many others. Every one of these events had different historical, philosophical and cultural origins, every one arose in particular local circumstances which will never be repeated. Only our ability to debase and destroy and dehumanize our fellow men has been – and will be – repeated again and again: our transformation of our neighbours into 'enemies', our reduction of our opponents to lice or vermin or poisonous weeds, our re-invention of our victims as lower, lesser or evil beings, worthy only of incarceration or expulsion or death.

The more we are able to understand how different societies have transformed their neighbours and fellow citizens from people into objects, the more we know of the specific circumstances which led to each episode of mass torture and mass murder, the better we will understand the darker side of our own human nature. This book was not written 'so that it will not happen again', as the cliché would have it. This book was written because it almost certainly will happen again. Totalitarian philosophies have had, and will continue to have, a profound appeal to many millions of people. Destruction of the 'objective enemy', as Hannah Arendt once put it, remains a fundamental object of many dictatorships. We need to know why – and each story, each memoir, each document in the history of the Gulag is a piece of the puzzle, a part of the explanation. Without them, we will wake up one day and realize that we do not know who we are.

Appendix: How Many?

Although the Soviet Union contained thousands of concentration camps, and although millions of people passed through them, for many decades the precise tally of victims was concealed from all but a handful of bureaucrats. As a result, estimating their numbers was a matter of sheer guesswork while the USSR existed, and remains a matter of educated guesswork today.

During the era of sheer guesswork, the Western debate about the statistics of repression – just like the more general Western debate about Soviet history – was tainted, from the 1950s onwards, by the politics of the Cold War. Without archives, historians relied variously on prisoners' memoirs, defectors' statements, official census figures, economic statistics, or even minor details which somehow became known abroad, such as the number of newspapers distributed to prisoners in 1931.[1] Those more inclined to dislike the Soviet Union tended to choose the higher figures of victims. Those more in clined to dislike the American or Western role in the Cold War chose the lower figures. The numbers themselves ranged wildly. In *The Great Terror*, his then groundbreaking 1968 account of the purges, the historian Robert Conquest estimated that the NKVD had arrested seven million people in 1937 and 1938.[2] In his 1985 'revisionist' account, *Origins of the Purges*, the historian J. Arch Getty wrote of merely 'thousands' of arrests in those same two years.[3]

As it turned out, the opening of the Soviet archives gave neither school complete satisfaction. The first sets of figures released for Gulag prisoners seemed at first to show numbers lying squarely in the middle of the high and low estimates. According to widely published NKVD documents, these were the numbers of prisoners in Gulag camps and colonies from 1930 to 1953, as counted on 1 January of each year:

1930	179,000
1931	212,000
1932	268,700
1933	334,300
1934	510,307
1935	965,742

1936	1,296,494
1937	1,196,369
1938	1,881,570
1939	1,672,438
1940	1,659,992
1941	1,929,729
1942	1,777,043
1943	1,484,182
1944	1,179,819
1945	1,460,677
1946	1,703,095
1947	1,721,543
1948	2,199,535
1949	2,356,685
1950	2,561,351
1951	2,525,146
1952	2,504,514
1953	2,468,524 [4]

These numbers do reflect some things that we know, from many other sources, to be true. The inmate figures begin to rise in the late 1930s, as repression increased. They dip slightly during the war, reflecting the large numbers of amnesties. They rise in 1948, when Stalin clamped down once again. On top of all that, most scholars who have worked in the archives now agree that the figures are based on genuine compilations of data provided to the NKVD by the camps. They are consistent with data from other parts of the Soviet government bureaucracy, tallying, for example, with data used by the People's Commissariat of Finance.[5] Nevertheless, they do not necessarily reflect the whole truth.

To begin with, the figures for each individual year are misleading, since they mask the camp system's remarkably high turnover. In 1943, for example, 2,421,000 prisoners are recorded as having passed through the Gulag system, although the totals at the beginning and end of that year show a decline from 1.5 to 1.2 million. That number includes transfers within the system, but still indicates an enormous level of prisoner movement not reflected in the overall figures.[6] By the same token, nearly a million prisoners left the camps during the war to join the Red Army, a fact which is barely reflected in the overall statistics, since so many prisoners arrived during the war years too. Another example: in 1947, 1,490,959 inmates entered the camps, and 1,012,967 left, an enormous turnover which is not reflected in the table either.[7]

Prisoners left because they died, because they escaped, because they had short sentences, because they were being released into the Red Army or because they had been promoted to administrative positions. As I've written, there were also frequent amnesties for the old, the ill and for pregnant women – invariably followed by new waves of arrests. This massive, constant movement of prisoners meant that the numbers were in fact far higher than they seemed to be at first: by 1940, eight million prisoners had already passed through the camps.[8] Using the inflow and outflow statistics available, and reconciling a variety of sources, the only complete reckoning I have seen estimates that eighteen million Soviet citizens passed through the camps and colonies between 1929 and 1953. This figure also tallies with other figures given by senior Russian security officials during the 1990s. According to one source, Khrushchev himself spoke of seventeen million passing through the labour camps between 1937 and 1953.[9]

Yet in a deeper sense, this figure is misleading too. As readers will also by now be aware, not every person condemned to forced labour in the Soviet Union actually served out his time in a concentration camp run by the Gulag administration. For one, the figures above exclude the many hundreds of thousands of people who were sentenced to 'forced labour without incarceration' for workplace violations. More importantly, there were at least three other significant categories of incarcerated forced labourer: prisoners of war, post-war inhabitants of filtration camps, and above all the 'special exiles', who included kulaks deported during collectivization, Poles, Balts and others deported after 1939, and Caucasians, Tartars, Volga Germans and others deported during the war itself.

The first two groups are relatively easy to count: from several reliable sources, we know that the number of POWs exceeded four million.[10] We also know that between 27 December 1941 and 1 October 1944, the NKVD investigated 421,199 detainees in filtration camps, and that on 10 May 1945, over 160,000 detainees were still living in them, engaged in forced labour. In January 1946, the NKVD abolished the camps and repatriated a further 228,000 to the USSR for further investigation.[11] A total of about 700,000 seems, therefore, a fair guess.

The special exiles are somewhat harder to count, if only because there were so many different exile groups being sent to so many different places at so many different times for so many different reasons. In the 1920s, many of the Bolsheviks' early opponents – Mensheviks, Social Revolutionaries and the like – were exiled by administrative decree, which meant they were not technically part of the Gulag, but were certainly being punished. In the early 1930s, 2.1 million kulaks were exiled, although an unknown number, certainly in the hundreds of thousands, were sent not to Kazakhstan or Siberia, but to other parts of their native province or to bad land at the edges of their collective farms: since many seem to have escaped, it is hard to know whether to count them or not. Much clearer is the position of the national groups exiled during and after the war to the 'special exile' villages. Equally clear, yet much easier to forget, are odd groups like the 17,000 'former people' expelled from Leningrad after Kirov's murder. There were also Soviet Germans who were not physically deported, but whose villages in Siberia and central Asia were turned into 'special settlements' – the Gulag came to them, as it were – as well as babies born to exiles, who surely count as exiles too.

As a result, those who have tried to collate the many statistics that have been published about each of these different groups have come up with slightly different numbers. In *Ne po svoei vole*, published by Memorial in 2001, the historian Pavel Polyan has added up the numbers of special exiles and got a figure of 6,015,000.[12] In a survey of archival publications, Otto Pohl, on the other hand, counts just over seven million special exiles from 1930 to 1948.[13] He gives the post-war figures for people living in 'special settlements' as follows:

October 1945	2,230,500
October 1946	2,463,940
October 1948	2,104,571
1 January 1949	2,300,223
1 January 1953	2,753,356[14]

Still, on the principle that the low estimate will satisfy the more fastidious, I have decided to choose Polyan's number: six million exiles. Adding the numbers together, the total number of forced labourers in the USSR comes to 28.7 million.

I realize, of course, that this figure will not satisfy everybody. Some will object that not all of those arrested or deported count as 'victims', since some were criminals, or even war criminals. Yet although it is true that millions of these prisoners had criminal sentences, I do not believe that anything close to the majority were actually 'criminals', in any normal sense of the word. A woman who has picked a few pieces of grain from a field which has already been harvested is not a criminal, nor is a man who has been late to work three times, as was the father of the Russian General Aleksandr Lebed, who received a camp sentence for precisely that. For that matter, a prisoner of war who has been deliberately kept in a forced-labour camp many years after the war has come to an end is not a legitimate prisoner either. By all accounts, the number of genuine professional criminals in any camp was tiny – which is why I prefer to leave the numbers as they are.

Others, however, will be unsatisfied with this figure on different grounds. Certainly in the course of writing this book, I have been asked the same question many, many times: Of these 28.7 million prisoners, how many died?

This answer is complicated too. To date, no completely satisfactory death statistics for either the Gulag or the exile system have yet appeared.[15] In the coming years, some more reliable numbers may emerge: at least one former MVD officer has personally taken it upon himself to comb methodically through the archives, camp by camp and year by year, trying to compile authentic numbers. With perhaps somewhat different motives, the Memorial Society, which has already produced the first reliable guide to the numbers of camps themselves, has set itself the task of counting the victims of repression too.

Until these compilations appear, however, we have to rely upon what we have: a year-by-year account of Gulag death rates, based on the archives of the Department of Prisoner Registration. This account seems to exclude deaths in prisons and deaths during transport. It has been compiled using overall NKVD reports, not the records of individual camps. It does not include special exiles at all. Nevertheless, I record it here, reluctantly:

1930	7,980 (4.2%)
1931	7,283 (2.9%)
1932	13,197 (4.81%)
1933	67,297 (15.3%)
1934	25,187 (4.28%)
1935	31,636 (2.75%)
1936	24,993 (2.11%)
1937	31,056 (2.42%)
1938	108,654 (5.35%)
1939	44,750 (3.1%)
1940	41,275 (2.72%)
1941	115,484 (6.1%)
1942	352,560 (24.9%)
1943	267,826 (22.4%)
1944	114,481 (9.2%)
1945	81,917 (5.95%)
1946	30,715 (2.2%)
1947	66,830 (3.59%)
1948	50,659 (2.28%)
1949	29,350 (1.21%)
1950	24,511 (.95%)
1951	22,466 (.92%)
1952	20,643 (.84%)
1953	9,628 (.67%)[16]

Like the official prisoner statistics, the table also shows some patterns which can be reconciled with other data. The sudden spike in 1933, for example, surely represents the impact of the famine which killed six to seven million 'free' Soviet citizens as well. The smaller rise in 1938 must reflect the mass executions which took place in some camps that year. The major rise in death rates during the war – nearly a quarter of prisoners in 1942 – also tallies with the memoirs and recollections of people who lived through the camps in that year, and reflects the wider food shortages throughout the USSR.

Yet even if and when these numbers are improved, the question 'How many died?' will still be difficult to answer with ease. In truth, no death figures compiled by Gulag authorities can ever be considered completely reliable. The culture of camp inspection and reprimand meant, among other things, that individual camp commanders had a vested interest in lying about how many of their prisoners died: both archives and memoirs indicate that it was common practice in many camps to release prisoners who were on the point of dying, thereby lowering camp death statistics.[17] Although exiles moved around less frequently, and were not released when half-dead, the nature of the exile system – prisoners lived in distant villages, far from regional authorities – means that statistics on exile death rates can never be considered completely reliable either.

More importantly, however, the question itself has to be asked a bit more carefully. 'How many died?' is in fact an imprecise question, in the case of the Soviet Union, and those who ask such a question should first consider what it is that they really want to know. Do they want to know, for example, simply how many died in the camps of the Gulag and in the exile villages in the Stalinist era, from 1929 to 1953? If so, a number based on archival sources is available, although even the historian who compiled it points out that it is incomplete, and does not cover all categories of prisoner in every year. Again, I reluctantly cite it: 2,749,163.[18]

Even if it were complete, however, this figure still would not reflect all of the victims of the Stalinist judicial system. As I say in the Introduction, the Soviet secret police did not, for the most part, use their camps in order to kill people. When they wanted to kill people, they carried out mass executions in forests: surely these are victims of Soviet justice too, and there were many of them. Using archives, one set of researchers cites a figure of 786,098 political executions from 1934 to 1953.[19] Most historians consider this more or less plausible, but the haste and chaos which accompanied mass executions may well mean that we will never know. Yet even this number – which, in my view, is actually too precise to be reliable – still does not include those who died on the trains to the camps; those who died during interrogation; those whose executions were not technically 'political' but were nevertheless carried out on spurious grounds; the more than 20,000 Polish officers who died in the Katyń massacres; and, most of all, those who died within a few days of release. If that is the number we really want, then it will be higher – probably far higher – although estimates will again vary greatly.

But even these numbers, I've found, do not always provide the answer to what people really want to know. Much of the time, when I am asked 'How many died?' what the questioner really wants to know is how many people died, unnecessarily, as a result of the Bolshevik Revolution. That is, how many died in the Red Terror and the Civil War, the famines which followed in the wake of the brutal policy of collectivization, the mass deportations, the mass executions, the camps of the 1920s, the camps of the 1960s through the 1980s – as well as in the camps and mass murders of Stalin's reign. In that case, the numbers are not only far larger, but they really are a matter of pure conjecture. The French authors of *The Black Book of Communism* quote a figure of twenty million deaths. Others cite numbers closer to ten or twelve million.[20]

A single round number of dead victims would be extremely satisfying, particularly since it would allow us to compare Stalin directly with Hitler or with Mao. Yet even if we could find one, I'm not sure it would really tell the whole story of suffering either. No official figures, for example, can possibly reflect the mortality of the wives and children and ageing parents left behind, since their deaths were not recorded separately. During the war, old people starved to death without ration cards: had their convict son not been digging coal in Vorkuta, they might have lived. Small children succumbed easily to epidemics of typhus and measles in cold, ill-equipped orphanages: had their mothers not been sewing uniforms in Kengir, they might have lived too.

Nor can any figures reflect the cumulative impact of Stalin's repressions on the life and health of whole families. A man was tried and shot as an 'enemy of the people'; his wife was taken to a camp as a 'member of an enemy's family'; his children grew up in orphanages and joined criminal gangs; his mother died of stress and grief; his cousins and aunts and uncles cut off all contact from one another, in order to avoid being tainted as well. Families broke apart, friendships ended, fear weighed heavily on those who remained behind, even when they did not die.

In the end, statistics can never fully describe what happened. Neither can the archival documents upon which so much of this book has been based. All of those who have written most eloquently on the subject of the Gulag have known this to be true – which is why I would like to give one of them the last word on the subject of 'statistics' and 'archives' and 'files'.

In 1990, the writer Lev Razgon was allowed to see his own archival file, a thin collection of documents describing his arrest and the arrests of his first wife, Oksana, as well as several members of her family. He read through it, and later wrote an essay on its contents. He reflected eloquently on the contents of the file; on the sparsity of the evidence; on the ludicrous nature of the charges; on the tragedy which befell his wife's mother; on the opaque motives of his father-in-law, the Chekist Gleb Boky; on the strange absence of repentance on the part of those who had destroyed all of them. But what struck me most about his experience of working in the archives was his description of how ambivalent he felt when he had finished reading:

I have long since stopped turning the pages of the file and they have lain next to me for more than an hour or two, growing cold with their own thoughts. My guardian [the KGB archivist] is already beginning to cough suggestively and look at his watch. It's time to go. I have nothing more to do here. I hand over the files and they are negligently dropped again into the shopping bag. I go downstairs, along the empty corridors, past the sentries who do not even ask to see my papers, and step out into Lubyanka Square.

It's only 5 p.m., but it is already almost dark and a fine, quiet rain falls uninterruptedly. The building remains beside me and I stand on the pavement outside, wondering what to do next. How terrible that I do not believe in God and cannot go into some quiet little church, stand in the warmth of the candles, gaze into the eyes of Christ on the Cross and say and do those things that make life easier to bear for the believer . . .

I take off my fur hat, and drops of rain or tears trickle down my face. I am eighty-two and here I stand, living through it all again . . . I hear the voices of Oksana and her mother . . . I can remember and recall them, each one. And if I remained alive, then it is my duty to do so . . .[21]

Notes

Full details of published and unpublished memoirs, works of literature, reference works, archives and interviews cited in the Notes in abbreviated form can be found in the relevant section of the Bibliography. All references to memoirs are to the English translated version, except where the Russian title of a work is given.

Introduction

1. Quoted in Cohen, p. 39.
2. Leggett, pp. 102–20.
3. Okhotin and Roginsky.
4. See Appendix for a fuller discussion of these statistics.
5. Rigoulot, *Les Paupières Lourdes*, pp. 1–10.
6. Quoted in Johnson, p. 243.
7. Quoted in Revel, p. 77.
8. Amis; John Lloyd, 'Show Trial: The Left in the Dock', *New Statesman*, 2 September 2002, vol. 15, issue 722, pp. 12–15; 'Hit and Miss', *Guardian*, 3 September 2002.
9. Thurston; Robert Conquest, 'Small Terror, Few Dead', *The Times Literary Supplement*, 31 May 1996.
10. This happened to the author in 1994. The phrase 'too anti-Soviet' is a direct quote from a letter. *The Times Literary Supplement* eventually ran a much shortened version of the review.
11. 'Neither Here nor There' (review of *Between East and West*, New York, 1994), *The New York Times Book Review*, 18 December 1994.
12. For a full discussion of this issue see Malia.
13. Webb and Webb, p. 31.
14. Quoted in Conquest, *The Great Terror*, p. 465.
15. See Klehr, Haynes and Firsov; and Klehr, Haynes and Anderson, for the archival history of the American Communist Party.
16. Quoted in N. Tolstoy, *Stalin's Secret War*, p. 289.
17. See Thomas, pp. 489–95, and Scammell, *Solzhenitsyn: A Biography*, for details. The attempt to portray Solzhenitsyn as an alcoholic (Scammell, pp. 664–5) was particularly clumsy, since he was known for his dislike of alcohol.
18. Pipes, pp. 824–5.
19. Overy, pp. 112 and 226–7; Moskoff.
20. L. Ginzburg, p. 36.

21. Kozhina, p. 5.
22. Kaczyńska, p. 15.
23. Kennan, pp. 74–83.
24. Chekhov, p. 371.
25. Kaczyńska, pp. 16–27.
26. Popov, pp. 31–8.
27. Kennan, p. 242.
28. Kaczyńska, p. 65–85.
29. Anisimov, p. 177.
30. GARF, 9414/1/76.
31. Kaczyńska, pp. 44–64.
32. Ibid., p. 161.
33. Chekhov, p. 52.
34. Kaczyńska, pp. 161–74.
35. Sutherland, pp. 271–302.
36. Adams, pp. 4–11.
37. Volkogonov, *Stalin*, p. 9.
38. This photograph appears, among other places, in Figes.
39. This photograph appears in Volkogonov, *Trotsky*.
40. Bullock, pp. 28–45.
41. Volkogonov, *Stalin*, p. 9.
42. Kotek and Rigoulot, pp. 97–107; Okhotin and Roginsky, pp. 11–12.
43. I elaborated upon this definition in a 'A History of Horror'.
44. Geller, p. 43.
45. Quoted in Kotek and Rigoulot, p. 92.
46. This account of the prehistory of concentration camps comes from Kotek and Rigoulot, pp. 1–94.
47. Kaczyńska, pp. 270–85.
48. L. Tolstoy, pp. 408–12.
49. See Martin, *The Affirmative Action Empire*, for a full discussion of Stalin's attitude towards 'enemy' ethnic groups.
50. Arendt, pp. 122–3.
51. Bullock, p. 24.
52. Weiner, 'Nature, Nurture and Memory in a Socialist Utopia'.
53. Bullock, p. 488.
54. Sereny, p. 101.
55. I am grateful to Terry Martin for helping me to clarify this point.
56. Shreider, p. 5.
57. Lynne Viola makes this point about kulak exiles.
58. See Applebaum, 'A History of Horror', for more details.

Part I: The Origins of the Gulag, 1917–1939

1 Bolshevik Beginnings

1. From *Stekla vechnosti*, pp. 172–3.
2. Likhachev, *Vospominaniya*, p. 118.
3. Pipes, pp. 336–7.
4. See, for example, Service, *Lenin*.
5. Pipes, pp. 439–505; Figes, pp. 474–551.

6. Geller, pp. 23 and 24.
7. Jakobson, pp. 18–26.
8. *Dekrety*, vol. II, pp. 241–2, and vol. III, p. 80. Also Geller, p. 10; Pipes, pp. 793–800.
9. Jakobson, pp. 18–26; Decree 'On Revolutionary Tribunals', in *Sbornik*, 19 December 1917, pp. 9–10.
10. Hoover, Melgunov Collection, Box 1, Folder 63.
11. Okhotin and Roginsky, p. 13.
12. RGASPI, 76/3/1 and 13.
13. Jakobson, pp. 10–17; Okhotin and Roginsky, pp. 10–24.
14. *Dekrety*, vol. I, p. 401.
15. Hoover, Melgunov Collection, Box 1, Folder 4.
16. Anonymous, *Vo vlasti Gubcheka*, pp. 3–11.
17. Hoover, Melgunov Collection, Box 1, Folder 4.
18. Lockhart, pp. 326–45.
19. S. G. Eliseev, 'Tyuremnyi dnevnik', in *Uroki*, pp. 17–19.
20. Okhotin and Roginsky, p. 11.
21. Geller, p. 43.
22. Ibid., p. 44; Leggett, p. 103.
23. Initially, the Cheka were put in charge of the camps in conjunction with the Central Collegium for War Prisoners and Refugees (*Tsentroplenbezh*). Okhotin and Roginsky, p. 11.
24. Leggett, p. 108.
25. Decree 'On Red Terror', in *Sbornik*, 5 September 1918, p. 11.
26. Ivanova, *Labor Camp Socialism*, p. 13.
27. *Istoricheskii Arkhiv*, no. 1, 1958, pp. 6–11; Geller, p. 52.
28. According to the historian Richard Pipes, Lenin did not want his name associated with these first camps, which is why the decrees were issued not by the *Sovnarkom*, a body he chaired, but by the Central Executive Committee of the Soviets (Pipes, p. 834).
29. *Dekrety*, vol. V, pp. 69–70 and 174–81.
30. RGASPI, 76/3/65.
31. Hoover, Melgunov Collection, Box 11, Folder 63.
32. Anonymous, *Vo vlasti Gubcheka*, pp. 47–53.
33. Izgoev, p. 36.
34. Bunyan, pp. 54–65.
35. Geller, pp. 55–64; Bunyan, pp. 54–114.
36. Okhotin and Roginsky, pp. 11–12; see also Jakobson for a full account of the institutional changes in the 1920s, as well as Lin.
37. RGASPI, 17/84/585.
38. For examples of these discussions see Hoover, Fond 89, 73/25, 26 and 27.
39. Volkogonov, *Lenin*, p. 179.
40. Service, *Lenin*, p. 186.
41. Hoover, Nicolaevsky Collection, Box 9, Folder 1.
42. Ibid., Box 99; RGASPI, Fond 76/3/87; *Genrikh Yagoda*, p. 265.
43. Razgon, p. 266.
44. Hoover, Nicolaevsky Collection, Box 99.
45. Ibid.
46. *Letters from Russian Prisons*, pp. 1–15.
47. Ibid., pp. 20–28.
48. Ibid., pp. 162–5.
49. Ibid.; Melnik and Soshina.
50. *Letters from Russian Prisons*, pp. 162–5.
51. Melnik and Soshina.

52. RGASPI, 17/84/395.
53. Doloi.
54. Guberman, pp. 72–4.
55. Bertha Babina-Nevskaya, 'My First Prison, February 1922', in Vilensky, *Till My Tale is Told*, pp. 97–109.
56. RGASPI, 76/3/149.
57. RGASPI, 76/3/227; Hoover, Fond 89, 73/25, 26 and 27.

2 'The First Camp of the Gulag'

1. *Ekran*, no. 12, 27 March 1926.
2. For a description of the geography of Solovetsky, the various islands and their development, see Melnik, Soshina, Reznikova and Reznikov.
3. 'Solovetskaya monastyrskaya tyurma', Solovetskoe Obshchestvo Kraevedeniya, *Vypusk*, VII, 1927 (SKM).
4. Ivan Bogov, *Izvestiya Arkhgubrevkoma i Arkhgubkoma RKP (b)*, 4 May 1920 (SKM); also quoted in Brodsky, p. 13.
5. GARF, 5446/1/2. See also Nasedkin's reference to Dzerzhinsky in GARF, 9414/1/77.
6. For example, see Solzhenitsyn, *Gulag Archipelago*, vol. II, pp. 25–70.
7. See Jakobson for an account of the prison systems of the 1920s.
8. GARF, 9414/1/77.
9. Juri Brodsky, pp. 30–31; Olitskaya, vol. I, pp. 237–40; Malsagov, pp. 117–31.
10. Olitskaya, pp. 237–40.
11. Hoover, Nicolaevsky Collection, Box 99; and Hoover, Fond 89, 73/34.
12. *Letters from Russian Prisons*, pp. 165–171.
13. Juri Brodsky, p. 194.
14. Shiryaev, pp. 30–37.
15. Volkov, p. 53.
16. Juri Brodsky, p. 65.
17. Likhachev, *Kniga bespokoistv*, pp. 98–100.
18. Juri Brodsky, p. 190.
19. Ibid., pp. 195–7.
20. Solzhenitsyn, *Gulag Archipelago*, vol. II, p. 54.
21. Chukhin, *Kanaloarmeetsi*, pp. 40–44; also Chukhin, 'Dva dokumenta'. Chukhin explains that these documents, reprinted in full, were a part of 'criminal investigation number 885'. They are known to come from the Petrozavodsk FSB archive, where Chukhin worked.
22. Klinger, p. 210; also reprinted in *Sever*, vol. 9, September 1990, pp. 108–12. The mosquito torture is also mentioned in archival documents – see *Zvenya*, vol. I, p. 383 – as well as in memoirs. See *Letters from Russian Prisons*, pp. 165–71; Volkov, p. 55.
23. Chukhin, 'Dva dokumenta', p. 359; Likhachev, *Kniga bespokoistv*, pp. 196–8.
24. Juri Brodsky, p. 129.
25. Tour guides on the Solovetsky islands relate this story. It is also found in Solzhenitsyn, *Gulag Archipelago*, vol. II, pp. 37–8.
26. Tsigankov, pp. 196–7.
27. Likhachev, *Kniga bespokoistv*, p. 212.
28. GARF newspaper and journal archives: *SLON*, vol. III, May 1924.
29. Shiryaev, pp. 115–32; Likhachev, *Kniga bespokoistv*, pp. 201–5. Also books and journals in SKM.
30. *SLON*, vol. III, May 1924 (GARF).

31. *Solovetskie Ostrova*, vol. 12, December 1925 (SKM).

32. Conversation with SKM director Tatyana Fokina, 12 September 1998. See also, for example, *Solovetskie Ostrova*, 1925, nos. 1–7, and 1930, no. 1; or the bulletins of the *Solovetskoe obshchestvo kraevedeniya*, in the collection of the museum and the collection of AKB. See also Dryakhlitsin.

33. *Solovetskie Ostrova*, vol. 9, September 1925, pp. 7–8 (SKM).

34. Reznikova, pp. 46–7.

35. *Solovetskii Lager*, vol. 3, May 1924 (SKM).

36. Reznikova, pp. 7–36; Hoover, Melgunov Collection, Box 7, Folder 44.

37. Nikolai Antsiferov, 'Tri glavy iz vospominanii', in *Pamyat*, vol. 4, pp. 75–6.

38. Klinger, pp. 170–77.

39. Ibid., pp. 200–201; Malsagov, pp. 139–45; Rozanov, p. 55; Hoover, Melgunov Collection, Box 7.

40. Tsigankov, pp. 96–127; Hoover, Melgunov Collection, Box 7.

41. *Istoriya otechestva v dokumentakh, Volume 2: 1921–1939*, pp. 51–2.

42. Jakobson, pp. 70–102.

43. Krasilnikov, 'Rozhdenie Gulaga', pp. 142–3. This is a collection of reprinted documents on the foundation of the Gulag, all of which come from the archives of the President of the Russian Federation, normally closed to researchers.

44. NARK, 689/1/(44/465).

45. NARK, 690/6/(2/9).

46. RGASPI, 17/3/65.

47. Okhotin and Roginsky, p. 18.

48. Ivanova, *Labor Camp Socialism*, pp. 70–71.

49. GAOPDFRK, 1051/1/1.

50. Jakobson, p. 121; conversations in 1998 and 1999 with Nikita Petrov, Oleg Khlevnyuk and Juri Brodsky. *Solovki*, the Italian edition of Brodsky's book, does not mention Frenkel.

51. For example, Klementev; S. G. Eliseev, 'Tyuremnyi dnevnik', in *Uroki*, pp. 30–32.

52. Shiryaev, p. 138.

53. Chukhin, *Kanaloarmeetsi*, pp. 30–31.

54. Gorky, *Belomor*, pp. 226–8.

55. GAOPDFRK, 1033/1/35.

56. Duguet, p. 75.

57. Solzhenitsyn, *Gulag Archipelago*, vol. II, p. 76.

58. Malsagov, pp. 61–73.

59. Shiryaev, pp. 137–8; Rozanov, pp. 174–91; Narinsky, *Vremya tyazhkikh potryasenii*, pp. 128–49.

60. Rozanov, pp. 174–91; Shiryaev, pp. 137–48.

61. Frenkel's prisoner registration card, Hoover, St Petersburg Memorial Collection.

62. Chukhin, *Kanaloarmeetsi*, pp. 30–31; Solzhenitsyn, *Gulag Archipelago*, vol. II, p. 78.

63. See 'Posetiteli kabinetu I.V. Stalina', *Istoricheskii Arkhiv*, no. 4, 1998, p. 180.

64. Hoover, St Petersburg Memorial Collection.

65. NARK, 690/6/(1/3).

66. Baron, pp. 615–21.

67. NARK, 690/3/(17/148).

68. Ibid.

69. Kulikov, p. 99.

70. GAOPDFRK, 1033/1/15.

71. Nogtev, 'USLON', pp. 55–60; Nogtev, 'Solovki', 1926, pp. 4–5.

72. Juri Brodsky, p. 75.

73. Solovetsky's deficit is cited in Khlevnyuk, 'Prinuditelnyi trud'; also GAOPDFRK, 1051/1/1.
74. Baron, p. 624.
75. GAOPDFRK, 1033/1/35.
76. Juri Brodsky, p. 75.
77. Ibid., p. 114.
78. Ibid., p. 195.
79. NARK, 690/6/(1/3)
80. Chukhin, 'Dva dokumenta'.
81. Juri Brodsky, p. 115.
82. *Letters from Russian Prisons*, pp. 183–8.
83. Hoover, Fond 89, 73/32.
84. Ibid., 73/34.
85. *Letters from Russian Prisons*, pp. 218–20.
86. Krasikov, p. 2.
87. *Letters from Russian Prisons*, p. 215.
88. Hoover, Fond 89, 73/34, 35 and 36.
89. Hoover, Nicolaevsky Collection, Box 782; Melgunov Collection, Box 8.
90. Hoover, Nicolaevsky Collection, Box 782, Folder 6.
91. Ibid., Folder 1.
92. *Letters from Russian Prisons*, p. 160.

3 1929: The Great Turning Point

1. Stalin interviewed by Emil Ludwig, 1934, in Silvester, pp. 311–22.
2. Likhachev, *Kniga bespokoistv*, pp. 183–9.
3. Solzhenitsyn, *Gulag Archipelago*, vol. II, p. 63; Figes, pp. 400–405 and 820–21.
4. Juri Brodsky, pp. 188–9.
5. Likhachev, *Kniga bespokoistv*, pp. 183–9.
6. Volkov, p. 168.
7. Khetso, p. 245.
8. Solzhenitsyn, *Gulag Archipelago*, vol. II, pp. 62–3; Khetso, pp. 243–54; Juri Brodsky pp. 185–8.
9. Chukhin, *Kanaloarmeetsi*, p. 36.
10. Gorky, *Sobranie sochinenii*, vol. XI, pp. 291–316. All Gorky quotes on Solovetsky come from this source.
11. Khetso, pp. 244–5.
12. Tolczyk, pp. 94–7. My interpretation of Gorky's essay is based upon Tolczyk's astute observations.
13. Tucker, *Stalin in Power*, pp. 125–7.
14. Payne, pp. 270–71.
15. Tucker, *Stalin in Power*, p. 96.
16. *Sbornik*, pp. 22–6.
17. See accounts in Tucker, *Stalin in Power*, and Conquest, *Stalin*, as well as Getty and Naumov.
18. See Conquest's *Harvest of Sorrow*, still the most comprehensive English account of collectivization and the famine. Ivnitsky's is an account that makes reliable use of archives. Like the exiles, the kulaks await their true chronicler.
19. Ivnitsky, p. 115; Zemskov, 'Spetsposelentsy', p. 4.
20. Getty and Naumov, pp. 110–12; Solomon, pp. 111–29.

21. Jakobson, p. 120.
22. Krasilnikov, 'Rozhdenie Gulaga', pp. 143–4.
23. Ibid., pp. 145–6.
24. Ibid., p. 145.
25. Nordlander, 'Capital of the Gulag'.
26. Krasilnikov, 'Rozhdenie Gulaga'; Jakobson, pp. 1–9.
27. Jakobson, p. 120.
28. Khlevnyuk, 'Prinuditelnyi trud'; Krasilnikov, *Spetspereselentsy v Zapadnoi Sibiri, vesna 1931 g.–nachalo 1933 g.*, p. 6.
29. GARF, 5446/1/54 and 9401/1a/1; Jakobson, pp. 124–5.
30. Harris.
31. Jakobson, p. 143.
32. See, for example, Kotkin, for a description of how plans for another Stalinist project – the Magnitogorsk steelworks, which had nothing to do with the Gulag – also went awry.
33. Evgeniya Ginzburg, for example, received a non-working prison sentence as late as 1936. See E. Ginzburg, *Journey into the Whirlwind*.
34. Chukhin, *Kanaloarmeetsi*, p. 25.
35. Tucker, *Stalin in Power*, p. 64.
36. Quoted in Bullock, p. 374.
37. Volkogonov, *Stalin*, pp. 127 and 148.
38. Moynahan, photographs on pp. 156 and 157, for example.
39. Tucker, *Stalin in Power*, p. 273.
40. Jakobson, p. 121.
41. Lih, Naumov and Khlevnyuk, p. 211; also Krasilnikov, 'Rozhdenie Gulaga', pp. 152–4; Khlevnyuk, 'Prinuditelnyi trud'.
42. Khlevnyuk, ibid., p. 74.
43. Jakobson, p. 121.
44. Khlevnyuk, 'Prinuditelnyi trud', pp. 74–6; Jakobson, p. 121; Hoover, St Petersburg Memorial Collection.
45. There are many examples in Stalin's '*osobaya papka*' (personal file) in GARF, 9401/2. Delo 64 contains an extensive report on Dalstroi, for example.
46. Nordlander, 'Origins of a Gulag Capital', pp. 798–800.
47. *Genrikh Yagoda*, p. 434.
48. Protocols of the Politburo, RGASPI, 17/3.
49. Volkogonov, *Stalin*, pp. 252, 308–9 and 519.
50. GARF, 9401/2/199 (Stalin's personal file).
51. RGASPI, 17/3/746; Nordlander, 'Capital of the Gulag'.
52. Nordlander, ibid.
53. Kaneva, p. 331.
54. Okhotin and Roginsky, p. 34.
55. *Genrikh Yagoda*, pp. 375–6.
56. Terry Martin suggested this to me in an email exchange in June 2002.

4 The White Sea Canal

1. Cited in Baron, p. 638.
2. Dallin and Nicolaevsky, pp. 218–19.
3. Bateson and Pim.
4. Dallin and Nicolaevsky, p. 219.
5. Ibid., p. 221.

6. Ibid., p. 220.
7. Ibid., p. 220; Jakobson, p. 126.
8. Dallin and Nicolaevsky, p. 220.
9. GARF, 5446/1/54 and 9401/1a/1.
10. GARF, 9414/1/2920.
11. Jakobson, p. 127.
12. Kitchin, pp. 267–70.
13. Jakobson, pp. 127–8.
14. GAOPDFRK, 26/1/41.
15. Gorky, *Belomor* (translation of *Kanal imeni Stalina*), pp. 17–19.
16. Ibid., p. 40.
17. Lih, Naumov and Khlevnyuk, pp. 225 and 212.
18. Makurov, p. 76. This is a collection of documents selected from the Karelian archives.
19. Okhotin and Roginsky, p. 163.
20. Baron, pp. 640–41; also Chukhin, *Kanaloarmeetsi*.
21. Makurov, p. 86.
22. Gorky, *Belomor*, p. 173.
23. Makurov, pp. 96 and 19–20.
24. Baron, p. 643.
25. Makurov, pp. 37 and 197.
26. Ibid., pp. 43–4.
27. Ibid., p. 197.
28. Chukhin, *Kanaloarmeetsi*, p. 121.
29. Makurov, p. 19–20.
30. Chukhin, *Kanaloarmeetsi*, p. 12.
31. Makurov, pp. 72–3.
32. Chukhin, *Kanaloarmeetsi*, pp. 127–31.
33. Tolczyk, p. 152.
34. Baranov, pp. 165–8.
35. Gorky, *Belomor*, pp. 46 and 47.
36. Ibid., pp. 158 and 165.
37. Pogodin, pp. 109–83; Geller, pp. 151–7.
38. Gliksman, p. 165.
39. Ibid., pp. 173–8.
40. GARF, 9414/4/1; *Perekovka*, 18 January 1933.
41. GARF, 9414/4/1; *Perekovka*, 20 December 1932–30 June 1934.
42. Solzhenitsyn, *Gulag Archipelago*, vol. I, p. 102.

5 The Camps Expand

1. *Kuznitsa*, March–September 1936 (GARF journal collection).
2. Khlevnyuk, 'Prinuditelnyi trud', pp. 75–6.
3. Nicolas Werth, 'A State against Its People: Violence, Repression and Terror in the Soviet Union', in Courtois et al., p. 154. An account of the incident, as recalled by an anonymous prisoner who met some survivors in the Tomsk prison, also appears in *Pamyat*, vol. I, pp. 342–3; also Krasilnikov, *Spetspereselentsy v zapadnoi Sibiri, 1933–1938*, pp. 76–119.
4. Elantseva. This article is based on archives found in the Tomsk Central State Archive of the Russian Federation, Far East.
5. Ibid.; Okhotin and Roginsky, p. 153.
6. N. A. Morozov, *GULAG v Komi krae*, p. 104.

7. Kaneva. My account is based on Kaneva's, which is in turn based on documents in the archives of the Komi Republic, as well as memoirs in the collection of Memorial.

8. Ibid., pp. 331 and 334–5.

9. GARF, 9414/1/8.

10. Mitin, pp. 22–6.

11. Exhibition at the Vorkuta Kraevedcheskii Muzei; also 'Vorkutinstroi NKVD' (MVD document of January 1941), in the collection of Syktyvkar Memorial, Komi Republic; Okhotin and Roginsky, p. 192.

12. Kaneva, p. 339.

13. Nadezhda Ignatova, 'Spetspereselentsy v respublike Komi v 1930–1940 gg', in *Korni travy*, pp. 23–5.

14. Ibid., pp. 25 and 29.

15. N. A. Morozov, *GULAG v Komi krae*, pp. 13–14.

16. Kaneva, pp. 337–8.

17. Nadezhda Ignatova, 'Spetspereselentsy v respublike Komi v 1930–1940 gg', in *Korni travy*, pp. 23–5.

18. Kaneva, p. 342.

19. Ibid.

20. Stephan, *The Russian Far East*, p. 225.

21. Nordlander, 'Capital of the Gulag'; I am indebted to David Nordlander's work on Kolyma – so far the only comprehensive, archive-based Western study of Kolyma – for the account of Kolyma's history in this section and elsewhere.

22. Ibid.

23. Viktor Shmirov of the Perm Memorial Society, conversation with the author, 31 March 1998.

24. Shmirov, 'Lager kak model realnosti'.

25. Stephan, *The Russian Far East*, p. 225.

26. Nordlander, 'Capital of the Gulag'.

27. Ibid.

28. Stephan, *The Russian Far East*, p. 226.

29. Nordlander, 'Capital of the Gulag'.

30. Stephan, *The Russian Far East*, p. 227.

31. Kozlov, 'Sevvostlag NKVD SSSR'.

32. Stephan, *The Russian Far East*, p. 226.

33. Conquest, *Kolyma*, p. 42.

34. Sgovio, p. 153.

35. Shalamov, *Kolyma Tales*, p. 369.

36. Kozlov, 'Sevvostlag NKVD SSSR', p. 81; Nordlander, 'Capital of the Gulag'.

37. M. Ioffe, pp. 66–71.

38. Kozlov, 'Sevvostlag NKVD SSSR', p. 82.

39. E. Ginzburg, *Within the Whirlwind*, p. 201.

40. Ibid.

41. GARF, 9414/1/ OURZ, in the collection of A. Kokurin.

42. Khlevnyuk, 'Prinuditelnyi trud', p. 78.

43. Ibid.; Okhotin and Roginsky, pp. 376, 399 and 285.

44. Okhotin and Roginsky, p. 38.

6 The Great Terror and Its Aftermath

1. Akhmatova, p. 103.
2. Bacon, pp. 30 and 122. Bacon compiled his figures from various sources, adding together all of the different categories of forced labourers. See Appendix for further discussion of statistics.
3. Solzhenitsyn, *Gulag Archipelago*, vol. I, p. 24.
4. Unless otherwise footnoted, this account of the Great Terror comes from Conquest, *The Great Terror*; Khlevnyuk, *1937*; Getty and Naumov; and Martin, 'The Great Terror'.
5. Getty and Naumov, p. 472.
6. *Trud*, no. 88, 4 June 1992; reprinted in Getty and Naumov, pp. 472–7; many similar documents are found in Sabbo, pp. 297–304.
7. Sabbo, pp. 297–304.
8. Kokurin and Petrov, *Lubyanka*, p. 15.
9. Veronica Znamenskaya, 'To This Day', in Vilensky, *Till My Tale is Told*, pp. 141–9.
10. Yurasova.
11. GARF, personnel files. Also Kokurin and Petrov, *Gulag*, pp. 797–857.
12. GARF, 8131/37/99.
13. This account of Berzin's arrest comes from Nordlander's 'Capital of the Gulag' and 'Magadan and the Evolution of the Dalstroi Bosses'.
14. Conquest, *The Great Terror*, pp. 182–213.
15. Yelena Sidorkina, 'Years under Guard', in Vilensky, *Till My Tale is Told*, p. 194.
16. GARF, 9401/12/94.
17. Conquest, *The Great Terror*, p. 298.
18. Geller, pp. 151–7.
19. Ivanova, *Labor Camp Socialism*, p. 96.
20. Kokurin and Petrov, *Gulag*, pp. 863–9.
21. Ivanova, *Labor Camp Socialism*, pp. 95–6; Makurov, pp. 183–4.
22. Rossi, *The Gulag Handbook*, p. 180.
23. Ibid., p. 60; Volkogonov, *Stalin*, p. 279.
24. Rossi, *The Gulag Handbook*, pp. 36 and 497; *Sbornik*, pp. 86–93.
25. Larina, p. 182.
26. Levinson, pp. 39–42.
27. Gorky, *Belomor*, p. 341.
28. Weiner, 'Nature, Nurture and Memory in a Socialist Utopia'.
29. Herling-Grudziński (referred to by his English name Gustav Herling throughout the text), p. 10.
30. Ivanova, *Labor Camp Socialism*, p. 95.
31. Rossi, *The Gulag Handbook*, p. 449.
32. Leipman, p. 38.
33. Nordlander, 'Capital of the Gulag'.
34. Makurov, p. 160.
35. Chukhin, *Kanaloarmeetsi*, p. 120.
36. Shmirov.
37. Quoted in Shmirov, ibid.
38. *Trud*, no. 88, 4 June 1992, reprinted in Getty and Naumov, pp. 479–80; N. A. Morozov, conversation with the author, July 2001.
39. Papkov.
40. GARF, 9414/1/ OURZ, in the collection of A. Kokurin.
41. This was Prikaz 00447, analysed by N. Petrov and A. Roginsky, 'Polskaya operatsiya NKVD, 1937–1938 gg', in Guryanov, pp. 22–43.

42. *Memorialnoe kladbishche Sandormokh*, pp. 3 and 160–67 (a collection of documents about the executions of Sandormokh). Another source cites the date of the NKVD order on the repression of prisoners as 16 August 1937 (Binner, Junge and Martin).

43. Florenskii, pp. 777–80, from Chirkov.

44. *Memorialnoe kladbishche Sandormokh*, pp. 167–9.

45. Hoover, Nicolaevsky Collection, Box 233, Folder 23; also N. A. Morozov, *GULAG v Komi krae*, p. 28.

46. Conquest, *The Great Terror*, pp. 286–7.

47. FSB archive, Petrozavodsk, Fond 42, pp. 55–140: Akt Zasedaniya Troiki NKVD KSSR no. 13, 20 September 1937, in the collection of Yuri Dmitriev, Petrozavodsk Memorial.

48. Conquest, *The Great Terror*, p. 438.

49. Getty and Naumov, pp. 532–7.

50. Ibid., p. 562.

51. E. Ginzburg, *Journey into the Whirlwind*, p. 256.

52. N. A. Morozov, *GULAG v Komi krae*, pp. 28–9.

53. Nordlander, 'Capital of the Gulag', pp. 253–7.

54. Makurov, p. 163.

55. Khlevnyuk, 'Prinuditelnyi trud', p. 79.

56. Ivanova, *Labor Camp Socialism*, pp. 105–107.

57. Nordlander, 'Capital of the Gulag'.

58. Khlevnyuk, 'Prinuditelnyi trud', p. 73.

59. Nordlander, 'Capital of the Gulag'.

60. GARF, 9401/1/4240.

61. Solzhenitsyn, *The First Circle*, pp. 25 and 29.

62. Golovanov; Raizman, pp. 21–3.

63. Kokurin, 'Osoboe tekhnicheskoe byuro NKVD SSSR'.

64. Khlevnyuk, 'Prinuditelnyi trud', p. 79.

65. GARF, 7523/67/1.

66. GARF, 9414/1/24 and 25.

67. GARF, 7523/67/1.

68. GARF, 8131/37/356, 7523/67/2 and 9401/1a/71.

69. Knight, *Beria*, pp. 105–106.

70. Khlevnyuk, 'Prinuditelnyi trud', p. 80.

71. Zemskov, 'Zaklyuchennye', p. 63; Bacon, p. 30.

72. Zemskov, 'Arkhipelag Gulag', pp. 6–7; Bacon, p. 30.

73. Okhotin and Roginsky, p. 308.

74. Ibid., pp. 338–9.

75. Ibid., pp. 200–201, 191–2 and 303.

76. Vasileevna, interview with the author.

77. The phrase 'camp-industrial complex' is used by M. B. Smirnov, S. P. Sigachev, and D. V. Shkapov, the co-authors of the historical introduction to Okhotin and Roginsky.

Part II: Life and Work in the Camps

7 Arrest

1. N. Mandelstam, pp. 10–11.

2. Robinson, p. 13.

3. Agnew and McDermott, pp. 145 and 143–9.

4. Gelb.

5. Martin, *The Affirmative Action Empire*, pp. 328–343.
6. Lipper, p. 35; Stephan, *The Russian Far East*, p. 229.
7. Conquest, *The Great Terror*, pp. 271–2.
8. Stajner, p. 33.
9. Martin, 'Stalinist Forced Relocation Policies'.
10. Several versions of this poem exist in Russian. This is based loosely on one found in Evtushenko.
11. Okunevskaya, p. 227.
12. Starostin; GARF, 7523/60/4105.
13. Razgon, p. 93.
14. GARF, 9401/12/253.
15. Weissberg, pp. 16–87.
16. Serebryakova, pp. 34–50.
17. Lipper, p. 3.
18. Starostin, pp. 62–9.
19. Wat, pp. 308–12.
20. Dolgun, pp. 8–9.
21. Okunevskaya, pp. 227–8.
22. Solzhenitsyn, *Gulag Archipelago*, vol. I, p. 8.
23. Gagen-Torn, p. 58.
24. Hoover, Fond 89, 18/12, Reel 1.994.
25. V. Petrov, p. 17.
26. N. Mandelstam, pp. 9 and 8.
27. Naimark, *The Russians in Germany*, pp. 69–140.
28. RGVA, 40/1/71/323.
29. Głowacki, p. 329.
30. E. Ginzburg, *Journey into the Whirlwind*, p. 45.
31. Yelena Sidorkina, 'Years under Guard', in Vilensky, *Till My Tale is Told*, pp. 194–5.
32. Razgon, p. 56.
33. Zhenov, p. 44.
34. Shikheeva-Gaister, pp. 99–104.
35. GARF, 9410/12/3.
36. Joffe, pp. 90–91.
37. Solzhenitsyn, *The First Circle*, pp. 533–4.
38. Hoover, Polish Ministry of Information Collection, Box 114, Folder 2.
39. Milyutina, pp. 150–51.
40. Solzhenitsyn, *The First Circle*, p. 547.
41. Gnedin, pp. 68–9.
42. Dolgun, p. 11.
43. Vogelfanger, pp. 4–5.
44. Bershadskaya, pp. 37–9.
45. Adamova-Sliozberg, p. 16.
46. Walter Warwick, unpublished memoir. My thanks to Reuben Rajala for this text.
47. Kuusinen, p. 135.
48. *Miranda* v. *Arizona*, 384 US 436 (1966).
49. N. Werth, 'A State against Its People: Violence, Repression and Terror in the Soviet Union', in Courtois et al., pp. 193–4.
50. Gorbatov, p. 118.
51. Hoover, Sgovio Collection, Box 3.
52. Sgovio, p. 69.
53. Hoover, Sgovio Collection, Box 3.

54. Finkelstein, interview with the author.

55. Durasova, p. 77.

56. N. Petrov and A. Roginsky, 'Polskaya operatsiya NKVD, 1937–38 gg', in Guryanov, pp. 37–8; N. Petrov, 'Polska operacja NKWD'.

57. N. Petrov and A. Roginsky, ibid., pp. 24–5.

58. Iwanow, p. 370.

59. N. Petrov, 'Polska operacja NKWD', pp. 27–9.

60. Ibid., pp. 24–43 and 32.

61. Hoover, Fond 89, 18/12, Reel 1.994; Getty and Naumov, pp. 530–37.

62. Conquest, *The Great Terror*, pp. 130 and 131.

63. V. Tchernavin, pp. 156–63.

64. Narinsky, *Vospominaniya*, p. 60.

65. Khrushchev's secret speech, reprinted in Khrushchev, p. 585.

66. Jansen and Petrov.

67. Gnedin, pp. 24–31.

68. Conquest, *The Great Terror*, p. 121.

69. Shentalinsky, p. 26.

70. Hava Volovich, 'My Past', in Vilensky, *Till My Tale is Told*, p. 251.

71. E. Ginzburg, *Journey into the Whirlwind*, p. 94.

72. Hoover, Polish Ministry of Information Collection, Box 114, Folder 2.

73. V. Tchernavin, p. 162.

74. Dolgun, pp. 37–8, 193 and 202.

75. Gorbatov, pp. 109–10.

76. Razgon, p. 73.

77. Pechora, interview with the author.

8 Prison

1. GARF, 9401/1a/14.

2. GARF, 9401/1a/128.

3. Sobolev, p. 66.

4. Garaseva, pp. 96–101; for a history of the Lubyanka building, see Sobolev, pp. 11–79.

5. Panin, p. 24.

6. Sergeev, pp. 232–8.

7. Gnedin, pp. 24–31.

8. Butyrsky and Karyshev, pp. 20–21.

9. Garaseva, pp. 96–101.

10. Chetverikov, p. 35.

11. Dolgun, p. 62. The Nazi leader Albert Speer made a very similar 'walk', over many years, in his cell in the Allied prison at Spandau.

12. E. Ginzburg, *Journey into the Whirlwind*, pp. 193 and 267.

13. Finkelstein, interview with the author.

14. GARF, 9413/1/17, 9412/1/25 and 9413/1/6.

15. GARF, 8131/37/360.

16. GARF, 8131/37/796, 1250 and 1251.

17. Zabolotsky, pp. 310–31.

18. Buber-Neumann, p. 36.

19. GARF, 9401/1a/14.

20. Buber-Neumann, p. 33.

21. Trubetskoi, p. 261.

22. Nadezhda Grankina, 'Notes by Your Contemporary', in Vilensky, *Till My Tale is Told*, p. 119.
23. Yasny, pp. 1–50.
24. Dolgun, p. 15.
25. See, for example, Gorbatov, p. 111, or Zarod, p. 45. Yakov Efrussi entitled his prison memoirs *Kto na 'E'?* (*Who Starts with 'E'?*).
26. Vesyolaya, pp. 30–33.
27. Bershadskaya, pp. 37–9.
28. Vesyolaya, pp. 30–33.
29. Buber-Neumann, pp. 36 and 37.
30. Adamova-Sliozberg, pp. 17 and 8.
31. Shalamov, *Kolyma Tales*, pp. 200–216.
32. Shikheeva-Gaister, pp. 99–104.
33. Bystroletov, p. 115.
34. Pechora, interview with the author.
35. GARF, 9489/2/31.
36. Weissberg, p. 278.
37. Lipper, pp. 7–10.
38. Zarod, p. 39.
39. Finkelstein, interview with the author.
40. Razgon, p. 223.
41. Hoover, Polish Ministry of Information Collection, Box 116, Folder 2.
42. Shalamov, *Kolyma Tales*, p. 215.
43. Olitskaya, pp. 180–89.
44. E. Ginzburg, *Journey into the Whirlwind*, pp. 71–2.
45. Dolgun, p. 95.
46. Vesyolaya, p. 312.
47. Zhigulin, p. 53.
48. Shalamov, *Kolyma Tales*, pp. 200–216.
49. Ibid., pp. 213 and 216.

9 Transport, Arrival, Selection

1. Sutherland, p. 136.
2. E. Ginzburg, *Journey into the Whirlwind*, p. 205.
3. Sgovio, pp. 129–35.
4. Khachatryan, interview with the author.
5. E. Ginzburg, *Journey into the Whirlwind*, p. 100.
6. GARF, 8466/1/23.
7. Anonymous, conversation with the author, Vilnius, September 1991; Fidelgolts.
8. Głowacki, pp. 320–405.
9. Bardach, p. 156.
10. Dostoevsky, p. 170.
11. Finkelstein, interview with the author.
12. Buca, p. 26.
13. Finkelstein, interview with the author.
14. Larina, p. 149.
15. Gliksman, pp. 230–31.
16. Panin, p. 36.
17. Ptasnik, pp. 846–54.

18. Noble, p. 71.
19. Tiif, p. 125.
20. Buca, p. 29.
21. Znamenskaya, pp. 20–22.
22. Karta, Kazimierz Zamorski Collection, Folder 1, Files 1253 and 6294.
23. Zabolotsky, p. xx.
24. Bershadskaya, pp. 47–9.
25. E. Ginzburg, *Journey into the Whirlwind*, p. 229.
26. Yakovenko, pp. 176–9.
27. Gagen-Torn, pp. 69–72.
28. Hoover, Polish Ministry of Information Collection, Box 114, Folder 2.
29. Ibid., Box 110, Folder 2.
30. Ptasnik, p. 853.
31. Armonas, pp. 40–44.
32. Sandratskaya, unpublished memoir.
33. Kaufman, pp. 228–33.
34. Karta, Kazimierz Zamorski Collection, Folder 1, File 1253.
35. Stephan, *The Russian Far East*, pp. 225–32.
36. Tvardovsky, pp. 249–51.
37. Sgovio, pp. 135–44.
38. Conquest, *Kolyma*, p. 20.
39. Karta, Kazimierz Zamorski Collection, Folder 1, File 1253.
40. Nerler, pp. 360–79.
41. Karta, Kazimierz Zamorski Collection, Folder 1, File 15876.
42. Hoover, Polish Ministry of Information Collection, Box 113, Folder 9.
43. Sgovio, p. 140.
44. Conquest, *Kolyma*, p. 24; E. Ginzburg, *Journey into the Whirlwind*, pp. 351–3.
45. Conquest, *Kolyma*, p. 25.
46. Ibid., pp. 25–7; Golovanov.
47. Nordlander, 'Capital of the Gulag', pp. 290–91; Conquest, *Kolyma*, p. 25.
48. Olitskaya, pp. 229–33.
49. E. Ginzburg, *Journey into the Whirlwind*, p. 353.
50. Karta, Kazimierz Zamorski Collection, Folder 1, Files 6294, 15882 and 15876.
51. Sgovio, p. 143.
52. Kuusinen, p. 150.
53. Lipper, pp. 92–5.
54. Karta, Kazimierz Zamorski Collection, Folder 1, File 1722.
55. Elena Glink, 'Kolyma Tram', in Vilensky, *Osventsim bez pechei*, pp. 10–16.
56. Bardach, pp. 191–3.
57. Karta, Kazimierz Zamorski Collection, Folder 1, File 1253.
58. GARF, 9401/1/614.
59. GARF, 9401/1a/61.
60. GARF, 9401/1a/64.
61. GARF, 9401/2/171 and 199.
62. GARF, 8131/37/2063.
63. GARF, 8131/37/2041.
64. Gagen-Torn, pp. 69–72.
65. Ekart, p. 44.
66. Yakovenko, pp. 176–9.
67. Solzhenitsyn, *Gulag Archipelago*, vol. II, pp. 495–6.
68. Zhenov, p. 74.

69. Armonas, p. 137.
70. Gursky, unpublished memoir.
71. Chirkov, p. 22.
72. Colonna-Czosnowski, p. 53.
73. GARF, 9414/1/2743.
74. Olitskaya, pp. 234–44.
75. Adamova-Sliozberg, p. 47.
76. Smirnova, interview with the author.
77. Andreevna, interview with the author.
78. Bardach, p. 227.
79. Hoover, Polish Ministry of Information Collection, Box 114, Folder 2.
80. Ulyanovskaya and Ulyanovskaya, pp. 356–65.
81. Shalamov, *Kolyma Tales*, p. 341.
82. Shiryaev, pp. 31–7.
83. For example, GARF, 9489/2/25.
84. Weissberg, p. 92.
85. Gliksman, p. 240; Adamova-Sliozberg, p. 48.
86. Yakir, p. 117.
87. E. Ginzburg, *Journey into the Whirlwind*, p. 365.
88. GARF, 5446/1/54.
89. GARF, 9401/12/316.
90. Bien, unpublished memoir.
91. Gliksman, pp. 218–21.
92. Gagen-Torn, p. 149.
93. Herling-Grudziński, p. 27.
94. Gliksman, pp. 246–8.

10 Life in the Camps

1. Vilensky, reprinted by permission of the author.
2. Okhotin and Roginsky, pp. 137–525.
3. Okunevskaya, p. 391.
4. GARF, 5446/1/54 and 9401/12/316.
5. GARF, 9489/2/20.
6. GARF, 9401/12/316.
7. GARF, 9414/6/24.
8. Rossi, *The Gulag Handbook*, p. 137.
9. Buber-Neumann, p. 75.
10. GARF, 9401/12/316.
11. Rossi, *The Gulag Handbook*, p. 130.
12. Sofsky, p. 55.
13. GARF, 9489, the Dmitlag archives (9489/2/31, for example).
14. GARF, 9401/12/316.
15. GARF, 9401, in the collection of the author.
16. GARF, 8131/37/361.
17. GARF, 8131/37/542.
18. GARF, 9401/1a/136 and 9401/1/4240.
19. Guberman, p. 33.
20. Adamova-Sliozberg, p. 48.
21. Finkelstein, interview with the author.

22. Zarod, p. 103.
23. Kuts, p. 165.
24. Lvov, unpublished memoir.
25. Herling-Grudziński, p. 29.
26. Sofsky has also written about prisoners' time and space in *The Order of Terror*. I have borrowed the idea from him.
27. Frid, p. 136.
28. GARF, 9401/12/316.
29. Zarod, pp. 99–100.
30. Frid, p. 136.
31. Zarod, p. 102.
32. GARF, 9401/12/316; Zarod, p. 102.
33. Rossi, *The Gulag Handbook*, p. 370.
34. Nordlander, 'Capital of the Gulag', p. 158; Mitin.
35. Olitskaya, pp. 234–44; Nordlander, 'Capital of the Gulag', p. 159.
36. Olitskaya, pp. 234–44.
37. GARF, in the collection of the author.
38. GARF, 9401/1a/127.
39. GARF, 9401/1a/128; Berdinskikh, pp. 24–43.
40. N. A. Morozov, *GULAG v Komi krae*, pp. 72–5.
41. Bondarevsky, p. 44.
42. Pavel Galitsky, 'Etogo zabyt nelzya', in *Uroki*, pp. 83–5.
43. MacQueen.
44. Hoover, Polish Ministry of Information Collection, Box 114, Folder 2.
45. GARF, 9414/1/2741.
46. Zarod, p. 104.
47. Mirek, *Zapiski zaklyuchennogo*, p. 116.
48. Herling-Grudziński, p. 113.
49. Lipper, p. 214; Zarod, pp. 104–5.
50. GARF, 9489/2/11.
51. Quoted in Zhigulin, p. 121.
52. Sulimov, pp. 45–55.
53. Sieminski, p. 45.
54. GARF, 8131/37/543.
55. GARF, 9414/1/2887.
56. GARF, 9414/1/496, an order of June 1951, setting up a camp 'according to the Gulag plan'.
57. GARF, 9414/6/24.
58. Evstonichev, p. 88.
59. Sulimov, p. 53.
60. GARF, 8131/37/4547.
61. Buber-Neumann, p. 75.
62. GARF, 9401/1a/274.
63. Andreevna, interview with the author.
64. GARF, 9401/1a/141.
65. Lipper, p. 131.
66. Filshtinsky, interview with the author.
67. Arginskaya, interview with the author; GARF, 9401/1a/274.
68. Hoover, Polish Ministry of Information Collection, Box 114, Folder 2.
69. Petrus, pp. 58–65.
70. Pechora, interview with the author.

71. Pechora, interview with the author; Bulgakov, interview with the author.
72. Arginskaya, interview with the author.
73. Pechora, interview with the author; Petrus, pp. 58–65.
74. Rozina, pp. 67–75.
75. Smirnova, interview with the author.
76. Ibid.
77. Sgovio, p. 186.
78. Vardi, pp. 93–150.
79. GARF, 9414/6/24 and 25.
80. Solzhenitsyn, *Gulag Archipelago*, vol. II, p. 268.
81. Rozina, pp. 67–75.
82. Vogelfanger, p. 67.
83. Okunevskaya, p. 391.
84. Golovanov, pp. 110–15 and 122.
85. Petrus, pp. 58–65.
86. Colonna-Czosnowski, p. 113.
87. GARF, 9414/4/1 (*Perekovka* of 30 June 1934).
88. Karta, Archiwum Wschodnie, V/AC/183.
89. GARF, 5446/1/54; Rossi, *The Gulag Handbook*, p. 14.
90. GARF, 9401/1/713.
91. Waydenfeld, p. 132.
92. Shalamov, *Kolyma Tales*, p. 132.
93. GARF, 9489/2/20.
94. GARF, 8131/37/357.
95. GARF, 8131/37.
96. GARF, 9401/1a/16.
97. GARF, 9489/2/20.
98. Arginskaya, interview with the author.
99. Sitko, interview with the author.
100. Filshtinsky, interview with the author.
101. Zhigulin, pp. 174–8.
102. Pechora, interview with the author.
103. GARF, 9414/3/9.
104. Shalamov, *Kolyma Tales*, pp. 337–8, 338–9 and 340.
105. Sgovio, p. 175.
106. Shalamov, *Kolyma Tales*, p. 341.
107. Rozina, pp. 67–75.
108. Shalamov, *Kolyma Tales*, p. 336.
109. Levinson, pp. 39–40.
110. Armonas, p. 123.
111. Sitko, interview with the author.
112. Sulimov, p. 43.
113. GARF, 9489/2/15.
114. GARF, 9401/1/713.
115. GARF, 9401/1a/128.
116. GARF, 9401/1a/140.
117. GARF, 9401/1a/189, 9401/1/713, 9401/1a/141 and 119.
118. GARF, 9489/2/20/109–113.
119. Kedrovy Shor, in the collection of the author.
120. Narinsky, *Vospominaniya*, p. 138.
121. Ibid., pp. 136–7.

122. Kedrovy Shor, in the collection of the author; GARF, 9489/2/5.
123. GARF, 9489/2/19.
124. Gliksman, p. 301.
125. GARF, 9401/1a/189.
126. V. Gorkhova, 'Raport vracha', in *Uroki*, pp. 103–5.
127. Alin, pp. 185–91.
128. V. Petrov, pp. 216 and 178.
129. Yakovenko, pp. 180–81.
130. Samsonov, *Zhizn prodolzhaetsya*, pp. 70–71.
131. GARF, 9414/1/25.
132. GARF, 9489/2/10.
133. GARF, 8131/37/809, 797 and 1251.
134. Kedrovy Shor, in the collection of the author.
135. GARF, 8131/37/361.
136. E. Ginzburg, *Journey into the Whirlwind*, pp. 386–9.
137. E. Ginzburg, *Within the Whirlwind*, p. 65.
138. Kedrovy Shor, in the collection of the author.
139. GARF, 8181/37/4544.
140. Veselovsky, p. 131.
141. Alin, pp. 185–91.
142. Zarod, p. 100.
143. Ibid., p. 140.
144. Shalamov, *Kolyma Tales*, p. 74.
145. V. Petrov, p. 99.
146. Sgovio, p. 161.
147. Zarod, p. 100.
148. Panin, pp. 74 and 162.
149. Pechora, interview with the author.

11 Work in the Camps

1. Reprinted in Cohen, pp. 96–7.
2. GARF, 9414/6 (photo albums).
3. Okhotin and Roginsky, pp. 137–476.
4. GARF, 9414/6/8.
5. E. Ginzburg, *Journey into the Whirlwind* and *Within the Whirlwind*.
6. Sitko, interview with the author.
7. Filshtinsky, p. 37.
8. GARF, 9489/2/9.
9. Pryadilov, pp. 113–14.
10. Weissberg, p. 96.
11. Solzhenitsyn, *One Day in the Life of Ivan Denisovich*, p. 49.
12. Vernon Kress, 'Novyi pioner, ili, Kolymskaya selektsiya', in Vilensky, *Osventsim bez pechei*, pp. 62–70.
13. Zorin, interview with the author.
14. Mindlin, pp. 52–7.
15. Sofsky, p. 168.
16. Pechora, interview with the author.
17. See, for example, photographs in the Memorial Archive.
18. Rossi, *The Gulag Handbook*, p. 255.

19. E. Ginzburg, *Journey into the Whirlwind*, pp. 405 and 407.
20. Ulyanovskaya and Ulyanovskaya, pp. 356–65.
21. V. Petrov, pp. 208 and 178.
22. Zarod, p. 114.
23. Bardach, pp. 233–4.
24. Sulimov, p. 57.
25. Filshtinsky, p. 38.
26. Bystroletov, p. 162.
27. Bardach, pp. 232–3.
28. GARF, 9401/1a/141.
29. GARF, 8131/37/4547.
30. See, for example, Zhenov, p. 69.
31. Lipper, p. 135.
32. George Victor Zgornicki, from a tape sent to the author, April 1998.
33. V. Petrov, p. 178.
34. Filshtinsky, p. 39.
35. GARF, 9401/1/713.
36. V. Petrov, p. 208.
37. Zarod, p. 114.
38. Bardach, p. 233.
39. Olitskaya, pp. 234–44.
40. Weissberg, p. 63.
41. Ekart, p. 83.
42. Usakova, interview with the author.
43. Dolgun, p. 185.
44. GARF document in the author's possession, no reference.
45. Razgon, p. 155. Examples of primitive saws are on display in the local history museum in Medvezhegorsk.
46. Hoover, Polish Ministry of Information Collection, Box 114, Folder 2.
47. Ibid.
48. Nordlander, 'Capital of the Gulag', p. 170.
49. GARF, 9414/4/3.
50. Nordlander, 'Capital of the Gulag', p. 182.
51. Dagor, p. 10.
52. Maksimovich, pp. 91–100.
53. A. Dobrovolsky; Okhotin and Roginsky, pp. 220–21 and 341–3.
54. GARF, 9414/6/23.
55. *SLON*, vol. I, 1924 (from GARF collection).
56. Chukhin, *Kanaloarmeetsi*, pp. 127–31.
57. Sgovio, p. 184.
58. GARF, 9401/1/567.
59. GARF, 9401/1a/68.
60. Feldgun, unpublished memoir.
61. GARF, 9401/1/567.
62. Herling-Grudziński, pp. 157–8.
63. Wigmans, p. 127; Korallov, interview with the author.
64. GARF, 9401/1/2443.
65. GARF, 9401/1/567.
66. GARF, 9414/1/1442.
67. Filshtinsky, pp. 163–9.
68. GARF, 9414/1/1441.

69. Ekart, p. 82.
70. GARF, 9414/1/1440.
71. GARF, 9414/4/145.
72. Kotkin, p. 232.
73. Andreevna, interview with the author.
74. Trus, interview with the author.
75. Ekart, p. 82.
76. Hoover, Polish Ministry of Information Collection, Box 114, Folder 2.
77. Herling-Grudziński, p. 155.
78. GARF, 9414/1/1460.
79. GARF, 9414/1/1461; Okhotin and Roginsky, p. 195.
80. GARF, 9414/1/1461.
81. Vladimir Bukovsky, conversation with the author, March 2002.

12 Punishment and Reward

1. Reprinted in Rossi, *The Gulag Handbook*, p. 460.
2. Kaufman, p. 249.
3. Herling-Grudziński, p. 199.
4. GARF, 9401/12/316.
5. Kuusinen, pp. 201–2.
6. Razgon, pp. 139–40.
7. GARF, 9401/1/713 and 9401/12/316.
8. Bardach, pp. 213–15.
9. Herling-Grudziński, pp. 199 and 200.
10. Ulyanovskaya and Ulyanovskaya, p. 358.
11. Herling-Grudziński, p. 200.
12. GARF, 9489/2/5.
13. Nordlander, 'Capital of the Gulag', pp. 230–31.
14. Adamova-Sliozberg, p. 66.
15. Svetlana Dointsena, director of the local history museum in Iskitim, conversation with the author, 1 March 1999.
16. I. Samakhova, 'Lagernaya pyl', in *Vozvrashchenie pamyati*, vol. I, pp. 38–42.
17. GARF, 5446/1/54.
18. GARF, 9401/12/316.
19. Ibid.
20. GARF, 9401/1/3463.
21. See, for example, Chirkov, pp. 54–5; Maksimovich, pp. 82–90.
22. GARF, 8131/37/542.
23. GARF, 9489/2/20.
24. Bystroletov, pp. 377–8.
25. Rozina, p. 65.
26. Armonas, pp. 123–6.
27. Gorbatov, p. 121.
28. Bystroletov, pp. 385–6.
29. A. Morozov, pp. 101–3.
30. There is an example of this in the collection of documents from Kedrovy Shor, in the author's possession.
31. GARF, 9401/12/316.
32. A. Morozov, pp. 171–5.

33. Bystroletov, p. 169.
34. Ulyanovskaya and Ulyanovskaya, p. 403.
35. Zhenov, pp. 104–6.
36. GARF, 9489/2/5.
37. Herling-Grudziński, p. 93.
38. Golovanov, p. 128.
39. Koroleva, interview with the author.
40. Yasny, pp. 52–3.
41. Bystroletov, p. 391.
42. Herling-Grudziński, p. 92.
43. Gogua, unpublished memoir.
44. Herling-Grudziński, p. 95.
45. Solzhenitsyn, *The First Circle*, p. 221; Thomas, pp. 175–7.
46. Mazus, pp. 34–7.
47. Herling-Grudziński, p. 95.

13 The Guards

1. RGASPI, 119/7/96.
2. Viktor Shmirov, conversation with the author, 31 March 1998. Shmirov is the director of the Perm Gulag Museum.
3. See GARF, 9414/4/29 for a list of White Sea Canal administrators excluded from the Party for, among other things, having sex with prisoners.
4. NARK, 865/1/(10/52).
5. Kuperman, unpublished memoir.
6. Ivanova, *Labor Camp Socialism*, p. 154.
7. See, for example, GARF, 9414/4/10.
8. GARF, 9401/1a/61 and 9401/1/743.
9. Kuzmina, pp. 93–9.
10. GARF, 9401/2/319.
11. GARF, 9414/3/40.
12. Razgon, pp. 201–10.
13. N. Petrov, 'Čekisti e il secondino'. (The author read the manuscript in Russian.)
14. Ibid. There were exceptions, of which the career of Viktor Abakumov is one. He started his career in the Gulag, yet worked his way up the ladder to become head of SMERSH (Soviet counter-intelligence). See Ivanova, *Labor Camp Socialism*, pp. 141–2.
15. Ivanova, ibid., p. 145.
16. I am grateful to Terry Martin for pointing this out.
17. Melgunov, p. 241. Also see N. Petrov, 'Čekisti e il secondino'.
18. Ivanova, *Labor Camp Socialism*, p. 140.
19. Ibid., p. 150.
20. GARF, 9401/1/743.
21. N. Petrov, 'Čekisti e il secondino'.
22. Smirnova, interview with the author.
23. Kokurin and Petrov, *Gulag*, pp. 798–857.
24. RGASPI, 119/3/1, 6, 12 and 206; 119/4/66.
25. N. Petrov, 'Čekisti e il secondino'.
26. GARF, 9414/4/3.
27. GARF, 9401/1/4240.
28. Ivanova, *Labor Camp Socialism*, p. 163.

29. See, for example, GARF, 9414/3/40 and 9401/1/743.
30. Ivanova, *Labor Camp Socialism*, pp. 143 and 161.
31. GARF, 9489/2/16.
32. GARF, 9414/3/40.
33. GARF, 8131/37/357.
34. GARF, 8131/37/2063.
35. Vasileevna, interview with the author.
36. GARF, 9401/1a/1.
37. GARF, 9401/1a/10, 9489/2/5 and 9401/1a/5.
38. GARF, 9401/1a/6.
39. Nordlander, 'Capital of the Gulag', p. 183.
40. Pechora, interview with the author.
41. Roeder, pp. 128–30.
42. Kuchin, *Polyanskii ITL*, pp. 10–16.
43. Ivanova, *Labor Camp Socialism*, pp. 159–60.
44. Ibid., p. 160.
45. Stajner, pp. 241–2.
46. Ivanova, *Labor Camp Socialism*, p. 160.
47. MacQueen.
48. GARF, 8131/37/2063 and 9401/12/316.
49. Kuusinen, p. 173.
50. E. Ginzburg, *Journey into the Whirlwind*, pp. 376–8.
51. Sgovio, pp. 247–8.
52. Nordlander, 'Capital of the Gulag'.
53. Rotfort, pp. 78–80.
54. Razgon, p. 214.
55. Vogelfanger, pp. 147 and 178.
56. Kopelev, *Khranit vechno*, pp. 372–5.
57. Nordlanger, 'Capital of the Gulag', p. 277.
58. Razgon, p. 228.
59. Starostin, pp. 83–8.
60. GARF document in the author's possession, no reference.
61. Ibid.
62. This is the argument in Goldhagen.
63. Smirnova, interview with the author.
64. Andreevna, interview with the author.
65. Arginskaya, interview with the author.
66. GARF, 8131/37/100.
67. R. Medvedev, p. 282.
68. Razgon, p. 221.
69. Gorchakov, *L-1-105*, pp. 156–7.
70. Pryadilov, pp. 81–95.
71. GARF, 8131/37/1253.
72. Levinson, p. 40.
73. Zhigulin, p. 154.
74. Sandratskaya, unpublished memoir, p. 51.
75. Gnedin, p. 117.
76. Berdinskikh, p. 22.
77. GARF, 9489/2/20 and 9401/1a/61.
78. Bulgakov, interview with the author.
79. GARF, 8131/37/809.

80. Zhigulin, p. 157.
81. Berdinskikh, p. 22.
82. Dyakov, p. 65.
83. Lipper, pp. 241–3.
84. Ivanova, *Labor Camp Socialism*, p. 149.
85. Ulyanovskaya and Ulyanovskaya, p. 316.
86. Kozlov, 'Sevvostlag NKVD SSSR', p. 89.
87. Weiner, 'Nature, Nurture and Memory in a Socialist Utopia'.
88. Zhigulin, p. 157.
89. Stajner, p. 69.
90. Buber-Neumann, p. 125.
91. Shreider, p. 193.
92. MacQueen.
93. Anna Zakharova, 'The Defense of a Prison Camp Official', in Cohen, p. 143.
94. Anonymous interview with the author.
95. Hochschild, p. 65.
96. MacQueen.
97. Razgon, p. 214.
98. GARF, 8131/37/809.
99. Berdinskikh, p. 28.
100. Zarod, p. 94.
101. GARF, 8131/37.

14 The Prisoners

1. Dostoevsky, p. 29.
2. E. Ginzburg, *Within the Whirlwind*, pp. 266–3.
3. Gorbatov, p. 125.
4. Ekart, pp. 71–4.
5. M. Ioffe, pp. 8–9.
6. Razgon, p. 184.
7. Colonna-Czosnowski, p. 109.
8. Varese, pp. 162–4.
9. Abramkin and Chesnokova, I, pp. 7–22.
10. Ibid.
11. Dostoevsky, p. 35.
12. Abramkin and Chesnokova, p. 10.
13. Razgon, p. 185.
14. Dolgun, pp. 139–60.
15. Korallov, interview with the author.
16. Abramkin and Chesnokova, p. 9.
17. Korallov, interview with the author.
18. Varese, pp. 146–50.
19. N. Medvedev, pp. 14–16.
20. Ibid.
21. Shalamov, *Kolyma Tales*, p. 411.
22. Solzhenitsyn, *Gulag Archipelago*, vol. II, p. 445.
23. Zhigulin, p. 136.
24. Berdinskikh, pp. 291–315.
25. Hoover, Polish Ministry of Information Collection, Box 114, Folder 2.

26. A. Akarevich, 'Blatnye slova', *Solovetskie Ostrova*, February 1925, no. 2 (SKM).

27. Guberman, pp. 72–3.

28. GARF, 9489/2/15.

29. Shalamov, *Kolyma Tales*, p. 7.

30. Feldgun, unpublished memoir.

31. Berdinskikh, p. 132.

32. Solzhenitsyn, *Gulag Archipelago*, vol. II, p. 441.

33. Sgovio, pp. 165–9.

34. GARF, 8131/37/1261.

35. D. Likhachev, 'Kartezhnye igri ugolovnikov', *Solovetskie Ostrova*, 1930, no. 1., pp. 32–5 (SKM).

36. Finkelstein, interview with the author.

37. Herling-Grudziński, p. 18.

38. Hoover, Polish Ministry of Information Collection, Box 113, Folder 2.

39. Gorbatov, pp. 140–41.

40. Colonna-Czosnowski, pp. 126–31.

41. Antonov-Ovseenko, *The Time of Stalin*, p. 316.

42. Varese, p. 159.

43. Finkelstein, interview with the author.

44. Zemskov, 'Zaklyuchennye v 1930-e gody', p. 68.

45. Dugin, 'Gulag glazami istorika'; Zemskov, ibid., p. 65.

46. Adamova-Sliozberg, 'My Journey', in Vilensky, *Till My Tale is Told*, p. 2.

47. Elletson, p. 2.

48. Kuchin, *Polyanskii ITL*, pp. 37–8.

49. Ekart, p. 69.

50. E. Ginzburg, *Within the Whirlwind*, pp. 334–5; Razgon, p. 93.

51. Razgon, p. 93.

52. Shalamov, *Kolyma Tales*, pp. 258–9.

53. Warwick, unpublished memoir.

54. Frid, p. 235.

55. Federolf, p. 123.

56. Purizhinskaya, interview with the author.

57. Trus, interview with the author.

58. Gagen-Torn, p. 77.

59. Razgon, p. 138.

60. Ekart, p. 192.

61. Leipman, p. 69.

62. Ekart, pp. 67–8.

63. Noble, p. 121.

64. Leipman, p. 89.

65. Ekart, p. 191.

66. Dostoevsky, p. 51.

67. Chukhin, *Kanaloarmeetsi*, pp. 164–7.

68. GARF, 9489/2/5.

69. Herling-Grudziński, p. 25.

70. S. I. Kuznetsov.

71. Polonsky.

72. MacQueen.

73. Panin, p. 187.

74. Stajner, p. 203.

75. Solzhenitsyn, *Gulag Archipelago*, vol. III, p. 401.

76. Hoover, Adam Galinski Collection.
77. Wat, p. 147.
78. Khachatryan, interview with the author.
79. Buca, p. 122.
80. Negretov, interview with the author.
81. Korallov, interview with the author.
82. Sitko, interview with the author.
83. Purizhinskaya, interview with the author.
84. GARF, 9414/1/206 (nationality statistics for 1954).
85. V. Petrov, pp. 119–37.
86. Trus, interview with the author.
87. Federolf, p. 234.
88. Gagen-Torn, p. 205.
89. Andreevna, interview with the author.
90. Pechora, interview with the author.
91. Larina, p. 159.
92. Solzhenitsyn, *Gulag Archipelago*, vol. II, p. 330.
93. Dyakov, pp. 60–67.
94. Solzhenitsyn, *Gulag Archipelago*, vol. II, pp. 351–2.
95. Shentalinsky, pp. 163–5.
96. Andreevna, interview with the author.
97. Gagen-Torn, p. 208.
98. Kuusinen, p. 202.
99. Solzhenitsyn, *Gulag Archipelago*, vol. II, pp. 65–6.
100. Ulyanovskaya and Ulyanovskaya, p. 300.
101. Arginskaya, interview with the author.
102. Gagen-Torn, p. 208.

15 Women and Children

1. Vilenksy, *Till My Tale is Told*, pp. 53–4.
2. For example, Vilensky, interview with the author.
3. Buber-Neumann, p. 38.
4. Herling-Grudziński, p. 136.
5. Ibid., pp. 134–5.
6. Levinson, pp. 72–5.
7. GARF, 9401/1a/107.
8. See, for example, Alin, pp. 157–60, and Evstonichev, pp. 19–20.
9. Statistics compiled from various sources, GARF. I am grateful to Aleksandr Kokurin for them.
10. 'Not Part of My Sentence: Violations of the Human Rights of Women in Custody'.
11. Shalamov, *Kolyma Tales*, pp. 415–31.
12. Sgovio, pp. 173–4.
13. Abramkin and Chesnokova, p. 18; Marchenko, *To Live Like Everyone*, p. 16.
14. Yakir, pp. 46–7.
15. Ulyanovskaya and Ulyanovskaya, pp. 388–91 and Lvov, unpublished memoir.
16. Ulyanovskaya and Ulyanovskaya, ibid.
17. Hoover, Polish Ministry of Information Collection, Box 114, Folder 2.
18. Frid, pp. 186–7.
19. Lvov, unpublished memoir.

20. Hoover, Polish Ministry of Information Collection, Box 114, Folder 2.
21. Pechora, interview with the author.
22. Andreevna, interview with the author.
23. Solzhenitsyn, *Gulag Archipelago*, vol. II, p. 233.
24. Filshtinsky, interview with the author.
25. Hava Volovich, 'My Past', in Vilensky, *Till My Tale is Told*, p. 260.
26. Lvov, unpublished memoir.
27. Buca, pp. 134–5.
28. Razgon, pp. 163–4.
29. Solzhenitsyn, *Gulag Archipelago*, vol. II, p. 233.
30. Herling-Grudziński, p. 135.
31. Frid, p. 187.
32. Ibid., pp. 187–8.
33. Zhigulin, pp. 128–33.
34. Vogelfanger.
35. Sitko and Pechora, interviews with the author.
36. Kaufman, p. 223.
37. Sitko, interview with the author.
38. Solzhenitsyn, *Gulag Archipelago*, vol. II, pp. 248–9.
39. Ibid., p. 249.
40. NKVD operational order of 15 August 1937, reprinted in *Sbornik*, pp. 86–93.
41. GARF, 9401/1a/66.
42. Kaufman, pp. 188–9.
43. Natalya Zaporozhets, in Vilensky, *Dodnes tyagoteet*, pp. 532–9.
44. Vilensky et al., *Deti Gulaga*, p. 428.
45. Ibid., pp. 41–2.
46. Hoover, Polish Ministry of Information Collection, Box 114, Folder 2.
47. Vilensky et al., *Deti Gulaga*, p. 117.
48. For example, the amnesty for women with children in 1945 specifically excluded political prisoners, as did a similar one in 1948. GARF 8131/37/4554; 9401/1a/191; and 9401/1/743.
49. Khachatryan, interview with the author.
50. Lahti, unpublished memoir. I am grateful to Reuben Rajala for this manuscript.
51. Joffe, p. 124.
52. Frid, p. 184; GARF, 9414/1/2741.
53. Andreevna, interview with the author.
54. Yakovenko, p. 196.
55. Hava Volovich, 'My Past', in Vilensky, *Till My Tale is Told*, pp. 260–64.
56. GARF, 9414/6/44 and 45.
57. E. Ginzburg, *Within the Whirlwind*, p. 3.
58. GARF, 9401/2/234.
59. GARF, 8313/37/4554 and 1261.
60. Vilensky et al., *Deti Gulaga*, p. 150.
61. Joffe, pp. 127–35.
62. GARF, 8313/37/4554.
63. Anonymous, interview with the author.
64. GARF, 8313/37/4554.
65. E. Ginzburg, *Within the Whirlwind*, pp. 3–11.
66. Although the anonymous nursery administrator I spoke to denied that this happened, many, many memoirists speak of mothers being separated from their children. Susanna Pechora says that in the special camps, it was standard practice.
67. Vilensky et al., *Deti Gulaga*, pp. 241–2.

68. Armonas, pp. 156–61.
69. Vilensky et al., *Deti Gulaga*, p. 320.
70. Bazarov, p. 362.
71. Ibid., pp. 370–76.
72. Vilensky et al., *Deti Gulaga*, p. 144.
73. GARF, 9401/1a/20.
74. Vilensky et al., *Deti Gulaga*, p. 248.
75. Ibid., p. 247.
76. GARF, 9401/1a/20.
77. Yakir, p. 31.
78. Anonymous, *Ekho iz nebytiya*, pp. 289–92.
79. Yurganova, interview with the author.
80. Hochschild, p. 87.
81. Pechora, interview with the author.
82. Lahti, unpublished memoir.
83. GARF, 9414/1/27.
84. Serge, p. 28.
85. Bazarov, p. 383.
86. GARF, 9414/1/42 and 9401/1a/7; Solzhenitsyn, *Gulag Archipelago*, vol. II, pp. 447–51.
87. Vilensky et al., *Deti Gulaga*, p. 11.
88. GARF, 9414/1/42; Bazarov, pp. 385–93.
89. Razgon, p. 162.
90. GARF, 9412/1/58.
91. GARF, 9401/1a/62 and 7.
92. GARF, 8131/37/4553.
93. GARF, 9401/1a/57.
94. Yakir, pp. 32–62.
95. Kmiecik, pp. 70–74.
96. Vilensky et al., *Deti Gulaga*, pp. 283–93.
97. Conquest, *The Great Terror*, p. 274.
98. GARF, 8131/37/2063.
99. GARF, 9414/1/27.
100. Kmiecik, pp. 93–4.
101. GARF, 9401/1a/81.
102. GARF, 8131/37/2063.
103. Kmiecik, pp. 114–17.
104. GARF archives, in the collection of the author.
105. GARF, 9414/4/1; from the newspaper *Perekovka*, 1 June 1934.
106. GARF, 9412/1C/47.
107. GARF, 9401/1a/107.
108. GARF, 9401/1a/7/84.
109. GARF, 8131/37/4547.
110. Razgon, pp. 162–3.
111. Ibid., p. 162.
112. Solzhenitsyn, *Gulag Archipelago*, vol. II, p. 457.
113. Wigmans, p. 90.
114. Klein, *Ulybki nevoli*, pp. 20–25.
115. See Vilensky et al., *Deti Gulaga*, for excerpts from these memoirs.

16 The Dying

1. Gagen-Torn, p. 244.
2. Rossi, *The Gulag Handbook*, pp. 107–8 and p. 476.
3. GARF, 9414/3/40.
4. Herling-Grudziński, p. 51.
5. Sgovio, p. 177.
6. Tamara Petkevich, 'Just One Fate', in Vilensky, ibid., pp. 223–4.
7. Shalamov, samizdat publication, translated with the help of Galya Vinogradova. While the author has good reason to believe this is the work of Varlam Shalamov, some work may have incorrectly circulated in the Soviet Union under his name.
8. Sgovio, pp. 162 and 160–61.
9. Bardach, p. 236.
10. Efrussi, 'Dokhodyagi', in Vilensky, *Osventsim bez pechei*, p. 59.
11. Herling-Grudziński, p. 136.
12. Gilboa, pp. 53–4.
13. Bardach, p. 235.
14. GARF, 8131/37/797.
15. N. Mandelstam, p. 263.
16. Gnedin, pp. 80–86.
17. Merridale, p. 261.
18. Todorov, *Facing the Extreme*, p. 37.
19. Rotfort, pp. 40–41.
20. Eizenberger, pp. 38–9.
21. Mindlin, p. 60.
22. E. Ginzburg, *Within the Whirlwind*, p. 91.
23. Todorov, *Facing the Extreme*, p. 63.
24. GARF, 8131/37/809.
25. Buca, p. 150; Berdinskikh, p. 28.
26. Vogelfanger, p. 80.
27. GARF, 8131/37/809.
28. GARF, 8131/37/542.
29. Merridale, p. 265.
30. Buca, p. 152.
31. Shalamov, p. 281.
32. GARF, 9414/1/2809.
33. GARF, 9414/1/2771.
34. Herling-Grudziński, p. 149.

17 Strategies of Survival

1. Shalamov, *Neskolko moikh zhiznei*, p. 391.
2. Vogelfanger, p. 206.
3. Zorin, interview with the author.
4. Quoted in Todorov, *Facing the Extreme*, p. 32.
5. Buca, p. 79.
6. Olitskaya, pp. 233–4.
7. Usakova, interview with the author.
8. Herling-Grudziński, p. 68.

9. Levi, p. 97.
10. Bettelheim, pp. 169–71.
11. Colonna-Czosnowski, p. 118.
12. Shalamov, *Kolyma Tales*, pp. 405–14.
13. This is Todorov's observation. Todorov, *Facing the Extreme*, p. 35.
14. Quite a lot has been written about *tufta* in the USSR. See Fitzpatrick, *Everyday Stalinism*; Berliner; Ledeneva; and Andreev-Khomiakov.
15. Frid, pp. 134–6.
16. Dyakov, p. 54.
17. Anonymous, interview with the author.
18. Cohen, pp. 140–47.
19. Yasny, p. 51.
20. Ulyanovskaya and Ulyanovskaya, pp. 360–61.
21. Borin, pp. 234–6.
22. Shister, interview with the author.
23. V. Petrov, p. 179.
24. Herling-Grudziński, p. 37.
25. Razgon, p. 155.
26. Solzhenitsyn, *Gulag Archipelago*, vol. II, p. 218.
27. Usova, unpublished memoir.
28. Karta, Kazimierz Zamorski Collection, Teczka 1, File 6107 (Halina Storożuk).
29. Frid, pp. 134–6.
30. E. Ginzburg, *Journey into the Whirlwind*, p. 416.
31. Sgovio, pp. 167–75.
32. S. Fomchenko, 'Pervye desyat', in *Uroki*, p. 225.
33. P. Galitsky, 'Etogo zabyt nelzya', in *Uroki*, pp. 83–5.
34. Samsonov, *Zhizn prodolzhaetsya*, pp. 70–71.
35. Maksimovich, pp. 91–100.
36. Zorin, interview with the author.
37. Finkelstein, interview with the author.
38. Ibid.
39. Adamova-Sliozberg, pp. 50–51.
40. Rossi, *The Gulag Handbook*, pp. 247 and 255.
41. Maksimovich, pp. 91–100.
42. Klein, *Ulybki nevoli*, pp. 60–61 and 73.
43. GARF, 8131/37/1261, 797 and 1265.
44. GARF, 9414/1/28.
45. Filshtinsky, pp. 15–22.
46. Sofsky, p. 130.
47. Solzhenitsyn, *Gulag Archipelago*, vol. II, pp. 253, 254 and 252.
48. Bien, unpublished memoir.
49. Solzhenitsyn, *Gulag Archipelago*, vol. II, pp. 252–3.
50. Petrov, pp. 48–96.
51. GARF, 9489/2/19.
52. Razgon, p. 154.
53. GARF, 9401/12/316.
54. GARF, 8131/37/356.
55. Razgon, pp. 222–31; Solzhenitsyn, *Gulag Archipelago*, vol. II, p. 255.
56. Filshtinsky, pp. 120–21.
57. Yasny, pp. 50–51.
58. Berdinskikh, p. 113.

59. Ibid., pp. 113–14.
60. Solzhenitsyn, *Gulag Archipelago*, vol. II, pp. 360–66.
61. Ibid., pp. 260–61.
62. Mukhina-Petrinskaya.
63. Panin, p. 176.
64. Razgon, p. 153.
65. Ibid., p. 156.
66. Shalamov, *Kolyma Tales*, p. 405.
67. Kopelev, pp. 142–4.
68. E. Ginzburg, *Within the Whirlwind*, p. 108.
69. Sgovio, p. 206.
70. Eizenberger, pp. 67–8.
71. Okunevskaya, p. 280.
72. Aleksandrovich, p. 11.
73. Rozsas, p. 282. I am grateful to Janos Rozsas for sending me this material.
74. Solzhenitsyn, *Gulag Archipelago*, vol. I, p. 279; Reshetovskaya, pp. 121–2.
75. GARF, 9414/1/2736.
76. GARF, 9489/2/25.
77. Gliksman, p. 300.
78. Herling-Grudziński, pp. 101–2.
79. Bien, unpublished memoir.
80. GARF, 8131/37/356, 809 and 356.
81. Papkov, p. 57.
82. GARF, 9489/2/25.
83. Aleksandrovich, pp. 11 and 22.
84. GARF, 8131/37/4547.
85. GARF, 9489/2/25.
86. Shalamov, *Kolyma Tales*, pp. 408–10.
87. Colonna-Czosnowski, pp. 102–7.
88. Dolgun, p. 240.
89. Finkelstein, interview with the author.
90. Okunevskaya, p. 336.
91. Aleksandrovich, p. 12.
92. GARF, 8131/37/4547 and 542.
93. Vogelfanger, pp. 71–2.
94. Gliksman, pp. 211–12.
95. Buca, p. 150.
96. GARF, 8131/37/356.
97. Lipper, p. 251.
98. GARF, 8131/37/809.
99. Trus, interview with the author.
100. GARF, 9414/1/2739.
101. For example, GARF, 9489/2/18.
102. E. Ginzburg, *Within the Whirlwind*, p. 8.
103. Dolgun, p. 239.
104. Bardach, p. 259.
105. Vogelfanger, pp. 68 and 162.
106. GARF, 9414/1/2771.
107. GARF, 9489/2/5/474.
108. Zhigulin, p. 153.
109. Kudryavtsev, p. 288.

110. Lipper, pp. 257–8; Herling-Grudziński, p. 102; Aleksandrovich, pp. 24–5; Marchenko, *My Testimony*, pp. 140–42.
111. Frid, p. 137.
112. Dolgun, p. 273; Lipper, pp. 257–8.
113. Aleksandrovich, p. 24.
114. Herling-Grudziński, pp. 80–82.
115. Zhigulin, p. 151.
116. Bardach, pp. 332–3.
117. Lipper, p. 258.
118. Bystroletov, p. 407.
119. Dolgun, pp. 176–9.
120. Todorov, *Facing the Extreme*, pp. 47–120.
121. Federolf, p. 224.
122. Z. Marchenko, unpublished memoir. I am grateful to Zoya Marchenko for giving me her work.
123. Kekushev, pp. 84–5.
124. Panin, p. 79.
125. Bardach, pp. 207–8.
126. Adamova-Sliozberg, pp. 8–9.
127. S. I. Kuznetsov, p. 613.
128. Chetverikov, p. 35.
129. Bardach, pp. 122–39.
130. E. Ginzburg, *Within the Whirlwind*.
131. Gagen-Torn, p. 161.
132. Shalamov, from samizdat publication; translated with the help of Galya Vinogradova. While the author has good reason to believe this is the work of Varlam Shalamov, some work may have incorrectly circulated in the Soviet Union under his name.
133. Scammell, *Solzhenitsyn*, p. 284.
134. Pashnin, pp. 103–17.
135. Cherkhanov, unpublished memoir; Ulyanovskaya and Ulyanovskaya, p. 300.
136. Zorin, interview with the author.
137. Kopelev, p. 154.
138. Zarod, p. 118.
139. K. Golitsyn, pp. 267–8.
140. Dolgun, pp. 206–7.
141. Andreevna, interview with the author.
142. Tvardovsky, pp. 272–5.
143. Klein, *Ulybki nevoli*, pp. 70–71.
144. Feldgun, unpublished memoir.
145. GARF, 9489/2/20.
146. Sgovio, pp. 168–9.
147. Feldgun, unpublished memoir.
148. E. Sudakova, 'Otryvok iz vospominanii', in *Uroki*, pp. 132–7.
149. Panin, p. 79.
150. Chirkov, pp. 96–7.
151. Herling-Grudziński, p. 156.
152. Okunevskaya, p. 352.
153. Starostin, pp. 88–92.
154. Joffe, p. 139.
155. Głowacki, pp. 317–18.
156. Finkelstein, interview with the author.

157. E. Ginzburg, *Journey into the Whirlwind*, p. 292.
158. Wat, p. 142.
159. Dolgun, pp. 141–7.
160. Bardach, p. 190.
161. Colonna-Czosnowski, pp. 120–21.
162. Gagen-Torn, 'Rukopis', in *Pamyat Kolymy*, pp. 23–5.
163. Smirnov, conversation with the author, February 2001.
164. Herling-Grudziński, pp. 139–40.
165. Arginskaya, interview with the author.
166. Ulyanovskaya and Ulyanovskaya, pp. 356–65.

18 Rebellion and Escape

1. Rawicz, p. 96.
2. Solzhenitsyn, *Gulag Archipelago*, vol. III, p. 97.
3. Zhigulin, p. 192.
4. Shalamov, *Kolyma Tales*, pp. 343–79.
5. MacQueen.
6. Herling-Grudziński, pp. 125–9.
7. V. Petrov, pp. 104–7.
8. Rossi, *The Gulag Handbook*, p. 204; Solzhenitsyn, *Gulag Archipelago*, vol. III, p. 161.
9. Solzhenitsyn, ibid., pp. 197–9.
10. A. Morozov, p. 187.
11. Solzhenitsyn, *Gulag Archipelago*, vol. III, pp. 197–9.
12. Kusurgashev, pp. 34–6; Rossi, *The Gulag Handbook*, pp. 204–5.
13. GARF, 9401/1a/552 and 64.
14. Stajner, p. 78.
15. Zhigulin, pp. 191–212.
16. Rossi, *The Gulag Handbook*, p. 406.
17. GARF, 9401/1a/185.
18. GARF, 9401/1a/7.
19. Malsagov.
20. V. V. Ioffe, 'Bolshoi pobeg 1928-ogo goda', in *Solovetskie Ostrova*, vol. II, pp. 215–16 (GARF).
21. GARF, 9414/1/8.
22. V. Tchernavin, p. 357; T. Tchernavin.
23. *Gulag*, BBC documentary, produced by Angus MacQueen, 1998.
24. Chukhin, *Kanaloarmeetsi*, pp. 188–92.
25. GARF, 9401/1a/5.
26. Makurov, p. 6.
27. GARF, 9401/1a/5 and 6.
28. Makurov, pp. 38–9.
29. Rossi, *The Gulag Handbook*, pp. 310–11.
30. Kozlov, 'Sevvostlag NKVD SSSR', p. 81.
31. GARF, 9401/1a/20.
32. GARF, 9401/1a/128; Kuchin, *Polyanskii ITL*, p. 148.
33. Poleshchikov, p. 39.
34. GARF, 9414/1/2632; Kuchin, *Polyanskii ITL*, p. 148.
35. Shalamov, *Kolyma Tales*, p. 345; Rossi, *The Gulag Handbook*, p. 342.
36. Rossi, ibid., p. 310.

37. Lvov, unpublished memoir.
38. V. Tchernavin, p. 319.
39. Buber-Neumann, p. 112.
40. Solzhenitsyn, *Gulag Archipelago*, vol. III, p. 140.
41. GARF, 9401/1/2244.
42. Buca, p. 33.
43. GARF, 9401/1a/64.
44. Bardach, pp. 106–21.
45. Solzhenitsyn, *Gulag Archipelago*, vol. III, p. 204.
46. Solzhenitsyn, ibid.; Yuri Morakov (former MVD officer), conversation with the author, November 1999.
47. Morakov, ibid.
48. GARF, 9414/4/10.
49. GARF, 9401/12/319.
50. Shalamov, *Kolyma Tales*, pp. 80–85.
51. GARF, 9401/1a/552.
52. GARF, 9401/1a/64 and 9401/12/319 among others.
53. Buca, pp. 123–7.
54. Vilensky, interview with the author.
55. Sgovio, p. 177.
56. Dvorzhetsky, p. 48.
57. Dolgun, p. 338.
58. C. A. Smith.
59. One of the most prominent Russian students of the Gulag, Veniamin Ioffe, the director of St Petersburg Memorial, tried to find Rawicz's files and failed. He was further thrown into doubt after carrying on a correspondence with the late author, which he felt was unconvincing.
60. Herling-Grudziński, pp. 124–5.
61. Ibid., pp. 194–5.
62. Ivanova, *Labor Camp Socialism*, p. 45.
63. Petrus, p. 61.
64. Ratushinskaya, pp. 21–2.
65. Petrus, p. 63.
66. Osipova, pp. 87–109; Serge, p. 71.
67. V. M. Poleshchikov, unpublished monograph, in the author's collection; Rossi, *The Gulag Handbook*, p. 120.
68. Osipova, pp. 109–34; M. Baitalsky, 'Trotskisty na Kolyme', in *Minuvshee*, vol. 2, 1990, pp. 346–57.
69. Vilensky, *Soprotivlenie v GULAGe*, p. 158.
70. Kravchenko, p. 341.
71. The following account comes largely from Mikhail Rogachev, 'Bunt nad Usą', *Karta*, no. 17, 1995, pp. 97–105, and from conversations with Rogachev in July 2001. There are also some details from Poleshchikov, pp. 37–65; Ivanova, *Labor Camp Socialism*, pp. 54–5; Osipova, pp. 167–82.
72. Ivanova, ibid., p. 45.

Part III: The Rise and Fall of the Camp-Industrial Complex, 1940–1986

19 The War Begins

1. Sitko, untitled poem, from *Tyazhest sveta*, p. 11.
2. Stajner, p. 101.
3. Razgon, p. 210.
4. E. Ginzburg, *Within the Whirlwind*, pp. 26–42.
5. Warwick, unpublished memoir.
6. GARF, 9414/1/68; *Imet silu pomnit*, p. 166.
7. E. Ginzburg, *Within the Whirlwind*, p. 28.
8. Gogua, unpublished memoir.
9. Hoover, Polish Ministry of Information Collection, Box 114, Folder 2.
10. Adamova-Sliozberg, p. 63.
11. GARF, 9401/1a/107.
12. Herling-Grudziński, p. 197.
13. Kokurin and Morukov, 'Gulag: struktura i kadry', *Svobodnaya Mysl*, no. 7; Kokurin and Petrov, *Gulag*, p. 441.
14. Bacon, p. 149.
15. Ibid., p. 148.
16. Ivanova, *Labor Camp Socialism*, p. 94.
17. GARF, 7523/4/37, 39 and 38.
18. L. Ginzburg, p. 14; Overy, pp. 104–8.
19. GARF, 9401/2/95, 94 and 168.
20. Overy, p. 77.
21. Juri Brodsky, p. 285.
22. This is what I was told on the islands by at least three people, including the director of the Solovetsky museum.
23. Makurov, p. 195.
24. Guryanov, Kokurin and Popiński, pp. 8–10. *Drogi śmierci*, published by the Karta Institute, consists of a collection of documents from Soviet archives, along with mostly unpublished memoirs from Karta's Archiwum Wschodnie ('Eastern Archive'), concerning the fate of prisoners in eastern Poland during the early days of the war.
25. Bacon, p. 91; Guryanov, Kokurin and Popiński, pp. 10–26.
26. Guryanov, Kokurin and Popiński, pp. 10–26.
27. GARF, 9414/1/68.
28. Guryanov, Kokurin and Popiński, p. 40.
29. Ibid., pp. 90–91.
30. Sabbo, pp. 1128–32.
31. Bacon, pp. 88–9.
32. M. Shteinberg, 'Etap vo vremya voiny', in *Pamyat Kolymy*, 1978, p. 167.
33. Guryanov, Kokurin and Popiński, p. 90.
34. GARF, 9414/1/68.
35. M. Shteinberg, 'Etap vo vremya voiny', in *Pamyat Kolymy*, 1978, pp. 167–71.
36. GARF, 9414/1/68.
37. Bacon, p. 91.

20 'Strangers'

1. In Taylor-Terlecka, pp. 56–7. Translated with the help of Piotr Paszkowski.
2. Razgon, p. 138.
3. Ibid.
4. Głowacki, p. 273.
5. Sabbo, p. 754.
6. Sword, p. 13.
7. Guryanov, pp. 4–9.
8. Martin, 'Stalinist Forced Relocation Policies', pp. 305–39.
9. Lieven, *The Baltic Revolution*, p. 82.
10. Głowacki, p. 331.
11. Hoover, Polish Ministry of Information Collection, Box 123; also Głowacki, p. 331.
12. GARF, 5446/57/65.
13. RGVA, 40/1/71/323.
14. Ptasnik.
15. Sabbo, pp. 804–9.
16. Gross and Grudzińska-Gross, p. 77.
17. Ibid., p. 68.
18. Ibid., p. 146.
19. Ibid., pp. 80–81.
20. Ibid., p. xvi.
21. Conquest, *The Soviet Deportation of Nationalities*, pp. 49–50.
22. Martin, 'Stalinist Forced Relocation Policies'.
23. Conquest, *The Soviet Deportation of Nationalities*, pp. 34–5.
24. Lieven, *The Baltic Revolution*, pp. 318–19.
25. Naimark, *Fires of Hatred*, p. 95.
26. Pohl, 'The Deportation and Fate of the Crimean Tartars'; Naimark, ibid., pp. 99–107.
27. Naimark, ibid., pp. 98–101.
28. Martin, 'Stalinist Forced Relocation Policies'.
29. Pohl, 'The Deportation and Fate of the Crimean Tartars', pp. 11–17.
30. Lieven, *Chechnya*, p. 319; Naimark, *Fires of Hatred*, p. 97.
31. Lieven, ibid., p. 320.
32. Pohl, 'The Deportation and Fate of the Crimean Tartars', pp. 17–19; Lieven, ibid., pp. 319–21.
33. Lieven, ibid., pp. 318–20; Naimark, *Fires of Hatred*, pp. 83–107.
34. Zagorulko (a large collection of documents from various archives, published under the auspices of the Federal Archive Services, GARF, TsKhIDK and Volgograd University, with the financing of the Soros Foundation).
35. Overy, p. 52.
36. Sword, p. 5.
37. Pikhoya, *Katyn*, p. 36.
38. See Czapski, which describes the Polish government's efforts to find the officers.
39. Sword, pp. 2–5.
40. Beevor, pp. 409–10.
41. Ibid., p. 411.
42. Zagorulko, pp. 31 and 333.
43. Ibid., pp. 25–33.
44. S. I. Kuznetsov, pp. 618–19.

45. The figures are from Overy, p. 297, and come from a Soviet document of 1956. Another Soviet document of 1949, reprinted in Zagorulko, pp. 331–3, contains similar numbers (2,079,000 Germans, 1,220,000 non-Germans, 590,000 Japanese and 570,000 dead).

46. Gustav Menczer, head of the Hungarian Gulag survivors' society, conversation with the author, February 2002.

47. Bien, unpublished memoir.

48. Knight, 'The Truth about Wallenberg'.

49. Andrzej Paczkowski, 'Poland, the Enemy Nation', in Courtois et al., pp. 372–5.

50. 'Kuzina Gitlera', *Novaya Izvestiya*, 3 April 1998, p. 7.

51. Noble.

52. Zagorulko, p. 131.

53. Ibid., p. 333. There were about 20,000 POWs in the Gulag.

54. Ibid., pp. 1042 and 604–9.

55. Ibid., pp. 667–8.

56. Ibid., p. 38.

57. Naimark, *The Russians in Germany*, p. 43.

58. Zagorulko, pp. 40 and 54–8.

59. *Vostochnaya Evropa*, p. 270.

60. Ibid., pp. 370 and 419–22.

61. GARF, 9401/2/497.

62. Zagorulko, pp. 40 and 54–8. Most POWs were released by the early 1950s, although 20,000 remained in the USSR at the time of Stalin's death.

63. Sitko, *Tyazhest sveta*, p. 10.

64. Bethell, p. 17.

65. Ibid.

66. Ibid., pp. 166–9.

67. Ibid., pp. 103–65.

68. Ivanova, *Labor Camp Socialism*, p. 43.

69. Pohl, *The Stalinist Penal System*, p. 51.

70. Pohl, ibid., pp. 50–52.

71. GARF, 7523/4/164.

72. GARF, 9401/1a/135.

73. GARF, 9414/1/76.

74. GARF, 9401/1a/135, 9401/1/76 and 9401/1a/136.

75. Ivanova, *Labor Camp Socialism*, p. 43.

76. Kruglov, pp. 66, 256 and 265.

77. Vilensky, interview with the author.

78. Ivanova, *Labor Camp Socialism*, p. 43.

79. GARF, 9414/1/76.

80. Described in Joffe, pp. 199–200.

81. Klein, *Ulybki nevoli*, pp. 396–403.

82. Hava Volovich, 'My Past', in Vilensky, *Till My Tale is Told*, p. 259.

83. Wallace, p. 137.

84. Ibid., p. 117.

85. GARF, 9401/2/65; Sgovio, p. 251; Wallace, pp. 33–41.

86. Wallace, ibid.; Sgovio, ibid.

87. Vera Ustieva, 'Podarok dlya vitse-prezidenta', in Vilensky, *Osventsim bez pechei*, pp. 98–106.

88. Wallace, pp. 127–8.

89. Sgovio, p. 245.

90. Wallace, pp. 33–41.
91. Sgovio, p. 252.
92. Wallace, p. 205.

21 Amnesty – and Afterwards

1. In Taylor-Terlecka, p. 144. Translated with the help of Piotr Paszkowski.
2. GARF, 9414/1/68; Zemskov, 'Sudba kulatskoi ssylki', pp. 129–42; Martin, 'Stalinist Forced Relocation Policies'.
3. GARF, 9401/1/743.
4. Bacon, p. 112.
5. The number of prisoners in forestry camps dropped from 338,850 in 1941 to 122,960 in 1944. Okhotin and Roginsky, p. 112.
6. Sgovio, p. 242.
7. Gorbatov, pp. 150–51.
8. Committee on the Judiciary (Testimony of Avraham Shifrin).
9. Gorbatov, pp. 169, 174–5 and 194.
10. GARF, 7523/64/687 and 8–15.
11. See, for example, Overy, pp. 79–80.
12. E. Ginzburg, *Within the Whirlwind*, p. 30.
13. GARF, 9414/1/1146.
14. Mindlin, p. 61.
15. GARF, 9414/4/145.
16. Bacon, pp. 135–7, 140–41 and 144.
17. GARF, 9414/1/68.
18. Sword, pp. 30–36.
19. Ibid., p. 48.
20. Herling-Grudziński, p. 190.
21. Karta, Anders Army Collection, V/AC/127.
22. Karta, Kazimierz Zamorski Collection, Folder 1, Files 15885 and 15882.
23. Herling-Grudziński, p. 228.
24. Waydenfeld, pp. 195–334.
25. Zarod, p. 234.
26. Janusz Wedów, 'Powitanie Wodza', in Taylor-Terlecka, p. 145.
27. Czapski, p. 243.
28. Sword, pp. 60–87.
29. *Slave Labor in Russia*, p. 31.
30. Djilas, p. 114.
31. Kotek and Rigoulot, p. 527.
32. Ibid., pp. 549 and 542.
33. Ibid., pp. 539–43 and 548–56.
34. Ibid., pp. 543–4.
35. Ibid., pp. 544–8; also Andrzej Paczkowski, 'Poland, the Enemy Nation', in Courtois et al., pp. 363–93.
36. Kotek and Rigoulot, pp. 565–72.
37. Todorov, *Voices from the Gulag*, p. 124.
38. Ibid., pp. 123–8.
39. Kotek and Rigoulot, p. 559.
40. Naimark, *The Russians in Germany*, pp. 376–97.
41. Todorov, *Voices from the Gulag*, pp. 39–40.

42. Saunders, pp. 1–11; Kotek and Rigoulot, pp. 619–48.
43. Ogawa and Yoon, p. 15.
44. Ibid., p. 3.
45. Alla Startseva and Valeriya Korchagina, 'Pyongyang Pays Russia with Free Labor', *Moscow Times*, 6 August 2001, p. 1.

22 The Zenith of the Camp-Industrial Complex

1. From *Sred drugikh imen*, p. 64.
2. E. Ginzburg, *Within the Whirlwind*, p. 279.
3. See Zubkova.
4. Service, *A History of Twentieth-Century Russia*, p. 299.
5. GARF, 9401/1/743 and 9401/2/104.
6. Kokurin and Petrov, *Gulag*, p. 540.
7. Ivanova, *Labor Camp Socialism*, pp. 95–6.
8. Service, *A History of Twentieth-Century Russia*, p. 299; Ivanova, 'Poslevoennye repressii'.
9. Andrew and Gordievsky, p. 341.
10. Ivanova, 'Poslevoennye repressii', p. 256.
11. Ivanova, *Labor Camp Socialism*, pp. 48–53.
12. Operation WRINGER, HQ USAF Record Group 341, Box 1044, Air Intelligence Report 59B-B-5865-B. Records of this debriefing operation are kept in the National Archives, Washington, DC. I am grateful to Major Tim Falkowski for bringing this story to my attention. The US Air Force considers this story plausible, but has not yet confirmed it for certain.
13. Nikolai Morozov told me this story. Komi Memorial has interviewed the inhabitants of Sedvozh, looking for oral evidence, but has found only one man who has heard the whole story, second-hand. Lyuba Vinogradova found the reference to the Scotsmen at RGVA, but the document itself was missing. RGVA was not willing to provide further information.
14. Bacon, p. 24.
15. Nicolas Werth, 'Apogee and Crisis in the Gulag System', in Courtois et al., pp. 235–9.
16. Ivanova, *Labor Camp Socialism*, p. 55–6.
17. E. Ginzburg, *Within the Whirlwind*, p. 283.
18. Ibid., pp. 290–91.
19. Ibid., p. 291.
20. Adamova-Sliozberg, p. 71.
21. Razgon, p. 220.
22. Ivanova, *Labor Camp Socialism*, pp. 55–6.
23. Ibid., p. 56.
24. Kokurin and Morukov, 'Gulag: struktura i kadry' (part 14), *Svobodnaya Mysl*, no. 11, November 2000.
25. Kuts, p. 195.
26. Bulgakov, interview with the author.
27. Kuts, p. 165.
28. Pechora, interview with the author.
29. Ivanova, *Labor Camp Socialism*, p. 61.
30. Kokurin and Petrov, *Gulag*, pp. 555–67; Kokurin, 'Vosstanie v Steplage'.
31. Kokurin, 'Vosstanie v Steplage'; Ivanova, *Labor Camp Socialism*, p. 55.
32. Abramkin and Chesnokova, p. 10.
33. GARF, 9401/1a/270.
34. E. Ginzburg, *Within the Whirlwind*, p. 103.
35. Abramkin and Chesnokova, pp. 10–11.

36. Zhigulin, pp. 135–7.
37. Buca, pp. 59–61.
38. Georgi Feldgun, unpublished memoir.
39. Sitko, interview with the author.
40. Zhigulin, pp. 135–7.
41. GARF, 9401/1/4240.
42. See, for example, Ilya Golts, 'Vorkuta', in *Minuvshee*, vol. 7, 1992, pp. 317–55.
43. Craveri and Khlevnyuk.
44. Ivanova, 'Poslevoennye Repressii'.
45. Kokurin and Morukov.
46. Craveri and Khlevnyuk, p. 186.
47. Ivanova, *Labor Camp Socialism*, p. 125.
48. Ivanova, 'Poslevoennye repressii', p. 272.
49. Craveri and Khlevnyuk, p. 183.
50. Craveri.
51. Nicolas Werth, 'Apogee and Crisis in the Gulag System', in Courtois et al., pp. 239–40.
52. Craveri and Khlevnyuk, p. 183.
53. Ivanova, *Labor Camp Socialism*, p. 125.
54. See, for example, Klein, *Ulybki nevoli*, p. 61.
55. Berdinskikh, p. 56.
56. Craveri and Khlevnyuk, p. 185.
57. Ibid., p. 186.
58. Knight, *Beria*, pp. 160–69.
59. Naumov and Rubinstein, pp. 61–2.
60. Ibid., p. 62.
61. Adamova-Sliozberg, p. 79.
62. Filshtinsky, p. 114.

23 The Death of Stalin

1. Quoted in Conquest, *Stalin*, p. 312.
2. Aleksandrovich, p. 57.
3. Ulyanovskaya and Ulyanovskaya, p. 280.
4. Andreevna, interview with the author.
5. E. Ginzburg, *Within the Whirlwind*, p. 357.
6. Negretov, interview with the author.
7. Stajner, p. 358.
8. Berdinskikh, p. 204.
9. E. Ginzburg, *Within the Whirlwind*, p. 360.
10. Aleksandrovich, p. 57.
11. Adamova-Sliozberg, p. 80.
12. Roeder, p. 195.
13. Vasileevna, interview with the author.
14. Khrushchev, vol. I, pp. 322–3.
15. E. Ginzburg, *Within the Whirlwind*, p. 357.
16. Knight, *Beria*, p. 185.
17. Ivanova, *Labor Camp Socialism*, p. 124.
18. Naumov and Sigachev, pp. 19–21 (APRF, 3/52/100).
19. Knight, *Beria*, p. 185.

20. Ibid.
21. Naumov and Sigachev, pp. 28–29 (GARF, 9401/1/1299).
22. Knight, *Beria*, pp. 188–94.
23. Ivanova, *Labor Camp Socialism*, p. 124.
24. For analyses of Beria's motives, see Khlevnyuk, 'L. P. Beriya'; Pikhoya, *Sovetskii Soyuz*, p. xxx; Knight, *Beria*, pp. 176–200.
25. Knight, ibid., pp. 194–224.
26. Dolgun, p. 261.
27. Aleksandrovich, p. 57.
28. Zorin, interview with the author.
29. Filshtinsky, interview with the author.
30. Armonas, pp. 153–60.
31. Pechora, interview with the author.
32. Trus, interview with the author.
33. Usakova, interview with the author.
34. Zorin, interview with the author.
35. Khachatryan, interview with the author.
36. GARF document, order from 3 September 1955, in the collection of the author.
37. Bulgakov, interview with the author; Ilya Golts, 'Vorkuta', *Minuvshee*, vol. 7, 1992, p. 334.

24 The *Zeks*' Revolution

1. Quoted in Vilensky, *Dodnes tyagoteet*, p. 216.
2. See, for example, E. Ginzburg, *Within the Whirlwind*, pp. 359–63; Dolgun, pp. 261–2; Hoover, Adam Galinski Collection.
3. Bulgakov, interview with the author.
4. Panin, p. 306.
5. Ilya Golts, 'Vorkuta', *Minuvshee*, vol. 7, 1992, p. 334.
6. For a description of the Ukrainian underground's attitudes to informers see Burds.
7. Panin, pp. 308–10.
8. Sitko, *Gde moi veter?*, pp. 181–90.
9. Craveri, p. 323.
10. Kosyk, p. 56.
11. GARF, 9413/1/159.
12. N. A. Morozov, *Osobye lagerya MVD SSSR*, pp. 23–4.
13. Ibid., pp. 24–5; Noble, p. 143.
14. Noble, p. 143.
15. GARF, 9413/1/160.
16. GARF, 9413/1/160; N. A. Morozov, *Osobye lagerya MVD SSSR*, p. 27.
17. Noble, p. 144.
18. GARF, 9413/1/160.
19. Buca. Buca was clearly there: aspects of his account tally with the official reports. What I doubt is his leading role.
20. Kosyk, pp. 61 and 56–65.
21. Vilensky, interview with the author.
22. Bulgakov, interview with the author.
23. Kuts, p. 198.
24. GARF, 9413/1/160.

25. Ibid.

26. Hoover, Adam Galinski Collection.

27. Buca, pp. 271 and 272.

28. Noble, p. 162.

29. Berdinskikh, pp. 239–40.

30. 'Materialy soveshchaniya rukovodyashchikh rabotnikov ITL i kolonii MVD SSSR, 27 Sent–1 Okt 1954', in the collection of Memorial.

31. Morozov and Rogachev.

32. GARF, 9401/1/4240.

33. GARF, 9413/1/160 and 159.

34. This account of the Kengir uprising was put together through a comparison and synthesis of several sources. A collection of archival documents concerning the uprising was compiled and annotated by Aleksandr Kokurin ('Vosstanie v Steplage'). The Italian historian Marta Craveri has written the most reliable account of the uprising to date, using these documents and others, as well as interviews with participants (Craveri, 'Krizis Gulaga', p. 324). A more uneven account of the uprising was also put together using Ukrainian opposition sources in Volodymyr Kosyk's *Concentration Camps in the USSR*. I also made use of several written accounts of the uprising, notably Lyubov Bershadskaya's *Rastoptannye zhizni*, pp. 86–97, and N. L. Kekushev's *Zveriada*, pp. 130–43, as well as the documents and memoirs published in the periodical *Volya* (2–3), 1994, pp. 307–70. I interviewed Irena Arginskaya, who was present in Steplag during the uprising as well. Solzhenitsyn's account, also put together from interviews with participants, appears in *The Gulag Archipelago*, vol. III, pp. 285–331. If not specifically footnoted, all descriptions of events are based on these sources. I have adhered to Craveri's chronology.

35. This is Marta Craveri's observation.

36. Solzhenitsyn, *Gulag Archipelago*, vol. III, p. 209.

37. *Volya*, (2–3), 1994, p. 309.

38. Bershadskaya, p. 87.

39. Ibid., pp. 95–7.

25 Thaw – and Release

1. Reprinted in Cohen, p. 184.

2. Craveri and Khlevnyuk, p. 187.

3. Negretov, interview with the author.

4. 'Materialy soveshchaniya rukovodyashchikh rabotnikov ITL i kolonii MVD SSSR, 27 Sent–1 Okt 1954', in the collection of Memorial. Ivanova, *Labor Camp Socialism*, p. 66; Okhotin and Roginsky, pp. 58–9; Kovalchuk-Koval, p. 299; Filshtinsky, interview with the author.

5. Smirnova, interview with the author.

6. GARF, 9401/2/450.

7. Ibid.

8. Khrushchev, p. 559.

9. Ibid., pp. 559–618.

10. Ibid., p. 351.

11. K. Smith, pp. 131–74.

12. GARF, 9401/2/479.

13. GARF, 9401/2/479; Craveri, p. 337; Ivanova, *Labor Camp Socialism*, p. 67.

14. Ivanova, ibid., pp. 67–8; Craveri and Khlevnyuk, p. 189.

15. Ivanova, ibid.; Craveri and Khlevnyuk, pp. 188–9.
16. Andreev-Khomiakov, pp. 3–4.
17. Kusurgashev, p. 70.
18. Vera Korneeva, quoted in Solzhenitsyn, *Gulag Archipelago*, vol. III, p. 454.
19. Zorin, interview with the author.
20. E. Ginzburg, *Within the Whirlwind*, p. 211.
21. Korol, p. 189.
22. GARF, 9489/2/20.
23. Efron, *Miroedikha*, pp. 127–8.
24. Usakova, interview with the author.
25. S. S. Torbin, *Vospominaniya*, Memorial Archive, 2/2/91; Korol, p. 190.
26. GARF, 9414/3/40.
27. Ilya Golts, 'Vorkuta', *Minuvshee*, vol. 7, 1992, pp. 352–5.
28. Sgovio, p. 283.
29. A. Morozov, pp. 381–2.
30. Hoover, Fond 89, 18/38.
31. Bulgakov, interview with the author.
32. Antonov-Ovseenko, *The Time of Stalin*, p. 336.
33. K. Smith, p. 133.
34. Cohen, p. 36.
35. K. Smith, p. 135; Hochschild, pp. 222–3.
36. K. Smith, p. 138.
37. Adamova-Sliozberg, pp. 84–6.
38. Rotfort, p. 92.
39. Herling-Grudziński, p. 236.
40. Andreevna, interview with the author.
41. Solzhenitsyn, *Cancer Ward*, p. 202.
42. Cohen, p. 115.
43. Antonov-Ovseenko, *The Time of Stalin*, pp. 332–6.
44. Cohen, p. 26.
45. Antonov-Ovseenko, *The Time of Stalin*, pp. 332–6.
46. Cohen, p. 135.
47. Razgon, p. 50.
48. Yuri Dombrovsky, p. 77. Translated with the help of Galya Vinogradova.
49. Solzhenitsyn, *Gulag Archipelago*, vol. III, p. 455.
50. Koroleva, interview with the author.
51. Pechora, interview with the author.
52. Aksyonov, p. 382.
53. Quoted in Adler, p. 141.
54. Vilensky et al., *Deti Gulaga*, p. 460.
55. Adler, p. 145.
56. Olga Adamova-Sliozberg, 'My Journey', in Vilensky, *Till My Tale is Told*, p. 70.
57. Adler, p. xx.
58. Merridale, p. 418.
59. Cohen, p. 38.
60. Rothberg, pp. 12–40.
61. The most complete account of Solzhenitsyn's life is Michael Scammell's biography, *Solzhenitsyn*. Unless otherwise footnoted, all biographical information about him comes from there.
62. Scammell, *Solzhenitsyn*, p. 415.

63. Ibid., pp. 423–4.
64. Ibid., pp. 448–9.
65. Ibid., p. 485.
66. Sitko, *Gde moi veter?*, p. 318.
67. Rothberg, p. 62.
68. Dyakov, pp. 60–67.

26 The Era of the Dissidents

1. Reprinted in Cohen, p. 183.
2. Sobolev et al., p. 68.
3. *Prisoners of Conscience in the USSR*, pp. 48–53.
4. Committee on the Judiciary (Testimony of Avraham Shifrin).
5. GARF, 9410/2/497
6. Committee on the Judiciary (Testimony of Avraham Shifrin).
7. R. Medvedev, p. ix.
8. *Sobranie dokumentov samizdata*, AS 143. (This is a collection of samizdat documents gathered by RFE-RL from the 1960s onwards. The documents were not 'published', but rather photocopied, bound, numbered and placed in a few major libraries.)
9. *Prisoners of Conscience in the USSR*, pp. 18–23.
10. *Sobranie dokumentov samizdata*, AS 127.
11. *Prisoners of Conscience in the USSR*, pp. 18–23.
12. Reddaway, *Uncensored Russia*, p. 11.
13. Joseph Brodsky, pp. 26–7.
14. Rothberg, pp. 127–33.
15. Hoover, Joseph Brodsky Collection, Transcript of the Brodsky Trial.
16. Ibid.
17. Browne, p. 3.
18. Cohen, p. 42; Reddaway, *Uncensored Russia*, p. 19.
19. Hopkins, pp. 1–14.
20. *Prisoners of Conscience in the USSR*, p. 21.
21. Browne, p. 9.
22. Litvinov, *The Trial of the Four*, pp. 5–11.
23. Browne, p. 13.
24. Thirty years later, Chornovil, then a leading figure in the Ukrainian independence movement, became independent Ukraine's first ambassador to Canada. Before he left, I interviewed him in Lvov, in 1990.
25. Reddaway, *Uncensored Russia*, pp. 95–111.
26. Ibid., p. 19.
27. Info-Russ, #0044 (see Archives in Bibliography). This is where Vladimir Bukovsky has posted the documents he obtained while carrying out research for the trial of the Communist Party, described later in this book. The documents later became the subject of his 1996 book, *Moskovskii protsess*, published in French and Russian. Some are also stored at Hoover, Fond 89.
28. Reddaway, *Uncensored Russia*, p. 24.
29. Ibid., pp. 1–47; also *Chronicle of Current Events*.
30. Hopkins, p. 122.
31. Ratushinskaya, p. 67.
32. Marchenko, *My Testimony*, p. 17.
33. Ibid., pp. 220–27.

34. Sitko, interview with the author.

35. Ratushinskaya, pp. 60–62.

36. Viktor Shmirov, conversation with the author, 31 March 1998.

37. Fedorov, interview with the author.

38. Marchenko, *My Testimony*, p. 349.

39. Fedorov, interview with the author.

40. Ratushinskaya, pp. 174–5.

41. Fedorov, interview with the author.

42. Marchenko, *My Testimony*, p. 68.

43. E. Kuznetsov, p. 169.

44. *Chronicle of Current Events*, no. 32, July 1974.

45. Bukovsky, *To Build a Castle*, p. 45.

46. Marchenko, *My Testimony*, pp. 90–91; E. Kuznetsov, pp. 165–6.

47. *Chronicle of Current Events*, no. 6, February 1969, quoted in Reddaway, *Uncensored Russia*, p. 207.

48. *Chronicle of Current Events*, ibid., quoted in Reddaway, ibid., pp. 20–216.

49. Marchenko, *My Testimony*, p. 69.

50. Sharansky, p. 236.

51. Marchenko, *My Testimony*, p. 115; Tokes, p. 84.

52. Sharansky, p. 235; Ratushinskaya, pp. 165–78.

53. *Sobranie dokumentov samizdata*, AS 2598.

54. Daniel, p. 35.

55. Marchenko, *My Testimony*, pp. 65–9.

56. *Sobranie dokumentov samizdata*, AS 2598.

57. *Chronicle of Current Events*, no. 32, July 1974.

58. Litvinov, *The Trial of the Four*, p. 17.

59. Reddaway and Bloch, p. 305; Yakir.

60. *Chronicle of Current Events*, no. 28, December 1972.

61. Commission on Security and Cooperation in Europe (Testimony of Aleksandr Shatravka and Dr Anatoly Koryagin).

62. *Chronicle of Current Events*, no. 33, December 1974.

63. Viktor Shmirov, conversation with the author, 31 March 1998.

64. *Sobranie dokumentov samizdata*, AS 3115.

65. Bukovsky gave an account of his experience at a Warsaw press conference in 1998. The text appears on the Info-Russ Web site (see Archives in Bibliography).

66. Bukovsky, *Moskovskii protsess*, pp. 144–61.

67. Reddaway and Bloch, pp. 48–9; Seton-Watson, pp. 257–8.

68. Bukovsky, *To Build a Castle*, p. 357.

69. Reddaway and Bloch, pp. 176, 140 and 107.

70. Info-Russ, #0202.

71. Reddaway and Bloch, p. 226.

72. Nekipelov, p. 132.

73. Reddaway and Bloch, pp. 220–21; Nekipelov, p. 132.

74. *Prisoners of Conscience in the USSR*, p. 190; photograph on p. 194.

75. Reddaway and Bloch, p. 214.

76. *Prisoners of Conscience in the USSR*, pp. 197–8.

77. 'Three Voices of Dissent', *Survey*, no. 77 (Autumn 1970).

78. Nekipelov, p. 115.

79. Reddaway and Bloch, p. 348.

80. Ibid., pp. 79–96.

81. Ibid., pp. 178–80.

82. Info-Russ, #0204.
83. Ibid.

27 The 1980s: Smashing Statues

1. Reprinted in Reavey, pp. 8–9.
2. Beichman and Bernstam, pp. 145–89.
3. *Prisoners of Conscience in the USSR*, pp. 20 and 119; Alekseeva.
4. Beichman and Bernstam, p. 182.
5. Reagan, pp. 675–9.
6. Berdzenishvili, interview with the author.
7. Ibid.
8. Bukovsky, *To Build a Castle*, p. 408.
9. Ibid.
10. Berdzenishvili, interview with the author.
11. Ratushinskaya, p. 236.
12. Walker, p. 142.
13. Reddaway, 'Dissent in the Soviet Union'.
14. Gorbachev, p. 24.
15. Remnick, p. 50.
16. Ibid., pp. 264–8.
17. K. Smith, pp. 131–74; Remnick, p. 68.
18. Remnick, pp. 101–19; K. Smith, pp. 131–74.
19. *USSR: Human Rights in a Time of Change*.
20. 'Lata dysydentów', *Karta*, no. 16, 1995.
21. 'On the Death of Prisoner of Conscience Anatoly Marchenko', Amnesty International Press Release, May 1987 (ML).
22. Ibid.
23. The closure of the camps does not, for example, figure in Walker's *The Waking Giant*; Matlock's *Autopsy on an Empire*; Brown's *The Gorbachev Factor*; or Kaiser's *Why Gorbachev Happened*. The important exception is Remnick's *Lenin's Tomb*, which includes a chapter on the last prisoners of Perm-35.
24. Paul Hofheinz, former Moscow-based reporter, conversation with the author, 13 February 2002.
25. Matlock, p. 275.
26. Remnick, p. 270.
27. Walker, p. 147.
28. Info-Russ, #0128.
29. Ibid., #1404.
30. Ibid., #0130.
31. *USSR: Human Rights in a Time of Change*.
32. 'The Recent Release of Prisoners in the USSR', Amnesty International Press Release, April 1987 (ML).
33. Ibid.
34. Amnesty International Weekly Update Service, 8 April 1987 (ML).
35. Berdzenishvili, interview with the author.
36. Amnesty International Newsletter, June 1988, vol. XVIII, no. 6 (ML).
37. 'Four Long-Term Prisoners Still Awaiting a Review', Amnesty International Press Release, April 1990; also Amnesty International Newsletter, October 1990, vol. XX, no. 10 (ML); Klymchak was released by the end of the year.

38. Matlock, p. 287.
39. 'Russian Federation: Overview of Recent Legal Changes', Amnesty International Press Release, September 1993 (ML).
40. Matlock, p. 295.
41. Quoted in Cohen, p. 186.

Epilogue: Memory

1. Razgon, *Nepridumannoe*, p. 27.
2. K. Smith, pp. 153–9.
3. Aleksandr Yakovlev, Chairman of the Russian Presidential Commission on Rehabilitation of the Victims of Political Repression, conversation with the author, 25 February 2002.
4. Merridale, pp. 407–8.
5. Gessen.
6. Aleksandr Yakovlev, conversation with the author, 25 February 2002.
7. I described this incident in 'Secret Agent Man', *Weekly Standard*, 10 April 2000.
8. About 130 skeletons were discovered in the cellar of a West Ukrainian monastery in July 2002, for example. *Moscow Times*, 18 July 2002.
9. Anne Applebaum 'Secret Agent Man', *Weekly Standard*, 10 April 2000.
10. Olga Adamova-Sliozberg, 'My Journey' in Vilensky, *Till My Tale is Told*, p. 16.
11. Andrew Alexander, 'The Soviet Threat was Bogus', *Spectator*, 20 April 2002.
12. Vidal.

Appendix: How Many?

1. Bacon, pp. 8–9.
2. Conquest, *The Great Terror*, p. 485.
3. Getty, p. 8.
4. Zemskov, 'Arkhipelag Gulag', pp. 6–7; Getty, Ritterspoon and Zemskov, Appendixes A and B, pp. 1048–9.
5. Getty, Ritterspoon and Zemskov, p. 1047.
6. Bacon, p. 112.
7. Pohl, *The Stalinist Penal System*, p. 17.
8. Pohl, ibid., p. 15; Zemskov, 'Gulag', p. 17.
9. The best summary to date of the debate about the post-1991 statistical revelations can be found in Bacon, pp. 6–41 and 101–122: the eighteen million is his figure, based on turnover rates and available statistics. For the record, Dugin claims that 11.8 million people were arrested between 1930 and 1953, but I find this hard to reconcile with the eight million known to have been arrested by 1940, particularly given the huge numbers arrested and released during the Second World War (Dugin, 'Stalinizm: legendy i fakty').
10. Overy, p. 297; Zagorulko, pp. 331–3.
11. Pohl, *The Stalinist Penal System*, pp. 50–52; Zemskov, 'Gulag', pp. 4–6.
12. Polyan, p. 239.
13. Pohl, *The Stalinist Penal System*, p. 5.
14. Pohl, ibid., p. 133.
15. Although some have been published. See Getty, Ritterspoon and Zemskov, pp. 1048–9.
16. GARF, 9414/1OURZ. These figures were compiled by Aleksandr Kokurin.
17. Berdinskikh, p. 28.
18. Pohl, *The Stalinist Penal System*, p. 131.

19. Getty, Ritterspoon and Zemskov, p. 1024.
20. Courtois et al., p. 4.
21. Razgon, pp. 290–91.

Bibliography

Memoirs and Works of Literature

Adamova-Sliozberg, Olga, *Put*, Moscow, 1993

Aituganov, I. P., *Krugi ada*, Kazan, private publication, 1998

Akhmatova, Anna, *The Poems of Akhmatova*, ed. and trans. Stanley Kunitz and Max Hayward, Boston, 1967

Aksyonov, Vasily, *Generations of Winter*, New York, 1995

Aleksandrovich, Vadim, *Zapiski lagernogo vracha*, Moscow, 1996

Alin, D. E., *Malo slov, a gorya rechenka*, Tomsk, 1997

Amalrik, Andrei, *Involuntary Journey to Siberia*, trans. Manya Harari and Max Hayward, New York, 1970

Amster, Gerald, and Asbell, Bernard, *Transit Point Moscow*, New York, 1984

Andreeva, Alla, *Plavanye k Nebesnomu Kremlyu*, Moscow, 1998

Andreev-Khomiakov, Gennady, *Bitter Waters: Life and Work in Stalin's Russia*, Boulder, CO, 1997

Anonymous, *Ekho iz Nebytiya*, Novgorod, 1992

Anonymous, *Vo vlasti Gubcheka: vospominaniya neizvestnogo protoiereya*, Moscow, 1996

Antonov-Ovseenko, Anton, *Vragi naroda*, Moscow, 1996

Antsiferov, Nikolai, 'Tri glavy iz vospominanii', *Pamyat*, vol. 4, pp. 75–6

Armonas, Barbara, *Leave Your Tears in Moscow*, Philadelphia and New York, 1961

Astafyeva, Olga, *V goda slepye: stikhi*, Moscow, 1995

Bardach, Janusz (with Kathleen Gleeson), *Man is Wolf to Man: Surviving Stalin's Gulag*, London, 1998

Belousov, Viktor, *Zapiski dokhodyagi*, Ashkhabad, Turkmenistan, 1992

Belyashov, V. M., *Zhizn pereselentsev na Urale*, Severouralsk, 1991

Berger, Joseph, *Nothing But the Truth*, New York, 1971

Bershadskaya, Lyubov, *Rastoptannye zhizni*, Paris, 1975

Bondarevsky, Sergei, *Tak bylo*, Moscow, 1995

Borin, Aleksandr, *Prestupleniya bez nakazaniya: vospominaniya uznika GULAGa*, Moscow, 2000

Brodsky, Joseph, *Less Than One*, New York, 1986

Buber-Neumann, Margarete, *Under Two Dictators*, trans. Edward Fitzgerald, London, 1949

Buca, Edward, *Vorkuta*, trans. Michael Lisinski and Kennedy Wells, London, 1976

Bukovsky, Vladimir, *To Build a Castle – My Life as a Dissenter*, New York, 1978

Burkhuis, L., *Chuzhoi spektakl: kniga vospominanii*, Riga, 1990

Buxhoeveden, Baroness Sophie, *Left Behind: Fourteen Months in Siberia During the Revolution, December 1917 – February 1919*, London, New York and Toronto, 1929

Bystroletov, Dmitri, *Puteshestvie na krai nochi*, Moscow, 1996

Cederholm, Boris, *In the Clutches of the Cheka*, trans. F. H. Lyon, London, 1929

Chetverikov, Boris, *Vsego byvalo na veku*, Leningrad, 1991

Chirkov, Yuri, *A bylo vse tak*, Moscow, 1991

Colonna-Czosnowski, Karol, *Beyond the Taiga: Memoirs of a Survivor*, Hove, Sussex, 1998

Czapski, Józef, *The Inhuman Land*, trans. Gerard Hopkins, London, 1987

Czerkawski, Tadeusz, *Byłem żołnierzem generała Andersa*, Warsaw, 1991

Daniel, Yuli, *Prison Poems*, trans. David Burg and Arthur Boyars, London, 1971

Darel, Sylva, *A Sparrow in the Snow*, trans. Barbara Norman, New York, 1973

Djilas, Milovan, *Conversations with Stalin*, trans. Michael Petrovich, New York, 1962

Dmitriev, Helen, *Surviving the Storms: Memory of Stalin's Tyranny*, trans. Cathleen A. McClintic and George G. Mendez, Fresno, CA, 1992

Dolgun, Alexander, *Alexander Dolgun's Story: An American in the Gulag*, New York, 1975

Domańska, Lesława, Papiński, Marian, and the Małachowski family, *Tryptyk Kazachstański*, Warsaw, 1992

Dombrovsky, Yuri, *Menya ubit khoteli, eti suki*, Moscow, 1997

Dorogi za kolyuchuyu provoloku, vol. 3, Odessa, 1996

Dostoevsky, Fyodor, *The House of the Dead*, trans. David McDuff, London, 1985

Durasova, S. G., 'Eto bylo strashnim sobytiem', *Istoricheskii Arkhiv*, no. 6, 1999, pp. 69–84

Dvorzhetsky, Vatslav, *Puti bolshikh etapov*, Moscow, 1994

Dyakov, Boris, 'Povest o perezhitom', *Oktyabr*, no. 7, July 1964, pp. 49–142

Efron, Ariadna, *Miroedikha*, Moscow, 1996

Efron, Ariadna, *Pisma iz ssylki*, Paris, 1985

Efrussi, Yakov, *Kto na 'E'?* Moscow, 1996

Eizenberger, Andrei, *Esli ne vyskazhus – zadokhnus*, Moscow, 1994

Ekart, Antoni, *Vanished without Trace: Seven Years in Soviet Russia*, London, 1954

Evstonichev, A. P., *Nakazanie bez prestupleniya*, Syktyvkar, 1990

Evtushenko, Evgeny, ed., *Strofy veka: antologiya russkoi poezii*, Minsk and Moscow, 1995

Federolf, Ada, *Ryadom s Alei*, Moscow, 1996

Fehling, Helmut, *One Great Prison: The Story behind Russia's Unreleased POWs*, Boston, 1951

Fidelgolts, Yuri, *Kolyma*, Moscow, 1997

Filshtinsky, Isaak, *My shagaem pod konvoem: rasskazi iz lagernoi zhizni*, Moscow, 1997

Finkelberg, M. F., *Ostavlyayu vam*, Yaroslavl, 1997

Fisher, Lipa, *Parikmakher v GULAGe*, trans. Zelby Beiralas, Tel-Aviv, 1977

Fittkau, Gerhard, *My Thirty-Third Year*, New York, 1958

Florensky, Sv. Pavel, *Sochineniya*, vol. IV, Moscow, 1998

Frid, Valery, *58-1-2: Zapiski lagernogo pridurka*, Moscow, 1996

Gagen-Torn, Nina, *Memoria*, Moscow, 1994

Garaseva, A. M., *Ya zhila v samoi beschelovechnoi strane*, Moscow, 1997

Gessen, Masha, 'My Grandmother, the Censor', *Granta* 64, London, January 1998

Gilboa, Yehoshua, *Confess! Confess!*, trans. Dov Ben Aba, Boston and Toronto, 1968

Ginzburg, Evgeniya, *Journey into the Whirlwind*, trans. Paul Stevenson and Max Hayward, New York, 1967

Ginzburg, Evgeniya, *Within the Whirlwind*, trans. Ian Boland, New York and London, 1981

Ginzburg, Lidiya, *Blockade Diary*, trans. Alan Meyers, London, 1995

Gizatulin, R. Kh., *Nas bylo mnogo na chelne*, Moscow, 1993

Gliksman, Jerzy, *Tell the West*, New York, 1948

Gnedin, Evgeny, *Vykhod iz labirinta*, Moscow, 1994

Golitsyn, Kirill, *Zapiski Knyazya Kirilla Nikolaevicha Golitsyna*, Moscow, 1997

Golitsyn, Sergei, *Zapiski utselevshego*, Moscow, 1990

Gorbachev, Mikhail, *Memoirs*, New York, 1996

Gorbatov, Aleksandr, *Years Off My Life*, trans. Gordon Clough and Anthony Cash, London, 1964

Gorchakov, Genrikh, *L-1-105: Vospominaniya*, Jerusalem, 1995

Gorchakov, Genrikh, *Sudboi nalozhennye tseli*, Jerusalem, 1997

Gordeeva, Valeriya, *Rasstrel cherez poveshenie*, Moscow, 1995

Gorky, Maxim, *Sobranie sochinenii*, Moscow, 1962

Grachev, Yu. S. V., *Irodovoi bezdne: vospominaniya o perezhitom*, Moscow, 1993

Gross, Jan Tomasz, and Grudzińska-Gross, Irena, eds, *War through Children's Eyes*, Stanford, CA, 1981

Guberman, Igor, *Shtrikhi i portrety*, Moscow, 1994

Herling-Grudziński, Gustaw, *A World Apart*, trans. Andrzej Ciołkosz, London, 1951

Ievleva, Valentina, *Neprichesannaya zhizn*, Moscow, 1994

Imet silu pomnit, Moscow, 1991

Intaliya, Moscow, 1995

Ioffe, Mariya, *Odna noch*, New York, 1978

Ishutina, Elena, *Narym: dnevnik ssylnoi*, New York, 1965

Izgoev, Aleksandr, 'Pyat let v sovetskoi Rossii', *Arkhiv Russkoi Revolyutsii*, vol. X, Berlin, 1923

Joffe, Nadezhda, *Back in Time: My Life, My Fate, My Epoch* [*Vremya nazad*], trans. Frederick S. Choate, Oak Park, MI, 1995

Kalachev, Konstantin, *V kruge tretem*, Moscow, 1999

Kaminskii, R. I., *Minuvshee prokhodit predo mnoyu*, Moscow, 1955

Kaufman, A. I., *Lagernyi vrach*, Tel Aviv, 1973

Kekushev, N. L., *Zveriada*, Moscow, 1991

Kersnovskaya, Evfrosiniya, *Naskalnaya zhivopis*, Moscow, 1991

Khrushchev, Nikita, *Khrushchev Remembers*, trans. Strobe Talbott, London, 1970

Kitchin, George, *Prisoner of the OGPU*, London, New York and Toronto, 1935

Klein, Aleksandr, *Ditya smerti*, Syktyvkar, 1993

Klein, Aleksandr, *Odin sredi odinokikh*, Syktyvkar, 1995

Klein, Aleksandr, *Ulybki nevoli*, Syktyvkar, 1997

Klementev, V. F., *V bolshevitskoi Moskve*, Moscow, 1998

Klinger, A., 'Solovetskaya katorga: zapiski bezhavshego', *Arkhiv Russkoi Revolyutsii*, vol. XIX, Berlin, 1929

Kmiecik, Jerzy, *A Boy in the Gulag*, London, 1983

Kopelev, Lev, *To Be Preserved Forever* [*Khranit vechno*; Ann Arbor, MI, 1975], trans. Anthony Austin, Philadelphia and New York, 1977

Korallov, Marlen, 'Kartserok – ne khuzhe drugikh', *Moskovskii Komsomolets*, 11 September 1993

Korol, M. M., *Odisseya razvedchika*, Moscow, 1999

Kovalchuk-Koval, I. K., *Svidanie s pamyatyu*, Moscow, 1996

Kozhina, Elena, *Through the Burning Steppe: A Memoir of Wartime Russia, 1942–43*, New York, 2000

Krapivsky, Semen, *Trizhdy rozhdennyi*, Tel-Aviv, 1976

Krasnopevtsev, Yuri, *Rekviem razluchennym i pavshim Stalinskoi repressii*, Yaroslavl, 1992

Kravchenko, Viktor, *I Chose Freedom*, London, 1947

Kress, Vernon, *Zekameron XX veka*, Moscow, 1992

Krzysztoń, Jerzy, *Wielbłąd na Stepie*, Warsaw, 1982

Kudryavtsev, F. F., *Primechaniya k ankete*, Moscow, 1990

Kusurgashev, G. D., *Prizraki kolymskogo zolota*, Voronezh, 1995

Kuts, V., *Poedinok s sudboi*, Moscow, 1999

Kuusinen, Aino, *The Rings of Destiny*, trans. Paul Stevenson, New York, 1974
Kuznetsov, Edward, *Prison Diaries*, trans. Howard Spier, New York, 1973
Larina, Anna, *This I Cannot Forget: The Memoirs of Nikolai Bukharin's Widow*, trans. Gary Kern, New York and London, 1993
Leipman, Flora, *The Long Journey Home*, London, 1987
Levi, Primo, *If This is a Man*, London, 1987
Levinson, Galina, ed., *Vsya nasha zhizn*, Moscow, 1996
Levitin-Krasnov, A. E., *Ruk tvoikh zhar*, Tel Aviv, 1979
Likhachev, Dmitri, *Kniga bespokoistv*, Moscow, 1991
Likhachev, Dmitri, *Vospominaniya*, St Petersburg, 1995
Lipper, Elinor, *Eleven Years in Soviet Prison Camps*, trans. Richard and Clara Winston, London, 1951
Litovtsi i Ledovityi okean, Yakutsk, 1995
Lockhart, R. Bruce, *Memoirs of a British Agent*, London and New York, 1932
Maevskaya, Irina, *Volnoe poselenie*, Moscow, 1993
Maksimovich, M., *Nevolnye Sravneniya*, London, 1982
Malsagov, S. A., *Island Hell: A Soviet Prison in the Far North*, trans. F. H. Lyon, London, 1926
Mamaeva, E. A., *Zhizn prozhit*, Moscow, 1998
Mandelstam, Nadezhda, *Hope against Hope*, trans. May Hayward, New York, 1999
Mandelstam, Osip, *Stekla vechnosti* (collected poems), Moscow, 1999
Marchenko, Anatoly, *My Testimony*, trans. Michael Scammell, London, 1969
Marchenko, Anatoly, *To Live Like Everyone*, trans. Paul Goldberg, London, 1989
Matlock, Jack, *Autopsy on an Empire*, New York, 1995
Mazus, Izrail, *Gde ty byl?*, Moscow, 1992
Medvedev, Nikolai, *Uznik GULAGa*, St Petersburg, 1991
Menshagi, V. G., *Vospominaniya*, Paris, 1988
Milyutina, T. P., *Lyudi moei zhizni*, Tartu, 1997
Mindlin, M. B., *Anfas i profil*, Moscow, 1999
Mirek, Alfred, *Tyuremnyi rekviem*, Moscow, 1997
Mirek, Alfred, *Zapiski zaklyuchennogo*, Moscow, 1989
Morozov, Aleksandr, *Devyat stupenei v nebytie*, Saratov, 1991
Mukhina-Petrinskaya, V., *Na ladoni sudby*, Saratov, 1990
My iz Gulaga (anthology), Odessa, 1990
Mysliwski, Wiesław, ed., *Wschodnie losy Polaków*, vols 1–6, Łomża, 1991
Narinsky, A. S., *Vospominaniya glavnogo bukhgaltera GULAGa*, St Petersburg, 1997
Narinsky, A. S., *Vremya tyazhkikh potryasenii*, St Petersburg, 1993
Nazvat poimenno (anthology), Gorky, 1990
Nekipelov, Viktor, *Institute of Fools*, trans. Marco Carynnyk and Marta Horban, London, 1980
Nikolskaya, Anna, *Peredai dalshe*, Alma-Ata, 1989
Noble, John, *I was a Slave in Russia*, New York, 1960
Numerov, Nikolai, *Zolotaya zvezda GULAGa: mezhdu zhiznyu i smertyu*, Moscow, 1995
Okunevskaya, Tatyana, *Tatyanin den*, Moscow, 1998
Olitskaya, Elinor, *Moi vospominaniya*, vols I and II, Frankfurt am Main, 1971
Orlov, Aleksandr, *Tainye istorii stalinskikh prestuplenii*, New York, 1983
Pamyat Kolymy, Magadan, 1990
Panin, Dmitri, *The Notebooks of Sologdin*, New York, 1973
Pashnin, Evgeni, 'Venchannye kolyuchie provoloki', *Vybor*, Moscow, January–March 1988, No. 3
Petrov, Vladimir, *It Happens in Russia*, London, 1951

Petrus, K., *Uzniki kommunizma*, Moscow, 1996

Petyla-2: vospominaniya, ocherki, dokumenty, Volgograd, 1994

Pogodin, Nikolai, 'Aristokraty', *Pesy sovetskikh pisatelei*, Moscow, 1954, pp. 109–83

Pol, I. L., *Oglyanus so skorbyu*, 1991

Polak, L. S., *Bylo tak: ocherki*, Moscow, 1996

Polonsky, V. V., 'Doroga v pyat let v Kazakhstan i obratno', *Istochnik*, 1/1996, pp. 66–77

Pomerants, Grigori, *Zapiski gadkogo utenka*, Moscow, 1998

Porshneva, G. I., *Ya vse zhe zhiv*, Moscow, 1990

Pryadilov, Aleksei, *Zapiski kontrrevolyutsionera*, Moscow, 1999

Ptasnik, Zofia, 'A Polish Woman's Daily Struggle to Survive', *The Sarmatian Review*, vol. XXI, no. 1, January 2002, pp. 846–54

Ratushinskaya, Irina, *Grey is the Colour of Hope*, trans. Alyona Kojevnikov, London, 1988

Rawicz, Slavomir, *The Long Walk*, New York, 1984

Razgon, Lev, *True Stories* [*Nepridumannoe*, Moscow, 1989], trans. John Crowfoot, Dana Point, CA, 1997

Reshetovskaya, Natalya, *Sanya: My Life with Alexander Solzhenitsyn*, trans. Elena Ivanhoff, Indianapolis, 1975

Robinson, Robert, *Black on Red: My 44 Years Inside the Soviet Union*, Washington, DC, 1988

Roeder, Bernhard, *Katorga: An Aspect of Modern Slavery*, trans. Lionel Kochan, London, 1958

Romanov, Grand Duke Gavril Konstantinovich, *V mramornom dvortse*, Dusseldorf, 1993

Rosenberg, Suzanne, *A Soviet Odyssey*, Toronto, 1988

Rossi, Jacques, *Qu'elle était belle cette utopie*, Paris, 1997

Rotfort, M. S., *Kolyma – krugi ada*, Ekaterinburg, 1991

Rozina, Anna, *U pamyati v gostyakh*, St Petersburg, 1992

Rozsas, Janos, 'Iz knigi "Sestra Dusya" ', *Volya*, 2–3, 1994

Ruta, U., *Bozhe kak eshche khotelos zhit*, London 1989

Sadunaite, Nijole, *A Radiance in the Gulag*, trans. Revd Casimir Pugevicius and Marian Skabeikis, Manassas, VA, 1987

Samsonov, V. A., *Parus Podnimayu*, Petrozavodsk, 1993

Samsonov, V. A., *Zhizn prodolzhaetsya*, Petrozavodsk, 1990

Serebryakova, Galina, *Huragan*, trans. Józef Łobodowski, Paris, 1967

Sgovio, Thomas, *Dear America*, Kenmore, NY, 1979

Shalamov, Varlam, *Kolyma Tales*, London, 1994

Shalamov, Varlam, *Neskolko moikh zhiznei*, Moscow, 1996

Sharansky, Natan, *Fear No Evil*, trans. Stefani Hoffman, London, 1988

Shelest, Georgi, 'Kolymskie zapisi', *Znamya*, no. 9, September 1964, pp. 162–80

Shikheeva-Gaister, Inna, *Semeinaya khronika vremen kulta lichnosti*, Moscow, 1998

Shipovskaya, E. A., *Ispoved rytsarya sveta*, Moscow, 1998

Shiryaev, Boris, *Neugasimaya lampada*, Moscow, 1991

Shreider, Mikhail, *NKVD iznutri*, Moscow, 1995

Siemiński, Janusz, *Moja Kołyma*, Warsaw, 1995

Sitko, Leonid, *Gde moi veter?*, Moscow, 1996

Sitko, Leonid, *Tyazhest sveta*, Moscow, 1996

Smith, C. A., *Escape from Paradise*, London, 1954

Snegov, Sergei, *Yazyk, kotoryi nenavidit*, Moscow, 1991

Solzhenitsyn, Alexander *Cancer Ward*, trans. Nicholas Bethell and David Burg, New York, 1995

Solzhenitsyn, Alexander, *The First Circle*, London, 1996

Solzhenitsyn, Alexander, *The Gulag Archipelago*, 3 vols, New York, 1973

Solzhenitsyn, Alexander, *One Day in the Life of Ivan Denisovich*, trans. H. T. Willetts, London, 1996

Sred drugikh imen (poetry anthology), Moscow, 1991

Stajner, Karlo, *Seven Thousand Days in Siberia*, Edinburgh, 1988

Starostin, Nikolai, *Futbol skvoz gody*, Moscow, 1992

Stypułkowski, Zbigniew, *Invitation to Moscow*, London, 1951

Sulimov, Ivan, *Ekho prozhitykh let*, Odessa, 1997

Taylor-Terlecka, Nina, ed., *Gułag polskich poetów: od Komi do Kołymy* (poetry anthology), London, 2001

Tchernavin, Tatiana, *Escape from the Soviets*, New York, 1934

Tchernavin, Vladimir, *I Speak for the Silent*, Boston and New York, 1935

Tiif, O., 'Iz vospominanii i zametok, 1939–1969', *Minuvshee*, vol. 7, 1992, p. 125

Tolstoy, Leo, *Anna Karenina*, trans. Rosemary Edmund, London, 1978

Trubetskoi, Andrei, *Puti neispovedimy*, Moscow, 1997

Trubetskoi, Sergei, *Minuvshee*, Moscow, 1991

Tvardovsky, I. I., *Rodina i chuzhbina*, Smolensk, 1996

Ulyanovskaya, Nadezhda, and Ulyanovskaya, Maya, *Istoriya odnoi semyi*, New York, 1982

Uroki gneva i lyubvi: sbornik vospominanii o godakh repressii, St Petersburg, 1993

Vardi, Aleksandr, *Podkonvoinyi mir*, Berlin, 1971

Veselovsky, B. V., *Skrytaya biografiya*, Moscow, 1996

Vesyolaya, Zayara, *7–35 Vospominaniya*, Moscow, 1990

Vilensky, Simeon, ed., *Osventsim bez pechei*, Moscow, 1996

Vilensky, Simeon, ed., *Till My Tale is Told* [*Dodnes tyagoteet*, Moscow, 1989], Bloomington and Indianapolis, IN, 1999

Vilensky, Simeon, et al., *Deti Gulaga: 1918–1956*, Moscow, 2002

Vins, Georgi, *Evangelie v uzakh*, Kiev, 1994

Vitzhum, Hilda, *Torn Out By the Roots*, trans. Paul Schach, Lincoln, NB, and London, 1993

Vogeler, Robert, *I Was Stalin's Prisoner*, New York, 1951

Vogelfanger, Isaac, *Red Tempest: The Life of a Surgeon in the Gulag*, Montreal, 1996

Voitolovskaya, Adda, *Po sledam sudby moego pokoleniya*, Syktyvkar, 1991

Volkov, Oleg, *Vek nadezhd i krushenii*, Moscow, 1990

Vremya i sudby (anthology), Moscow, 1991

Wat, Aleksander, *My Century: The Odyssey of a Polish Intellectual*, ed. and trans. Richard Lourie, Berkeley, CA, 1988

Waydenfeld, Stefan, *The Ice Road*, Edinburgh and London, 1999

Weissberg, Alexander, *Conspiracy of Silence*, London, 1952

Wigmans, Johan, *Ten Years in Russia and Siberia*, trans. Arnout de Waal, London, 1964

Wu, Harry, *Bitter Winds*, New York, 1994

Yakir, Pyotr, *A Childhood in Prison*, New York, 1973

Yakovenko, M. M., *Agnessa*, Moscow, 1997

Yasny, V. K., *God rozhdeniya – devyatsot semnadtsatyi*, Moscow, 1997

Zabolotsky, N. A., 'Istoriya moego zaklyucheniya', *Minuvshee*, vol. 2, 1986

Zajdlerowa, Zoe, *The Dark Side of the Moon*, ed. John Coutouvidis and Thomas Lane, London, 1989

Zarod, Kazimierz, *Inside Stalin's Gulag*, Lewes, Sussex, 1990

Zernova, Ruf, *Eto bylo pri nas*, Jerusalem, 1988

Zhenov, Georgi, *Sanochki*, Moscow, 1997

Zhigulin, Anatoly, *Chernye kamni*, Moscow, 1996

Znamenskaya, A. N., *Vospominaniya*, St Petersburg, 1997

Unpublished Memoirs

Baitalsky, Mikhail, Memorial Archive, 2/1/8
Bien, George, Hoover Institution
Cherkhanov, P. D., Memorial Archive, 2/1/127
Feldgun, Georgi, collection of Novosibirsk Memorial
Gogua, I. K., Memorial Archive, 1/3/18
Gursky, K. P., Memorial Archive, 2/1/14–17
Kogan, Mark, Memorial Archive, 2/2/46–7
Kuperman, Yakov, M., Memorial Archive, 2/1/77
Lahti, Suoma Laine, collection of Reuben Rajala
Lvov, E. M., Memorial Archive, 2/1/84
Marchenko, Zoya, in the author's collection
Martyukhin, Lev Nikolaevich, collection of Simeon Vilensky (Vozvrashchenie)
Neapolitanskaya, V. S., Memorial Archive, 3/3/39
Sandratskaya, Mariya, Memorial Archive, 2/105/1
Shreider, M. P., Memorial Archive, 2/2/100–102
Torbin, S. S., Memorial Archive, 2/2/91
Usova, Zinaida, Memorial Archive, 2/1/118
Warwick, Walter, collection of Reuben Rajala
Zgornicki, George Victor, tape sent to the author, April 1998

Works of Reference

Abramkin, V. F., and Chesnokova, V. F., *Ugolovnaya Rossiya, tyurmi i lagerya*, vol. I, Moscow, 1993
Adams, Bruce, *The Politics of Punishment: Prisoner Reform in Russia, 1863–1917*, DeKalb, IL, 1996
Adler, Nanci, *The Gulag Survivor*, New Brunswick, NJ, 2002
Agnew, Jeremy, and McDermott, Kevin, *The Comintern*, New York, 1997
Alekseeva, Lyudmila, *Istoriya inakomysliya v SSSR*, Moscow (online at www.memo.ru/history/diss/books)
Amis, Martin, *Koba the Dread: Laughter and the Twenty Million*, London, 2002
Anders, Władysław, *Bez ostatniego rozdziału: wspomnienia z lat 1939–1946*, Newtown, Montgomeryshire, 1949
Andrew, Christopher, and Gordievsky, Oleg, *KGB: The Inside Story*, New York, 1990
Anisimov, Evgenii, *The Reforms of Peter the Great: Progress through Coercion in Russia*, Armonk, NY, and London, 1993
Antonov-Ovseenko, Anton, *Lavrentii Beriya*, Krasnodar, 1993
Antonov-Ovseenko, Anton, *The Time of Stalin*, New York, 1980
Applebaum, Anne, 'A History of Horror', *The New York Review of Books*, 18 October 2001
Applebaum, Anne, 'Inside the Gulag', *The New York Review of Books*, 15 June 2000
Arendt, Hannah, *The Origins of Totalitarianism*, New York, 1951
Artizov, A., et al., *Reabilitatsiya, kak eto bylo: dokumenty*, Moscow, 2000
Averbakh, I. L., *Ot prestupleniya k trudu*, Moscow, 1936
Bacon, Edwin, *The Gulag at War*, London, 1994
Baranov, Vadim, *Gorkii bez grima*, Moscow, 1996
Baron, Nick, 'Conflict and Complicity: The Expansion of the Karelian Gulag, 1923–1933', *Cahiers du Monde Russe*, 42/2–4, April–December 2001, pp. 615–48

Bateson, Edward, and Pim, Sir Alan, *Report on Russian Timber Camps*, London, 1931

Bazarov, Aleksandr, *Durelom, ili, Gospoda kolkhozniki*, Kurgan, 1988

Bazunov, V. V., and Detkov, M. G., *Tyurmy NKVD-MVD SSSR v karatelnoi sisteme sovetskogo gosudarstva*, Moscow, 2000

Beck, F., and Godin, W., *Russian Purge and the Extraction of Confession*, trans. Eric Mosbacher and David Porter, London, 1951

Beevor, Antony, *Stalingrad*, London, 1998

Beichman, Arnold, and Bernstam, Mikhail, *Andropov: New Challenge to the West*, New York, 1983

Berdinskikh, Viktor, *Vyatlag*, Kirov, 1998

Berliner, Joseph, *Factory and Manager in the Soviet Union*, Cambridge, 1957

Besançon, Alain, *The Rise of the Gulag: Intellectual Origins of Leninism*, New York, 1981

Besançon, Alain, *Le tsarevitch immolé*, Paris, 1991

Bethell, Nicholas, *The Last Secret*, New York, 1974

Bettelheim, Bruno, *The Informed Heart*, London, 1991

Binner, Rolf, Junge, Marc, and Martin, Terry, 'The Great Terror in the Provinces of the USSR: A Cooperative Bibliography', *Cahiers du Monde Russe*, 42/2–4, April–December 2001

Blandy, Charles, *The Meskhetians: Turks or Georgians? A People without a Homeland*, Camberley, 1998

Bobrick, Benson, *East of the Sun: The Conquest and Settlement of Siberia*, London, 1992

'Borba za GPU', *Sotsialisticheskii Vestnik*, no. 14–15, August 1933

Brackman, Roman, *The Secret File of Joseph Stalin*, London and Portland, OR, 2001

Brodksy, Juri, *Solovki: Le Isole del Martirio*, Rome, 1998

Brodksy, Juri, and Owsiany, Helena, *Skazani jako szpiedzy Watykanu*, Warsaw, 1998

Brown, Archie, *The Gorbachev Factor*, Oxford, 1996

Browne, Michael, ed., *Ferment in the Ukraine*, Woodhaven, NY, 1971

Bukovsky, Vladimir, *Moskovskii protsess*, Paris, 1996

Bullock, Alan, *Hitler and Stalin: Parallel Lives*, London, 1993

Bunyan, James, *The Origin of Forced Labour in the Soviet State*, Baltimore, 1967

Burds, Jeffrey, 'AGENTURA: Soviet Informants' Networks and the Ukrainian Rebel Underground in Galicia, 1944–1948', *East European Politics and Societies*, 11/1, Winter, 1997, pp. 89–130

Butyrsky, Fedor, and Karyshev, Valeri, *Moskva tyuremnaya*, Moscow, 1998

Cahiers du samizdat, vols I–XV, from 1972, Brussels (LOC)

Celmina, Helene, *Women in Soviet Prisons*, New York, 1985

Chekhov, Anton, *A Journey to Sakhalin*, trans. Brian Reeve, Cambridge, 1993

Chornovil, Vyacheslav, *The Chornovil Papers*, New York, 1968

Chronicle of Current Events, nos 28–64 (1972–82) Amnesty International Publications, LOC

Chukhin, Ivan, 'Dva dokumenta komissii A. M. Shanina na Solovkakh', *Zvenya*, vol. I, Moscow, 1991, pp. 359–81

Chukhin, Ivan, *Kanaloarmeetsi*, Petrozavodsk, 1990

Ciesielski, Stanisław, *Polacy w Kazachstanie w latach 1940–1946*, Wrocław, 1996

Cohen, Stephen F., ed., *An End to Silence: Uncensored Opinion in the Soviet Union*, New York and London, 1982

Commission on Security and Cooperation in Europe, One Hundredth Congress, First Session, 15 May 1987 (Testimony of Aleksandr Shatravka and Dr Anatoly Koryagin)

Committee on the Judiciary, Hearings before the Subcommittee to investigate the Administration of the Internal Security Act and other Internal Security Laws of the Committee on the Judiciary, US Senate, Ninety-Third Congress, First Session, 1 February 1973 (Testimony of Avraham Shifrin)

Committee on Un-American Activities, US House of Representatives, Eighty-Sixth Congress, Second Session, 4 April 1960 (Testimony of Adam Galinski)

Conquest, Robert, *The Great Terror: A Reassessment*, London, 1992

Conquest, Robert, *Harvest of Sorrow*, London, 1988

Conquest, Robert, *Kolyma: The Arctic Death Camps*, New York, 1978

Conquest, Robert, *The Soviet Deportation of Nationalities*, London, 1960

Conquest, Robert, *Stalin: Breaker of Nations*, London, 1993

Courtois, Stephane, et al., eds, *The Black Book of Communism*, trans. Jonathan Murphy, Cambridge, 1999

Craveri, Marta, 'Krizis Gulaga: kengirskoe vosstanie 1954 goda v dokumentakh MVD', *Cahiers du Monde Russe*, XXXVI (3), July–September 1995, pp. 319–44

Craveri, Marta, and Khlevnyuk, Oleg, 'Krizis ekonomiki MVD (konets 1940-x–1950-e gody)', *Cahiers du Monde Russe*, XXXVI (1–2), January–June 1995, pp. 179–90

Dagor, K., 'Magadan', *Sovietland*, no. 4, April 1939

Dallin, Alexander, and Firsov, F. L., eds, *Dmitrov and Stalin: 1934–1943, Letters from the Soviet Archives*, New Haven and London, 2000

Dallin, David, and Nicolaevsky, Boris, *Forced Labour in Soviet Russia*, London, 1948

Dawidowicz, Lucy, *The War against the Jews, 1933–1945*, London, 1990

Dekrety sovetskoi vlasti, Moscow, 1957

Deutscher, Isaac, *Stalin: A Political Biography*, London, 1949

Dobrovolsky, Aleksandr, 'Mertvaya doroga', *Otechestvo*, vol. V, 1994, pp. 193–210

Dobrovolsky, I. V., ed., *Gulag: ego stroiteli, obitateli, i geroi*, Moscow, 1998

Doloi, Yuri, *Krasnyi terror na severe*, Arkhangelsk, 1993

Dorofeev, Oleg, 'Kuzina Gitlera', *Novaya Izvestiya*, 3 April 1998, p. 7

Dryakhlitsin, Dmitri, 'Periodicheskaya pechat Arkhipelaga', *Sever*, vol. 9, 1990

Dugin, Aleksandr, 'Gulag glazami istorika', *Soyuz*, 9 February 1990, p. 16

Dugin, Aleksandr, 'Stalinizm: legendy i fakty', *Slovo*, no. 7, 1990, p. 40

Duguet, Raymond, *Un bagne en Russie rouge*, Paris, 1927

Ebon, Martin, *The Andropov File*, New York, 1983

Ekonomika Gulaga i ego rol v razvitii strany, 1930-e gody: sbornik dokumentov, Moscow, 1998

Elantseva, O. P., 'Kto i kak stroil BAM v 30-e gody', *Otechestvennye Arkhivy*, no. 5, 1992, pp. 71–81

Elletson, Howard, *The General against the Kremlin: Alexander Lebed, Power and Illusion*, London, 1998

Fainsod, Merle, *How Russia is Ruled*, Cambridge, 1962

Figes, Orlando, *A People's Tragedy: The Russian Revolution, 1891–1924*, London, 1996

Filene, Peter, ed., *American Views of Soviet Russia*, Homewood, IL, 1968

Fireside, Harvey, *Soviet Psychoprisons*, New York and London, 1979

Fitzpatrick, Sheila, *Everyday Stalinism*, New York, 1999

Fitzpatrick, Sheila, *Stalin's Peasants: Resistance and Survival in the Russian Village after Collectivization*, New York, 1994

Foucault, Michel, *Discipline and Punish: The Birth of the Prison*, trans. Alan Sheridan, New York, 1978

Gelb, Michael, 'Karelian Fever: The Finnish Immigrant Community During Stalin's Purges', *Europe-Asia Studies* 45, no. 6, 1993, pp. 1091–116

Geller, Mikhail, *Kontsentratsionnyi mir i sovetskaya literatura*, London, 1974

Genrikh Yagoda: Narkom Vnutrennikh Del SSR, generalnyi komissar gosudarstvennoi bezopasnosti: sbornik dokumentov, Kazan, 1997

Getty, J. Arch, *Origins of the Great Purges*, Cambridge, 1985

Getty, J. Arch, and Manning, Roberta, eds, *Stalinist Terror: New Perspectives*, Cambridge, 1993

Getty, J. Arch, and Naumov, Oleg, eds, *The Road to Terror: Stalin and the Self-Destruction of the Bolsheviks, 1932–1939*, New Haven and London, 1999

Getty, J. Arch, Ritterspoon, Gabor T., and Zemskov, Viktor, 'Victims of the Soviet Penal System in the Pre-war Years', *American Historical Review*, October 1993

Gilbert, Martin, *The Holocaust: The Jewish Tragedy*, London, 1978

Giżejewska, Małgorzata, *Polacy na Kołymie: 1940–1943*, Warsaw, 1997

Głowacki, Albin, *Sowieci wobec Polaków: na ziemiach wschodnich II Rzeczypospolitej, 1939–1941*, Łódź, 1998

Goldhagen, Daniel, *Hitler's Willing Executioners*, New York, 1996

Golovanov, Yaroslav, 'Katastrofa', *Znamya*, January 1990, pp. 107–50; also February 1990, pp. 104–49

Gorky, Maxim, ed., *Belomor [Kanal imeni Stalina]*, New York, 1935

Gross, Jan Tomasz, *Revolution from Abroad: The Soviet Conquest of Poland's Western Ukraine and Western Belorussia*, Princeton, 1988

Guryanov, Aleksandr, ed., *Repressii protiv polyakov i polskikh grazhdan*, Moscow, 1997

Guryanov, Aleksandr, Kokurin, Aleksandr, and Popiński, Krzysztof, eds, *Drogi śmierci*, Warsaw, 1995

Harris, James R., 'Growth of the Gulag: Forced Labour in the Urals Region, 1929–1931', *The Russian Review*, no. 56, April 1997, pp. 265–80

Hill, Christopher, ed. (for Amnesty International), *Rights and Wrongs: Some Essays on Human Rights*, London, 1969

Hochschild, Adam, *The Unquiet Ghost: Russians Remember Stalin*, New York, 1994

Hopkins, Mark, *Russia's Underground Press*, New York, 1983

Hosking, Geoffrey, ed., *The Road to Post-Communism: Independent Political Movements in the Soviet Union, 1985–1991*, London, 1992

Hosking, Geoffrey, *Russia: People and Empire, 1552–1917*, London, 1997

Inside Soviet Slave Labour Camps, 1939–1942: An Analysis of Written Statements by 9,200 Former Prisoners, Washington, DC, 1952

Ioffe, Veniamin, 'FSB: delo i slovo', *Novye etyudy ob optimizme*, St Petersburg, 1995, pp. 120–61

Istoriya otechestva v dokumentakh, Volume 2: 1921–1939, Moscow, 1994

Ivanova, Galina M., *Labor Camp Socialism*, trans. Carol Flath, Armonk, NY, and London, 2000

Ivanova, Galina M., 'Poslevoennye repressii i GULAG', *Stalin i kholodnaya voina*, Moscow, 1998, pp. 245–73

Ivnitsky, N. A., *Kollektivizatsiya i raskulachivanie, nachalo 30-kh gg*, Moscow, 1996

Iwanow, Mikołaj, *Pierwszy naród ukarany*, Warsaw and Wrocław, 1991

Jakobson, Michael, *Origins of the Gulag: The Soviet Prison Camp System, 1917–1934*, Lexington, KY, 1993

Jansen, Marc, and Petrov, Nikita, *Stalin's Loyal Executioner: People's Commissar Nikolai Ezhov*, Stanford, CA 2002

Johnson, Paul, *The Intellectuals*, London, 1988

Kaczyńska, Elżbieta, *Syberia: największe więzienie świata (1815–1914)*, Warsaw, 1991

Kaiser, Robert, *Why Gorbachev Happened*, New York, 1991

Kalbarczyk, Sławomir, *Wykaz łagrów sowieckich*, Warsaw, 1997

Kaneva, A. N., 'Ukhtpechlag, 1929–1938', *Zvenya*, vol. I, Moscow, 1991, pp. 331–54

Kapuściński, Ryszard, *Imperium*, London, 1994

Karlov, S. V., and Tuguzhekova, V. N., *Repressii v Khakasii*, Abakan, 1998

Karta (historical journal), vols 1–31, Warsaw, 1991–2001

Kennan, George, *Siberia and the Exile System*, London, 1981

Kerber, L. L., *Stalin's Aviation Gulag*, Washington, D C, and London, 1996

Khetso, Geir, *Maksim Gorkii: sudba pisatelya*, Moscow, 1997

Khlevnyuk, Oleg, 'L. P. Beriya: predely istoricheskoi "reabilitatsii"', in G. A. Bordyugov, ed., *Istoricheskie issledovaniya v Rossii. Tendentsii poslednikh let*, Moscow, 1996, pp. 139–54

Khlevnyuk, Oleg, 'Prinuditelnyi trud v ekonomike SSSR: 1929–1941 gody', *Svobadnaya Mysl*, no. 13, 1992, pp. 73–84

Khlevnyuk, Oleg, 1937: *Stalin, NKVD i sovetskoye obshchestvo*, Moscow, 1992

Klehr, Harvey, Haynes, John Earl, and Anderson, Kyrill, eds, *The Soviet World of American Communism*, New Haven and London, 1998

Klehr, Harvey, Haynes, John Earl, and Firsov, Fridrikh, *The Secret World of American Communism*, New Haven and London, 1995

Klimovich, Rygor, *Knets Gorlaga*, Minsk, 1999

Knight, Amy, *Beria: Stalin's First Lieutenant*, Princeton, 1993

Knight, Amy, 'The Truth about Wallenberg', *The New York Review of Books*, vol. XLVIII, no. 14, 20 September 2001, pp. 47–50

Knight, Amy, *Who Killed Kirov?*, New York, 1999

Koestler, Arthur, *Darkness at Noon*, trans. Daphne Hardy, New York, 1941

Kokurin, Aleksandr, 'Gulag: struktura i kadry', a series of articles appearing in *Svobodnaya Mysl*, from 1997 to 2002. From 1997 (article 1), Kokurin's co-author was Nikita Petrov; from 2000 (article 10) his co-author was Yuri Morukov

Kokurin, Aleksandr, 'Osoboe tekhnicheskoe byuro NKVD SSSR', *Istoricheskii Arkhiv*, no. 1, 1999, pp. 85–99

Kokurin, Aleksandr, 'Vosstanie v Steplage', *Otechestvennye Arkhivy*, no. 4, 1994, pp. 33–82

Kokurin, Aleksandr, and Morukov, Yuri, 'Tunnel pod Tatarskim prolivom: neosushchestvlennyi proekt', *Istoricheskii Arkhiv*, no. 6, June 2001, pp. 41–78

Kokurin, Aleksandr, and Petrov, Nikita, *Gulag, 1917–1960: dokumenty*, Moscow, 2000

Kokurin, Aleksandr, and Petrov, Nikita, *Lubyanka: spravochnik*, Moscow, 1997

Korni travy: sbornik statei molodykh istorikov, Moscow, 1996

Kosyk, Volodymyr, *Concentration Camps in the USSR*, London, 1962

Kotek, Joel, and Rigoulot, Pierre, *Le siècle des camps*, Paris, 2001

Kotkin, Stephen, *Magnetic Mountain*, Berkeley, CA, 1995

Kozlov, A. G., *Ogni lagernoi rampy*, Magadan, 1992

Kozlov, A. G., 'Sevvostlag NKVD SSSR: 1937–1941', *Istoricheskie issledovaniya na severe dalnego vostoka*, Magadan, 2000

Krasikov, N., 'Solovki', *Izvestiya*, no. 236 (2271), 15 October 1924

Krasilnikov, S. A., 'Rozhdenie Gulaga: diskusii v verkhnikh eshelonakh vlasti', *Istoricheskii Arkhiv*, no. 4, July/August 1997, pp. 142–56

Krasilnikov, S. A., et al., eds, *Spetspereselentsy v Zapadnoi Sibiri, 1930 g.–vesna 1931 g.*, Novosibirsk, 1992

Krasilnikov, S. A., et al., eds, *Spetspereselentsy v Zapadnoi Sibiri, vesna 1931 g.–nachalo 1933 g.* Novosibirsk, 1993

Krasilnikov, S. A., et al., eds, *Spetspereselentsy v Zapadnoi Sibiri, 1933–1938*, Novosibirsk, 1996

Kruglov, A. K., *Kak sozdavalas atomnaya promyshlennost v SSSR*, Moscow, 1995

Kuchin, S. P., *Istoriya goroda Krasonyarsk-26: 'Granitnyi iz 505'*, Zheleznogorsk, 1994

Kuchin, S. P., *Polyanskii ITL*, Zheleznogorsk, 1999

Kulikov, K. I., *Delo SOFIN*, Izhevsk, 1997

Kuzmina, Marina, *Ya pomnyu tot vaninskii port*, Komsomolsk-na-Amure, 2001

Kuznetsov, S. I., 'The Situation of Japanese Prisoners of War in Soviet Camps (1945–1956)', *Journal of Slavic Military Studies*, vol. 8, no. 3, pp. 613–18

Lebedeva, Natalya, *Katyn: prestuplenie protiv chelovechestva*, Moscow, 1994

Ledeneva, Alena, *Russia's Economy of Favors: Blat, Networking and Informal Exchange*, Cambridge, 1998

Leggett, George, *The Cheka: Lenin's Political Police*, Oxford, 1981

Letters from Russian Prisons, International Committee for Political Prisoners, New York, 1925

Levye esery i VChK: sbornik dokumentov, Kazan, 1996

Lieven, Anatol, *The Baltic Revolution*, New Haven and London, 1993

Lieven, Anatol, *Chechnya: Tombstone of Russian Power*, New Haven and London, 1998

Lih, Lars, Naumov, Oleg, and Khlevnyuk, Oleg, eds, *Stalin's Letters to Molotov*, New Haven and London, 1995

Lin, George, 'Fighting in Vain: NKVD RSFSR in the 1920s', Ph.D. dissertation, Stanford University, 1997

Lipshits, Evgeniya, *Dokumentalnyi urod XX veka*, Tel Aviv, 1997

Litvinov, Pavel, *The Demonstration in Pushkin Square*, trans. Manya Harari, London, 1969

Litvinov, Pavel, *The Trial of the Four: The Case of Galanskov, Ginzburg, Dobrovolsky and Lashkova*, trans. Janis Sapiets, Hilary Sternberg and Daniel Weissbort, ed. Peter Reddaway, New York, 1972

MacQueen, Angus, 'Survivors', *Granta* 64, Winter 1998, pp. 38–53

Maksheeva, V. N., ed., *Narymskaya khronika, 1930–1945*, Moscow, 1997

Makurov, V. G., *Gulag v Karelii: sbornik dokumentov i materialov, 1930–1941*, Petrozavodsk, 1992

Malia, Martin, 'Judging Nazism and Communism', *The National Interest*, no. 64, Fall 2002, pp. 63–78

Martin, Terry, *The Affirmative Action Empire: Nations and Nationalism in the USSR*, Ithaca, NY, 2001

Martin, Terry, 'Stalinist Forced Relocation Policies: Patterns, Causes and Consequences', in *Demography and National Security*, Myron Weiner and Sharon Russell, eds, New York, 2001

Martin, Terry, 'Un'interpretazione contestuale alla luce delle nuove richerche' ('The Great Terror: A Contextual Interpretation in Light of New Research'), *Storica*, 18/2000, pp. 22–37

Medvedev, Roy, *Let History Judge*, trans. Colleen Taylor, New York, 1972

Melgunov, Sergei, *The Red Terror in Russia*, London and Toronto, 1926

Melnik, A., and Soshina, A., 'Zayavleniya politzaklyuchennykh Petrominska i Solovkov', *Zvenya*, vol. I, Moscow, 1991, pp. 245–51

Melnik, A., Soshina, A., Reznikova, I., and Reznikov, A., 'Materialy k istoriko-geograficheskomu atlasu Solovkov', *Zvenya*, vol. I, Moscow, 1991, pp. 303–30

Memorialnoe kladbishche Sandormokh: 1937, 27 oktyabrya – 4 noyabrya (Solovetskii etap), St Petersburg, 1997

Merridale, Catherine, *Night of Stone: Death and Memory in Russia*, London, 2000

Minuvshee, a series of bound history anthologies, published first in Paris, later in Moscow, from the late 1980s and through the 1990s

Misiunas, Romuald, and Taagepera, Rein, *The Baltic States: Years of Dependence: 1940–1990*, Berkeley and Los Angeles, 1993

Mitin, V. A., 'Vaigachskaya ekspeditsiya (1930–1936 gg.)', *Gulag na severe i ego posledstviya*, Arkhangelsk, 1992

Mora, Sylwester (S. Starzewski), and Zwierniak, Piotr (Kazimierz Zamorski), *Sprawiedliwość sowiecka*, Rome, 1945

Morozov, N. A., *GULAG v Komi krae, 1929–1956*, Syktyvkar, 1997

Morozov, N. A., *Osobye lagerya MVD SSSR v Komi ASSR (1948–1954 g)*, Syktyvkar, 1998

Morozov, N. A., and Rogachev, M. B., 'Gulag v Komi ASSR', *Otechestvennye Arkhivy*, no. 2, 1995, pp. 182–7

Moskoff, William, *The Bread of Affliction: The Food Supply in the USSR during World War II*, Cambridge, 1990

Moynahan, Brian, *The Russian Century*, New York, 1994

Naimark, Norman, *Fires of Hatred: Ethnic Cleansing in Twentieth-Century Europe*, Cambridge and London, 2001

Naimark, Norman, *The Russians in Germany*, Cambridge, 1995

Naumov, V., and Rubinstein, Joshua, eds, *Stalin's Secret Pogrom*, New Haven and London, 2001

Naumov, V., and Sigachev, Y., eds, *Lavrentii Beriya, 1953: dokumenty*, Moscow, 1999

Nerler, P., 'S gurboi i gurtom: khronika poslednego goda zhizni O. E. Mandelshtama', *Minuvshee*, vol. 8, 1992

Nevsky, G. V., et al., eds, *Pokayanie: martirolog*, vols 1–3, Syktyvkar, 1998

Nogtev, A., 'Solovki', *Ekran*, no. 2 (39), 1926, pp. 4–5

Nogtev, A., 'USLON: ego istorii, tseli i zadachi', *Solovetskie Ostrova*, no. 2–3, February/March 1930

Nordlander, David, 'Capital of the Gulag: Magadan in the Early Stalin Era, 1929–1941', Ph.D. dissertation, UNC Chapel Hill, 1997

Nordlander, David, 'Magadan and the Evolution of the Dalstroi Bosses in the 1930s', *Cahiers du Monde Russe*, 42/2–4, April–December 2001, pp. 649–65

Nordlander, David, 'Origins of a Gulag Capital: Magadan and Stalinist Control in the Early 1930s', *Slavic Review*, 57, no. 4, Winter 1998, pp. 791–812

'Not Part of My Sentence: Violations of the Human Rights of Women in Custody', Amnesty International Report, Amnesty International USA, XX, 1999

Obozy koncentracyjne OGPU w ZSRR, Warsaw, 1998

Ogawa, Haruhisa, and Yoon, Benjamin H., *Voices from the North Korean Gulag*, Seoul, 1998

Okhotin, N. G., and Roginsky, A. B., eds, *Sistema ispravitelno-trudovykh lagerei v SSSR, 1923–1960: spravochnik*, Moscow, 1998

Olhovych, Orest, ed., *An Interview with Political Prisoners in a Soviet Perm Camp*, trans. Taras Drozd, Baltimore, 1975

Organy Gosudarstvennoi Bezopasnosti SSSR v Velikoi Otechestvennoi Voine: sbornik dokumentov, tom I: Nakanune, Moscow, 1995

Osipova, Irina, *Khotelos by vsekh poimenno nazvat*, Moscow, 1993

Overy, Richard, *Russia's War*, London, 1997

Paczkowski, Andrzej, ed., *Powrót żołnierzy AK z sowieckich łagrów*, Warsaw, 1995

Pamyat – a series of bound history anthologies, published from the late 1970s in the US and Paris

Papkov, S. A., 'Lagernaya sistema i prinuditelnyi trud v Sibirii i na Dalnem Vostoke v 1929–1941 g.', *Vozvrashchenie pamyati*, vol. III, pp. 40–57

Parrish, Michael, *The Lesser Terror: Soviet State Security, 1939–1953*, Westport, CT, and London, 1996

Payne, Matthew, *Stalin's Railroad: Turksib and the Building of Socialism*, Pittsburgh, 2001

Petrov, Nikita, 'Čekisti e il secondino: due diversi destini', *Nazismo, Fascismo e Comunismo*, Milan, 1998, pp. 145–64

Petrov, Nikita, 'Polska operacja NKWD', *Karta* 11, 1993, pp. 24–43

Petrov, Nikita, and Skorkin, K. V., eds, *Kto rukovodil NKVD: 1934–1941*, Moscow, 1999

Piesakowski, Tomasz, *The Fate of Poles in the USSR, 1939–1989*, London, 1990

Pikhoya, R. G., *Sovetskii Soyuz: istoriya vlasti, 1945–1991*, Novosibirsk, 2000

Pikhoya, R. G., et al., eds, *Katyn: dokumenty*, Moscow, 1999

Pipes, Richard, *The Russian Revolution*, New York, 1990

Pohl, J. Otto, 'The Deportation and Fate of the Crimean Tartars', a paper presented at the Fifth Annual World Convention for the Association for the Study of Nationalities, published online at www.iccrimea.org/jopohl.html

Pohl, J. Otto, *The Stalinist Penal System*, Jefferson, NC, and London, 1997

Poleshchikov, V. M., *Za semyu pechatyami*, Syktyvkar, 1995

Polyan, Pavel, *Ne po svoei vole: istoriya i geografiya prinuditelnykh migratsii v SSSR*, Moscow, 2001

Popov, V. P., 'Neizvestnaya initsiativa Khrushcheva (o podgotovke ukaza 1948 g. o vyselenii krestyan)', *Otechestvennye Arkhivy*, no. 2, 1993, pp. 31–8

Popova, T. U., *Sudba: rodnykh L. Martova v Rossii posle 1917 goda*, Moscow, 1996

'Posetiteli kabineta I. V. Stalina', *Istoricheskii Arkhiv*, no. 4, 1998, p. 180

Prisoners of Conscience in the USSR: Their Treatment and Conditions, Amnesty International report, 1975

Raizman, D., *Maldyak v zhizni koroleva*, Magadan, 1999

Rapoport, Yakov, *The Doctors' Plot: Stalin's Last Crime*, London, 1991

Reagan, Ronald, *An American Life*, New York, 1990

Reavey, George, ed. and trans., *The New Russian Poets, 1953–1968: An Anthology*, London and Boston, 1981

Reddaway, Peter, 'Dissent in the Soviet Union', *Problems of Communism*, 32/6, November–December 1983, pp. 1–15

Reddaway, Peter, *The Forced Labour Camps in the USSR Today: An Unrecognized Example of Modern Inhumanity*, International Committee for the Defence of Human Rights in the USSR, 1973

Reddaway, Peter, *Uncensored Russia: Protest and Dissent in the Soviet Union*, New York, 1972

Reddaway, Peter, and Bloch, Sidney, *Psychiatric Terror: How Soviet Psychiatry is Used to Suppress Dissent*, New York, 1977

Remnick, David, *Lenin's Tomb*, New York, 1994

Revel, Jean-François, *The Totalitarian Temptation*, trans. D. Hapgood, London, 1977

Reznikova, Irina, *Pravoslavie na Solovkakh*, St Petersburg, 1994

Rigoulot, Pierre, *Des Français au Goulag, 1917–1984*, Paris, 1984

Rigoulot, Pierre, *Les Paupières Lourdes*, Paris, 1991

Rogovin, Vadim, *1937*, Moscow, 1996

Rossi, Jacques, *The Gulag Handbook*, trans. William Burhans, New York, 1989

Rothberg, Abraham, *The Heirs of Stalin: Dissidence and the Soviet Regime, 1953–1970*, Ithaca, NY, and London, 1972

Rousset, David, *Police-State Methods in the Soviet Union*, International Commission Against Forced-Labour Camps, Boston, 1953

Rozanov, Mikhail, *Solovetskii kontslager v monastire*, Moscow, 1979

Rubinstein, Joshua, *Soviet Dissidents*, Boston, 1980

Ruud, Charles, and Stepanov, Sergei, *Fontanka 16: The Tsar's Secret Police*, Montreal, 1999

Sabbo, Hilda, ed., *Voimatu Vaikida/Nevozmozhno molchat*, Tallinn, 1996

Saunders, Kate, *Eighteen Layers of Hell*, New York, 1966

Sbornik zakonodatelnykh i normativnykh aktov o repressiyakh i reabilitatsii zhertv politicheskikh repressii, Verkhovnyi Sovet Rossiiskoi Federatsii, Moscow, 1993

Scammell, Michael, *Solzhenitsyn: A Biography*, New York and London, 1984

Scammell, Michael, ed., *The Solzhenitsyn Files*, Chicago, 1995

Sereny, Gitta, *Into That Darkness*, London, 1974

Serge, Victor, *Russia Twenty Years After*, trans. Max Shactman, New Jersey, 1996

Sergeev, I. N., *Tsaritsyno, Sukhanovo: lyudi, sobytiya, fakty*, Moscow, 1998

Service, Robert, *A History of Twentieth-Century Russia*, London, 1997

Service, Robert, *Lenin: A Biography*, London, 2000

Seton-Watson, Hugh, *The Russian Empire, 1801–1917*, Oxford, 1990

Shentalinsky, Vitaly, *The KGB's Literary Archive*, trans. John Crowfoot, London, 1993

Sherbakova, I. L., ed., *Nakazannyi narod: repressii protiv rossiiskikh nemtsev*, Moscow, 1999

Shmirov, Viktor, 'Lager kak model realnosti', speech made at the conference 'Sudba Rossii v kontekste mirovoi istorii dvadtsatogo veka', Moscow, 17 October 1999

Silvester, Christopher, ed., *The Penguin Book of Interviews*, London, 1993

Slave Labor in Russia, American Federation of Labor, excerpts from the report of the International Labor Relations Committee of the 66th convention of the American Federation of Labor, San Francisco, CA, 6–16 October 1947

Slovar tyuremno-lagerno-blatnogo zhargona, Moscow, 1992

Smith, Kathleen, *Remember Stalin's Victims*, Ithaca, NY, 1996

Sobolev, S. A., et al., *Lubyanka, 2*, Moscow, 1999

Sobranie dokumentov samizdata, Radio Liberty Committee, Munich, Germany (LOC)

Sofsky, Wolfgang, *The Order of Terror: The Concentration Camp*, trans. William Templer, Princeton, 1997

Soina, E. G., *K istorii pobega solovetskikh uznikov v Finlyandiyu: novye materialy*, unpublished manuscript

Solomon, Peter, *Soviet Criminal Justice Under Stalin*, Cambridge, 1996

Stalin's Slave Camps, Brussels, International Confederation of Free Trade Unions, 1951

Stephan, John, *The Russian Far East: A History*, Stanford, 1994

Stephan, John, *Sakhalin: A History*, Oxford, 1971

Strods, Dr Heinrich, 'The USSR MGB's Top Secret Operation "Pirboi" ', Riga, the Occupation Museum of Latvia. Originally published in *Genocidas ir rezistencija*, no. 2, 1997, pp. 66–76.

Sutherland, Christine, *The Princess of Siberia*, London, 1985

Sword, Keith, *Deportation and Exile: Poles in the Soviet Union, 1939–48*, New York, 1994

Teatr Gulaga, Moscow, 1995

Thomas, D. M., *Alexander Solzhenitsyn: A Century in His Life*, London, 1998

Thurston, Robert, *Life and Terror in Stalin's Russia, 1934–1941*, New Haven and London, 1996

Todorov, Tzvetan, *Facing the Extreme*, trans. Arthur Denner and Abigail Pollak, New York, 1996

Todorov, Tzvetan, *Voices from the Gulag*, trans. Robert Zaretsky, University Park, PA, 1999

Tokes, Rudolf, *Dissent in the USSR*, Baltimore, 1975

Tolczyk, Dariusz, *See No Evil: Literary Cover-Ups and Discoveries of the Soviet Camp Experience*, New Haven and London, 1999

Tolstoy, Nikolai, *Stalin's Secret War*, New York, 1981

Tolstoy, Nikolai, *Victims of Yalta*, New York, 1977

Tsigankov, Anatoly, ed., *Ikh nazvali KR*, Petrozavodsk, 1992

Tucker, Robert, *Stalin as a Revolutionary: 1879–1929*, New York, 1973

Tucker, Robert, *Stalin in Power: The Revolution from Above*, New York, 1990

Tuguzhekova, V. N., and Karlov, S. V., eds, *Repressii v Khakasii*, Abakan, 1998

Uimanov, V. N., ed., *Repressii: kak eto bylo*, Tomsk, 1995

USSR: Human Rights in a Time of Change, Amnesty International publications, October 1989

'USSR Labour Camps', Hearings before the Subcommittee to investigate the Administration of the Internal Security Act and other Internal Security Laws of the Committee on the Judiciary, US Senate, Ninety-Third Congress, First Session, 1 February 1973

Varese, Frederico, *The Russian Mafia*, Oxford, 2001

Vidal, Gore, *The Last Empire*, London, 2002

Vilensky, Simeon, ed., *Soprotivlenie v GULAGe*, Moscow, 1992

Viola, Lynne, 'The Role of the OGPU in Dekulakization, Mass Deportations, and Special Resettlement in 1930', *Carl Beck Papers in Russian and East European Studies*, no. 1406, 2000

Vlast i obshchestvo v SSSR: politika repressii (20–40-e gg.), Moscow, 1999

Volkogonov, Dmitri, *Lenin: Life and Legacy*, trans. Harold Shukman, London, 1994

Volkogonov, Dmitri, *Stalin: Triumph and Tragedy*, trans. Harold Shukman, London, 1991

Volkogonov, Dmitri, *Trotsky: The Eternal Revolutionary*, trans. Harold Shukman, London, 1996

Vostochnaya Evropa v dokumentakh rossiiskikh archivov, 1944–1953: tom I, 1944–48 (collection of documents published by the Institute for Slavic and Balkan Studies), Moscow and Novosibirsk, 1997

Vozvrashchenie k pravde (collection of documents from the Tver archives), Tver, 1995

Vozvrashchenie pamyati, vols I–III (historical anthology), Novosibirsk, 1991, 1994, 1997

Walker, Martin, *The Waking Giant: The Soviet Union under Gorbachev*, London, 1986

Wallace, Henry, *Soviet Asia Mission*, New York, 1946

Webb, Sidney, and Webb, Beatrice, *Soviet Communism: A New Civilisation?*, London, 1936

Weiner, Amir, *Making Sense of War*, Princeton, NJ, and Oxford, 2001

Weiner, Amir, 'Nature, Nurture and Memory in a Socialist Utopia: Delineating the Soviet Socio-Ethnic Body in the Age of Socialism', *The American Historical Review*, vol. 104, no. 4, October 1999, pp. 1121–36

Werth, Nicolas, *Les procés de Moscou*, Brussels, 1987

Werth, Nicolas, *Rapports secrets soviétiques, 1921–1991*, Paris, 1994

Yurasova, D., 'Reabilitatsionnoe opredelenie po delu rabotnikov Gulaga', *Zvenya*, vol. I, Moscow, pp. 389–99

Zagorulko, M. M., ed., *Voennoplennye v SSSR: 1939–1956*, Moscow, 2000

Zaron, Piotr, *Ludność polska w Związku Radzieckim w czasie II wojny światowej*, Warsaw, 1990

Zemskov, V. N., 'Arkhipelag Gulag: glazami pisatelya i statistika', *Argumenty i Fakty*, no. 45, 1989

Zemskov, V. N., 'Gulag (istoriko-sotsiologicheskii aspekt)', *Sotsiologicheskie Issledovaniya*, no. 6, 1991, pp. 4–6

Zemskov, V. N., 'Spetsposelentsy (po dokumentam NKVD-MVD-SSSR)', *Sotsiologicheskie Issledovaniya*, no. 11, 1990, pp. 3–17

Zemskov, V. N., 'Sudba kulatskoi ssylki (1934–1954 gg)', *Otechestvennaya Istoriya*, 1, 1994, pp. 118–47

Zemskov, V. N., 'Zaklyuchennye v 1930-e gody: sotsialno-demograficheskie problemy)', *Otechestvennaya Istoriya*, no. 4, July/August 1997

Zubkova, Elena, *Russia after the War: Hopes, Illusions and Disappointments, 1945–1957*, trans. Hugh Ragsdale, Armonk, NY, 1998

Zvenya (historical anthology), vol. I, Moscow, 1991

Archives

AKB – Arkhangelsk Local Lore Library, Arkhangelsk
APRF – Archive of the President of the Russian Federation, Moscow
GAOPDFRK – State Archive of Social-Political Movements and the Formation of the Republic of Karelia (former Communist Party archives), Petrozavodsk
GARF – State Archive of the Russian Federation, Moscow
Hoover – Hoover Institution on War, Revolution and Peace, Stanford, CA
IKM – Iskitim Local Lore Museum Collections, Iskitim
Info-Russ – Vladimir Bukovsky's document collection
[http://psi.ece.jhu.edu~kaplan/IRUSS/BUK/GBARC/buk.html]
Karta – The Karta Society, Warsaw
Kedrovy Shor – Archives of the Kedrovy Shor *lagpunkt*, Intlag, in the author's collection
Komi Memorial – Archive of the Memorial Society, Syktyvkar
LOC – Library of Congress, Washington, DC
Memorial – Archive of the Memorial Society, Moscow
ML – Marylebone Library, Amnesty International Documents Collection, London
NARK – National Archives of the Republic of Karelia, Petrozavodsk
RGASPI – Russian State Archive of Social and Political History, Moscow
RGVA – Russian State Military Archive, Moscow
St Petersburg Memorial – Archives of the Memorial Society, St Petersburg
SKM – Solovetsky Local Lore Museum Collections, Solovetsky islands
TsKhIDK – Centre for Preservation of Historic Document Collections, Moscow
VKM – Vorkuta Local Lore Museum Collections, Vorkuta

Interviews

Anonymous ex-director of camp orphanage (Moscow, 24 July 2001)
Anna Andreevna (Moscow, 28 May 1999)
Anton Antonov-Ovseenko (Moscow, 14 November 1998)
Irena Arginskaya (Moscow, 24 May 1998)
Olga Astafyeva (Moscow, 14 November 1998)
David Berdzenishvili (Moscow, 2 March 1999)
Viktor Bulgakov (Moscow, 25 May 1998)
Zhenya Fedorov (Elektrostal, 29 May 1999)
Isaak Filshtinsky (Peredelkino, 30 May 1998)
Lev Finkelstein (London, 28 June 1997)
Lyudmila Khachatryan (Moscow, 23 May 1998)
Marlen Korallov (Moscow, 13 November 1998)
Natasha Koroleva (Moscow, 25 July 2001)
Paulina Myasnikova (Moscow, 29 May 1998)
Pavel Negretov (Vorkuta, 15 July 2001)
Susanna Pechora (Moscow, 24 May 1998)
Ada Puryzhinskaya (Moscow, 31 May 1998)
Alla Shister (Moscow, 14 November 1998)
Leonid Sitko (Moscow, 31 May 1998)
Galina Smirnova (Moscow, 30 May 1998)
Leonid Trus (Novosibirsk, 28 February 1999)
Galina Usakova (Moscow, 23 May 1998)

Olga Vasileevna (Moscow, 17 November 1998)
Simeon Vilensky (Moscow, 6 March 1999)
Danuta Waydenfeld (London, 22 January 1998)
Stefan Waydenfeld (London, 22 January 1998)
Maria Wyganowska (London, 22 January 1998)
Valentina Yurganova (Iskitim, 1 March 1999)
Yuri Zorin (Arkhangelsk, 13 September 1998)

Glossary

The Political Police

Cheka – *Chrezvychainaya komissiya* (Extraordinary Commission): secret police during the civil war era

GPU – *Gosudarstvennoe politicheskoe upravlenie* (State Political Administration): secret police during the early 1920s, successor to the Cheka

MGB/KGB – *Ministerstvo/Komitet gosudarstvennoe bezopasnosti* (Ministry of/Committee on State Security): secret police in charge of internal and external surveillance in the post-war era

MVD – *Ministerstvo vnutrennikh del* (Ministry of Internal Affairs): secret police in charge of gaols and camps in the post-war era

NKVD – *Narodnyi komissariat vnutrennikh del* (People's Commissariat of Internal Affairs): secret police during the 1930s and the Second World War, successor to OGPU

OGPU – *Obedinennoe gosudarstvennoe politicheskoe upravlenie* (Unified State Political Administration): secret police during the late 1920s and early 1930s, successor to GPU

Okhrana – tsarist-era secret police

Foreign Words and Institutions

balanda: prison soup

banya: a Russian steam bath

Barbarossa: Hitler's invasion of the Soviet Union – Operation Barbarossa – on 22 June 1941

beskonvoinyi: a prisoner who has the right to travel within different camp divisions without an armed guard

besprizornye: Soviet street children. Most were orphans, products of the civil war and collectivization

blatnoe slovo: thieves' jargon (see *urka*)

Bolsheviks: the radical faction of the Russian Social Democratic Labour Party, which under Lenin's leadership became the Russian Communist Party in 1918

bushlat: a long-sleeved prisoners' or workers' jacket lined with cotton wadding

Central Committee: the chief policy-making body of the Communist Party of the Soviet Union. In between Party congresses, it met two or three times a year. When it was not in session, decisions were taken by the Politburo, which was technically a body elected by the Central Committee

chifir: extremely strong tea. When ingested, produces something resembling a narcotic high

collectivization: policy of forcing all peasants to abandon private farming, and to pool all of their land and other resources into a collective, pursued from 1929 to 1932. Collectivization created the conditions for the rural famine of 1932–4, and permanently weakened Soviet agriculture

Comintern: the Third (Communist) International, an organization of the world's communist parties, formed in 1919 under the leadership of the Soviet Communist Party. The Soviet Union shut it down in 1943

Council of People's Commissars (or *Sovnarkom*): theoretically the ruling government body, the equivalent of a ministerial cabinet. In practice, subordinate to the Politburo

dezhurnaya or *dnevalnyi*: in normal parlance, a concierge. In a camp, the man or woman who stays behind in the barracks all day, cleaning and guarding against theft

dokhodyaga: someone on the verge of death; usually translated as 'goner'

dom svidanii: literally 'House of Meetings', where prisoners were allowed to meet their relatives

etap: prisoner transport

feldsher: a medical assistant, sometimes trained and sometimes not

glasnost: literally 'openness'. A policy of open debate and freedom of speech launched by Mikhail Gorbachev in the 1980s

Gulag: from *Glavnoe upravlenie lagerei* (Main Camp Administration), the secret police division which managed the Soviet concentration camps

Izvestiya: the Soviet government newspaper

Karelia: the Republic of Karelia, in the north-west corner of the Soviet Union, bordering Finland

katorga: tsarist term for forced labour. During the Second World War, the Soviet regime also adopted the word to describe strict-regime camps for war criminals

kolkhoz: a collective farm. Peasants were forced to work on them after the policy of collectivization was put into practice in 1929–31

kolkhoznik: inhabitant of a *kolkhoz*

Kolyma: the Kolyma River valley, in the far north-eastern corner of Russia, on the Pacific coast. Home to one of the largest camp networks in the USSR

Komi: the Republic of Komi, the north-eastern section of European Russia, west of the Ural mountains. The Komi people are the indigenous inhabitants of the Komi Republic, and speak an Ugro-Finnic language

Komsomol: Communist Party youth organization, for young people aged fourteen to twenty-eight. Younger children belonged to the Pioneers

kontslager: Russian for concentration camp

Kronstadt rebellion: a major uprising against the Bolsheviks, led by the sailors of the Kronstadt naval base, in 1921

kulak: traditionally, a prosperous peasant. In the Soviet era kulak came to mean any peasant accused of opposing Soviet authority or the collectivization policy. Between 1930 and 1933, over two million kulaks were arrested and deported

kum: the camp administrator responsible for managing the informers' network

KVCh: *Kulturno-vospitatelnaya chast*, the Cultural-Educational Department of each camp, responsible for the political education of the prisoners, as well as theatrical and musical productions

lagpunkt: the smallest camp division

laogai: Chinese concentration camp

Leningrad/St Petersburg: the same city. Founded in 1712 by Peter the Great, St Petersburg briefly became (the more Russified) Petrograd in 1914, when Russia went to war with Germany, and was then renamed Leningrad after Lenin's death in 1924

makhorka: rough tobacco smoked by Soviet workers and prisoners

maloletki: juvenile prisoners

mamka: female prisoner, the mother of a child born in prison

Memorial: organization founded in the 1980s to count, describe and assist the victims of Stalin. Now one of the most prominent human rights advocacy groups in Russia, as well as the premier historical research institute

Mensheviks: the non-Leninist wing of the Russian Social Democratic Workers' Party. After the Bolshevik Revolution, the Mensheviks tried to become a legal opposition, but their leaders were sent into exile in 1922. Many were later executed or sent to the Gulag

monashki: religious women, of various faiths. Literally 'nuns'

nadziratel: prison or camp guard

naryadchik: the camp clerk responsible for assigning prisoners to work tasks

NEP: *Novaya ekonomicheskaya politika* (New Economic Policy) – Soviet economic policy launched in 1921. Briefly brought back petty capitalism (private shops and traders). Lenin viewed it as a 'strategic retreat', and Stalin abolished it altogether

norm: the amount of work a prisoner would be required to do in a single shift

normirovshchik: the camp clerk responsible for setting work norms

Novyi Mir: Soviet literary magazine, the first to publish Solzhenitsyn

NTS: *Narodno-trudovoi Soyuz*, the 'people's workers' party', an underground political grouping which opposed Stalin, with branches in the USSR and abroad

obshchie raboty: literally 'general work'. In a camp, usually unskilled physical labour such as cutting trees or digging ditches

osoboe soveshchanie: 'special commission'. Committees used to sentence prisoners during periods of mass arrest, from the late 1930s

osobye lagerya: 'special camps'. These were set up for especially dangerous political prisoners in 1948

otkazchik: someone who refuses to work

otlichnik: an outstanding worker

OUN: *Organizatsiya Ukrainskikh Natsionalistov*, the Organization of Ukrainian Nationalists, West Ukrainian partisans who fought against the Red Army during and after the Second World War

parasha: a slop bucket in a prison cell or barracks

pellagra: a disease of starvation

People's Commissar: head of a government ministry

perestroika: a (failed) programme of restructuring the Soviet economy, launched by Mikhail Gorbachev in the 1980s

Politburo: the Political Bureau of the Central Committee of the Communist Party. In practice, the Politburo was the most important decision-making body in the USSR: the government – the Council of People's Commissars – had to do its bidding

Pravda: the newspaper of the Soviet Communist Party

pridurok (plural *pridurki*): a prisoner who is not on 'general work', but has an easier or more specialized job

psikhushka: psychiatric hospital for political dissidents

refusenik: a Soviet Jew who had asked to emigrate to Israel, but had been turned down

rezhim: prison regime

samizdat: illegal underground publications. An ironic pun on 'Gosizdat', the name of the state publishing house

scurvy: a disease of malnutrition, from lack of vitamin C. Among other things, results in night blindness and loss of teeth

sharashka: special prison where imprisoned scientists and technicians carried out secret assignments. Invented by Beria in 1939

SHIZO: from *shtrafnoi izolyator*, a punishment cell within a camp

SLON: *Severnye lagerya osobogo naznacheniya* (Northern Camps of Special Significance). The first camps set up by the political police in the 1920s

Social Revolutionaries: a Russian revolutionary party, founded in 1902, which later split into two groups, Left and Right. Briefly, the Left SRs participated in a coalition government with the Bolsheviks, but later fell out with them. Many of their leaders were later executed or sent to the Gulag

Sovnarkom (or Council of People's Commissars): theoretically the ruling government body, the equivalent of a ministerial cabinet. In practice, subordinate to the Politburo

spetslagerya: concentration camps set up by the Soviet Military Administration in occupied Germany after 1945

sploshnye nary: a long, unseparated wooden plank bed – a sleeping shelf – on which many prisoners slept at once

Stakhanovite: a worker or peasant who has overfulfilled the required work norm. Named after Aleksei Stakhanov, a miner who cut 102 tons of coal instead of the norm of seven in a single shift in August 1935

starosta: literally 'elder'. In prison cells, camp barracks and train cars, the *starosta* was responsible for keeping order

Stolypin wagon or *Stolypinka*: nickname for a railway car used for prisoner transport, in fact a modified passenger car. Named, unfairly, in honour of Pyotr Stolypin, Prime Minister of tsarist Russia from 1906 until his assassination in 1911

suki: literally 'bitches'. Camp slang for criminal prisoners who collaborated with the authorities

taiga: northern Russian landscape, characterized by pine forests, wide rivers, open fields

Thaw: brief period of reform following Stalin's death. Launched by Nikita Khrushchev's speech to the Twentieth Party Congress in 1956, and effectively halted by his successor, Leonid Brezhnev, in 1964

tovarishch: 'comrade'. A term of respect in the USSR

troika: three Soviet officials who, in lieu of courts, sentenced prisoners during periods of mass arrest, starting in 1937

trudosposobnost: work capability

tufta: in a camp, a method of cheating on work norms in order to receive a larger food ration

tundra: Arctic landscape, where the earth is permanently frozen. Only the surface melts briefly in summer, creating a swamp, a few shrubs and grasses, but no trees

udarnik: a worker or peasant who has overfulfilled the required work norm. After 1935, the term 'Stakhanovite' was more common

urka: a professional criminal; also known as *blatnoi* or *vor*

vagonki: double-decker bunks in camp barracks, for four people

vakhta: the headquarters of the camp armed guard, stationed at the entrance into the camp compound

valenki: felt boots

Vlasovites: followers of General Vlasov, who fought with the Nazis against the Red Army during the Second World War

VOKhR: from *voenizirovannaya okhrana*, armed guard. The armed guards in a camp

vor: a professional criminal; also known as *urka* or *blatnoi*

Wehrmacht: Hitler's military forces

zek: from z/k, an abbreviation for *zaklyuchennyi*, or 'prisoner'

zemlyanka: a house or barracks built in a hole in the ground; an earth dugout

zona: a concentration camp. Literally, the area within the barbed wire

Text and Illustrations Permissions

Text

Illustrations

Index

Library of Congress, 409
Lice and bedbugs, 195–7
Lieberman, 274
Life in the camps, 12, 179–206. *see also*
   Survival strategies
  absurdity of, 225–7
  barracks, 189–95
  bathing, 195–8
  dying prisoners, 307–15, 342
  food situation, 199–206
  freedom of movement, 183
  initiation process, 172–8
  outside contacts, 233–40
  in post-Stalin era, 480–87
  punishment regime, 229–33, 236, 486–7
  rules for living (*rezhim*), 185–8
  Solzhenitsyn's portrayal of, 466–70
  space in which prisoners lived (*zona*),
    181–5
  White Sea Canal camps, 78–9
Likhachev, Dmitri, 28, 44, 46, 47, 59, 267,
   496
Lipper, Elinor, 132, 155, 168, 190–91, 215,
   255, 343, 345
Litvinov, Pavel, 479
Livingstone, Ken, 7
Locals' attitudes towards prisoners, 356–7
Lockhart, Robert Bruce, 31, 96
Loginov (KVCh officer), 224, 406
Loginov, Aleksei, 257, 258
Lokchimlag camp, 101, 229
Long Walk, The (Rawicz), 355, 362–3
Losev, A. F., 79
Lovech camp, 412
Lu Fa, 367
Lubyanka prison, 149, 152–4, 471
Lukashenka, Aleksandr, 504
Lunts, Danil, 489
Lwów mass murder, 377

Magadan, 100, 218
Magnitogorsk camp, 225
Makeev, Aleksei, 447
Malenkov, Georgi, 243, 465
Malsagov, S. A., 73, 358
Mandelstam, Nadezhda, 127, 133, 312
Mandelstam, Osip, 28, 130–31, 133, 166,
   205
Marchenko, Anatoly, 345, 480–81, 482,
   484, 485, 486, 497–8
Marchenko, Zoya, 346

Martin, Terry, 72
Maslennikov, General I. I., 441, 442–3
Mazus, Izrail, 239–40
McCarthy, Joseph, 8
Medical care, 194, 337–46
Medvedev, Nikolai, 264–5
Medvedev, Roy, 253, 463, 473, 495
Medvedev, Zhores, 473, 488, 490
Medvedkov, 73
Medvezhegorsk camp, 182
Meetings with relatives, 237–40
Mein Kampf (Hitler), 21
Melnikova, Polina, 313
Memoria (Gagen-Torn), 307
Memorial Society, 10, 210, 350, 497, 505,
   506, 518, 519
Memorials and debates regarding Soviet
   past, 504–14
Mengele, Joseph, 19
Merekov, Aleksei, 319
Merridale, Catherine, 312, 465, 507, 508
Meyerhold, Vsevelod, 144
Mikoyan, Anastas, 460–61
Milyutina, T. P., 137
Mindlin, M. B., 210–11
Minlag camp, 290, 291, 434–5, 436, 440,
   443
Mishakova, Olga, 462–3
Mishkina, Galina, 435
Mkrtchyan, Beniamin, 191, 210
Mollison, Theodor, 19
Molotov, Vyacheslav, 69–70, 76, 77, 106,
   333, 373, 465
Mordovia camps, 428–9, 472, 481, 484, 494
Moroz, Vladimir, 303
Morushko, Pan, 444
Moscow–Volga Canal, 71–2, 83
Mosquitoes, 45, 212–13
Motylova, Tamara Lazarevna, 338
Muksalma camp, 40–41
Music in camps, 187, 350–51
Muslim exiles, 389
Muslim prisoners, 276–7
Mussolini, Benito, 69
MVD. *see* Cheka/OGPU/NKVD/MVD/KGB
'My Generation' (Frolovsky), 415

Nagy, Imre, 412
Narinsky, A. S., 201
Nasedkin, V. G., 42, 224, 244, 378, 396,
   404, 406